Houghton Mifflin Company
Boston

New York
Atlanta
Geneva, Illinois
Dallas
Palo Alto

Principles of Theatre Art

Second Edition

H. D. Albright
Cornell University

William P. Halstead
University of Michigan

Lee Mitchell
Northwestern University

Preface

The present volume is intended primarily as a text for a first course in the art of the theatre — whether this be titled Dramatic Production, The Elements of the Theatre, An Introduction to Drama and the Theatre, or another of the many variants appearing in college and university announcements. It is, therefore, addressed to the beginner; it presupposes a genuine interest in plays and play production, though not necessarily actual production experience. As its title suggests, it attempts to explain and to justify the aesthetic process by which plays are translated into theatrical terms and are projected from a stage to an audience. Though it supplies in full measure the "facts" of dramaturgy as well as of rehearsal and performance, it seeks throughout to focus on the principles which underlie theatre practice and theatre technique.

The book assumes that some of its readers are interested principally in developing appreciation and rational enjoyment of the dramatic art; others, a background for detailed and specialized study of one of its facets; and still others, the basis for professional training as teacher, director, or other artist of the theatre. In the belief that for each of these groups the forest is more important than the trees, the writers have provided a relatively complete and balanced coverage of all the elements of drama and the theatre, with special emphasis on their interrelationship.

Because the director's task impinges on and draws together the work of all his fellow-artists, somewhat more space has been devoted to direction than to other aspects of production. The essential nature of the dramatic composition serves as an introduction to, and basis for, the remainder of the book; and the objectives and conditions of production — for pre-modern as well as contemporary playscripts — are set forth in considerable detail. A special effort is made to correlate the work of the designer with that of the actor and the director, and to establish historical as well as aesthetic distinctions in the use of the stage space.

Classroom exercises and projects for the student, based on the content of the several chapters, are offered in an appendix. Other supplementary sections include notes on costume and make-up, and a series of bibliographies. The more than sixty drawings, most of them full-page, are the work of Lee Mitchell.

To their many collaborators — especially those who supplied photographs for the volume — the writers are grateful. Apart from their families, who were patient as well as helpful, the authors wish to mention the following in particular: Mel Beaudette, George Crepeau, Gifford Wingate, Mrs. C. C. Arnold, and Miss Gretchen Roeschlaub. To their students, both graduate and undergraduate, who have joined with them in bringing to life more than two hundred productions, they owe a great deal more than they are here able to express. Finally, their indebtedness to their own teachers and colleagues, and to other writers on contemporary dramatic production, will be apparent to many readers, even though it cannot be fully and specifically acknowledged anywhere on these pages.

H. D. A.
W. P. H.
L. M.

Note to Second Edition

As an important feature of the Second Edition, the writers have introduced considerable new material, particularly material on open staging — i.e., on wrap-around stages and especially on arena and thrust stages. Some of this is, of course, historical in coverage, some descriptive and expository; much of it treats designing and directing for the open stage.

In addition, more than half the original photographs have been replaced, as well as a number of the line drawings. The five sets of theatre plans which followed the original Chapter 13 have been replaced by more recent plans of various types. The bibliographies have been updated, and the projects and exercises have been adapted to suit the several topics that have been newly introduced. The focus throughout remains on the nature and scope of the various facets of contemporary theatre art, with special emphasis on their interrelationship.

The writers are grateful, both personally and professionally, to those who have supplied photographic or other material for either edition of the volume.

H. D. A.
W. P. H.
L. M.

Contents

Preface, *iii*
List of Figures, *ix*
List of Plates, *xi*

SECTION ONE · DRAMA

1 Drama as Art, *3*
Four Characteristics of Drama
The Elements of Drama

2 The Dramatic Composition, *7*
Kinds of Composition
Formalities of Composition
The Elements of Composition

3 Plot, *17*
Kinds of Plots
The Episode
Articulation of Plot
Plot Conflicts
Dilemma
Irony
Suspense and Surprise

4 Characterization, *30*
Aesthetic Acceptability
Identification
Consistency of Character
Motivation
Revelation
Contrast and Conflict

5 Language, *41*
Requirements of Dramatic Language
Poetic Language
Prosaic Language
Some Forms of Dramatic Language

6 Thought, *56*
The Nature of Thought in the Drama
The Channels through Which Thought Is
  Expressed

7 Drama and Audience, *63*
Immediate Effect
Levels of Perception and Effect
Aftereffects
Change in Effect
Five Tests of Quality

SECTION TWO · ACTING

8 Purpose and Method in Acting, *79*
Objectives in Performance
The Actor's Dual Nature
"Systems" of Acting
Preparation vs. Performance
Study and Memorization

9 Movement and Gesture, *90*
The Nature of Stage Pantomime
Conventionalization in Pantomime
The Actor in Space
General "Rules" for Stage Behavior
Movement on the Open Stage
Physical Requirements for the Actor

10 Voice and Speech, *111*
Audibility and Intelligibility
Reading for Meaning

The Nature of Emphasis
Speaking in a Context
Insuring Credibility

11 **Characterization,** *125*
Completeness in Characterization
Analyzing a Role
Selection and Adaptation
Enrichment
Imagination and Belief

12 **A Perspective on the Whole,** *136*
The Actor and His Audience
Aesthetic Balance
Continuity and Growth
The Actor and His Fellows

SECTION THREE · THEATRE AND STAGE

13 **Methods of Organizing the Theatre
     Structure,** *147*
Arena Staging
Formal Staging
Simultaneous Staging
Multiple Staging
Theatrical Staging
Actualistic Staging

14 **The Proscenium Theatre,** *172*
The General Structure
The Auditorium
Behind the Proscenium
Revolts from the Pattern

15 **The Open Theatre,** *208*
The Open Stage
Origins
Influence of the Shakespearean Festivals
The Thrust Stage
Open Theatres
Some Open Theatres of Modest
     Dimensions
Virtues and Disadvantages
Some Combinations

SECTION FOUR · DESIGN

16 **The Nature and Function of Design,** *225*
A Definition of Design
The Nature of Design
The Function of Design

17 **Aesthetic Factors in the Design,** *234*
The Appropriateness of the Design to the
     Script
The Appropriateness of the Design to the
     Director's Interpretation
The Need for Individuality
Visual Unity

18 **Physical Factors in the Design,
     1: Setting and Lighting,** *243*
The Kinds of Stage Action
The Place of Performance
The Technical Demands of the Script

19 **Physical Factors in the Design,
     2: Costume,** *267*
Style
Mobility
The Costume and the Actor

20 **Principles of Spatial Composition,** *286*
Line
Light and Shade
Color

21 **Principles of Temporal Composition,** *310*
Duration
Variation
Accumulation

SECTION FIVE · DIRECTION

22 **The Function of the Director,** *323*
The Director as Administrator
The Director as Leader
The Director as Interpreter

23 The Visual Stimuli, *339*
Stimuli Provided by the Actor
Stimuli Provided by the Influence of Design on the Actor

24 The Auditory Stimuli, *372*
Characteristics of Voice and Speech
Other Auditory Stimuli Provided by the Actor
Stimuli Supplied by Other Media

25 Patterning the Visual and Auditory Stimuli, *394*
Emphasis and Subordination
Style
Atmosphere
Picturization
Balance
Proportion
Unity

Progression
Rhythm

26 Directing for the Open Stage, *436*
Directing the Movement
Other Directorial Principles
Inherent Advantages and Difficulties

27 The Director's Relationship with His Associates, *442*
With the Playwright
With the Audience
With the Actor
With the Designer and Production Heads
The Other Side of the Picture

28 The Conduct of Rehearsals, *458*
Casting
The First Reading of the Play
The Period of Analysis
Rehearsals
Performances

Appendix A: Projects and Exercises for the Student, *491*
Appendix B: On the Art of Costuming, *508*
Appendix C: A Note on Make-up, *516*
Appendix D: Selected Bibliographies, *523*

Acknowledgments for Photographs, *537*
Index, *539*

Figures

1. Gross Bodily Attitude   85
2. Common Directions to the Actor   87
3. Dressing to the House   91
4. Effects of Position on the Acting of a Scene   93
5. Two "Broken" Entrances   95
6. Character Build-up   97
7. Types of Imposed Movement   101
8. Development of a Confrontation   102
9. Open and Closed Positions   105
10. The Actors' Facings   107
11. Gesturing   108
12. Starting and Finishing a Cross on the Upstage Foot   113
13. The Counter   114
14. Comparative Dimensions of Ancient, Renaissance, and Modern Theatres   152
15. The Orchestra-Pit Elevator   175
16. Basic Seating Plans   177
17. Types of Seating Slopes   178
18. Reflection of Sound   181
19. Cubage of a Proscenium Stage   183
20. Some Standard Scenic Units   184
21. Three Kinds of Act Curtains   187
22. The Forestage   189
23. Some Devices to Speed Scene Changing   191
24. Lighting Units   195
25. The Parts of a Box Set   201
26. The Parts of a Wing-and-Drop Set   203
27. Pictorial and Sculptural Action   245
28. Same Setting as Seen from Orchestra and from Balcony Seats   249
29. Draped and Fitted Costumes   269
30. Costume Accents   273
31. Costume Accessories   274
32. Drapery in Motion   278
33. Convergence   288
34. Enclosure   289
35. Intersection and Opposition and Some Combinations   291
36. Balance   292
37. Repetition   295
38. Comparative Angles of Illumination   296
39. The Spectrum Band   300
40. Relative Visibility of Hues   302
41. Warm and Cool Color-Groups   305
42. Selective Reflection of Color   307
43. Cross-Coloring of Light   309
44. Temporal Progression   315

45. Three Ways of Directing Attention to One Character in a Group   345

46. Methods of Recording Stage Action   347

47. Methods of Recording Stage Action   351

48. Provisions for an Inconspicuous Entrance Downstage Near Center   355

49. A Setting Providing Three Playing Levels and Three Playing Depths

50. Wedge-Shaped Platform Designed to Force Action Toward Proscenium   360

51. Stage Movement (*Arsenic and Old Lace*)   361

52. Stage Movement (*Born Yesterday*)   362

53. Stage Movement (*The Winslow Boy*)   363

54. Acting Areas   365

55. A Setting Designed to Provide One Strong Dominant Position   400

56. Subordination of Minor Characters   403

57. Subordination of Minor Characters   404

58. Awkward and Graceful Costume   407

Sections and ground plans of the following five significant theatre plants appear in Chapter 13:

Stratford Shakespearean Festival Theatre, Stratford, Ontario   167

The Community Theater, Western Springs, Illinois   168

Theater Arts Building, University of California at Los Angeles   169

Tyrone Guthrie Theatre, Minneapolis, Minnesota   170

Vivian Beaumont Theater, Lincoln Center for the Performing Arts, New York City   171

Plates

Frontispiece

    J. B.

1. *Caesar and Cleopatra*   } between

2. *Camelot* (above); *The King and I* (below)   20–21

3. Four studies from *The Inspector-General*

4. Studies from *Oedipus Rex* (above); *Billy Budd* (below, left); and *West Side Story* (below, right)

5. Studies from *Julius Caesar* (below); *King Lear* (above, left); and *Galileo* (above, right)   132–133

6. *A Company of Wayward Saints* (above); *Oliver!* (below)

7. Indian Snake Dance (above); Greek theatre at Delphi (below)

8. Model of Valenciennes Mystery Play (above); Old Globe theatre, San Diego (below)

9. Theatre at Drottningholm (above); design by de Loutherbourg (below)   148–149

10. Stage at Siena, 1560 (above); at London, 1596 (below, left); at Ghent, 1539 (below, right)

11. Quin as Coriolanus (above, left); Garrick and Mrs. Pritchard in *Macbeth* (above, right); *The School for Scandal* (below)   164–165

12. Design by Duke of Saxe-Meiningen (above); *The Return of Peter Grimm* (below)

13.   Appia setting for *King Lear* (above); Craig setting for *Hamlet* (below)

14.   Copeau's theatre, Le Vieux Colombier (above); *From Morn to Midnight* (middle); *The Adding Machine* (below)

between 180–181

15.   *The Birds*

16.   *The Heiress* (above); *High Ground* (middle); *Dark of the Moon* (below)

17.   *The Beaux' Stratagem* (above); *The Trojan Women* (below)

204–205

18.   Passion Play at Oberammergau, 1910 (above); *Death of a Salesman* (below)

19.   *Ion* (above); *Oedipus Rex* (below)

20.   *Papa Is All* (above); *Southern Exposure* (below)

21.   *The Cherry Orchard* (above); *The Government Inspector* (below)

220–221

22.   Two treatments of *Macbeth*

23.   *The Caucasian Chalk Circle* (above); *The Threepenny Opera* (below)

24.   *H. M. S. Pinafore* (above); *The Pirates of Penzance* (below)

244–245

25.   *The Shewing Up of Blanco Posnet* (above); *The Lady from the Sea* (below)

26.   *Lysistrata* (above); *West Side Story* (below)

260–261

27.   *The Jest* (above); *The Voice of the Turtle* (below)

28.   *Henry V*

29.   *Coriolanus* (above); *Henry V* (below)

428–429

30.   *Angel Street* (above); *Jeb* (below)

Section One

Drama

1 | Drama as Art

Four Characteristics of Drama
The Elements of Drama

In the vocabulary of the English-speaking world, the word "drama" may be used to mean one of three quite different but related things. First, in its broadest and most general sense, it may be used to mean that art which is concerned with plays as written and performed. In another sense it may be used to mean the dramatic composition, a creation presenting, through language and pantomime, a sequence of events intended to be acted on a stage. Finally, it may mean that branch of literature which encompasses such compositions.

The principal subject of this section is the dramatic composition — what it is, its parts, its various kinds, and the qualities which make one composition better or worse than another. The dramatic composition will be considered here, however, not as a work of art complete in itself but as one element in the whole art of the drama which is seen by the audience. We shall consider the dramatic composition as the scheme or plan according to which the play is performed. An analogy may help to make this point clear. The present study will be like that of a musical composition, not of the score only, as written down and read in print, but of the whole musical composition as written, played by musicians, and heard by an audi-

ence. The analogy may perhaps be made clearer by comparing drama with several other arts of which music itself is one.

FOUR CHARACTERISTICS OF DRAMA

Considering drama as an art and comparing it with other arts such as music, painting, and architecture, one is able to note many ways in which it differs from or resembles each of the others. This comparison reveals four characteristics of drama, which, taken together, distinguish it from other arts and also describe its own peculiar artistic make-up.

The first and most conspicuous characteristic is its *temporal* nature. For drama exists primarily in time. Each performance is a distinct work of art, and although many of the elements such as composition and décor remain fundamentally unchanged throughout the life of one production, each performance varies in quality so that one may be much better and another much worse than the average. Every actor is aware of the truth of this. If one compliments him on a performance, the first thing he says is: "Which night did you see it?" In this respect, drama is like music, which reaches its

3

highest quality only in its best performance and which varies in quality from performance to performance. But drama and music are both quite unlike painting and architecture, whose works, once completed, remain unchanged sometimes for centuries.

Drama is a fugitive art. Its best performance occupies only a few hours and then is gone forever. From the point of view of the theatre artist its characteristic effects must be achieved within the narrow limits of time which circumscribe a single performance. From the point of view of the spectator it defies study at leisure such as might be spent on a painting. The impression it makes on the mind and emotions of the beholder is not complete until the performance is concluded. It is complete then in the sense that thereafter it can be examined only in retrospect. When a work seems great in performance, it is often quite difficult for one to describe this greatness to another who has not witnessed the very same performance. Thus one sometimes finds violent disagreement over the merits of a given production between members of the audience who happened to have witnessed the performance on different occasions.

The second characteristic of drama is that it is *mimetic*. That is to say, it re-creates, reproduces, or represents. What it re-creates, of course, is human life in speech and action. The thoughts, feelings, decisions, and actions of human creatures constitute the principal material from which the work of art is fashioned. The re-creation of the these things lies at the heart of the mimetic art. In drama the activity of human beings is portrayed or acted out. Other terms sometimes used to describe this process are "imitation" and representation," but each of these has other connotations which confuse its meaning, while the term *mimetic* means but this one thing and is less likely to be misconstrued.

Sometimes segments of life are re-created with great fidelity to detail. At other times, life as re-created in drama is unlike anything one might experience outside the theatre, but yet appeals to the observer because it is true to some broad concept of how life is or ought to be. In either case, truth to life is a condition of its acceptance as a work of art. The characters and their actions, no matter how "unreal," must be plausible and must coincide to some degree with what people in general do, might do, or ought to do or say.

One sees at once how sharply this mimetic characteristic sets drama off from other arts. For one cannot truthfully say that mimesis is characteristic of any other art. Painting and sculpture are only occasionally mimetic, as in portraiture or similar representations of life. Both are more commonly decorative; they please the eye but represent nothing definitely human. Music may, on occasion, re-create recognizable sounds of life, such as the song of birds or the ripple of water, but it does not have to do so in order to please, and it does so infrequently.

But with drama, truth to life is a condition of its acceptance as art. If it is untrue it is rejected by the audience and thereby fails of its purpose. If its material is not human life, it is either not understood or else understood so differently by every member of the audience that confusion results. Attempts at non-human or "abstract" drama abundantly demonstrate this. In sum, drama is mimetic, or it is not certain of being drama at all.

The third characteristic of drama is that it is *interpretative*. The ultimate work of art, the performance, is not an original creation; it is an interpretation performed according to a previously created scheme or composition. Only the original creation possesses any durability. The complete and final work of art which springs from it is fugitive in the extreme. Yet to the audience in the theatre the performer is the center of interest, for it is by his art that the original composition emerges. The better the performance the more readily one believes that the speeches and actions are the performer's own, and the more easily the playwright is forgotten. To those most familiar with the art the finest instance is the superb performance. It is not primarily Shakespeare, Ibsen, Molière, or Chekhov who is esteemed, nor yet *Hamlet, Ghosts, Tartuffe,* or *The Cherry Orchard,* but Barrymore's *Hamlet,* Duse's *Ghosts,* Coquelin's *Tartuffe,* and Stanislavski's *Cherry Orchard.*

Really great plays are few; superb performances of them are fewer still. In the greatest there is a kind of incandescence which illuminates the whole, giving it greater meaning and feeling and bringing it at times almost unbearably close to life itself. It has often been said of Chekhov that one did not really know his work until one had seen it performed by Stanislavski's company. Similar statements have been made of each of the others mentioned above.

This characteristic drama shares with music. Not every work of Beethoven or Verdi is comparable to the Beethoven or Verdi as performed under the direction of Toscanini. Lovers of Brahms's music say that there is no Brahms equal to that performed by Pablo Casals.

The final characteristic relates to the form of drama. Drama as manifested in the performance is a *synthesis,* or blend, or fusion, of distinct elements into a complex whole. Fundamentally, the synthesis consists of the art of the playwright plus the art of the performer, but the typical production is a synthesis not only of these but of many more arts which may include those of director, designer, composer, and choreographer as well.

A superior synthesis gives heightened value to a production the separate elements of which, taken separately, may each be of no more than modest quality. The better the synthesis the more difficult it becomes to judge the particular drama other than as a whole and the more difficult it becomes to distinguish the various elements which comprise the work. On the other hand, the better the quality of the various elements involved, the more offensive an incomplete or imperfect synthesis is likely to be. In any case, it may be said truthfully that the quality of the performance is conditioned by the degree to which the synthesis approaches perfection.

Summing up, one may say that the drama as art is distinguished by four characteristics. First, it is *temporal* in its nature, for it exists primarily in time, within narrow limits of time, and only once at a time. Second, it is *mimetic* in its treatment of its material, for its material is human life, which it re-creates in speech and action. Third, it is *interpretative* in its means, for it is performed according to a plan or composition previously created, and it exists fully only in performance. Finally, it is *synthesized* in its form, for the performance comes into being only through the synthesis of a variety of distinct arts: playwriting, directing, design, acting, and sometimes many more.

THE ELEMENTS OF DRAMA

In the preceding pages the elements of the performance were designated as script, acting, directing, and design. These vary somewhat according to the point of view from which they are perceived. From the point of view of the audience the elements are perceived simultaneously, are interrelated, and are of varying importance to the whole. But from the point of view of the theatre worker they are more likely to be conceived of in the order in which they are developed and gradually blended into the whole work.

The audience experiences only the whole work of art, perceiving most strongly those things to which its attention is guided by the interpreter and recalling most vividly the high points of the performance. In so far as the audience is aware of the elements involved, the order of their importance as experienced and recalled will probably give acting first place, for it is the actor's personality and art to which the audience most strongly responds. Often this response mistakes the actor for the character whom he impersonates and credits him with spontaneous origination of the thoughts which he voices and the decisions upon which he acts. The better the actor the more likely the audience is to do this. After acting, the element most vividly perceived is usually the language, especially those bits of language in which ideas or feelings are particularly well expressed. The third most vividly perceived element is usually the design. This is because the visual sense of the average spectator is generally the keenest of his senses, so that what he sees impresses him readily and is easily recalled. Somewhere after these come the elements of plot and theme, or thought. These vary greatly among individual members of the audience, for the capacity to assimilate all the relevant factors in a sequence of impressions is dependent upon the mentality of the individual and upon his experience both with life and with temporal art. A curious fact is that a high degree of pleasure to the individual is often possible even when the plot and theme are imperfectly perceived. But the effect of drama is unquestionably better when both perception and recall of all elements of the work are strong and clear.

In contrast to the audience view of the drama is the view of the theatre worker, who sees the art as it were with a double vision, viewing it simultaneously in terms of its effect as a whole and as a problem of synthesis involving the various elements in the order of development from their inception to their final realization in performance. The principal elements seen from this point of view are: the composition — that is, the plot, characterization, language, and thought; the acting, including the adaptation of the composition to the stage, the directing, and the actor's work in itself; and the design, or visual scheme, involving setting, costume, properties, and lighting.

It is with the point of view of the theatre worker that we turn now to the first element of the synthesis: the dramatic composition.

2 | The Dramatic Composition

Kinds of Compositions
Formalities of Composition
The Elements of Composition

The composition, also called the "script," or the "playscript," is the written plan or scheme according to which a drama is performed. As such it can be compared to the score of a symphony or the assembled drawings for an architectural work. In a drama, the number and kinds of characters, the language in which they express themselves, their actions, and the consequences of their actions are all determined by the original composition. Moreover, the composition is usually the primary factor in determining the kind of drama which the audience will experience and the form in which they will experience it. Whether it will be serious or light, compact or rambling — these alternatives, together with many others, are generally settled in advance by the intent of the author.

In point of time, the composition is necessarily the first element of the synthesis to develop. All the other elements, such as acting, directing, and design, are dependent upon it, develop out of it, and are incapable of existing apart from it. Until the play has been written, it cannot be designed, directed, or acted.

In addition to being first in time, the composition is also the most stable element of the synthesis, for once completed it is capable of retaining its substance indefinitely. While the other elements are durable only to the extent of one production or even of one performance, the composition may endure for generations, outlasting innumerable different productions.

KINDS OF COMPOSITIONS

In art as complex as drama it is not practicable to attempt to classify in detail all the many kinds of compositions which have been developed. But looking at it in a rather broad and general way, from the single viewpoint of the author's intention — in so far as it is apparent in his work — the student can discern several distinct kinds of compositions. The principal kinds are those which are distinguished according to the author's purpose, his attitude toward his subject, and his treatment of his material.

The Author's Purpose

Some plays are written with the primary purpose of stirring an audience to overt action in behalf of some social or political cause. Such a play is Clifford Odets' *Waiting for Lefty*, which ends with a question to which, when the play has been properly performed, the audience responds vigorously. The primary purpose of this play is persuasion. Many another play is composed primarily in order to demonstrate some theory or to teach some sort of lesson. The sixteenth-century *Everyman* is such a play. When the dramatic composition is aimed primarily toward persuasion, demonstration, instruction, or other ends equally achievable by other means than drama, it is termed *heteronomous*. The success or failure of such a play is determined above all by the effectiveness of its persuasion or instruction. The term means literally "subject to the laws of another." *Waiting for Lefty* and *Everyman* are heteronomous plays. Their success is determined in the one case by the principles which govern successful persuasion, and in the other by the principles which determine effective instruction.

The other kind of drama is called *autonomous*. The term means "self-governing." When applied to art it means a composition developed primarily according to effects peculiar to that art. In drama these would be the effects peculiar to drama independent of other purposes. Molière's farce, *Les Fourberies de Scapin*, is a good example of autonomous drama, for it is constructed wholly to delight an audience, with no other apparent end. Another play of this kind is Shakespeare's *Twelfth Night*.

Dramas which are entirely autonomous or clearly heteronomous are naturally rare. Although aimed toward persuasion, a play must still observe many of the necessities of dramatic art in order to arouse interest and hold attention. On the other hand, much of the best drama is also instructive in morality, psychology, and many other subjects. However, any play is bound to be *primarily* either autonomous or heteronomous in intent, and it is not usually difficult to determine which.

Of each kind the extreme examples are likely to display pronounced virtues and weaknesses. The virtues are always the virtues of singleness of purpose. The weaknesses are usually deficiencies. In the heteronomous work these deficiencies are usually of an artistic nature, and in the autonomous

work, of intellectual content. For example, the play whose primary purpose is to provoke thought often seems incomplete or an act or so too long. Sometimes the epilogue, intended to focus the attention upon the thought content, seems like an addition rather than a necessary part of the whole play. By contrast, the strictly autonomous work, although highly amusing or intensely exciting during its performance, often seems inconsequential in retrospect and lacking in social or philosophical significance.

In new plays, especially those showing pronounced originality, the author's purpose is sometimes so difficult to determine that one is tempted to believe he may have composed the play with no other purpose than to confuse and irritate his audiences. This very irritation, however, is occasionally one of the earliest indications that a masterpiece is at hand. Not until one has seen a play several times, preferably in different productions by different directors and actors, can one say that one understands it. Even Shakespeare, whose plays are well understood today, puzzled and annoyed many critics whose ideas were based on their acquaintance with classical dramatists. A hundred and fifty years after Shakespeare's death no less a critic than Samuel Johnson was saying of him: "He sacrifices virtue to convenience, and is so much more careful to please than to instruct, that he seems to write without any moral purpose."[1] One can see from this that understanding an author's purpose does not come quickly or easily. One should never rush to judgment. In order to understand a play one must first understand its author.

The Author's Attitude

The second division of kind is according to

---

[1] "Preface to Shakespeare." Reprinted in *European Theories of the Drama*, rev. ed., ed. Barrett H. Clark and Henry Popkin (Crown Publishers, 1965), p. 185.

the playwright's attitude toward his material. His material is life, and his attitude toward it, as manifested in the composition at hand, may be serious, light, bitter, mocking, or facetious.

Serious drama is primarily emotional both in its intent and in its principal effect. The author's emotional identification with his material produces a similar identification on the part of the audience witnessing his work. The intellectual effect, if any, is usually an aftereffect emerging gradually with recollection of the performance. If the emotional involvement is deep and strong enough the aftereffects are likely to persist and more and more meanings to emerge as the details are recalled.

The highest level achieved by serious authorship is *tragedy*. Both actions and characters seem to possess a significance greater than that afforded by the performance itself. Of course, good tragedy, like the best in any art, is uncommon. More common is a less impressive species of serious drama generally called simply "drama," from the French *drame*. Its appeal is on a lower level than that of tragedy. It may be emotionally moving and it may be thought-provoking too, but its scope is smaller. The out-reaching significance of tragedy is absent in "drama," which does not seem as profound, as big, or as important. A good example of modern "drama" is Tennessee Williams' *Glass Menagerie*. We can see the difference in scope as soon as we compare it with Sophocles' *Antigone* or Shakespeare's *King Lear*.

The most common variety of serious drama is called *melodrama*. Originally this was a specific kind of cheap thriller, the more emotional moments of which were heightened with offstage music. Today the term is appropriate to any play featuring excitement, suspense, and violent action and appealing relatively little to the mind. Emlyn Williams' popular *Night Must Fall* and *In Abraham's Bosom* by Paul Green are good modern instances of melodrama.

There are many kinds of light drama, and they can be differentiated according to level of intellectual appeal. The lowest form, of course, is *farce* (for example, *Hotel Paradiso*), which gains its effect mainly through vigorous physical activity and broad, easily understood jokes. The highest form is *satire* (Gogol's *The Inspector-General*, for instance), in which the action is fundamentally plausible and the characters quite lifelike. Satire affords us the particular delight of recognizing the absurdities of people very much like ourselves and those we know. The difference between the best farce and the best satire is a difference in quality of effect, but both make the foibles and incongruities of human life apparent to the observer.

Between the two extremes of farce and satire lie all the varieties of light drama ordinarily grouped under the generic term "comedy." Among these are "high comedy," which is chiefly marked by a sophisticated treatment of the material (Noel Coward's *Blithe Spirit*, for example); "comedy of manners," which deals more particularly with social foibles and affectations (Richard Brinsley Sheridan's *The School for Scandal*); and "domestic comedy," which treats lightly the incongruities of everyday life as seen in family relationships, adolescence, petty worries, or minor parental problems (*You Can't Take It With You*, by Kaufman and Hart).

Most drama which has appeared since the Middle Ages, epecially in English, is neither wholly serious nor wholly light, but a mixture. As a rule, the drama is composed so that a serious action and a light one run side by side, alternating in their demands upon the audience. Sometimes two sets of characters are presented, one to be taken seriously while the other, being comical, lightens and relieves the seriousness of the first set. For example, in the medieval *Second Shepherds'*

Play the comical shepherds' action is followed by the serious presentation of the Nativity. In the popular melodrama of the last century, *Uncle Tom's Cabin*, the emotional scenes involving Uncle Tom, Eva, and Eliza are periodically relieved by the appearance of the comical lawyer, Marks.

A rarer mixture of serious and light drama is achieved when a playwright succeeds in composing a work which hovers between the two, presenting characters and actions which are successively amusing and moving throughout the play. In such works the emotional appeal is delicate rather than deep and the comic effect is deft rather than broad. Shakespeare achieves a brilliant mixture of the two in many of his romances (*The Merchant of Venice*, for example). Tennessee Williams has done it pretty well once or twice and Eugene O'Neill did it successfully in *Ah, Wilderness!*

In the past decade, many playwrights, sensing that a subject may be so complex that it can be understood only when seen from more than one viewpoint, have expressed ambivalent attitudes in highly original ways. A subject may have a serious side and a comical side, both of which must be appreciated for complete understanding.

Inconsistency and contradiction are certain to appear when a subject is shown from several viewpoints — reverently and irreverently, or seriously and mockingly — and shifts of attitude are more likely to puzzle and confuse an audience than to clarify the subject for them. Nevertheless, the risk is one which the playwright must often take. Life is not always simple; intelligent people know it is not simple, and they will reject a too-simple representation of life more readily than they will reject one which is merely hard to follow.

The impetus for this kind of experiment seems to have come principally from the plays of Bertolt Brecht, which began to be widely known only a generation ago. Brecht's attitude toward his material was fundamentally serious, but he believed that audiences could appreciate the full significance of his plays only if they were forced to maintain a detached and objective view of the action. To achieve this detachment, he tried to prevent growth of sympathy for his characters by using a number of devices associated with nonserious drama since the time of Aristophanes: buffoonery, direct address, extradramatic action, and interpolated ballads.

The Author's Treatment of His Material

The third division of kind is made according to the way the author treats the material at his disposal. Two extremes are clearly apparent, and each has accounted for many masterpieces. One may be called *intensive*, and its opposite, *extensive*. In certain great periods of theatre history the prevalent taste inclined strongly toward one or the other; and the majority of practicing dramatists tended to compose works predominantly of one kind.

Intensive drama is characterized by pronounced compression and streamlining of the material and a high moment-to-moment clarity in performance. The successive incidents which make up the play are closely related and show a minimum of superfluities. Each character introduced and every word uttered advances the action or illuminates the issues. The resulting drama is, in consequence, both highly concentrated and greatly intensified. Most of the works of the Greeks represent life re-created in this fashion, and for this reason the term "classical" has come to mean highly compressed drama. The French playwrights of the seventeenth century, chiefly Molière, Racine, and Corneille, produced masterpieces of similar kind, and at the close of the nineteenth century, Ibsen duplicated their success in *Ghosts* and *Hedda Gabler*.

In contrast, extensive drama is distinguished by its richness, complexity, and variety. The relationships of incidents and characters, except as they vary the effect, may become apparent only upon conclusion of the work, or even in retrospect. The characteristic impression one gains is of great abundance and diversity, of a vast area of life encompassed within the several hours' experience of the performance.

Most chronicle and historical plays tend toward the extensive. As an art, extensive drama seems particularly agreeable to the tastes and inclinations of England and America. Shakespeare, of course, composed in this form with great success, working always with a bold hand and a prodigal freedom of plot and characterization, lavishing two or three plots on a single drama and introducing many characters mainly for variety or contrast. A long list of subsequent extensive dramas could be cited, including Eugene O'Neill's *Marco Millions*, Ibsen's *Peer Gynt*, Brecht's *Mother Courage*, and Peter Shaffer's *Royal Hunt of the Sun*.

FORMALITIES OF COMPOSITION

Life as re-created in the theatre is necessarily more vivid and more coherent than the daily life which most members of the audience experience. Life itself contains much that is tedious and repetitive and much that is chaotic and meaningless. In drama, accident and chance are less conspicuous than in life, while cause and effect are usually more so. The playwright, in common with the novelist and the painter, re-creates life with a greater definiteness of form and a better sense of order. It is the ability to do this that makes the playwright an artist.

Vividness and coherence are gained through a variety of artistic devices, called *formalities* of composition, which give form to the mimetic presentation of life on the stage. Every art has its own formalities. A painting has its enclosing frame. A musical composition has its dominant key. Drama, too, has a great many formalities, but only a few important ones will be named and described here: the formalities of composition for heightening unity of effect, for increasing dramatic impact, and for economizing exposition.

Unifying Devices

Unity of effect is especially important in temporal art. The audience is not free to study the work at leisure, but must accept it as presented at a given time and place with the successive impressions in a predetermined sequence. The various incidents and characters must therefore seem to belong together, and the successive impressions gained from them must seem to add up to something. When no relationship of effects is perceived and when the impressions add up to nothing, the audience is likely to lose patience during the performance and feel unsatisfied when it is over.

The effect of oneness, or unity, is often achieved by using one or another of several formalities of composition, or some combination of them. A common device is relating all incidents to the actions of a single character. Many historical dramas have been composed around incidents true or apocryphal in the lives of persons as different as Socrates, Mary Stuart, Galileo, Abraham Lincoln, and Joan of Arc. Fiction and legend have furnished such favorites as Robin Hood, Till Eulenspiegel, and Sinbad the Sailor. Sometimes the various incidents have no relationship to each other beyond the fact that they all happened to the same person.

Another formality is the restriction of a drama to a single occurrence, showing its critical moments together with its causes and immediate consequences. This is the means by which Arthur Miller gives unity to his *Death of a Salesman*. He does not show the whole life of Willy Loman the salesman, but only those incidents in his life which help to explain his suicide. Similarly, Martínez Sierra's *Cradle Song* is limited to the single occurrence of the adoption of a foundling girl by a convent of nuns, followed by their giving her up to marriage when she is grown. In Ibsen's *Ghosts* the central action is a mother's attempt to protect her son from the consequences of his father's profligacy. During the course of the drama the reasons for her attempt are revealed and the play ends with her failure. In each of these works attention is narrowed to a single action with only as much detail as is necessary to make it fully understood. In each instance the action sequence is logically and finally completed as the play ends. This is unlike life, where many unrelated actions proceed concurrently and where finality is never assured. But it is more understandable than life, more coherent, and more satisfying to experience.

A third unifying device is singularity of locale — that is, having all the visible action occur in one place. Many actions may be shown and they may be related only by the fact of all of them occurring in the same place. A good instance of this is Vicki Baum's *Grand Hotel*, in which a great diversity of characters and actions occupy about twenty-four hours in many rooms of a large European hostelry. Elmer Rice's *Street Scene* exhibits a similar diversity during the passage of one day on the sidewalk in front of a New York tenement. These two, which first appeared in successive seasons, were followed by a great number of plays localized on transatlantic liners, through trains, passenger planes, and various sorts of hotels. The formality of singular locale is also widely employed as a means of heightening the unity of many dramas already excellent in other respects and as different one from an-other as Jonson's *Alchemist*, Racine's *Phaedra*, and Shaw's *Candida*.

Thinking of singular locale one naturally thinks of Greek tragedy. None of these has been cited here because, of all that survive to us, only one, the *Oresteia* of Aeschylus is a complete work. Each of the others is but one part of a three-part whole. In the *Oresteia*, moreover, the locale does not remain the same throughout.

The last device for heightening unity is the compression of time. In many dramas the action is shown as taking place within successive days, or in one day, or, more rarely, even during a space of time no greater than that actually occupied by the performance. Also, many a dramatist compresses the imagined time of the whole action sequence so that the events which in life would be separated by weeks or months seem to proceed without interruption. This effect of uninterrupted progression, contrary to probability, is called "dramatic time." Shakespeare habitually composes in this fashion. In his *Macbeth*, for instance, the eighteen years' reign seems to pass in a few days, and characters refer to events of years before as if they had happened the night before. In his *Julius Caesar*, Cassius and Brutus meet and quarrel and make up; Brutus passes the night sleeplessly; then, as day breaks, he rallies his forces for a battle which is immediately joined. By sundown he is defeated and in flight. There is no break in the action from sundown to succeeding sundown, although, according to those present, the meeting of Cassius and Brutus takes place many days' march from the battlefield.

This compression of time, whether as literal as Racine's or as free as Shakespeare's, makes the action more lifelike rather than less so, particularly during performance, and the inconsistencies if any are often discoverable only by close study of the script. One reason for this may be that time itself is relative. For in life it moves, not at a steady pace, but swiftly or slowly according to the excitement or ennui of the moment. In retrospect, especially when cause and effect are clearly apparent, successive events seem closer together.

All the devices mentioned above have been known and used since antiquity. During the Renaissance three of the four were codified under the title of "the three unities" of action, place, and time. Many playwrights have employed all of these successfully in a single play. Not all, of course, have achieved great, or even successful, plays in consequence, for the "unities" are only devices for improving the form of a drama. Their use affords no guarantee of quality.

Devices for Increasing Impact

A few of the devices for increasing the impact of a drama are worth noting. These are devices which make the language more vivid or more to the point than the language of everyday life, or which increase the emotional effect of speech. They will be discussed in somewhat greater detail in Chapter 5.

Probably the commonest vivifying device is the composition of interlinked dialogue, or *stichomythia,* as it is called when written in verse.[2] In this a sequence of short speeches is linked together by successive repetitions of phrase or thought. The effect is strongest when the lines are brief and of equal duration. In verse drama the lines usually have each the same number of accentuated syllables, and sometimes they are even further connected by end-riming one with another. This is not the way people speak in life. It is neater, sharper, and more apt. It makes the kind of dialogue one would like to be able to carry on in life, but which one generally thinks of only after the occasion for it has passed.

[2] For an example see page 51.

Another device which increases the vividness of a drama is the inclusion of a speech carefully composed so as to express the principal point or points of view with maximum effect. Nearly every play one can recall contains at least one of these and many of them are masterpieces of expression which retain their values even when separated from the situations to which they apply. Hamlet's soliloquy beginning "To be or not to be" is one of these. Charlie's speech at the end of Miller's *Death of a Salesman* is a good recent example.

An increase in sympathy is often gained by having a character address himself directly to the audience. Clifford Odets uses this with tremendous effect in *Waiting for Lefty,* as does Saroyan in *Hello Out There* and Tennessee Williams in *The Glass Menagerie.* The device is by no means a new one, having been a favorite of dramatists from the days of Roman comedy, but it continues to seem novel whenever it is encountered and to give both freshness and impact to the play in which it occurs.

Devices for Economizing Exposition

The compression of the visible action of a drama into a two or three hours' performance always necessitates the establishment of a certain amount of antecedent action in order that the audience may know at least who the principal characters are and have an idea of what sort of play to expect. Since this material is likely by its nature to lie outside the immediate action sequence and since the giving of it is likely to be more on the order of narrative than drama, the inclination of the author is to accomplish it as economically as possible. Two devices in particular are often employed toward the solution of the problem. One is the use of the *prologue.* The other is the use of a *chorus.* By using a prologue the author is able to tell the audience directly the things it needs to know, and thereafter to proceed with the action of the play. Sometimes the prologue is balanced at the other end of the play with an epilogue by means of which he is able to tell them what they ought to have observed, thereby diminishing the risk that some significant aspect of his subject might be overlooked. Of similar value is the device of the chorus, which supplies necessary information or pertinent comment during the course of the performance. Often its function is expanded to include that of the prologue as well. The most distinct and formal choruses are those in Greek tragedy, occasionally imitated in modern works, as in T. S. Eliot's *Murder in the Cathedral.* The blending of chorus and prologue is effected in *The Glass Menagerie* through Tom's commentary, and in *Our Town* through the Stage Manager's.

Another device for economizing on exposition is the use of *character types.* These are characters who, in appearance, manner, or speech, are readily recognizable either from resemblance to characters frequently seen on the stage or to certain kinds of people common in everyday life. Since they are quickly recognized, the necessity of introducing and explaining them is obviated and the play is able to get under way the sooner. Medieval audiences seem to have been familiar with the type-characters of the Devil, Herod, and many another figure of religious legend. In the last half of the nineteenth century the villain and hero of melodrama were easily identified at the outset so that the dramas in which they figured were able to proceed immediately to the succession of thrilling incidents which comprised the melodramatic play.

Terminal Devices

There remain two more formalities which are frequently seen though difficult to classify. The purpose of each is the same: to bring the action to a satisfying conclusion, giving a sense of completion and finality to the end of the play. One of these is to repeat in the final scene the situation, characters, locale, or lines with which the performance began. The effect of this device is to round out the play as if the action, moving in a circle, had returned to its starting point. It is most useful in a play like Elmer Rice's *Street Scene,* where the action is extremely diffuse, and it supplies an impression of coherence which the action itself often lacks. The other device is to introduce some new and hitherto concealed fact which makes further action unnecessary. Sometimes the information is brought by a new character. Sometimes an unperceived and unanticipated turn of events, plus delayed exposition, brings about an abrupt but satisfying conclusion. This device is usually more effective during the performance than it is in retrospect, and although it may be thrilling at the moment it may afterward seem illogical and contrived. This kind of ending has come to be called the *deus ex machina,* from Euripides' fondness for concluding his plays by the introduction of gods supposedly let down from above by some sort of machinery in order to rescue his mortal characters from predicaments otherwise insoluble.

THE ELEMENTS OF THE COMPOSITION

The elements of a dramatic composition are generally thought of as those parts of the written work which are integral to the whole. The number and kind may vary according to the nature of the composition and to the specifications for performance set down by the dramatist. As many as seven elements may be present in his composition, and as few as three.

The three elements always present are: plot, characterization, and language. These are the basic elements. A fourth, thought, is usually present in some degree, increasing in its importance as the scope and seriousness of the work increases. Two more, music and dance, are one or the other, or both, integral in certain compositions. For example, music is integral in Shakespeare's *Twelfth Night;* both music and dance are integral in his *Tempest.* Design becomes an element of the composition when the author's descriptions condition the visual scheme of the play. It is an element of Shaw's *Candida,* for that work is so composed that visualization according to any scheme other than that which Shaw has specified is all but impossible. It is not an element of any composition of Molière's, for that author describes no visual scheme.

The basic elements of plot, characterization, and language are inseparably related. Although one or another may dominate in a particular play, the dominance is always relative, for all three are essential to any composition ordinarily thought of as dramatic. *Volpone* may be admired particularly for its plot, *The Cherry Orchard* for its characterization, and *The Cocktail Party* for its language, but in each instance the other elements are not only strongly present but closely interwoven in the whole.

The *plot* is the scheme of action. Parenthetically it must be added that "action" is not here thought of as mere physical activity, but as what the characters do. What they do may be to fight, fall in love, make decisions or evade them, voice their secret thoughts, or harangue either other characters or the audience. The plot is the scheme which determines what actions are included in the play and the order in which they follow one another. A given action is included because it is in some way relevant to the whole. It takes place early or late in the play because it is there that it contributes the most to the progression of events and to the necessary impression of cause and effect; were it to occur elsewhere, the progression would be confused instead of clear, and the impression of cause and effect obscured. Plot, then, is the scheme of action which includes

selection, arrangement, and progression of events from the beginning to the end of the play.

Characterization is the dramatist's representation of the people whose lives and actions constitute the play. Real life is only partially human. It also includes the actions of time, natural phenomena, and miracles of Divine intervention. But the dramatist concentrates his mimetic skill on the representation of human beings and shows all other forces of life in terms of their effect upon human beings. Characterization principally shows why individual human beings do what they do. The audience is made acquainted with a character by what he tells them of himself, what another character says of him, by some decision that he makes, or by some physical act which he performs. Certain probabilities of his behavior are thus established. When next this character is confronted with the necessity for action the alternatives are limited.

In its simplest terms, the relationship between plot and characterization may be stated thus: plot is mainly what the characters do; characterization shows *why* they do it. The influence of characterization upon the representation of cause and effect now becomes clear. Two plays employing the same plot may differ greatly in quality according to the quality of the characterization; one may be a shallow and impermanent thriller, the other a profound and enduring masterpiece.

The *language* of the drama is for the most part the expression of the character's decisions, beliefs, and emotions. Sometimes it is the expression of the author's thoughts for which the character functions as mouthpiece. However, in performance the thoughts must be accepted as the character's own, for if the audience becomes aware that the character's expressions are not original and spontaneous the play is less convincing. Some authors, such as Barrie, and Shaw also, spend a good deal of language upon extra-dramatic description of mood, locale, and character. Such descriptions are more on the order of literature than drama, for they are intended primarily for reading. They are integral to the performance only to the extent that they take shape in the design or influence the interpretation.

Language is not to be thought of as distinct from action. The saying that "actions speak louder than words" is inapplicable to the drama, where the opposite is as often true. In our definition of action as what a character does, speech *is* action, for it is one of the things that human beings do which is re-created on the stage. In drama an irrevocable decision is as often expressed in language as in physical activity, and the verbal expression of belief or feeling frequently precedes the physical expression and sometimes supplants it entirely.

Aptness and vividness of language beyond the probabilities of everyday life is characteristic of the greatest drama of every period of theatre history.

From time to time various studies of the art of the drama have inclined to exalt one element or another at the expense of the remaining ones. Such studies have a limited usefulness to the theatre artist — director, actor, or designer — whose greatest effort is always directed toward discovering the true relationship between all the elements of a particular composition. For only upon full understanding of this relationship can intelligent and truthful interpretation be based.

3 | Plot

Kinds of Plots · The Episode
Articulation of Plot · Plot Conflicts
Dilemma · Irony · Suspense and Surprise

In the preceding chapter, *plot* was defined as "the scheme of action which includes the selection, arrangement, and progression of events from the beginning to the end of the play." By this definition the plot also determines where the beginning and end will be in relation to the subject presented. For example, Shakespeare's *King Richard II* and Gordon Daviot's *Richard of Bordeaux* both show the same historical character and many of the same incidents of his reign, but Shakespeare's play begins with the duel between Bolingbroke and Mowbray and ends with Richard's death, while Daviot's play begins many years earlier, in Richard's minority, and ends with his final imprisonment. Here are two plays on the same subject, but with different plots. Similarly, John Drinkwater's *Abraham Lincoln* and Robert Sherwood's *Abe Lincoln in Illinois* show, in the one instance, the principal events of Lincoln's presidency, and, in the other, his pre-presidential development.

KINDS OF PLOTS

There are three kinds of plots: simple; complex; and compound. Aristotle, writing of Greek tragedy in the fourth century before Christ, notes the existence of the first two of these, the simple and the complex. The third kind, the compound, comes into being eight-

een centuries later and is brought to its highest point of development by Shakespeare in England and Lope de Vega in Spain.

The *simple plot* is one which represents a direct progression of events from some acceptable starting point to some predictable conclusion, with no major deviation from expectation. All of the historical plays mentioned above, with the possible exception of *Richard II*, are constructed on this plan. Aristotle cites a Prometheus play, probably Aeschylus' *Prometheus Bound*, as an example of the simple plot from his time. Innumerable others could be cited from more recent drama. Among these would be the English *Everyman*, Marlowe's *Doctor Faustus*, Martínez Sierra's *Cradle Song*, O'Neill's *Emperor Jones*, Romains' *Doctor Knock*, Shaw's *Saint Joan*, and Sidney Howard's *Paths of Glory*.

Simple plots dealing with historical personages and events gain their effect partly from familiarity of the audience with the outcome. The others depend either upon vividness of episode or logic of progression. The best of the simple-plot dramas produce a feeling of inexorable progression toward a predestined conclusion.

The *complex plot* is one in which the outcome is different than the expectation, the progression being complicated by one or more unexpected shifts of direction. The

17

classic example of this is Sophocles' *Oedipus the King,* where the messenger from Corinth, bringing news which promises to dispel Oedipus' fears, instead confirms them. Shakespeare effects some amusing reversals in *A Midsummer Night's Dream* through a magical love charm administered by Puck. At the outset, Hermia loves Lysander and is loved by him and by Demetrius as well. Helena loves Demetrius, but is loved by no one. Puck causes Lysander to fall in love with Helena, so that each of the four loves one who in turn loves another. On the second try, Puck succeeds only in causing Demetrius also to love Helena, and then both youths love the bewildered Helena, leaving Hermia out in the cold. On Puck's third and final try the mix-up is straightened out, and the play ends with the four lovers forming two couples, with Hermia and Lysander as one pair and Helena and Demetrius as the other.

A familiar reversal, brilliantly composed, is the one in the trial scene of *The Merchant of Venice* when Shylock, after having rejected all pleas for mercy, prepares to exact the contractual penalty of a pound of flesh from his debtor, Antonio. At the last instant, when it seems that nothing can save Antonio, Portia points out that the contract allows flesh, but no blood. This puts Shylock in the position of having to collect his penalty without bloodshed, and since this is impossible, Antonio's life is saved. In Gogol's *Inspector-General* a delightful reversal is accomplished by means of a letter which, when read aloud, reveals that all of the officials of the town have been fleeced by an itinerant dandy whom they mistook for an Imperial Inspector they had been expecting. Then, as they fall to blaming each other, their quarrel is interrupted by the appearance of a soldier who announces the arrival of the real Inspector. An original and powerful reversal is effected by Pirandello in his *Henry IV* when a psychiatrist, attempting to shock Henry out of his delusions of grandeur,

instead causes him to commit a crime from which he escapes by retreating into his former delusions.

The complex plot is most satisfying when the various changes in its course are not only different from expectation but also more logical. The effect is better when the changes come rather more toward the end than the beginning of the play. Sometimes a masterly reversal brings the progression to a close. This kind of conclusion is seen in *The Inspector-General,* in *Macbeth,* and in *Tartuffe.*

The *compound plot,* as its name implies, is a combination of two or more progressions of events compounded in such a way as to produce a satisfying whole. Sometimes the different threads of action are distinct throughout the play, achieving totality of effect by the manner in which they balance one another. In other instances, distinct plots are interwoven so closely that a change of course in any, changes the course of all.

The compound plot cannot be distinguished from the simple and complex plots except by the multiplicity of its actions. A compound plot may be composed of two plots, both of which are simple and direct in their progressions, or of two plots both of which are complex, or of two plots one of which is simple and the other of which is complex. When more than two plots are compounded the possible combinations of simple and complex increase accordingly.

Of double-plot compositions, one of the simplest in overall plan is Shakespeare's *The Winter's Tale.* Here the two plots are given in succession. The first one is serious and the second is light. Together they produce a very agreeable balanced whole. In Heywood's *A Woman Killed with Kindness,* two plots are carried forward simultaneously, one of them beginning with a catastrophe but emerging finally to a happy outcome, while the other, beginning happily, ends tragically. In Lope de Vega's *The Sheep Well,* the events leading up to the peasants' revolt are counterpoised by the events leading to the defeat of their oppressor by the King of Castile so that in the end the peasantry come under the protection of the royal victors. The compounding of one plot within another is effected by Maxwell Anderson in his *Joan of Lorraine.* Here a play about Joan of Arc is contained within a plot representing a struggle between actress and director over the interpretation of the role of Joan.

Since unity of effect demands that multiple plots possess either aesthetic or causal relationship, it is often difficult to discern the various plots of a work having three or more of them. This is particularly true when the cause-and-effect progression involves many threads of action, and the better the compounding the more difficult it becomes to distinguish the various plots involved. Shakespeare employs multiple plots frequently, and his works include several of the best compound plots in all literature. One of his best is that in *The Tempest,* where the three plots, of the conspiracy of Antonio and Sebastian against Alonso, of that of Caliban and Stephano against Prospero, and of Prospero's simultaneous purgation of his enemies and betrothal of his daughter, all move forward side by side and are resolved together in one great final scene. A clever, though less elaborate, compounding of plots is achieved by Farquhar in *The Beaux' Stratagem.* Here two romantic plots, one treating the Aimwell-Dorinda love affair and the other presenting the Archer-Mrs. Sullen courtship, are developed along with the Boniface-Gibbet plot and all are resolved together.

THE EPISODE

Since the human organism is capable of perceiving but one thing at a time, every plot, of whatever kind, consists of a *series* of events, or incidents, or episodes. In drama the terms "incident" and "episode" are used synonymously to designate one of the actions in the series of actions comprising the plot. "Episode" is a Greek word originally applied to that part of a drama which advances the plot, as distinguished from that part, usually choral interlude, song, or dance, which does not. "Incident" is from the Latin word for "happening" and is generally thought of as an occurrence forming one part of some larger sequence of events. To illustrate how the events form a series, one might take the hypothetical example of a drama on the subject of the first World War. In the course of a three-hour performance it is manifestly impossible to present all of the happenings of four years and many campaigns, but the assassination of the Archduke Francis Ferdinand at Sarajevo, which precipitated the struggle, might be given as the initial incident, and the decision of the Germans to ask for an armistice as the concluding one. In between, a variety of events might be re-created, such as the unfortunate decision of von Moltke to modify his strategy during the invasion of France, the decision of Joffre to defend Verdun regardless of cost, Wilson's declaration of war, the Czar's abdication, and so on. All these separate happenings would be episodes in the chronological progression of events from Sarajevo to the armistice.

In most compositions the episodes are distinguished one from another by the appearance of new characters or by principal characters leaving the scene or retiring from participation in the action. For example, the first five episodes of *Macbeth* are as follows:

1. Enter the Weird Sisters. They say that a battle is in progress, agree to meet again when it is over, and disappear.
2. Enter Duncan, with his sons and several of his men. They meet a wounded soldier who describes the course of the battle up to its climax, but faints, and is helped away.
3. Enter Ross, bringing the news that Duncan's forces, under the leadership of Macbeth and

Banquo, have won out. Duncan sends Ross to greet Macbeth with a new title, and all leave, rejoicing.

4. Enter the Weird Sisters, to their promised meeting. They weave a spell and then await the coming of Macbeth.

5. Enter Macbeth and Banquo. They see the Sisters, question them, and receive equivocal greetings which disturb both men. But when they attempt to question further, the Sisters vanish.

There is a definite limit to the number of episodes which can be contained in any given plot. This limit is fixed by three factors operating conjointly. They are: (1) the capacity of the mind to perceive and remember; (2) the complexity of the plot; (3) the duration of the performance. Individual members of the audience differ, of course, in the number of episodes which they can assimilate, but if the total number is greater than can be grasped by any significant proportion of the audience, the effect of the performance is seriously weakened. The more complex the plot the harder it becomes to follow the progression of episodes, so that a plot with many deviations in its course is more likely to succeed if the number of its episodes is less than that of some more direct progression. Finally, the two or three hours which embrace the time that one audience can usually be kept in the theatre limits the number of episodes to as many as can be clearly perceived within that time.

ARTICULATION OF PLOT

In the sequence given above, from *Macbeth*, three threads of plot are introduced: the Sisters' spell-casting; the perpetuation of Duncan's dynasty; the relationship of Macbeth and Banquo. The fifth episode brings the first and third threads together, not to be separated again until the very end of the play. Up to the fifth episode, however, the relationship between the various parts of the progression is not yet clear, and it is as much as one can do to identify the characters and discover what they are concerned about at the moment. As the performance continues, its course will become clearer; now it is like a symphony of which only a few notes have been sounded and whose melodic structure is as yet unrevealed.

Were the play to continue with additional episodes and new threads of action without revealing any relationship between them, the most patient audience would eventually lose interest in the proceedings. But since the plot has been laid out according to a prefigured scheme of relationships, the effect of the first five episodes upon later ones will soon become apparent. Looking back, then, one will realize that none of the first five could have been dispensed with, nor could the order in which the episodes have been given be any different and still be as good. For in a plot as well articulated as *Macbeth's*, each episode has its repercussions which affect later episodes. Thus the episodes are linked together to produce a continuous chain of cause and effect.

In a printed playscript the articulation of the plot is most easily discerned by taking first some episode toward the end of the composition and then searching backward for its incidental causes. Except for the opening event, the best individual episodes are often those with the most convincing causes. An episode which has no antecedent — anywhere but at the beginning — is likely to confuse the progression. An episode which has no consequence is superfluous. Sometimes an individual episode may be effective although the causes for it are unconvincing, in which case the plot is said to be poorly articulated.

Very few compositions are perfectly articulated. Even *Oedipus the King* has been criticized on this point, in regard to the episode

PLATE 1. **A University Production of Shaw.** A scene from *Caesar and Cleopatra*, showing adroit use of curtains combined with steps and levels. (*West Virginia University: director, Charles D. Neel; designer, Joe E. Ford; lighting, Clarke Crandall.*)

PLATE 2. **Modern Musicals on the University Stage.** Simple but striking treatments of *Camelot* (above) and *The King and I.* (Above, *University of Hawaii: director, Robert Soller; designer, Diana Martin.* Below, *University of Kansas: director, Lewin Goff; settings, Virgil Godfrey; costumes, Herb Camburn.*)

in which the Corinthian messenger reveals to Oedipus his origin as a foundling. This is criticized on the basis that it is an improbable coincidence that the man who comes from the Corinthian court with the news of the death of Oedipus' foster parents would have been the very same shepherd who rescued the infant Oedipus from exposure so many years before. But this coincidence does not seem as farfetched in performance as it does in the script, and it can in fact only be discovered by the closest scrutiny, so that this criticism is, practically speaking, unjustified. For the ultimate test of a plot is in how it seems to the spectator both during the performance and in recall of the performance, not how it seems when read.

Devices of Articulation

The cause-and-effect chain is not of course the only factor in articulating the episode sequence. Beginning with the Greeks, certain technical devices have been employed to this end, mostly by the authors of intensive single-plot plays, and usually with pronounced success. One of these devices is that which the French call *liaison:* having one or more characters from an episode remain on stage through the succeeding episode, so that all the episodes within each act are linked by characters carried over from episode to episode. This practice can be seen most clearly in the plays of Racine and most of those of Molière and Corneille. It is similar to the general practice of the Greeks in beginning one episode with a character or two who had figured in the episode immediately preceding, of using the leader of the chorus to link episodes, and of keeping the chorus on stage throughout the play.

Another articulatory device — although it may not seem so at first glance — is the division of the play into acts, signified in performance by the emptying of the stage or the closing of the curtain, and sometimes by an intermission. This pause, whether long enough for spectators to stretch their legs or as short as a minute, is comparable to the pause in a symphony which marks the end of a movement. It separates the whole sequence into several distinct parts, making comprehension easier than if the entire sequence were presented as an undivided whole. It also allows the audience time to *add up* the impressions which it has gained so far, and thus improves the funding process.

There are numerous theories as to the proper position of the act divisions in relation to the climactic moments of the play. Most of these theories are difficult to apply to specific performances because of the fact that few theatre workers or critics can be found who will agree as to which particular moments are climactic. Today many a four- or five-act play is performed with but one division instead of three or four without seeming to impair comprehension of the whole. In others, divisions seem to be dictated primarily by the necessities of lowering the curtain or dimming the lights to obscure changes of scenery. Along with this goes the tendency of designers to reduce the interruption to a minimum, and, on occasion, by clever planning of the scene change, to eliminate the interruption entirely. Theory and practice are therefore, in performance, often at odds and sometimes unrelated.

The closing of the act curtain briefly to indicate a lapse of time is a device currently popular among playwrights. This is a device of articulation, but one of rather negative value since it interrupts the progress of the play more often because of the ineptitude of the author than the necessities of the plot. Better playwrights in earlier times, such as Shakespeare, Molière, and Sophocles, have been able to construct plots without such interruptions, and not, as some think, because they lacked act curtains, but because they possessed a skill in plotting which made this device unnecessary.

Variety and Contrast of Episode

It is the practice of most playwrights to vary the successive episodes as greatly as possible in mood, activity, and duration. In some plays this results in episodes sharply contrasted one to another. This is good, for unless the differences between episodes are properly emphasized the progression is in danger of failing to sustain interest. Moreover, after the play has progressed to a certain point the episodes may begin to seem alike, producing a sort of "this-is-where-I-came-in" feeling.

To avoid such an effect, the playwright tends to follow a quiet episode with a lively one, a long episode with a shorter one, and, in mixed drama, a serious episode with a light one. The possible differences in duration, mood, and activity are so numerous that it is seldom necessary to alternate between any given two of these; and this is in fact undesirable, since if the pattern of the progression becomes very apparent the interest of the audience is likely to diminish. Shakespeare's romances generally show a remarkable amount of variation from episode to episode, with those of most delicate mood followed by ones of earthy comedy or bitter conflict, to be followed in turn by music, dance, or legerdemain, with no two episodes in an entire composition being exactly alike in any important respect.

When the differences are as great as this, the variety and contrast continually refreshes interest, as in *The Tempest* where the opening episode of the storm at sea is followed by a quiet scene between Prospero and Miranda. Similarly, in *Julius Caesar*, where a gentle and leisurely exchange between Brutus and Lucius is followed by the hair-raising appearance of Caesar's ghost, and this in turn by a quarrel between the four generals of the opposing armies.

Dramas with choral interludes make the variation of the progression easier because the change in style from episode to chorus and back again provides contrasts which would otherwise have to be developed among the episodes themselves. Evidence of this is seen in *Murder in the Cathedral* and in *The Ascent of F.6*, where choruses intervene between all episodes in the sequence. A similar contrast is gained by the Stage Manager's periodic intervention in *Our Town*.

Shakespeare, like many Elizabethans, employs parallel episodes to telling effect. In some cases the episodes are alike in nearly every respect but the characters involved, but more often the similarities provide the basis for striking contrasts. For example, the episode in *The Tempest* in which Caliban enters carrying a burden of wood is followed by one in which Ferdinand enters similarly laden, affording a strong contrast between the lowest and the noblest creatures presented. Also, the episode in which Sebastian and Antonio plot the death of Alonso is followed immediately by the one in which Caliban and Stephano plan the murder of Prospero. In *Julius Caesar*, the episode in which Portia pleads with Brutus to tell her the cause of his behavior is followed at once by one in which Calpurnia makes a similar plea to Caesar, thus setting off the differences between the two couples. Later in the play the speech of Brutus to the Roman populace is followed by Antony's contrasting speech with its contrasting consequences. In *Macbeth*, Macduff's reception of the news of his wife's death is paralleled by Macbeth's receipt of the news of Lady Macbeth's death, and the reactions of the two men to similar tidings emphasizes the difference in their personalities.

PLOT CONFLICTS

A great deal has been written on the subject of conflict as a factor in dramatic effect.

While it is true that the representation of human conflicts — of belief, of purpose, and of feeling — is capable of employment to greater effect in drama than in any other art, the insistence upon conflict as an essential of drama makes necessary the rejection on the one hand of many masterpieces such as *Everyman* and *Peer Gynt* as "not fundamentally dramatic," and on the other the stretching of the definition of "conflict" to the point that it becomes practically meaningless.

Today the insistence upon conflict, like the insistence upon the three unities in the seventeenth century, is a continual source of trouble to definers. Plays which lack conflict, while acknowledged as masterpieces, can only be cited as exceptions "which prove the rule." This is a patent fallacy. A rule is a statement of fact to which a minimum of exceptions exist. Exceptions do not prove a rule. They disprove it.

Conflict in drama is but one manifestation of the phenomenon of contrast which gives vividness to all artistic creations. In painting the use of opposing lines and contrasting hues produces a more vivid picture. In music the use of contrapuntal themes produces a more varied and more vivid composition But there are still many great paintings in which opposition of neither line nor color is conspicuous, and monophonic compositions in music are capable of quality equal to those in polyphony. One must recognize the limitations of conflict as a factor in drama, therefore, in order to understand its position in relation to the whole work. There are many kinds of conflict possible in drama, and the subtlest of them shade imperceptibly into mere devices for accentuation. The principal ones are the conflicts developed in plotting and those developed in characterization. The plot conflicts will be discussed now; the others will be taken up in the chapter on characterization.

A plot conflict is that sense of struggle which is developed when several lines of action point each toward some outcome which is incompatible with the others. If the indicated outcome of one is to be achieved, the others cannot be. The only alternative is that the conflicting progressions cancel out one another, for if reconciliation is effected the conflict is likely to seem, in retrospect, pointless.

The two principal kinds of plot conflicts are the *direct conflict* and the *sequential conflict*. The direct conflict is seen in the plot in which the purposes of two or more persons or groups are directly opposed. Instances of this are numerous. One of the best is that in Ibsen's *An Enemy of the People* in which Dr. Stockmann's insistence that the pollution of the town's water supply be made known is opposed by his brother's determination either to suppress the Doctor's report or to discredit it. In Maxwell Anderson's *Mary of Scotland*, Mary's objective of unifying her subjects is opposed by Queen Elizabeth, whose safety depends upon her ability to keep the Scots at each others' throats instead of England's. In Calderón's *Mayor of Zalamea* the intention of the Mayor to try a soldier charged with rape is opposed by the Colonel who demands that the soldier be handed over for court-martial. In all of these plots the purposes of two forces are in such direct opposition that the objective of one can be achieved only at the expense of the other.

The sequential conflict is easy to recognize in a play, but somewhat more difficult to describe. Basically it may be described as one purpose overtaking another so that the objective of the first is superseded by that of the second. Jonson employs this kind of conflict several times, notably in *Volpone* and *The Alchemist*. In *Volpone*, Mosca takes advantage of an opportunity to dispossess Volpone while the latter is pursuing the torment of those whom he has deceived. In *The Alchemist*, of the three rogues who have been fleecing their greedy and gullible neighbors, two of them plan in addition to rob their fellow, believing that he cannot prevent them without incriminating himself. In Ibsen's *Hedda Gabler,* Hedda's desire to control Lövborg is overtaken by Judge Brack's determination to possess her. In *The Inspector-General* of Gogol, the purpose of the civic officials to bribe Khlestakov into a good report of them is superseded by Khlestakov's tardy but profitable deception of them. In *A Streetcar Named Desire,* Blanche's attempt to alienate her sister from a plebeian husband is overtaken by the husband's disclosure of Blanche's unsavory past.

Both kinds of conflicts usually demand that the opposition culminate in an episode in which the conflicting purposes are revealed to each other. This episode is often called the "obligatory scene" because, when the conflict is strongly developed, its omission is likely to be disappointing to an audience. When the conflict is direct, this episode can come early or late in the progression, according to the requirements of the plot. In *An Enemy of the People* it is one of the first episodes. In *Mary of Scotland* it is the last. In the sequential conflict the nature of the development is such that this episode cannot usually occur much before the end of the play. It is often the last or next to last, and in any case its completion marks the end of expectation and usually brings the progression finally to a halt.

DILEMMA

The course of the plot seldom moves forward very evenly, nor is it usually intended that it should. Sometimes the progression is checked by a fork in the path along which it is moving. Diverging courses are then presented, only one of which can be pursued. The previous construction of the plot renders a choice of alternatives not only desirable but absolutely inescapable. In addition to

this the choice is likely to be an extremely difficult one, for the alternatives presented are generally either equally attractive or equally repellent. The situation thus posed is familiar to theatregoers everywhere. It is the *dilemma.*[1]

A well-constructed dilemma is capable of producing one of the strongest as well as one of the most typical of dramatic effects. There are several reasons for this. One is that difficult decisions confront every human being many times during his life, with immediate and often awesome personal consequences, so that one not only takes interest in similar difficult choices represented on the stage but also gains, no doubt, a certain pleasure from not having to share the consequences. Another reason is that the dramatic plot can be constructed in such a way as to uncover the dilemma suddenly, achieving considerable impact, and yet hold the outcome in concealment. The novelist, who also constructs dilemmas, not only lacks control over tempo but is powerless to conceal the outcome from any reader who, overexcited by the very skill with which the dilemma has been presented to him, skips pages until he finds the solution. In music the factor of choice between two possible themes cannot be established until each has been partly sounded, so that although the resolution can be concealed the dilemma itself cannot be made much of a surprise.

Dilemma always checks the progression. Sometimes the check is temporary, with dramatic interest heightened by the way in which the choice is presented or prepared for. More rarely, the plot is constructed in

[1] Unequal alternatives do not constitute a dilemma, for there exists in them nothing to impede the progression. Unless, of course, the choice is blind, as with Bassanio in *The Merchant of Venice,* where in his choice of the caskets an attractive alternative is opposed to a very unattractive one, with all means of distinguishing between them carefully masked. In such cases the outcome is a matter of chance, since neither reason nor emotion is capable of shaping the choice.

such a way as to terminate in a dilemma, and the subsequent choice concludes the play. Rarest of all is the dilemma which brings the progression to a complete and final stop, ending the play with the choice unmade.

An instance of the unsolved dilemma is seen in Ibsen's *Ghosts*. With the onset of Oswald's madness, Mrs. Alving is confronted with the necessity of deciding whether to accept the prospect of spending the rest of her life attending the idiocy of the son upon whom all her hopes had rested or to carry out her promise to him to administer the lethal drug. As she hesitates, the final curtain falls. Ibsen's *Hedda Gabler* also ends with an unsolved dilemma when Hedda, forced to choose between yielding to Judge Brack's advances or having her share in Lövborg's death revealed, evades the choice by shooting herself.

Of terminal dilemmas, one of the best is that in Jonson's *Volpone*, where the principal character is confronted with the choice between confession of his chicanery or dispossession of his wealth. He confesses, and throws himself upon the mercy of the court, which promptly strips him of his ill-gotten gains and commits him to life imprisonment. Another good dilemma terminates Galsworthy's *Escape*. Matt, the fugitive convict, is given shelter by a priest who hides him in his sacristy. Presently a constable appears, with several parishioners, in search of Matt. One of them asks the priest directly whether he has seen the convict. As the priest hesitates, Matt is faced with the choice either of escaping at the sacrifice of the priest's integrity or of protecting the priest by giving himself up. He steps out of his hiding place and surrenders, thus ending the chase and bringing the play to a close.

Often the audience is aware of the dilemma long before the characters are, so that interest grows as the inevitable choice approaches. This is the case in Maxwell An-derson's *Winterset*. We know that Miriamne is the sister of Garth Esdras and we know that the exposure of Garth's part in the death of Mio's father is Mio's main purpose in life. When Mio falls in love with Miriamne we know that it is only a matter of time until he discovers whose sister she is and is thus faced with the choice between having his revenge and having her. Somewhat similar is the dilemma posed by Arthur Miller in the first act of *All My Sons*. The father is certain that his eldest son is dead and knows that sooner or later the mother must realize it. But the mother clings to her belief that the son is still alive and will eventually return home, for, as she tells the father, if the son is ever proved dead then it is also true that it was his father who killed him. The audience is shown the dilemma approaching throughout the first act; then, as the mother states her position, the progression is checked and the act curtain falls.

Not all dilemmas are as tragic as those noted above. The dilemma which faces Bob Acres in *The Rivals* is delightful, and it becomes more so as the action progresses. Acres is determined to behave like a gentleman if it kills him. But when he has been egged into challenging his rival to a duel he finds himself faced with a situation in which the only alternatives seem to be either a possibly fatal encounter or the admission of his ungentlemanly cowardice. One of the funniest dilemmas in all drama is the one in *Scapin* in which the miserly father is confronted with the choice between losing his only son or yielding a large sum to ransom him. The loss of the money is fully as painful as the prospect of losing his son, so that the old man can only stamp about and mutter to himself, quite incapable of decisive action.

In comedy it seldom matters whether a dilemma is placed early or late in the progression. It is but one of many situations capable of comic effect, and can be followed by others equally diverting. In serious drama the position of a dilemma is an important factor in its effectiveness, for the closer it is to the end of the play the more effective it is likely to be. Thus, when a series of dilemmas are woven into the plot, the last one is — all other things being equal — usually the best. But if only one dilemma is constructed and that one placed early in the progression, it is easily overshadowed by later events so that it may come to seem in retrospect rather less important than when it occurred. The dilemma in *All My Sons* is of that kind. It makes a gripping first act, but when the play is over one is at a loss to see how it ties in to the conclusion. What has happened is that the dilemma has been used as a device to assist the exposition, with the result that the thrilling first act is achieved at the expense of a less exciting conclusion.

IRONY

Fundamentally, irony consists of action, speech, or character which is better understood by the audience than by the personages involved. The actions and expressions of the characters, prompted by their impulses and beliefs, are witnessed by an audience possessed of knowledge which the characters do not have. The spectator is thus able to foresee mistakes, penetrate pretensions, and apprehend absurdities in the behavior represented on the stage. The result is that the play becomes more meaningful to the spectator than to the creatures whom it concerns.

The use of irony is not peculiar to drama. It is found in every art, literary and pictorial, in which human life is represented. The nature of dramatic irony is such, however, as to make possible a much higher degree of irony than can be achieved through any other medium of expression.

A good example of this is found in Euripides' *Trojan Women.* The play begins with a prologue between Athene and Poseidon in which she draws from him a promise to destroy the victorious Greeks with a storm as soon as their home-bound ships are well out to sea. Throughout the succeeding episodes, as we watch the consequences of the exultant victors' greed and vanity we know that their triumph is to be short-lived. This is dramatic irony at its best.

Sophocles' *Oedipus the King* is often cited as an instance of the masterly use of irony, for the audience sees beyond every action while the characters remain plausibly unaware of the meaning of their actions until the final episode. Oedipus' limp, from which he gets his name, and the fact that his wife is much older than he, are immediately apparent to all as he describes his fear of the prophecy that he should marry his mother and pursues the rumor regarding the crippled royal infant whom the shepherd saved from exposure. Yet the single-mindedness with which he pursues his course prevents him from connecting himself with the evidence which every member of the audience can see.

A most amusing irony is achieved in the court sequence of Jonson's *Volpone.* The righteous judges, intent upon impartial justice, are on the verge of rewarding the wicked and punishing the innocent when a quarrel causes the rogues to denounce each other and reveal the truth. Right is thus finally done, and the judges take the credit, although as far as they were concerned justice is quite accidental. Another delightful irony is developed in *Tartuffe* when Orgon, after having discovered Tartuffe's hypocrisy, finds himself incapable of convincing Madame Pernelle of the truth, having previously convinced her otherwise. We, the audience, know what a rogue Tartuffe is, but Madame Pernelle, having once been persuaded of his piety, clings obstinately to her convictions and refuses to consider the evidence against him.

Plots based upon historical or legendary

events are richest in opportunities for irony, since the audience attends the play already knowing the outcome of the activities represented and is equipped to judge the significance of the action against knowledge of its consequences. Thus, for example, Napoleon's decision to invade Russia is made more dramatic by our knowing of the terrible retreat from Moscow, and Abraham Lincoln's goodbye to his neighbors at Springfield gains poignancy from our knowledge that he will never return alive.

Irony is by no means limited to the plot of a play. Irony of character — seeing through the motives of the individual represented — and irony of speech — utterances having opposite meanings for the audience from those intended by the speaker — are equally common and extremely effective. Both of these will be treated in subsequent chapters.

SUSPENSE AND SURPRISE

Suspense and surprise are both primarily temporal effects, usually dependent upon timing; and this is true as much in performance as in the construction of the plot.

Suspense is developed when a decisive action is delayed or when the space of time between an action and its consequence is protracted. Expectation is thus aroused as a means of increasing interest in the progression, then sustained for as long as the plot and the conditions of performance will permit. When conflict is a feature of the plot, the approach of the obligatory scene is capable of arousing considerable suspense. When a dilemma is created, until the impending choice is made the progression is suspended and interest intensified. When irony is employed there is often considerable suspense pending the characters' realization of the facts which the audience already knows.

Sometimes suspense is aroused in antici-pation of some foreseen event, and the feelings aroused may be those of dread or mere impatience. Both of these are present in the duel scene in *Hamlet,* where, although the outcome is known to practically every spectator, yet the sequence is so cleverly constructed that the resolution is several times postponed, each time to increased suspense.

In *The Imaginary Invalid,* Argan is persuaded to feign death in order to test the affection of his wife. When, being assured of his demise, she begins to rejoice instead of mourn, and to load his name with epithets, we know that he must eventually abandon his ruse and confront her with his living presence. As he postpones this inevitable action our delight increases. O'Neill, often a master of theatrical effect, constructs a sequence of great suspense in *Mourning Becomes Electra* by causing Lavinia to place a box of poison which she has found in her father's deathbed upon his body as it lies in its coffin awaiting burial. Lavinia knows that sooner or later her mother must see the box there and realize that the means of the father's death is known.

There are many plays in which suspense is built up by withholding some revelation the exact nature of which is vague, so that curiosity and fear combine to powerful effect. For example, *The Innocents,* by William Archibald, developed a high degree of suspense of this sort by repeated suggestions of the presence of some incomprehensible and evil power dominating the lives of two children. This building of suspense by implication is common in all kinds of drama, from melodramas as crude as *Dracula* to works as subtle as Maeterlinck's *Death of Tintagiles.* In many cases the moments of suspense are better managed than is the unavoidable revelation. The reason for this is that when a strong appeal is made to the imagination a point is easily reached at which hardly any discovery is likely to be equal dramatically to the possibilities which have been created by the overstimulated imagination of the spectator, so that disappointment inevitably follows the discovery that was intended as a climax. Fear of the unknown is common to all mankind; knowledge, no matter how terrible, can seldom equal that fear in emotional power. Now and then a playwright will avoid this danger by leaving the discovery incomplete. Maeterlinck, in *Tintagiles*, and in other plays in which he invokes this dread of the unknown, wisely avoids completely revealing the source of the suspense.

Like any other surprise, a dramatic surprise is necessarily both unexpected and sudden. But it is also much more besides. The happening which is sudden and unlooked for, while it may be surprising, is not always dramatic; it may be merely startling, and of no further significance. Accidents are often surprising, but they are often undramatic.

A surprise becomes dramatic when, in addition to being sudden and unexpected, it is also relevant to the events which precede and follow it, when it is, in other words, an integral part of the progression. It becomes more dramatic when it occurs at an especially opportune or critical moment in the course of events, as in *Macbeth* when Macbeth proposes a toast to the absent Banquo and Banquo's ghost appears. It becomes most dramatic when it is the opposite of what is expected and is at the same time more logical, as in Corneille's *Cinna* when Augustus, confronting the friends who had sworn to assassinate him, pardons them. One has been led to expect, when Augustus discovered the treachery of the friends whom he had favored, that his punishment would be dreadful. But it is more consistent with the Augustus we have been shown that he would pardon them, and he does so, to our great surprise.

The timing is best when the surprise is accomplished as quickly as the apprehension of the audience will allow. The judgment of this is an important factor in the art of the performer, for each audience varies in its ability to keep up with events.

Plot surprises are generally designed to produce an unexpected turn in the course of events. The discovery of Phaedra's posthumous letter in Euripides' *Hippolytus*, and the burning of Lövborg's manuscript in Ibsen's *Hedda Gabler*, are both good examples of this. Sometimes an unusually well planned surprise effects a complete reversal, as in *All My Sons* when the mother's casual boast that the father has never been sick a day in his life exposes the very secret they had been guarding. Sometimes the surprise consists of a revelation which creates a dilemma, bringing the progression to a suspenseful halt. This happens in the trial scene of *The Merchant of Venice* when Portia calls Shylock's attention to the fact that his bond allows no bloodshed.

Some surprises are achieved by directing the attention of the audience away from some relevant fact and then reintroducing it at a critical moment. This is what Jonson does in *The Alchemist* when he brings back Dapper, who had been concealed in the privy many scenes earlier, and in the interval had been forgotten by both audience and characters. Gogol does the same thing when he has the real Inspector announced at the end of *The Inspector-General*. A similar surprise, but pathetic instead of comical, is effected by Chekhov in *The Cherry Orchard* by having old Firs reappear after the family has left the house. Firs has been out of sight since the previous act and pretty well forgotten; his reappearance comes as a distinct shock, especially when we realize that he is ill and, being locked in the vacant house, will probably die there.

Sometimes an action is repeated in such a way as to create expectation either that it will be the same as the first time or that it will be different, and then the expectation is countered. In *Romeo and Juliet*, having seen one fight between the Montagues and the Capulets which ended without fatalities, we watch Mercutio's facetious challenge to Tybalt expecting another fight of the same kind, but instead Mercutio is killed. In *Doctor Faustus* the impressive conjuration of Mephistophilis is duplicated by a comic scene in which Robin and Rafe, toying with Faustus' magical books, are surprised by the appearance of Mephistophilis. The tone of the second scene is so different from that of the first that nothing indicates that the results will be the same, so that when the devil appears, in a rage at being summoned frivolously, it is both surprising and amusing.

4 | Characterization

Aesthetic Acceptability · Identification
Consistency of Character · Motivation
Revelation · Contrast and Conflict

The whole subject of characterization is an exceedingly complex one because of the intricate relationship between composition and performance. In performance the behavior and speech of the character seem spontaneous. Only a flaw in the writing or acting will permit even momentary recognition of the fact that what the actor is saying and doing has been predetermined by the author. Yet, if the author has created a witty character the actor would hardly care to make him seem otherwise. If the character is composed with the intention of repelling the audience the actor cannot make him attractive without marring the author's work.

One might compare the actor's performance to a building and the author's intention to the plan for that building. Close study of the plan will reveal the kind of structure intended, the complexity of it, its style, and the materials and labor needed for its realization. For the time being the subject of characterization will be dealt with, not in the whole, but in part; in particular the first part: the author's plan.[1]

Certain aspects of character are clear in any dramatic composition. One of these is *aesthetic acceptability* — that is, the extent to which the character is recognizably human, interesting to watch, and presentable

within the limitations of performance, such as the practical limit of two hours, more or less, and the artistic limits of the actor's art. Another aspect is *identification* — the distinguishing of the character as some certain kind of person and as an individual being. A third factor is *consistency* — the way in which the various manifestations of personality, actions and speech, principally, fit together. A fourth factor is *motivation* — the way in which the author has accounted for the character's behavior. Fifth and last is the matter of *revelation*. Character, on the stage as in life, is never static. For one thing, it cannot be comprehended completely at first, but becomes understandable gradually as more and more of it is seen. Also, human character undergoes continual modification under the impact of successive experiences, so that even once it is understood it does not stand still, but sometimes improves and sometimes deteriorates. Beyond all these aspects is the further matter of contrast and balance among the characters represented in the composition.

AESTHETIC ACCEPTABILITY

Beyond the obvious requirements of performability, the first principle of dramatic characterization is *vitality*. The most stageworthy character is not merely as much alive

[1] Characterization from the standpoint of the actor is treated more fully in Chapter 11.

as those around us, but much more so. This vitality is what distinguishes him from the human beings whom we see and hear in daily life and it is what makes him often more interesting than they. The evidence of this is the fact that the most notable creations of dramatic authorship are all creatures of more than ordinary capacities for thought, feeling, and expression. The unbounded imagination of Faustus, the audacity of Scapin, the unscrupulousness of Richard III, the tenacity of Oedipus, the impetuousness of Romeo — these are the primary sources of their fascination for us.

Many great characterizations exhibit striking combinations of impressive qualities. Dr. Stockmann is reckless, impulsive, and stubborn. Bob Acres is impressionable and imaginative to a high degree. Some creations, such as Cleopatra, are so diverse as to exceed the mimetic powers of all but the most gifted performer.

If one were forced to describe the character of Cleopatra in a word, one would probably say that she seems, above all, extremely "feminine," for though her nature is contradictory and changeable yet it possesses an overall consistency which seems describable only by that adjective. Hers is a characterization which is true to life in general. It represents more than one woman of one place and time; in many ways it seems to represent not only a woman, but womankind. This is what is known as a *generalized* character.

Many a great characterization is of this sort. Some are highly convincing, not only as individuals but as the embodiment of qualities common to all men and women, or at least recognizable to all. Marlowe's Faustus is such a one. Hamlet is another. Many a character of Molière's represents the epitome of some widely shared human failing. Creations of this caliber are understandably rare, for they are the products of genius which sees further and understands better

than ordinary mortals can ever hope to do. Through them the ungifted spectator, incapable even of understanding fully the human beings about him, is able to understand the humanity re-created in the drama.

The generalized character is most common in classical tragedy and the best examples of it are still seen there. It is also found in Roman and neoclassical comedy, often admirably conceived and presented.

All human beings possess both general and particular characteristics. The general characteristics are those which the person shares with others of his kind, such as masculinity, which he shares more or less with all men, or youth, which he shares with all of his own age and immaturity. The particular characteristics are those which he does not share, which belong to him only, and which serve to differentiate him from others of the same sex, age, and so on.

At the opposite extreme from the generalized character is the *particularized* character whose principal appeal springs from his individuality. Usually he represents some unusual quality of being, or unusual combination of qualities, and his impulses and habit of mind are quite different from those of others of his kind as well as from those of the other characters in the play. Cyrano de Bergerac is such a character. Dogberry in *Much Ado About Nothing* is another. Bob Acres in *The Rivals* usually strikes one as a unique creature when even moderately well performed.

The particularized character is most commonly encountered in comedy, in extensive drama, and in modern works purporting to give rather literal and detailed representations of life. Gregers Werle and Old Ekdal in *The Wild Duck* are especially good examples of particularized characters. Chekhov's characters are often highly particularized and are as a rule much more interesting as individuals than as representations of general humanity. Bernard Shaw has created a number of particularized characters. The dustman, Doolittle, in *Pygmalion,* is one of the best. The best characterizations of Tennessee Williams are also often particularized to a high degree.

The opposite tendencies of generalization and particularization do not provide categories according to which all characters can be classified. Rather, they should be thought of as extremes which relatively few characterizations fully exemplify, while the majority, although tending usually toward one or the other, lie somewhere along the scale which terminates at the one extreme in generalization and at the other in particularization.

IDENTIFICATION

The fact that the composition must be performed within a space of several hours' time makes it difficult to develop each character fully. This difficulty increases in proportion to the complexity of the plot and the number of characters involved. The author, in consequence, is often inclined to employ characters who represent readily recognizable kinds of human beings. A descriptive phrase or two or a familiar action is all that is needed to make such characters known to the audience. Because they are typical of well-known creatures, they are called *types.*

Types and Stereotypes

The henpecked husband, the lovesick adolescent, the obnoxious child, the gossipy neighbor, the elderly miser, and the blustering bully are all familiar types. Shakespeare's famous "seven ages" speech describes a succession of popular types according to age. Of bad men, there have always been the two favorite types: the "black rogue," immoral and thoroughly evil, and the "golden rogue," amoral but lighthearted and likeable.

Altogether there are probably more of these types than could be named. Many of the best ones appear in drama of every epoch since theatre art began. Others which have been popular in certain countries or particular times have never gained widespread recognition.

A stereotype is a type which has become fixed or conventionalized in its representation through repeated duplication by successive playwrights. It is a copy of a copy, an imitation of a type which has proved especially popular on the stage, and thus more truly an imitation of theatrical character than of life.

Some common stereotypes today are the gruff but kindly old man, the prostitute with a heart of gold, and the clumsy inarticulate lover. From time to time certain groupings of stereotypes appear in play after play. For some years now the hard-boiled sergeant, the green rookie, the soldier from Texas, and the soldier from Brooklyn have been practically indispensable to any play about modern warfare. In movie westerns, the deft sharp-shooting cowboy, his comical side-kick, the cunning persistent villain, and the brave virtuous maiden almost invariably comprise the principal characters.

Stereotypes result from creative effort of a lower order than that which goes into the re-creation of true types. It is always easier to copy the work of some other artist than it is to imitate living creatures. One of the weaknesses of theatre art is its tendency to copy theatrical characters somewhat more readily than character as it exists in life, as if there were no difference between the two. As long as a stereotype is capable of provoking applause and attracting paying customers, many playwrights find it difficult to believe that it is not actually superior to a true creation.

The popularity of a stereotype, fortunately, is usually short-lived, and those which our grandfathers applauded seem ridiculous now, even to the most undiscriminating theatregoer. One reason for this is that as the characteristics which first made it popular on the stage are copied again and again they lose freshness and eventually become tiresome. Another reason is that as the successive copies emphasize the theatrical elements more and more, the character bears less and less relationship to life until it reaches the point where it is no longer sufficiently true to life to be acceptable as representative of humanity.

Description of Character

There are only four ways in which a character can be described to an audience in the theatre. These are: (1) by what other characters in the play say about him; (2) by what he says of himself; (3) by what he does; (4) by his appearance.

In the plays of the Greeks and the Romans one finds nearly every principal character named, usually with some additional information, before he comes upon the stage. Often the character is glimpsed approaching and as those on stage recognize him they name him and ask each other why he comes or wonder what his message or prophecy to them will be. More recent dramas often provide for abundant description of a character before he appears, but the provision is by no means as conventional as in classical drama and the necessity for identifying each principal character is accomplished in a greater variety of ways. Of description prior to appearance, the most famous instance is in Molière's *Tartuffe*, where the first two acts consist mainly of argument as to the sincerity of Tartuffe, with Tartuffe himself not appearing until the play is nearly half over. Sometimes the comment of other characters describes a person who is on the stage at the time so that the audience views the character, as it were, through the eyes of interested observers. Shakespeare does this in *Julius Caesar* when he has Caesar and Antony discuss Cassius, who stands just out

of hearing, in another part of the stage. There is a very amusing scene in *The Imaginary Invalid* in which Dr. Diafoirus proudly describes his son while the boy stands by, beaming.

The simplest form of self-description occurs in the *naive soliloquy* in which a character addresses himself directly to the audience, identifying himself to them, describing his relationship to the other characters, or telling what he is about to do. This kind of soliloquy is common in classical comedy and in the drama of the Orient. It is used frequently in modern drama too, but it is not as conventional today as it was in earlier periods. Recent instances are seen in Thornton Wilder's *Our Town* and Tennessee Williams' *Glass Menagerie*. Shakespeare uses the naive soliloquy often. Autolycus in *Winter's Tale* and Iago in *Othello* afford two good instances from among the many whom he describes by this means. From classical drama one instance will suffice: Poseidon in *The Trojan Women*.[2]

It is a curious fact that what a character tells the audience about himself is usually taken at face value, while the description he gives of himself to other characters is not as likely to be believed by the audience until his actions and the comments of the others support his assertions.

Ben Jonson's principal characters usually describe themselves early in the play. With only a little help from Mosca, Volpone describes himself completely before the initial episode is over. In *The Alchemist*, Sir Epicure Mammon describes himself to Surly by telling what he will do when his investments have made him rich.

We are still thinking, of course, of the initial description of character. There are many instances of characters describing themselves under the pressure of events during some climactic moment of the play, but

---

[2] For further discussion of the soliloquy, see pages 54–55.

these self-revelations usually amount to a good deal more than identification and will therefore be considered in detail farther on.

Since the curiosity and interest of the audience is generally keenest at the time of a character's first appearance, the earliest actions of a character are usually given the greatest weight as evidence of his nature. What follows tends to be interpreted in the light of what was first seen. For this reason the first action of an important character is often the action most significant to his characterization, and, in the hands of a great playwright, carefully composed. Hedda Gabler's first action in deprecating Aunt Julia's bonnet describes Hedda as a person both thoughtless and cruel and gives warning that the effect of her personality upon the other simpler creatures of the household is not likely to be a happy one. King Lear's first action in giving his kingdom to the most vocal of his three daughters casts immediate doubt upon his wisdom. The first action of Iago in arousing Brabantio from bed with a lewd description of his daughter's elopement is highly informative. Thereafter, nothing that is said in praise of Iago is convincing, for what has been seen contradicts the testimony of the other characters.

The significance of a character's external appearance varies inversely in proportion to the worth of the play in which he appears, for the lowest level of drama places the greatest emphasis on externals, while the best drama relies the least on external appearance, especially in characterization. In any case, appearance is more closely related to the design of a production than to its composition.

CONSISTENCY OF CHARACTER

Once a character has been identified to an audience the human need for order and coherence demands that his subsequent actions accord with the idea of the character as initially presented. For a comical character to turn serious or a shallow one to become profound invites confusion. For a noble character to speak facetiously offends one's sense of decorum as well as of consistency.

In this respect drama is different from life. The human being whose actions are consistent with his self-description is rarely encountered in life. Moreover, the opinions of others as to his character vary in reliability according to the knowledge and judgment of the individual observer and may therefore be inconsistent with his nature as experienced at first hand. Also, a person may act in one way at one time and in another way at another time. Except at the most superficial level, inconsistency of behavior in those around us is a continual source of pain. Perhaps this is why inconsistency, though lifelike, is generally unacceptable in drama, for drama is most satisfying when it makes sense of the human behavior which it shows us.

There are two main lines of consistency in drama: consistency of type, and consistency according to the *donnée*. The French word, *donnée*, means "given" — that which is given as the starting point, like the rules of a game. If the *donnée* of a character is comical, his behavior must continue to be amusing, or at least not strikingly otherwise. If his *donnée* is sober and profound, this too must be observed throughout the presentation of him. If a character is presented as stupid and dull-witted, for him to behave with sagacity or make wise observations would violate not only artistic consistency but plausibility. Jeppe in *Jeppe of the Hill* and Christopher Sly in *The Taming of the Shrew* may dress as lords, but they must still behave like louts and not like noblemen, for it is improbable that the assumption of costly clothes would make either of them a superior being. Evidence of this is seen in the familiar Cinderella plot, where the test of the playwright's skill is his ability to make the metamorphosis plausible to his audience. Shaw's *Pygmalion* has such a plot, and actresses complain bitterly about the difficulty of making the Eliza of the last act consistent with that of the first.

Consistency to type is more easily maintained because many of the more familiar types are compounded of contradictory elements, thus allowing a wide latitude of behavior. Cleopatra is both cunning and reckless. Oedipus is persistent and yet beset with doubts. But Cleopatra cannot become manly nor Oedipus cowardly without shocking us, for femininity in the one and courage in the other are basic to the type.

Of course there are some inconsistencies which are not only accepted but applauded because, although they fail to accord with the nature of the character as established, they satisfy deeply rooted wishes or beliefs of the audience as to what *ought* to be. It is not probable that a man as meek as the husband in Noel Coward's *Fumed Oak* would really be as independent as he turns out to be, nor is it probable that after having been bullied by wife and mother-in-law for so many years he would ever be able to speak to them as he finally does. Nevertheless it is delightful to hear him declare his independence because it is something he ought to have done long ago. It is not probable that Edmund in *King Lear* or Iachimo in *Cymbeline* would renounce his villainies and repent his crimes. But a man who has done wrong ought to repent, so that repentance in each case is gladly accepted by the audience.

MOTIVATION

In the life around us we see what people do, but we seldom see why. We see activities which are the results of decisions previously made, but the decisions themselves and the reasons for them are usually no more than partially glimpsed and are often the subjects of wonder and conjecture. Were the human activity we see on the stage no clearer than this, it would be as hard to understand as life itself and probably incapable of holding our interest. But drama is not life. It is a simulation of life in which we see not only the actions of humans but the causes of their behavior. If the behavior is presented without its causes, it seems not to make sense. The presentation then becomes inadequate and the actions shown are thought of as lacking motivation. The more important the action, the more keenly this lack is felt. Unmotivated activity — that is, activity the reason and purpose of which is obscure — is likely to be dismissed as insignificant or rejected as incomplete.

There are two main kinds of motivation: ethical and pathetic; and there are innumerable combinations of the two. *Pathetic motivation* is motivation by means of those factors in human behavior which are involuntary, such as emotion, impulse, instinct, and conditioned response. *Ethical motivation* is motivation by means of those factors which are voluntary, such as reason, will, faith, or belief in some principle. Interesting combinations of the two occur when a character passionately believes in something or when he is influenced in his reasoning by instinct or conditioning.

Ethical motivation is most clearly apparent in the characters inhabiting tragedy and satire. In the great tragedies profound principles of human behavior are often at stake, so that the question of whether the principles according to which a particular character acts are right principles becomes very important. When Creon in Sophocles' *Antigone*, after giving his views on the relationship of the individual to the state, says: "These are my principles, and according to them is the decree which I have made," he reveals himself as an ethically motivated character, and the principles which he has voiced determine his subsequent decisions and are at the same time tested by the consequences of those decisions. In *Death of a Salesman,* Willy Loman states his belief that popularity and wealth bring happiness, and this belief determines his behavior with disastrous consequences to him and his family. Dr. Stockmann in *An Enemy of the People* is motivated by the conviction that truth is stronger than prejudice, a conviction which he maintains although the actions of all his friends contradict it. The psychiatrist in Pirandello's *Henry IV* acts according to his stated belief that once a man knows the true causes of his fears he can thereafter face life with equanimity.

Pathetic motivation tends to be somewhat more vivid and at the same time easier to understand, since it springs from emotions and impulses which are common to all human beings. It has the further advantage of accounting readily for that intensity of feeling which is often thought of as "dramatic." It is not surprising therefore that characters thus motivated are so often the favorites of actors as well as audiences. Human emotion is capable of more effective and more complete communication than are the processes of the mind or will, and it is easier to share emotion than belief. Not all actors have intellects capable of comprehending a Brutus or a Creon, but all have feelings. All members of an audience have feelings which may be appealed to, but not all have minds capable of reasoning clearly or following a logical argument. The ability to feel is native to all; the ability to think is developed by practice, and developed to widely different degrees by different individuals. Medea, Phaedra, Cleopatra, and Juliet have been the favorite roles of innumerable actresses, all being characters of more than ordinary intensity of feeling. Of more recent creations, Hedda Gabler, Anna Christie, and Blanche in *A Streetcar Named Desire* have proved successful in this category. For the men there have always been Cassius in *Julius*

Caesar and Iago in *Othello,* two roles in which the actor rarely fails regardless of the success of the play as a whole.

Othello himself is an instance of compounded ethical and pathetic motivations. Early in the play striking evidence is presented of Othello's ability to control his emotions and to make sound judgments without regard to his personal feelings. Then as his jealousy is aroused, his persistent effort to reason and judge impartially is weakened by his increasing emotional involvement until finally he discovers that he has committed an appalling crime under the belief that he is doing right.

It is in satire, however, that the various combinations of ethical and pathetic motivation are most highly developed. Usually the beliefs of the characters are contradicted by their actions or by the course of events, or their reasoning is transparently false, and this without the characters being aware of the incongruity. A capital instance of this is the Puritan, Tribulation Wholesome, in *The Alchemist,* whose piety is strongly influenced by his greed for money. In *The Rivals,* Bob Acres' faith in dueling as a means of proving himself a devil of a fellow is belied by his lack of courage. In *Doctor Knock,* the Doctor's dedication to the advancement of medical science is controverted by his determination to amass a fortune.

Within the last century certain discoveries relating to man's animal origin have put emphasis on those qualities which cause him to behave like an animal — hunger, sex, fear, and the like — frequently obscuring the more important question of why he behaves like a man. This emphasis has produced a number of extremely interesting and theatrically effective characters, but in plays which seem curiously pointless in comparison with those in which ethical motivation has received more attention. An interesting instance of this is O'Neill's *Mourning Becomes Electra,* in which all of the characters are pathetically motivated, by contrast with Aeschylus' *Oresteia,* in which all the characters are ethically motivated. Interesting, too, is the fact that the O'Neill play ends on a somber note of futility while that of Aeschylus ends in rejoicing. In Maeterlinck's *Pelléas and Mélisande* all of the characters are pathetically motivated, driven by their emotions toward a catastrophe which they can foresee but cannot avoid. In Chekhov's works, both serious and comic, the motivation is almost entirely pathetic. In the Capeks' *Insect Comedy,* life is presented as a matter entirely of instinct and conditioning, no character possessing either control or direction of his activity, and the presentation of various aspects of insect life which resemble those of human beings aims at the conclusion that man is not after all very different from the lowest orders of life.

From this it can be seen that the study of motivation is one of the most interesting aspects of the director's or actor's work. A whole book could be written on the subject. For the time being our only object is to call attention to the importance of motivation and to describe its nature from the point of view of the playwright.

REVELATION

On the stage, as in life, character is never static. One reason for this is that the performance, being a creation in time, can at the outset show only a little of each character as it appears and must of necessity make up the sum of what is known of each, bit by bit, as the play progresses. Each speech and each action adds to the audience's knowledge of the character, so that when the play ends the knowledge is as complete as the whole play requires, or as the author is able to make it. Thus the character is revealed. No character in drama can be comprehended fully and completely in the first instance of its appearance without sacrificing interest in its subsequent actions. For this reason the playwright tends to reveal character gradually so that interest will increase, or at least be sustained, to the end of the play.

In many plays, and in particular in comedies, the successive appearances of a character merely add to what is already known of him or confirm the initial impression which he has created. Often this is crudely done, as in works of inferior quality where, after one has witnessed a few examples, one knows pretty much what will follow. But the process of revelation by simple addition can also be delightful, as in the comedies of Molière, where the characters end up unchanged to all practical purposes by what has happened to them, yet each has behaved throughout so like himself that the action has been a joy to watch.

In life, of course, people do change continually, both in response to various pressures of the world around them and according to ideas which they develop to guide their behavior. Sometimes character improves. Sometimes it disintegrates. But it is never really static. Under extreme pressure or the impact of crisis the change is more marked. Of a person who has survived some terrible experience we often hear it said: "He will never be the same again," and we know this to be true.

It is in serious drama that the revelation of character is most likely to serve the double function of adding to one's knowledge at the same time as it shows and explains some great change in a character. Creon changes from an arrogant man to a humble one as a result of events in *Antigone.* Blanche DuBois in *A Streetcar Named Desire* changes from an insecure and high-strung spinster to a lunatic living in a world of fantasy. Romeo changes from a youth into an adult, and Juliet from a girl into a woman. Othello changes from a confident, moderate man into a creature of impulse torn with doubts. The ability to reveal change in character without sacrifice of consistency has always been one of the marks of genius in playwriting and most especially so when the change is both profound and fully motivated.

No genius is required for the concoction of one or another of two stock changes which have been favorites of audiences since the days of Menander. One of these is the "turning worm" change. The other is the "Cinderella" change. Both, when moderately well contrived, seem to reveal a character "as he really is" though the character revealed is generally quite different from the one seen earlier in the play. Both tend to be effected abruptly, and as closely as possible to the end of the play. The "turning worm" change employs a meek and much-abused character who finally reveals himself as not meek at all but the strongest character of the group shown. This is the kind of change which Noel Coward has employed in *Fumed Oak*, George S. Kaufman in *The Butter and Egg Man*, and Garson Kanin in *Born Yesterday*. The "Cinderella" change is more superficial and consists not so much in change of character but in the withholding by the playwright of certain basic facts about the character's position in society in order to reveal these facts late in the play for surprise effect. The result, though, is usually that of a change in the character as we know it, together with the impression that the character is finally revealed as it really is. What is usually seen here is a character whose family position, occupation, or social status prevents her from enjoying her due recognition for virtue or intelligence until the discovery of certain facts suddenly proves her to be something better, as for example, not a peasant but a princess, not a clerk but an heiress, and so on.

A popular variation of the "Cinderella" plot causes a character to be disguised as another of much higher rank or greater renown. In this guise his true qualities, up to now unrecognized, become apparent. The climax usually occurs when the imposture is revealed. *Kismet* and *If I Were King* and *The Prisoner of Zenda* are romantic versions of this kind of "Cinderella" plot. Versions in which comic effect is gained by a lowly or stupid character being passed off as a noble or an intellectual are Molière's *Doctor in Spite of Himself*, Holberg's *Jeppe of the Hill*, Shaw's *Pygmalion*, and Shakespeare's Induction to *The Taming of the Shrew*.

There are certain changes which occur in life which cannot usually be shown on the stage without violating our need for consistency. A comical character cannot usually turn serious, or a serious character comical, without offending and confusing the audience. A stupid character cannot usually turn intelligent, or an intelligent one stupid. For a good man to turn bad is also much more difficult on the stage than in life, and can be made acceptable only with the greatest skill in motivation; for such a change, though it may be lifelike, conflicts with our idea of what ought to be.

CONTRAST AND CONFLICT

Closely related to the vitality of characterization are the degrees of contrast among the characters presented. The more sharply the characters are contrasted one with another, the more vivid each becomes and the richer the total effect is likely to be. This seems to be equally true of comedy and tragedy and of all styles of drama.

The most readily recognized contrasts are those in which two or more characters, similar in some way, are at the same time strongly differentiated. In classical and neoclassical comedy the frequent pairing of characters provides many such contrasts. In *The Menaechmi* the twin brothers, seemingly identical at first, turn out to be quite distinct persons. In Molière's *Scapin* the two servants, Scapin and Silvestre, are decidedly different, the one clever and deft, and the other stupid and bungling. In *Julius Caesar* we see Brutus, Cassius, Antony, and Octavius, all about as different one from another as human beings can be, yet all are patricians and all are soldiers. In *The Cherry Orchard* there is the landowner Gaev and the landowner Lopakhin, the one impractical and irresponsible and the other shrewd to the core, and in the same play the selfless old servant, Firs, is contrasted with the vain young servant, Yasha.

The commonest contrasts, as one might expect, are developed simply from difference in personality and the things which make up personality, such as intelligence, temperament, and courage. The above are all contrasts of personality, and are to be found in nearly every play.

A more subtle differentiation is seen in contrasts of mood among characters, as when, in *Tartuffe,* at the very moment when Orgon is at the depth of his desperation and chagrin there enters the cheerfully blunt M. Loyal; or in *Romeo and Juliet,* where in one scene we see the just-married Romeo in sober mood, Tybalt malicious and vengeful, and Mercutio more flippant than ever.

Contrasts in character make both characters and play more vivid and hence more readily acceptable. Yet vividness of character contrast is by no means a mark of quality, for it is to be found in drama of all kinds, in the greatest as well as in the most fugitive of potboilers. For of all aspects of the playwriting art, this is the one most easily mastered. Many a play has enjoyed success which has consisted of almost nothing more than the presentation of a number of strikingly contrasted characters. Such plays are naturally popular with actors and often hardly less so with audiences. *You Can't Take It with You* and *The Man Who Came to Dinner* are good examples of this.

Conflict develops when the contrasts are so pronounced that they cannot coexist. As has already been indicated in an earlier chapter, when this occurs there are only two alternatives: one or more of the characters must change or be destroyed. Unless of course some miracle takes place, such as the appearance of a messenger from the King, as in *Tartuffe;* or a benevolent uncle, as in *The School for Scandal;* or the King himself as judge, as in *The Mayor of Zalamea.* Conflict of character is usually rooted in differences of personality, but it often extends beyond such differences into conflicts of purpose and conflicts of motivation.

Conflicts of purpose are comparatively common and can be developed from nothing more than two or more persons intent upon disparate ends, as are Trock and Mio in *Winterset.* Mio is determined to prove that his father died innocent; Trock is determined to prevent the truth of the Romagna case from coming out. Similarly, in a now familiar example, the Colonel in *The Mayor of Zalamea* insists that his soldiers shall not be subject to civil law, while Crespo, the mayor of the village, is determined that the crime of Captain Alvaro be punished.

More profound are conflicts of motivation because they embrace both conflicts of personality and conflicts of purpose, yet go deeper than either into the reasons for the differences. Conflicts of motivation spring, as one might expect, from the two main kinds of motivation. Ethical conflicts develop when the beliefs of characters are opposed. In *All My Sons* the father believes that a man owes first thought to the welfare of his own family while his son believes that the welfare of the community and country in which he lives transcends that of the individual family. The pathetic conflict exists when the emotions or temperaments of characters are in direct opposition, as in *Julius Caesar,* when the four generals meet for a parley on the battlefield and fling recriminations at one another, or in the famous lovers' quarrels in *The White Devil* and *Antony and Cleopatra.*

In addition to ethical and pathetic con-

flicts, there are also many varieties of conflicts developed from opposition of ethical
to pathetic, although this kind of conflict is
generally less clear than that in which the
motivations are similar. In comparing the
three possibilities, one may say that conflicts
of ethical versus ethical are likely to be the
more impressive and the more lasting in
effect, while those of pathetic versus pathetic
are likely to be the more vivid at the moment of performance, and that mixed conflicts may fall anywhere between.

Most conflicts are bilateral, involving two
main characters or lines of opposition. Three-
or four-sided conflicts are less often seen but
are generally richer and more satisfying. An
excellent example of three-sided conflict is
the one in Shaw's *Saint Joan,* where the
ethical motives of Joan, the Bishop, and the
Duke of Warwick are contrasted.

All in all, contrast of character in drama
is closely related to the principle of variety
and contrast which intensifies and enriches
all art, though there are some significant differences in the way this principle operates.
In drama, contrasts are sought for and developed to a far greater degree than in music
or painting. In both of the latter there are
degrees beyond which contrasts cannot be
developed without causing pain to the ear
and the eye. In music, contrasts of sound
emerge as discords and dissonances which
may actually hurt one's ears. In painting,
certain contrasts of color are all but unendurable to the beholder. Comparable limits
seem not to exist in drama where as a rule
the stronger the contrasts — in character at
least — the more truly "dramatic" the result.

5 | Language

Requirements of Dramatic Language
Poetic Language · Prosaic Language
Some Forms of Dramatic Language

The language of the drama is distinguished by the fact that its primary appeal is to the ear. It must be heard to be fully appreciated. In this respect it differs from language of other kinds and other purposes. Printed language, as in a book or on a poster, is seen rather than heard; it appeals primarily to the eye. A well-composed book is pleasant to read. A well-designed poster catches the eye. By contrast, dramatic language is rather more pleasant to hear than to see and is designed to catch the ear. Moreover, it often lingers in the mind's ear, as music does, long after it has been heard.

This is not to say that the language of drama is not also readable, for it often is. But although it must be speakable, it is under no compulsion to be readable. The proof of this is found in the great number of plays whose language in performance is thrilling yet often quite difficult to read. In fact, plays seldom make easy reading, and those that do so are sometimes disappointing in performance. Some plays which do make good reading do so by accident. Shakespeare's language, whether read or heard, is unexcelled, yet we know that he did not intend his plays to be read. He seldom permitted their publication until after they had been performed on the stage, and it is highly improbable that he could have been as careless of their performance as he was of their appearance in print.

THE REQUIREMENTS OF DRAMATIC LANGUAGE

The distinguishing fact of its auditory appeal imposes upon dramatic language two cardinal necessities. The first of these is oral effectiveness. This means that the language must be such as an actor can speak easily and can manipulate to maximum dramatic effect. The second necessity is auditory effectiveness. This means that it must be the kind of language that an audience can really enjoy listening to and can understand without difficulty.

Oral Effectiveness

In order to be effectively spoken, language must recognize the virtues and limitations of the human voice. For example, emotion is expressed in speech mainly by the way in which a speaker utters vowel sounds. In the best dramatic language, therefore, vowels are arranged in such a way as to allow the actor considerable leeway in voicing these sounds, sustaining them when necessary or coloring them with emotion. Good acting speeches seem to be composed with a strong sure feeling for the possibilities afforded the speaker by the arrangement of vowels. Choice of words on the part of the author is thus often as much a matter of sound as of sense, the finest dramatic speeches being unusually felicitous combinations of both.

Certain consonants, if poorly arranged, mar the sound of language. In English the worst of these is the "s" sound, for few persons are able to pronounce it clearly, and when it occurs with any great frequency it gives an unpleasant hissing effect to the speech. It is this quality in everyday English which makes our language sound to the Spaniard or the Italian like the hissing of geese. Another difficult sound is the consonant "r," which looks so much better in print than it sounds when spoken. One difficulty with this sound is caused by the wide regional variations in its pronunciation and another by the fact that its pronunciation is undergoing continual change. For example, the actors for whom Shakespeare wrote uttered their "r"s with a soft roll somewhat as the back-country Irishman does today, so that certain of Shakespeare's speeches must once have sounded much better than they usually do today. Consider what the original effect must have been in Macbeth's famous line:

> This my hand will rather
> The multitudinous seas incarnadine,
> Making the green one red.

For the actor, one of the greatest stumbling blocks in the English language arises where the consonants "t" and "d" are grouped closely together, for to pronounce each such consonant in a series of them not only hampers the flow of speech but also artificializes it, while to omit any of these makes the speech difficult for the listener to follow. Combinations such as "mended deeds" or "entreat to" are hard to pronounce, and although they occur most often in the work of poorer playwrights, no play is entirely free of them.

Probably the most striking difference between spoken and written language lies in the phrasing. In written language, punctuation and length of phrase are related to the reader's comprehension. In spoken language punctuation provides necessary pauses for breathing, principally for the periodic intake of breath. In recent times novels have been written without any punctuation whatever and yet have been quite readable. But speech without punctuation is an impossibility. Length of phrase in spoken language must be such that the basic unity of expression can be conveyed in one breath. If the length exceeds this limit, the speaker must either force his breath and thus weaken his control of the phrase, or else break up the unit with inappropriate breathing pauses. This difference between written and spoken language can be seen by comparing some work written to be read, such as Milton's *Lycidas*, with one written to be spoken, such as Marlowe's *Doctor Faustus*. One discovers that *Lycidas* is not capable of being spoken effectively by any person of normal lung capacity, for its phrases are much longer than can be uttered without pausing for intake of breath. *Doctor Faustus,* by contrast, is surprisingly easy to speak; its phrases appear to be long, but when one speaks them he finds that the necessary pauses are very conveniently placed.

Auditory Effectiveness

The best oral language is composed in such a way that its meaning is readily grasped by the hearer at the same time that his ear is pleased by the sound.

Most of the devices which make language pleasant to hear are based on the repetition of certain sounds according to some distinct pattern. This gives to the language a sense of order which raises it above the level of everyday speech. Two of the commonest devices in dramatic language, both poetic and prosaic, are *alliteration* — the repetition of initial sounds, and *assonance* — the ordered repetition of vowels. Alliteration is heard in the opening lines of Marlowe's *Doctor Faustus:*

Not marching now in fields of Thrasimene,
Where Mars did mate the Carthaginians. . . .

and in the prose of Farquhar's lines:

Sir, I have now in my cellar ten tun of the best ale in Staffordshire; 'tis smooth as oil, sweet as milk, clear as amber, and strong as brandy; and will be fourteen year old the fifth day of next March. . . .[1]

Assonance may consist of a repetition of initial vowel sounds, as in:

. . . if you don't come back stark mad with rapture and impatience — if you don't, egad, I will marry the girl myself.[2]

More often, however, the pattern is composed of similar, but not identical vowels, as in:

Lo! he is fallen, and around great storms and
  the outreaching sea.
Therefore, O man, beware![3]

Alliteration and assonance seem to possess a natural affinity for each other and thus are found more often in combination than separately. Notice, for example, how the alliteration of "b" is combined with the assonance of "o" and "e" in the following speech:

My bounty is as boundless as the sea,
My love as deep; the more I give to thee
The more I have, for both are infinite.[4]

Repetition — by saying the same thing two ways, one after the other — is common in the everyday speech of every tongue, for it is one of the simplest and easiest ways of making meaning clear orally. The more nearly alike the phrases in structure and sound, the easier the meaning is to grasp and the more pleasant it is to hear. In dramatic language, therefore, repetitive balance is often developed to considerable effect. Thus we have in the opening lines of *The Glass Menagerie* Tom's statement: "I have tricks in my pocket — I have tricks up my sleeve," and in the final lines of *Doctor Faustus*, the famous

Cut is the branch that might have grown full
  straight
And burned is Apollo's laurel bough. . . .

A cumulative balance is often achieved by means of a series of phrases of similar construction, and sometimes by repeating phrases of identical length beginning with the same word. Romeo's death speech in the final scene of *Romeo and Juliet* affords examples of both of these:

Eyes, look your last!
Arms, take your last embrace! and, lips, O you
The doors of breath, seal with a righteous kiss
A dateless bargain to engrossing death!
Come, bitter conduct! Come, unsavoury guide!

Sometimes cumulative and repetitive phrases are combined in one speech, consisting of a series of phrases of similar construction framed at beginning and ending by sentences of similar sense. Mrs. Malaprop's famous speech from *The Rivals* (I, ii), on the education of young women, gives an excellent instance of this:

. . . I would by no means wish a daughter of mine to be a progeny of learning; I don't think so much learning becomes a young woman; for instance, I would never let her meddle with Greek, or Hebrew, or algebra, or simony, or fluxions, or paradoxes, or such inflammatory branches of learning — neither would it be necessary for her to handle any of your mathematical, astronomical, diabolical instruments. — But, Sir Anthony, I would send her, at nine years old, to a boarding school, in order to let her learn a little ingenuity and artifice. Then, sir, she should have a supercilious knowledge

---

[1] *The Beaux' Stratagem*, Act I, Scene i.
[2] *The Rivals*, III, i.
[3] *Oedipus the King*, Epilogue. Murray translation.
[4] *Romeo and Juliet*, II, ii, 133.

in accounts; — and as she grew up, I would have her instructed in geometry, that she might know something of the contagious countries; — but above all, Sir Anthony, she should be mistress of orthodoxy, that she might not mis-spell and mis-pronounce words so shamefully as girls usually do. . . .

From the hearer's standpoint, one of the most effective kinds of balanced repetition occurs when the phrases are similar in sound but opposite in sense. This is called *antithesis*. The device is widely used in poetry, though by no means limited to poetic speech. A well-contrived antithesis is rarely heard in everyday speech, for few persons have either the command of language or the quickness of wit to develop an antithesis extemporaneously. The device is especially effective, therefore, in dramatic language. Here is an example from *The Glass Menagerie*, from the same speech quoted above:

I am the opposite of the stage magician. He gives you illusion that has the appearance of truth. I give you truth in the pleasant disguise of illusion.[5]

The languages of various nationalities differ greatly both in general dramatic effectiveness and in the kinds of drama for which they can best be employed. Compared to other languages, English is characterized by its large and rather loose vocabulary. The most commonly used terms in English have in nearly every instance numerous connotations and levels of meaning. The result is a language rich in suggestion and implication and therefore especially effective for imaginative description or the expression of emotion but considerably less exact than some others. In oral English it is quite difficult to be precise in meaning without borrowing terms from some other more exact tongue such as Greek or Latin or French, none of

[5] Acting edition (Dramatists Play Service, 1945), p. 3. Reprinted by permission of Random House, Inc.

which blends well with spoken English and none of which is easy for the ear to grasp. Actors throughout the English-speaking world abhor roles which require them to pronounce phrases from any of these tongues.

A special difficulty in oral English arises from the fact that the language contains a great many words which are identical in sound but quite different in sense, with the result that the hearer can distinguish meaning only by close attention to context. Some of these are "hair" and "hare," "heart" and "hart," "dear" and "deer," "marry," "Mary," and "merry."

POETIC LANGUAGE

Dramatic language at its best always seems to originate with the character who utters it, with the result that the hearer accepts the language as the character's natural way of speaking. Poetic language gives the impression less of a mode of expression than of a character unusually well-spoken; of a character imaginative and emotional, fascinating to listen to and more than ordinarily vivid in his speech. The audience in the theatre, unlike the reader of a book, is generally unable to distinguish poetry from prose by the verbal form in which it is cast. What the audience experiences when it hears poetic language is a richer and more vivid kind of speech, a fuller and more complete expression of a character's thought and feelings. In drama three qualities of language combine to produce this impression of richness. They are: imagery, rhythm, and diction.

Imagery

Vividness of poetic language springs mainly from the images it creates in the mind of the hearer. Often this consists simply in the way in which the speech is contrived. Othello's "Keep up your bright swords, for the dew will rust them" makes the command emphatic, giving it at the same time a touch of disdain and also suggesting the glitter of bared blades. Lady Macbeth's "All the perfumes of Arabia will not sweeten this little hand" suggests a stench of ineluctable persistence. Both of these are, at first hearing, fundamentally simple expressions, but each, though simple, possesses a vividness which causes the line to echo, as it were, in the mind of the hearer. Imagery has a way of extending the simple meaning of a speech like the ripples radiating from a stone dropped into a pond or the overtones of a bell reverberating after the note is struck.

Two of the most characteristic kinds of poetic imagery are *comparison* and *substitution*. Objects are described and ideas are crystallized by relating them to sensations which produce a more intense and more lasting impression than could be produced by plain statement. The relationship is established by comparison with some more vivid or more familiar thing or by substitution of one term for another. All of these comparisons and substitutions are called figures of speech. Together they constitute the bulk of the imagery of language.

Comparison is most clearly recognizable by the presence of terms such as "like," "than," and "as of." The figures of speech employing these terms are called *similes,* from the Greek "to liken." For example, Faustus exclaims to Helen of Troy:

O, thou art fairer than the evening air
Clad in the beauty of a thousand stars . . .[6]

The heart of the sentence is "O, thou art fair." The simile begins with "than." The comparison is between Helen's fairness and the beauty of the starlit evening, and several reverberating images result: the clear twilight; the brilliance of the night in fine weather; the peacefulness of that hour when the day's work is done and the landscape is quiet with the first stars emerging in the sky. In *The Trojan Women,* Hecuba recalls the

[6] *Doctor Faustus,* xiv, 106.

approach of the fleet of the invading Greeks with these words:

O ships. . . . O hurrying beat
Of oars as of crawling feet. . . .[7]

Here the simile marked by "as of" invokes the picture of many-footed beasts, perhaps sea monsters or giant centipedes. At the same time it suggests the regular rhythm of the oar-driven advance of the vengeful enemy. In *Romeo and Juliet* (II, ii, 117), Juliet voices her misgivings by saying:

I have no joy in this contract tonight.
It is too rash, too unadvis'd, too sudden;
Too like the lightning which doth cease to be
Ere one can say 'It lightens.'

Here the expression of foreboding is crystallized by the simile of the lightning, the comparison being set off with "like." The image invoked compounds the impressions of the suddenness, the vividness, and the transience of lightning with the memory of the stunning impact of the lightning flash and the feeling of sultry night charged with impending storm.

The vivifying of an expression by the substitution of one image for another less striking one is called *metaphor.* Comparison is invoked, as in simile, but is as a rule more subtle, tending rather to suggest or imply similarity. The substitution is always made in the direction of greater concreteness. Sometimes it may consist of the substitution of a part for a whole, as in Cleopatra's:

. . . Now no more
The juice of Egypt's grape shall moist this lip.[8]

Sometimes it consists of the substitution of some general idea for some particular object, as when Romeo, placing the slain Paris in the grave, says:

Death, lie thou there, by a dead man interred.[9]

[7] Murray translation, line 122.
[8] *Antony and Cleopatra,* V, ii, 284.
[9] *Romeo and Juliet,* V, iii, 87.

Peculiar also to poetic language is personification — the attributing of qualities of life to abstractions or inanimate objects — as when Marullus asks the Commoners in *Julius Caesar* (I, i, 49):

Have you not made universal shout
That Tiber trembled underneath her banks
To hear the replication of your sounds
Made in her concave shore?

Here the inanimate river Tiber is given the qualities of human fear, trembling at the noise of thousands of voices shouting. Similar is Romeo's description of daybreak:

Night's candles are burnt out and jocund day
Stands tip-toe on the misty mountain-tops.[10]

"Jocund day" pictures the day as merry and, in this instance, as inappropriately and unfeelingly gay, coming to hurry the parting of the lovers.

Rhythm

The recurrence of certain accents, of certain sounds, or of certain inflections establishes the rhythm of spoken language. All speech has some sort of rhythm, but in poetic speech the rhythm is highly developed and usually shaped to support the nature of the speech of which it is a part. In dramatic language the rhythm is not as a rule fixed into a specific pattern but arranged rather to provide the speaker with considerable opportunity to reinforce the emotion and meaning of the language by rhythmic means.

Rhythm may be light and tripping, as it is in the speech of the comic Dromio of Ephesus in *The Comedy of Errors* (I, ii, 43):

Return'd so soon? Rather approach'd too late!
The capon burns, the pig falls on the spit;
The clock hath strucken twelve upon the bell —
My mistress made it one upon my cheek;
She is so hot, because the meat is cold;
The meat is cold because you come not home. . . .

There are many ways of delivering the above

speech and a variety of emphases are possible, but any pattern of emphasis or inflection is bound to produce a light, flippant effect. There is no way of making the speech otherwise without departing wholly from the spirit of the scene. Contrast this with Mephistophilis' invocation in *Doctor Faustus* (ix, 46):

Monarch of hell, under whose black survey
Great potentates do kneel in awful fear,
Upon whose altars thousand souls do lie,
How am I vexed with these villains' charms!

The second speech has much greater sweep and dignity. The cadences are longer, larger, and more impressive. Compare this in turn with the surge and beat of the Herald's speech in *Agamemnon* as he describes the Greek fleet caught in a storm:

Night and the horror of the rising wave
Came o'er us, and the blasts that blow from
    Thrace
Clashed ship with ship, and some with plunging prow
Vanished, as strays by some ill shepherd driven.[11]

Shakespeare's rhythms, especially in the more highly emotional scenes, are remarkably flexible, affording the actor a wide variety of inflections and emphases. Yet the rhythmic possibilities are very pronounced, so that whatever choices are made, the actor speaking the lines is carried along as it were on the flow of the language. The following lines are very close to everyday speech. The language is simple and straightforward; there is no especially poetic imagery. Except for the strong rhythm, it could hardly be called poetic. But what rhythm and what power it has!

You all do know this mantle. I remember
The first time ever Caesar put it on.
'Twas on a summer's evening in his tent,
That day he overcame the Nerveii.
Look, in this place ran Cassius' dagger through.

---

[10] *Romeo and Juliet,* III, v, 9.

[11] Morshead translation, lines 653 ff.

See what a rent the envious Casca made.
Through this the well-beloved Brutus stabb'd;
And as he pluck'd his cursed steel away
Mark how the blood of Caesar follow'd it. . . . [12]

Diction

"The perfection of style," says Aristotle, speaking of language in tragedy, "is to be clear without being mean." [13] That is to say, without being common, or colloquial.

The question of diction in dramatic language is especially acute because of the fact that the language must seem to issue naturally from the character who speaks it. In order to be effective as heard it must seem spontaneous. Yet the very nature of poetic language is such that it goes beyond everyday speech toward a kind of expression which is more highly ordered, more rhythmic, more vivid, and richer in emotion and meaning.

The problem of the dramatic poet is one of finding a mode of expression capable of conveying his meaning without seeming artificial when heard in the mouths of his stage characters. The poet is faced, one might say, with a perpetual dilemma. On the one hand is language which is capable of adequate expression, but which, while it might read well enough, seems affected and strange when spoken. The character uttering it will sound "bookish" and insincere, as if he were quoting some one else rather than voicing his own thoughts and feelings. On the other hand is the language which people speak in everyday life. This language is fully acceptable when heard and it does not call attention to itself. But it is also generally incapable of expressing great thoughts or profound emotions. The poet who employs everyday language will have to do without what would have been his finest speeches and to substitute, as the movies do, "meaningful" silences.

[12] *Julius Caesar*, III, ii, 175.
[13] *Poetics*, XII, Butcher translation.

A popular solution to this problem has always been through recourse to archaic diction — the language of some earlier generation than our own. The archaism may consist of terms now obsolete, of forms of address such as "thee" and "thou," or of idioms no longer current. The use of language of earlier times has a tendency to give dignity to speech, along with a certain remoteness. The dignity springs from the association of such language with certain great works such as the King James Bible and the plays of Shakespeare. The remoteness comes naturally from the fact that it is no longer current.

Therefore if a play deals with characters either of some earlier age or of some strange place, archaic diction becomes acceptable. In a poetic play written today a medieval hero, a modern Chinese peasant, or an African prince can be allowed the use of thee's and thou's and considerable archaic elegance in his speech without any member of the audience feeling that his language is affected or pompous, for the character is remote in time or place from his hearers. A certain remoteness of language thus becomes appropriate.

Archaic diction, however, always faces the hazard that certain expressions may be unfamiliar to the majority of the listeners and therefore ineffectual; the sound of the language may be impressive but the sense may not always be clear enough to register fully.

Many modern playwrights seem to achieve their best poetic language in plays set in earlier times, particularly in Elizabethan or medieval days, for it then becomes possible to resort to archaic speech of a kind already established by writers of acknowledged greatness whose language is familiar to the audience.

The development of poetic language in plays of contemporary setting is much more difficult, for no tradition exists to support the rich coloring of image and sound necessary to full expression. Only a few modern playwrights seem to have succeeded in this. T. S. Eliot has done it several times, and most recently in *The Confidential Clerk*. W. H. Auden and Christopher Isherwood seem to have done it fairly well in *The Ascent of F.6*. It is interesting to compare these works with the less successful attempt of Maxwell Anderson in *Winterset*.

The problem of diction is by no means confined to poetic drama written in English. Much of the best of drama is that which is translated into English from other tongues, and the question is always present as to whether the translation should be made into contemporary English or into archaic English. Those who attempt to translate ancient Greek or Latin plays, for example, into the English of today reason that since the plays were originally written in the language of their own times they should be translated into the language of ours. The result is usually satisfactory when the play concerned is a comedy but is generally less happy when imperial tragedy is the subject, for the essential dignity and grandeur is often lost in the process. More satisfying results in tragedy have generally been achieved when the drama of other times in other tongues has been translated into the somewhat archaic diction which we associate with earlier ages and with our own classics.

PROSAIC LANGUAGE

It is only in comparatively recent times that prose has been employed very effectively or very widely in drama. Earlier dramatists habitually inclined toward colorful language; and although they did not always use verse forms, they did nevertheless tend toward vivid imagery and rhythmic language whether they wrote in verse or in prose. In short, the language of early drama is fundamentally poetic and it is seldom possible to tell from hearing it spoken whether it is written in verse or prose.

Prosaic language imitates everyday speech. In general it avoids highly colored images and pronounced rhythms, aiming rather toward the idiom and the impression of formlessness of the language we hear about us.

The difference between prose and poetry is like the difference between drawing and painting. The beauty of a drawing may be its clarity, as in a steel engraving; or in the way in which a few artful lines suggest so much more than is actually shown, as in a charcoal sketch. Its beauty is peculiar to its nature. It is not the beauty of rich or subtle color, but of clarity; not of fullness and sweep, but of suggestion. The beauty of prose is not that of opulence and depth; it is that of the surface, usually clearly shown, often suggesting, but not showing, depths beneath.

At its best, prosaic language combines a high degree of colloquial impact with a tendency toward implication and understatement. To the extent that it reproduces the more striking idioms of everyday expression it is forceful and convincing. In understatement it is successful to the degree that it succeeds in convincing the hearer that a great deal more could have been said. The little that has been given him causes his mind to go on working, filling in what has not been expressed. From what has been said he imagines what a character must feel, and in the process feels it himself. A good example of this is a scene in *The Three Sisters* between Baron Tusenbach and Irina. The Baron and Irina are to be married on the following day, but the Baron has been challenged to a duel. Irina does not know about the challenge. Now here he is on his way to a duel which will probably end in his death, and he is saying goodbye to her:

Baron: Dear, I'll be back shortly.
Irina: Where are you going?
Baron: I must go into the town, and then . . . to see my comrades.

Irina: That's not true. Nickolay, why are you
so absent-minded today? What hap-
pened yesterday near the theatre?

Baron: I'll be back here in an hour and with you
again. Goodbye my darling. . . . Those
papers of yours you gave me are lying
under the calendar on my table.

Irina: I am coming with you.

Baron: No, no! (He starts to go, quickly, but
when he reaches the gate he stops.) Irina!

Irina: What is it?

Baron: I didn't have any coffee this morning.
Ask them to make me some. (He goes
out quickly.)[14]

There are many different kinds of prose,
according to the character, station, and occupation of the speaker, the subject matter
of the speech, and the general style of the
play. Among these the principal kinds are
three: formal, colloquial, and vernacular.

Formal prose is prose which is grammatically correct and complete as to syntax.
Formal prose is sometimes called "literary
prose" because it more nearly resembles the
language men write than that which they
actually speak. Wrongly used in drama it
sounds false and stilted. But there are many
occasions in which formal prose is more
effective, mainly because it is usually easier
to understand when heard. The complete
sentence gives the listener more leeway in
grasping the meaning at the same time that
grammatical correctness makes misunderstanding less likely.

In plays where ideas are important, the
basic ideas are often expressed in prose more
formal than that of the rest of the play or of
the same character's other lines. Notice the
way in which Tennessee Williams puts the
lines of his interlocutor in *The Glass Menagerie* into rather formal prose, while the
same character's lines in the play proper are

[14] *The Plays of Anton Tchekov* (Modern Library),
p. 177. Reprinted by permission of Random House,
Inc.

considerably less formal. Thornton Wilder
does the same thing with his stage-manager-
chorus in *Our Town.*

Often one character in a play will speak a
prose more formal than the others. Usually
this happens when the one character is meant
to be set off in some way from the others. It
may be because he utters lines of greater significance, as Joan does in Shaw's *Saint Joan.*
Or it may be because he must seem in some
way remote or foreign, like Irene in *Idiot's
Delight.* Foreigners, especially educated
ones, are easily made more convincing when
given language somewhat more formal and
correct than the others. This practice has
the further advantage of avoiding the difficulties encountered in dialects, which may be
equally convincing but are seldom as easy
to understand when heard.

Colloquial prose is the language as actually spoken, barring localisms, slang, and
occupational idioms. Colloquially, a character would say, "I haven't got any," or "I've
got to go," instead of the more correct and
more formal, "I have none," or "I have to
go." Colloquial speech is characterized by
such contractions as "I've" for "I have,"
"don't" for "do not," "can't" for "cannot," and
so on. It is the speech of the character of
our own time and nationality. As such it is
already so familiar to our ears that it needs
no further description here.

Vernacular is the spoken language of some
particular locale, occupation, or social class.
It bears practically no relationship to formal
language, for it is often ungrammatical and
imperfect of syntax. Its effectiveness lies in
its impact. Good vernacular speech more
than makes up in force what it loses in dignity. At its best it is extremely vivid, and in its
idiom it sometimes approaches the imagery
of poetic speech. Some examples may help
to make this clear.

The first example is that of a local vernacular. The play is Lynn Riggs' *Green Grow the*

Lilacs, and the language is that of rural Oklahoma:

Why, my name's Curly. Thought you knowed. Curly McClain. Born on a farm in Kansas. Cowpuncher by trade and by profession. I break broncs, mean 'uns. I bull-dog steers. I ain't never been licked, and I ain't never been shot. Shot *at,* but not *shot.* I got a good disposition, too, and when anything seems like to me it's funny, why I let loose and laugh till my belt breaks in two and my socks fall down.[15]

The second example is of occupational vernacular. Here is the idiom of the sailor, Ruth's father in Ruth Gordon's *Years Ago:*

This Castle Square Company strikes me as a kind of *fresh-water* craft. . . . Next time you try, go after somethin' seaworthy. . . . Somethin' that has a A1 ratin' in Lloyd's. . . . And don't sail from no rivermouth port. Back water ain't good for a sailor and it ain't good for theatrical personages neither.[16]

The third example is the vernacular of class rather more than of locale or occupation. The speech is from the fourth scene of *The Green Pastures.* Cain, a field hand, is telling how Abel happened to get killed:

Lawd, I was minin' my own business and he come monkeyin' aroun' wit' me. I was wukkin' in de field an' he was sittin' in de shade of de tree. He say "Me, I'd be skeered to git out in dis hot sun. I be 'fraid my brains git cooked. Co'se you ain't got no brains so you ain' in no danger." An' so I up and flang de rock. If it miss 'im all right, an' if it hit 'im, all right. Dat's de way I feel.[17]

SOME FORMS OF DRAMATIC LANGUAGE

Aristotle was able to classify and describe the forms of language employed in the

[15] Reading edition (Samuel French, 1931), p. 64. Reprinted by permission of Samuel French, Inc.

[16] (Viking Press, 1947), p. 134. Reprinted by permission of The Viking Press, Inc.

[17] Marc Connelly, *The Green Pastures* (Farrar & Rinehart, 1929), p. 37. Reprinted by permission of Rinehart and Company. Originally published by Farrar & Rinehart, Inc.

tragedy of his time. But between his time and our own the drama has so greatly increased in its variety that such a classification is probably impossible. Moreover, the numerous forms overlap and blend together in such profusion that distinction between them is often hopeless.

For the purposes of this discussion it will suffice to note a few of the outstanding forms of dramatic language. These are all forms of language which achieve their highest development in drama. They are: dialogue, set speech, *bon mot,* soliloquy, and the various embellishments.

Dialogue

The commonest form of dramatic language is dialogue: conversation between two or more persons. The sharpest, most effective dialogue is usually that which takes place between two characters, but dialogue between three or more is capable of greater variety and of being sustained longer. Dialogue involving more than five characters is likely to be somewhat diffuse, for five is generally the largest number that a listener can keep track of without conscious effort. Modern playwrights tend to develop dialogue involving larger numbers of characters than did earlier playwrights. They also employ dialogue for a greater variety of purposes than earlier dramatists.

First, a sample of terse dialogue from Episode I of Clifford Odets' *Waiting for Lefty.* The scene is between a cab driver and his wife. He has just come home from his day's work.

Joe: Where's all the furniture, honey?

Edna: They took it away. No installments paid.

Joe: When?

Edna: Three o'clock.

Joe: They can't do that.

Edna: Can't? They did it.

Joe: Why, the palookas, we paid three-quarters.

Edna: The man said read the contract.

Joe: We must have signed a phoney . . .

Edna: It's a regular contract and you signed it.

Joe: Don't be so sour, Edna . . . (Tries to embrace her.)

Edna: Do it in the movies, Joe — they pay Clark Gable big money for it.[18]

The highest development of dialogue, technically speaking, is linked dialogue, or *stichomythia.* Sophocles seems to have been the first to bring this form to its full development and his practice has been imitated by playwrights ever since. The term is used to describe dialogue in verse in which the lines are of equal length, with a word, a phrase, or an idea repeated in successive speeches in such a way as to form a kind of overlapping or linkage. An example of stichomythia from Sophocles' *Antigone* may help to make this clear. The exchange takes place between Creon, the king, and his son, Haemon.

Haemon: What if I am young? Think not of my youth, but of the worth of what I say.

Creon: Is it worthy to honor a traitor?

Haemon: Certainly not. No one honors a traitor.

Creon: Antigone is guilty of treason.

Haemon: The Thebans, to a man, think otherwise.

Creon: Are my subjects telling me how I should govern?

Haemon: Who is talking like a youth now?

Creon: Am I not to rule as I think best?

Haemon: No country is ruled by one man only.

Creon: Does not the country belong to its monarch?

Haemon: If it does, that monarch rules only a desert.[19]

In the original Greek, these lines are of equal length and identical meter. However, the carry-over of phrase is apparent, and this is the thing which gives stichomythic dialogue its particular effect.

A famous example of linked dialogue marks the first meeting of Romeo and Juliet. Here the lines are not only linked but rimed, and in addition composed in the form of a sonnet:

Romeo: If I profane with my unworthiest hand
This holy shrine, the gentle fine is this:
My lips, two blushing pilgrims ready stand
To smooth that rough touch with a tender kiss.

Juliet: Good pilgrim, you do wrong your hand too much,
Which mannerly devotion shows in this;
For saints have hands that pilgrims' hands do touch,
And palm to palm is holy palmers' kiss.

Romeo: Have not saints lips, and holy palmers too?

Juliet: Ay, pilgrim, lips that they must use in prayer.

Romeo: O, then, dear saint, let lips do what hands do!
They pray; grant thou, lest faith turn to despair.

Juliet: Saints do not move, though grant for prayers' sake.

Romeo: Then move not, while my prayer's effect I take.
Thus from my lips, by thine my sin is purg'd.[20]

Equally clear, but less formal, is the linkage in the dialogue between Constance, Tony, and Mrs. Hardcastle in Act III of *She Stoops to Conquer.* Here the linkage is accomplished by means of one word in each speech which provides the key to the responding speech and also reoccurs in the response. Constance has asked Mrs. Hardcastle to turn over certain heirlooms which the old lady has been keeping for her, and

[18] *Six Plays of Clifford Odets* (Modern Library), pp. 7–8. Reprinted by permission of Random House, Inc.

[19] Episode III, lines 729–739.

[20] *Romeo and Juliet,* I, v, 97 ff.

Mrs. Hardcastle is pretending they are mislaid.

Mrs. H: Don't be alarmed, Constance. If they are lost, I must restore an equivalent. But my son knows they're missing, and not to be found.

Tony: That I can bear witness to. They are missing, and not to be found, I'll take my oath on it.

Mrs. H: You should learn resignation, my dear. See me, how calm I am.

Constance: People are generally calm at the misfortune of others.

Mrs. H: We shall find them. And, in the meantime, you shall make use of my garnets till your jewels are found.

Constance: I detest garnets.

Mrs. H: The most becoming things in the world to set off a clear complexion. You shall have them. I will get them at once. (*Exit.*)

Constance: Was ever anything so provoking — to mislay my own jewels and force me to wear her trumpery!

Tony: Don't be a fool. If she gives you the garnets, take what you can get. The jewels are your own already. I have stolen them out of her bureau drawer, and she does not know it yet.

Linked dialogue is not peculiar to the drama of any particular period or nationality, for it occurs as often in modern as in ancient drama. The principal difference between the two is that in modern drama the lines are less evenly balanced, so that an effect more closely resembling everyday speech is achieved. As an example of this, notice the linkage in the following dialogue from Ibsen's *An Enemy of the People,* between Mrs. Stockmann, Captain Horster, and Billing (Act I):

Mrs. S: Do you expect to set sail soon, Captain Horster?

Captain: I expect to be ready to sail next week.

Mrs. S: I suppose you'll be going to America?

Captain: Yes. America is on our itinerary.

Mrs. S: Then you won't be able to vote in the election.

Captain: Is there an election coming up?

Billing: Didn't you know?

Captain: No. I don't usually have much to do with elections.

Billing: But aren't you interested in local affairs?

Captain: No, I don't know anything about politics.

Billing: Just the same, everybody ought to vote.

Captain: Even if he doesn't know what the voting is all about?

Billing: Doesn't know! What do you mean? A community is like a ship. Every citizen ought to be ready to take command when the situation calls for it.

Captain: That might be all right on shore. It would certainly never do on shipboard.

The Set Speech

The "set speech" is a speech, addressed by one character to another, or to a group, which is set off somewhat from the dialogue by its greater length, more careful composition, and especial appropriateness. The best set speeches crystallize the spirit of the scene or the play in memorable language. It is a rare play that has no set speeches. The best of them provide us with some of the finest moments which the art of the drama affords.

Beyond the fact that the set speech embodies a particularly apt expression of something close to the heart of the play, there is no clear classification of this phenomenon to be made. Some set speeches describe a character with great vividness. Others are narrative in nature, putting before our eyes a picture of an action which is more vivid than if the action had actually been seen by us. Still others occur as invocations, prayers, or apostrophes. Of somewhat similar nature are the speeches delivered as speeches: Antony's funeral oration in *Julius Caesar* and Lincoln's farewell to his neighbors in *Abe Lincoln in Illinois.* Finally there are those set speeches, usually placed close to the end of a play, which summarize the underlying thought or emotion and give to the whole the necessary sense of significance and completeness.

An excellent example of the set speech describing a character is to be found in Act III of Sidney Howard's *The Silver Cord*, near the end of the play. The speaker is Mrs. Phelps, the overpossessive mother. The speech is narrative in form, but before it is complete we have a full-length portrait which shows us very clearly the sort of woman Mrs. Phelps is, and at the same time tells us why.[21]

Of the straight narrative speech we have many splendid examples. Some of the best are those in Greek tragedy, in the Messengers' descriptions of the offstage catastrophe. Those in Euripides' *Hippolytus* and Sophocles' *Oedipus the King* and *Antigone* are particularly fine.

Invocation or apostrophe finds its finest expression, as one might expect, in poetic drama. Witness the speech of Faustus to Helen of Troy, when, at his request, Mephistophilis causes her to appear to Faustus in the flesh, as she appeared in life:

Was this the face that launch'd a thousand ships,
And burnt the topless towers of Ilium?
Sweet Helen, make me immortal with a kiss.
Her lips pluck forth my soul; see where it flies!
Come, Helen, come, give me my soul again.
Here will I dwell, for heaven be in these lips,
And all is dross that is not Helena.
I will be Paris, and for love of thee,
Instead of Troy, shall Wertenberg be sack'd;
And I will combat with weak Menelaus,
And wear thy colors on my plumed crest;
Yea, I will wound Achilles in the heel,
And then return to Helen for a kiss.
O, thou art fairer than the evening air
Clad in the beauty of a thousand stars;
Brighter art thou than flaming Jupiter
When he appear'd to hapless Semele;
More lovely than the monarch of the sky

In wanton Arethusa's azur'd arms;
And none but thou shalt be my paramour.[22]

The summary speech may be an expression of character and feeling such as Cleopatra's "Give me my robe, Put on my crown. I have immortal longings in me." [23] Or it may be a recapitulation such as Essex' in the last scene of Maxwell Anderson's *Elizabeth the Queen:*

If we'd met some other how we might have been happy —
But there's an empire between us! . . .

Sometimes it is a splendid summary of the issues which have formed the action of the play. An instance of this is Ladvenu's speech in the epilogue of Shaw's *Saint Joan:*

At the trial which sent a saint to the stake as a heretic and a sorceress, the truth was told; the law was upheld; mercy was shown beyond all custom; no wrong was done but the final and dreadful wrong of the lying sentence and the pitiless fire. At this inquiry from which I have just come, there was shameless perjury, courtly corruption, calumny of the dead who did their duty according to their lights, cowardly evasion of the issue, testimony made of idle tales that could not impose on a ploughboy. Yet out of this insult to justice, this defamation of the Church, this orgy of lying and foolishness, the truth is set in the noonday sun on the hilltop; the white robe of innocence is cleansed from the smirch of the burning faggots; the holy life is sanctified; the true heart that lived through the flames is consecrated; a great lie is silenced; and a great wrong set right before all men.[24]

The Bon Mot

Bon mot is a French term for an expression which is especially apt, appropriate, true, or all three at once, and which is at the same time terse and pithy.

Of all the language effects in drama, the *bon mot* is often the most delightful. It de-

---

[21] Acting edition (Samuel French, 1926), p. 89.

[22] *Doctor Faustus,* xiv, 93 ff.
[23] *Antony and Cleopatra,* V, ii, 283.
[24] *Nine Plays* (Dodd, Mead, 1946), p. 1133. Reprinted by permission of The Public Trustee and The Society of Authors.

lights both the mind and the ear at the moment that it is heard. It is easily recalled and it is as pleasurable in recall as on its first hearing. It is also highly quotable. Moreover, when one is experiencing a play for a second time the now familiar *bon mot* is heard with increasing pleasure.

There are three main kinds of *bon mots*, according to their construction. These are: aphorisms, epigrams, and rejoinders.

The aphorism is a terse saying embodying some readily recognized truth or established principle. A famous example is Shakespeare's "All is not gold that glitters." Others are Euripides' "A lover once will always love again," and Bulwer-Lytton's "The pen is mightier than the sword." All these are from poetic drama; and, while it is true that poetic drama lends itself more readily to aphorism than prose does, we often find aphorisms in prose drama such as *Death of a Salesman*, when Charlie says, "The only thing you got in this world is what you can sell."

The epigram is similar to the aphorism in that it is also terse and embodies a truth. However, it goes beyond the simple aphorism in that it invokes some antithesis or play on words. In the best epigrams two ideas are set off against each other and the language in which they are expressed is managed in such a way as to sharpen the contrast between them. Such is Oscar Wilde's "A cynic is one who knows the price of everything and the value of nothing." Similar is Clemence Dane's "A woman marries a man expecting to change him, a man marries expecting the woman to remain the same, and both are disappointed."[25] Finally, there is Shakespeare's:

Cowards die many times before their deaths;
The valiant never taste of death but once.[26]

The rejoinder consists of an especially apt or telling reply to some question or statement. The effect may spring from the fact

[25] This line originally was heard in the first production of *A Bill of Divorcement*. It is not in the printed version.
[26] *Julius Caesar*, II, ii, 32.

that the reply is both apt and unexpected, from some subtle irony, or from the way in which it combines answer with aphorism. Both apt and unexpected is Richard's reply to Mowbray in *Richard of Bordeaux* when Mowbray asks, "Richard, is there no one you trust?" Richard answers, "Yes. Four thousand archers paid regularly every Friday." Somewhat similar in effect is the rejoinder which Shaw puts in the mouth of Caesar in his *Caesar and Cleopatra*. Being told that the great library of Alexandria is burning, and with it the memory of mankind, Caesar answers, "A shameful memory. Let it burn." A satiric rejoinder — one of the best — occurs in Molière's *Doctor in Spite of Himself*. The make-believe doctor, feeling for a heartbeat on his patient's right side, is reminded that the heart is on the left. To this he replies in his most impressive bedside manner: "So it was formerly. But now we have changed all that." A rejoinder having somewhat the character of an epigram occurs in Giraudoux' *The Enchanted* when the Supervisor, cautioning Isabel that her interest in the Ghost may endanger her imminent marriage, says, "Your husband may not like to have an invisible friend come between you." To which Isabel answers, "So many invisible things come between a husband and wife — do you think one more will matter?"[27]

The Soliloquy

Soliloquy ("speaking alone") is used in drama to describe a speech which is delivered either when a character is alone on the stage or when, in the presence of other characters, his speech is not addressed to them and is usually not heard by them. In drama of the last century or so, soliloquies are often given as if the character were thinking aloud. In earlier drama soliloquies generally provide for direct communication between the character and the audience.

Any soliloquy is likely to be primarily one

[27] (New York: Random House, 1950), p. 71. Reprinted by permission of Random House, Inc.

or another of two kinds according to whether its principal purpose is the communication of fact or the description of thought and feeling. The first of these, the soliloquy whose primary purpose is to put the audience in possession of facts relevant to the plot or to characters other than the speaker, is called the *naive soliloquy*. An example of this is Brush's soliloquy in Plautus' *Menaechmi* telling how he lost track of Menaechmus I (III, i):

Here I am over thirty years old, but I never got into a worse mess than I did today. I pushed into the middle of the assembly like a darn fool and while I was watching the goings-on, Menaechmus slipped away from me. . . .

Another is Trinculo's first speech from Shakespeare's *The Tempest* (II, ii, 18):

Here's neither bush nor shrub to bear off any weather at all, another storm brewing. I hear it sing i' th' wind. Yond same black cloud, yond huge one, looks like a foul bombard that would shed his liquor. If it should thunder as it did before, I know not where to hide my head. . . .

Early drama, especially comedy, contains innumerable naive soliloquies. In later drama they become less common as the playwrights devise less obvious means of conveying necessary information to the audience.

The second kind, the soliloquy whose primary purpose is the description of thought or feeling, is called the *sophisticated soliloquy*, for it is capable of much higher development than the soliloquy which merely gives information. The best known and most quoted soliloquies are practically all of this kind: Hamlet's "To be or not to be . . ."; Hecuba's "Up from the earth, O weary head . . ."; Macbeth's "If it were done when 'tis done, then 'twere well/ It were done quickly . . ."; and many others. The greatest of the sophisticated soliloquies occur in tragedy and are expressions of profound thought or feeling.

Writers of realistic drama in the generation following Ibsen eschewed the soliloquy on the ground that it was not lifelike, but neither they nor any others have ever found a means of conveying a character's thought and emotion with comparable dramatic effect.

Embellishments: Malapropisms and Puns

Embellishments include all those uses of the language which lend brilliance to the scene or which set off some character and yet are in no way essential to either. These include odd or amusing expressions, clever distortions of phrases, and plays upon words.

One of the most delightful forms of embellishment is the *malapropism,* so called from the name of a character in *The Rivals*, Mrs. Malaprop. An example of the malapropism is Dogberry's "Is the whole dissembly appeared?" in *Much Ado About Nothing*. In this the substitution of "dissembly" for "assembly" produces a sentence whose meaning is the exact opposite of that which Dogberry intends. The comic effect is ironic because the audience recognizes the misuse of the word while Dogberry does not. At another point in the play Dogberry exclaims, "Comparisons are odorous," meaning "odious" of course. Mrs. Malaprop's own misuse of the language is justly famous, as when she cautions her maid: "If you ever betray what you are entrusted with, you forfeit my malevolence forever, and your being a simpleton shall be no excuse for your locality," or when she promotes her ward's marriage plans, saying to Sir Anthony, "I hope you will represent her to the captain as an object not altogether illegible."

The commonest embellishments of all are *puns*. These are so well known that it is scarcely necessary here to describe them. There was a time, in the infancy of our language, when the endless possibilities for punning afforded by the many instances of words with similar sound but opposite meaning intrigued both playwrights and audiences. That time is now long past. Today puns seem to annoy audiences more readily than they amuse them and are for that reason generally avoided.

6 | Thought

The Nature of Thought in the Drama
The Channels through which Thought is
Expressed

The nature of drama as a simulation of life makes the thought content of a play a matter of considerable importance. How important the thought is depends upon how serious the play is. In farce the thought is inconsequential, for the view of life in a farce is flippant; in tragedy the quality of the thought — according to the view of life intended — is of first importance. But in both farce and tragedy the human activity which the author re-creates must be re-created according to *some* idea of what life is or ought to be, and it must provide some acceptable explanation for the behavior of the characters represented.

THE NATURE OF THOUGHT IN THE DRAMA

Most serious dramas are marked by the presence of some pervading idea or "theme," and it is according to this idea of life that the action is developed and the characters motivated. In Aeschylus' trilogy, the *Oresteia*, the pervading thought concerns the nature of justice, divine and human. In answer to the question "what is justice?" there is unfolded a chain of events illustrating the idea that justice is a community, not an individual, responsibility, and that if enduring justice is ever to be achieved the wronged persons may neither judge nor punish. In sharp contrast to this stands the theme of Sartre's *The Flies,* which represents the same events as the *Oresteia.* In *The Flies* the thought is that life is as it seems only. Standards of justice are seen as mere creations of the individual man's mind, existing only in his mind. According to this view, man is responsible to nothing but his own conscience, which provides a more dependable guide for his behavior than the time-honored customs of the community. A third treatment of the same story, O'Neill's *Mourning Becomes Electra,* takes a still different view of the very same series of events and makes no attempt to cope with any question of justice or right. Instead, man is represented as the victim of subconscious impulses over which he has no control. Since he is not a free creature, he is not responsible for his actions and cannot be judged.

In most serious drama viewpoints are necessary on both moral and ethical questions. A particular work may be concerned more with one than the other, but the two are at one and the same time both distinct and also inseparable.

The *moral viewpoint* is that which concerns the individual human being whose actions are shown and explained to the audience. His actions are usually explained in terms of his own ideas of what is brave or cowardly, generous or selfish, and right or wrong. In Eliot's *Murder in the Cathedral* the morality

56

of martyrdom is explained and the two sides of it are shown, the one side being that of the martyr, Thomas à Becket, and the other being that of his murderers. Both give their reasons for their actions and the reasons are compared and contrasted. In Galsworthy's *Escape* the responsibility of an individual for payment for a crime he has committed is shown and the question of what right he has to expect help and sympathy from others is explored and answered.

The *ethical viewpoint* concerns the relation of people to each other and to the community in which they exist. Questions are raised such as those concerning loyalty, duty to family, duty to country, humanitarianism in the treatment of the weak or the under-privileged, and the responsibility of a ruler or leader to those who follow him. There are many different ethical codes. The military code, for example, involves obedience, exact execution of orders, the treatment of enemy wounded, and many other questions not prominent in any civilian ethical code. Business ethics involve fair value, fair competition, and the truthful representation of goods for sale. The professional ethics of the doctor and the lawyer involve secrecy in regard to a client's affairs and impose strict conditions governing the acceptance and rejection of cases. No two ethical codes are wholly compatible. The many conflicts between the various codes under which man functions provide some of the greatest material for serious drama. In Arthur Miller's *All My Sons* there is a conflict between a man's duty to his family and his duty to his country. In this play the father believes that his family comes first, but his son insists that his duty to his country is more important. In *Billy Budd* military ethics are placed in conflict with the humane ethics of civilian life, and a good man is hanged for striking an officer who had wronged him severely. In Galsworthy's *Justice* the ethics of legal procedure are questioned by showing a case in which

they produce the opposite of the effect for which they were intended.

The importance of the author's thought is greater the more serious his work. It is especially important in tragedy because actions of profound consequence demand explanation. One must know why. Also, most tragedies show human suffering, physical or mental, or both. In life, suffering is something which all human beings experience and which most of them learn sooner or later to endure. But the *representation* of suffering is unendurable to us unless we know its causes and understand its purpose. The suffering which we witness on the stage must not be pointless. It may be justified by a great and noble purpose which makes it worth while, it may be deserved because of some previous evil-doing, or it may be compensated for eventually by comparable happiness. But it must in any case add up to something. Merely to represent life with accuracy is not enough in serious drama. For the work to be satisfying it must give not only a faithful representation of life but one which makes sense to those who see it.

This is almost as true of satire as it is of tragedy. Satire represents the failings of human beings — their selfishness, their cowardice, their greed, and their vanities. Because it represents common aspects of human behavior specifically as failings, these failings must be portrayed in relation to some idea of what *ought* to be. Not many men are brave, but all agree that a man ought to be brave. Not all men are honest, but all believe that a man ought to be honest, and honesty is everywhere admired and respected. Not many of us are truly generous in our treatment of others; most are selfish. But a man ought to be unselfish. It is against such universally accepted standards of what ought to be that the actions of ordinary human beings are measured in satiric drama. When they fall short of the standard the action is both amusing and instructive. To achieve such effect the standard itself must above all be perfectly clear.

The necessity for re-creating human activity according to some clear standard of behavior explains why the number of truly great dramas is not larger. The ability to understand life is rare. The ability to understand it and also re-create it vividly according to that understanding is one of the distinctions of genius. Many a play has been composed which was both serious and profound and yet missed greatness because its author was either unable to comprehend or incapable of explaining the activity which he re-created. John Webster, a contemporary of Shakespeare whose tragedies are generally regarded as second only to Shakespeare's own, falls short on this score. His plots are gripping, his characters interesting, and his language extraordinarily vivid. Yet his plays fail to satisfy because his characters seem to suffer and die to no purpose. Webster himself seems pessimistic. He seems to believe that love is fugitive, loyalty the pose of sycophants, and honor a delusion of the simpleminded. As a result, the life he represents is pointless. It is full of feverish activity of no significance.

In our own day, Eugene O'Neill often approached greatness in his dramas and yet missed, in part because of his inability to make sense of the activity he represents. In various works he attempted various explanations as if searching for some standard against which to measure his characters and their actions, but he never succeeded in finding one which fully satisfied.

Thought has less weight in the lower forms of drama, such as farce, fantasy, tragicomedy, and melodrama. In these the emphasis tends to shift from thought to action, thrills, and sentiment. Moral and ethical questions are evaded or ignored and thought content reduced to well-phrased, easily remembered sayings which aim to simplify rather than clarify whatever issues are present. The re-sult is a presentation which delights and entertains at the moment it is being experienced but which leaves no one pondering its significance after the performance is over.

THE CHANNELS THROUGH WHICH THOUGHT IS EXPRESSED

The author's thought is evident in four aspects of his work: plotting, characterization, language, and the use of symbols. One can study any one of these and glimpse the thought behind it. In his *plotting* his thought appears in the way he represents cause and effect. In substance he is saying: "Such and such causes produce such and such effects," and he then proceeds to demonstrate his point. Assuming that the activity he shows us is in itself interesting, if his explanation of it is plausible, we leave the theatre satisfied. In his *Death of a Salesman* Arthur Miller shows us a man at the point of realizing that his life is a failure and beginning to wonder what has gone wrong. Then through a series of flash backs he shows us the causes of the failure. Presently his explanation becomes clear: Willy Loman had put his faith in the wrong values. That Willy's values are widely believed in also becomes clear, leaving us with the troubling thought that many of our acquaintances may be heading for the same end as Willy has now reached.

In Ben Jonson's *Volpone* Mosca's final attempt to cheat his master results in the exposure of his own and Volpone's deception as well as that of the would-be heirs. The exposure comes about by accident at the very moment that the court is about to acquit Mosca of all the charges against him. The representation of cause and effect in this instance reveals several themes. One is that greed and malice ultimately reveal themselves and the other is that justice owes as much to accident as to intent.

The second channel through which

thought is expressed is *characterization*. Everyone forms, from experience and observation, his own ideas of what man is, what kinds of men there are, how men respond to stress, and what things affect them most strongly. Like everyone else, dramatists differ widely in their experience and observation of character and in the degree to which they are influenced by the prevalent thought of their times. Yet each must portray the various characters which he shows us according to some idea of what man is and how he functions. It is not surprising, therefore, that the underlying thought in this respect should vary greatly and yield many interesting contrasts.

Pirandello, for example, presents character as something which exists principally in the opinion of others. A man is what others think he is. He is honest only to the extent that others believe him so. He is a hero only if generally accepted as such. If all others believe him insane, why, then he must be, and no matter how vigorously he asserts his reason he can only be laughed at if no others are convinced of his sanity.

This is the exact opposite of the thought of Molière, to whom man is what he is, no matter what others may take him for. To Molière the fact that a man is respected in no way alters the fact that he may be both a fool and a fraud. Nor does his integrity prevent him from being taken for a fool when the situation is reversed. Molière goes further than this. He shows again and again that man does not change; nothing improves his basic nature; he is capable of learning neither from his own experience nor from the advice of others; the mistakes which he makes he is certain to repeat. Molière's old men are different from his young men principally in being more set in their ways; they are clearly no wiser.

The thought of Sophocles is still different. He believes that man's character is shaped according to his power of self-determination, independent of the opinions of others, moderated to avoid extremes, and tempered to complete control of impulse and emotion. He believes that man is capable of wisdom but that wisdom is achieved only through suffering, for each man in his own way.

Shakespeare's thought seems to be that man's nature is determined primarily by his birth and upbringing — the better these are the greater his capacity for growth. He also believes that man is capable of great change under stress, that there is always a right and a wrong choice available so that when a man chooses right his character improves and when he chooses wrong his character deteriorates accordingly.

Many playwrights think of man as a creature not possessing control of his own character nor capable of resisting exterior influences, thus being the unwilling victim of instinct and environment. Eugene O'Neill shows his characters as such victims, sometimes of instinct as in *The Emperor Jones,* sometimes of emotion as in *Mourning Becomes Electra,* and sometimes of environment as in *Anna Christie* and *Beyond the Horizon.*

The thought value in characterization can usually be determined by asking several questions. The first is: Is mankind represented as being, in general, self-determined, with each character shaped according to its own ideas? If one asks this question of the characters of Sophocles the answer is usually "yes." If one asks it of the characters in Arthur Miller's plays, the answer is again usually "yes." If one asks it of the characters in *Mourning Becomes Electra* or *Strange Interlude,* the answer is definitely "no," for the characters in both plays are shaped by their impulses and emotions. The second question is: Is mankind represented as capable of actual change — either improvement or deterioration — of character? The results of this question will be interesting because there will be almost no correspondence between them and the "yes" and "no" answers to the first question, not over any large number of plays at least. The third question is the most interesting of all: What and how many kinds of men are represented? Some playwrights are capable of representing only small and petty creatures, some only great spirits. The best playwrights, of course, often reveal an astonishing range of characterization, showing extremes of meanness and magnanimity in the characters of a single play.

Hardly less important to the thought of the playwright in regard to character is the thought of the actor. Even a great play cannot achieve its true greatness on the stage unless the actor shares the author's understanding of human nature. This helps to explain why *Oedipus* and *Macbeth,* both masterpieces in characterization, in performance so seldom equal our expectations. Oedipus is a high-principled character and as such is often beyond the comprehension of an actor who has no strong principles of his own. Macbeth is a man with an extremely sensitive conscience; an actor without conscience often lacks the means of understanding him. In contrast, immoral and unscrupulous characters are generally performed with considerable success because their basic qualities are within the comprehension of everyone. Everyone is familiar with such qualities as deception, cowardice, greed, and ambition because they are things which every man feels at some time or other. Iago, Tartuffe, Richard III, Cassius, and Medea are as a result seldom performed without success. Even though the play as a whole may fail, these characters seem certain to fascinate audiences no matter who impersonates them.

Characters of high moral and ethical perception, on the other hand, frequently fail to come to life. As performed on the stage such characters often seem colder, less human, and less interesting than in the script. A convincing Brutus is as rare as a convincing Cassius is common. Othello is seldom as fascinating as Iago is. Cordelia in *King Lear*, Hermione in *The Winter's Tale*, and Celia in *Volpone* all tend to be less interesting in performance than in reading. That this is in large part due to the inadequate understanding of the performer seems a logical conclusion.

The third channel of thought is *language*. Although action is often considered the essence of dramatic art as distinct from other arts, the final mark of quality in drama is vivid verbal expression. Thought of profound or complex nature is not expressible with comparable effect by any means other than language. It is not surprising therefore that in the greatest drama the thought which is expressed first through the channels of plot and characterization is always crystallized ultimately in the language.

There are usually a number of places in such a play where the thought of the author comes through with especial clarity. One of these is the prologue. When the chorus of *Romeo and Juliet* first mentions the "star-crossed lovers" we begin to know how the author views the action which he is about to present and also how we as the audience should see it. When the prologue of *The Alchemist* speaks of showing us the vices of the time for our instruction and delight we learn two things: that the author views his characters as vicious and that he intends us to learn to avoid their example.

The epilogue, or the final lines of the play when there is no epilogue, often sum up the author's thought or the characters and actions which he has shown us. A good example of this is the last sentence of Sophocles' *Antigone* in which a restatement of the famous Solonic maxim ("Wisdom through suffering") states the significance of the tragedy which we have witnessed: "The boasts of proud men are punished with great affliction; thus man in old age through suffering finally gains wisdom."

In plays employing a chorus — *The Glass Menagerie, Our Town,* Drinkwater's *Abraham Lincoln, Murder in the Cathedral,* most Greek plays — the thought of the author is often quite clearly stated and the significance of the main action of the play pointed out and explained. In most cases the choruses also expand the significance of the action shown, giving a larger meaning than it would otherwise convey.

The aphorisms or *sententiae* in a play when studied as a whole sometimes reveal the author's thought with surprising clarity. During performance these trenchant lines impress us singly; often it is not until one has gone back to the script and compared them and aligned them in sequence that one realizes that they form a cumulative pattern clearly designed to impress certain ideas on the audience. One good example of this can be seen in *Romeo and Juliet* by taking only a few of the many *sententiae* of that play in the order in which they occur. The first is slipped in between the ecstatic lines of the balcony scene, already quoted:

. . . I have no joy in this contract tonight.
It is too rash, too unadvis'd, too sudden;
Too like the lightning, which doth cease to be
Ere one can say "It lightens." [1]

The next is in Friar Laurence's reply to Romeo's haste: "Wisely and slow. They stumble that run fast." [2] A third comes a few scenes later with the Friar's:

These violent delights have violent ends
And in their triumph die, like fire and powder,
Which, as they kiss, consume.[3]

Far less explicit but often more powerful in the expression of thought is the imagery which pervades the language of a play, arousing in the hearer a wealth of significant association. The two *sententiae* just quoted from *Romeo and Juliet* — similes evoking

images of lightning and the explosion of gunpowder — are but two of a series of similar images recurring throughout the play and closely related to the explosion and violent and deadly action which is represented. In *Macbeth* a curious thread of imagery is woven into the language of the play from beginning to end, all of it having to do with clothing, fabric, and the fit of clothing. The total impression which results from this is that of a man trying to wear robes that are not his and which fit him poorly. In Marlowe's *Doctor Faustus* the predominant imagery is astronomical, being developed around the stars, their constellations and movements, meteors, and comets. The cumulative effect of these is to suggest to the mind the image of the night skies, in all their vastness and beauty. In *Oedipus* the various figures of speech relating to blindness add up to the amazing total of eightyeight, sixty of them coming before Oedipus blinds himself and twenty-eight afterward. The idea of blindness is never absent for long.

The fourth channel of thought is *symbolism.* A symbol is a material object which represents something immaterial. In drama it may be some object featured in the action in such a way as to suggest certain meanings or emotional states not actually shown or described, or it may be some object referred to repeatedly until eventually it acquires special significance for the audience. Occasionally, though rarely, the symbol is developed from some sound or smell.

The best modern drama is replete with symbols employed to powerful effect. One of the best of these is Eilert Lövborg's manuscript in *Hedda Gabler.* Hedda, Thea, and Lövborg himself refer to it as his and Thea's "child." One of the greatest scenes in modern theatre occurs when Hedda destroys this manuscript, saying as she does so: "I am burning your child, Thea! Burning it, curlylocks! Your child and Eilert Lövborg's!" An-

---

[1] II, ii, 117.   [2] II, iii, 94.
[3] II, vi, 9.

other is the orphanage in *Ghosts,* which Mrs. Alving has built with the intention of making up in this way for her husband's wrongdoing. During the dedication ceremony it catches fire and is destroyed. At the same time she discovers that her son is the victim of an incurable disease inherited from his father. One could go on through the entire canon of Ibsen's plays and describe symbol after symbol of similar effectiveness, for few of his works are without them.

Many a play takes its title from some object employed for symbolic effect: Chekhov's *The Sea Gull* and *The Cherry Orchard;* Maeterlinck's *The Blue Bird;* Tennessee Williams' *The Glass Menagerie, A Streetcar Named Desire, The Rose Tattoo,* and *Camino Real.* These are only a few titles from a vast list.

Chekhov, whose plays in performance produce an almost perfect impression of unordered and actualistic representation of life, employs some of the most effective symbolism yet achieved. One of these is the sound of the breaking harp string in *The Cherry Orchard.* The final occurrence of it at the very end of the play is extremely moving.

Symbolism provides a channel through which the dramatist is able to infer and suggest meanings not communicable through any other aspect of his art. In some ways it can be compared to the metaphor in language or to the dominant imagery in a poetic play. But in many other ways it goes far beyond either of these in the peculiarly

dramatic power which it is capable of generating. The metaphor creates an instant of insight with gradually widening repercussions. The dominant image creates an overtone which pervades the play and gains significance as one recalls it afterward. But symbolism at its best, as with the manuscript in *Hedda Gabler* or the harp string in *The Cherry Orchard,* culminates in a moment of highly theatrical impact and gives to each member of the audience a vivid and hairraising glimpse of forces in life which are generally sensed, often feared, and vaguely understood.

One interesting thing about symbolism is that although it is found in drama of all ages and nationalities, it reaches its highest development in the most realistic drama of recent times. Perhaps earlier dramatists, writing poetically with a wealth of poetic devices with which to express their thoughts, felt no need for symbols, or if they did, found them already available in metaphor. Perhaps modern dramatists, composing in prose shaped to the less expressive nature of everyday discourse, found symbolism the only means of extending their meanings beyond the limitations of their self-confining idiom. In any case, as things stand at present, the most effective symbolism still exists in the most prosaic drama. That which has been employed in modern poetic drama has not as a rule been as successful and has often seemed to create a good deal more smoke than light.

7 | Drama and Audience

*Immediate Effect · Levels of Perception
and Effect · Aftereffects · Changes in Effect
Five Tests of Quality*

With drama the ultimate test of quality is its effect in performance. Great drama is drama of great effectiveness; it provokes thought, arouses laughter, or stirs the emotions to an extraordinary degree. As the performance takes shape moment by moment it calls forth a perceptible response from its audience which becomes increasingly definite as the play progresses. As this response develops, a reciprocity is established between performer and audience which enhances the whole experience for all involved: audience, actor, and playwright, too, if he be alive and present.

Among theatre people there is a saying that the audience is the better half of the play. What they mean by this is that the drama is at its best when its performance is supported by a responsive audience. Everyone who works in the theatre certainly knows how the same play can achieve at one time, with a sensitive audience, an inspired and brilliant performance, while at another time, with a dull audience, it falls woefully short of the brilliance which all know to be potential in it. The ideal audience is a rare phenomenon. When it occurs, actors immediately recognize it and reach heights of artistry seldom achieved otherwise. The dramatist watching his work performed at such a time sees nuances of thought and feeling which he had not known were possible,

and his creation, like a child coming of age, acquires an independent life of its own. It is his creation, but at the same time it is much more than his. With a poor audience, one which does not listen closely, one which is restless, one which is sluggish in response, the actor labors under a tremendous burden and ends the evening exhausted without the feeling of having accomplished much. The dramatist at the same time rails at the audience as a collection of dullards, and if his work fails, he blames its failure on the inability of the audience to recognize the true value of his creation.

There are dramas, acknowledged masterpieces, which cannot endure any but an inspired performance. Only from that rare combination of perfect performance and perfect audience does inspiration arise. The competent, the imaginative, the knowing performance is not quite enough. Only competence plus imagination plus knowledge plus the inspiration of an ideal audience is capable of bringing forth a performance as great as one knows it ought to be. When such a performance is achieved, the drama in question is not only as good as one expected and hoped for but incomparably better. Dramas which require such inspired performance are the cause of many notable failures but also, on occasion, of those rare triumphs of dramatic art which seem to beggar all de-

63

scription. *The Cherry Orchard* is such a drama. Racine's *Phaedra* is another.

When one has experienced one great performance of a great play the memory of it becomes a thing to treasure; one gains great pleasure from discussing the play with others or from describing its performance. Reading it can never be the same, for the page is alive with the memory of the emotion and thoughts which the performance aroused.

A great play is not a simple thing, nor is the experience of it simple or easy to analyze. Drama is the most complex of all the arts and its effect upon us is many-sided. In order to discuss it in terms of effect it is necessary to separate one effect from another, to study them one by one, and then to reassemble the various effects into some sort of order. The logical first step is to describe what happens during performance.

IMMEDIATE EFFECT

Like the musical composition, the dramatic composition is capable of being realized fully only in performance. In order to be properly understood and appreciated, it must be perceived in motion as it unfolds moment by moment. What the spectator perceives must be perceived on the instant. In the best drama, this instantaneous perception is marked by three qualities, all peculiarly dramatic: intensity, impact, and funding. Intensity of perception renders the action clearer, more vivid, and more memorable than any comparable occurrence in life. Perception is intensified when a play arouses acute emotion or increases understanding to an extraordinary degree. Impact in drama is the quality of being forceful, striking, or startling. Perception is greatly heightened by the suddenness with which an action occurs or by the force with which an idea is driven home. Funding is the cumulative effect which develops as perception is added to perception.

Intensity of Perception

Dramatic intensity is one of the qualities which raises the performance-experience above everyday life. One experiences the simulated life of the drama with greatly increased perceptions of almost unlimited variety. There is the intense pleasure generated during the famous table scene in *Tartuffe* as Elmire's plan of unmasking Tartuffe by allowing him an opportunity to seduce her gets out of hand and as her husband, whom she has hidden within hearing, expecting him to interrupt, fails to emerge from his hiding place. The pleasure in this instance is intensified by the suspense generated by Orgon's delayed emergence together with the absurdity of his wife's predicament. There is the intense excitement of the duel in *Hamlet* as the contest is protracted when the score is tied and it begins to look as if Hamlet might win after all over both Laertes' poisoned foil and the King's poisoned cup. There is the intense dread in Maeterlinck's *Death of Tintagiles*, created by fearful references to the hideous unseen queen and the certainty that something terrible is about to happen to the young prince. There is the intense sympathy for Hecuba in *The Trojan Women* as she takes in her arms the body of the dead Astyanax, her last grandchild, executed at the orders of the triumphant Greeks. There is the intense pain one suffers upon witnessing Creon's horrible retribution in *Antigone*. And there is the intense delight which one enjoys upon experiencing the balcony scene in *Romeo and Juliet* with its splendid representation of perfect lovers, perfect in their expression of their love.

Impact

Impact in drama is force and suddenness combined in one action to powerful effect. The climax of the trial scene in *The Merchant of Venice* is so contrived as to achieve, in any even moderately good performance, a tremendous impact, for, when every stratagem and delay seems to have failed, Portia suddenly reveals the flaw in the deed and stops Shylock from carrying out his revenge. The banquet scene in *The Tempest* builds to a powerful climax when, after music, dance, and spectacle, as Alonso's men begin to eat, the banquet vanishes in a clap of thunder and Ariel confronts them in the guise of an avenging harpy. Impact is the essence of the great scene in Sophocles' *Electra* in which Aegisthus, having been brought the supposed corpse of his enemy, triumphantly whips off the covering, only to discover that the murdered victim is not his enemy but his wife. In *The Glass Menagerie* Tom's symbolic smashing of the glass as he hurls himself from the house is overwhelming. All of these are instances of moments of greatly heightened perception achieved in each case by means of a single forceful device. The main devices for increasing impact have already been discussed in the first chapter of this section.

Funding

The performance-experience consists of a series of perceptions, added one to another as the performance progresses, culminating in a total impression of the whole. This cumulative process is called "funding." It is basic to the experience of both drama and music.

In its earlier moments the performance is perceived in the form of details only, interesting in themselves perhaps, but as yet without significance. As the play progresses, the earlier perceptions have greater and greater effects upon later ones. Thus the performance-experience as it develops becomes gradually richer and more significant.

Event by event and perception by perception the total experience is built up. Connections between events come to light. Cause and consequence become related. The vari-

ous threads binding the whole together begin to be apparent. By the time the conclusion is reached the total organization of the work ought to be clear.

The experience is satisfying in the degree to which the successive perceptions "add up" to produce a sense of completeness. If one misses some important point along the way, the conclusion is likely to be unsatisfactory. If the author has omitted or muddled some essential point or the performers failed to make all points clear, these omissions and failures cause a faulty funding, with consequent dissatisfaction to the audience.

LEVELS OF PERCEPTION AND EFFECT

Every audience is composed of individuals representing many different levels of perception. These levels can be differentiated according to age, education, intellect, emotional sensitivity, and experience both of life and of dramatic art. The person of keen intellect grasps many meanings not noticed by the person of average mentality. The person of more than ordinary emotional sensitivity experiences a higher degree of pleasure and pain than the average member of the audience. Middle-aged and elderly persons may be profoundly moved by dramas which to teen-agers are no more than superficially thrilling, or they may be profoundly bored by works which their offspring regard as epoch-making. The better-educated members of the audience are more likely to understand references to particular persons or places, to history, mythology, medicine, law, and economics. They are also more likely to understand phrases in French or German which may have been introduced into the dialogue. The person possessing a wide firsthand experience of life is likely to be more critical of inferior drama and more appreciative of great drama, although he may have no way of distinguishing in advance of the performance between the one and the other. Of all these, the habitual theatregoer is likely to be the most appreciative of the artistry of the performer and to be able to recognize most readily the performance of unusual brilliance.

Many plays are written and performed for the benefit of some rather distinct level of perception. To cite an extreme example, children's theatre plays are intended to reach only the level of children of some particular age bracket. *Goldilocks and the Three Bears,* amusing and exciting though it is to children between four and seven years, is often tedious to eighth-graders and unendurable to teen-agers. *Treasure Island,* on the other hand, which eighth-graders enjoy, is by turns unintelligible and unbearably exciting to younger children.

The plays of Racine, like those of most of the serious dramatists of his generation in France, are generally comprehensible only to persons of highly cultivated and rather specialized tastes in drama. Persons whose intellect, education, and experience of drama fall short of the requirement often find Racine's best works quite unappealing. A similar situation prevails in regard to the many great comedies of the Restoration. To habitual theatregoers and especially to the older and more urbane among them, a great many of the Restoration comedies are delightful. To many others they may seem frothy and inconsequential. Pirandello's plays, compounded as they are of enigmas and paradoxes, demand such intellectual agility on the part of their audiences as to make them capable of enjoyment by comparatively few persons. To others they seem only confusing, fatiguing, and eventually boring — a lot of to-do about nothing. Some of the best recent English playwrights appeal mainly to individuals possessing considerable education — one might almost say to the "educated" class, if such a class exists. Among these playwrights are many of the most highly esteemed composers of social, moral, and ethical "problem" plays: Shaw, Galsworthy, Maugham, and Eliot.

Beyond these, there is still another group of works appealing mainly to habitual theatregoers — plays whose greatest appeal is to a certain specialized perception which has been sharpened by continual theatre attendance and consequent familiarity with prominent theatre personages. Most of these plays are about theatre people. One of the most recent is *Light Up the Sky.* Before that there was Ruth Gordon's *The Leading Lady,* Kaufman and Ferber's *The Royal Family,* Kaufman's *The Butter and Egg Man,* Sheridan's *The Critic,* and Beaumont and Fletcher's *The Knight of the Burning Pestle.*

Certain species of drama tend to register their best effects at certain levels of perception. Comedies of wit, for example, are generally enjoyed most by persons of rather quick apprehension and better-than-average education. The best satires, also, seem capable of full appreciation only by persons of considerable maturity and experience of life. Others may occasionally enjoy them, but not usually to the same degree, for many of their most delightful nuances are likely to be over the heads of the younger and less experienced members of the audience. The knowledge that a play can be good and at the same time out of the reach of its audience affords many a playwright considerable consolation, especially when his work seems unappreciated, for then he can rationalize his failure with the belief that he wrote the right play but attracted the wrong audience for it.

Actually, the fact that a particular play appeals mainly to some particular level of perception bears no consistent relation to its quality as a work of art, for among the many works of specialized appeal are found some of the world's worst as well as the world's greatest dramas. If the appeal is to the least discriminating members of its audience it is likely to be a poor work. If the appeal is to the most mature and the most discriminating it may be quite narrow and the play still be a very great one.

Great breadth of appeal, on the other hand, is one of the most reliable earmarks of greatness. The play which registers at many different levels of perception simultaneously is a rare achievement. Most of Shakespeare's plays do this. *Macbeth,* for example, is as thrilling to teen-agers as it is moving to adults. It possesses a great deal more significance, of course, for the adult than it does for the youth, and it means more to the person with wide experience both of life and of drama. But the most interesting thing about it is that it affects all levels of perception strongly according to the full capacities of each. What is true of Shakespeare is equally true of Molière. *The Imaginary Invalid* and *Scapin* delight the young and the uneducated as much as they do the oldster with several college degrees.

AFTEREFFECTS

A play seldom ends when the performance is concluded. Like a piece of music, it lives on for some time in the memory of the spectator. If it has been a good play and well performed, it may live thus for many years. The more intense the pleasure during the performance and the greater the impact, the more vivid the memory is likely to be. The richer the work and the more meanings it possesses, the longer this memory is likely to persist.

In some ways the memory of a play is like an echo, or perhaps the sound of a bell. A large bell has not one but several sounds. The first sound is caused by the clapper striking the lip of the bell. This is followed by the reverberation of the sound from lip to lip inside the bell. While this is taking place, the vibration of the outer rim of the bell spreads a different tone, and this is followed in turn by a third sound caused by

the vibration of the narrow upper part of the bell. Eventually these various sounds blend together, and the reverberation continues for some seconds, then gradually decreases in volume. Eventually the sound becomes inaudible, although it is quite difficult to say at what moment it actually ceases to exist. If the bell is a very fine one, the reverberations seem to linger in the air for a long time after the stroke of the clapper. The aftereffects of a play are very much like these lingering reverberations. They do not occur all at once, but one after another, with each seeming to give rise to the following one and to blend with it. In drama these aftereffects are of three kinds: first, afterimages of sight and sound; second, the reflections on the meaning of the actions seen and heard; and finally, the comparison of these afterimages and thoughts with those aroused by other plays in any way comparable.

Afterimages

The most vivid afterimages are usually those created by certain high points in a play when the action is momentarily arrested, and they remain in the mind like pictures: the shocking image of the "blood-bolter'd Banquo" confronting Macbeth; the brilliant entrance of the victorious Fortinbras and his officers into the corpse-strewn hall in *Hamlet;* the disclosure of the murdered Clytemnestra in Sophocles' *Electra;* the revelation of Helen of Troy in *Doctor Faustus;* the picture of Jeppe in *Jeppe of the Hill,* suspended from the gallows and believing himself dead; the spectacle of the absurd two-headed "beast" formed by Caliban and Trinculo in *The Tempest* when they try to conceal themselves under Caliban's skimpy cloak.

Images of movements or actions tend to be somewhat less easily remembered, but they seem also to be capable of arousing more emotion when recalled, probably because they generally occur in the memory as part of some continuum which at the time aroused sympathy or delight: the expression on Tartuffe's face when he realizes that it is not Elmire but her husband whom he holds in his affectionate embrace; Rageneau's description of the duel in *Cyrano de Bergerac,* illustrated with a spit from the fireplace, the half-roasted fowl sliding back and forth as he flourishes the supposed weapon; Caesar's long movement across the stage, as he staggers away from the conspirators who have attacked him toward the shelter of his friend Brutus, not knowing that Brutus stands ready to deal him the final fatal thrust; Horace's painful climb up the stairs in *The Little Foxes;* Laura blowing out the candles one by one at the end of *The Glass Menagerie.*

Sound images seem to be less generally retained, perhaps because most individuals possess relatively weaker memories for auditory than for visual sensations. On occasion, however, auditory sensations can be extremely persistent, even though one may not be able to recall the exact sound or melody. One of these is the tom-tom beat which accompanies the action of *The Emperor Jones.* Another is the "memory" music in *The Glass Menagerie.* The sound of the breaking harp string in *The Cherry Orchard* may haunt some members of the audience for months after the performance.

It is interesting to note that the sound of spoken phrases is not usually very accurately remembered. Now and then one may remember a particularly good phrase or epigram or riming couplet, but more often one remembers the meaning of a phrase more clearly than the exact words or the inflection given the words by the actor.

Does one recall one's emotions? Is there any distinct afterimage of fear, pity, or joy? Probably not. What happens more likely is that one retains an afterimage of the sound or sight or movement which aroused the original emotion — the stimulus, in other words — and upon recalling this, one experiences somewhat the same emotion as was caused by the original stimulus.

Reflection

After experiencing a performance, especially the performance of a drama which one has enjoyed more than usual, he tends to continue for some time afterward recalling its high points and reflecting on its meanings. This same reflection also occurs after reading a play, but not as a rule to anything like the same degree. Reflecting on the meanings of a play one has seen is often a pleasure; reflecting on the meanings of a play one has merely read is by comparison more often a chore. This is because in the latter instance one lacks material for that vivid image-recall which makes reflection pleasant and easy.

There is some difference between the intellectual aftereffects of comedy and those of tragedy. In comedy one views the action with a degree of detachment which makes possible immediate delightful recognition of the absurdities, inconsistencies, and ironies of the action witnessed. The pleasure of reflection is principally a matter of recalling the incidents which caused delight, and, by recalling them, also reliving the pleasure of the moment.

Tragedy, together with serious drama of all kinds, generally produces two effects, one after the other — an immediate effect and an aftereffect of somewhat different nature. In serious drama one is usually emotionally involved in the more important actions of the play. One experiences fear or sorrow or pity along with the characters, and while he may grasp the general significance of the experience at this time, many of the meanings do not become clear until after the performance is over. The deeper the emotion one feels during the performance the less likely he is to be actively thinking while it is going on. The thought comes later. For it is well known that emotions and intellect do not function simultaneously. Man's nature is such that it is quite impossible for him to think clearly while in the grip of strong feeling.

The most interesting thing about serious

drama, therefore, is not merely the intensity of the emotions which it arouses but the amount of thought it provokes after the performance is over. One finds oneself then wondering what the outcome might have been if things had been only a little different: if Friar Laurence's letter to Mantua had been delivered; if, in *A Streetcar Named Desire*, Stanley had not prevented Blanche from marrying Mitch; if, in *The Cherry Orchard*, Lopakhin had been able to bring himself to propose to Varya. After seeing *The Glass Menagerie* one is haunted with the thought of what will become of Amanda and Laura without Tom to support them, for it is impossible to imagine either as being able to shift for herself. Similarly, after the final curtain of *A Doll's House* one wonders how Nora will manage without husband or home and whether she will be able to remain away from her children forever. Such afterthoughts continue after the performance is over as if the play had been an actual happening and not at all a thing which the performers enact every evening, and it is perhaps one of the best tributes to the quality of a work that one should think of it in this fashion.

This extension of the action beyond that witnessed on the stage is the commonest intellectual aftereffect. It is not the only one, however.

Thinking over the performance one often finds himself searching for additional reasons for the behavior witnessed. In *Hedda Gabler*, for example, as one reflects on the character of Hedda a surprising number of motives become apparent which may have passed unnoticed at the time, and as a result a more complete Hedda gradually emerges. Sometimes this search ends in a paradox. What has been seen cannot be explained, yet in its very inexplicability it seems remarkably true to life. Such a paradox emerges from one's contemplation of the character of Cleopatra in Shakespeare's *Antony and Cleopatra;* one cannot be sure where her sincerity leaves off

and her deception begins, and this very uncertainty makes her seem all the more feminine and lifelike.

Sometimes in reflecting on the performance, one discovers additional explanations for what he has seen, or is able to add up the reasons given in such a way as to make the whole play more comprehensible. In *An Enemy of the People*, Dr. Stockmann's errors of judgment become more apparent the more one thinks about them. In *Antigone*, Creon's inability to temper his principles to the demands of the immediate situation becomes increasingly tragic in retrospect.

Frequently reflection reveals parallels and ironies which may have escaped notice in the performance. During the performance of *Hamlet* one may view Hamlet, Laertes, and Fortinbras simply as young men each of whom is pursuing his own course. But afterward one may reflect on the similarities between them in that each is intent upon avenging a wrong done his father. Then striking differences become apparent, for Hamlet is seeking a legitimate means of righting his wrong, while Laertes seizes the first opportunity without regard for fairness or justice. Fortinbras, on the other hand, creates his own opportunities regardless of cost or difficulty. In Somerset Maugham's *The Circle* one comes gradually to realize how very much Elizabeth's elopement resembles Kitty's, how ineffectual has been the example of the older couple in preventing Elizabeth from making the same mistake, and how likely it is that in twenty years Elizabeth and Teddy will be what Kitty and Hughey are now.

Comparison

The final aftereffect of a good performance is the inevitable comparison of it with other performances of similar plays, or possibly even with other performances of the same play. In the first instance the comparison reveals differences in quality between the various compositions. In the second instance it brings to light differences in the quality of acting, staging, and design. In each case there must be some foundation for the comparison in the likenesses of subject, of thought, or of management of plot and language. One can scarcely see Cocteau's *The Infernal Machine* without comparing it with Sophocles' *Oedipus the King,* nor Sartre's *The Flies* without recalling Aeschylus' *Oresteia* and O'Neill's *Mourning Becomes Electra.* Anderson's *Joan of Lorraine* reminds one of Shaw's *Saint Joan* and Schiller's *Maid of Orleans.* E. P. Conkle's *Prologue to Glory* brings to mind Sherwood's *Abe Lincoln in Illinois* and John Drinkwater's *Abraham Lincoln;* Racine's *Phaedra* demands comparison with Euripides' *Hippolytus;* Daviot's *Richard of Bordeaux* reminds one of Shakespeare's *Richard II.* In all of the above instances two or more authors have dramatized the identical characters from history or legend.

Similar plots provide the basis of comparison between Marlowe's *Doctor Faustus* and Goethe's *Faust;* between Noel Coward's *Fumed Oak* and Somerset Maugham's *The Breadwinner;* between McEnroe's *The Silver Whistle* and Savoir's *He;* between Sutton Vane's *Outward Bound* and Anderson's *High Tor;* between Barrie's *Dear Brutus* and Shakespeare's *The Tempest;* between *The Prisoner of Zenda* and *The Prince and the Pauper;* between *The Dybbuk* and *The Enchanted;* between Anderson's *Wingless Victory* and Euripides' *Medea.*

The more one reflects on the subject and the plot of a play the more instances come to mind of other similar works. As they do, the differences, particularly the differences in quality between them, become more readily apparent.

CHANGES IN EFFECT

The impression which a play makes on the minds of the various members of the audience may be very strong but it is nevertheless subject to many modifications as time goes on. Sometimes the memory enhances the work and subsequent reflection confirms the first impression until, in the memory, the play becomes better. Bakst is supposed to have said that it would be impossible to revive any of his earlier productions without repainting the scenery, for people remembered them as being so colorful that in order to equal this memory the settings would have to be much brighter than they originally were. Sometimes a production seems outstanding until another better one supersedes it. Leslie Howard's *Hamlet* was generally praised until John Gielgud's production of the same play appeared in New York. Then the people who had seen both began to compare the two and many who had praised Howard's performance began to deprecate it and say that it barely scratched the surface of what it might have been.

It is comparatively seldom that a good play will be overshadowed thus by a second and better production of the same work, but even without such a happenstance a number of factors will, in time, combine to alter the effect of even the best dramas. The principal of these factors are familiarity, timeliness, and changes in language and taste.

Changes Due to Familiarity

As one becomes more familiar with a particular drama, either from seeing a number of different productions of it or from seeing it and studying the script and reading or hearing about it, a number of interesting changes take place. Some qualities, dependent upon novelty, are lost forever after the first acquaintance. Others, dependent upon understanding, often combine to improve the work as familiarity increases.

Losses in effect due to familiarity are for the most part related to the temporal nature of drama. Particular temporal effects of surprise and suspense suffer the most rapid deterioration. For the play which the dramatist originally wrote was intended to be seen always for the first time by audiences unaware of the outcome and incapable of foreseeing the surprises in store for them. The carefully planned reversals, the artful disclosure of concealed relationships, the last-minute rescues, the surprise endings, were all planned to arouse certain responses from audiences possessed of childlike innocence of the work in question. Once the play has been seen or read, that innocence is lost forever.

Some of the world's best comic plots have been used by so many playwrights over so many hundreds of years that familiarity has worn them quite threadbare. Among these are many of the love-intrigue and mistaken identity plots of Plautus and Terence. Originally these must have seemed delightfully ingenious and novel, but repeated use of them by fourth-rate playwrights has ruined them permanently. These same plots still appear regularly on the modern stage, but rarely in plays of much merit.

Puzzles and riddles lose their dramatic power even more completely than ingenious plots do. One can enjoy some small measure of suspense or surprise while seeing a familiar play, but one gains no pleasure from familiar riddles except possibly the pleasure of watching them skillfully unfolded. The riddles of the three apparitions in *Macbeth* must once have stirred audiences to a degree now almost impossible to imagine. Their effect is totally different today, when every schoolboy knows their answers.

But what one loses in temporal effect is often more than compensated for by gains in understanding. Nothing emphasizes the difference in quality between the best drama and the most inferior as much as thorough understanding. For as one knows a play better, one becomes quicker and more confident in placing it among the best and worst plays one has known. Timeworn plots, stereotyped characters, and trite expressions, as they become familiar, reveal their faults

like shabby costumes exposed to bright daylight. At the same time plays of genuine merit, as one comes to know them better, become more admirable rather than less so.

In the best drama there are many more qualities than can be appreciated in one experience. Successive experiences of a work of true merit bring to light additional details and subtleties with each new viewing. Moreover, once one knows the outcome of a play, many speeches and actions reveal an irony of which one could not have been aware when first seeing the work, and the recognition of these ironies adds materially to the pleasure of understanding.

Good lines and well-composed speeches, especially those not depending greatly upon impact for their effect, become things to look forward to. Finally, familiarity brings with it a great increase in the clarity of a drama which is especially appreciated when the work is one of more than ordinary complexity. Shakespeare's triple-plot plays are considerably easier to follow when one knows them. Arthur Miller's *The Death of a Salesman,* made up of flash backs and fade-outs blending past with present, with the symbolic appearances of Uncle Ben along the way, is much clearer the second time one sees it than the first. Chekhov's *The Cherry Orchard* on first acquaintance is likely to seem somewhat aimless, although if the performance is a good one it will be fascinating to watch. But subsequent performances reveal dimensions in characterization, together with a pattern and purpose in the whole work, to an astonishing degree.

Changes in Timeliness

Almost all plays are composed under the influence of some ideas or interests which happen to be timely at the moment. While this timeliness endures, the play gains from it. Then, as new ideas develop and interests change, the quality of timeliness gradually disappears. If the play then continues to live, it lives more and more on its merits as a work of art. No doubt Shaw's *Saint Joan* gained a great deal from the interest attending the sanctification of Joan which took place about the time that it first appeared on the stage. Ibsen's *A Doll's House* and *Ghosts* appeared at a time when the subject of women's suffrage was being widely argued. Today when universal suffrage is accepted as a matter of course and many more grounds for a woman's leaving home are everywhere allowed, the issues which made these two plays vital are much less urgent. O'Neill's *Strange Interlude* was first produced at a time when the theories of Sigmund Freud were making deep impressions on the thinking of well-read people. Now that the Freudian theories have been assimilated, this play provides a much less authentic-seeming explanation of human behavior than it did when first written.

War plays suffer greatly from changes in popular interest. Between the first and second world wars a strong pacifist sentiment prevailed. During this time there appeared some of the best war plays ever written. One of the best was Sidney Howard's *Paths of Glory*, which showed, through a succession of trenchant and moving episodes, the fate of three soldiers condemned and executed in exemplary punishment of a regiment which had failed in an attack. During the second world war this play became unproduceable, for people then were involved in a desperate struggle for existence and few were willing to accept a representation of warfare which did not idealize this struggle. After the war, popular sentiment never returned to the pacifist beliefs which had prompted Howard in writing this play. Now, though the work is artistically as good as it ever was, its attitude is at odds with general taste, with the result that it is seldom seen on the stage. Other war plays have scarcely fared better. *What Price Glory?*, once regarded as a vivid and realistic representation of military life, seems now to present that life in much too colorful a light. *Journey's End,* commercially one of the most successful war plays ever produced, now seems effete and immature. Anderson's *The Eve of St. Mark* fails from similar causes. *Command Decision,* a very successful work which appeared shortly after the end of the second world war, is already losing much of its lustre and sinking slowly to the level of innumerable duty-versus-honor plays of similar make-up.

Of all the species of topical drama, plays capitalizing on interest in some current political or social crisis lose value the most quickly. *Waiting for Lefty,* which dramatizes the decision of a group of cab drivers to strike for higher pay, was very timely during the depression when thousands were barely able to earn enough to keep body and soul together. It is much less vital now, when cabs seem almost impossible to find outside of a few mid-city taxi stands and when cab fares are so high that few can afford them. Today the thought of any cab driver starving is exceedingly difficult to accept. Ben Hecht's *A Flag Is Born* was a strong plea for recognition of Israel at the time when that country was fighting for its life against the Arabs and Egyptians. Today, when the Arabs and Egyptians are still smarting from their defeat, while the nation of Israel flourishes, the issue of independence is no longer as vital.

One of the most striking examples of loss of timeliness was the fate of the play *The Greatest of These,* by Max Wylie. The play dealt with the struggle of India for freedom from British rule. As it was a pretty good play, it might ordinarily have been expected to have enjoyed moderate success. But the week that it opened in Chicago, Britain in a surprise move granted India its sovereignty. All at once Indian freedom became a dead issue and *The Greatest of These* closed shortly after.

Changes in Language and Taste

The language in which a play was originally written may at one time have been extraordinarily expressive and striking, but spoken language is a living thing which from generation to generation changes its form. Eventually expressions fall into disuse and as they do so, their presence in the language of a play creates an obscurity.

The more colloquial the language, the quicker it loses brilliance, and becomes at some points unintelligible and at others quaint and outdated. This change in effect is most apparent in plays written a generation or so ago. The slang of our grandparents, long since worn out, is as amusing to us as their manners and their dress.

Plays of more than a few generations' age, especially if written in formal language, may sound somewhat stilted, but they may at the same time gain a certain dignity from the archaic flavor of their lines. Inevitably some of their lines will become unintelligible when heard, while now and then an expression whose meaning has changed will produce on the audience a different or even an opposite effect from that which its author intended.

Changes in taste are difficult to describe but distinct in their effect on the reception of the play. *The Second Mrs. Tanqueray* was once thought a very good play, but it now seems distinctly Victorian in its general make-up. It has become a kind of museum piece more noted for the way in which it displays the peculiarities of society of time past than for its virtue as a drama. The same is certainly true of *The Green Hat*, which was one of Katharine Cornell's greatest successes in the mid-nineteen-twenties, for it shows a group of characters and a way of life which one can now hardly believe existed. Yet it was widely credited less than thirty years ago when Iris March's romantic peregrinations drew the sympathies of countless audiences.

Plays performed first in one country and then in another sometimes undergo peculiar changes due to differences in audience taste. One of the most interesting cases of this kind occurred with *Tobacco Road*. When this play was offered on Broadway, it was received as a rather unusually rough and sensational bit of realism with no significance beyond the fact that its outspoken language and sordid characterization caused the greatest stampede of sensation-seeking audiences in the history of the American theatre. When the same play was produced in Australia, the supposed sensationalism practically escaped notice. The Australians, being by nature outspoken, were rather unaffected by the representation of those actions which shocked Americans. Instead, the work was viewed by the Australians as an interesting and authentic picture of lower-class farm life in the United States.

Tastes in drama of distinct mode or manner are quickly exhausted as the success of one work is followed by a host of imitations of similar character until the vein is exhausted. Many a species of drama once prevalent and enthusiastically approved has become practically extinct. Among these are the sentimental comedies of the eighteenth century none of which survive except as curiosities in anthologies of drama, the heroic tragedies of the seventeenth century of which no more than a half-dozen titles are now even recognizable, and the heroic romances of the nineteenth century whose plots and characters have passed into opera and musical shows.

FIVE TESTS OF QUALITY

The most practical skill which one can acquire in regard to theatre art is skill in distinguishing good drama from bad, or, to put it more accurately, the better from the worse. Among the thousands of plays to be read and hundreds of performances to be seen, a lifetime is far too short for one to waste any time on inferior works when superior ones are available. Moreover, for directors and actors the best plays afford both a richer opportunity for the practice of the art and a deeper sense of achievement.

Perhaps this is why whenever a particular play is discussed the talk sooner or later turns to the question of value. This discussion of value generally ranges back and forth between questions concerning the quality of the various elements and questions of general merit. Questions regarding the quality of various elements of the work are likely to sound something like this: Was the plot original? Was it well contrived? Were the characters true to life? Were they types or stereotypes? Was the language expressive and appropriate? Was the language consistent as to style? Was the thought clear? Was it significant? Questions of general merit are likely to shape up quite differently: How good is the play? What makes a play good instead of bad? How does one recognize a good play when it comes along? In answering such questions one always has one's own experience to guide him, and the wider one's experience, the firmer his basis of comparison. Evaluation is, after all, mainly a matter of comparison. Beyond this, one can always refer to the judgments of others of greater experience and keener discrimination.

Few can be content, however, with such general guidance as experience and authority afford, for one's own experience is always increasing, and as it increases, his judgments undergo repeated modification. Also, at times, experience accumulates much faster than it can be assimilated. Experience is continually ripping up, remodelling, and rebuilding the conclusions already arrived at, so that a man who relies solely on experience is perpetually dependent upon standards which are either incomplete or in progress of overhaul. Nor is dependence upon authority of others wholly satisfactory.

For one thing, authorities seldom entirely agree. For another, most people prefer rather to make their own judgments than to accept those of others already made. The authority of others, therefore, is for reference rather than absolute guidance.

The following five tests of quality are proposed as subjective standards against which one may measure the worth of a drama as soon as the experience of the performance has settled somewhat. All they guarantee is that he who uses them will be helped in deciding how good the work is in comparison to other works seen. The person with wide reading-knowledge of drama and much theatregoing experience is bound to arrive at different conclusions than the one who has read only a few plays and seen one or two on the stage. But each should at least end up knowing why the drama he saw seemed good or bad as the case might be.

First Test: Intensity of Pleasure at Moment of Perception

"Pleasure" as used here includes all the vicarious sensations experienced while watching a performance: delight, anxiety, sympathy, and so on. One of the marks of good drama is that it causes one to perceive more clearly than in life and to feel more intensely. The more intensely one enjoys a work, the better it is, providing it holds up when checked against the other four criteria.

Second Test: Duration of Pleasure in Retrospect

The better a drama is, the longer one continues to enjoy it after the performance is over. It is by this standard that one is able to distinguish between the superficial thrill of melodrama and the profound emotion of tragedy, for the thrill caused by the former, although it may be intense at the moment of perception, does not last very long after the performance is over. In contrast, the emotion aroused by a great performance of a great work may last indefinitely. This is because the better work has more to it; the emotion aroused is more complex. In retrospect one both thinks and feels. Who can recall the climaxes of *Electra* or *Hamlet* as first seen (assuming of course that the performance was good) without feeling something of the pleasurable shock which they caused?

Third Test: The Quality of the Afterimpression

This is a very important test because only the best dramas meet it entirely; all others fall short in varying degrees. A great play leaves one feeling definitely and unmistakably satisfied and it usually also leaves one seemingly wiser and with a more complete sense of well-being than before the performance. Moreover, this satisfaction continues for some time afterward — perhaps forever.

Inferior plays do not produce this effect. One may come away from the performance with the feeling that something was missing, that there was too much going on, or too little, that there was one act too many or one act too few. Shaw's plays often leave one with the feeling that there was one act too many; O'Neill's with the feeling that there was one act too few even though their performance may have required six hours. Ibsen's plays sometimes leave one at the immediate end of the play feeling that they have ended some minutes too soon, but afterward as one reflects on them they become more satisfying. Some plays, like *Waiting for Lefty* and *A Flag Is Born,* leave one wanting to do something definite but the impulse quickly evaporates and afterward one can recall the performance without wanting to do anything at all. Some plays leave one depressed. Tennessee Williams' plays do this when their performances have been good. This is because Williams seldom resolves the issues which he raises. It is depressing to witness suffering without being shown the reasons for it.

Fourth Test: Quality of Pleasure upon Witnessing a Second Performance

It often happens that one remembers a drama with pleasure and looks forward to seeing it again only to be disappointed upon discovering that it is not nearly as good as it originally seemed. When one sees a play the second time the effects of surprise and suspense are much less pronounced, so that if the work in question lacks depth or subtlety, disappointment is inevitable. Many a play, which when first seen seemed great, on second seeing turns out to be quite ordinary. The loss is not worth lamenting. As one's discrimination increases there are certain to be many such losses.

On rare occasions one's second experience of a play is infinitely more pleasurable than the first and he discovers all sorts of interesting details which he had not noticed before. One knows what is ahead moment by moment, and he is no longer closely restricted to following the course of action, so that he is able to glimpse ironies and undertones which surround the progress of the plot. Such an experience is possible with many of Sophocles' plays, most of Shakespeare's, some of Ben Jonson's, and a goodly number of Molière's. It is one of the most reassuring signs of their greatness.

Fifth Test: Comparison of the Pleasure with That Caused by Similar Compositions

This test becomes increasingly reliable as one's experience of drama improves. One play seems good only until one has seen another similar but better one. Or if the play of the moment turns out to be similar to another which was better, one can easily rank it accordingly. A number of possible comparisons come to mind, but at this point it is probably better that each man make his own.

These five tests, taken together, can at least establish the relative quality of any given drama one may see performed. Not only that, but they can also be applied, with very slight adaptation, to the evaluation of drama which one may read but not yet have seen on the stage. The principal adaptation would be to alter the fourth test to "quality of pleasure upon reading a play the second time."

These are, of course, not the only standards one ought to employ. As one's experience increases he will encounter as many standards as there are writers on the subject of that uniquely rich and complex art which is drama. It is to be hoped that all will help each of us toward the discovery and enjoyment of works of finest quality and guide him toward the proper understanding of their elements. Since one cannot within the span of a lifetime know all art or all drama, he can at least aim to know the best.

Section Two

Acting

8 | Purpose and Method in Acting

Objectives in Performance • The Actor's Dual Nature • "Systems" of Acting • Preparation vs. Performance • Study and Memorization

The director of a dramatic production has for his central objective — in its simplest terms — the projection to an audience of the form, purpose, and meaning of a playwright's manuscript. The director's principal medium of expression in achieving this projection is *the actors* — individually and collectively, and in their relations to each other as well as to the setting in which or before which they move and speak. Some of these relationships are of course physical, some psychological; some are developed in space, some in time; some are directly prescribed by the playwright, some creatively imagined by the actor and his director or designer, as a part of the overall plan of production.

It is important to remember, in any case, that the key elements throughout are a manuscript, some actors, and an audience; and that the basic function of the actor is to serve as a sort of middleman between script and observer, in a process of projecting theatrical values *from* a playwright *to* an assembled group of spectators and listeners. The fully functioning actor, then, is normally not merely "performing" in and for himself, not merely "putting on an act," as he might if he were a magician or a pantomimist in a music-hall entertainment or at a fraternity get-together. Nor is he indulging in mere dramatic

play, as children might do when they play at make-believe in the rumpus room or show off their costumes to the neighbors at Halloween time. Indeed, acting — that is, as an art — enters into the picture precisely at the point when the actor consciously focuses on creating a controlled effect in the mind and spirit and imagination of a body of spectators.

In such a process, so conceived, the actor's freedom is no greater than his responsibility. His every decision, his every insight, his every motivation is conditioned by the requirements of the playscript on the one hand, and by the very real needs of the audience on the other. The deepest and most abiding satisfactions for the actor-artist are therefore not purely subjective or selfish ones, since they are attuned to purposes and values quite outside himself. This is not to say that there are no "personal" satisfactions for the serious actor, but only that these should be peripheral and incidental. It is to say that the sensitive actor conceives his creative task as predominantly interpretative and communicative; that he gears his rehearsal and performance to the play's scale of values; and that he operates within the framework of a plan of production at once larger and more significant than his own individual patterns or intentions.

As other chapters of the present volume will suggest, a production in the contemporary theatre is a co-operative enterprise of tremendous proportions, concerned with a shifting complexity of light, color, mass, sound, and movement. It is in the nature of the actor's task to assimilate his own individual design into the production's larger one, giving it vitality and concreteness without weakening its unity and coherence. His task is thus many-sided and complex, requiring constant adjustment to the methods and procedures of his colleagues in production. Moreover, it allows of no single approach or formula of preparation. It demands flexibility of both voice and body, responsiveness of both intellect and emotion. It assumes insight as well as technique, imagination as well as judgment. It deals with inner content as well as outward form.

OBJECTIVES IN PERFORMANCE

Within such a frame of reference, what are the qualities inherent in a good performance? In the course of his analysis and rehearsal, what ultimate values should the student-actor keep in view? Is it not possible to set down — before he has begun — an overview of what he should have accomplished, once he has reached the end of his job?

A first principle has already been implied: *a good performance is rooted deeply in the play from which it springs.* Its patterns of action, of dialogue, and of character are not only congruous one with the other, but are uniquely suited to a particular playscript. A good performance is composed not of random bits from other roles, other plays, and other productions, but of carefully integrated details characteristic of the style and form of the manuscript at hand. There are as many lovers (or scoundrels or cynics or fools) as there are plays into which such characters have been written; but only one will do for a given performance with its given circumstances. The Cleopatra that Shaw intended will not pass in Shakespeare; the Elizabeth of Anderson's *Mary of Scotland* cannot be palmed off in his *Elizabeth the Queen.* The physicians in *The Doctor in Spite of Himself* or other plays of Molière and in Romains' *Doctor Knock,* despite certain surface similarities, cannot readily be traded from production to production.

On the other hand, a generalized "depiction" of character, however appropriate in style and mood, is not enough. The successful performer does something more than to set character. He develops a character in action; as experienced directors like to phrase it, he plays the play. He is not acting in a vacuum; or, to change the figure, he is not merely picturizing an individual personality. He is intensely aware throughout his performance of the ebb and flow of plot and action, of the interplay of scene and situation, of the way in which his drama moves forward structurally. The successful performance registers contrast; climax; growth and development.

In the second place, *a good performance is continuously clear.* Such a performance is never fuzzy or uncertain in outline. It does not allow of inconsistency in motivation or in emotional tone. The performer is always and everywhere in character, steering a middle course between a barren and obvious simplicity, and an extreme and confusing complexity, of detail. Though a good performance is not without surprises, these are necessarily appropriate, believable, and satisfying ones for the judicious spectator. Patterns of movement, of speech, and of characterization are in such a performance happily blended into an organic unity of effect and of impact.

Aside from its positive values, a good performance is scrupulous in avoiding potentially negative distractions. Awkward or restless movement, apparent self-consciousness in voice or pronunciation, a sense of straining for effect — any of these can disturb the proper focus of a part and distort the clear line of its development. Handicaps due to indistinct utterance, excessively low volume, or poor projection are of course more obvious, even to the untrained observer. And a missed opportunity in the theatre, whether it is concerned with establishing a positive effect or with controlling a potentially negative one, may be lost forever. If a lecturer, for example, feels that he has failed to make a necessary point, he can retrace his steps, restate his theses, compensate for missed opportunities. If, on the stage, a character is fuzzily set at the beginning of an act, or if an expository unit is clouded over because of mismanagement of one sort or another, the matter may never be wholly clarified until several additional scenes have gone by.

Plays of such widely divergent manner and point as the contemporary *Male Animal* and the Elizabethan *Twelfth Night* or *As You Like It* can of course be thus handicapped in performance. A set of fumbled cues and a badly centered delivery on the part of the kid sister in the first act of *The Male Animal* can, despite considerable effort on the part of the rest of the cast, so befog the relationships between the Turners and the demon alumnus or the aging football star that most of the first-act overtones are lost on a third of the audience. For those spectators who are not, perhaps, already clear in their minds about Shakespeare's habit of masquerading his heroines as personable young men, the art of costume or of make-up cannot immediately compensate for expository passages that are anything less than firmly and clearly projected.

Thirdly, *a good performance is continuously interesting.* Within the limits of overall unity and consistency, the successful actor searches constantly for fresh and varied appeals to audience interest. For the performer who is sensitive to nuances of character and interpretation, any good manuscript affords dozens of opportunities to vary the tempo, the volume, or the general flavor of his line reading, and to support such contrasts with shifts in gross bodily attitude as well as in minor detail. The good performer is aware that original impressions, however interesting or even startling, soon lose their strength; and that fresh holds on audience attention must be established with planned, though varied, persistence. Under ideal circumstances, a scene gets more interesting, rather than less, as it develops — an achievement which a good start will make possible but which it cannot guarantee.

To assure the full projection of such planned appeals to interest and attention, the skilled performer has gone one step farther: he has so controlled the normal flow of his acting that any significant changes in his patterns, either visual or auditory, are set off in clear contrast to the fundamental background. If he has allowed himself to shift or sidle through most of a scene, he knows that later movements will as a result have less audience impact, for good or ill, than they could otherwise have had. Even characters centrally motivated as active and dynamic, and perhaps brash as well — such as Lorraine Sheldon or the zany comedian in *The Man Who Came to Dinner,* and Melantius or Amintor in *The Maid's Tragedy* — must so manage the scope and the frequency of their movements that they do not seem merely restless or nervous throughout, and that their sequences of pointed activity can register against a stabler background. Similarly, the effect of a shock or setback on a less aggressive character cannot be adequately stressed in performance unless it is contrasted with a previously established pattern of relative stability or ease in behavior and in line reading.

Both clarity and interest, then, have demanded a controlled performance. It is not paradoxical to suggest that *a good perform-*

ance must seem to be spontaneous, as well. Despite the repetition, the routine, the hard work that have gone into weeks of preparation, the final presentation seems fresh and unrehearsed. Patterns of voice and movement that are allowed to seem stale cannot at the same time be expressive. The successful actor calls upon every reserve of vitality, every degree of concentration, to vivify, at the moment of performance, the reactions which he has so carefully planned and learned in the course of his rehearsals. Overlaid with meaning and color by a fully active imagination, his lines seem genuinely responsive to the inner life of the scene, and his actions seem to flow easily from its given circumstances. As a great actor, William Gillette, has put it, a good performance suggests the "illusion of the first time."

The actor's air of spontaneity is improved if he is accomplishing his task without apparent strain. There is no waste motion, no squandered breath, no excess of energy about a top performance. The experienced actor never suggests that he is working too hard, and the laymen in the audience are never aware of the effort involved. Sequences that may earlier have seemed forced or labored have been eased and remotivated in rehearsal, so that complicated actions and difficult lines can be brought to their maximum of effect with an economy of effort. The performer's mastery and control are ever-present, but they are assimilated into the all-encompassing vitality of a fresh and individualized portrayal.

Finally, *a good performance is a team performance.* The twentieth century has been called The Age of the Director, just as the eighteenth is referred to as The Age of the Actor. Other observers remind us that "the play's the thing," to a degree and in a sense that are unique with our time. Certainly individual virtuosity, per se, of such a nature as to call special attention to itself rather than to the ensemble, is foreign to our con-

temporary climate of aesthetic opinion. Actually, it is not that we have come to undervalue or understress the actor, but that we have focused our interest and our expectations in terms of an acting group. The performer is, if anything, more "important" than ever before, but he is important in terms of organic unity and consistency in an entire production. The able performer, then, stands out vividly, though he stands out as one of a team. He realizes that he alone cannot carry a modern production, and that, personally and professionally, he has more to gain than to lose by responding freely to the interplay designed by his director. When it comes to the final test of performance, a play moves forward on the basis of not merely the individual characterizations or virtuoso achievements alone, however vital or stirring these may be, but principally on the basis of group actions and reactions, group rhythms, group responses, and group developments.

THE ACTOR'S DUAL NATURE

These, then, are the actor's ultimate objectives, as his task is conceived in the contemporary theatre. If he is to achieve these objectives in performance — that is to say, achieve *all* of them — he must manage somehow to serve a dual function. In effect, the actor is asked to be two performers at once: an interpreter as well as an instrument of interpretation. Unlike most other creative or interpretative artists, the actor is at once artist and medium. Some artists work on, and project through, clay or marble or canvas; the pianist or violinist works with a responsive but nonetheless lifeless instrument which stands, as it were, between him and his listeners. Even the puppeteer communicates through an intermediary, a means outside himself.

To express this duality another way, let us say that a stage performer must "act" as both an *actor* and a *character*. In most plays, certainly in most contemporary plays, the actor is primarily a character; and he is intended to think a character's thoughts, feel a character's emotions, and look at his fellows through a character's eyes. From the standpoint of an audience, he is normally expected to be consistent and believable as an individualized personage in the fictional world of the drama. The spectators, on the whole, expect the actor-as-actor to be assimilated into the actor-as-character, and — so far as they are consciously aware — the performer looks, speaks, and moves like the dramatically real personage they conceive him to be. From Oswald in *Ghosts* and Treplev in *The Sea Gull* to Oscar or Ben Hubbard in *The Little Foxes* and Willy Loman in *Death of a Salesman,* the basic expectation is that the performer will project his "acting" primarily in terms of characterization.

But there is in every successful actor at the moment of performance a sort of second man, who looks out for the actor without interfering with the character. The second man, the actor-as-actor, checks on the planned pattern of his own speech and action, makes adjustments to compensate for unexpected variations in his interplay with other characters, and carefully notes the ebb and flow of audience reaction. He is aware of the timing of his crosses, the precision of his byplay, the relative strength of his climaxes. He is concerned lest a too literal absorption in the character he is projecting may distort the director's overall design.

The two — actor-as-actor and actor-as-character — must normally be in balance. If the actor is completely lost in the character, the resulting performance may be uncontrolled and unreliable. In an extreme case of this sort, planned patterns of speech and movement, on which the performer's partners have long since come to depend, may be so seriously disturbed as to ruin an entire scene or act. While the rest of the company are frantically trying to compensate for distortions in dialogue and in space relations, and hastily attempting to predict where the next cue is coming from, normal teamwork goes by the board, and much of the scene's flavor and air of conviction is dissipated. If on the other hand the performer focuses too strongly on his acting at the expense of his character, his performance may well be artificial and unconvincing. When patterns of visual and auditory stimuli, planned throughout the rehearsal period, show through too obviously in performance and call special attention to themselves, most productions tend to lose both their spontaneity and their credibility. In such instances individual performances become lifeless and mechanical, lacking, as they then do, the "art that conceals art."

The point, therefore, is that every successful performer must operate simultaneously on *both* levels — but that his focus as an actor must remain in suitable proportion to his focus as a character. The relative focus proper to each is variable, depending on the nature and style of the play and the production. It is likely that in some types of comedy, for example, the actor may need to concern himself somewhat less with character as such and somewhat more with the timing and precision of his auditory and visual patterns in their own right, though he must normally be careful to neglect neither. Such relatively strong emphasis on acting-as-acting will be required also in nonactualistic productions of one sort or another, such as those of the expressionistic *From Morn to Midnight* or *The Adding Machine,* highly stylized versions of pre-modern dramas (e.g., *Everyman*), and most stagings of *Pelléas and Mélisande* or *The Tents of the Arabs.* In some cases there will be rather subtle shifts in focus from one level of acting to the other, between scenes in the same production. The distinction here is clearly one of degree: though the performer can normally slight neither aspect of his dual function, he must be acutely aware of the relative emphasis which he is placing on each.

"SYSTEMS" OF ACTING

One of the most elusive and confusing problems for the young actor is that of choosing — as he sometimes thinks he must — between "systems" of playing a part. He discovers early in his training and experience that there are many systems, many concepts, many approaches, and of course many names. The advice which is offered him ranges from "feel-the-emotion" to "think-the-thought" and from "live-the-part" to "suggest-the-part"; from "Be natural" to "Focus on technique." If he has read more widely in contemporary sources than in earlier ones, he may have been influenced by the many Russian advocates and apologists, stemming principally from Stanislavski and the Moscow Art Theatre.

Historically, most systems of acting group themselves into one or the other of two schools of opinion: a psychological school of "inner response" and a mechanical school of "external technique." In brief, the advocates of external technique believe that trained actors and directors can set up a more or less dependable system of bodily attitudes and gestures which, when combined with a rather arbitrary and mechanical mode of line delivery, can express emotion and thought and can project these to an audience. The student is urged to concern himself about outer techniques, external manifestations, assumed behaviors, and the like; whether or not he "feels" the emotion or "thinks" the thought is in this view largely irrelevant, since if the external patterns are correct there will be a suitable reaction in the audience. The danger in using such an approach, or at least in using it to the exclusion of any other, is that the results may be stiff and mechanical, stereotyped and unconvincing. Even in the hands of a relatively skilled performer, it sometimes leads to excesses of insincerity and artificiality. It is especially weak as a basic system for the educational theatre, since it lays so much stress on external and mechanical analysis, so little on the development of comprehension and insight in the student-actor.

Supporters of the system of inner response, on the other hand, incline to the opinion that if the "thought" of the character or the playwright is properly assimilated, perfect vocal and bodily expression can automatically follow. An overly strict adherence to such an approach brings the young actor no nearer a solution to his problem than did the other system, per se. The student-actor, particularly the beginner, needs a good deal more to guide him than the disarmingly simple admonition to focus on the inner content, and then to move and speak as his mind and feelings will him to do. In the first place, the individual actor's moving and speaking must be tied into a larger pattern, if they are to function clearly and interestingly and significantly on the stage. Moreover, a planned heightening and exaggeration of effect are often required, to supplement normal reactions and to fit these into the imaginative, conventionalized reality of the drama. Not infrequently, certain external traits of character outside the range of the young actor's normal behavior, and possibly the range of his experience as well, must be acquired experimentally. And finally, a number of vocal or physical disabilities or shortcomings may come between the actor's inner comprehension and its outward perfect expression. The psychological approach, in short, is in some ways a system without a technique.

Clearly, neither of these systems, in its extremest form, will serve the actor adequately at every point in his analysis, preparation, and performance. Developing a role is a continuing *process*, not a sudden seizure or revelation or inspiration; and no single sys-

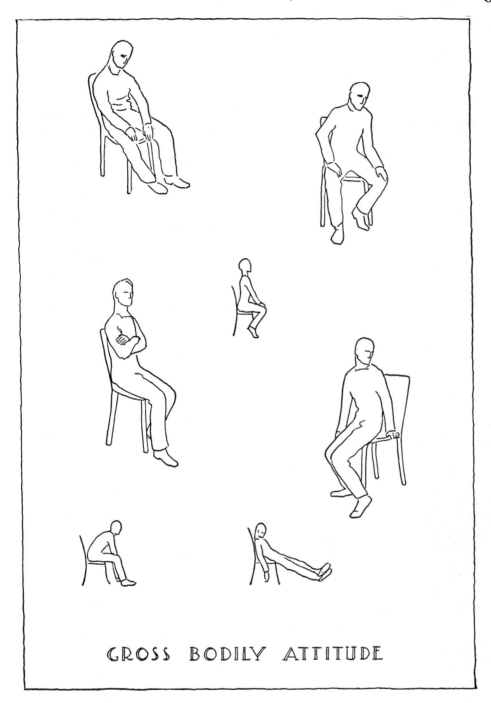

CROSS BODILY ATTITUDE

Figure 1. Bodily action is of course fundamental to expression, and in many cases it may be preliminary to verbalization.

tem or approach can serve as a kind of formula for such a process, or for all of the steps along the way.

PREPARATION VS. PERFORMANCE

What actually happens in practice is that the typical actor uses *both* the psychological and the mechanical approach, to the degree and at the time that each serves him best. With the guidance and often with the assistance of the director, he first creates a basic conception of his character, then imaginatively adapts his voice and body to suit that conception, and ultimately motivates the conception by bringing his real and imagined experience to bear on the character he has thus conceived. As Kjerbühl-Petersen has suggested, the artistic work of the actor is divided into several phases, separated as to time.[1] It is important to distinguish between what the actor does, and how he does it, *at various stages of study and rehearsal*, and what he must do *in performance*. While he is still trying to understand the character, his approach is normally quite different from his approach later on, when he is attempting to play the role in public.

For example, the actor will need at some point, usually fairly early in the rehearsal period, to reach a sort of emotional identification with his Hamlet, his Cyrano, or his Willy Loman. He will need to react personally — and often with tremendous immediacy and directness — to more or less real emotional values and situations; he will need to grieve, perhaps to weep, to laugh and be delighted. These basic and very genuine emotional responses, however, do not and cannot carry over, as such, into the later stages of his work. They cannot be actually and literally reproduced with dependable regularity, partly because of the strain they

would impose on the actor and partly because of the lack of control they would induce in him. The actor's own personal emotions, in short, cannot be expected wholly to guide him at the moment of performance. They must be looked upon, rather, as a base, a point of departure, for the rich and vivid characterization he hopes ultimately to develop.

With his immediate and personal reactions as a frame of reference, then, the actor now moves into another stage of what has already been described as a continuing process. At this point, he needs to experiment, objectively and perhaps somewhat mechanically, with various patterns of speech and behavior. He needs to examine his own emotional reactions, as such, and his own physical attitudes, as such; he is forced to test and choose, pointing up certain values and results, but suppressing others. Through a process of selection, and in part by trial and error, he must gradually build up — in voice, in movement, and in characteristic detail generally — a planned pattern of meanings and effects that can be correlated with the style and form of a particular playscript and that can be made to register with an audience in a theatre. At a still later stage, the actor can make this pattern essentially habitual, and can repeat it from day to day. Finally, by means of imaginative concentration at the moment of performance, he can lend it freshness and expressive power.

It is evident, in any case, that such considerations as "assuming a posture," "betraying an emotion," or "feeling a part" are one thing at the time of analysis or in an experimental rehearsal, quite another in actual performance. It is evident also that a clear recognition of the several steps or stages in preparing a part is a necessary element in the trained actor's approach to his task. Naturally enough, the steps overlap, as it were; there can be, and need be, no cut-and-dried division between the analytical

[1] Lorenz Kjerbühl-Petersen, *Psychology of Acting* (The Expression Co., 1935), tr. Sarah T. Barrows, p. 201.

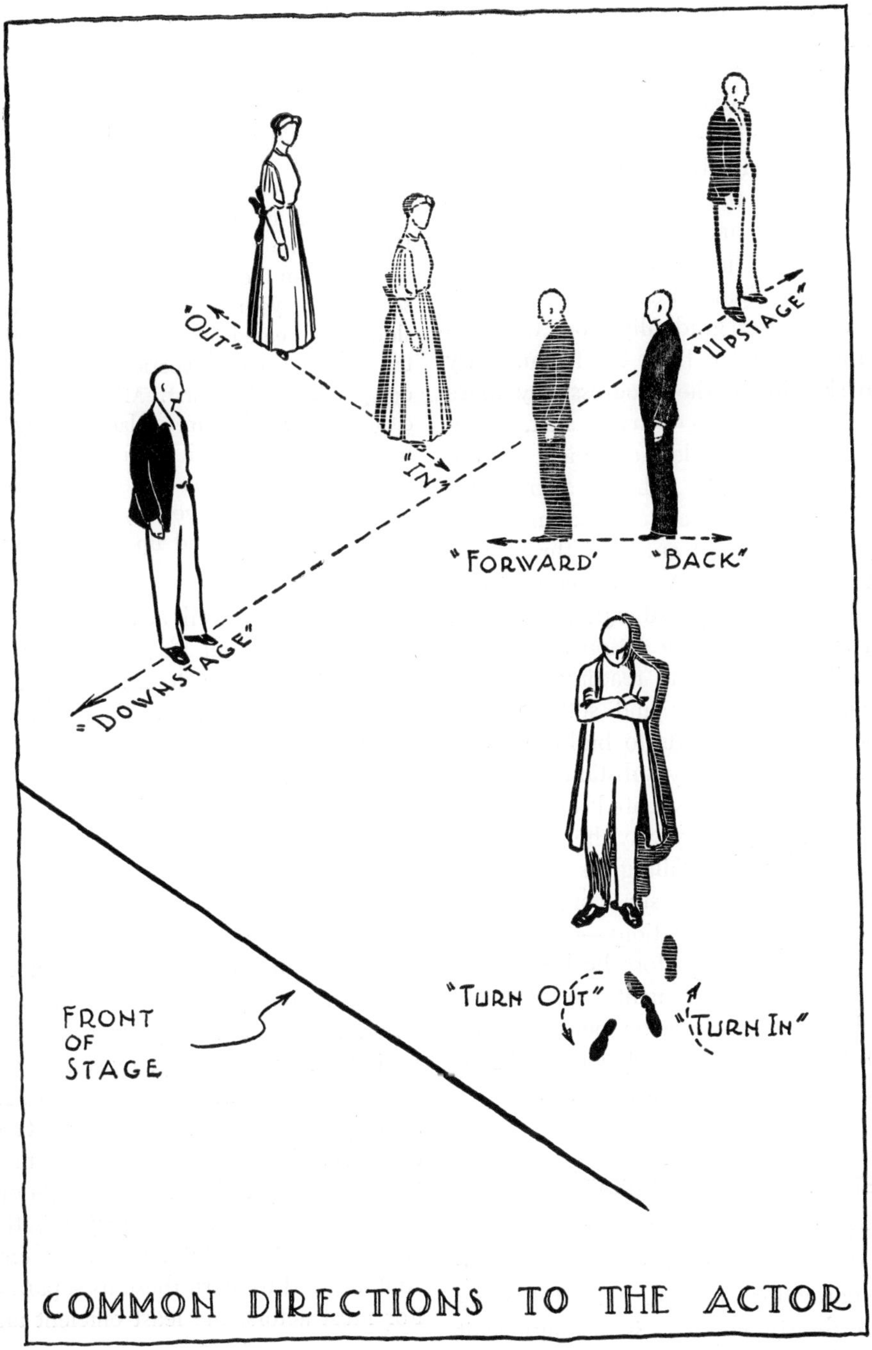
"OUT"
"IN"
"UPSTAGE"
"FORWARD'
"BACK"
"DOWNSTAGE"
"TURN OUT"
"TURN IN"
FRONT
OF
STAGE
COMMON DIRECTIONS TO THE ACTOR

Figure 2. Directions for the actor's movements and positions on the stage have for the most part become standardized.

and the creative, the intellectual and the emotional, the preliminary and the final, in building a character. But not everything can be accomplished at once, and it is best to take first things first — and to take the remainder in a relatively orderly sequence.

On the whole, the entire process of analyzing, preparing, and playing a part — from the earliest reading of the manuscript through to the final rehearsals before performance — moves gradually from the general to the particular, from the fragmentary and the sketchy to the progressively more complete. What is necessary at first, therefore, is a relatively clear-cut view of the *broad outlines* of the whole: a basically sound conception which can be modified, refined, perfected, and enriched throughout the rehearsal period. As the actor moves from preliminary study and experimentation, through blocking out the action and establishing suitable voice and reading patterns, to developing character and setting characteristic detail, he needs to build progressively on an increasingly substantial framework; and if he has slighted any of his earlier obligations in any way, he may be in some difficulty as to fulfilling his later ones. Moreover, if he seriously confuses the *sequence* of these obligations — e.g., if he tries to perfect details before he has set his basic patterns of movement, or attempts specifically to build character before he has clarified his basic point of view — he is merely being inefficient and wasteful.

STUDY AND MEMORIZATION

The principles here set forth for preparation in general apply specifically to study and memorization, per se. The following advice for the student-actor is as simple as it is substantial:

Know what you are after from the beginning, at least in broad outline; but don't try to do *everything at once.* Don't let your patterns of speech and action develop at random, out of odds and ends of other roles or recent unselected off-stage experiences; don't let them just "happen." From personal study and analysis, and from consultation with your director, set up an accurate *first impression* of the sort of thing you are aiming at. If your mind-set in relation to the play, the part, and the director's design is warped from the start — or if you *have* no mind-set — then your learning must inevitably be slow, misdirected, and wasteful. On the whole, try to do what the experienced director tries to do; put first things first. Minor details may fall easily and readily into place during later rehearsals if the broad outlines and the skeletal structure of your job are clarified during the earlier ones. . . . If you try to learn everything at once, you may end up by learning nothing at all.[2]

The actor is well advised, on the other hand, to relate all his learning of separate units within a play to the larger context in which they appear. Various portions of the work should be considered (and "learned") as aspects of a total situation, not as separate items to be taken up in isolation. Individual lines of dialogue are best considered in the light of the scene of which they are a part; individual scenes in relation to the actor's part as a whole; and individual parts as organic and functional units in the play.

As a corollary, it is best to memorize "by wholes," or certainly by large units. During periods of actual study, most trained actors concentrate on entire scenes or acts, focusing sharply on the progression and interrelation of ideas. Before they begin to memorize, they are likely to break up the acts or scenes into unified and coherent major sections, according to their intellectual or emotional content; and to learn these as separate units. For most actors, the least efficient and least

[2] H. D. Albright, *Working Up a Part*, 2nd ed. (Houghton Mifflin, 1959), p. 128. The quotation is from Appendix C, entitled "Suggestions for Study and Memorization."

rewarding system of memorization is to begin at the beginning line by line and speech by speech, learning by rote. Such a scheme promises minor results at once, but is likely to take longer in the end; and it usually develops stereotyped and inexpressive readings.

Indeed, it is often as dangerous to memorize one's lines too early in the rehearsal period as it is to memorize them too late.[3] The simplest, most efficient, and most natural way of learning them is to "set" them only after one has begun to know the play, to understand the characters and the dramatic situations, and to correlate speech with action. At this point the dialogue is easier to learn than at any time earlier — and harder to forget. The actor can now learn by context, and is not dependent on auditory or visual memory alone. Since he can associate each speech with its related stage position and gross bodily attitude — and with the positions and attitudes of other characters, as well as with the flow and cadence of the several scenes — he can learn them with genuine assurance, and can deliver them in later rehearsals with interpretative skill and insight. Lines that are memorized too early

[3] The exact schedule for learning lines depends in large part on the nature of the play and of the production. On this point, see Chapter 28.

and by rote must frequently be relearned before the dress rehearsal.

To follow through on this "contextual" type of learning, the actor must of course maintain the same approach to private practice sessions that he has developed for the group meetings. On the whole, he should study and rehearse the various units in his play essentially as they are ultimately to be used in performance. If, between scheduled rehearsals on stage, he breezes through his patterns of movement or mumbles over his lines with no thought of expressive content or of correlation with fellow-actors and the scene, he is establishing habits that are irrelevant to the central task — and he must certainly expect to break down from time to time under the varied stimuli of group rehearsals. None of us can learn to act a role unless we practice *acting* it, in rehearsals at home as well as on the stage.

One final point in this connection is of special importance: only concentrated study and practice will serve the purposes of play production. Active attention, critical alertness, and conscious effort are indispensable throughout all types of rehearsals. Irrelevancies, interruptions, and divided interests are wasteful of time and energy. In general, unless the actor is rehearsing with a wide-awake mind, he might better not be rehearsing at all.

9 | Movement and Gesture

The Nature of Stage Pantomime • Conventionalization in Pantomime • The Actor in Space • General "Rules" for Stage Behavior Movement on the Open Stage • Physical Requirements for the Actor

Bodily action, as the French actor Talma once observed, is "language" in another form. As an instrument of expression, and of communication between player and audience, it holds in the contemporary theatre at least equal rank with voice and speech. Indeed, a certain kind of primacy might be established for bodily action, in that it rises at times above the normal limitations of spoken language and registers "meanings" directly, somewhat in the fashion of music.

In ordinary daily life, bodily action is of course fundamental to expression, and in many cases it may be preliminary to verbalization. Most people first reveal their intentions — and establish general meanings — in bodily attitudes and reactions, especially those of the head and face; and only later do they add vocally somewhat more detailed impressions and qualifications. In clearly manifest actions or impulses to action, they register tensions of worry or fright; they suggest defiance or surrender; they indicate indecision, depression, anger, or despair. And in at least a general way an observer knows what they are thinking and what they are likely to do. (See Figure 1.)

On the stage, the actor is under special obligation to use both instruments of expression — that is to say, bodily action as well as spoken language — in his constant

striving for clarity and vividness. The actor must inevitably appeal to both the eye and the ear of his audience, and he is likely to be at his best and his most effective when he is properly correlating the two modes of appeal. Functionally, the two are not separable, though it is convenient and clarifying to examine them in isolation as a first step toward fuller understanding.

THE NATURE OF STAGE PANTOMIME

When pantomime — i.e., the expression of meaning in terms of bodily action alone — is transferred to the stage, it should, as they say, be larger and clearer than life. It need seldom be downright crude or unsubtle, but it can rarely be fuzzy, indeterminate, or incomplete. By definition, pantomime is overt and perceptible; and in the theatre there can be no half-measures in this regard. It is safe to say that there is no such thing as a partially successful (i.e., partially clear and partially meaningful) pantomimic action on the stage: if it is not both purposeful and effective, and wholly so, it is not successful at all. A character's impulse, in pantomime as in speech, must be "readable" from the stage, or it is wasted.

In the most obvious terms, this is particularly true of big theatres, big productions,

Figure 3. The actor's pantomime is projective in that it is played toward the house, even in representational productions.

big effects. In the outdoor theatres of ancient Greece, or in some of the large English houses of the eighteenth century, only relatively positive and unrestrained patterns could possibly be projected to the huge audiences of thousands of spectators. Such pageant-plays of our own time as *The Lost Colony* must be conceived, and for the most part produced, in broad strokes. In a less obvious way, however, the point at issue applies no less inescapably to the comparatively intimate naturalism of most plays since Ibsen. Either explicitly, or perhaps by implication or symbolism, it is still the business of the actor to make outwardly evident and perceptible the human values and relationships which, with whatever subtlety or restraint, the author has written into the play.

To begin with, the actor must recognize that effective stage pantomime is *selective and unified.* It is a truism that the detailed realities of daily life must undergo a process of selective simplification if they are to serve the expressive needs of an art object. Such details are so numerous, so varied, and so complex as to be almost meaningless until they are functionally organized and clarified. Out of the dozens of random bits of action or gesture that might possibly apply in a given situation, it is necessary to choose only the most telling and the most typical, and rigorously to exclude all the others. A limited number of selected details, intelligibly conceived and strikingly presented, will make possible the unity and coherence demanded by all artistic endeavor.

Unified bodily action is of course purposeful bodily action. "No movement without a purpose" is common enough advice; and the wise student-actor takes it literally. The notion of dramatic immobility, however, too often seems to strike the untrained player as a contradiction in terms. Bobbing and nodding, shifting his weight, backing up as he completes a line, fiddling with hand props and furniture, he manages to leave an impression of restlessness and uncertainty, but

of nothing more. To complete the confusion, he frequently and regularly shifts his basic position on stage with no apparent aim. Unless such actions, large and small, can be assimilated into a purposeful pattern, they should quite evidently be discarded entirely.

It is not proposed, on the other hand, that the player should normally seem static or repressed. Merely barren and inexpressive inactivity is a poor substitute for purposeless movement. What the actor must learn to do is to select a few pointed and characteristic details from all that may occur to him, and to make the most of the relatively few he has retained. He must limit the multiplicity and complexity of his actions. He need not repress his physical vitality, but he must direct it into useful and meaningful paths. A unity that is too simple is dull and uninteresting; but one that is too varied and complex leaves us restless or confused. When too many unrelated or loosely related details are placed in a still life, a sculpture, or a stage picture, we cannot perceive it as a unity, and we are bewildered as to its meaning and intention as well as dissatisfied with its effect.

Good stage pantomime, moreover, is *heightened and projected.* Short of downright exaggeration and overacting, the skillful player uses all the resources at his command to capture (and to hold) the interest as well as the understanding of his spectators. To selective simplification, in short, he adds enlargement. In so doing, he attempts to rise above the potential distractions beyond the footlights that so bedevil every house manager, and to meet his group-audience on terms that recognize the spaces and distances involved. As every experienced director has learned to his cost, plays — even modern and relatively "intimate" ones — are not written to be acted in a closet. Bodily actions that are not firm and deliberate, heightened beyond the commonplace reality of normal existence, just do not carry in a theatre.

Half a gesture on the stage, it is recorded,

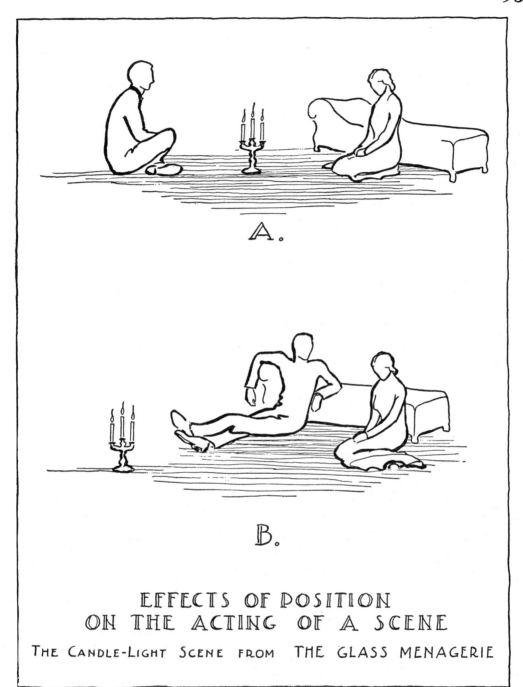

A.

B.

EFFECTS OF POSITION
ON THE ACTING OF A SCENE
THE CANDLE-LIGHT SCENE FROM *THE GLASS MENAGERIE*

Figure 4. The actor's very position in space takes on meaning in relation to other actors and to the pattern of the whole.

is often worse than none. An uncertain or indeterminate movement, if it reaches the audience at all, usually carries a false suggestion of timidity or weakness. Actions that are inhibited or cut off abruptly, rather than followed through, are usually unclear as well as unnatural in their effect. Similarly, gestures or small movements that are executed by one part of the body while the rest of the body remains relaxed and inexpressive have a negative value on the stage. In general, stage actions need to be so clear and complete, so definitely enlarged beyond the normal, that they seem real and natural to an audience; if they are allowed to remain literally and objectively real, they may not reach the audience at all.

The actor's pantomime is of course projective in another sense, in that it is unobtrusively though unmistakably played toward the house, even in so-called representational productions.[1] Though the players may seem to be unaware of the audience, may appear to be unconscious of projecting their voices and "opening out" their movements toward the house, they have concentrated throughout the rehearsal period on those very objectives. This type of projection, like the enlargement already referred to, is more frank and less subtle in nonillusionistic productions, particularly in revivals of some types of pre-modern plays. That it is less extreme or obtrusive in contemporary pieces, and perhaps more difficult, does not, however, make it of any less consequence. (See Figure 3.)

CONVENTIONALIZATION IN PANTOMIME

The degree to which stage pantomime can or must be conventionalized in various types of productions is a complicating factor of central importance. At one extreme in characterization is the stereotyped use of tradi-

[1] The "representational" concept is discussed elsewhere in the volume; see especially Chapter 12.

tional signs: the curled lip, the furrowed brow, the eyes rolled up into the head, the palm applied to the forehead, and the like. At the other extreme is no sign at all, a pattern of attitudes and gestures so "natural" and restrained as to be devoid of perceptible or at least of discriminable meaning; or perhaps so specialized and untypical as to lack immediacy and normal intelligibility. As an instrument of expression, the human body has tremendously varied and flexible resources. How are we to insure in this expressiveness a proper and adequate degree of universality?

The ceremonial rites and dances from which drama itself has doubtless evolved were markedly conventionalized, and the pantomime on which they so largely depended was rigidly codified. Much of the medieval drama, both within and without the church, was strongly pantomimic — as, ultimately, was the improvised comedy of the *commedia dell'arte* groups. Pantomime has always been more readily codified than spoken language and, in part for that reason, has always been more readily understood by all levels, types, and races of people.

The actors and teachers of the seventeenth, the eighteenth, and especially the nineteenth century attempted from time to time to systematize and universalize pantomimic action as it applied to standard drama. One of the best-known of these attempts was made by François Delsarte (1811–1871), who in effect catalogued bodily attitudes in terms of a wide range of moods and emotions, intentions and meanings. Thus, to portray "Vehemence," the feet are apart, and the weight rests upon the advanced foot, the heel of which is raised. For "Defiance," the head is advanced and the feet are apart; the weight is on the foot that is behind, while the other foot is thrown diagonally forward. Each finger has its separate function, and there are nine "inflections" of the hand, forming a projected globe and its radii. The torso

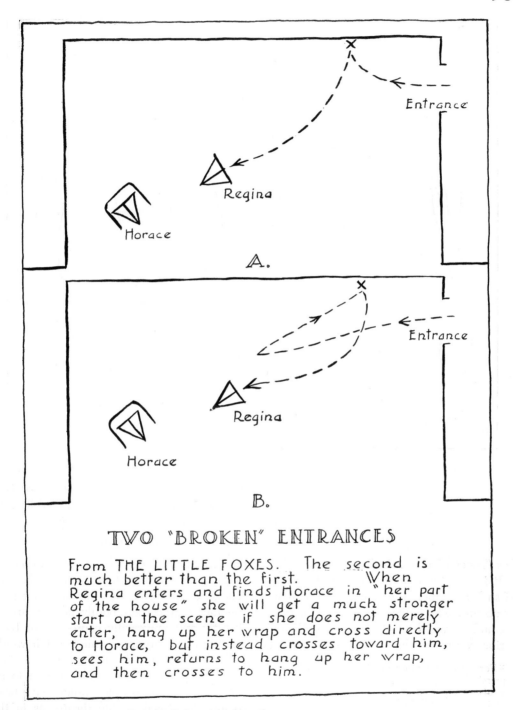

TWO "BROKEN" ENTRANCES

From THE LITTLE FOXES. The second is
much better than the first. When
Regina enters and finds Horace in "her part
of the house" she will get a much stronger
start on the scene if she does not merely
enter, hang up her wrap and cross directly
to Horace, but instead crosses toward him,
sees him, returns to hang up her wrap,
and then crosses to him.

Figure 5. Within the director's larger plan, the
actor must exercise a considerable degree of
freedom and responsibility.

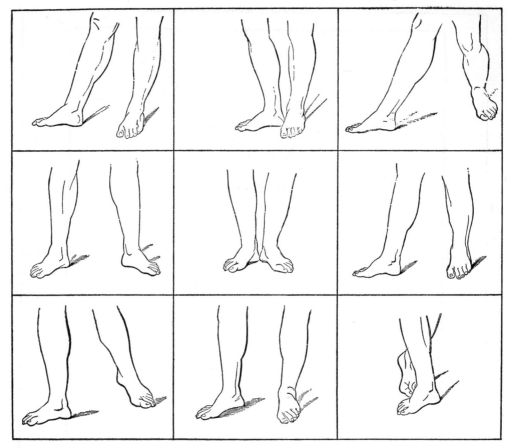

Chart from *Delsarte System of Oratory.* The interpretative "attitudes" indicated are: (top row, left to right) Defiance, Force, Terror; (middle row, Intoxication, Childhood, Hesitation; (bottom row) Vehemence, Transitive, Ceremony.

has "zones of expression" — and so on.[2]

It is only too easy in our time to dispose of such an elaborate system as crude, naive, or absurd. The individualized and "natural" methods to which most of us currently subscribe were developed in large part to

[2] For these and other details in the "science of expression" see the collection entitled *Delsarte System of Oratory* (Edgar S. Werner, 1893), particularly the work by l'Abbé Delaumosne, translated by Frances A. Shaw. A chart (originally copyrighted in 1882) from the Delsarte volume is reproduced above.

counteract the very clichés of pantomime and characterization that such cataloguing tended to produce. But this does not alter the fact that certain bodily actions are so directly and universally expressive of basic emotions or attitudes of mind that it would be foolish to ignore them. Some such actions are perhaps instinctive, and common to all times, places, and peoples; others have been so long identified, in the theatre as in the other arts, with certain attitudes of mind and

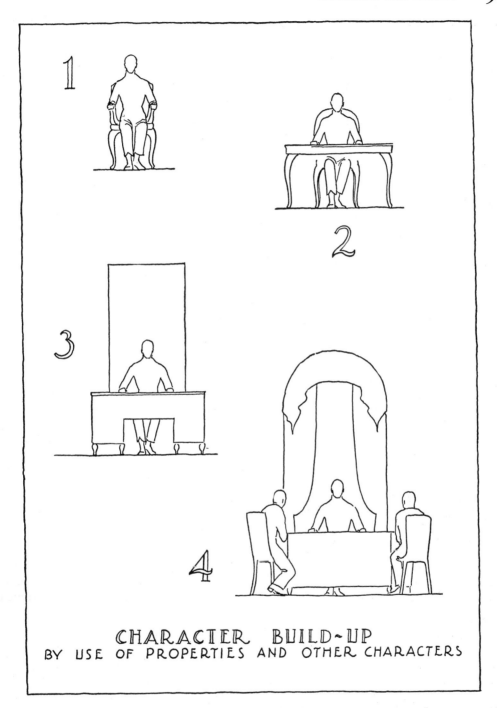

CHARACTER BUILD-UP
BY USE OF PROPERTIES AND OTHER CHARACTERS

Figure 6. Properties and their arrangement, as well as architectural features, may be used to strengthen the actor.

spirit as to have acquired a legitimate symbolic or conventional value.

Through varying climates and periods of aesthetic opinion, the astute critic has always recognized these values. George Henry Lewes, for example — even while he was attacking nineteenth-century clichés and stereotypes as substitutes for what he called sympathetic expression — still wrote as follows:

When we are told that [Edmond] Got "merely behaves just as a warm-hearted man would behave on suddenly receiving the news of a dear friend's death," we ask what warm-hearted man? A hundred different men would behave in a hundred different ways on such an occasion, would say different things, would express their emotions with different looks and gestures. The actor . . . must be typical. His expressions must be those which, while they belong to the recognised symbols of our common nature, have also the peculiar individual impress of the character represented. It is obvious, to anyone who reflects for a moment, that nature is often so reticent — that men and women express so little in their faces and gestures, or in their tones, of what is tearing their hearts — that a perfect copy of almost any man's expressions would be utterly ineffective on the stage. It is the actor's art to express in well-known symbols what an individual man may be supposed to feel, and we, the spectators, recognising these expressions, are thrown into a state of sympathy. . . . As to any minute fidelity in copying the actual manner of murderers, misers, avengers, broken-hearted fathers, etc., we really have had so little experience of such characters, that we cannot estimate the fidelity; hence the actor is forced to be as typical as the poet is.[3]

So far as pantomimic action is concerned, credibility is tied to immediate recognition; and both are tied — even in strongly illusionistic productions — to a degree of conventionalization. To say that individuals differ considerably in their ways of express-

ing the same emotion is not to say that any way at all will be clear and believable in the theatre. There are scores of ways to die or, as in Lewes's example, to receive the news of death, but only a relative few of these have been accepted throughout the years by actor and spectator alike as suitable communicative symbols. Acceptance varies with modes and forms of theatrical production, and with the shifting fashions of time and place. But each audience accepts, and understands and believes, substantially the same type of expressive bodily action: that which is selectively simplified, heightened, and to a degree conventionalized.

THE ACTOR IN SPACE

The present discussion has thus far been limited to what the actor does — and "means" — as an individual, principally in pose and gesture. Actually, he rarely functions solely as an individual, since his very position in space takes on meaning in relation to other actors, to furniture and its arrangement, to wall openings and other architectural features in the setting, and of course to the compositional pattern of the whole. (See Figure 4.) Once he begins to make larger movements, to establish new and shifting and dynamic relationships with his fellow-actors and his surroundings, he is potentially expressive in a way that has so far been barely implied.

In a stimulating section of *The Stage Is Set,* the professional designer, Lee Simonson, has vividly suggested the expressive value of movement on the stage.

Imagine that you are about to rehearse a comedy, the first act of *Arms and the Man.* Forget Shaw's stage-directions for the moment and take the act after Bluntschli has broken into Raina's bedroom and she has decided not to rouse the house. . . . Here are two people quietly talking to each other. Now select your ideal players, [but] keep them seated. They may recite the

---

[3] George Henry Lewes, *On Actors and the Art of Acting* (Brentano's, n. d.), pp. 133–134.

lines flawlessly, achieve every comic innuendo, laugh and weep to perfection. But keep them seated. The effect will be not of an incident lived but of a reading, a perfect piece of elocution with gestures attached. Keep them standing but never allow them to move from the same spot, and the effect will be the same.

You meet what seems to be a simple problem by telling your two players to move about as they have a mind to. Immediately you discover how subtle the problem is. . . . You find yourself obliged to set the essential parts of your scene: a window leading from a balcony (through which the artillery officer can break in), the young lady's bed, a door leading to the rest of the house, a table or tables to hold two essential properties, a candle and a photograph of the young lady's fiancé. Now begin to move your actors, and it will not be long before you discover that the positions of these two openings and the few pieces of furniture determine not only how your actors move but also the implications of everything they say, and after a while, the entire mood of the scene.

. . . Raina blows out the candle and goes to bed. Where will the candle be? Next to the bed seems the obvious place. But that cannot be set until the director has made up his mind what Raina does when she discovers a man silhouetted against her window and lights the candle again. If the candle is within easy reach the lady will be discovered in bed by the soldier. If the rest of the act were purely melodramatic this might be an excellent arrangement, for the soldier could then threaten the lady at the pistol's point. It might do equally well if the act were entirely romance of the blood-and-thunder variety, and Bluntschli a long-lost lover, banned by the family and determined either to force himself into Raina's bed or to drag her off with him down the balcony. But the act is nothing of the sort. Its words are a comedy of *rapprochement* between a terrified young woman and a terrified young soldier, who find they have both been needlessly afraid of each other and finally take each other for granted.[4]

The actor's movements in space — i.e., in a context of surroundings — are thus one of his primary concerns. It is true that some of the basic decisions as to meaningful space relations have already been made for him. The designer and in particular the director have set, in the floor plans for the production and in the blocking out of broader movements and positions, certain limits and conditions on his choice of physical action.[5] Within this larger plan, however, the actor must exercise a considerable degree of interpretative freedom and responsibility. (See Figure 5.) Much of the timing, the motivation, and the characteristic detail, for example, is left to the actor; and he is accountable for most of the primary decisions as to pantomime as well as characterization. In supplying (and controlling) the larger patterns of movement, the director is attempting to "see" the production as a whole. Even with the best of intentions, and despite a certain amount of skill and experience, actors do get in each other's way, do blanket each other's lines, do play important bits from unemphatic positions, and do develop awkward or misleading stage pictures. Responsibility for planning, clarifying, and perfecting relationships in space must thus inevitably be shared.

In approaching the diverse and complex problems of stage movement, it is helpful to recognize certain fundamental distinctions. Many of these will be treated, directly or indirectly, in the section on Directing; but at least a brief expository coverage is in point here. In the first place, purposeful movement on the stage can be either *inherent* or *imposed* — on the one hand, inherent in the plot and prescribed by the dramatist as essential to the action; on the other, imposed by the actor or director (and occasionally by the playwright himself) to fulfill special interpretative or characteristic functions.

Such actions as the dueling in *Hamlet* and

[4] Lee Simonson, *The Stage Is Set* (Harcourt, Brace, 1932), pp. 274–275. By permission of the publishers.

[5] The interrelationship of responsibility, as between actor and director, is further discussed under Direction; see especially Chapter 27.

Nora's dancing in *A Doll's House* are inherent movement, as are the sequences of eating and drinking in *The Wild Duck.* Most entrances and exits are in this category, along with prescribed actions near a window opening on a street, and the like. These may of course be adapted to suit an individual setting or an individual directorial design, but cannot ordinarily be omitted or slighted without serious loss in clarity and point.

Imposed movement may be suggested by the author, it may need to be adapted or developed, and it may have to be devised practically from start to finish by the director and the actors. The cumulative effect of imposed movement — plus the detailed "business" which accompanies it — is largely what determines the special tone, flavor, and significance of a given scene or a given production. The "action" of a good performance often depends less on the plot movements prescribed by the playwright than on the nuances and subtleties of movement and space relations that can be invented by the skilled interpreter. Movements of clear-cut and perhaps violent action are, contrary to the layman's common belief, relatively easy to plan and rehearse. The fire scene in *Ghosts,* the stabbing of Polonius in *Hamlet,* the third-act curtain in *R.U.R.* — these, and others like them, require neither the ingenuity and insight nor the time and care in rehearsal that are needed for the day-by-day patterning of meanings and overtones in "ordinary" scenes.

Some types of imposed movement are selected to insure pleasing and, on the whole, balanced stage pictures. Movements for essentially pictorial effect (and movements to compensate for others that might unbalance or otherwise destroy a pictorial effect) are relatively common in most plays; they offer no special problems, though they can rarely be crude or obvious in their execution. Movement imposed to relieve monotony or strain is another common type. Long

and rather static scenes, like scenes of unusual tension, often require easing, in terms of planned actions that will afford relief without at the same time breaking the continuity and forward movement. On a somewhat higher level, though not unrelated to the types already described, are movements imposed to secure and hold attention. The player and his director must be co-conspirators in focusing attention on the new, the meaningful, and the important — at the expense, if possible, of the old, the irrelevant, or the insignificant. (See Figure 7.)

Almost any movement on the stage is either "strong" or "weak" in attention value. In the Elizabethan and other audience-centered theatres,[6] physical proximity to the audience was a strong value in itself; positions or actions near the stage pillars or well down on the forestage were, all other things being equal, more emphatic than those near the curtains of the study. On the contemporary stage there is normally less value in sheer proximity, though downstage positions are likely to be stronger than upstage positions in themselves, unless other factors are operating. Levels raised from the stage floor, areas brightly lighted or otherwise specially treated, and positions on which other actors are focusing are usually granted more than normal strength.

Within the several areas, and in the playing space as a whole, advancing movements are ordinarily stronger than retreating ones; and movements downstage or toward stage center, from sitting to standing positions, and from a stair or ramp to stage level tend to be stronger than their opposites. Thus, at the second-act curtain of *Kind Lady,* there is a tremendous accumulation of power and impact as the several members of a gang of thieves rise, descend, move downstage, and close in from the side — on the helpless and lonely woman of the house, who is downstage center, with her back to the audience.

[6] See Section III, on Theatre and Stage.

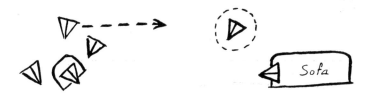

Figure seated on arm of sofa, alone, leaves heavy effect on right; if balance is clearly indicated, upstage figure on right eases over to left in course of the discussion.

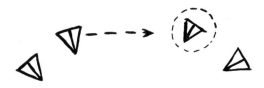

If figure on left is required to cross to figure on right later, upstage figure can prepare to compensate by moving left somewhat earlier.

TYPES OF IMPOSED MOVEMENT

Figure 7. Some types of imposed movement are selected in order to insure pleasing and on the whole balanced stage pictures.

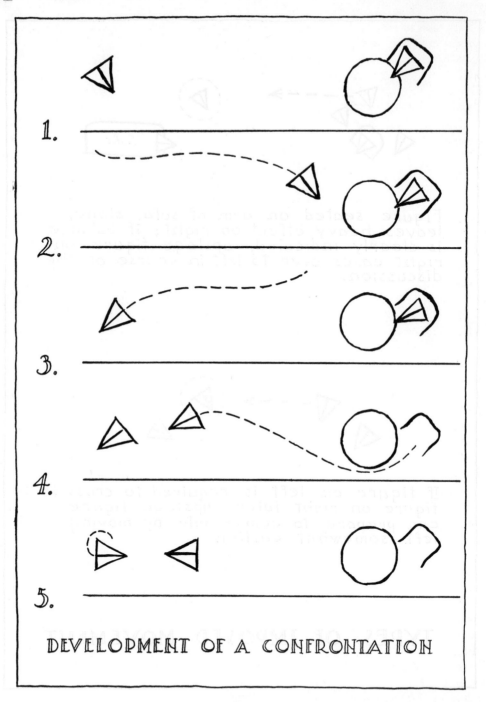

DEVELOPMENT OF A CONFRONTATION

Figure 8. Antagonists, as individuals or groups, must "act out" their conflicts in space if they are to be clear and meaningful.

Closely akin to movement for emphasis is movement imposed to suggest changes of attitude or relationship. Among the most obvious of these would be actions to show change from opposition to agreement, or vice versa; or to indicate intervention between two opposing groups. Antagonists, as individuals or groups, must "act out" their conflicts in space if they are to be immediately clear and meaningful. They must face up to their opponents, turn or move away if they cannot or will not prolong the discussion, advance and draw back and advance again as they develop their arguments or propositions in earnest. Other characters must intervene in space as well as in idea, or must desert one group to take sides — quite literally — with another.

To cite but a single example, in this case of individual rather than group antagonists: in Act I of *Milestones,* John Rhead and Sam Sibley play a so-called confrontation scene.[7] Several issues are at stake here. These men are in opposition both personally and professionally, and they represent in a larger way the liberal and the conservative of every generation, within the play itself and in the world as we know it outside. From the beginning of the scene, the two men are psychically "distant," though John in particular tries from time to time to close the gap between them. He can fully act out this changing relationship to his antagonist only by introducing appropriate changes in his stage positions. Contrariwise, Sam is for the most part postponing, dodging, evading, and he will generally need to avoid advancing or approaching movements until well on into the scene, when he is finally committed to standing up to John. In the meantime, as either character threatens to burst out in anger, or on the other hand relaxes and controls himself momentarily, he will need to supply physical action (i.e., action not specifically called for in the stage directions of

the play) that can enlarge on the speeches involved and underline their significance. In short, as the various stages in the development of their disagreement are established, these must be embodied in space as well as marked off in time.

In most plays, such opposition — with any accompanying intervention or change — is much more likely to be psychological rather than physical in its original impulse. The point in question here covers a great deal more than the gross activity of actual fisticuffs or swordplay, or attempted arrests, suicides, kidnapings, and the like. The issue is normally one of visually dramatizing the psychological values and interrelationships involved — of translating into spatial terms and visual situations the inner conflicts of a scene. Here again the most turbulent or even violent oppositions are often the easiest to handle. Much more difficult and time consuming is the embodiment of countless subtler impulses from scene to scene, at a tea table, in an ordinary living room, on the slope of a quiet hill.

Other types and functions of stage movement will be suggested throughout this volume, as for example movement to set character or indicate frame of mind or spirit. It is worth noting with respect to all the types discussed, here or elsewhere, that they are not to be thought of as mutually exclusive. Indeed, economy of time and motion — as well as freshness and expressive power — dictates that several functions should ordinarily be combined in a single movement or group of movements. The player or director who too laboriously spells out illustrative action one letter at a time, as it were, is misconceiving the potentialities of the physical stage.

GENERAL "RULES" FOR STAGE BEHAVIOR

In working out both his individual pantomime and his positions and relationships in space, the player has available to him cer-

---

[7] See Figure 8; and, in connection with the recording of stage movement, Figures 46 and 47.

tain traditional "rules" for movement — particularly on the proscenium stage. Strictly speaking, these are not rules at all, since if they are applied with formula-like precision, they may do as much harm as good. However, they do serve as a convenient point of departure for actor and director, and they do save a good deal of time if they are approached intelligently and taken for what they are — reliable basic guides to conventional stage action. Some of them relate principally to economy of time and effort, others to avoidance of distraction, still others to spatial composition in general; most of them are concerned with opening out the production toward the house.[8]

Typically, the actor on a proscenium stage plays one-half or three-quarters front. (See Figure 10.) As a result, he often stands or sits with the foot that is away from the audience advanced slightly; he usually gives the audience a relatively full view of his face; and he ordinarily faces the audience as he turns from side to side. He does not hesitate to break this general rule, particularly in strongly realistic production modes, if he has sufficient justification for doing so, but he habitually recognizes its basic soundness. As a corollary, he tries to handle such properties as a pipe or a telephone receiver with his upstage hand, so as not to cover his face, and normally avoids crossing his body with gestures by either arm. Thus, he tends to pick up a book from a table or replace it elsewhere with the arm nearest the piece of furniture concerned, and to pass a book to a fellow-actor with the hand nearest the other actor. On entering a standard door in a side wall of the set, he tends to open the door with the upstage hand, turn slightly toward the house as he enters, and close the door with his downstage hand. (See Figure 11.)

In relating himself to other characters, he

[8] Special problems arise, of course, in Open Staging; see the pages immediately following, and Chapter 26.

is constantly aware of potential lines of sight. Two actors in ordinary conversation may be standing on a line roughly parallel to the footlights (and opening out, as suggested above). In order to throw a bit more emphasis on one than the other, or perhaps for the sake of sheer variety, they may move to positions on a line diagonal to the footlights. In normal situations, they must not angle their diagonal so close to the vertical that the downstage actor *covers* the upstage actor from any sizable portion of the audience. Roughly speaking, the closer they are to each other in space, the less leeway they have in stationing themselves up or down of each other. On the other hand, the closer they are to stage center, the more leeway they have in this respect.

Movement about the stage is best made in relatively straight lines, using the shortest path from point to point. Shallow curves are of course required from time to time, as when furniture or other actors bar the most direct path or when characterization dictates such patterns. For the most part, wide curves may falsely suggest weakness, uncertainty, or undue preoccupation with the movement, per se; and wide curves usually consume too much time. In moving from one area to another, the actor typically steps out with the foot nearest the point to which he is going, so that he moves directly and economically and avoids the general effect of tangled legs and feet. (See Figure 12.)

Important crosses are ordinarily made downstage of the furniture and the other actors, unless such a route would too obviously suggest avoidance of the shortest path. Crosses meant to pass relatively unnoticed, on the other hand, should, if possible, be made upstage of most groupings, where they will have less claim on audience attention. It is frequently necessary for one actor to compensate for other actors' necessary crosses by adjusting his own position in relation to a group. If he finds himself in the direct path

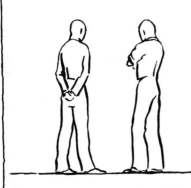

CLOSED POSITIONS

The Characters are facing toward each other and away from the audience. Uncommon except as a means of subordinating minor characters in a grouping.

OPEN POSITIONS

These characters are facing toward each other and also toward the audience. This is the most usual facing, for the principals in a grouping.

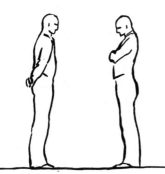

PROFILE POSITIONS

These are facing each other directly without favoring audience at all. Seldom used except for confrontations of rather high intensity.

OPEN AND CLOSED POSITIONS

Figure 9. Many traditional "rules" for movement and position are concerned with opening out the production toward the audience, especially in a proscenium playhouse.

of another player's cross, for example, he may have to give way just a bit, and then unobtrusively take up an adjusted position after the cross. (See Figure 13.)

He will need also to "dress the stage" generally — that is to say, take such a position in relation to the furniture and other actors as to insure a normally pleasing and varied but well-balanced composition. He need not be overly formal about this, but he will want to keep the grouping roughly in balance unless some other arrangement is clearly indicated. In particular, he should avoid helping to form a straight and evenly-balanced line of characters from one side of the stage to the other. Although the director is chiefly responsible for such arrangements, the actors should use all their knowledge, skill, and common sense in helping to work out the picturization of the action, and should otherwise conserve the director's time and energy.

MOVEMENT ON THE OPEN STAGE

Most of the "rules" offered on the preceding pages do not apply, of course, to the open stage.[9] In the full arena, for example, the actor is *always* open to some portion of his audience. The one-half or three-quarter front positions so crucial to the proscenium stage are largely meaningless in this case. Similarly, covering is inevitable so long as there are at least two characters in the acting area. For this reason, the actor often uses a curved rather than a straight-line approach when advancing to meet another actor across a cleared space; the moving actor is thus open at least briefly to more of his audience, and at the same time he partially avoids covering the other actors.

Since it is patently impossible to maintain a frontal relationship with the whole audience, as in the proscenium playhouse, the

[9] See Chapters 15 and 26.

actor can attempt only to face the highest percentage possible. Thus, if he is at the edge of an arena stage and also in front of an open aisle, he is facing possibly 90 per cent of his audience — no doubt the maximum possible. Again at the periphery but midway between open aisles, he can face perhaps 75 per cent. It should be noted that when he is drawn to the center, which might be expected to be a strong area, he can maintain face-to-face contact with only 50 per cent of the house. (See page 177.)

Typically, there are few "strong" or "weak" positions, per se, on an open stage. In some compositions, center-stage (in effect "upstage") has a certain strength value. But audience attention focuses largely on movement. The sheer direction of a movement — relatively significant on a proscenium stage — is in itself rarely strong or weak in open staging. The actor must depend on length or duration of movement, tempo or rhythm, and vitality or animation.

Matters of this kind are more fully discussed in Chapter 26, but an additional general observation or two should be useful at this point. A character who must be out of focus for the moment cannot subordinate himself by merely turning away (or retreating to a weak area), as he can on a conventional stage. He must usually sit or lie at a relatively low level, or move off the playing area altogether — to the front of an open aisle in an arena or to the "ditch" of a thrust stage. It is especially important that such characters maintain a vital interest in the proceedings, listening intently, reacting clearly though quietly, and helping to point attention where it is required.

Since the back of the head or torso is rarely as interesting or expressive as the front, an actor on the thrust or arena stage must turn with considerable frequency to face varying quadrants of his audience. From his first "enter and turn" to his last "tour of the

PROFILE

¾ FRONT

FULL FRONT

¾ BACK

FULL BACK

THE ACTORS' FACINGS

Figure 10. On the conventional stage, the actor usually plays three-quarters front unless there is sufficient justification for doing otherwise.

This is better than
This

This is better than
This

This is better than
This

• GESTURING •
GESTURES ARE USUALLY MADE WITH UPSTAGE ARM

Figure 11. In both planning and execution, gestures — like other and larger actions on a proscenium stage — should keep the actor open to the house.

apron,"[10] the typical performer faces some of his audience all the time, and all of it some of the time — though, to complete the pattern, he cannot face all of it all of the time. This rotation, inherent in the nature of open staging, is unavoidable, though it can be handled with subtlety and variety and can be motivated in part. In any case, some viewers hold it to be a principal drawback in open staging.

PHYSICAL REQUIREMENTS FOR THE ACTOR

Two basic physical qualities may be set forth as prerequisite to full and free expression on the stage: bodily *responsiveness* and bodily *control*. The first is often described in terms of sense-awareness. Most beginning actors fail to appreciate the technical importance of their awareness of — and their memory of — experience with the five senses. As a result, they seem to lack "contact" with people and things about them. They move, sit, and talk as though detached in some way from the living presence of their fellow-actors and from the functional environment which surrounds them. Only too frequently,

they move about the room as though they were sleep-walking: they do not appear to see the doors, the furniture, or the other persons on the stage. They handle a heavy object as though it were light as a feather, carry a book as though it were a box of high explosives, use a telephone as though it were something they did not recall having seen before. An actress, playing a housewife, performs as though the well-worn furniture in her own living room were new and strange, touches it or sits down in it as though it belonged to somebody else.[11]

In so complex and varied an activity as the theatre, an acutely developed sense-awareness can in itself hardly guarantee success in

all types of roles in all modes of production, though it can safely be said that most successful actors have cultivated this quality to a high degree. The beginner is therefore urged to practice sense-exercises with considerable regularity, perhaps as a matter of weekly routine.[12] He may commence with drills in simple recall (e.g., touching fur or velvet, hearing the rustle of a mouse or the buzz of a mosquito, tasting vanilla ice cream or pumpkin pie), focusing on the inner experience rather than on his outward reaction to it. Once he has cultivated, to at least some degree, a retentive and discriminating memory of sense-experiences, he will need to "sense-and-react" in his drills; at this point he should try to recreate the "feel" of his sensations as vividly as possible, and respond outwardly to the inner stimuli. Ultimately, it is of course wise to develop brief pantomimic exercises, relating the specific sensations to a simple context.

The actor who seems sensuously "dead" on the stage may be just not concentrating his physical and mental resources on the task at hand. Indeed, the untrained observer frequently underestimates the degree of alertness and vitality which most acting demands. Prompt and vivid responses are absolutely indispensable to a sense of conviction; and the player who is physically ill or weary, or only half concentrating on the interplay of his scene, is in difficulty before he starts. It is not paradoxical to suggest that it takes considerable energy adequately to portray a dull or inert character on the stage.

[10] See page 437.
[11] Albright, *Working Up a Part*, p. 29.

[12] The following are typical examples of exercises of this type:
Imagine that you SEE: an approaching storm, with occasional flashes of lightning; a searchlight against the dark sky; a childhood friend, after many years; an injured pet; a careening cyclist who has lost control; an unexpected gift of great value.
Imagine that you SMELL: a delicate perfume; exhaust from a diesel; gasoline; turpentine; sun-dried laundry; lilacs; honeysuckle; shellac; oil paint; burning glue.

The apparently unresponsive player, on the other hand, may be an inhibited player, unduly concerned about "going too far" or "wearing his heart on his sleeve." The acquired social inhibitions of even a short lifetime may make an otherwise promising young person temporarily incapable of dramatic expression. Bodily action and gesture in the theatre, and the sense-reactions on which they are based, must ordinarily be free responses, with no implications of self-consciousness.

Nothing that has been said in relation to full responsiveness, however, should be taken to suggest lack of control. Freedom or energy that is undisciplined is likely to be distracting as well as meaningless on the stage. While the spectator may be dulled by inhibited playing, he becomes merely tired and confused when he is asked to face up to constant and unrestrained activity.

The actor's physical discipline is therefore utilitarian. At its base is a cultivated ability to relax. Expressive movement, as well as efficient voice production, requires freedom from undue strain and tension. Overtension produces special pressures in the back and the shoulder, irrelevant constrictions in the throat and the midsection, and an awkward stiffness in arms and legs. Generally speaking, it brings into play whole groups of muscles which would not ordinarily be concerned in a specific pose or gesture, and thus restricts the flexibility of the entire organism. Relaxation brings poise; and poise means freedom to move or react with a minimum expenditure of effort, and a maximum degree of co-ordination and control. A constantly and dynamically changing stage picture calls special attention to players who let themselves get caught off balance, or who move with jerky shifts of body weight.

The most suitable training for the prospective actor is therefore that which cultivates his muscular co-ordination, his rhythmic sense, and his overall control. Isolated exercises which tend to develop muscle systems and parts of the body separately and without regard to their function in the organism as a whole have usually proved to be of dubious value. Eurhythmic training, some types of dancing, and certain forms of athletics have traditionally been recommended as the most adequate means of physical development for work on the stage. Swimming, tennis, boxing, gymnastics, and especially fencing are usually indicated, since these activities tend to subordinate the part to the whole.

10 | Voice and Speech

*Audibility and Intelligibility • Reading for
Meaning • The Nature of Emphasis • Speaking in a Context • Insuring Credibility*

AUDIBILITY AND INTELLIGIBILITY

The first requirement for stage dialogue is a simple and obvious one: audibility. With speech, as with movement, the actor seeks to communicate meaning; but auditory "meanings" that cannot be heard are merely annoying to an audience in the theatre. Good voice production and good articulation are therefore central to the actor's task. Neither one of these can guarantee intelligent and responsive reading of dramatic dialogue, but both are in a sense prerequisite to such reading. Both in turn (and especially voice production) depend on good breathing.

Experienced actors and teachers of acting, though they sometimes differ as to the details, are in general agreement on the advisability of predominantly diaphragmatic breathing for voice production. That is to say, it is best to achieve the necessary enlargement of the chest cavity chiefly by diaphragmatic action (which is naturally accompanied both by expansion at the waistline and by a slight raising of the lower ribs), and to depend on a minimum action in the upper chest. Certainly there is less overall effort involved in diaphragmatic as opposed to chest breathing; and it is likely to offer less interference with either normal or characterized posture and action on the stage. It is probable also that emphasis on diaphragmatic breathing best assures the full and deep breathing required for tone production. The relatively shallow breathing needed for ordinary conversation in living room, classroom, or office will simply not give adequate support for a tone that must project beyond the footlights. Shallow breathing, with the inadequate breath reserves that inevitably accompany it, results in a voice that lacks firmness and body, as well as variety and staying power.

Diaphragmatic breathing, moreover, coordinated as it is with the action of the abdominal muscles, can assure not only deep but controlled breathing. In exhalation during vocalization, a good tone must be supported against the use of surplus breath and against sudden fluctuations in breath pressure. This is most readily accomplished by slightly delaying the lowering of the chest structure, which has been raised in some degree during inhalation, and by using the muscles of the abdominal wall to regulate the flow of outgoing breath. A clear and firm tone, as opposed to a breathy or fluctuating one, uses relatively little outgoing air. Even the actor who has breathed deeply enough, and consequently has stored up potential reserve power, can still produce weak or fuzzy tones if he uses too much breath; and he will at the same time be wasting his reserves, which are so necessary in sustaining long and continuous passages in the dialogue.

111

Adequate breathing for singing or speaking demands a feeling of strength, of security, and above all of control, at the waistline. The beginning actor soon discovers that he can develop such control only by conscious, and fairly persistent, experimentation and exercise. Weak, breathy, or blurred tones must normally be replaced by firm and clear ones; and the latter must be developed in practice until they become habitual. As with other corrective measures, this kind of self-training should ordinarily not be attempted during rehearsal or performance. Full concentration on interpretative and creative values during the actual playing of a scene does not allow of special attention to breath and breath control, or to any other essentially technical matter; and for this reason the actor should seek this sort of training before and between rehearsals.

Some teachers see an additional advantage in predominantly diaphragmatic breathing as opposed to chest breathing, in that the muscles concerned in the former are farther removed from those of the larynx and throat than are the muscles of the upper chest, and thus less likely to interfere with vocalization. In any case, full, smooth, and free response in the vocal cords must be unimpeded by tensions from without. A good tone, by the standards of the actor, is one that seems to flow easily through the throat, as if there were nothing there to interrupt it. If there is undue strain in the throat during vocalization, the result is likely to be an excessively high pitch; and if the muscles of the throat are tensed to the degree that the resonating surfaces are excessively hardened, the tone may develop a harsh or strident quality as well. On the contrary, an "open," relaxed throat contributes to mellowness and richness of tone.

Several other factors generally lead to improved quality, among them a controlled and balanced nasal resonance. The sounds [m], [n], and [ŋ] (orthographically represented as *m, n,* and *ng*) depend primarily on nasal resonance — i.e., in the formation of these sounds, the soft palate does not block off the nasal passages, and the sounds make full use of these passages as resonators. If, on the other hand — because of weak or sluggish action of the soft palate — these passages are not blocked off during the formation of normally *non*-nasal sounds, such as certain of the vowels, the result is what is popularly described as "overnasality" or a "nasal twang." There is a fairly wide range as to the amount of nasal resonance considered suitable in various sections of the country; and some actors feel that a slight nasalization of ordinarily non-nasal sounds gives them color and carrying power. For the most part, however, the typical untrained voice is likely to be handicapped by too much nasal resonance rather than by too little. Full use of the nasal resonance chambers is of course demanded on [m], [n], or [ŋ]; but for other sounds the chambers of the mouth and lower throat should be used predominantly. Flexibility and accuracy in action, so as to assure such discrimination in the use of the resonators, can be developed or restored through exercise.

For several generations, vocal teachers have counseled placement of the tone "against the teeth," or out "in front of the mouth." While this concept doubtless has an essentially psychological or figurative basis rather than a physiological or scientific one, it has apparently proved helpful in many cases. Certainly the clear vowel [a] (as in "father") can be produced, or can seem to be produced, abnormally far back in the throat, so that it vibrates "as though muffled with cotton." If, on the other hand, one focuses psychologically on placing the same sound "against the teeth" or "in the mask," he can readily deliver a more vibrant and brilliant tone.

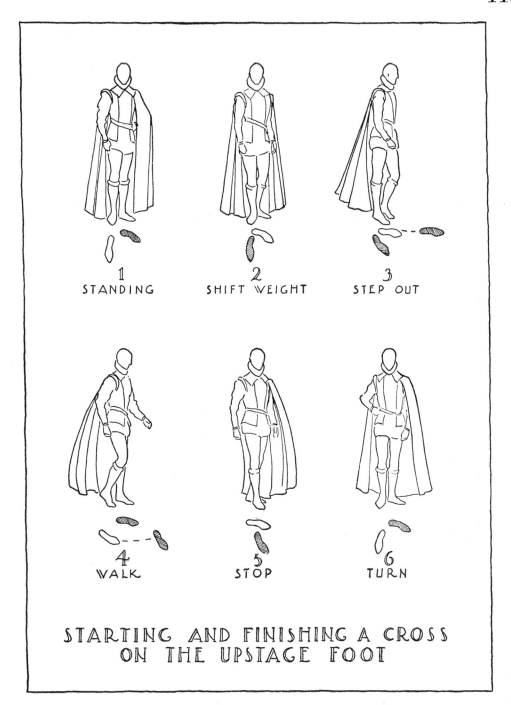

Figure 12. In order to move directly and economically, the actor steps out with the foot nearest the point to which he is going.

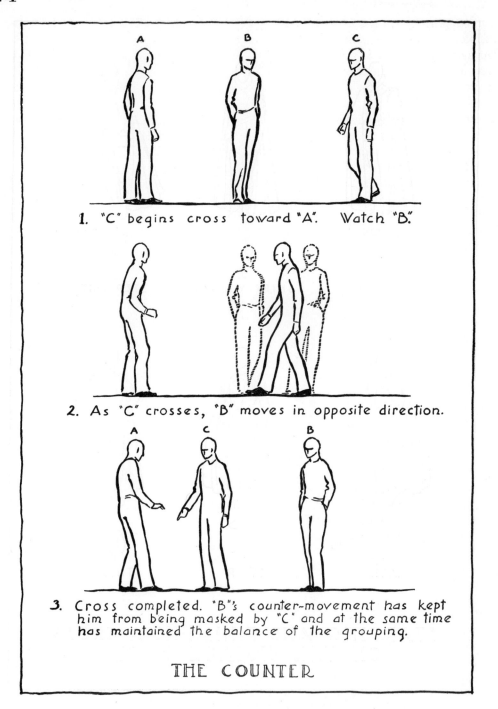

1. "C" begins cross toward "A". Watch "B".

2. As "C" crosses, "B" moves in opposite direction.

3. Cross completed. "B"'s counter-movement has kept him from being masked by "C" and at the same time has maintained the balance of the grouping.

THE COUNTER

Figure 13. Actors must often compensate for other actors' crosses by adjusting their own positions in relation to the group.

On a somewhat more literal plane, it is possible that such a concept of forward placement has proved important chiefly because most of the consonants and many of the vowels are concerned with relatively precise activity at the front of the mouth. The actor's articulation for purposes of the stage must — short of overprecision and artificiality — be clearer and more exact than it need be in ordinary conversation. When a member of a theatre audience claims that he cannot hear, it may be that what he really means is that he cannot understand. If such is the case, no amount of shouting will remedy the matter.

Rapid, jerky, staccato speech, whether it is due to generally poor physical co-ordination or to special nervous tensions of the moment, is obviously a serious liability for the actor — as, at another extreme, are sluggish lips and tongue or a tight jaw. "Natural" articulation for the stage has a heightened, slightly exaggerated clarity that makes for easy audibility and intelligibility under performance conditions. Unless the tempo and rhythm of an actor's lines are definitely though imperceptibly slowed down as compared with everyday standards, they will ordinarily *seem* to be too fast on the stage. Vowels in particular (as well as some of the continuant consonants) must be well sustained, since they lend to the voice much of its quality, its carrying power, and its emotional expressiveness; and certain weak consonants (e.g., those normally indicated as *f*, *p*, and *t*, and [θ] as in "thing") must be articulated clearly.

Adequate projection, in short, depends on an ample and well-supported breath supply; on an open throat, a rather careful moulding of the tone by mouth and lips, and some slowing of speech tempos and rhythms; and on free functioning of the vocal cords. The commonest danger signs are special tensions in the throat, undue rises in pitch, and a metallic or strident quality in the tone generally.

There are, of course, a few special problems with respect to intelligibility on an open stage. The need of an actor to be understood by spectators who are behind him, and who can not see his lips or read his features, requires him to articulate and to project his voice as clearly as in a traditional theatre of similar seating capacity. The difficulty often lies with the individual actor, particularly if he is unaccustomed to playing on an open stage. Since in the arena, for example, he has the security of knowing that no one of his auditors is very far away from him at any time and that he is free of the acoustical problems that sometimes plague a proscenium playhouse, he often mistakenly assumes that projection (as well as articulation) will "take care of itself."

A special case in this connection is the professional actor who has most recently been employed in a succession of film roles. When he is invited to play on an open stage, he may have become so used to letting the engineers and sound men worry about his audibility that he may adequately project only three-fourths of his time.

For the most part, however, vocal stimuli and vocal controls are handled almost exactly as they might be in a comparable proscenium playhouse. Only slight adaptations are necessary if one is to apply traditional principles to the arena or to other forms of the open stage.

READING FOR MEANING

But speech sounds are only the stuff of which meanings can be made and by which meanings can be communicated. Put together in sequence, speech sounds form words; and sequences of words, in turn, form the basic unit of oral communication: the *thought group*. That is to say, dramatic meaning does not move forward in a succession of single sounds, as sounds, or of single words, as words, but progresses in terms of groups of words expressing single ideas. And in some respects the actor's central job — so far as dialogue is concerned — is to locate, to fuse, and to project such thought groups, as they relate to each other and to the whole speech or scene.

Naturally enough, a single word does on occasion function as a complete thought unit — as with "yes" or "no"; "one" or "ten"; "go" or "stay." For the most part, however, people do not communicate by means of isolated words, but by means of organized clusters of words; and each of these expresses an idea or a relatively complete part of an idea. An actor may be reading a speech like King Duncan's "This castle hath a pleasant seat," or a somewhat briefer and less formal one, like "Magnificent spot!" The number of words actually used has varied between five and two. However, in each case the oral unit, and the unit of thought, has been not the separate words, but the entire word cluster itself. In speaking such a line, the actor does not think first and separately of *this,* then of *castle,* then of *hath,* and so on; he thinks of all the words in the cluster, fused as a single idea. To break up such a thought group into separate words or into unnecessarily small partial groups would be to deliver a reading that was as unnatural in its effect as it was difficult to follow. If the basic unit was a part of a longer sentence or sequence of sentences, the difficulty would be compounded.

The number of words functionally combined in a cluster need not be looked upon as fixed or unvaried. Depending on the communicative circumstances (e.g., if a line is motivated as strong or impressive, or if it is addressed to someone who may have difficulty in comprehending), the groups may properly be many and relatively short. Under opposite conditions, they may of course be fewer and relatively long. In any case, the grouping should normally follow psychological or motivational patterns rather than strictly grammatical ones; it should be based, as it were, on sense rather than syntax. A typical thought group usually contains from four or five to a dozen or more words, smoothly tied together and embodying a single idea that may be held in the speaker's and the listener's consciousness for at least a brief period of time.

During delivery, each such thought group is naturally set off from its neighbors by a shorter or longer pause. The length of the pause is dictated by the value which the actor wishes to set on the idea he has just completed and the time it takes him — psychologically speaking — to move on to the next one. The break may range in time from an almost imperceptible hesitation to what is known within the profession as "the grand pause." Neither its timing nor its placing should ordinarily be determined by any such consideration as lack of reserve breath, or failure to look ahead in the context; only the logic and the coherence of the passage involved are relevant in this connection. In effect, the pause serves as a sort of oral punctuation, unifying the inner content of the successive groups in themselves, and at the same time separating each group from its fellows and allowing the listeners to recognize interrelationships of meaning.

This last-named function is a vitally important one, since it is on *relations* between ideas that much of the forward movement in a passage of dialogue depends. If everything is made emphatic, nothing really emerges as emphatic, since meaningful distinctions are blurred and no sense of development or progression is established. On the whole, prominence must usually be given to *new* ideas at the expense of those which have been previously introduced; to ideas that express *change* or *contrast* (and in some cases *parallel value*) in relation to others; and to *main* ideas as opposed to parenthetical or subordinate ones. In each case, the mind must focus on significant, idea-carrying words or phrases, relegating the others to the background of attention.

To begin with the first classification listed above: it is essential to give positive stress to new material and to skip lightly over *echoes* of what has already been said or established. In the following quotation, the notion of "rain" is introduced at once, and is then echoed several times, always in the same language:

In all the world there is no rain like Paris rain. Even in that city of superlatives rain is a fiercely isolated phenomenon, something that is quite detached from the common diuturnities. London in November drizzles. . . . But Paris is different, vividly different. Rain in Paris is an event, not a routine.[5]

Below, however, the idea of "practical" or "practicality" is first introduced without the use of any such word as *practical,* and is then echoed several times in one form or another of the word itself:

To mention the poets as holding the key to our problem of individualism may well beget a smile from hardheaded men. But heads hardened beyond a point become blocks. Disdain of the poets reveals a mind with only the empty pride of practicality but without the means to be really practical in things social. It is not practical to defeat one's ends by the means one uses to achieve them. An individualism which actually develops only a few individuals and salves other individuals with the mere anarchistic hope that they are well off since you are — this is a seepage theory of welfare which has every element of wishful thinking. Such utopianism does not become practical men.[6]

In reading either example aloud, the echoes must be properly subordinated, and

prominence must be given to each new point as it first appears in the author's progression of meaning. Nothing new must be implied by the repetition of an old idea, lest new distinctions in relation to that idea be blurred or obscured. Similarly, if in a dramatic sequence an actor fails to stress an idea that is new, or falsely stresses one that is not, he merely beclouds the meaning and probably ends up by deceiving his listeners. If a scene is to move forward, the matter of echoing — or, as some actors prefer to call it, back reference — demands constant alertness on the part of the speakers, lest they bury the new in a false concern for the old. It is worth remarking that pronouns are by definition "back references," and are normally not to be given special focus.

Contrasts or parallels must always be clearly, though not crudely or obtrusively, marked by the speaker — an accomplishment that is not always easy to insure, especially when the units concerned are separated by long intervening passages, or when more than one set of parallels or contrasts is immediately involved. Proper focus on ideas which are logically or intrinsically important, at the expense of the merely subordinate or parenthetical, is less commonly a difficulty for most actors. In some cases, however, especially in the reading of verse, a main idea may be contained in a grammatically subordinate construction, and will need special treatment lest it be lost or blurred. A special class of subordinate units are those whose meaning is naturally implied from the context. Thus a schoolboy, in his preoccupation with words, as such, might assert that the fire "continued to *burn* for several hours," though the mature and wary speaker would assume that fire "burns" and slide easily over such implied matter.

THE NATURE OF EMPHASIS

In these, and in all other matters of focus or emphasis in line reading, it is best not to

[5] From "Paris Rain and London Rain," by Joseph Auslander. By permission of *The Christian Science Monitor.*

[6] Reprinted from *The Promise of American Politics* by T. V. Smith by permission of The University of Chicago Press. Copyright 1936 by University of Chicago.

look upon the process as a mere stressing of chosen words. On the contrary, it should be regarded as a means of giving new (or contrasting or important) *ideas* prominence, or of bringing them into the forefront of attention. This is ordinarily a rather subtle operation, coloring an entire sentence or thought group, and rarely concentrating its effect on individual smaller units. The beginning actor is well advised to think of "plugging" ideas or concepts rather than words or phrases, per se. If he sets his mind to putting an exact shade of meaning into a fairly large unit, then the stressing of individual portions of that unit may well take care of itself.

What he needs to avoid in particular is an undue dependence on punching or pounding as a mode of being emphatic. Anyone who equates emphasis with percussion can hit (in his own view) all the right words, but still manage to express all the wrong meanings. In expressive communication, ideas are brought into prominence by natural changes in pitch, in intonation, and timing (or in a blending of several or all of these), and rarely by stress alone. Overconcern with mere force, on the other hand, may destroy the meaning as well as the natural sound or rhythm of a line.

It is of course true that some words (on occasion, indeed, certain syllables) do carry a good deal more of the meaning than others, and that if these key units are assimilated by the listener, he will understand the whole, since the remainder of the original sentence or sentences will be suggested by the rhythm, the melody, or the context in general. But this is a matter of extreme subtlety and delicate proportion, dependent only in relatively small part on force or percussion. As an example, it may be useful to examine the following speech by Ellen Creed, in Act I, Scene ii of *Ladies in Retirement:*

Ellen: You're quite right about my sisters. They are — peculiar. I don't wonder they've got on your nerves. I think perhaps they've got on mine, too, and that's why I said what I did.

But, you see, I love them. I love them intensely — just because they are so helpless. They're almost a religion with me. You're quite right, though, Leonora. They can't stay here. They must go. . . . [7]

Properly read in their context, the following portions of Ellen's speech could register the essence of the whole:

. . . right . . . sisters . . . peculiar . . . nerves . . . mine, too . . . said . . . love . . . intensely . . . are so helpless . . . religion . . . right . . . stay here . . . go.

These portions would not carry the essence of the speech, however, if they were looked upon as "the emphatic words" and were then stressed by pounding, at the expense of companion values in pitch, intonation, timing, and rhythm. If, in the last two sentences quoted, both *stay here* and *go* were arbitrarily and mechanically made "emphatic" in this way, the result would patently be nonsense for all concerned.

Nor would it be helpful, in the case of "They can't stay here," to press arbitrarily on *can't,* for example, on the ground that this word is the most emphatic one, logically and intrinsically, as the sentence is set down on the page. If this scheme were valid, then the sense of any passage would best be projected in reading aloud by exerting special force on such individual units as "must," "will," "no," "not," "but," "if," "especially," "utterly," and the like. In practice, reading of this sort is choppy in its effect, and actually neither clear nor emphatic. The sense of such words, which are logically strong as they appear on the printed page, must ordinarily be assimilated into the intent of the whole and must color the effect of the entire line, as it is ultimately delivered on the stage.

Any device for assuring that the actor is speaking and communicating meanings rather than pronouncing and reciting words is a good device; any device that substitutes

[7] (Dramatists Play Service, 1941), p. 39. By permission of the publishers.

for meaning a mechanical application of stress — or, for that matter, of intonation or voice quality — is likely to be a bad one, in the long run. Most good actors have at some time or other been aided by the very simple (and quite ancient) device of "bridging" — that is to say, the interpolation of explanatory material in order to clarify the meaning of a passage as it appears in the playscript. Between sentences, or between basic units of the same sentence, the actor "thinks into" a speech characteristic words and phrases that indicate appropriate focus and suggest appropriate implications. The following examples may serve to illustrate the possibilities.

Why leave it to me? (Well, I'll tell you why!)
Why leave it to me? (It's none of my affair.)
Why leave it to me? (This is always the way it turns out.)
Why leave it to me? (I don't think I can handle it.)

This is a first-class opportunity. (I see that, now.)
This is a first-class opportunity. (Surely you can't object?)
This is a first-class opportunity. (The others were phonies.)
This is a first-class opportunity. (It's worse than the rest have been.)

In rehearsal, it may be necessary to *speak* in such phrases, later dropping them when fully expressive readings have been achieved. In any case, no mere trick of expression, and in particular no mechanical application of pressure or accent, would serve in either case to give these lines the precise shade or focus of meaning that such "bridging" can give them.

SPEAKING IN A CONTEXT

Here, as elsewhere, the particular phraseology in which a line may be written is for the actor only a partial indication of its full-est and richest communicative possibilities. Above all, the actor must resist assuming that all communicated meanings are somehow purely intellectual meanings, based on the immediate logical content of the speech concerned. In the theatre, a logically "correct" reading may still be unsatisfactory. If it is delivered as though barren of all feeling, it may seem arbitrary or dull; if it is given in a mood which the author did not intend, it may be inaccurate or misleading in its effect. In addition to his awareness of grouping and group relations, and of various factors in emphasis, the actor must be acutely responsive to specific *attitudes* and to particular *emotional values* inherent in his lines. He must, in short, read from a context.

Only occasional lines in a typical play are flat statements of fact, without emotional color or significance, even in predominantly expository passages. Most dramatic lines are intended to stimulate, not merely to inform; many of them, indeed, will not "make their point" if they are treated factually or literally. The logical sense-meaning of a speech is of course the basis of its communicative effect, and if this basic sense-meaning is absent or distorted, the resulting reading, it is true, may be mere sound and fury. But full communication in the theatre is achieved only when such sense-meanings are overlaid with contextual values, growing out of character and situation.

Pointer readings on a gauge are perhaps the ultimate in immediate, scientific, factual reference; yet even these can not, in some backgrounds, be merely informative. A gauge-reading of "fifteen" must assuredly have one communicative effect if the danger point is twenty pounds of pressure, quite another if the danger point is known to be fourteen. Obviously, two characters can utter identical phrases, but mean entirely different things. That is to say, communication varies not only in terms of sense-meanings or dictionary-meanings, or even conventional grammar and syntax, but in terms of the intent, the attitude, the tone, and the mood of a given character in a given situation. Regardless of the exact language in which a speech is cast, the value which an actor sets on a phrase or a sentence must grow out of — and in performance must suggest — the character's immediate purpose, the attendant or preceding circumstances, and the general function of the scene. The actor's most persistent query, "What do I mean?", must be stretched to include a good deal more in dramatic dialogue than surface logic. With this basic question are fused others such as these: "How do I feel about all this at the moment? How did that line or that action or that decision affect me as a character? How can I show that I am affected? What must I make my own line *say*, if I am to reply in this context?"

An apparently bland line like "Ask Mr. Luton if he wouldn't mind coming here for a moment" is hardly unusual in modern dramatic literature, and it is ordinarily not expected to carry rich overtones of meaning. Placed in Act II of Somerset Maugham's *The Circle*, however, such a line can no longer be read as though it had only surface value or significance:

Footman: Yes, sir.
Arnold: Tell Mr. Luton to come here at once.
Elizabeth: Ask Mr. Luton if he wouldn't mind coming here for a moment. . . .
Footman: Very good, madam.[8]

Since Elizabeth has just faced her own husband, Arnold, with the news that she is about to go away with Teddy Luton, and since Arnold in his fury is summoning Teddy to throw him out of the house, a commonplace reading of "Ask Mr. Luton if he wouldn't mind . . ." would scarcely make its point.

Both on and off the stage, more than one servant has told her mistress, "I'm as good

    [8] Acting edition (Samuel French, 1948), pp. 45–46. By permission of the publishers.

as you are," usually with standard implications. When — on "The Island" in Barrie's *The Admirable Crichton* — the normal roles are reversed and Lady Mary is goaded into making the identical remark to Tweeny, who happens to be her maid, the reading demands more than standard implications.

These are fairly obvious examples of shifts in surface value because of context; any well-written play would exhibit others, as well as many less obvious (though no less significant) ones. If a character is asking a boon from a friend, a relative, or a debtor, he does not — regardless of the specific language he is called upon to use — ask it with quite the same flavor as from someone else. If he insists or affirms, he does so differently a third or a fourth time, compared with the first or the second. In some cases (as in classic tragedy, whose audience can be expected to have foreknowledge of the outcome), the irony in the protagonist's lines provides an overlay of special meaning. In others, the special communicative values derive from the locale or milieu in which an otherwise matter-of-fact speech may be delivered; if two lovers, rivals, or enemies were to confront each other in physical circumstances which duplicated or reflected circumstances in their past relationship, the dialogue would need to take on new and added values. A wide variety of other similar possibilities might readily be listed here.

The influence of playing in a dramatic context can be examined in still another way: an individual character is for the most part not speaking by and to himself, as though delivering a single continuous passage; he is "answering back" to others who are themselves part of the situation. The meaning values in his readings, therefore, are varied and ramified not only by the contextual background in general, but by the specific interaction of character on character, speech on speech, reply on reply. The echoes, parallels, or emphases which a single actor chooses to recognize derive not alone from the logic (or emotion or attitude) of his own character; they derive as well from a reaction to the logic (or emotion or attitude) of his partners. The pace or the pitch level which he selects as clearest and most valid under the circumstances must depend in part on its relation to those of other characters in the scene. A passage which might seem to be just a bit too hurried or high-pitched in a scene with one group of characters might well turn out to need even faster pace and wider pitch range if it had to be read in a different set of character relationships.

It is thus the special responsibility of individual players within a group to avoid either conscious or unconscious imitation of their fellows in pitch, volume, tempo, intonation, and the like. It is only too easy for one actor to "take his level" from others in the same scene, a tendency he must regularly suppress. If the others are fully acting out their roles, they may, for example, be relatively loud and strident of speech or relatively slow and deliberate in delivery; yet the indicated motivations for his particular character may require quite the opposite. When surface details in the readings of other characters are allowed to exert a direct influence on his own, he is bound to weaken or distort the individualized quality of his characterization and to blur the outlines of the scene as a whole. Similar temptations to imitate are to be avoided in pronunciation also, as in the case of an American character in the midst of a group with South British standards, or of a colloquial pattern set against relatively formal ones. Group clarity depends to a substantial degree on the maintenance of such planned and motivated contrasts.

INSURING CREDIBILITY

The level of "naturalness" often rises, too, in direct proportion to the sharpness of contrast in the readings, and to the vividness of the give-and-take between characters. Players who give a clear-cut impression that they are in active communication with each other — however quiet or however violent the scene may rightly be at the moment — are likely to seem most real. Several devices for quickening this communicative sense, and for developing what might be called oral contact, are available to the actor, and they are especially useful during the early and middle stages of rehearsal. The best of these are simple and direct in their operation, and do not call for mechanical distortion of any kind. If the actor is generally responsive to various factors in the context, yet seems insufficiently "alive" in his exchanges with other characters, it is possible that he needs only to enlarge or intensify his natural reading patterns. It may be that the readings he has developed up to that point are accurate enough and are faithful to the given circumstances, but that their range of variety must be widened. Using his already-developed normal patterns as a base, he therefore enlarges the perhaps overly mild distinctions inherent in these. Contrasts in pitch, volume, and tempo are intensified; changes in melodic pattern are subtly exaggerated; pauses are strengthened; and in general, the effect of "answering back" is heightened.

When it is intelligently applied, such a device can make a more or less colorless, though otherwise correct, reading ring true; it is one mode of defense against the spectator's perennial complaint, "I couldn't believe a word of it!" In other cases — as with language which is unusual or unfamiliar to the actor concerned, or which expresses what are to him unusual or unfamiliar sentiments — a temporary paraphrase is likely to be helpful. Such speeches can be phrased in more familiar or more colloquial language and rehearsed in this form until vivid and convincing expression is achieved; and the tone or the flavor read into the paraphrase can usually then be transferred to the original language. Bridging — introduced in an earlier section as a device for reading in special overtones of meaning — can also be utilized to achieve unique vividness and flavor, otherwise lacking in certain lines or speeches, and to develop oral contact between actors in a group.

In later stages of rehearsal, when lines may tend to become a routine matter, it is especially difficult to maintain this lively human quality. Constant repetition is allowed to dull the perceptions, and stereotyped recitations gradually take the place of the ebb and flow of vivid speech. Functional desires and purposes, of which the actor may once have been acutely aware, are weakened or lost; attention lags; and even listening becomes a formality. The player seems merely abstracted. At this point, the vitality of the earlier give-and-take must somehow be restored. The actor must focus, with the utmost concentration, on convincing his partner of the significance and value of what he has to say. Without completely losing sight of other objectives, he must concentrate for a time on *arousing belief*. At the moment of utterance, a rich awareness of the inner content of his speeches must be coupled with a vivid urge to communicate, to convince, to excite. Stanislavski wrote in this connection of "infecting" one's partner.[9] He recognized, too, that the result itself can be infectious, in the sense that exciting belief in someone else intensifies belief within the speaker. Conviction breeds conviction on the stage; and genuine conviction on the stage usually carries to the house.

There remains one other factor of central importance in establishing and maintaining credibility; this is best described as a *conversational quality* in the dialogue. Most of the sense of conviction which an actor strives so hard in other ways to attain cannot be consistently maintained unless most signs of

9 E.g., in *Building a Character,* Chapter 8.

false elegance, artificiality, and affectation are rigorously excluded from his delivery. He will need to recognize from the beginning that overpreciseness and exaggerated syllabification are faulty signs of either correctness or clarity of English speech. An overly exact enunciation, in which each word or syllable is given equal value, is on the contrary just as bad as a slovenly enunciation; for the actor, it is in some ways worse. In addition to being unnatural and uninteresting, overprecision destroys normal word grouping and interferes with proper focus on important points in the dialogue.

It is a commonplace of English phonetics that the "best" conversational speech recognizes normal weakening of vowels in unaccented syllables. Unlike French, for example (whose pattern of accent requires a relatively even touch on the successive syllables in a unit, with a slightly heavier pressure only on the last), English speaking is characterized by a wide degree of contrast between accented and unaccented syllables, and by a weakened — and often shortened — form of the vowel in unstressed positions. Thus, the "o" vowels in *locomotive* have several different degrees or gradations of value when this word is pronounced normally and naturally by an English-speaking person; the vowel sound in *you* or *do* is graded in value according to the position and stress of the syllable which it forms; the vowels in *a, the,* or *and* are usually pronounced in weakened form; and so on. When such examples as these are arbitrarily (and incorrectly) given full value, regardless of their unaccented position, the result is monotonous, artificial, and unconvincing. Not infrequently, the effect is that of a foreign-born speaker, as yet not wholly familiar with the rhythms and accents of the English language.

Other related handicaps to credibility are "spelling" pronunciations, and pronunciations based on false elegance. Normal pronunciation simply does not include the "t" sound in

Christmas and *hasten,* the "th" in *clothes,* and the like. Nor does it include, for example, such affectations as "tryooth" for *truth,* or the indiscriminate use of the so-called broad "a." On a somewhat different basis, repetitious or singsong inflections of any kind will obviously interfere with conversational quality. Variations of both pitch and tempo should ordinarily seem free and spontaneous in spoken, as distinguished from recited, dialogue. For this reason, planned pauses and changes of pace — valuable for easing an otherwise stilted passage — can readily become stereotyped, if extreme care is not taken in utilizing them.

Generally speaking, any pattern which calls undue attention to voice or pronunciation per se and therefore distracts attention from the actor's sense of conviction is a potential trouble-maker.

11 | Characterization

Completeness in Characterization · Analyzing a Role · Selection and Adaptation Enrichment · Imagination and Belief

One of the central functions of the actor is to realize and embody character in action, and to do so as fully and as vividly as possible. Though plot may be, as Aristotle insisted, "the First Principle" of the drama, character and plot have — throughout the history of drama as well as of dramatic criticism — necessarily been closely tied in practice. It is true that the bare outlines of the plot of *Hamlet* or *Macbeth* can arouse in us a certain curiosity and excitement, if merely because of the variety and the violence of the incidents involved; yet it is a critical commonplace that we are truly absorbed in the action of either play only when we know something about the persons involved and care something about what may be happening to them. Incidents, as such, take on significance and value only when they are meaningfully related to human desires and motives. That is a principal reason why so many cut-down versions of Shakespeare (and, for that matter, so many thirty-minute radio adaptations of standard modern works) have proved unsatisfying. When there is barely time to present what has happened, there is no time to suggest why; and it is the "why" that makes the difference.

COMPLETENESS IN CHARACTERIZATION

From the standpoint of both playwright and actor, there are varying levels of completeness in characterization. As the characters appear in the manuscript, some of them are well-rounded and individualized; others are typed; and a few are essentially without characteristic qualities of any kind, being in effect mouthpieces of the author. The student who is relatively unfamiliar with the long history of drama since Aeschylus, and who bases his judgment principally on post-Ibsen forms and on post-Ibsen theories of production, is likely to assume that all characters must be projected strictly as individuals. Actually, as an earlier section of this volume has already indicated,[1] the range — i.e., both in the playwright's conception and in his execution — is rather wide. In many plays, particularly those of complicated plot and large casts, there are various levels of completeness in characterization.

In such plays, two or three characters may be developed as three-dimensional, four or five may be lightly sketched, and others may be presented as mere shadows. Even Ibsen, devoted by temperament and policy to naturalistic detail in characterization, achieved fullness and richness in a bare majority of instances. Among Ibsen's smaller-cast plays, *Ghosts* and one or two others offer mostly fully-rounded figures; and *The Wild Duck*, despite a sizable number of parts, achieves a remarkable uniformity in the thoroughness

[1] See especially pages 31–33.

with which the major and minor characters are drawn. For the most part, however, Ibsen and other modern playwrights have, like their predecessors, turned to readily available and easily recognizable patterns for their minor and middle-range characters.

So long as he stays within the scope of the author's basic style and purpose, the actor has a certain freedom — indeed, a certain obligation — to fill in the bare outlines which are offered him by typed and shadowed roles. Physically and psychologically, intellectually and emotionally, it is required that he supply from his own resources details which the author has merely suggested or has not indicated at all. Beginning with general considerations of age, station, occupation, nationality, state of health, and the like, and moving on through personal traits of speech, posture, or movement, the actor tends to complete the embodiment merely outlined by the playwright. Such roles as Chrysalde, Arnolphe's confidant in *The School for Wives;* Lucentio in *The Taming of the Shrew;* Le Bret in *Cyrano;* Jim O'Connor in *The Glass Menagerie;* and Ivy and Violet in *The Family Reunion* — all these, though representing a wide range of dramaturgical form and style, are very lightly sketched by the author. Unless they are rounded out with characteristic detail and revealing motivation, supplied in large part by the actors preparing the roles, they will seem unnecessarily weak and flat, if not unclear, in the playing.

But there is an obverse to the coin of thus completing the author's indicated characterization. In any well-written play, there is a necessary scale of centers of interest and there are necessary limits to the proportionate focus of attention which each center of interest can be allowed. If a competent playwright has written into his script a series of descending levels of individualized characterization, it is important that both actors and director respect these levels, modifying the relationships between them only after serious consideration. An overzealous player — having, perhaps, badly learned the principles and techniques of one of the Russian systems of character building — may make a minor character or scene so strong in attention value as to dwarf a major one, and may thus distort the intended balance and proportion of an entire act.

Occasionally, of course, the playwrights themselves are uncertain or confused as to where the allowable interest (i.e., between two or more characters) properly lies. In Clifford Odets' *Rocket to the Moon,* the author seems to develop a markedly growing interest in Cleo as the play moves forward. As a result, an actress preparing this role would ultimately wonder whether she should not conceive of Cleo as the central figure in the action. Yet in the early scenes the predominant focus is clearly on another character, and the specific intentions of the playwright seem to shift and blur throughout the course of the play. In an instance such as this, even a clear-cut interpretative decision by the producing group may be insufficient to stabilize and clarify a performance of the work. In other instances — e.g., Ibsen's *The Wild Duck* — there are, so to speak, parallel centers of interest, several of which can be developed to a relatively high degree of completeness without seriously distracting from the central one. Nonetheless, the roles of Gregers and Hedvig (and to a lesser degree that of Old Ekdal), if they are played too vividly and with overattention to characteristic detail, are in danger of weakening the impact of Hialmar and therefore of the play as a whole.

ANALYZING A ROLE

The player's obligation to deliver an interesting and individualized characterization, then, should not exceed his obligation to satisfy his playwright's intention and his director's interpretative design. Such matters as these had better be settled upon early rather than late. Many of the basic decisions which a particular actor shares with other actors and with the director are treated in Section V, especially in connection with "The Period of Analysis." [2] It is sufficient here to summarize these group considerations, as a preliminary to examining the individual player's responsibility in relation to them. They may be discussed for present purposes under the headings of plot and plot structure; thematic content; and atmosphere and style.

Based as it usually is on conflict and contrast, the plot line of a play typically develops a series of major and minor climaxes, few of which can be played for full clarity and effectiveness unless they are recognized from the beginning of the rehearsal period. On a concrete and personal level, dramatic conflicts are exemplified by individual protagonists and antagonists, and by persons or groups related or attached to these. In such realistically plotted and balanced pieces as Galsworthy's *Strife*, Roberts (representing the striking men) and John Anthony (chairman of the company) are boldly set forth and contrasted as opponents in an arbitrary struggle; in most plays the basic conflict is not so sharply outlined. In some cases the conflict is developed by means of complicating traits within a single character, as (in O'Neill's *The Emperor Jones*) between Jones's desires and pretensions and his own fears and superstitions. On a more abstract and universal level, the conflicts in a dramatic action tend to symbolize forces in the protagonist's world — social, economic, or other. In *Strife*, mentioned above, the personal stories of Roberts and Anthony are blended with a broader conflict of capital and labor. A whole range of other dramas of "social awareness," from *The Weavers* to

2 See pages 464–468; see also under "The Director as Interpreter" in Chapter 22.

Waiting for Lefty, focus similarly on class differences; and in some instances a group, rather than an individual, actually serves as the play's protagonist.

The units of action — that is to say, the episodes or structural scenes — on which the playwright has based his plot development are of special concern for the producing group. The limits of such scenes are ordinarily set by the entrance or exit of major characters or major groups of characters, especially as such exits or entrances mark off a recognizable dramatic unit. There is frequently a change of mood, tempo, and focus at the beginning of these scenes; and each can be found to carry a purpose, flavor, and point of its own, as contrasted with preceding and following units. The forward movement of the action is delayed, held in suspension, or quickened in most instances. In others, there is a distinct reversal — either a reversal of direction, so far as the plot line is concerned, or a reversal of control, in terms of individual characters.

In deciding on the limits of these structural units, the production group should avoid the extremes of either unusual length or unusual brevity. If the separate units are conceived of as too long, then the larger unit of which the scenes are a part (e.g., an act) may lack variety and color, as well as clarity of development; if the scenes are made to be arbitrarily short, the act may lack unity and coherence, since it will appear to be unnecessarily choppy and broken. Failure to settle at a fairly early stage on clearly defined structural divisions of this sort can greatly handicap both actors and director in later rehearsals. Only by working in terms of such a pattern of organization can the various stages in the development of the action be borne in mind and projected in rehearsal and performance.

Frequently more decisive than plot in determining the special quality of a dramatic composition is its "thought" or "meaning" or "theme." Always elusive and rarely explicit, the thematic material cannot necessarily be encompassed in a specific statement — though it is important for all engaged in a production to go as far as possible toward expressing the play's central meaning in simple and precise language. Examples of this process are offered on pages 332–333, in relation to plays ranging from the *Oedipus* to *Death of a Salesman*. Since the group opinion in such matters will ultimately affect all the individual interpretations of the several roles, this is another decision which cannot be long postponed. Where there is a wide difference in reaction and judgment, the director will need to set a basic interpretation on which all can depend and from which all can work.

A number of great plays weave together several dramatic threads in terms of a single dominant idea; in this sense, *Lear*, for example, and perhaps *Antony and Cleopatra* as well, is symphonic. The overly tidy and logical (though at the same time dull) simplicity which John Dryden attempted to give the latter fable in *All for Love* is well known. The central theme of many plays is, of course, simple; and in some cases it is merely frail. Speaking generally, one can only say that the relative focus on theme differs widely from script to script, and that it is as gross an error to underestimate this focus as to overstress it at the wrong place and time. So far as the actor is concerned, the following is a helpful overview of the problem:

It is best not to look upon finding the theme as a mere exercise in intellectual gymnastics. In some cases you may not wish to call the process "finding a theme" at all, and you may not be able or willing to force your idea about the play into [a] specific statement. . . . In other cases you may wish to identify or combine the process with a search for the author's purpose in writing the play, or the author's life-attitude or world-attitude as he has expressed it in this play and possibly in others. You may prefer, as some

people do, to call what you are looking for the play's "core" or *"leit-motif"* or "Idea." But — with your director, of course — you usually cannot avoid some decision as to *what the play is fundamentally about*, as to what essential and unique characteristics set it apart from other plays of broadly similar plots and situations.[3]

The emotional tone, or atmosphere, of a production is another intangible, difficult to describe — though easy to recognize in performance, particularly if it is "right." Certainly one can say that a single spirit must pervade every dramatic production, lending to it an ultimate unity of effect and an emotional quality proper to its theme and its action. This dominant atmosphere — which, difficult though it may be to capture in words, must be thoroughly agreed upon by all concerned in a dramatic enterprise — should never be seriously violated. It is, for example, an interpretative truism that in comedy, no matter how "serious" affairs may appear to be at the moment, a generally and unmistakably optimistic tone must prevail. Here again, in planning their work, the players must balance their obligation to certain roles against their obligation to the play; and their obligation to a single scene against their obligation to the entire production.

The immediate function of emotional tone in a performance is the establishment in the audience of a prevailing mood suitable to the context of a given play. Tone is a matter of *treatment;* and, if it is kept at all consistent throughout the rehearsal period, it can later exert a subtle but recognizable control over the responses of the spectators, leading them unobtrusively to accept the values which the director has set for his interpretation. Some of the auditory and visual patterns which a director may impose on his actors, as a means of intensifying the atmosphere of a particular production, are indicated on pages 411–415, in Section V.

[3] Albright, *Working Up a Part*, p. 15.

It should be obvious that much the same plot material can be dealt with — by playwright or performer — sentimentally or skeptically, seriously or trivially, tragically or comically; basically similar themes may be treated with sharp satire, gentle humor, or dry wit. The sustained atmosphere of a well-planned performance can be the hallmark which distinguishes the individuality of one serious playwright from that of another, the unique spirit of a past age from that of the present, or the peculiar quality of one national culture from that of its contemporaries. The capturing of this dominating atmosphere — allowing for any necessary variety and contrast — is therefore a group responsibility of the first magnitude.

The personal decisions which an individual actor makes in analyzing his role, then, must reflect an awareness of the group decisions arrived at in respect to plot, theme, and tone. In actually beginning work toward a given characterization, it is best to lay out a preliminary and basic plan which can later be modified, added to, and refined. That is to say, whether the part in itself as it appears in the script is highly individualized or not, it is still a good policy to develop, at a relatively early stage in the process, a kind of generalized image of the character, and to add detail later as the part may require and allow. Ultimately, as we have seen, every permissible degree of individualization is desirable, in typed and shadowed roles as well as in three-dimensional ones. On the other hand, a truly unique character on the stage would be a monstrosity: in his effect upon an audience, he would vary between the merely bizarre and the unintelligible. In the theatre, if not in life, every "individual" character is in one way or another a variant from a recognizable class or group, professional, social, economic, or other. Every "individual" trait is in some sense a variant from a recognizable pattern, personal, cultural, racial, or otherwise. Playwrights in every age have not hesitated to simplify and universalize their characters in terms of such classifications; and actors have found convenience as well as logic in the categories of "leading man and leading lady," "the juveniles," "the heavy," "the comedian," "the soubrette," and the like. For most actors various forms of typification are helpful (if not, indeed, essential) as a preliminary framework for developing a rounded characterization in rehearsal and performance.

With an experienced actor, and one relatively familiar with the various facets of the character concerned, the generalized conception on which he plans to base his later work may be arrived at quickly and directly; with others, the process may be lengthy and involved. In any event, a rough plan for organizing and recording the main features of the role should be drawn up at this point. In a standard plan of this sort, the character's general bearing, as suggested by nationality, station in life, occupation, and other similar factors, might well come first. Considerations of age, physical strength and vitality, present state of health, and the like, could come next. To these one would add also items like the character's intellectual and moral disposition, as indicated generally in the manuscript, and his customary mode of emotional response to problems that concern him. To be sure, not all of these elements can be fully assimilated at once; but facing up to them promptly will tend to make the work easier (and the results more substantial) later on.[4]

In connection with this general analysis, some consideration should be given to objective details. How, for example, ought the character — as thus far conceived — to stand and move and speak? Would he ordinarily be self-possessed, confident, bold; discreet,

[4] It is best to relate all such considerations, as early as possible, to plans for make-up and costume. Sections on both these items have been included as appendices to the present volume.

circumspect, cautious; uncertain, indecisive, weak? How, then, would he carry himself? Wear his clothes? How sweeping would he make his gestures? Would he stride freely across the stage? How would he normally sound? Typically, what would be his quality of voice; his range of pitch and volume? In supplying even tentative answers to such queries as these, the player must be at his most observant, his most imaginative, and his most inventive.

SELECTION AND ADAPTATION

Fundamentally, there is only one source for the answers: the player's own resources. The help which he gets from his directors, his teachers, and his fellow-workers can be suggestive and stimulating; and he would not wish to do without it. But their experience of life is not his, and they cannot create for him an external image which he can believe in and which he can successfully project. In searching for characteristic details, he may depend on his own past experience, his imagination, his intuition. He may draw on his family, his friends; pictures, engravings, news photographs; novels, short stories, essays. He may turn to the courtroom, the concert hall, the ball park. He may observe the patrician and the *nouveau riche*, the employed and the unemployable, the garrulous as well as the inarticulate.

These and a host of other opportunities can be used to observe and record the outward signs of human character and intention. A distinctive frown or twinkle, an unusual way of carrying the neck or the shoulders, a characteristic mode of resting the hands on the hips or of holding a cup or a newspaper, a special kind of stride or shuffle — all are grist to the mill. Each, stored up in the memory and later modified for use on the stage, can help to give a dramatic character the appearance, the flavor, or the point that is required. To be sure, the actor is not ad-

vised to note such details so that he may some day merely imitate or reproduce them as a kind of novelty act or trick, or as a kind of superficial decoration which he can apply to the outer surface of the character he is conceiving. But he is urged to record them with accuracy and discrimination, so that he may later modify and combine them for use in motivated expression.

However, out of the infinite number of potential choices — in gesture and voice, attitude and manner — considerable selectivity is not only possible but mandatory. Multiplicity and complexity of detail may be "true to life," to be sure; but in acting (as in the other arts) unimportant, confusing, and unnecessary details must be rigorously screened out. Many actions in ordinary living are desultory and commonplace, even meaningless. Others are made up of unrelated trifles which cannot be composed into a significant design. The indicated technique for the actor is to choose only the most telling and most typical details from the many that are available, and then to make the most of the relatively few that remain.

As an inherent part of selection and emphasis, it is necessary also to adapt specific habits and traits, observed in others, for use in the theatre. The general circumstances of theatrical presentation, and the particular blocking of a given production in a given setting, in themselves prescribe certain adaptations. No matter how "real" it would be for some characters to speak quietly and to execute overly dainty gestures and movements, their words and actions would still have to be made intelligible to an audience. The simplest patterns of movement — sitting, rising, pacing, turning — may require adaptation on the stage if the actor is to avoid awkwardness inappropriate even for a character intended to seem awkward. In the living room at home, a characteristic movement might be made in any one of several directions, with no loss or gain in general expressiveness; on the stage, the areas to and from which a movement is made (and the movement's relation to the overall grouping at the moment) help to determine both its strength and its point. Scenes of eating and drinking, of violent movement, or of extreme emotional intensity obviously require adaptation on the part of the actors concerned, if they are to speak and gesture meaningfully and with proper timing in relation to their fellows.

Other adaptations are indicated because of a player's own voice, physique, and personality. A distinctive tone of voice or manner of wearing the hair or of gesturing with a flip of the wrist that might be suitable for one individual might not do at all for another in an identical or similar role. The differences between the Barrymore Hamlet and the Evans or Gielgud Hamlet go deeper than deliberate choice as to "interpretation"; each artist was in a measure forced to use characteristic detail which suited his body, voice, and stage presence. Again, the habitual postures and gestures which a given actor can choose for his character depend for their full effectiveness on what the other actors on stage may be planning to do. Too much repetition of the same patterns will cancel out their clarity and significance for all the actors involved, and too much contrast between patterns may violate the unity and coherence of the ensemble. The relationships between character and character are always determined to some extent by whether the actors playing the roles are constitutionally heavy, loud, energetic, fast moving, or whatever; and, if one actor's character is to be lazier or less meticulous than another's, mutual adaptation will be necessary on a personal as well as an aesthetic level.

Finally, and perhaps most important, adaptations from real-life observation will be required because of the nature and purpose of the role. Reference has already been made to the general influence of plot, theme, and atmosphere, as these condition the choice of characteristic detail. Separable from such influences, though at the same time functionally related to them, is what many actors call the character's *super-objective:* the central drive which underlies his actions, thoughts, and attitudes throughout the play, and the central drive by which his final climactic action can be explained or justified. Once it is established that Hialmar (again in Ibsen's *The Wild Duck*) is a man who will ultimately drive his daughter to suicide because of his passionately self-centered view of himself and his role in the family circle, the actor has a set of criteria for choosing and adapting external details of behavior. In the earlier portions of the action, the player can emphasize patterns of conduct which reveal Hialmar's basic attitude, and can apply the test of consistency and relevancy to other patterns. In Ibsen's play, he will sooner or later discover that what may appear to be inconsistent is not actually so; and if he searches deep enough he will find that what appears to be irrelevant can be made relevant — the opening of a letter, for example, or the eating of a piece of bread.

ENRICHMENT

In earlier sections on movement and speech,[5] the point has already been stressed that outer forms of communication — gestures, gross bodily attitudes, intonations, tempos of delivery — tend to change as inner *purpose* changes. On the stage as in our day-by-day existence, the nature and the meaning of an action are shaped by its intention. On the simplest level of stage behavior, the "how" of a bit of business inevitably stems from the "why." A character lifts aside a heavy desk to see what is hidden behind it, to try it in another position in relation to the light, or to test its strength and stability. An-

[5] See especially "Speaking in a Context," in Chapter 10.

other character sits in a chair because he badly needs a rest, because he wants to conceal a tear in the seat of his trousers, or because he wishes to annoy someone by appearing to be boorish. In each instance, the physical action takes both its form and its impact from the basic motivation, even though its general outlines have not varied appreciably.

To such simple cues for action, however, are usually added various *motivating circumstances,* which in themselves will further condition a character's external behavior. As a convenient example, let us assume a farewell scene between a young man and a young woman. If they can be conceived by the actors only as "any" young man and young woman, it is possible to characterize them in only the most general sense. Once various levels of preceding circumstances are established, however, the playing of the roles can be particularized and given color. The mere fact that they had once been lovers, or had once been married but were now divorced, or had — though unrelated by blood — grown up together as members of the same family would quite obviously dictate certain aspects of their conduct, as they made their farewells. And this conduct would be further modified by attendant circumstances — e.g., the presence in the same room of a third person exerting some form of psychological pressure on either of the two central characters in the scene.

Whatever "happens" on the stage, in short, necessarily derives its nature, form, and style from a dramatic *purpose* — an individual or characteristic need of one or more of the personages, an influence prescribed by given dramatic circumstances, or both. For the most part, a generalized purpose will not suffice: an action cannot be characterized by mere activity. The motivation (or, as some would describe it, the justification) for any movement or behavior pattern should be as specific as possible, and should of course be drawn directly from the actor's intimate knowledge of his character and the scene in which he is playing. In some instances a single motivation seems unalterably imposed by the context. In others, however, one motivation or type of motivation must be selected from several that are possible, in accordance with larger needs of the ensemble; and in still others a suitable motivation must be supplied by the actor if none seems clearly indicated. By this latter means, the simplest of crosses, or of risings or sittings, can be enriched and vivified. Thus, in a standard example, a character moves to the fireplace to find matches for his cigarette, to clear out the bowl of his pipe, or to warm himself momentarily by the fire. What he does not do is to walk vaguely or aimlessly from one point on the stage to another.

Where a choice of justifications is offered, the final decision may not be wholly in the hands of an individual player. It is true that a character's typical reaction to attack — counterattack, for example, or postponing the issue, or mending fences on the spot — is dictated in large part by the given requirements of the role. At the same time, the specific nature of his temporizing or of his immediate response can vary in tempo, in firmness, in volume, and in half a dozen other ways; and his choice in these matters is not infrequently determined by factors outside his own role. If the scene in question is already quite properly a slow one, it may not be feasible to add still another brake to the existing pace. If the scene is already loud and violent, then sheer volume, however justly motivated, will lack fullness of impact. If the scene is the first, or the third, or the second of a planned sequence, then the larger requirements of the director's design may be decisive. It is important to observe, however, that in any of these instances, just "Play it slower" or just "Play it louder" is much less helpful and pointed advice than: "Change the motivation."

PLATE 3. **Character Studies from *The Inspector-General.*** (Above) Left, Khlopov; right, Schpekin. (Below) Left, Lyapkin-Tyapkin; right, Khlestakov. (*Cornell University: director, H. D. Albright; costumes, Barbara Oliver.*)

PLATE 4. **Character Studies from Classic and Contemporary Drama.** Studies from *Oedipus Rex* (above), *Billy Budd* (below, left), and *West Side Story*. (Above, *University of Miami:* director, Delmar E. Solem; designer, Kenneth Kurtz; costumes, Ben Gutierrez-Soto. Below, left, *University of North Carolina:* director, Foster Fitz-Simons; designer, Millard McDonald. Below, right, *University of Denver:* director, Jerry Rumley; designer, Peter Vagenas.)

PLATE 5. **Character Studies from Shakespeare and Brecht.** Studies from *Julius Caesar* (below), *King Lear* (above, left), and *Galileo*. (Below, *Wayne State University: director, Leonard Leone; settings, Richard D. Spear; costumes, Judith Haugan; lighting, Gary M. Witt. Above, left, University of Miami: director, Delmar E. Solem; designer, Vincent Petti; costumes, Roberta Baker. Right, Wayne State University: director, Leonard Leone; settings, Richard D. Spear; costumes, Robert Pusilo; lighting, Gary M. Witt.)*

PLATE 6. **Period Studies in Commedia and 19th Century Locales.** *A Company of Wayward Saints* (above) and *Oliver!* (Above, University of Minnesota: director, Arthur Ballet; settings, Wendell Josal; lighting, Robert Baruch. Below, University of Kansas: director, Jack Brooking; settings, James Hawes; costumes, Chez Haehl.)

IMAGINATION AND BELIEF

One other point of major importance, touched upon briefly in earlier sections, should be considered in connection with character development: the level and the quality of *imaginative belief* which a superior performance demands.

The point at issue here is that belief in a part connotes a good deal more than belief in its actual or literal reality. Even the most realistically conceived plays, as we have seen, are selective in their detail. On the other hand, neither a part nor the play in which it appears need be strictly realistic in order to engender belief; otherwise only plays in such traditions as those of Ibsen or Galsworthy could be played with any degree of sincerity and conviction. Yet actors in every passing generation have found Shakespeare, Congreve, and Shaw imaginatively real, and audiences of varying kinds have believed in them. The "reality" involved is an aesthetic reality — dictated by the play and by its form and style — which a given audience will accept for a given performance.[6]

Dorimant, in *The Man of Mode*, appears on the contemporary stage in brocaded coat and velvet knee-breeches, in silk stockings and silver-buckled, high-heeled shoes. He indulges in direct asides or conventionalized soliloquies, and he is as unlike the character creations of Ibsen or Galsworthy as dramatic technique can make him. These factors, in themselves, do not deny him conviction. By contemporary standards he may be artificial; he is not unbelievable. He is consistent with himself, with the author's point of view, and with the play's basic conception. Though actualistically impossible, at least in our time, he is aesthetically probable. In fantastic or exotic pieces — e.g., *Lute Song* or *The Yellow Jacket*, adapted from Chinese modes, or *From Morn to Midnight* and *The*

[6] In this connection, see the early pages of Chapter 12.

Adding Machine, expressionistically conceived — the acting calls for unconventional rhythm, flavor, and style. Here again, the "truth" and "reality" are not based on the external commonplaces of everyday life, yet the sincerity and integrity of the author and the consistency of the character drawing allow for conviction and belief.

It may well be that a young actor, whose experience has been limited to contemporary dramas in a realistic mode, may find highly conventionalized parts temporarily beyond his range, since he will find it so difficult to believe in his role. It is entirely possible that such roles are indeed more difficult to play, generally, than those which are realistically conceived. Yet they offer no more hurdles to any player than a standard role which is incompletely or inconsistently motivated. Just as a single example, the part of Dickie Reynolds in *Accent on Youth* — though it appears in a frail and charming comedy of character in which actualistic motivations are quite properly a secondary consideration — is still cast in a realistic mode, based on objective truth and probability. But the Dickie of Act I and Act II is difficult to believe in terms of the Dickie of Act III; and if he is convincing to the actor in one place, he is highly improbable in another. From this point of view, at least, it is a great deal easier to find and express conviction in an unconventional role, and to handle it properly during performance, if only it is conceived consistently throughout the playscript.

It is usually held by those who should know best that in comedy (and especially in farce) the player must "stand outside" his character, in a sense not typical of acting in serious roles. If comedic values are to be recognized, understood, and appreciated by an audience, a rather specialized rapport must be maintained between it and the actor. That is to say, an actor in a comedy role, in addition to offering a character, offers a certain kind of comment or observation on human nature; and in a subtle way he shares the audience's awareness of and delight in the character's absurdities.

Compared with actors of serious roles, the comedy actor is not engrossed as fully — or, perhaps, not engrossed as fully in the same way — in strict identification with his character. Though he has based his work on a careful study of every facet of the person he is to represent, he tends to focus on certain angles or approaches or points of view, and to underplay most of the others. In a spirit of general good nature, he calls attention to the incongruity and disproportion apparent in a comic character, without stressing the inner difficulties that might cause us discomfort or even pain. As Athene Seyler has described it, comedy is "the sparkle on the water, not the depths beneath: the gay surface, the glint of sunlight." [7]

Comedic playing thus deals with a rather special kind of distortion or imbalance with regard to the "real" and the "true." Yet once an actor has chosen the particular angle from which to view his comic character, has settled on the nature as well as the degree of allowable distortion, he must present the resultant portrait with warm conviction. This, indeed, is one of the real secrets of the successful comedian: to *believe* in the distorted view of life which his character typifies. Having consciously drawn a character just a little out of balance, the comedian then consciously offers this picture as a true likeness. Having scaled his character's figure

[7] Athene Seyler and Stephen Haggard, *The Craft of Comedy* (Theatre Arts, 1946), p. 11. It is important to note, however, that Miss Seyler adds at once: "But . . . the waters must run deep underneath. In other words, comedy must be founded on truth and on an understanding of the real value of a character before it can pick out the high-lights. It is only when one thoroughly understands a person that one can afford to laugh at him." The actor and the student of acting will find this slim and unpretentious volume a source of rare insight into the problems of playing comedy.

disproportionately, he then — with considerable good will — presents it as correct and just and good.

In comedies as in serious pieces, then, and in various styles and modes of production, the skilled actor learns to accept his fictional situation on the stage as theatrically true and real. The factual and the immediate are gradually blended with the imagined and the imaginary, and all are treated as stimuli to action. Through Director Tortsov, in *An Actor Prepares,* Stanislavski speaks of using IF as a lever, to lift us out of everyday life onto the plane of imagination.[8] The player is urged to act, with deep artistic faith, "as if" his character's desires and frustrations and emotions were real. Other teachers and directors, though uncommitted to the particular "psycho-technique" which Stanislavski had developed, join him in stressing the importance and validity of the actor's sense of dramatic truth.

It is relatively unimportant that an actor can say to himself, "I believe my character to be capable of this or that action in everyday life"; it is essential that he believe the character capable of such an action in terms of the play. *Othello* affords a familiar example. When an actor playing Othello is registering anger or jealousy, it is not required — if, indeed, it is possible — that he feel these emotions personally. What is important is that he *imagines* anger or jealousy with great vividness, that he *believes* in them as they are conceived in the play, and that he *projects* them convincingly to the audience. The actor who indulges in real emotions at the time of performance, who feels the part in any sense of actuality, is, as we have seen in other contexts, both ineffective and unreliable.[9]

By the time performance has arrived, the "emotions" of an actor's characterization

[8] Especially in Chapters 4 and 8.

[9] In this connection, see "Preparation vs. Performance," in Chapter 8.

belong on the other side of the footlights. Professional theatre men of such widely divergent backgrounds and points of view as Stanislavski and Kjerbühl-Petersen agree thoroughly on this point. Stanislavski has frequently insisted [10] that the proper place for the actor to experience the agony of his role, to weep his heart out if necessary, is at home or in early rehearsals. When he comes on the stage to convey what he has been through emotionally, the audience is intended to be more affected than the actor; and he will need to conserve all his resources for his central task: to reproduce the "inner life of his character." Kjerbühl-Petersen recognizes that an audience, because of the acting, attributes certain emotions to the character represented, and notes that the use of emotion as basic material is universally characteristic of aesthetic creation. However,

. . . the work of art does not of course cherish the emotions in question as such: the block of marble does not feel the pain nor does the painted surface of the Crucified One, nor does the reverberating orchestra, but we, in conscious self-deception induced within us by the artist, attribute the appropriate emotion to the character portrayed; . . . this is done by a creative activity of the phantasy, in accordance with the associations present. It is not otherwise in dra-

[10] E.g., in *Building a Character*, pp. 69–70.

matic art: the character to be acted, often only a poetic fiction, is in itself as unemotional as the marble of the Laocoön. And though we assume that the actor truly experiences every feeling by which the fictitious character may seem to be animated, according to the purpose of the author, still it is none the less an illusion. Indeed these emotions of the actor, if they are not to remain his insignificant private property, must in every case be transferred by the audience to the character portrayed.[11]

A proper focus on the inner life to which Stanislavski has referred will, at the moment of performance, demand the actor's full attention: intense concentration, vivid sense-awareness, and above all a freely-functioning imagination are imperative. Even the naïveté of childhood, buried under layers of social education, can be restored if the imagination will have it so. The most sophisticated or perhaps cynical adult can develop belief, if only he "imagines strongly." Handicaps of voice or physique, perhaps even technical errors in character building, may go unnoticed by an audience absorbed in an interesting production; failures to maintain a sense of conviction are likely to be observed and remembered.

[11] *Psychology of Acting*, pp. 157–158. By permission of The Expression Co., Magnolia, Massachusetts.

12 | A Perspective on the Whole

The Actor and His Audience • Aesthetic Balance • Continuity and Growth • The Actor and His Fellows

THE ACTOR AND HIS AUDIENCE

In previous chapters of the present section and in other portions of this volume, attention has been focused on the actor's relationship to the production as a whole. It is necessary at this point to enlarge on some of these considerations, and to draw certain of them together in perspective. In addition, it is necessary to relate the actor to his audience in a rather special way.[1]

Basic to all such considerations is recognition of the factor of *aesthetic illusion*, common to all the arts. The actor in production does not actually deceive an audience into believing that a character rather than an actor is "living" on the stage. Such deception would be not only undesirable artistically, but doubtless impossible under normal conditions, except for the briefest of periods. Moreover, even if it were possible, it would not be as satisfying to the spectator, who gains an added and distinctive pleasure from appreciating the skill with which an artist-performer impersonates a character quite different from himself. The spectator's attitude is thus a blending of — or perhaps an alternation between — a consciousness of "reality" on the one hand and an awareness of "art" on the other. And his enjoyment

depends not only on the presence and the strength of an illusion, but on the influence of various elements working against actual deception.

Any deception involving the spectator in the modern theatre is therefore conscious and willing self-deception; in the familiar phrase, there is a "willing suspension of disbelief." In the theatre as in the other arts, the spectator experiencing an illusion is psychologically substituting, for the actual patterns of sight and sound which he literally observes, a "reality" which does not actually exist, or which exists only in his imagination. In this process, he is not the unwilling victim of an imposture perpetrated by the playwright and the actor. He is consciously playing a game of pretense, *considering* the art objects real though at the same time he knows they are not; and he does this because precisely that combination of life and art gives him the most pleasure. If the objects were of such a nature as to deny the possibility of his considering them real, there would be no illusion at all, and there would be a weakening of interest if not of enjoyment. If at the other extreme the illusion were so complete or so intense as to engender involuntary deception, the experience would not be pleasurable.

In keeping with these observations, a well-written play and an expert job of acting both

---

[1] On the influence of theatre architecture on the audience–actor relationship, see Chapter 13.

foster illusion but at the same time control it. In dramaturgy as in production, there are two related but disparate elements, one bringing the audience under the spell of illusion, the other reminding the audience not to go too far. At times the spectator blends the two types of elements within his consciousness; at other times he alternates in focus between them. On the one hand is the "content" of the play or the role, to some degree and in some sense taken from life. On the other is an artistic form or structure, somewhat conventionalized and even abstracted from actual living.

In the theatre, the nature of the architecture, the seating arrangements, and the decorations proclaim the fictional quality of the coming performance. The theatre programs, the gongs calling the audience to attention, the dimming lights, the curtain — all prepare for an illusion that is controlled. Under arena conditions, a spectator on one side of a theatre-in-the-round consciously accepts the intended illusion, while at the same time he is aware of the reactions of spectators seated in the first row across the circle from him. On every type of stage, time and space are conventionalized; a prompter can be seen or imagined in his box; there are act or scene breaks; and there is applause for a point well taken or a bit of action expertly brought off. All such illusion-controlling factors ultimately afford pleasure for the spectator, by preventing confusion in his attitude toward the actor and the actor's character.[2]

Within the drama itself, as has already been suggested, the effect of various formal elements tends constantly to counteract the illusion-sponsoring "content." Conversely, however, "the drama is an art-form ever tend-

ing to create the illusion that it is not a form. More surely than any other form it is the art that conceals art, that communicates an air of reality without necessarily being realistic."[3] For example, even rhythm and rime — and the nonactualistic diction of formal verse — can under some conditions sustain an aesthetic illusion no less intense than that of other patterns of speech. Thus, also, characters of many times, places, and nationalities speak the same language on stage; and in some plays soliloquies, asides, and set speeches do not in themselves destroy (though they may inhibit) illusion. Moreover, there are, as it were, degrees of illusion within verse plays. It is recognized that Shakespeare varied — however subtly — between strongly formal and strongly illusive effects from play to play, as well as from scene to scene within the same piece.[4] The several "levels of reality" in the T. S. Eliot verse dramas of the thirties require of the actor a nice discrimination between formal and conventionalized scenes or speeches on the one hand and relatively illusionistic portions, still in verse, on the other. In *The Family Reunion*, for example, not only the members of the chorus are set off from the other characters from time to time as to strength of illusion; Harry and Agatha in particular, and occasionally Mary and the dowager, are required clearly to shift their frame of reference to "reality" in some of the scenes.

It is clarifying to think of strongly illusionistic scenes or characters as *representational*, strongly formal or conventionalized ones as *presentational*. The former "represent" an image of life that may seem to exist at times independent of the theatre; they are

---

[2] Kjerbühl-Petersen's *Psychology of Acting* presents an unusually full and cogent treatment of various aspects of aesthetic illusion in acting; throughout the book the author relies heavily on such primary studies as that of Lange in *Wesen der Kunst*.

[3] William G. McCollom, "Illusion in Poetic Drama," in *The Journal of Aesthetics and Art Criticism*, V (March, 1947), 184.

[4] See, for example, William G. McCollom's "Illusion in Poetic Drama," cited above, and his "Illusion and Formalism in Elizabethan Tragedy" (unpublished thesis, Cornell University, 1944).

primarily stage-centered. Presentational plays or elements in plays, on the other hand, more frankly "present" a dramatic action or theatrical performance; they are primarily audience-centered. As a matter of degree, it is more obvious in presentational scenes that the stage is a stage, the actor an actor, and the theatre a theatre than is possible or desirable with representational ones. Ibsen and Chekhov, quite clearly, are strongly representational throughout, Congreve and Molière (and the avowed expressionists of recent years) strongly presentational.

But these distinctions are matters of proportion: each play is *sui generis,* each sets its own aesthetic laws. Regardless of its aesthetic or historical style and form, of its proportionate admixture of presentation and representation, every play and every role is capable of engendering illusion, if it is capable of theatrical performance. Aesthetic illusion, as it is here conceived, does not presuppose representation or Ibsenesque naturalism; it requires — on various levels and to varying degrees — the "willing suspension of disbelief" that has already been described. An experience of illusion in the theatre calls forth the spectator's inward (that is to say, his emotional and psychological and sensory) participation in the dramatic action; and kinds of dramatic writing other than strictly representational types are capable of stimulating such participation. In every instance, with all types of drama, degrees of focus on illusion-fostering elements as well as on illusion-controlling elements are present. The actor's handling of both kinds of elements must clearly follow the proportionate focus on each written into the playscript and designed into the production with which he is working.

AESTHETIC BALANCE

Still another mode of approaching the nature of theatrical illusion is the concept of *aesthetic distance* or *aesthetic detachment.*[5] For full artistic enjoyment of a potentially dramatic event, the notion of aesthetic distance assumes that an observer must remain somewhat detached and disinterested — not *un*interested, not aloof, not indifferent, though still not involved in an actual and personal sense. For example, if one is not involved personally in any way, he can assume an aesthetic attitude and maintain aesthetic distance in relation to the most violent of storms, the most tragic of auomobile accidents, the most destructive of fires; and, even more readily, in relation to a film or stage portrayal of such actions. He can react *in* the dramatic situation, so to speak, rather than *to* the situation. He is not disposed to do anything about it in a real-life sense, interrupt it, own it, change or control it, take actual part in it. The term "distance" is of course relative and more or less figurative; it is more psychological than physical, and it refers more to an attitude within the spectator than it does to his actual position in space.

On the stage, as in the field of art generally, extreme realism or uncontrolled illusion involves the danger of destroying this attitude of detachment, and for that reason technical conventions (comparable to the elevated stage, the proscenium arch, and the dimmed house lights of the contemporary theatre) have traditionally been employed to guard against the danger. The painter hangs his picture in a special frame, the sculptor mounts his statue on a special pedestal, and both artists place and light these objects carefully and set them off from the

[5] This concept has been variously described, as for example in Herbert Sidney Langfeld, *The Aesthetic Attitude* (Harcourt, Brace, 1920), Chapter 3; in Alexander Bakshy, *The Theatre Unbound* (Cecil Palmer, London, 1923); and in John Dolman's *The Art of Play Production* and *The Art of Acting* (Harper, 1928 and 1949). A useful anthology of modern aesthetic theories, including a brief critical summary, is: Melvin M. Rader, *A Modern Book of Esthetics* (Holt, 1935).

reality of their surroundings. The danger of actual (if only temporary) deception is naturally greater in the case of the art of the theatre, since the materials of a dramatic production are the living beings of the actors, rather than an inert pigment on the surface of a painting, or a piece of ivory, or a musical tone.

The proper balance between the degree of actual involvement and the degree of aesthetic detachment within the spectator cannot be looked upon by the actor as a *constant* balance. As we have seen, conditions in the style of the playscript as well as in the design of the production make such balance variable and relative. The nature of a given audience for a given play and production is another factor of recognized significance. As Dolman has indicated,

the degree of detachment necessary to an attitude of enjoyment is proportionate to the mentality and cultivation of the audience. Audiences of children or unsophisticated adults, with their less critical imaginations . . . , can enjoy a more intimate relationship with the actor and a greater sense of imaginative participation, without loss of aesthetic distance, than an audience of theatre-wise sophisticates. . . . Adult audiences which resent a soliloquy or aside speech in a modern realistic play have little difficulty in accepting the franker and more artificial asides of eighteenth-century comedy, for the very reason that they can assume a more imaginative and playful attitude toward the latter. It is extremely important to understand that these more robust and intimate audience attitudes do not imply a surrender of aesthetic distance, nor an exception to the principle of balance. . . . They simply mean that under different conditions the distance is differently measured.[6]

The exact nature and source of a spectator's aesthetic pleasure, within the context of balanced illusion and detachment, are matters about which one can only speculate.

[6] John Dolman, Jr., *The Art of Acting*, p. 29. By permission of Harper & Brothers, publishers.

One of the most interesting and possibly most useful theories in this connection is concerned with imitative responses which, it is assumed, are set up within the spectator. Many schools of psychology agree that an instinctive tendency to imitation plays a relatively large part in our behavior. As children we imitate, consciously or unconsciously, much of what we observe, though social inhibitions may later suppress at least the outer signs of this reaction. It is possible that as adults we similarly respond to objects and actions by "feeling ourselves into them," consciously or unconsciously. We would thus respond imitatively (and pleasurably, in this case) to an exceptionally graceful dancer or skater. Contrariwise, an awkward slack-rope walker or an inexpert acrobat who is balancing his partner at the end of a long pole can induce in us the most unpleasant imitative reactions. Even in less obvious instances, stimuli of the same general nature can be assumed to produce in the human organism some kind of bodily response, whether the stimuli are real or imagined. At times the reaction shows outwardly, in overt imitation; more frequently it is experienced unconsciously and inwardly as merely a motor set or attitude, or a relatively weak impulse to action.

In either of these cases, the muscular response is assumed to condition — if not to cause — the spectator's perception of such experiences as weight, form, smoothness, grace, and the like. In a process now widely known as "empathy," [7] the motor and other adjustments which the spectator makes within his own body are projected into the object he is observing, and seem to be a part or a characteristic of the object itself. The theory is essentially that of Lipps, whose "Einfühlung" has been translated and interpreted by Titchener and later writers as

[7] For a detailed discussion see Langfeld, *op. cit.*, especially Chapters 5 and 6, and Rader, *op. cit.*, Chapter 8.

"empathy"; a related conception, from Groos, is usually termed "inner mimicry."

Roughly speaking, in an empathic response the spectator imaginatively projects his consciousness into persons on the stage, and imaginatively identifies himself with theatrical objects or situations. For example, the grace of a line or the fitness of a character's motivation seems to be an attribute of the line or the motivation. Actually, the source of the spectator's pleasure or satisfaction lies in the ease of his adjustment to the line or the motivation. According to the theory of empathy, the perception of such qualities as grace or fitness is dependent solely on neither the object nor the observer, *per se,* but on the *relation* between the two. That is to say, the nature of a motor response or adjustment depends on two factors and their interrelationship: (1) the nature of the object observed; (2) the nature of the past experience and present attitude of the observer. The theory thus allows for intellectual as well as purely sensuous elements in art and the theatre; and allows for "objects" that exist in time and in space, in sound and in sight, in memory and imagination as well as in the physical world.[8]

In instances in which actors can apply the theory of empathy, they may then have one more explanation for — certainly they will have one more manifestation of — a breakdown in the aesthetic attitude of the audience. If a spectator's empathic adjustment is too difficult, or if a series of empathic adjustments is too difficult to unify, or if portions of the empathic adjustment are unpleasant, he is aware of confusion and dissatisfaction; and he may begin to think of something else, or to observe the object other than aesthetically. Clumsy movements or poorly co-ordinated bits of business on the part of individual actors can call forth an unpleasant response, and correspondingly distract the spectator's attention. The design of a grouping or the action pattern for an entire scene can be so complicated as to interfere with satisfactory

[8] Albright, *Working Up a Part,* p. 121.

empathic adjustment. Unrelated moods, styles, or ideas, placed crudely in juxtaposition, can result in an empathic jar or shock. With practically no exceptions, it is within the province and the power of an actor to control the empathy as well as the detachment of his audience, and to maintain a proper balance between them.

The dual role of the actor, as conceived in an earlier chapter,[9] is of special point in this connection. The delicate but variable balance between "actor" and "character" which exists in every scene parallels that between form and content in the play, between illusion-controlling and illusion-fostering elements in the production, between detachment and empathy in the audience. The sensitive actor is vividly aware of these interrelationships during actual performance. He operates, as it were, on two planes of consciousness; and he subtly shifts when necessary from one plane to the other without sacrificing — or calling undue attention to — either. Through neither accident nor design does he ever reach the point of destroying the spectator's experience of illusion, even in highly presentational scenes. Yet the illusion itself never gets out of hand, since he retains technical awareness and practical control.

CONTINUITY AND GROWTH

The control which the actor-as-actor exerts at any given moment, however, is only a single aspect of a larger view of the whole production. A good dramatic presentation — like other forms of art — is more than a sum of small and disparate pieces, loosely tied together in space or in time. Voice and speech, posture and movement, and characteristic details of interpretation are blended together indivisibly. There is in each competent performance on the modern

[9] See Chapter 8. Note also the treatment of audience "rapport" in Chapter 13.

stage an organic quality that is one of its distinguishing features.

Without involving oneself too deeply in the complications of Gestalt psychology and without accepting all of its implications, it is possible to recognize one central insight of the Gestaltists. This insight suggests that every human experience is a "conformation" of the individual parts and elements of this experience — and that if we allow ourselves to isolate any portion of it, this portion no longer possesses the same quality it had when it was still involved in the whole. A word uttered separately from its context is of a different quality from the same word operating within the conformation of a sentence; the quality is different both phonetically, from the standpoint of pronunciation, and interpretatively, from the standpoint of rhythm and intonation. Two lines of verse which are read independently of a longer speech from which they have been extracted are no longer the "same" lines of verse. A single scene which is out of scale with others in a dramatic sequence — a scene which has, to put it another way, lost sight of the super-objective of the whole — may as well be a scene from quite another play.

As a necessary condition of rehearsal for a long play, separate portions or aspects are focused on in turn and special drills are held in isolation. Especially in early sessions, moreover, the need to take roles apart tends to overshadow the instinct to put them back together. As a result, even the most conscientious actor may temporarily lose sight of the structural coherence that characterizes his role and his play. He has so thoroughly dissected his part that he is momentarily unable to organize its components into unity once again. During the later rehearsals such difficulties may be corrected by a restudy of the playscript, and by a conscious effort to grasp its structure, so that its several units may again be seen in proper relation to each other and to the whole. Especially revealing

and helpful at this stage is a reappraisal of the author's stage directions, and a reconsideration of the dramatic desires and objectives of the principal characters.

Actors trained under the Russian system frequently speak of the "unbroken line" that characterizes an effective movement or a well-delivered speech. That which is inconsistent or irrelevant has been removed; and, above all, the bits and pieces of which the speech or the movement is composed have been organized into a continuous, forward-moving pattern. The same conception (which in this case the Russians term the "through line of action") can profitably be applied to the pattern for an entire role. Each thematic thread, each individual scene, each minor climax is given proper value in its place; but each is scaled to suit the final climax and resolution required by the role. As a traditional rule of thumb has it, "the objective of a sonnet is the fourteenth line." For the individual actor, the objective of an act is its final speech; of a play, its final scene.

For this reason, it is important for the actor to learn to conserve as well as to build, to remember that between the first act and the last there are several scenes of mounting tension. If an Othello or a Lear were to throw all his physical and nervous energy into a performance during the earlier scenes, he would have no reserves to call upon later, in support of the unfolding of his passion or the accenting of a climax. In such a play as *Ladies in Retirement,* the actress playing Ellen Creed must be prudent and even calculating, not only in withholding certain outward evidence of her developing plans for later action, but in conserving her resources of temperament. If in either sense she squanders too much too early, then the audience and the other players must merely mark time for an entire scene or act. Even in playing a scene of emotional intensity, any actor must keep the end in view, lest he throw his role out of proportion.

It is a standard fault of inexperienced actors to shoot their bolts at the very beginning. They may be vivid and interesting, they may play with clarity and flavor, and they may promise rich characterizations — for one act. In some cases, they doubtless simply lack the technical resources to grow, to move forward, to develop; in others, it is a matter of failure to maintain a sense of proportion, an overall perspective, in respect to the roles. In any event, a sledgehammer attack at the start can be merely confusing to an audience. Even a potentially interested spectator is "cold" at the opening curtain, and is without intellectual and emotional orientation. For the most part it is best to establish audience contact on a relatively low level of intensity and then to raise the level gradually but insistently thereafter.

THE ACTOR AND HIS FELLOWS

Several other considerations are important to a proper perspective on the actor's obligations to the entire production. While these considerations do involve aesthetic values, they are primarily personal and ethical in nature. Some of them are concerned with rehearsal, some with performance; all are directly involved in an actor's relationships with his fellow-actors.

A successful production, from the standpoint of the players, is a collective, creative, and essentially pleasurable enterprise. Unless it is all of these, moreover, it may not be any of them. If even a few of the actors approach their tasks in an attitude of tedium or drudgery, it is unlikely that either teamwork or creativity can long prevail. The only workable approach for the conscientious actor is to be "serious" and "businesslike"; but these must not be equated with *long-faced* or *grim*. There is little solemnity, either real or imagined, at a good rehearsal. There is enthusiasm, excitement, satisfaction. On the other hand, there is a minimum of

irrelevant fraternizing, of half-hearted attention, or of superficial dabbling. Creativity flourishes best in an atmosphere of concentration and self-discipline. As we have seen everywhere in the present volume, any player in the modern theatre is only one unit in an extremely large and complex organization; and his attitude and behavior at rehearsals are a hallmark not only of his creativity but of his respect for responsible authority and his loyalty to a common cause. On the stage and in the theatre, individual effort can best be judged in terms of teamwork.

The individual actor's contributions to a pleasant and productive rehearsal [10] are easily described. In the first place, he is prompt and he is well prepared. He does not miss a rehearsal without previously arranged permission; he does not leave before his portion of the work is done. Whenever possible, he arrives ten or twenty minutes *before* he is scheduled to appear, so that he has time to check briefly on his preparation and to set his intellectual and emotional approach to the scene under consideration. He is prepared in general in that he has known the playscript as a whole from the time of the earliest readings; he is prepared specifically in that he has worked between rehearsal calls on the particular lines, the particular points, and the particular details on which the director has planned to focus. Without previous outside preparation on the part of individual actors, many types of group rehearsal would be chaotic and wasteful.

During the course of the rehearsal, moreover, the actor is concentrating clearly on the business at hand. Unless he has been temporarily excused, he should keep track of the development of other scenes and other characters, watching for clues with which to point up various aspects of his own role. To the notes (e.g., on positions, movements,

[10] The conduct of rehearsals, from the standpoint of the director, is discussed in Chapter 28.

and character relationships) which he has carefully recorded during blocking-out rehearsals, he should regularly add other observations, designed to enrich his own characterization and his own insight into the play's overtones. He should normally keep track of his own entrance cues, and should be ready to act — i.e., from the start — with a sure grasp of immediate context as well as preceding circumstances. Once on the rehearsal-room stage, he should of course stay imaginatively in character until well beyond his exit; and he should strive to deliver as accurate and as vivid a scene as he and his fellows are capable of at their present level of development. Many actors, unfortunately, tend to compensate for their own inertia and lack of preparation by overacting in rehearsal, and thus upset the precarious balance of an otherwise promising scene.

Finally, in most types of rehearsal, he should join with his director and his fellow-actors in maintaining a performance atmosphere. A performer's speeches must be fully voiced and expressively read throughout the rehearsal, and his postures, gestures, and movements must be followed through as planned and accurately projected. Otherwise he is wasting everybody's time, and postponing the precision and the refinement which all are so earnestly seeking. From the standpoint of the other actors, who are themselves dependent on consistent cues and reactions from their colleagues, an incomplete performance in rehearsal is upsetting and wasteful. From the standpoint of the director, such a performance delays the polishing process, confuses interpretative values, and raises false issues as to the soundness of the basic design.

By the time of the first performance, when details have been set and general polish has been achieved, each actor has one final obligation: to stick to the team patterns that have been mutually developed throughout the rehearsal period. The temptations that beset every player, even the most loyal and the most experienced, when he is faced with a particularly responsive audience (or, for that matter, a determinedly unresponsive one), are only too well known. The wine of audience appreciation is notoriously heady. An extra laugh here, a touch of unexpected applause there, a sentimentalized reaction somewhere else, and the weak-willed actor will be tempted to improve upon the author's and the director's planned interpretation. "Hamming," "mugging," and "tear-jerking" are cheap terms for what is after all a cheap operation, especially from the point of view of the other artists concerned. No audience can safely be allowed to rewrite an author's play or redesign an actor's patterns at will.

On the other hand, some adjustments are necessary and desirable from performance to performance. No two audiences (and, in the living theatre, no two performances) are quite alike; and the way in which an acting company unobtrusively adjusts to the specific reactions of a particular audience is a final test of its competence. The matter of holding for laughs is perhaps the most obvious example. According to a traditional rule of thumb, a skillful actor "waits for" but never "waits out" a laugh, though in some instances he deliberately kills a series of small ones in order to build for a bigger one later on. In either case he and his partners have not rushed doggedly ahead with the dialogue, but have honestly and legitimately adapted their timing to the specific requirements of an individual group of spectators. It is thus possible that a given scene may run five and a half minutes on Friday night and six and a half minutes on Saturday night, but that both may be "right" for particular audiences.

Such controlled adaptations are at the opposite pole from the cheap catering to audience excitement described earlier. In these instances the actor has not been stampeded into squeezing out an extra bit of attention for himself; he has maintained his poise under pressure, and has been faithful to the production's design. Minor shifts of focus or of timing may be necessary also in other circumstances — e.g., when for some audiences a very quiet scene threatens to go "cold" or "dead." Seasoned players react instinctively to such a difficulty, picking up the tempo and the vitality of the scene with deliberate care but not moving so rapidly as to interfere with clarity or conviction. Those who have lost their poise, on the other hand, may confuse speed with mastery. Terrified lest they lose their grip on the audience, they hurry over the passage, and end up by doing more harm than good. In the majority of such cases, only less hurry and more intensity can restore to a scene the values it once had attained in rehearsal. Most on-the-spot changes from the set patterns previously agreed upon, unless they are subtly and unobtrusively achieved, are unlikely to be successful, if only because the other actors cannot immediately cope with them.

In all considerations of this kind, an audience can properly be taken as a partner in a creative and imaginative enterprise, as the final stimulus that brings a dramatic performance to life. A certain amount of give and take, of adjustment to audience response, is not only possible but imperative in the theatre. An actor who is loyal to his colleagues will welcome from beyond the footlights every evidence of appreciation that is keyed to his author's intention and his director's design. He will nourish such responses, allowing them to stimulate his imagination and sustain his belief. At the same time, he will reject — and attempt to control, if not to kill — any responses that are foreign to the point, the spirit, and the intention of the production as he and his fellows have conceived it.

In the co-operative world of the theatre, no individual actor is entitled to a private system of ethics. No one member of the team has, after all, the *right* to mug or to ham, to be careless or inefficient, to be routine or inaudible in performance. None has the right to waste rehearsal time because he is ill prepared or is thinking of something else. As a member of the group, none has the right to be merely second-rate.

Section Three

Theatre
and Stage

13 | Methods of Organizing the Theatre Structure

Arena Staging • *Formal Staging*
Simultaneous Staging • *Multiple Staging*
Theatrical Staging • *Actualistic Staging*

Theatre structures differ widely in their basic architectural organization, a circumstance which in turn dictates the relationships between actor, stage, setting, and audience. The majority of theatre buildings now in use in America and Europe have as their key architectural feature a *proscenium arch* through which the audience views the performers at some distance, psychological as well as physical. The stage action is seen from one side only and is therefore planned as a sort of picture in motion displayed to the spectators in the frame of the proscenium. This arrangement of theatre space has predominated in the occidental world for about three hundred years, during which it has undergone only minor modifications.

In recent years, a number of theatres have been built embodying entirely different concepts of illusion and style. In consequence, a new form of theatre structure has come into being, distinguished by a single enclosure occupied by both actor and audience. The performers are virtually surrounded by spectators instead of being seen from one side only through a proscenium opening. This new form is called the *open theatre* because openness is its most striking feature.

This organization of theatre space around a central playing area is not really new when viewed in the perspective of history, for the open theatre prevailed everywhere in the western world from the birth of formal theatre in Greece in the fifth century B.C. to the beginning of modern times. The open theatre produces a more intimate physical relationship between actor and audience than the proscenium theatre, and because of the varying sight lines the stage action is likely to be developed as movement rather than picture. Currently the open theatre takes two main forms: the *arena*, in which the stage occupies the center of the enclosure with the audience on all four sides of the action, and the *thrust stage*, in which the acting area abuts one wall of the enclosure and extends into the middle of the auditorium with spectators on three sides.

The arena stage is the older of the two contemporary forms and has been used successfully for two decades in numerous commercial and semi-professional theatres, both in new structures specifically planned for arena staging and in halls originally designed for other uses converted later into arena theatres. In this country, all the theatres featur-

147

ing the thrust stage have been erected within the past decade, but their influence on the thinking of architects and stage directors has been considerably greater than that of any other form. (See Chapter 15.)

A quick look at the possible organizations of the theatre plant and at the ways they have been used in some periods of theatre history will provide an understanding of the aesthetic and practical bases of current theatre structures, and an understanding of the import of new proposals and developments. It also will reveal incidentally some of the anachronistic conventions and anachronistic structural features of modern theatre buildings.

The basic determinant in the relationship between actor, audience, and scenery in the theatre structure is found in the degree to which the locale of the action is defined and the way the locale is indicated. Six distinct methods of locating stage action can be identified in theatre history:

1. Action unlocalized: Arena Staging (as seen in primitive theatre).

2. Action vaguely located by a neutral background: Formal Staging (as seen in the classical Greek theatre).

3. Action located and shifted by the successive use of segments of a scenic background, with the individual segments sufficiently representational to identify the locales: Simultaneous Staging (as seen in the medieval mystery and morality performances).

4. Action located and shifted by moving to the different areas and levels of a complex nonrepresentational background: Multiple Staging (as seen in the Elizabethan theatre).

5. Action located and shifted by representational scenery used as a background for actors: Theatrical Staging (as seen in Italy in the Renaissance and in England in the Restoration and eighteenth-century theatres).

6. Action located and shifted by representational scenery used as an environment for actors: Actualistic Staging (as seen in most productions from the nineteenth century to the present).

In any formal classification of essentially developmental material, there are inevitably examples which do not exactly fit — because they are transitional, because they are purely eccentric, or because they so mix the characteristics of different classes that they defy arbitrary classification. In spite of these limitations, a system of classification does help to organize developmental material, so long as the classes are recognized primarily as general guides.

ARENA STAGING

The most primitive organization of theatre space is the pure (or complete) arena, which provides merely an unlocalized space for the action in the midst of the audience. This scheme is used for the dances and other precursors of theatre found in primitive races. The dances of the American Indians, for example, are performed among the tribe, whether they are incantation rites entreating the gods verbally or theatric rites showing the gods what is wanted by impersonation and representative action, as in the Buffalo Dance and the Antelope Dance. (See Plate 7.) The arena was the first form used in the Greek ceremonies which evolved into theatre. And nearly every time that the theatre died down and then was reborn, it reverted to the pure arena form at the beginning, even though it often developed very quickly a specialized pattern of organization. So it was with the Interlude players who were the ancestors of the Elizabethan companies, with the drama which arose in the Church at the end of the Middle Ages, and with the *commedia dell'arte.*

The primitive arena without scenery is accepted by the spectators either as the exact spot in which a ceremony takes place,

PLATE 7. **Arena and Formal Staging.** (Above) A miniature group portraying the Hopi Snake Dance (Arizona), and employing many conventions of the historical Arena Stage. (Below) The theatre at Delphi during a performance of *Prometheus Bound* with Hans Jacob Nilsen. (*Director, Linos Karzis.*)

PLATE 8. Simultaneous and Multiple Staging. (Above) A model of the Valenciennes Mystery Play, 1547. (*Model constructed by E. Bradlee Watson for the Dartmouth College Theatre Museum, from a contemporary drawing.*) (Below) The Old Globe Theatre of San Diego during a performance of *The Merchant of Venice*. (*Director, Philip Hanson; supervising director, Craig Noel; costumes, Robert Abel. Theatre constructed under the supervision of Thomas Wood Stevens.*)

PLATE 9. **Theatrical Staging.** (Above) The auditorium and stage of the theatre at Drottningholm, Sweden, built in 1766, and containing not only the original scenery, but the oldest scene-shifting machinery still in operation. (Below) An original maquette by P. J. de Loutherbourg, who designed "accurate" settings for David Garrick to replace the conventional ones of Theatrical Staging.

PLATE 10. **Drawings of Three Sixteenth-Century Theatres.** (Above) Italy: *L'Hortensio* performed at Siena, 1560; an early example of Theatrical Staging and of a temporary proscenium arch. (Below, left) England: A sketch of the Swan Theatre made from memory by DeWitt, a Dutch visitor, in 1596. (Below, right) Netherlands: Stage façade for the *landjuweel* at Ghent, 1539. Notice the resemblances between these last two examples of Multiple Staging.

or as a neutral space unlocalized in the minds of actor and spectator. It is possible that locale could be identified in an arena by means of the dialogue. But actor and dramatist have seldom so localized it. It also seems unlikely that a verbal identification would influence the visualization of the spectator, in the absence of a scenic element to which to attach the sense of locale.

An arena can be of any size, and so in itself it enforces no standard degree of visual or vocal projection. However, as in all theatres, the key actions of the play must be revealed to the entire audience.[3] To accomplish this in a true arena, a chorus of actors is often used, for the most part performing in unison. If an individual performs a key action, there are several ways to concentrate attention and to provide visibility for the action. The chorus may leave the arena, or may crouch down so that all can see this central figure easily; or the central figure may stand on a platform. In any case, the central actor either needs to make his pantomime so broad that its meaning is projected clearly by his back and by his profiles as well as his front; or he needs to turn in all directions, repeating the action — even if this be an artificial convention. It is customary during the Mass in the Catholic Church for the priest to repeat certain actions facing in different directions. A single action is sufficient from the theo-

[3] Nothing in history or psychology requires that a stage be elevated. The raised stage is a purely architectural convenience to overcome the deficiencies of the sight lines of an auditorium. When the spectators are few enough so that they can sit or stand in one of two rows of concentric circles, actors can perform on the ground. When the spectators are more numerous, but can be arranged on a slope so that all can see the playing area over the heads of those in front of them, there is no need to raise the actors. The stage at ground level is seen in primitive forms of theatre, and in the early forms of almost all theatre developments. Therefore, in classifying theatres, there need be no distinction between a theatre in which the action is on the ground and one which employs a platform.

logical standpoint, but the Church recognizes that the worshiper feels included in the ritual only when these actions are made in some approximation of his direction, and so by convention the actions are repeated to include the entire congregation. Primitive theatre recognizes the same psychological need, as when the central actor in some of the dances of the Far East moves about the perimeter of the arena repeating his action conventionally. The American Indians sometimes employ this convention when performing dances for tourists, but the genuine dances do not use it except as the religious significance calls for repetition facing different points of the compass.

This unlocalized arena surrounded by spectators encourages direct communication between actors and spectators, and even a physical mingling of the two groups, as when the demons in primitive dances attempt to frighten spectators. The performers are often considered to be acting as representatives of the audience. All the conventions of this staging method contribute to produce the closest possible actor-audience relationship.

Since the action is in the midst of the audience, the actors alternately face in various directions. Any patterned movement tends to be concentric — either circular or an alternation of centrifugal and centripetal.

The Arena Stage is a primitive form, but it is by no means limited to primitive use. *Prometheus Bound* and other early plays of Aeschylus, as well as dramas by his predecessors, were performed while the theatre at Athens was still in this unlocalized form.

FORMAL STAGING

"Formal Stage" is the term used for a playing space with a neutral background which in itself gives no specific representation of a locale, but which can be accepted by the audience as a definite locale when it is so identified in the dialogue. The audience surrounds the playing area on most sides. Seemingly, even the simplest cloth or architectural background permits the spectator to visualize a definitely localized action in this manner.

The addition of this neutral background is the second step in the development of most theatre forms. The actors of the *commedia dell'arte* hung an unpainted cloth on a frame behind their platform stage; the Interlude players erected their platform against one wall when they played in the courtyard of an inn; entertainers in banquet halls quickly shifted from their arena in the center of the hall completely surrounded by spectators, to a side where they could play against the background of a wall.

The most notable period of theatre using this Formal Staging technique for locating the action was the Greek tragic theatre in the sixth and fifth centuries B.C. Tragedy developed from the long poems *(dithyrambs)* which were sung by a chorus in honor of the god Dionysus in complete arenas such as market places.

When the popularity of the ceremonies at Athens increased so that there were more spectators than could see comfortably from a flat auditorium, the ceremonies were moved to an arena marked out at the base of a hollow in the side of a hill. The spectators could sit or stand on the hillsides and still surround the arena on approximately three sides. Here the first few of the great Greek dramas were performed in a circular arena called an *orchestra* ("a place to dance"). By convention the actors of a drama were limited to a chorus and two actors, and later to the chorus with its leader and three actors. But the playwrights wrote more than three roles in a play, and the actors played more than one part. All actors were men, who played men's and women's roles interchangeably.

A dressing room was needed nearby for the costume changes, and so about 465 B.C. a little wooden hut called a *skene* was erected just back of the orchestra in the Theatre of Dionysus at Athens. Because this, at the same time, supplied a scenic element to which a locale could be assigned, the Greek theatre suddenly changed from an unlocalized arena to a formal stage with a specified locale. (See Plate 7.)

The simple wooden wall of the *skene* developed in the following centuries into an elaborately ornamented stone façade several stories high. The name *proskenion* ("the front of the *skene*") was later applied to this façade.[4] This façade was not only neutral in appearance, but it was ordinarily used to represent a neutral locale — "before" a house, palace, or temple. Thus, a variety of action could be played there which would have been less convincing had the locale been more exactly defined.

The actors in the Greek theatre played in front of this formal façade, sometimes on a platform immediately in front of the façade, but more frequently in the orchestra. Here, then, it was possible to use the circular design of action as in the true arena. It was possible also to use a linear form, with the actors grouped in front of the neutral scenic background — though spectators at the sides would see a distorted version of this grouping. Also it was possible, as it had not been in the complete arena, for a key actor to take up a position near the back of the orchestra where his action could be seen simultaneously by all spectators. Therefore conventional repetition of action was not necessary in the Greek theatre.

It was customary in Greece to give four plays in one day as a contest between playwrights.[5] The audience accepted a shift of

---

[4] *Proskenion* was at first applied to the platform "in front of the *skene*," but to avoid confusion, its later meaning is used here.

[5] The first three formed a trilogy on a single subject. This trilogy can be considered a single play, as it is in Section I.

locale for each new play. Theoretically, then, the audience should have been prepared to accept the convention of a change of locale during the action of a single play, but few examples of dramas using this convention have been preserved.

Little movable scenery was used in the Greek theatre. A platform (*eccyclema* or *ekkuklema*) could be rolled out (or possibly pivoted) through one of the doors to reveal a throne or the body of someone killed offstage. There were other machines. *Pinakes* (panels) and *periaktoi* (revolving prisms) are described by Vitruvius.[6] Presumably these pieces of painted scenery were too small to change the overall appearance of the *skene,* but, by accepted convention, they may have shifted the locale of the action.

The enormous size of the auditorium (*cavea*) in the Greek theatres — the one at Athens, for example, accommodating 17,000 spectators — required tremendous vocal projection and enlargement of gesture. (See Figure 14.) Subtlety in voice or action would be effective for only a small fraction of the audience. The explicitness with which the dialogue often describes the actions of the characters suggests that the playwrights knew that the spectators would not see every detail. This does not mean that the acting style was necessarily bombastic or unmotivated, but merely that it was enlarged in the way that a speaker enlarges his technique when he addresses an audience of this size without mechanical amplification. Subtleties of thought and of emotional conflict could still be presented.

In spite of the physical distance of some spectators, there was close *rapport* between actor and audience. The chorus and the actors in the Greek tragedies performed in the midst of the audience, even after the *skene* was built. The first row of seats was separated from the orchestra by no more than a curb or a single step. The writing style of the tragedies at times demanded direct communication of actor to audience. The chorus and its leader spoke to the audience in narration and in comment on the action. It often stepped out of the historical period of the play to give advice to the contemporary audience or to plead the cause of the poet in the play contest. The characters often spoke while alone on the stage except for the chorus; since the chorus was often treated as representative of the audience, it seems likely that the actors sometimes addressed the audience and chorus together. They may sometimes have addressed the audience without the intermediary of the chorus. In the comedies, actors sometimes mingled with the spectators.

This direct address to the audience helped to produce a nonillusionary atmosphere. Other elements in the Greek theatre which contributed to a nonillusionary style include the poetic form of all dialogue, which often conformed to rigid and complex rhythmic forms; the familiarity of the plots, derived from widely known legends; and a relative absence of action. The Formal Stage played its part in helping to maintain aesthetic distance.[7]

Lest a modern reader, habituated to illusionistic theatre and inexperienced in the nonillusionistic style, feel that this style discouraged excitement and emotion, it is worth remembering that it was from seeing such performances that Aristotle formulated his theory that the pleasure of tragedy is in *catharsis* — the purging of personal emotions through the emotional response to the performance. Still today we respond emotionally to material presented in a nonillusionistic manner: to incidents described by speakers, to stories read aloud from a book, and to on-the-spot news accounts by radio reporters. So the emotions of a modern man can still be aroused by nonillusionistic pre-

---

[6] A Roman writer on architecture who attempted in about 15 B.C. to describe early Greek scenery.

[7] On this point, see the early pages of Chapter 12.

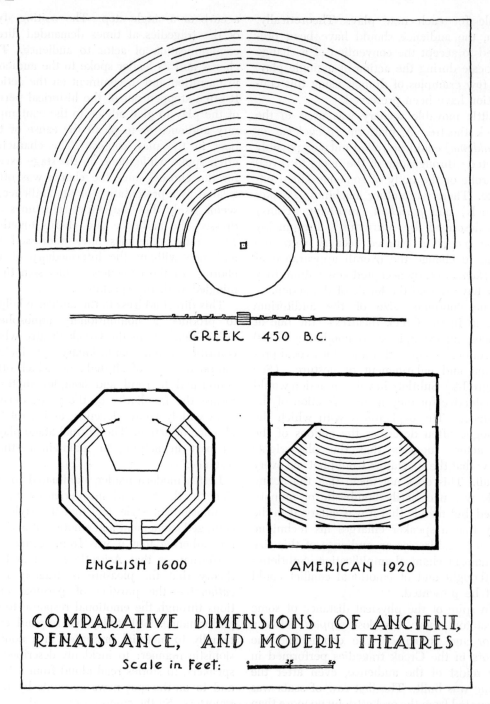

GREEK   450 B.C.

ENGLISH 1600   AMERICAN 1920

COMPARATIVE DIMENSIONS OF ANCIENT,
RENAISSANCE, AND MODERN THEATRES
Scale in Feet:

Figure 14. The historical trend is toward smaller theatres, but the economy of the commercial theatre often reverses this trend.

sentations when these use current conventions, and he probably would respond to them in the theatre as completely as did a Greek if he were habituated to the theatrical conventions involved.

SIMULTANEOUS STAGING

Simultaneous Staging is an organization of the scene in which several unrelated locales are represented at the same time around a common playing area used for all locales, and in which each incident is located by the way in which the actors relate themselves to one or more of the scenic units. Usually, the scenic unit which establishes a locale is depictive. For example, it may be a realistic building, it may be a section of a building, or it may be a compromise in which one feature of the building is represented in approximately real size with the rest of the building in miniature. The spectators surround the playing area on many sides. The limits of the playing space are often indefinite.

The most effective use of this scheme was in the medieval mystery and morality plays, which grew out of drama performed in the Church in the Middle Ages as a part of the Mass. Scenes from the Easter and Christmas stories were performed by priests in symbolic costumes around a bit of scenery placed at the altar. Over the centuries, the episodes in the service were multiplied. Each episode was played in a specific part of the church structure, or around a scenic element or a property symbolic of the locale.

In the thirteenth century, these plays were moved either to the church porch or to the churchyard, and laymen took over the acting from the priests. At the same time that the drama moved out-of-doors, the locales within a play sequence were increased in number; each locale was established by a *mansion* which consisted of a bit of scenery or a property. A common and neutral playing area *(platea)* was used in front of the mansions, but it was localized for each scene by the entrance of actors from a certain mansion or the movement of the actors to the mansion. Actor and spectator simply ignored the mansions that were not in use, and so found nothing illogical about a collection of buildings gathered from many countries, or in the juxtaposition of a realistic Hell Gate and a garden of Gethsemane suggested by realistic details.

The mansions were organized sometimes in a line (see Plate 8); sometimes around the circumference of a town square; and sometimes as a procession of *pageant-wagons* drawn into place in succession. In spite of the variation in the organization of the setting, in most instances the spectators were spread around a considerable circumference of the playing space. The actors were seen in a sculptural grouping rather than a linear design, just as in the staging methods described previously. There was little separation of spectators and actors in either a physical or a psychological sense.

The playlets were performed with great "realism," but a different kind of realism from that attempted today. Properties were genuine; scenery varied from extreme representation to pure conventional symbolization. The amateur actors strove for realistic physical action — the kind of realism they could best understand — in the same way that some beginning actors still find physical reality easier than mental and emotional reality, and so use more than the necessary physical effort in hitting, slapping, kicking, and whipping. In the mystery plays, ingenious methods were found to make fire and smoke come out of the nostrils of devils, to inflict convincing wounds, to make blood spurt, and to perform the Biblical miracles by legerdemain. Actors accepted terrific pain in order to give realism to flogging scenes. Occasionally actors playing the devils were burned by the gunpowder squibs and other fireworks burning in their ears and nostrils. And several actors of the parts of Jesus and some of the martyrs were killed accidentally during performances.

Further, the playlets were acted by local amateurs, probably supplemented by strolling players. In England, for example, each trade guild (somewhat equivalent to a modern craft union) performed the playlet most appropriate to its trade. It must have been difficult for a spectator to obtain much illusion while the local grocers performed "The Creation of Eve, with the Expelling of Adam and Eve out of Paradise." Low comedy incidents were inserted into the most reverent of the scripts, and in all periods low comedy has encouraged intercommunication of actor and spectator.

All these factors suggest that the performances of these mystery and morality plays may have been good "shows" for an unsophisticated audience, but that they afforded less aesthetic satisfaction than the dramas of other periods. Yet they were popular for over five centuries, and it is probable that some performances overcame all the obstacles and did produce a truly dramatic experience.

The staging method in itself is a useful one and has been employed successfully for other types of performance. For example, Simultaneous Staging persisted in the French theatre and some other Continental theatres long after the mystery plays, and eventually was framed behind a proscenium arch. Corneille wrote for this staging method.

MULTIPLE STAGING

The Elizabethan theatre found another method for the presentation of a sequence of different locales without interrupting the flow of the drama — a complex formal background with a number of playing spaces which could be used singly or in combination. The locale of the action was changed often; it was established sometimes by dia-

logue, sometimes by the way in which the parts of the stage were used; and it was often left without identification. The name "Multiple Staging" can be given to this organization of the theatre space, in order to emphasize the many different playing areas provided by the stage. In Simultaneous Staging, the locales are specifically depicted by representative scenery which is constantly in sight but which is ignored by the audience during those times when the actors do not use it. In Multiple Staging, in contrast, the background is formalized to the extent that it has no suggestion of a specific locale, and its individual scenic elements are used to represent several locales in sequence.

This theatre form was a spontaneous development in England from diverse origins. The form of the theatre building was copied from the inn yards and the bear- and bull-baiting pits where the Interlude players performed until they built theatres for themselves near London. George Kernodle [8] has traced the form and conventions of the stage to medieval and Renaissance art in general, and specifically to the *tableaux vivants* used in the outdoor street shows which were built to welcome royal visitors and for other celebrations. A similar theatre form developed in the Netherlands. (See Plate 10.)

Shakespeare referred to the theatre as a "wooden O." A theatre structure of this period was roughly thirty-five feet high and eighty feet square or octagonal, open to the sky. Two or three galleries extended most of the way around an open central pit where "the groundlings" stood. Into this pit projected a trapezoid-shaped open stage, wide at the back and narrowed to a blunt point at the center of the pit. The rear portion was covered by a canopy called the *shadow* or the *heavens*, which contained machinery for raising and lowering actors and properties. Doors at the rear corners of the stage

[8] *From Art to Theatre* (University of Chicago Press, 1944).

were the usual entrances to the forestage. Between the doors was a room which became an inner stage when its curtains were opened. In some theatres there was a curtained room of similar size above this. The curtains which closed off this upper room were hung a few feet behind the low balcony railing so that scenes could be played on this shallow lip while the curtains were closed. Side stages, windows, or balconies were often included on this second level. These arrangements of the second floor varied, and apparently spectators were sometimes allowed to sit there, just as they sat on stools at the sides of the stage floor. Some theatres had a room on a third level, ordinarily used for musicians, but which could be used in the action. (See Plates 8 and 10.)

The forestage was unlocalized, just as in the medieval mansion settings. The locale of a scene was often left unidentified. At other times, as we have seen, it took its locale from the dialogue. But frequently the locale was established by the conventions of the theatre. Kernodle has brought logic to these conventions by relating them to contemporary art. Renaissance artists, he points out, painted architectural exteriors almost exclusively. When they wanted these exteriors to be interpreted as interiors, they hung cloth in the background or they painted inner rooms seen through architectural exteriors by the conventional removal of a portion of the wall. The Elizabethan stage adopted these conventions. When the action used only the forestage and the side doors, the locale was assumed to be out-of-doors. Scenes in the inner stages were assumed to be indoors, and any time the curtains of the inner stage were open, the forestage was considered part of the interior. Even an entrance through the closed curtains instead of through a door was enough to indicate an interior locale; and the opening of the curtains during a scene could transport actors on the forestage from one room to another or from an exterior

to an interior locale without any movement by them. Other scholars have postulated even more specific conventional meanings for the use of the inner stages, and for other elements of the stage.

In the same way as in Simultaneous Staging, a property such as a rock was sometimes placed on the forestage, and ignored during some scenes but accepted as locating the action when the actors in a scene touched the property or grouped themselves about it. Some scenery was used, more often set-pieces than painted scenery — rocks, bushes, and thrones. It has been conjectured that the use of painted scenery increased in the seventeenth century.

The Elizabethan audience surrounded the stage on three sides, so that the grouping of actors was still sculptural. However, two or more levels of this stage could be used together for pictorial groupings. Both textual references and stage directions indicate that they were so used in court scenes, battle scenes, and other scenes of display, as well as for many scenes where dramatic effect is obtained from dialogue between actors on two levels, as in *Romeo and Juliet*, *Richard II*, and *Henry VI*, Part 1. Staging methods previously discussed could have grouped actors on varied levels for pictorial effect, but there is little suggestion within the dialogue, in descriptions, or in drawings, to indicate that they often did so.

Rapport between actor and spectator was strong in the Elizabethan theatre. In addition to spectators sitting on the sides of the stage, the groundlings in the pit crowded close around the edge of the stage, separated from it only by a low railing. This proximity of the actors to the front spectators is similar to that in earlier staging methods. The plays often encouraged audience participation. Low comedy invites this, and Shakespeare, Marlowe, and their contemporaries inserted farcical scenes into their most serious tragedies. A great deal of Elizabethan comedy is planned for direct address to the audience, and, in *The Knight of the Burning Pestle* and several other plays, characters at first pretend to be members of the audience and comment on the action. Obviously, prologues, epilogues, choruses, the soliloquy of the Duke of Gloucester which begins *Richard III,* and those of Edgar and Edmund in *King Lear,* are spoken directly to the audience. No distinction seems to be made between these and the introspective soliloquies of Hamlet and Macbeth, and so it can be assumed that they, too, were spoken as direct address to the audience.

On the other hand, this Elizabethan theatre gave opportunity for a modification of acting technique. In previous types of theatre, the auditoriums were vast, and the spectator in the rear was at a considerable distance from the actor, although the continuity of spectators in front of him avoided a psychological separation. In the Elizabethan theatre, for the first time, the typical auditorium was intimate. (See Figure 14.) The Fortune Theatre, for example, is thought to have held about twenty-three hundred spectators, yet they were assembled within a building eighty feet square and thirty-two feet high. An actor could stand at the front of the forestage and be in the center of this building. Only a few spectators in the corners of the top gallery were more than seventy feet from the actor. Most of them were much closer.

This was, then, a theatre in which intimate and subtle playing was possible. Shakespeare obviously wrote, for example, the Hamlet soliloquies and the two tender balcony scenes of *Romeo and Juliet* for an intimate style of acting. Other examples abound in Elizabethan drama.

But this subtle acting must have alternated with strong, full-blooded acting. The Elizabethans were a lusty race, and their playwrights did not limit themselves to intimate and introspective scenes. They required of their actors a tremendous amount of violent physical action — many duels, marches, battles, and scenes of torture. The rhetoric of Shakespeare, Marlowe, Kyd, and others invited strong, full-throated delivery (and some of it seems ludicrous when delivered in a tame and "natural" reading). While Shakespeare has Hamlet caution the Players against "o'erdoing," he also warns them, "Be not too tame neither." Just as in Greek drama, it can be assumed that the good actors were believable in their strong playing, though perhaps the poorer ones were not.

The Elizabethan theatre, then, was highly conventionalized, though less so than the staging techniques discussed previously. The permanent setting, the constant change of locale, the closeness of the audience, and the direct communication have been mentioned. In addition, tragedy was usually written in verse, and comedy often was. Contemporary dress was worn no matter what the historical period of the play. But conventions do not necessarily interfere with belief in a performance once they have been accepted by the audience. Modern audiences unaccustomed to the Elizabethan conventions respond with belief to some scenes in a good production of a play by Shakespeare. The Elizabethan audience, having accepted the conventions, responded with belief to a considerably larger proportion of a play, and the belief at these times was similar to the belief of a modern audience at a contemporary performance.

When the Puritans obtained power in the English Parliament in 1642, they closed the theatres. When the theatres were allowed to reopen in 1660, a new staging technique was introduced. Certain traditions were carried over from the Elizabethan drama and resulted in a distinct English literary tradition and in a few distinctive staging techniques. But essentially the Elizabethan stage form lay dormant for two hundred and fifty years. No other theatre permitting Multiple Staging was invented in England, though the method continued in the Spanish and the Flemish theatre for some time.

The ease with which locale could be changed on the Elizabethan stage without breaking the continuity of action encouraged playwrights to use many locales and to shift rapidly between them. Subsequent staging techniques employed a more definite representation of locale, and found these multi-scened plays a hardship, both in the quantity of scenery demanded, and in the waits for scene changes. Actually, these plays demand a stage fully as flexible as that of the Elizabethans.

THEATRICAL STAGING

Theatrical Staging is a method of locating action which attempts to depict a specific locale by means of scenery. However, this scenic locale is presented as a background for the action rather than as an environment for it; the actors play in front of the scenery rather than within it. The locale is often changed during the action by shifting the scenery in view of the audience. This is the first staging method discussed here which employs a proscenium arch and limits the spectators to a single side of the platform. This scheme is recognized universally as a distinct method of staging, and it has been given varied names related to historical periods, but has no overall descriptive designation which fits into the classification system used here. The term "Theatrical Staging" has been chosen for it because the method calls attention to the scenery as an artifice, and reminds the spectator that the action is taking place in a theatre.

The organizational schemes previously discussed use scenery only in a general way to establish locale for the stage action, and they often need dialogue or convention to identify it definitely. Scenery is sometimes used as decoration and embellishment in these schemes, but it is usually permanently installed through the play, and so attracts little attention after the initial display.

Theatrical Staging, on the other hand, depicts the locale in such literal terms that the nature of the room or exterior is recognized immediately. The only identification needed from dialogue is ownership and sometimes geographical site. Actualistic Staging, which is to be discussed next, also depicts the locale, but in addition it provides a true and believable environment for the action. When the locale is shifted in Actualistic Staging, the change of scenery is effected behind a curtain. This minimizes the theatrical and conventional aspect of the change of locale. Theatrical Staging, instead, displays the scenery as a theatrical convention, not quite lifelike. It usually employs *chiaroscuro* [9] painting on a flat surface. The locale is changed often, and the scenery is shifted in view of the audience. The scenery is meant to impress the spectator both by its beauty and by the mechanical ingenuity with which it is changed. The most distinctive difference from Actualistic Staging is that, in spite of the literal setting, the actors play in front of it and treat it as a background rather than as an environment.

Scenery in the modern sense was developed in Italy in the sixteenth century. As one phase of the Renaissance interest in the classics, the Italians performed the Latin plays of Plautus and Seneca, and then imitations of these. At the princely courts *intermezzi*, stressing singing and dancing, supplemented the plays, gradually replaced them, and eventually became opera and ballet.

The court painter was commissioned to provide the decorations for such a performance of Latin plays and *intermezzi*. Naturally he applied to the scenery the techniques of his easel art. The artists of this period

9 I.e., painting using strong emphasis on light and shade to create a three-dimensional illusion.

were fascinated by the contemporary discoveries in the laws of perspective as applied
to architectural painting, and consequently
the settings became exercises in architectural
perspective. A row of buildings in perspective was designed for each side of the stage
to give the illusion of a deep street scene on
a stage only thirty feet deep.

The first settings used houses executed
in three dimensions, but in what is now
called "forced" perspective, so that the dimensions of the buildings decreased rapidly
toward the back of the setting. As one contribution to this forcing of perspective, the
stage floor raked upward toward the back.
The designers became interested in changing the settings during the action. After
several experiments, they adopted single
wings set parallel to the front of the stage,
but painted to look like the two walls of a
building. One set of these wings could be
pulled offstage as another set was pushed on.
(See Plate 11.) Many sets of wings could
be arranged in packs for rapid scene changes.
The borders masking the top of the settings
were similarly arranged in packs, so that one
set of borders was lifted to reveal another
set. The backscenes were also changed,
either by lifting them as is done today, or,
when there was not sufficient height, by
splitting them in the center so that they
could be drawn to the sides in the same manner as were the wings.

Elaborate machinery was invented to
lower clouds, chariots, and couches to the
stage carrying actors and musicians, to raise
huge temples and mountains through trapdoors, and to operate other moving structures
with the assistance of rolling and revolving
platforms. Soon, machinery consisting of
ropes, pulleys, and huge wooden drums was
invented to move all of this scenery simultaneously.[10]

Since the mechanical changing of scenery
was part of the entertainment, there was no
impulse to use a front curtain in order to
conceal the changes. A curtain was sometimes used to hide the scenery (often including the proscenium arch) until the performance began. Once changing scenery was
used, it became a special feature and the
dramatist was encouraged to go out of his
way to change the locale so as to show off
the machinery. The apex of the elaboration
of scenery was reached in 1728 in Paris when
Servandoni devised in the *Salle des Machines*
of the Tuileries an entertainment wholly of
décor.

This Italian type of scenery was copied
throughout Europe, and was the type of
scenery employed in England during the
Restoration and the eighteenth century.
These two-dimensional settings would not be
believed by a modern audience accustomed
to three-dimensional illusion, but contemporary accounts describe them as miraculously "real."

Scenery was first presented in Italy on a
somewhat open stage in the banquet hall
of a prince, but very quickly it was found
expedient to place it behind a frame to conceal its edges (the *proscenium arch*, from a
slight misinterpretation of the Greek use of
the term *proskenion*). Kernodle finds evidence of many temporary and permanent
arches in the sixteenth century. This was a
natural borrowing from art. Illuminated
manuscripts, carvings, low-relief sculpture,
and paintings had for centuries used the
convention of a framing arch. (See Plate 10.)

Some designs used a simple arch. Some
substituted a "deep proscenium" with oblique
walls which continued the auditorium decoration and related it to the scenery. The
floor space within this deep proscenium

---

[10] The system of changing scene by pulling out
and up one set of wings, backdrops, and borders
(to reveal a second set) continued through the
eighteenth century, and an equipment of such
machinery built in 1766 is still in operation in
the Drottningholm Theatre near Stockholm. (See
Plate 9.)

provided a forestage on which the actors could play. Many theatres had, in addition, a projecting apron stage. The apron was especially deep in English theatres as a carry-over from the forestage of the Elizabethan theatre. In England, also, uniquely British "proscenium doors" gave direct entrance to the apron in front of the proscenium arch. (See Plate 11.) The actors in all theatres modeled after the Italian had the full depth of the stage in which to play, limited only by the awkwardness of walking on the raked floor. But the tradition of playing in the midst of the audience kept the actors on the apron, or in the first few feet behind the proscenium. Dim lighting and poor acoustics also contributed toward driving the actors forward.

The proscenium arch caused a revolution in the shape of the auditorium, and in the whole relationship between audience and stage. When scenery was arranged around three sides of a deep and narrow rectangle or trapezoid and placed behind an arch, the spectators could no longer spread around several sides of the playing space. In order to see this scenery they had to mass together in a narrow wedge not much wider than the proscenium itself. The way was paved for the further revolution in which the actors retreated behind the proscenium and isolated themselves psychologically as well as physically from the audience. The actual psychological revolution was delayed until the nineteenth century, but it was implicit in the space relationship established in the seventeenth century.

In the court theatres, the prince sat in the center of the auditorium at some distance from the stage; no one was seated in front of him. The honored guests were grouped beside the prince and behind him. The seats for the retainers were frequently in bleacher-like banks around three sides of the hall. Similar banks had been in use earlier to permit the retainers to watch the prince eat.

When public theatres were built (usually under princely patronage), this banquet hall tradition was imitated uncritically. For example, the auditorium floors were flat in the early theatres, though they were raked toward the back in later ones. The architects soon discovered that more people could be seated in the same volume of space if seats were added to the upper part of the hall; therefore they built two, three, four, and as many as seven shallow balconies around the auditorium, one above the other. These had to be supported by posts, and it became standard practice to continue the posts as partitions slanted backward at an angle related to the sight lines of the theatre. This produced *boxes*. The privacy offered by the boxes, plus the elevated position which permitted the occupants to see the audience and to be seen by it, made these boxes — which had the poorest view of the stage — the favorite seats, just as were the galleries in the contemporary Elizabethan theatre. Fortunately, this also solved the problem of the perfect view for the princely patron. He could be seated in the "royal box" in the center of the first level and no head would intrude between him and the stage; yet the entire floor below him could be filled with paying customers, as had been impossible in the banquet halls where the prince sat in the equivalent of tenth-row-center with no one seated in front of him. Such a royal box persists in many European theatres and in a few American ones.

In the first rectangular theatres modeled directly on the banquet halls, the sight lines were poor for the occupants of the boxes on the side and of the unpartitioned balconies above them. So the architects experimented with ovoid auditoriums. The "horseshoe" was the most successful modification of the ovoid, and is seen today in the Metropolitan Opera House and in many older European theatres.

In somewhat the same way tradition dulled

the imagination of the architects with regard to the stage house. Since the height of a stage in a banquet hall was limited by the height of the room, the stages in early theatres were built with comparably low ceilings, and the technicians continued to use clumsy methods of *tripping* backdrops (folding them as they were raised). This was rectified in later buildings by using tall stage houses which permitted drops to be flown flat.

Artificial illumination was first used in the theatre during the Renaissance because this was the first time that plays were given indoors. In the banquet halls, chandeliers and sconces of candles provided the basic lighting. When theatres were built, fixtures similar to these were installed in the auditorium and the stage, both of which were lighted to about the same intensity. Oil lamps could be substituted for candles, but were not usual until the eighteenth century, when wicks were improved to reduce the smoke.

Candles (and later lamps) were set in rows one above the other at the sides of the stage behind the proscenium and the wings. Less frequently, lights were placed across the front of the stage (*footlights* — or *floats*, when they were troughs of oil with wicks floating in them supported on corks), and overhead behind borders. Polished metal "basins" were often placed behind the candles as reflectors to increase their brightness. Pieces of colored glass or flasks of colored liquid could be placed in front of the candles. This use of open flames for illumination resulted in many theatre fires, and helps explain why theatres are scarce among older buildings which have survived.

The aesthetic effect of Theatrical Staging is contradictory. This contradiction indicates a difference in goal of designer and actor which neither recognized. The designer strove for "realism"; he designed what could have become a scenic environment for the actor. But the actor did not accept it as an environment. Habituated to playing in free communication with the audience, and in the midst of that audience, he had no impulse to retire within the environment, and so he played in front of the scenery. With his scenery thus treated as background, the designer in turn could use perspective tricks which would have been impossible had the actors retreated within his setting. So here was a possible environment to house psychologically isolated acting, but it was reduced by both actor and designer to a mere background.

In recognition of this contradictory attitude, it is possible to argue that the Theatrical Staging technique as exemplified by the theatres of the Italian Renaissance and the English Restoration was the fumbling beginning of Actualistic Staging, with the designer making a complete transition, and the actor waiting two hundred years to alter his technique to conform to the décor. However, Theatrical Staging produced a distinctive organization of the theatre space which was used for two hundred years, and it is worth recognizing as a distinct method.

The theatres of Italian Renaissance through English Restoration had a fairly large seating capacity, but, by the use of galleries, massed the audience into a relatively small cubic space. Therefore, no great enlargement of acting technique was required until theatre size increased still more in the eighteenth century. Any excesses of vocal or physical acting style in the period were by choice of the actor and playwright, and were not necessitated by the acting conditions. This reflects itself in the contrary waves of acting style between the florid style of Betterton and Quin and the so-called "realism" of Garrick and Kean. As in the Elizabethan theatre, the acting style was left to the choice of the actor rather than to conformity with the physical requirements of the theatre.

Using early eighteenth-century England as an example of acting style associated with Theatrical Staging, we may note that the verbal elegance and the self-conscious gesture and attitude of the period were reflected in the acting style of tragedy by self-consciously beautiful and dignified speech and action. Contemporary dress was worn by the actresses, but conventionalized tragic costumes became fashionable for the men. This consisted of a wide *tonnelet*, which was supposed to represent classical body armor, but more closely resembled the ballet skirt from which it was adapted, and a Roman helmet buried under a forest of plumes. This helmet was worn on top of a full-bottomed periwig. (See Plate 11.) The artifice of these attitudes and clothes may suggest isolation from the audience, but the sheer artificiality of the elegance was an indication to the audience that the actor was conscious of his technique and asked admiration rather than belief. To that extent it produced rapport.

Comedy acting, in a similar manner, encouraged rapport by means of leers, winks, and smirks, in addition to such direct address as the soliloquy,[11] the aside (a convention in which a character speaks to the audience without having the other characters seem to hear him), and the prologue and epilogue. These last had a new popularity, and were often spoken in personal terms by an actor rather than by a "character." And close rapport with the spectators was encouraged by playing at the front of the stage or on the apron.

Theatrical Staging was the first mode of theatre organization which encouraged a design of the stage action in the pictorial medium instead of the sculptural. The audience was assembled on one side, and all spectators looked at the stage groupings from the same direction. But, even though this type of design was used occasionally, picturization was discouraged by the tendency of the actors to play on the forestage, and by the presence in many theatres of spectators seated on stools at the sides of the stage.[12]

ACTUALISTIC STAGING

Locale is depicted in Actualistic Staging by a more or less believable environment. The actors play within this environment, and thereby separate themselves from the audience psychologically as well as physically. It is this separation of actor and spectator, rather than any new scenic device or architectural organization, which distinguishes this method from Theatrical Staging, and from all staging methods previously discussed. In Theatrical Staging, it was noted, the designer showed a tendency to create a believable environment; but the actors — for various reasons — did not treat it as such. The action in Actualistic Staging is stage-centered, and the actors, abandoning the long tradition of audience-centered action, attempt to establish the illusion that the spectator is accidentally viewing this action by some miracle that allows him to see through a wall.

The creation of an illusion of actuality has been to some degree the goal of most staging for the past two hundred years. What is accepted as an adequate degree of reality has varied during the period, so that included within Actualistic Staging is a range from two-dimensional painted cutouts to solidly constructed three-dimensional structures. But the organization of stage space established by the Romanticists in the late eighteenth century has continued unchanged into modern Realism. Romanticism and Realism

---

[11] If proof is needed, one has the speech of Mr. Puff in Sheridan's *The Critic* (1779): "The soliloquy always to the pit! That's a rule!"

[12] In the theatre designed for the *Comédie Française* in 1689, for example, the width of the playing space was reduced to less than fifteen feet by the rows of benches for spectators included in the architect's plans (A. M. Nagler, *Sources of Theatrical History* [Theatre Annual, 1952], pp. 285–286).

differ in the style of décor rather than in basic organization.

The Romantic Style

The first important variety of Actualistic Staging is that of Romanticism. This scenic style reflected the movement in art and literature which sought a return to nature and at the same time exalted the emotions. This often resulted in a choice of a literary subject from the "picturesque" past or from exotic "foreign climes." Romanticism asked the theatre to depict these historical and exotic locales, and to do so with "greater realism" — which meant a substitute for the conventionalized setting of exterior architecture (Theatrical Staging). The resulting style was a two-dimensional painter's realism. It produced a vogue for backdrops of "actual places" painted in realistic detail, and for "real" costumes. David Garrick (1717–79), as actor-manager, initiated the theatre movement in England.

His first step toward actuality was to abandon the "unreal" conventional costume of the tragic hero (the *tonnelet* with its wide stiff skirt, and the plumed helmet). He substituted "real" clothes: the embroidered coat, satin knee-breeches, and powdered peruke of his own eighteenth century. (See Plate 11.) These real clothes were used to dress interchangeably Able Drugger, Antony, Romeo, Macbeth, and Lear. Since the actresses had always worn contemporary gowns, this "innovation" of Garrick's undoubtedly improved the unity of the production. Later, Garrick went one step further and wore authentic period costumes; but apparently the rest of the cast did not, and so unity was violated once again.

Next Garrick imported de Loutherbourg from France in 1771 to provide scenery for his productions. De Loutherbourg was a romantic idealist, equally interested in detailed accuracy and emotional identification. A drop (or a set of cutout drops) by him became a huge easel painting accurately reproducing a locale mentioned by the playwright. If the setting included architecture, it was drawn in the style of contemporary landscape painting, instead of in the draftsman's technique of the Italian Renaissance. A front curtain now was used to conceal scene changes. The designs of de Loutherbourg which have been preserved indicate that this mania for realism through accurate reproduction of the actual place took precedence over any interpretation of the mood of an episode. The use of archeologically accurate costumes increased in the nineteenth century; these, like the scenery, were authenticated by scholars, but were designed without consideration for characterization and atmosphere. (See Plate 9.)

In order to permit a better view of the scenery, Garrick and de Loutherbourg drove the spectators from their stools at the sides of the stage. They concentrated the lighting back of the proscenium. The apron was not actually eliminated, but the new lighting discouraged its use and paved the way for the retreat of the actor behind the proscenium.

The Romantic period of the late eighteenth century and most of the nineteenth century was a transitional period in actor-audience relationship and in acting style. The actors gradually retreated behind the proscenium as the Garrick revolution spread and as his more "natural" style of comedy acting attracted imitators. But the acting in some comedy, and most tragedy and melodrama, continued to be audience-centered and "grand," and rapport continued between actor and spectator. A transition in acting and décor was under way during the vogue of the Romantic Style, but the revolution was not complete.

The Realistic Style

Once Romanticism had encouraged the audience to expect actuality in scenery and costumes, it became apparent that a true environment could not be achieved through the painter's two-dimensional technique.

The two-dimensional wing-and-drop scenic technique was least successful in depicting believable interiors, and so the first move toward three-dimensional environment was directed at the interior. To replace the wings standing parallel to the curtain line, flats were lashed together to make solid side walls; the acting area was thus inclosed in the three "walls" of a *box set.* (See Figure 25.) Mme. Vestris, a London theatre manager, used such a set in 1841. She is usually credited with the innovation, though there are rival claims of approximately the same date. Once the box set was invented, its realism increased rapidly. Eventually it acquired a ceiling, and *thicknesses* for doors and other openings to make the walls seem massive and solid. Thus the form which provides a majority of settings today was achieved over a hundred years ago.

In all previous staging methods, exterior locales were more easily imitated than interiors. In three-dimensional Realism, however, a believable environment was easier to achieve for interior settings. Such is the influence of scenic style upon playwriting that the drama reflected this scenic circumstance by going indoors. Interior settings became almost as predominant as were architectural exteriors in plays written for production under the previous staging methods.

Another advance toward actuality was made in the overall production. The scenic artists of Romanticism and early Realism strove for accuracy of details, and largely disregarded the effect of the whole. A desire for unified effect stimulated the theatrically-minded George II, Duke of tiny Saxe-Meiningen, to strive for ensemble playing, for integration of acting and décor, and for what is now called "director's design." In the period 1874–90, the Duke taught his permanent acting group to work for an integrated performance instead of for personal prominence. Particularly, he stressed the detailed planning of mob scenes so that a total impact of verisimilitude was achieved. He employed steps and platforms liberally in order to use the three-dimensional possibilities of the stage space, and in order to increase the opportunities for meaningful picturization. His designs are indicative of this desire for integration: they include the actors depicted at the dramatic climax. (See Plate 12.) He also attempted historical accuracy of settings and costumes. The Saxe-Meiningen company toured through Europe and created an indelible impression on theatre artists wherever it played. It especially influenced Stanislavski and Antoine, who were to become important leaders in the theatre at the turn of the century.

Opportunity for more "natural" treatment of stage lighting occurred in this same period. Previously, with candles and lamps, the goal of stage lighting had been to obtain enough light to make the actors and scenery visible; there was little opportunity to treat light as a part of the décor. But when gaslight was introduced onto the stage in 1817,[13] electric arclights in 1846, and electric bulbs in 1881, any degree of brightness could be supplied. *Gas-tables* and then electric *switchboards* and *controlboards* permitted this light to be selectively changed during the action. More use of colored light was possible with electric light because tinted gelatine could be used, since there was no longer danger of igniting it. An almost exact reproduction of natural light could be achieved, and light could be used in other ways as a part of the décor. Electric light also permitted the development of the *sky dome* or *cyclorama* of plaster or cloth lighted to simulate the sky — thereby reducing the need for painted backdrops. The ultimate in duplicating the phenomena of nature was the *effect machine,* which could throw photo-

[13] Gas was used to illuminate other rooms of theatres in 1815.

graphic images of moving clouds on the cyclorama.

The peak was reached in the specialized variety of Realism called Naturalism. In this extreme, every possible verisimilitude was introduced into the presentation: three-dimensional solidity of setting, representational lighting, the perfect reproduction of a recognizable room, the smell of bacon frying, the sight of real water flowing from a stage faucet, and the inaudibility of an actor talking with his back to the audience.

In America, David Belasco was the dean of the directors associated with such a style. Working with highly theatrical, sentimental plays (mostly of his own authorship), he directed and set them with consummate "naturalism." He exactly reproduced a Child's restaurant down to a cook flapping pancakes in the window; he cluttered the setting of *The Return of Peter Grimm* with hundreds of theatrically extraneous properties "because that was the way the room would be" (see Plate 12); he erected complete rooms beyond the entrances of a setting in order to help the actors acquire a strong sense of illusion as they traversed these extra rooms on their way to the stage; he expected actors to "engross themselves in their parts"; and he kept his electricians busy developing lighting equipment that would more nearly reproduce natural light.

Like the painted actuality of Romanticism, this extreme Naturalism defeated its purpose because it drew attention to the setting instead of providing merely an environment that strengthened the believability of the dramatic action. Its failure produced some violent reactions which will be discussed in a later chapter.

A less violent reaction was the modification of the style into what is called "selective" Realism, or other equivalent terms, where everything on the stage is either convincingly real or acceptable as symbolically real, but where a high degree of artistic choice is exercised in the objects to be included,

in the hope of producing identification, clarification, and intensification with the simplest possible means. "Selective" Realism is the prevailing style today. (See Plate 16.)

With few exceptions, however, the motion picture has retained the goal of Naturalism. A. Nicholas Vardac [14] believes that the motion picture is the culmination of the trend to actuality initiated by David Garrick, and that by carrying it further than is possible on the stage, the films have relieved the stage of the need to strive for it. Settings in other than the Realistic Style appear on Broadway and elsewhere with increasing frequency.

The need to provide a highly illusionistic environment for each locale in a play causes interruptions for scene changes. This mechanical problem has brought about an alteration in playwriting technique. Recognizing that any interruption of the action was likely to reduce the cumulative effect of the play, during most of the era of Realistic Staging playwrights avoided changes of locale within acts, and gradually reduced the acts themselves from five to two in order to reduce the number of major intermissions.

The theatre for Realistic Staging needs to be small enough so that the actor can speak and move on the same scale as in ordinary life and still be seen and heard by every spectator. The economy of the modern American commercial theatre makes this impossible, and therefore plays are performed in theatres that are too large for these special requirements. Adapting to this circumstance, the skillful actor learns to enlarge his action slightly, and acquires the technique of projecting his voice while still retaining all the inflectional patterns and variations of quality which are natural in unprojected speech. The unskillful actor either is inaudible, or breaks the illusion by "shouting."

With Realistic Staging, dramatic action retreated behind the proscenium; and the setting became the environment of the actor.

[14] *Stage to Screen* (Harvard University Press, 1949).

PLATE 11. **Drawings of Three Eighteenth-Century Performances.** (Above, left) The famous actor James Quin as Coriolanus in 1749. He wears the conventional acting costume of *tonnelet* and plumed helmet. (Above, right) David Garrick and Mrs. Pritchard in *Macbeth* in the second half of the century. Garrick abandoned the conventional acting costume in favor of "real" contemporary clothes. (Below) *The School for Scandal* at Drury Lane Theatre, London, 1777.

PLATE 12. **Two Styles of Actualism.** (Above) Design of décor and action by the Duke of Saxe-Meiningen for *Prinz von Homburg*. (Below) Naturalism in a scene from David Belasco's production of *The Return of Peter Grimm*.

The "realistic," "naturalistic," and "slice-of-life" dramas that were written in the late nineteenth century were meant to be seen as if through a keyhole. To assist this illusion of actuality, the actors stayed within the frame and in no way acknowledged the presence of a thousand spectators beyond the proscenium. In extreme uses of this technique, the proscenium was considered to be a "fourth wall" to the room: andirons were placed in the footlights and furniture was placed with its back to the curtain line; actors referred to pictures and other objects supposedly hanging on this imaginary wall; and they turned their backs to the audience. For the first time in the history of the theatre, actors retreated from the audience, set up a psychological as well as a physical barrier of distance between themselves and the audience, and attempted to live an isolated, stage-centered life.

This change was not made overnight. It developed in erratic steps from the time of Garrick to the early decades of the twentieth century, and reached its zenith at about the same time as the extreme in Naturalistic scenery. Since then, just as the scenic style has veered to "selective" Realism, so acting now seeks to be effective as well as believable.

This change in the theatre organization brought on by Realistic Staging and a comparable trend in playwriting was more drastic than former changes, because, in addition to the special alteration in the relationship between actor and spectator, it — at least until recently — resulted in a new standard for acting. As a part of the actor's psychological isolation, his highest goal became the ability to induce complete belief in the character he was playing and in the action in which he was participating. The highest praise that could be given to an actor changed from "I admired your performance," to "I believed you." Any evidence of conscious skill in the actor was considered a blemish.

This style of acting is appropriate to roles in the repertory of Realism, but the standard of naturalness as the primary test of acting ability has threatened to cut off the modern audience from a full enjoyment of the great plays written before Ibsen. These plays were written for a more self-conscious acting style and for a passion larger than that of ordinary contemporary life. When the modern theatre adapts these older plays to a strictly illusionistic mode, their effectiveness is reduced, and sometimes they become ridiculous. If, instead, an attempt is made to meet the demands of style and passion inherent in the play, American actors find it difficult to perform in this unfamiliar manner. Even when it is achieved, most audiences, trained in terms of Realistic Staging (especially in motion pictures and television) to believe that the highest goal of acting is to be "natural," find this highly emotional style unpleasant and ludicrous. Shakespeare alone of the great playwrights of the past seems to be able to move a modern audience when constricted by a "natural" style, but even his plays lose some of their spirit and passion in the process of being cramped by such an approach. This inability of Realistic Staging to project the great plays of the past is one cause for the current criticism of this whole method of organization of the stage space and of the associated acting technique.

For the first time in the theatre, the arrangement of the actors, and of the actors within the setting, demands pictorial design of action and grouping rather than sculptural design. Although this technique of design tends to produce a flatness of effect, it gives to the director a greatly increased opportunity to reinforce the dramatic action by meaningful picturization.

Six methods of locating the stage action and of organizing the theatre space have been distinguished here. All these methods blend into one another, and compromises between the methods are frequent. A new style of scenery and staging does not immediately drive its predecessors from the theatre; rather, they coexist for a period. Thus Belasco, Stanislavski, and others continued to strive for Naturalism long after "selective" Realism had gained wide acceptance and anti-illusionistic techniques were gaining some acceptance. Even today when "selective" Realism is predominant, designers occasionally return to a strongly illusionistic style and receive critical praise.

Each staging method arose spontaneously to satisfy a particular concept of theatre, acting, and playwriting. Once the method was accepted, its conventions in turn exerted an influence upon the acting, playwriting, and aesthetic objectives of the theatre. One example is the effect that Realistic Staging has had in shifting stage action indoors, and in reducing both the scene changes within acts and the number of act divisions.

At the time a new staging method develops, it is revolutionary in its influence, dictating changes of method in the other components. Once established as a tradition, however, the influence becomes reactionary, discouraging change.

The staging methods discussed here have differed in their mode of indicating locale, and in the details by which the parts of the theatre plant are interrelated. The basic actor-audience relationship and the fundamentals of acting remained constant until Actualistic Staging forced the actor to break off his long rapport with the audience and retreat into stage-centered isolation. Realistic Staging reached its zenith early in the twentieth century in Naturalism, and since that time its initial goal has been modified. Most of the modifications have been made as the result of the dissatisfaction of directors and designers with a mode of production which confined their artistry within the uncomfortably narrow conventions of the proscenium stage. To escape from this confinement, designers and directors often seemed willing to adopt any other mode no matter how radical, from the presenting of plays without act curtains to producing in open rooms where the performers were completely surrounded by spectators.

Realistic Staging is probably still the form of staging most commonly encountered, and the proscenium stage is likely to continue to be with us for a good many generations. But alongside the proscenium form, the "new" open form is becoming increasingly accepted. The new form has no proscenium arch and no formal physical separation of actor from audience. As in premodern times, the performer is often nearly surrounded by spectators. Open staging enhances many kinds of drama and indeed is adaptable to almost all. As many different plays are being produced successfully in open theatres today as on proscenium stages, and some of the best authors of our time are writing specifically for open stages.

The two forms will be treated in detail in Chapters 14 and 15. To illustrate some of the discussion, a series of plans for contemporary theatre plants is reproduced on the following five pages (167–171).

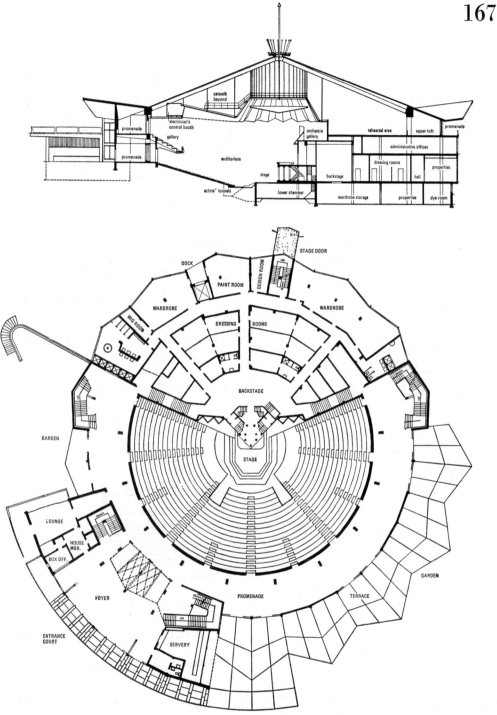

The Stratford Festival Theatre, Stratford, Ontario. This was the first major theatre in America to be built with a fully developed thrust stage. It was erected in 1957 around a stage originally designed by Tanya Moiseiwitsch for the production of Shakespearean plays in a large circular tent. In 1962 the stage which is shown here was modified to provide more widely spaced side entrances and fewer supporting piers for the upper stage. The architects were Rounthwaite and Fairfield.

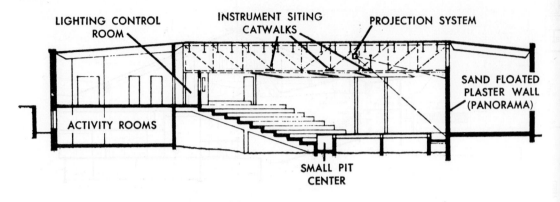

LIGHTING CONTROL ROOM

INSTRUMENT SITING CATWALKS

PROJECTION SYSTEM

SAND FLOATED PLASTER WALL (PANORAMA)

ACTIVITY ROOMS

SMALL PIT CENTER

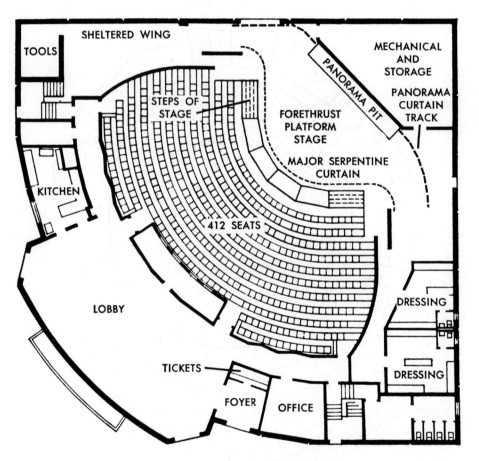

SHELTERED WING

TOOLS

MECHANICAL AND STORAGE

PANORAMA PIT

PANORAMA CURTAIN TRACK

STEPS OF STAGE

FORETHRUST PLATFORM STAGE

MAJOR SERPENTINE CURTAIN

KITCHEN

412 SEATS

DRESSING

LOBBY

DRESSING

TICKETS

FOYER

OFFICE

The Community Theatre, Western Springs, Illinois. From the moment of its opening in 1961, this building attracted international attention for its attractive proportions, easy operation, and extremely low cost — about one-third that of the most nearly comparable buildings. Gus Orth was the architect, James Hull Miller the consultant and guiding genius.

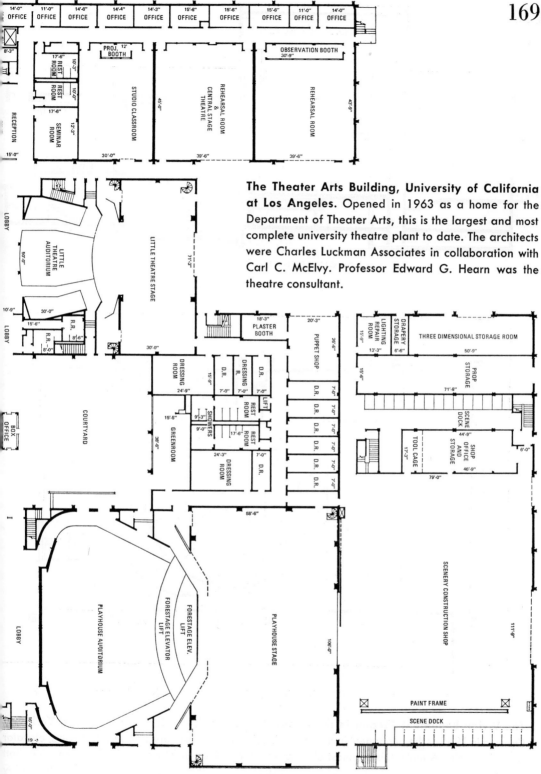

The Theater Arts Building, University of California at Los Angeles. Opened in 1963 as a home for the Department of Theater Arts, this is the largest and most complete university theatre plant to date. The architects were Charles Luckman Associates in collaboration with Carl C. McElvy. Professor Edward G. Hearn was the theatre consultant.

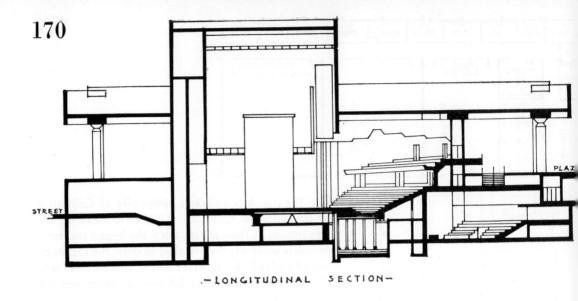

.—LONGITUDINAL SECTION—

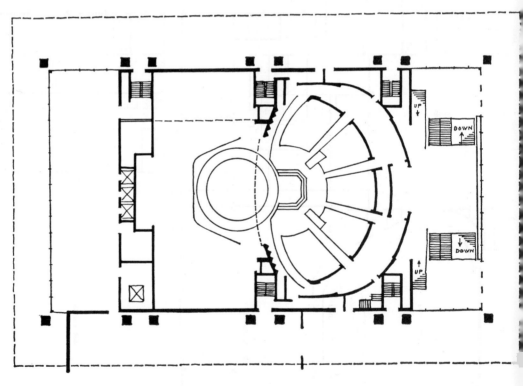

— COMPOSITE PLAN, LEVELS 3, 4, and 5 —

The Vivian Beaumont Theater in the Lincoln Center for the Performing Arts, New York City.
Opened in 1965 as the permanent home of the Lincoln Center Repertory Theater. Revolving, elevator
and sliding stages make this the most elaborately mechanized theatre plant in North America. Both
proscenium and open stages can be provided according to the requirements of the particular play.
Eero Saarinen was the architect, with Jo Mielziner as collaborating designer. (*Courtesy of Lincoln
Center for the Performing Arts, Inc.*)

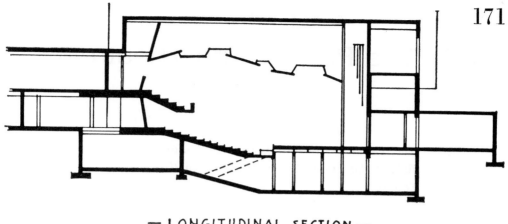

— LONGITUDINAL SECTION —

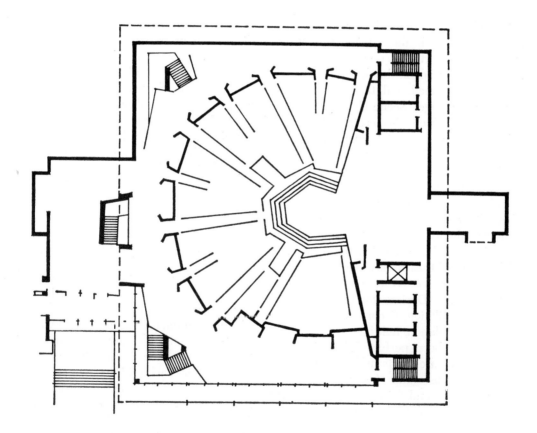

— PLAN — LOBBY AND STAGE FLOOR LEVEL —

The Tyrone Guthrie Theatre, Minneapolis. Opened in 1963, this theatre was intended to accommodate a resident company, a repertory predominantly classical, and 1,400 spectators seated as close to the stage as possible. The resemblance of this plan to that of the Stratford, Ontario, Festival Theatre is not surprising since Sir Tyrone Guthrie and Tanya Moiseiwitsch once again were the moving spirits. The architect was Ralph Rapson.

14 | The Proscenium Theatre

*The General Structure • The Auditorium
Behind the Proscenium • Revolts from the
Pattern*

Most theatres in use today are proscenium theatres, in which the audience is seated facing a large curtained opening. When the play is about to begin, the lights in the auditorium are dimmed and the curtain opens to reveal the stage. Scene changes occur in blackouts or when the curtain is closed. When it is time for an intermission, the curtain is closed and the auditorium lights are brightened. At the end of the play, the curtain is closed again, then opened and closed quickly several times for the curtain calls; when the curtain calls are completed, the auditorium lights are brought up full and stay on until the audience has left the theatre.

This form of theatre has been in common use throughout the Western world for over three centuries. During this time all of the details of ventilation, décor, acoustics, audience accommodation, lighting, and stage machinery have been perfected by successive generations of architects and engineers. As a result, the proscenium theatre today represents a familiar and fairly efficient form for the presentation of the vast majority of modern plays. Of course no one would claim that the proscenium theatre is perfect for all kinds of drama. Plays of earlier times, for example, written to be performed out-of-doors, often fit awkwardly into it. And more and more

contemporary playwrights call for entirely different actor-audience relationships. Nevertheless, the proscenium theatre is the one kind of theatre building found everywhere and with which every theatre worker is obliged to be familiar. The odds are that most of those now studying theatre art will spend most of their lives working in proscenium theatres. For this reason, detailed consideration of the proscenium theatre is basic to any discussion of theatre art as a whole, and the present chapter is devoted to it.[1]

THE GENERAL STRUCTURE

The most conspicuous architectural characteristic of the proscenium theatre is the way it joins two distinct enclosures by means of a proscenium arch in a common wall. The theatre structure is thus compartmented into two areas, one for the auditorium and one for the stage, each with its own special form and function. The spectators sit in the auditorium enclosure and watch the actors performing in the stage enclosure. The proscenium opening in effect frames the stage action.

[1] The open theatre and stage are discussed in the following chapter.

When structural steel and asbestos came into use about seventy-five years ago, the separation of actor and audience was further defined by fire laws requiring every theatre to have a fireproof partition to close the proscenium opening and protect the spectators in case of a conflagration on the stage. This "fire curtain" is always built into a fireproof wall and closes automatically when the temperature in the theatre rises above a certain point.[2] This separation came about as a result of theatre fires. It has produced a fundamental structural change from previous centuries without making much corresponding change in the appearance of the building. Most theatres of the sixteenth to eighteenth centuries were remodeled from banquet halls, tennis courts, and other rectangular halls, and remained essentially a single structure with a thin partition for the proscenium wall, which offered little or no protection from fire on stage.

So far as the audience is concerned, a theatre is primarily a place for entertainment. Its great attraction is the opportunity it affords for vicarious experience. The audience approaches the theatre with the expectation of glamour, excitement, or emotional vividness. The architect and the decorator try to sustain and increase this excitement and anticipation as the spectator moves through the theatre. One of the familiar architectural devices for this effect is spaciousness of lobby, foyer, and auditorium, as exemplified in the princely court theatres (where the entrance might be through the palace itself), many of the state and public theatres of Europe, the ANTA Theatre[3], the Radio City Music Hall, the Martin Beck

Theatre, and the Wisconsin Union Theatre. Serving the same general purpose are many additional devices of color and ornamentation such as the resplendent chandeliers of the Paris Opera, the Chagall murals in the new Metropolitan Opera House in Lincoln Center, and the heroic sculptures in the lobby of the New York State Theater. Another means for heightening the excitement of theatregoing is extreme novelty of form as seen in the Stratford (Ontario) Shakespearean Festival Theatre and the Tyrone Guthrie Theatre in Minneapolis. In smaller theatres architects sometimes take an opposite course and stress intimacy and comfort.

THE AUDITORIUM

When the theatre became semipublic and then truly public, a tier of balconies was added around three walls of the auditorium in order to crowd as many people as possible into the space and to keep the farthest spectator as close to the stage as possible. As has already been noted, the lower balconies were often partitioned as boxes. (See page 159.) For three centuries these balconies remained shallow and attached to three sides of the theatre, but when twentieth-century engineers developed steel beams which would support large balconies without pillars, the sections of the balconies at the rear of the auditorium were deepened until they now sometimes overhang half or more of the orchestra; side balconies, with their bad sight lines, were abandoned. Then it was found that one large, deep balcony supplied more good balcony seats than several shallow ones in overhanging tiers.

However, the tradition of boxes continued in spite of the abominable view of the stage which they afford, and many commercial theatres in use today have two or three boxes on each side of the proscenium at the level of each balcony. Even some theatres and

---

2 Building Code of the City of New York and that recommended by the National Board of Fire Underwriters. Since other cities ordinarily model their codes after them, there is considerable uniformity in the country.

3 Built as the Guild Theatre.

motion picture houses built in the past few years retain a decorative treatment at the sides of the proscenium in loving memory of the boxes.

In the twenties it was fashionable in non-commercial theatres to place all seats on one floor, but it was found that rear seats in a deep auditorium are less desirable than seats in a balcony.

The seating arrangement of sections divided by aisles running from front to rear has persisted for centuries. For safety in case of fire or panic, the building codes prescribe that no seat may be more than six seats from an aisle. Center sections are thereby limited to fourteen seats in a row. This scheme inevitably sacrifices some highly desirable seating space. French theatres attach collapsible seats on springs to the aisle seats, and fill the aisles with spectators. This type of seat sometimes is used in American buses.

Another seating plan, known as *Continental* because it was popularized in Germany in the twenties, is permitted in the United States under special conditions. This provides sufficient space between rows so that a seated person does not have to rise to let others pass, and it eliminates aisles. It accommodates nearly as many spectators in the same space as the more common mode.

Between the apron and the first row of seats there is often an *orchestra pit* sufficiently below the floor level to keep the heads and instruments of the musicians below the level of the stage, but not to prevent the conductor from seeing the stage action when he stands. It is difficult to decide the desirable size of this pit for a multi-purpose theatre. A small orchestra is often desirable with a straight play, especially in revivals of pre-modern plays. An orchestra of ten to twenty pieces is needed for musical comedies, and a much larger one for operas, operettas, and some elaborate productions of classics. Yet when a large pit

is not in use, the first row of seats is needlessly far from the stage. If an elevator is needed in the stage area because of basement storage, the pit is one place for it. This location permits the elevator to be used at stage level as a forestage for plays, concerts, and commencement exercises, as a pit for either a visible or concealed orchestra, and as a floor for additional auditorium seats when it is not otherwise needed. An elevator in the floor of the stage itself to connect the stage with basement shops, while permitting the use of trapdoors in this area, and useful for an occasional special feat of stagecraft, is often blocked by scenery or a *ground cloth* during a production.

Provisions for Seeing

When the first orchestra was marked off in Greece, the spectators stood around the circumference. For two thousand years the spectators spread themselves at least halfway around the stage. But with the development of spectacle in sixteenth-century Italy, the performance could be appreciated only from the front, and so the audience space was narrowed, and ultimately, with the triumph of Actualistic Staging, the space was reduced almost to the width of the proscenium, fanning out a little in the rear.

In the twentieth century, a new problem has arisen. The motion picture has accustomed the spectator to seeing approximately the same amount of detail from every seat in the house, and has made him critical of a theatre seat from which he sees less well than those near the front. Kenneth Macgowan [4] states that six hundred is the maximum number of spectators that can be seated near enough to the stage to obtain the nearly uniform impression from it that they are habituated to by motion pictures. For college,

[4] "Architecture for the Audience," in "Papers Presented at the Eighth Ann Arbor Conference: The Theatre" (University of Michigan College of Architecture and Design, 1950), p. 9. (Mimeographed.)

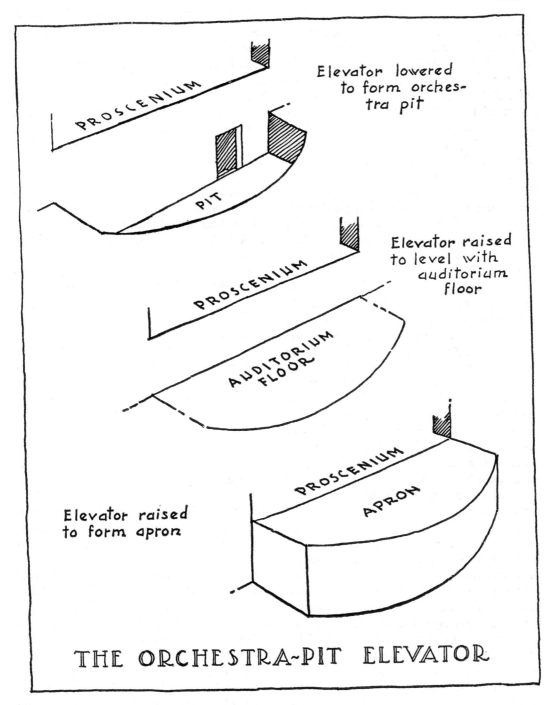

Elevator lowered to form orchestra pit

Elevator raised to level with auditorium floor

Elevator raised to form apron

THE ORCHESTRA-PIT ELEVATOR

Figure 15. When an elevator is needed in the stage area because of basement storage, the orchestra pit is an excellent place for it.

high school, and community theatres, three to seven hundred seats is a satisfactory size for an auditorium. The exact size is determined by the probable audience and by the number of performances considered desirable. But the high production costs in the commercial theatre make such a small theatre economically impractical, and so houses seating a thousand or more are used despite the limited vision from the rear seats.

The audience now demands good sight lines within the auditorium. Seats cannot be fanned out too far to the sides, particularly at the front of the house. A spectator may accept a partial view of the setting, but he complains if action is concealed from him. A deep auditorium can be twice as wide as the proscenium, but a small one cannot spread this much. Psychologically, seats in back corners seem farther from the stage than they actually are; Joseph Urban in the Ziegfeld Theatre eliminated such seats by designing an oval auditorium with the stage at one narrow end. The theatre at Carnegie Institute of Technology similarly has its stage in one of the sides of an oval. Other theatres have curved back walls. The impression of a tunnel is produced when side walls are flat, whether or not they are angled, so modern design curves them or breaks them in other ways such as by louvered entranceways.

To insure good visibility, the auditorium floor is ordinarily *raked*. Still better practice is to *dish* it — to rake it increasingly toward the back so as to provide increasing elevation between rows of seats as they are more distant from the stage. However, auditoriums are ordinarily designed to keep the degree of slope to that which permits ramped aisles without steps. Any steps are a danger in case of fire or panic, and irregularly placed single steps, such as would be required by a sharply dished floor, are prohibited. In order to reduce the necessary rake, an attempt is often made to seat spectators so that they look between the heads of the people in the row ahead. By using a staggered arrangement of seats which vary in width as much as two inches, this can be accomplished for seats in the center of a row, but aisle seats usually are lined up behind one another. Seats are set in curved rows so that every seat faces toward the upstage center of the stage.

The slope of the balcony needs to be steep enough to provide good vision, but not so steep as to be alarming. Care is taken that the spectators in the top of the balcony can see the back wall of the setting as well as all upstage action. Since the full height of the proscenium is seldom used, this balcony angle is determined from the usual height of settings. Balcony patrons also should be able to see the apron and any special forestage which is likely to be constructed.

Provisions for Hearing

The audience also demands to hear well. Even good amplification equipment adds a sizzling sound, and it can introduce unnaturalness by its sheer volume. This amplification is less serious in the motion picture theatre, where the visual image is enlarged proportionately.

Amplification should not be necessary in an auditorium of the size in which it is feasible to perform most plays. The Metropolitan Opera House, the Mormon Tabernacle in Salt Lake City, and Hill Auditorium in Ann Arbor are examples of large auditoriums in which the acoustics make amplification unnecessary.

Sound waves are reflected in a manner similar to light rays — reflected in a highly directional manner from a hard surface (as light is by a mirror), but diffused and absorbed by a soft or porous surface (as light is by a matte surface). Sound, however, can be amplified by repeated reflection in a small space (as light cannot); and there are other differences. It is desirable that the shape and texture of the walls behind the actor and immediately in front of him amplify his voice without distortion, and that

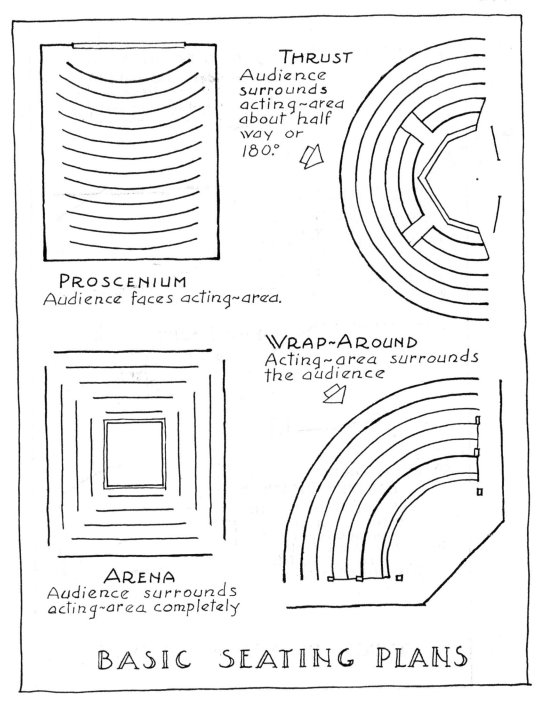

THRUST
Audience surrounds acting~area about half way or 180.°

PROSCENIUM
Audience faces acting~area.

WRAP~AROUND
Acting~area surrounds the audience

ARENA
Audience surrounds acting~area completely

BASIC SEATING PLANS

Figure 16. With wrap-around, arena, and thrust stages, all members of the audience are relatively close to the performers. Particularly in large proscenium theatres, sight lines and other factors complicate the problem.

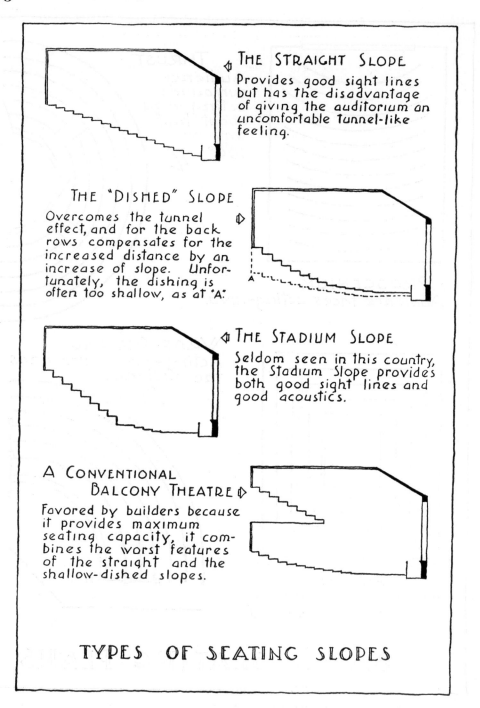

THE STRAIGHT SLOPE
Provides good sight lines but has the disadvantage of giving the auditorium an uncomfortable tunnel-like feeling.

THE "DISHED" SLOPE
Overcomes the tunnel effect, and for the back rows compensates for the increased distance by an increase of slope. Unfortunately, the dishing is often too shallow, as at "A."

THE STADIUM SLOPE
Seldom seen in this country, the Stadium Slope provides both good sight lines and good acoustics.

A CONVENTIONAL BALCONY THEATRE
Favored by builders because it provides maximum seating capacity, it combines the worst features of the straight and the shallow-dished slopes.

TYPES OF SEATING SLOPES

Figure 17. European architects have experimented more freely with arrangement of the auditorium than have American architects.

the walls beyond this be absorbent or be so designed that the sounds reflected by the surfaces are diffused rather than focused in such a way as to produce an echo. (See Figure 18, which points out additional acoustical considerations.)

Plaster absorbs little sound, wood absorbs more; cork, cloth, human bodies, and porous materials are still more absorbent. The rococo architecture of the eighteenth and nineteenth centuries provided endless broken surfaces which diffused the reflected sounds. Many surfaces were of wood. As a result, this decorative style resulted by chance in many theatres with good acoustics. The modern architectural style with its flat plaster surfaces is the most difficult possible style from the acoustical standpoint, and results in many acoustically bad theatres. The usual correction is the application of sound-absorbent materials to the walls and heavy carpeting to the floors. While this correction reduces echoes, it also reduces the volume; and it results, moreover, in duller sounds because it selectively absorbs the higher frequencies of the actors' voices. The need for acoustically perfect radio studios has led to ingenious solutions which can be copied in theatre architecture.

In the past, auditoriums have had different acoustics when empty, with sound reflected from the floor and from wooden seats, than when filled with sound-absorbent human bodies. Current practice is to install a type of upholstered seat which absorbs the same amount of sound as would a spectator sitting in the seat. This produces a constant value in the acoustics. The science of acoustics is so complex that even the experts make scale models for preliminary tests of their designs for auditoriums.

Other Provisions for Audience Comfort

Spectators in the past have endured hard and badly-shaped seats, bad ventilation, uneven temperature, and other discomforts, in return for the thrill of the theatre performance. But the motion picture palaces have accustomed them to comfort, and they now expect it in the theatre. This calls for well-shaped upholstered seats, and easy access to them. Rows of seats in theatres often have been so close together that a long-legged man is uncomfortable when he slouches the least bit, and there are balcony seats in some theatres in Europe in which a six-foot man cannot sit down. The Continental method of seating, explained earlier, solves the comfort problem as well as that of easy access.

Good ventilation, humidification, heating, and cooling systems contribute to comfort. Special attention is given to their silent operation — some theatres which have effective ventilating systems cannot use them during performances because of their noise.

Ideally, the theatre is soundproofed against all but the most extraordinary outside noise, and also against extraneous sounds within the structure itself. Sources of such noises include the greenroom, the dressing rooms, the shop, the rehearsal areas, the remote-control switches and dimmers, passages outside the fire exits, and the foyers and lobbies.

The decoration of the auditorium contributes to the psychological mood of the spectator. There was a tendency earlier in this century to make theatre interiors plain and dull so as not to distract from the stage. This was found needless, since the auditorium is dark while the curtain is up. Joseph Urban exploded this theory for all time by covering the walls of the Ziegfeld Theatre [5] with huge story-book figures and vivid backgrounds painted in primary colors and gold.

Provisions for Safety

The provisions of the building codes have been developed over the years to insure the safety of the theatre audience both from

[5] Joseph Urban, *Theatres* (Theatre Arts, 1929), in numerous illustrations.

fire itself and from panic caused by the sight or smell of smoke. To keep pace with the improvements in fire prevention provided by developments in steel and concrete building methods, these codes are occasionally revised to remove those restrictions which are no longer needed. While the codes are often slow in reflecting improved engineering, their provisions are never justifiably violated or evaded. Because its amateur crews are thoughtless in handling matches, other open flames, and electrical equipment, the school stage even more than a commercial theatre needs a fire curtain and other safety equipment. Yet many a school theatre is built without a fire curtain.

Most codes require that the fire curtain be raised in view of the audience just before the performance. The mechanism which lowers it automatically in case of fire, the mechanism for closing the other fire doors, and all safety devices are supposed to be inspected by the fire department at regular intervals. The code requires an adequate number of exits, clearly marked and free of obstruction at all times. Steps must be lighted and they may not be used at all in any place where people are likely to stumble on them. All exit doors are required to swing outward in the direction the audience moves when leaving the auditorium.

BEHIND THE PROSCENIUM

The size of the stage house of a well-planned theatre surprises many people — including architects. The acting area within a setting is seldom more than forty feet wide, twenty deep, and sixteen high. Seeing plays only from out front, spectators assume that the stage house needs to be only slightly larger than this, forgetting the offstage parts of the setting seen through entranceways and windows, and the area beyond and above this which is needed for storing and handling scenery and for the passage of the

actors and crew. Ordinarily, a good stage house has approximately the same cubic footage as the auditorium, as though the auditorium were tipped upright onto its front wall.

Historically, the stage house has not always been this large. In the days of flat wings and drops, there was not so much need for offstage space at the sides and back as in the present period of bulky plastic units. The stage today must accommodate varied types of scenery. Many of the theatres of the sixteenth through eighteenth centuries were remodeled from halls and the stage had to fit the space available. Since labor was cheap, efficiency was not important. However, when theatres were planned for the use of elaborately changing scenery, the stage house increased enormously. The *Salle des Machines*, built in 1660 in the Tuileries, had a 32-foot proscenium; and the stage was 132 feet deep. The stage of the Paris Opera today is of nearly comparable size: it is twice as wide as the auditorium; its normal depth is equal to the auditorium depth but this can be almost doubled by opening up a large practice room behind the stage; the stage house is twice as tall as the high-domed auditorium and has five floors below it for machinery. Many of the state theatres of Europe have comparable stage space.

The Work Space

With the increase in building costs in modern times, stage space often has been restricted in both commercial and noncommercial theatres. This is one of the reasons why so many Broadway theatres have been leased for radio, television, and motion pictures, and why the Alvin, the Martin Beck, the Music Box, the Winter Garden, the Imperial, the Majestic, and other houses with adequate stages are seldom without a tenant.

The commercial theatre can afford expensive mechanical devices for rapid scene changes, such as *sliding stages, elevator*

PLATE 13. **Expressional Design.** Appia and Craig believed that scenery should be expressive rather than meaningful or depictive, advocating relatively simple planes and masses, with a maximum of focus on the moving body of the actor. (Above) A setting for *King Lear* by Appia. (Below) A model by Craig for *Hamlet*.

PLATE 14. **Two Revolts Against the Conventions of Actualism.** (Above) The remodeling of Le Vieux Colombier by Louis Jouvet for Jacques Copeau, to reduce the separation of auditorium and stage, was a revolt against the proscenium arch. (Middle and Below) Expressionism, a revolt against actualistic conventions in general, attempted to objectify inner experience by reflecting or symbolizing a character's mental state. As a scenic mode, expressionism can in part be applied to realistic plays, but it fully matches the writing technique of *From Morn to Midnight* (middle) and *The Adding Machine.* (Middle, director, H. D. Albright; designer, Lawrence Voss. Below, director, Barnard Hewitt; designer, John McCoy. Both, Cornell University: A. M. Drummond, supervising director.)

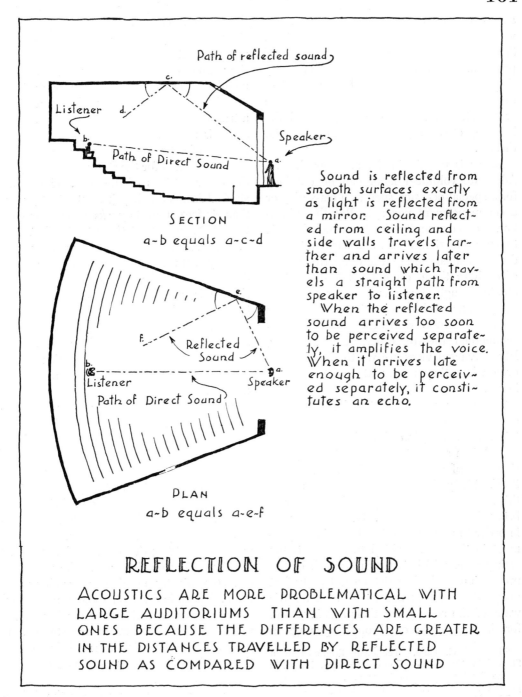

Path of reflected sound

Listener

Speaker

Path of Direct Sound

SECTION
a-b equals a-c-d

Reflected Sound

Listener

Speaker

Path of Direct Sound

PLAN
a-b equals a-e-f

Sound is reflected from smooth surfaces exactly as light is reflected from a mirror. Sound reflected from ceiling and side walls travels farther and arrives later than sound which travels a straight path from speaker to listener.

When the reflected sound arrives too soon to be perceived separately, it amplifies the voice. When it arrives late enough to be perceived separately, it constitutes an echo.

REFLECTION OF SOUND

ACOUSTICS ARE MORE PROBLEMATICAL WITH LARGE AUDITORIUMS THAN WITH SMALL ONES BECAUSE THE DIFFERENCES ARE GREATER IN THE DISTANCES TRAVELLED BY REFLECTED SOUND AS COMPARED WITH DIRECT SOUND

Figure 18. Sound waves are reflected like light waves, but differ from them in other ways, including the possibility of amplification.

stages, flown settings, jackknife stages, and various adaptations of the *revolving stage.* Some of these simplify the "live storage" problem. Educational and community theatres usually cannot afford special devices for scene changes, and so require more space at the stage level for the storage and the handling of scenery than does a commercial theatre.

Labor is unpaid in the amateur theatre. Adequate volunteer labor can be obtained for a special occasion such as a class play or a commencement pageant. But the educational or community theatre which has six to ten productions a year and has two to four dress rehearsals and four to ten performances of each of them, often finds it difficult to obtain enough crew members for a complicated show. While revolving and elevator stages are seldom worth their cost in a non-commercial theatre, other, less expensive, labor-saving devices are worth the expense, even when they necessitate a larger stage house.

The space requirements of a stage are enormous.[6] The space required for the curtains, *masking pieces,*[7] and lights of the proscenium area extends a few feet on each side and a few feet back of the proscenium itself. Many directors and designers keep this space as shallow as possible in order to bring the action forward. Others deepen it in order to mount additional lighting equipment in the area. Behind this space is the acting area, which is the full width of the proscenium and often sixteen to twenty feet deep. Surrounding this is the area for the walls of the setting, for their *bracing,*[8] and for the *backings* seen through openings in

the setting. These backings occupy a strip six to ten feet wide at the sides of the setting, and may extend fifteen feet or more behind the acting area in an exterior setting. A triangular clear space is needed behind this area if *light projections* are to be thrown on a translucent backdrop from the rear. Clear space is needed outside these areas for the passage of actors and the crew. In addition, space is needed for the storage of scenery for the other settings of the play. If flats are stacked in *docks,* they jut out slightly more than six feet. Laid in *packs* against the wall, they still may extend three to five feet from it. The weight and solidity of much modern scenery with its built thicknesses and its three-dimensional wood trim of mouldings, chair rails, and door frames, plus the recent increase in plays which call for changes of locale within acts, require that scenery walls be moved intact, carrying their bulky bracings. Levels, stairs, and complex three-dimensional pieces need to be moved on *wagons.* (See Figure 20.)

All these units require storage space. However, this space need not be the full height of the stage house. Edward C. Cole[9] and others recommend that a wagon room large enough to accommodate a full-stage wagon be built on each side of the proscenium. If these rooms are separated from the stage by large soundproof doors and have supplementary storage and work space, settings on wagons rolled into them can be changed during the actions on the stage. The workshop can conveniently provide one such wagon room. The other wagon room can be used for rehearsals, as a dance or music practice room, as a gymnasium, or for storage. If the structure contains a small laboratory theatre, the stage of this can do double duty as a wagon room.

Lee Simonson[10] recommends the follow-

---

[6] Edward C. Cole, "Technical Problems of a Stage," in "Ann Arbor Conference," pp. 19–25, is an excellent summary of these requirements. The present discussion is based upon this paper.

[7] *Masking:* concealing from the view of the audience any part of the stage not meant to be seen. (A *backing* — used outside a wall opening to suggest a hall, another room, a sky, *et al.* — is a form of masking.)

[8] As with *stage braces* — hardwood braces of ad-

justable length used to support scenery from behind.

[9] *Ibid.*

[10] "Theatre Planning" in *Architecture for the New Theatre,* edited by Edith J. R. Isaacs (Theatre Arts Books, 1935), p. 34.

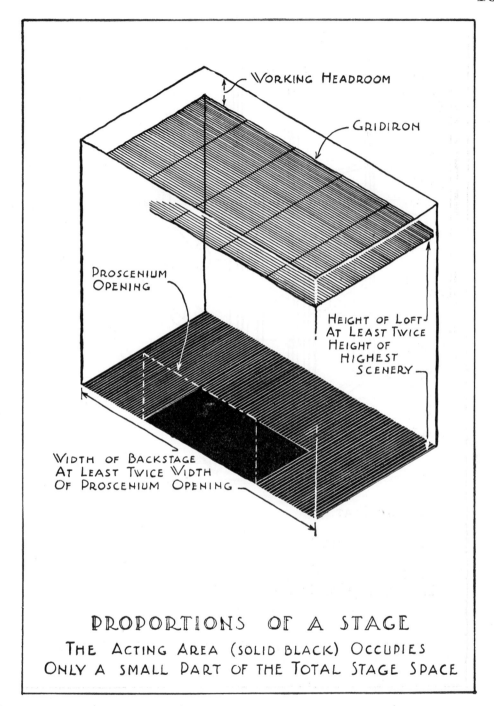

WORKING HEADROOM

GRIDIRON

PROSCENIUM OPENING

HEIGHT OF LOFT
AT LEAST TWICE
HEIGHT OF
HIGHEST
SCENERY

WIDTH OF BACKSTAGE
AT LEAST TWICE WIDTH
OF PROSCENIUM OPENING

PROPORTIONS OF A STAGE
THE ACTING AREA (SOLID BLACK) OCCUPIES
ONLY A SMALL PART OF THE TOTAL STAGE SPACE

Figure 19. The width, depth, and height necessary for the stage of a well-planned proscenium theatre surprise many people — including architects.

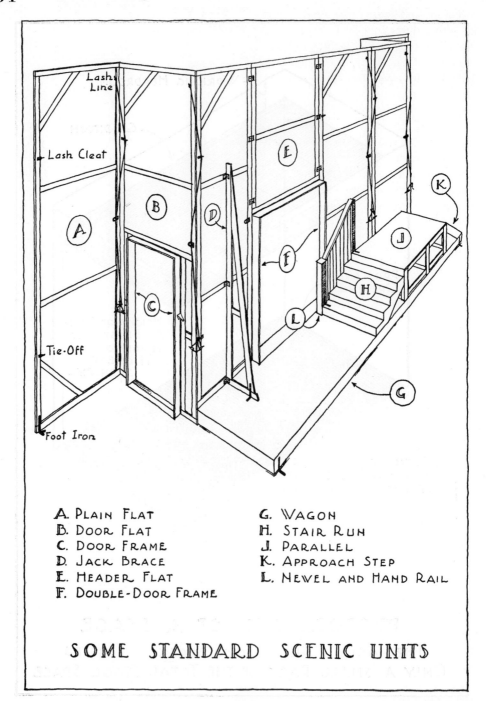

Lash Line

Lash Cleat

Tie-Off

Foot Iron

A. PLAIN FLAT
B. DOOR FLAT
C. DOOR FRAME
D. JACK BRACE
E. HEADER FLAT
F. DOUBLE-DOOR FRAME

G. WAGON
H. STAIR RUN
J. PARALLEL
K. APPROACH STEP
L. NEWEL AND HAND RAIL

SOME STANDARD SCENIC UNITS

Figure 20. This method of construction, which obtains maximum strength and stiffness from very light structure, has been standardized.

ing minimum and maximum dimensions for a stage with a thirty-foot proscenium: width, sixty to ninety feet; depth, forty-five to sixty feet; height of gridiron,[11] seventy-five to ninety feet, with working space above the gridiron. Most theatre workers endorse these recommendations, though some dimensions can be altered if equivalent space is provided in other ways. Cole's plan for full-stage wagons stored in adjacent rooms permits the depth and width of the stage house to be reduced, with a consequent saving in the span of the gridiron and roof beams. If the scene shop is connected to the stage by large doors to provide additional width or depth, the area of the stage floor can be reduced correspondingly.

Backstage there is as much unbroken wall space as possible. Only the absolutely necessary obstructions are allowed to infringe upon the stage area. A misplaced radiator or pipe can render fifteen feet of wall space practically unusable. Half a dozen such errors in arrangement can ruin a stage. Therefore the switchboard, the counter-weight system, and any necessary doors, windows, stairs, ladders, sinks, radiators, winches, pipes, fire extinguishers, and the like, are not scattered about, but are grouped systematically, preferably in corners. When the counterweight system and other protrusions reduce the wall space appreciably, crossbars (*guard rails*) are installed above head height to permit scenery to be stacked against the bars and still allow access to the equipment behind the scenery. No daylight is admitted to the stage house.

The Proscenium Arch and Its Equipment

Thirty-six to forty feet is the ordinary width of the proscenium in commercial houses, thirty to thirty-two in noncommercial

---

[11] The *gridiron* (or *grid*): a framework of beams, usually steel, near the top of the stage house; used to support the rigging needed for flying scenery. Discussed later in the present chapter.

theatres with small auditoriums. Some are twenty-eight, twenty-four, or less, but even twenty-eight begins to cramp scenery and action slightly. On the other hand, some schools have sixty- to eighty-foot prosceniums in their huge assembly halls, and these have to be masked down to a usable size, with side seats left unoccupied. Some directors prefer the wide stage of the commercial theatre. However, the amateur actor finds it difficult to acquire the professional actor's technique of filling this width by extending his movements, and he feels and looks more at ease on a narrower stage. In order to force the action forward where both voice and gesture project more easily, settings also are usually shallower in the noncommercial theatre than on Broadway. Many directors seek to stage all but the most elaborate plays in sets twelve feet or less in depth, and use angled settings when more visual spaciousness seems required, because this keeps at least parts of the setting shallow.

The height of the proscenium is usually determined by its decorative appearance from the auditorium, and often, therefore, is approximately three-fifths of its width. This produces an arch far higher than is desired for settings, and its full height is utilized only on rare occasions. The Cleveland Play House, however, has often employed its extremely high proscenium to display impressive settings thirty and more feet high.

A fireproof curtain rises and falls in smoke-proof steel slots just behind the proscenium arch. It is called the *asbestos*, though now it is often made of steel. In this country the steel is ordinarily painted to look like cloth, but in Germany it often is frankly corrugated metal.

Immediately behind the asbestos is an *act curtain*, which is usually called the *front curtain* even though it is the second one. This either *rises*, or *draws* on a *traveler* — a wood or metal track with a slot along the bottom enclosing little rollers or balls from which hang wire loops. A pair of curtains or *drapes* (from *drapery*) is snapped to these loops, and an endless rope is so *rigged* that it separates and draws together the two halves simultaneously. In musicals there may be a third *production curtain* (or *scene curtain*) behind the *house curtain* (act curtain).

Infrequent use is made of other types of curtains. The *tableau curtain* (or *tab*) is one which is pulled upward and outward toward the upper corners to hang as do cottage window curtains.[12] The Metropolitan Opera House uses one. A *French curtain* is lifted by a bottom batten with the curtain material piling up on it like a Venetian blind. The *contour curtain*, such as the one in the Radio City Music Hall, is a modification of this form; the lines are attached directly to the cloth, and can be operated individually to produce various shaped openings — though they seldom are. A *roll curtain* (or a *roll drop*) is a flat sheet of painted canvas attached at the bottom to a hollow cylinder about the size of a telephone pole. A rope wrapped around the cylinder starting from the back revolves the cylinder backward, and the drop is rolled around the cylinder, starting from the bottom, as the rope is pulled. This device was often used when the front curtain came into general use in the eighteenth century.

A secondary frame, consisting of a *teaser* and a pair of *tormentors*,[13] ordinarily reduces the proscenium in height and in width.

The teaser is a movable valance of drapery in folds (or a stiff panel of wood covered with cloth) which hangs laterally across the stage, and masks the top of the setting and the overhead lights. A *grand drape* looped in festoons may hang in front of the teaser in a very elaborate production. It is ordi-

narily tied off at a permanent height, while the teaser is raised and lowered to conform to the height of the setting. The grand drape is most frequently seen in a theatre playing vaudeville or in a motion picture house with a stage show. It is a direct descendant of the painted false prosceniums and of similar inner frames of decoration used from the seventeenth century onward. The movable teaser is a more recent development, probably necessitated by the variable heights of settings after the box set was introduced. (Some writers define "grand drape" as a synonym for "teaser," or as the overall name of teaser plus tormentor.)

When the proscenium doors of the English theatre were discarded in the eighteenth century, *tormentor doors* were substituted. The tormentors were made of two panels covered with canvas, hinged together so that they could stand by themselves without additional support, one panel set parallel to the teaser, and the other set at a right angle nearly touching the proscenium wall. The latter contained a tormentor door, which permitted the same type of entrance as the former proscenium door. This type of tormentor can still be seen in vaudeville theatres, but is seldom seen now in legitimate theatres. Tormentors of the same shape, but covered with free-hanging drapes, are used in many noncommercial theatres. More frequently seen is a flat tormentor parallel to the proscenium with a *lip* turned slightly upstage to mask a frame of wood or pipe on which spotlights are mounted, a *tormentor tower*. Both of these modern styles can be moved in and out to alter the width of the playing area.

The *right* and *left* designations on the stage are those of an actor standing on the stage facing the auditorium. The right side is traditionally the *prompt side* in America, even when the setting makes it preferable to prompt from the left. The left side is the *O.P. side* (or *opposite prompt*). British tradi-

[12] Complex variants on this are given various names, including *French drape* (not to be confused with *French curtain* mentioned in the text).

[13] While amusing origins can be conjectured for these terms, their derivation is unknown.

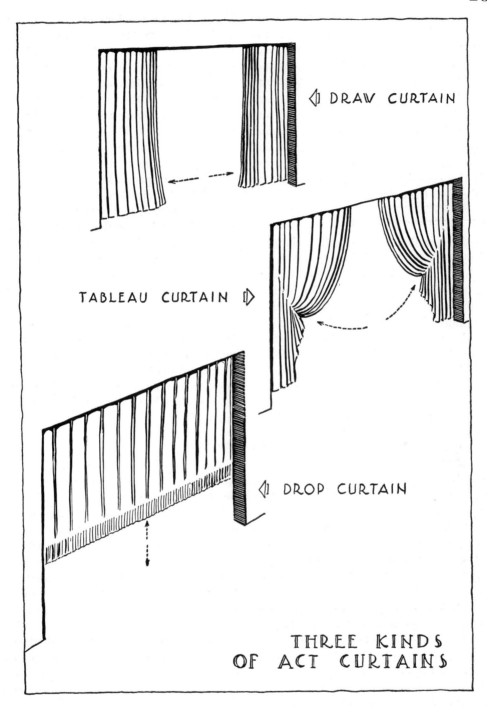

Figure 21. Drop curtains are currently used as front curtains where stage height permits, but other types are used as secondary curtains.

tion reverses this. Repertory theatres, where there is more need for prompting, put the bookholder in a *prompter's box* in the footlights. The prompter at the Metropolitan Opera House wields a baton in time with that of the conductor (watching him through a rear-view mirror), cues the singers, and supplies the words when they are needed. The prompter at the Comédie Française, and at some other European repertory theatres, reads the complete script in an undertone just ahead of the actors.

Plaster Cyclorama or Dome

The back wall of a stage is often plastered so that it reflects light diffusely, and so can be lighted as sky. It may be curved to form a plaster *cyclorama* (or *cyc*). For best effect, the cyc is curved vertically as well as horizontally, because this spherical shape keeps the spectator from identifying its exact distance from him unless he sees an edge. The ultimate form, a *sky dome*, approaches a quarter of a sphere so large that no spectator can see any of its edges. This construction is extensively used in Europe; the Goodman Theatre in Chicago has a complete dome. The sky dome was popularized by Mariano Fortuny in the early part of this century when modern lighting equipment had not been perfected, and was used in combination with his ingenious *Fortuny System* which produced diffused colored light by reflection from bands of varicolored silk. The less complete cyc has to be masked at the sides and top by painted scenery or drapes.

A cyclorama reduces the depth necessary for a stage because it achieves an illusion of depth much superior to scenery hung flat, and therefore it can be placed nearer to the spectator and the actor. It is placed as close to the proscenium as feasible, because the size of the stage background which a spectator can see through the proscenium expands rapidly with distance; each foot be-

tween the proscenium and the cyc enormously increases the necessary size of the cyc to create the same effect. Because it blocks rearstage storage, a cyclorama necessitates a corresponding increase in the storage areas in the *wings* at the sides of the stage. The cyc or dome reduces the flexibility of the stage because of the shallowness it creates, the limitation on the flying of scenery in the area it overhangs, and the elimination of rear storage space. It seriously limits the use of light projections because of the short *throw* permitted, and because the distortion of the image is irregular. It eliminates any possibility of projection from the rear. Many designers therefore prefer a cloth cyc which can be lifted out of the way when more playing depth is needed. Commercial productions sometimes obtain light diffusion almost equal to that of a plaster cyc by using gauzes in front of a cloth sky drop, and by supplementing the gauzes with chemical smoke. In spite of limitations, plaster cycloramas are popular in noncommercial theatres because they produce beautiful sky effects with minimum effort.

The Floor

The floor of the stage needs to be of soft wood so that nails and *stage screws* [14] can be driven into it easily.

Today the stage floor is flat, but until this century it was usually raked away from the audience, so that the terms *downstage* for the part nearest the audience and *upstage* for that farthest from it had a literal meaning in terms of height. This raked floor was a part of the system of built perspective of sixteenth-century Italy, and it persisted even when the box set made it meaningless and a nuisance. Some European opera houses still retain it. In the United States, a raked floor is sometimes laid temporarily upon the

---

[14] A screw or peg (with a handle permitting a firm hand grip), used principally to fasten a stage brace to the floor.

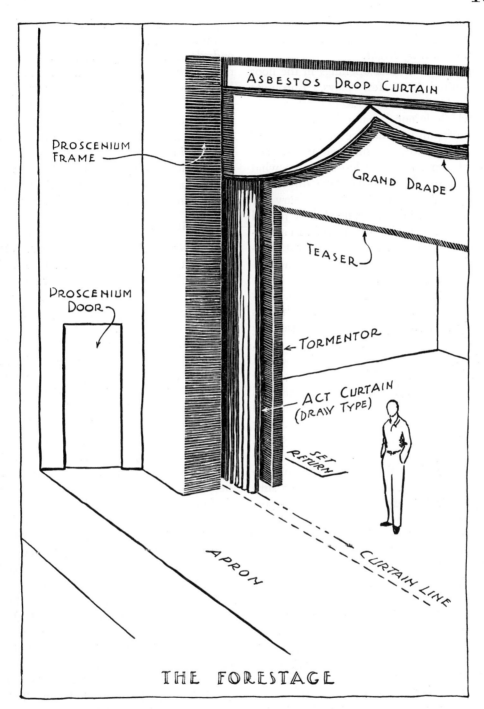

THE FORESTAGE

Figure 22. Most proscenium theatres today have only a token apron in contrast to the deep fore-stage traditional in earlier English theatres.

flat stage floor when sets are built in what is now called *forced perspective*, as in *No Exit* and *Clash by Night.*

Trapdoors and other openings in the floor are required by a few plays. Entrances through *traps* can add scenic interest to plays which do not demand them. But there is no uniformity in the size and location of the traps required for different plays. The designer can alter their location somewhat from that specified in the stage directions, but a prominent location is necessary for some of them, while others need to be placed inconspicuously at the side or back. In anticipation of these varied demands, most commercial and some noncommercial theatres have loose sectional flooring over the entire stage area to permit a trap anywhere. This necessitates a basement, the use of which is seriously restricted by fire laws because only a wooden floor separates it from the stage. The independent sections of flooring squeak even when they are thick, and splinter more than a solid floor. For these reasons, as well as the cost of floorbeams, traps are omitted from many stages and the dialogue of a play is altered to justify substitute business. Modern plays and modern staging call for fewer traps than the melodramas of the nineteenth century, and modern staging substitutes a realistic explanation whenever possible for the supernatural ghosts and apparitions of Elizabethan plays (in contrast to the eighteenth- and nineteenth-century ingenious and spectacular devices for emphasizing the supernatural).

The stage floor often extends in front of the proscenium and forms an *apron.* (See Figure 22.) This is an anachronism copied from the forestage of the Restoration. The apron is useful when the director wishes to break the proscenium line in revivals of plays of earlier periods, but more often, even in these, it is inconvenient. A truly effective forestage for a revival needs to be deeper than the permanent apron, and the curved

edge of most aprons makes it more difficult to build an extension than if the stage floor ends flush with the proscenium. Some commercial theatres are built without an apron, but a noncommercial theatre usually has one, and often has *proscenium steps* from stage to auditorium. These steps are a convenience at rehearsals, and can occasionally be used in the production of an older play. The Pasadena Playhouse and the Cleveland Play House have removable sections of steps which can cover the entire orchestra pit.

Moving Stages

Revolving, sliding, and *elevator* stages have all been used in Europe and occasionally in this country to speed scene changes. But they all require so much space or such expensive machinery that they are rarely installed in America.

Though each was proclaimed as an innovation when it was introduced in the nineteenth or twentieth century, all were used in the Italian theatres in the sixteenth and seventeenth centuries, and at least the revolving platform was used in the *tableaux vivants* in all countries. The Japanese Kabuki theatres have used the revolving stage since the eighteenth century. The *eccyclema* of the Greek stage may have been a revolving platform, and A. M. Nagler, in his *Sources of Theatrical History*,[15] quotes Pliny's description of two huge *revolving theatres* built in the first century B.C. in Rome. In most of these uses, however, the mechanical apparatus was a temporary one, built for a single production, in contrast to the devices now installed as permanent theatre equipment.

A full sliding stage is at least twice as wide as the proscenium opening and rolls on tracks to display one setting while settings are shifted on the concealed half. This requires a stage house at least three times the width of the proscenium. A stage of this

15 P. 21.

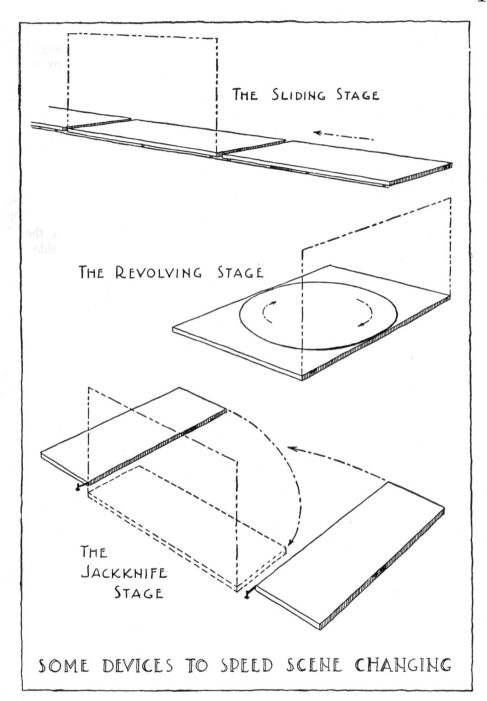

THE SLIDING STAGE

THE REVOLVING STAGE

THE JACKKNIFE STAGE

SOME DEVICES TO SPEED SCENE CHANGING

Figure 23. Mechanical equipment for scene shifting is designed not only for speed, but also to handle heavy and complex scenery.

type is usually operated by motors placed in the basement.

A modification of the sliding stage, as either a permanent or a temporary installation, is a wagon shaped like a sector of a circle or a segment of a ring, which moves in an arc so that the concealed half revolves toward the back of the stage house as it is rolled offstage. It can be contained in a slightly narrower stage house than the regular sliding stage, and is nearly as practical as the sliding stage because most settings are narrower at the back. Exciting use was made of this device by Albert Johnson in the outdoor pageant, *American Jubilee,* at the 1939 New York World's Fair. Four hundred continuous feet of scenery forty feet high was built on a 240° segment of a circle, and while it carried a cast numbering hundreds, it was "revolved" by a pull from a tractor to reveal hundred-foot segments in sequence.

Another adaptation of the sliding or rolling device is a group of independent wagon stages the size of the acting area. They are stored at the sides and back of the stage and are rolled into position one at a time. They either roll free or move on tracks, and are moved either manually or by internal motors. Norman Bel Geddes' plan for a *sinking stage* lowers the stage to the basement on an elevator to have full-stage wagons rolled on and off it.[16]

A variant of the sliding stage is a pair of *jackknife stages,* each of which revolves on a pivot at its downstage corner just behind the proscenium, so that while one is being viewed by the audience, the other rests in the wings with its back wall against the side wall of the stage. In *The Patriot,* Geddes flew a third complete setting to alternate with two such wagons. American stages are likely to have better depth than width, and are therefore more likely to be capable of accommodating the jackknife, which requires

only about sixteen to twenty feet on each side of the proscenium, instead of a width equal to the proscenium as is required for a sliding stage.

Full-stage elevators have been used to carry complete settings, but elevator sections of the stage floor are more frequently seen. These are a simple and quick way to create levels, and are installed in many European stages. Steele MacKaye created a sensation in 1880 when he used a double-deck elevator in the Madison Square Theatre for *Hazel Kirke.* This permitted the setting on one deck to be seen by the audience while the other was being changed either in the basement or in the flies.

To be fully efficient in scene shifting, a revolving stage needs to carry complete settings, including their side walls. If a turntable thirty feet in diameter is placed behind a thirty-foot proscenium, there is a fifteen-foot gap between the side of the proscenium and the edge of the turntable — so it cannot carry any part of the side wall of the usual interior setting. If the diameter of the turntable is increased to sixty feet, there is still a gap of about six feet where the side wall should be. Only when the diameter reaches approximately three times that of the proscenium is it able to carry a series of full interior settings. When storage space is added, this results in an extravagantly large stage. But stages with such turntables exist in London and on the Continent. Max Reinhardt and his designers were especially adept at the use of revolving stages, designing productions in which enormous exterior scenes of tremendous width and depth had interior settings hidden under hills or behind architectural exteriors.[17] *Stanislavsky Produces Othello* [18] gives rough sketches for a similarly complicated use of the Moscow Art Theatre turntable. The theatre at the State University of Iowa has a

---

[16] Norman Bel Geddes, *Horizons* (Little, Brown and Co., 1932), pp. 159–181. See also Isaacs, *op. cit.,* pp. 87–98.

[17] Hiram Kelly Moderwell, *The Theatre of Today* (Dodd, Mead, 1925), pp. 42–43.

[18] Trans. Helen Nowak (Geoffrey Bles, 1948).

permanent turntable. Radio City Music Hall has a turntable which is modest in size compared to the other dimensions of this stage. The Music Hall stage also contains elevators within the turntable to raise and lower sections of the floor.

Small temporary revolving platforms laid on top of the stage floor have been used for a number of musicals and for a few non-musical plays. For *Lady in the Dark* and other musicals, Harry Horner designed a pair of revolving wagons mounted on top of the stage floor. The turntables nearly touched the proscenium at each side, and met at upstage center. Thus half of each of the two interior settings was placed on each turntable (each filling about one-quarter of it) and a small *flipper* on one-half of the setting covered the crack between the two halves. Nearly half of each turntable was devoted to the dream sequences of the play and was left nearly bare to permit a view from the auditorium all the way to the back wall of the stage house. These sections used for the dream sequences also contained smaller turntables within the large ones for rapid sequences of small settings. For *The Great Waltz* at the Center Theatre, Albert Johnson overcame the inadequate size of the main turntable which bore the major part of each setting, by installing supplementary turntables filling the gap between the main one and the proscenium and carrying the side walls of the settings. A small turntable can carry full settings if its curve extends beyond the proscenium and touches it at each side — but then it cannot be turned while the curtain is down. Joseph Urban resolved this with plans for a theatre with a proscenium, front curtain, and small revolving stage all arching out into the auditorium.[19]

The Gridiron and Counterweight System

The *fly loft* (or *flies*) is the space in the stage house above the setting — out of sight

[19] Urban, *op. cit.*, pp. 29–34.

of the audience. Scenery is *flied* (or *flown*) there by *lines* of Manila rope or steel cable. Near the top of the flies is the *gridiron* (or *grid*) from which the lines hang. This consists of heavy beams, once thick wooden beams, but now usually steel I-beams, running from front to back, with *spreaders* between them. The beams are the direct support of the hanging scenery. The lines pass over pulleys (or *loft blocks*) on a beam or a pair of beams, then cross the gridiron toward a side wall, pass through a *head block* containing a separate *sheave* (usually pronounced "shiv") for each line, and then descend toward the stage floor.

The lines supporting the flown scenery can be operated manually either from the stage floor or from *fly galleries*. These are balconies extending from the side wall of the stage house, placed high enough so that scenery can be *stacked* beneath them in *packs* against the wall, or in *docks*. As many sets of lines as possible are installed, partly for the sake of quantity, but mainly so as to have a set of lines available at any stage depth that is needed.

The lines are *tied off* on a *pinrail*, a heavy wooden beam or metal pipe securely fastened to the fly gallery for protection against upward stress. The pinrail is pierced by holes into each of which fits a *belaying pin* which has an enlargement near one of its ends so that when it is dropped into the pinrail, part of it extends above and part below the pinrail. The ropes are looped so that they are secured by friction, much as one fastens an awning rope. When the scenery is to be *let in* or *taken out*, the pin can be removed so that all the wrappings of rope drop loose at once (though it is usually unwound instead). Placing the pinrail on a fly gallery removes the piles of loose rope from the stage floor, but this location limits the *flymen* to that duty alone, because it is seldom possible for them to climb and descend ladders or stairs to the fly gallery fast enough to be useful in other scene-shifting tasks.

In order to reduce the physical labor of flying, particularly of heavy scenery which would require the combined efforts of more flymen than can reach the lines at the same time, *counterweights* are tied into the lines. These are ordinarily canvas bags filled with sand. Many actors and stagehands have been injured by sandbags carelessly tied to, instead of into, the lines.

A *counterweight system* is substituted for manual flying in most modern theatres. An iron *pipe batten* is permanently attached to each set of lines. This is a length of pipe large enough to be inflexible, extending the approximate width of the proscenium — often with extension pipes which slide from inside the batten to lengthen it. Scenery is tied to these battens. (The term *batten* occurs in many connections, because it is the general term used for any horizontal board or pipe on the stage.) Lines of woven wire cable, after passing over the loft block and the head block, are attached to a counterweight *carriage* (or *cradle*, or *arbor*). The carriage is moved up and down by an independent continuous rope attached to its top and bottom and running through its own pair of sheaves at gridiron and floor level. Blocks of iron are inserted into the carriage to form a total weight approximately that of the scenery. Since the weights are equal, it follows that to move the scenery and the carriage up and down in compensating movement, physical effort is needed only to overcome inertia and friction.

The asbestos and the act curtain are counterweighted with carriages similar to those of the counterweight system, but independent of it. They are sometimes electrically operated, whereas the regular counterweight system is usually manually operated.

A spaced flooring of wood or steel slats placed on top of the gridiron beams and spreaders provides a safe floor on which

crewmen can walk, but the space between slats allows a *snatch line* to be installed at any point for the suspension of a special bit of scenery or property. Examples are the knife stuck in the ceiling in *The Thirteenth Chair* which falls on cue and imbeds itself in a table; and the plates, vases, and other objects which are tossed about the room in the final moment of *Blithe Spirit*, supposedly being thrown by the invisible ghostly wives as they vent their irritation on their mutual husband.

This flying system is outmoded — it is clumsy and inflexible. George C. Izenour is working at Yale University to develop a system using self-synchronous motor-driven loft blocks.[20] This would eliminate the need for lines at the side of the stage house, would make it possible to fly a drop hung diagonally, and would have other advantages. Another proposal is a horizontal gridiron which flies scenery to the side rather than upward into the fly loft. Plans for such a theatre have been published by Arch Lauterer.[21] For the Festival Theatre in Newport, Jean Rosenthal [22] has planned to achieve this by using industrial type monorail and lift devices.

The present flying system needs to hoist drops and the cyclorama out of sight of spectators in the front row. Recommendations for the height of the gridiron are often based on the height of the proscenium, but this is meaningless because that dimension is usually determined by the decorative scheme of the auditorium rather than by a consideration of the height of scenery. A backdrop or sky drop often needs to be thirty or more feet high to accommodate to the line of vision of people seated in the front row looking upward. If two such drops are used in

[20] "Ann Arbor Conference," p. 38.
[21] *Theatre Arts*, XXX (September, 1946), 538–544.
[22] "Notes on New Developments in Technical Equipment," in "Ann Arbor Conference," p. 41. She credits Lauterer with this innovation, though Frederick Kiesler had proposed at least the principle in *Theatre Arts*, XVII (June, 1931), 451.

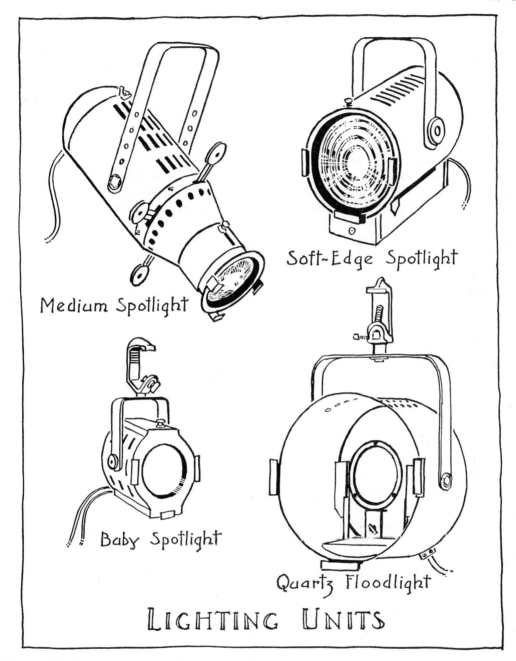

Medium Spotlight

Soft-Edge Spotlight

Baby Spotlight

Quartz Floodlight

LIGHTING UNITS

Figure 24. Three types and sizes of spotlights and one floodlight. (See page 197.) The example at upper left is an ellipsoidal spot, so named because of the nature and shape of its reflector. The Fresnel spot (at upper right) uses a relatively flat "cut" lens in contrast to the standard plano-convex lens.

a production, one needs to *clear* the other. A cloth cyclorama may be fifty or more feet high. It is ideal if this can be lifted to clear a backdrop behind it, but this convenience can be sacrificed. It should be possible, however, to lift the cloth cyc as much as eighteen feet so that sixteen-foot scenery mounted on a wagon can pass under it. Therefore, a realistic guide to the gridiron height is that it needs to be greater than twice that of the tallest backdrop that will be used, and greater than the cloth cyc plus eighteen feet.

Aesthetic objections to a tall, windowless stage house projecting above the rest of the theatre building now can be met under the revised Building Code of the City of New York [23] by building the theatre partly underground, and by adding floors of rooms above the auditorium to raise this height closer to that of the stage house.

Shops, Storage Space, and Greenroom

An educational or community theatre needs extensive shop and storage space. An overall economy is sometimes effected by placing a building-and-painting shop immediately behind a shallow stage and opening into it through a large arch filled by a soundproof lifting or rolling door which can be opened to deepen the stage. The use of a shop at the side as a storage space for wagons has been mentioned. Other double use of shop facilities is possible. Some producing groups build and paint scenery on the stage. This particular double use of space saves building costs, but it results in many inconveniences to both the technical staff and the rehearsal group.

Shops are needed for carpentry, painting, electrical work, property construction, and costume construction.

Storage is needed for drops, flats, other scenery, props, lighting equipment, and costumes, and for supplies of lumber, canvas, paint, glue, costume materials, and so on. The

[23] Revision of June 13, 1953.

shop and storage space can be combined in numerous ways; but there is seldom enough of either.

A scene shop needs to be large enough to permit the trial erection of a setting, with enough additional work space so that other construction and painting can continue. More floor space is needed in a school than in a commercial scenic studio because the amateur workers are less efficient and skillful in the use of the space than are experienced professionals, and because the shop needs to accommodate a large number of workers at certain peak periods. A commercial theatre has little use for shop space, because fire laws usually prohibit building scenery on the premises.

The shop needs as much continuous unbroken wall space as possible. All the necessary openings and protrusions are best grouped as compactly as possible in corners and in the narrower walls. Since painting is best done under artificial light similar to that of the stage, windows are a hindrance in a shop used for painting; but good ventilation is needed.

Greenroom is the name which has come down from the late Restoration period for the room where the cast and crew can relax near the stage as they await their cues. This is a useful room in which to assemble the cast at dress rehearsals for critiques away from the stage and auditorium, so that the technical staff can continue its work. It provides a place for actors to meet their friends after the performance without congesting the stage and the dressing rooms. If the room is of adequate size and shape, it can be used as a rehearsal hall when there is no performance or stage rehearsal in progress.

The behavior of actors varies in the pre-performance hour and in their offstage time during the play. Some like to joke, to tease, to sing, and to make noise generally. Others prefer to think about their roles, to review their latest criticisms, and even to review their lines. These latter actors are annoyed if their thoughts are constantly interrupted by the horseplay of the former, and the boisterous element feel that the quiet ones are "going Stanislavski." Careful assignment of dressing room companions is a help in this respect. When there is a commodious greenroom, the talkative members of the cast tend to gather there and to leave the worriers in comparative privacy. A plan for the building so that workrooms can serve as chorus dressing rooms allows the number of dressing rooms to be kept economical, and still provides dressing facilities for occasional large-cast shows.

Lighting Equipment

Spectators in the auditorium are seldom aware of the complexity of good stage lighting, and the extent to which it contributes to the effect of a play, especially by those almost imperceptible changes of lighting which shift audience attention from area to area and change the atmosphere of the design. More and more exact and detailed use is being made of lighting in both the commercial and noncommercial theatres. Izenour [24] points out that completely to control light in the theatre, one needs to be able to change at will the size, shape, direction, color, and intensity of each beam of light. Of these, intensity is as yet the only one which can be modified easily during a performance. There are European devices for changing color slides electrically, but their cost has discouraged their adoption in the United States. Control of lighting, therefore, is by no means complete, but it is infinitely superior to that of previous centuries, as noted in the preceding chapter.

Even though it remains inflexible during a performance, provision is made for at least a flexible *setup* of lighting equipment, both on the stage and in the beams and balconies

[24] "Ann Arbor Conference," p. 37.

of the auditorium. A good system for the control of intensity is needed.

Stage lighting equipment is still in an early phase of development. The volume of sale of stage lighting equipment has not encouraged extensive research by commercial firms aimed directly at theatre needs, especially when school architects continue to specify obsolete lighting equipment. Fortunately, the increase in advertising display lighting, illumination of public monuments, and illumination of night sports events in recent decades has encouraged research in lighting equipment which can also be applied to equipment for the stage, and for this reason improvements are being made.

Strip, flood, and *spot* are the three basic types of stage lighting equipment. A striplight is a row of relatively low-wattage lamps. Various kinds of strips are still used: footlights along the front of the apron, sunk nearly level with it; a series of *borderlights* hanging overhead at various stage depths, ordinarily just behind each drape border; and *horizon strips,* either permanent and sunk in a *cyc trough* where they can be covered by sections of flooring when not in use, or movable and often on casters. The horizon strips are used to light the lower part of the cyc or sky drop in order to supplement the basic lighting from the last borderlight, in order to provide variation of color to simulate a sunset or sunrise, or in order to lighten the sky realistically at the bottom. Such strips sometimes are used to light *ground rows* representing distant landscapes. Foots and borders are usually wired in three or four *circuits* by color.

A floodlight is a lamp enclosed in a metal box — square, triangular, or half-round, with one side open — backed by a reflector which may be a metallic mirror or just white paint. A floodlight is similar to a striplight in that the rays of light fall directly on the stage without being refracted, but the box enclosure restricts the shape of the beam somewhat. Ellipsoidal mirror reflectors for floods were perfected for outdoor lighting; these make the floods (often called *beam projectors*) highly *efficient* and make their beams almost as small and sharp as beams produced by a lens. Efficiency in stage lighting is determined by the percentage of the rays of light produced by a lamp filament which reach the stage, as distinguished from those rays which strike nonreflecting surfaces or which are absorbed in the process of reflection and refraction.

In a spotlight the lamp is enclosed in a *housing* which permits the rays to shine through a lens or lenses in only one aperture, the size and shape of which may be changed by shutters. The lens controls the direction of the rays, and ordinarily *refracts* (or *bends*) them into a more compactly focused beam. A "cut" or Fresnel lens throws a soft-edged beam. A plano-convex lens throws a hard-edged beam and is generally used in spotlights. A spherical mirror placed behind the lamp adds to the efficiency of the spot by reflecting some of the rays which strike the back of the housing. The rays which strike the unmirrored sides of the housing are still lost, and make the spotlight relatively low in efficiency. The ellipsoidal spotlight, known by such trade names as *Klieglite* and *Lekolite,* is more efficient than the ordinary spotlight because the ellipsoidal reflector is so designed that it reflects and uses practically all rays.

Spot-flood lamps are another product of industrial need for which stage use has been found. They are lamps with a reflecting surface on the inside of the bulb (behind the filament) and with a thickened front surface which partially focuses the rays.

The stage today is lighted chiefly by spots. On the proscenium stage, a row of them is hung on a *pipe* or *bridge* just behind the teaser. A bridge is a horizontal frame of pipes with a flooring which allows an electrician to stand on it to adjust spots during the setup, and also to operate a pivoting *follow-spot* from overhead during the performance. Additional spots are hung further upstage on battens, along the front of the balcony, and in false beams in the auditorium ceiling (*beam lighting*). Others may be mounted on *tormentor towers* of wood or pipe.

Ideally, light should strike the actor's face at a 30° to 45° overhead angle. Therefore *front lighting* from balcony and beams is likely to be used for the three or five independently lighted *areas* across the front of a proscenium stage, and teaser and tormentor spots are likely to be used for the upstage areas.

This spotlighting of each part of the playing area and of important units of scenery is *pulled together* by striplighting from foots, the first (or *X-ray*) border, and occasionally other borders, in order to prevent sharp changes of color or intensity as the actors pass from one area to another. Striplighting is also used to light the scenery and to counteract shadows which are too dark. These striplights are supplemented by flood-lighting from the wings to represent sunlight, moonlight, firelight, and light through a doorway, and for lighting the backings. Beam projectors are especially designed to give a sharply focused beam to simulate sunlight. The sky is lighted by the last border-light, supplemented by horizon strips or trough lights. Open-stage lighting practice is conditioned, of course, by special factors. These are discussed on pages 252–253.

Almost all light used on the conventional stage is tinted by glass, gelatine, or plastic color media. For best visibility, the actors need to be lighted evenly from all front angles; but such even lighting produces a flat effect. To restore plasticity, each acting area is lighted by two spotlights, one from each side. (See Figure 43, page 309.) Another point in this connection: contrasting hues are used in these spots in order to let color contrast suggest light and shade without requiring much actual difference in intensity. This *cross-lighting* is usually done with one warm and one cool color. Colored light is also used for realistic color effects such as sunlight, moonlight, fire, and so on.

The *house lights* of the auditorium and all stage lights are regulated from a single controlboard (or switchboard). This board contains a switch and a fuse for each circuit to which a lighting instrument may be connected.

A *dimmer* is used to decrease or increase the intensity *(voltage)* supplied to the lamp in an instrument. Bulky *resistance dimmers* (or *rheostats*) used to be standard, but *autotransformer, thyraton-reactor,* and *electronic* dimmers have been developed which are smaller, more efficient, and can *take* variable *loads* of wattage, as the resistance dimmer cannot. A dimmer is sometimes wired permanently into the circuit for each instrument. This is wasteful, because a production seldom needs more than half the instruments dimmed at the same time — e.g., second border circuits are seldom used, often only one footlight circuit is used in a production, not all the available spots and floods are used in any one lighting design, and some of the equipment is kept *full up* throughout its use and so needs no dimmer. It is cheaper to install a flexible board which permits a dimmer to be connected to any circuit which needs it and to install about half as many dimmers as circuits.

Since a resistance dimmer operates efficiently only when its load is within ten per cent of the wattage for which it is designed, and since the total wattage used on the stage is highly variable, a resistance-type electrical *master dimmer* is impossible. *Mechanical mastering* is the only device for dimming a number of circuits at the same time; ingenious gears interlock dimmers under the control of a master handle, or of a *wheel*

which can dim some lights and *heat* others at the same time. This has the disadvantage of dimming the brightest lights first and *picking up* the others as their *readings* are reached, so that the lighting of the scene may change considerably as it is dimmed. The newer types of dimmers with flexible loads permit electrical mastering which dims all lights proportionately by means of a bank of large dimmers jointly controlling the maximum load of the control board. In a board designed for flexibility, the individual dimmers of this bank of masters can be used at other times for control of the house lights, and for individual instruments.

Pre-set switches and dimmers permit the switchboard operator to set up several lighting designs and to energize them in turn by operating the appropriate *pre-set master switch.* By the double-checking which this also permits, a good many of the human errors made by inexperienced switchboard operators can be eliminated.

In order to save space and to reduce the fire hazard in the stage area, many of the larger switches and dimmers are placed in another part of the building and are operated by *remote control.* A small switch or dimmer on the board energizes a large magnetic switch, or a gear on a large dimmer. When all switches and dimmers are operated by remote control, a large number of circuits with their pre-sets can be grouped in a console no larger than a church organ console. This can be placed backstage, located like the traditional switchboard against the proscenium wall at the prompt side; on an overhead balcony backstage; in the orchestra pit; under a secondary prompter's box as at the Metropolitan Opera House; in a booth in the back of the auditorium; or in any other part of the auditorium. It even can be shifted between several of these locations.

Commercial theatres usually have minimum boards, and the production must carry its own *portable* dimmer banks, which add to backstage congestion.

Scenery

The types of scenic units are relatively few, though there are very many ways to use this scenery, and ways to combine different types. When the different painting techniques and colors and textures are also considered, the possibilities for variation become almost infinite. In spite of these possibilities, the influences of tradition and of fashion encourage uniformity, so that a truly novel setting is rare.

Types of Units. School theatres usually install a set of drapes which completely enclose the stage for concerts, assemblies, and lectures. The drapes hang from battens or travelers. They may be organized as a *drape cyclorama,* surrounding the stage on three sides like a box set; or as a *pair of drapes* and a series of *leg drapes,* all parallel to the curtain line. Both schemes use *drape borders* to mask the flies.

The drapes are often of natural-colored monk's cloth, but drapes of black or other dark velour are more adaptable. Such drapes are often used as a basic setting for plays, with various kinds of partial settings placed in front of them. When this scenery is kept away from the drapes and they are not touched by the actors in making entrances and exits, they become a mere neutral background, and the scenic effect, created by the inset scenery, is relatively uninfluenced by the color of the drapes. The lighter the color of the drapes, the more likely they are to assert themselves as a part of the setting.

Formalized exterior settings are sometimes made by festooning cloth in irregular folds as foliage, and by dropping folds or cylinders of cloth from behind these festoons to simulate tree trunks.

Flats are the light frames of wood covered with canvas, duck, or heavy muslin, used for most interior and exterior walls. (See Figures 20 and 25.) Usually constructed of $1'' \times 3''$ white pine, they are given maximum stiffness but the lightest possible construction. The carefully engineered method of construction is universal except for minute variations.[25] The flats may be *lashed* together, or they may be hinged. A *book* (or a *two-fold*) is a hinged pair of flats.

When settings with three flat walls were first introduced and named box sets, the spectators were able to see that the scenery and doors were only an inch thick. The current practice is for *thickness* to be added to those edges which the spectators see. A *casing* (or *frame,* or *box*) is added to the *door shutter,* and windows similarly are built solidly and with their normal depth. Thicknesses of wood or wallboard are hinged or nailed to other visible edges. Cornices, mouldings, chair rails, baseboards, and other three-dimensional *wood trim* are attached temporarily. *Backings* are set up behind openings to prevent a view of the backstage and to give a realistic illusion of adjacent rooms or an exterior.

Many settings use as a ceiling an enormous flat large enough to cover all but the front few feet of a setting. This space is left uncovered so that teaser spots can throw their beams into the setting. Organizations which always play in one theatre often build this ceiling in permanent form, and sometimes cover its reverse side for use as a sky drop. Other types of ceiling cover the setting as completely, but fold in such a way that they can pass through a loading door.

Platforms, steps, and ramps are sometimes constructed solidly, but with the economical methods employed in stage carpentry instead of those of the house carpenter, who builds for constant use over many years and so uses six times as much lumber as the stage

[25] The oldest movable scenery in existence — that built about 1770 for the Drottningholm Theatre in Sweden — has essentially the same construction.

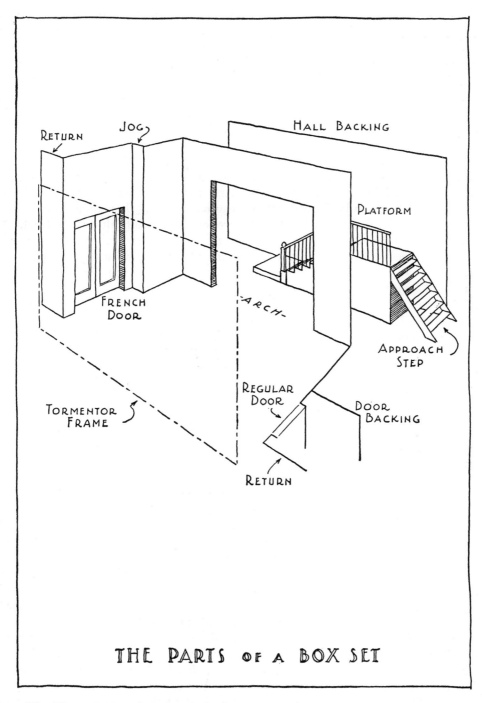

THE PARTS OF A BOX SET

Figure 25. The majority of settings in both commercial and noncommercial theatres are now box sets, first introduced about 1840.

carpenter for the same structure. (See Figure 20.) An active producing group which reuses scenery constantly builds *parallels* for platforms and independent *platform tops* for flooring. This equipment can be folded for storage. A parallel consists of four or more light frames which are hinged as a parallelogram so that they fold to a thickness of three or four inches and a length equal to a side plus an end. Ramps and complex structures like rocks and uneven ground are, whenever possible, organized into planes of standard size in order that they can be formed out of sloping parallels of standard size with irregularities superimposed.

Three-dimensional objects such as trees, bushes, rocks, and some interior objects are constructed of light wooden frames covered by *chicken wire* (hardware stores call it "poultry netting") and cloth. Smaller objects are molded either directly or by means of plaster of Paris negative casts, out of *paper mash (papier mâché)* or *laminated paper.*

Wagons to shift heavy and complex scenic units are solidly built platforms one step high, mounted on large rubber-tired, ball-bearing casters. The wagons can be of any size up to one which can carry a complete setting, though the factor of inertia makes it difficult to start the movement of large ones. Though wagons may be built for a specific production, they are planned as part of the permanent equipment. The temporary revolving stages placed on top of the regular stage floor are made up of a number of small wagons bolted together. They can be operated by internal motors, manually, or by a continuous rope operated by a windlass.

Casters can be mounted on any heavy scenic unit, and can accomplish the same purpose as a wagon. A castered framework called a *jack* is sometimes attached to a scenic unit such as a wall to hold it firmly upright. A *tip jack,* on the other hand, is attached in such a way that when the wall is in position in the setting it rests on its own base but can be lifted or tipped onto the jack and rolled away on casters attached to the jack.

Wing-and-drop scenery is sometimes used instead of three-dimensional scenery and box sets. In previous centuries it was painted realistically in the hope that it would be accepted as three-dimensional. Today it often is painted decoratively and its two-dimensional construction tacitly admitted. Exteriors are often done in this technique because convincing three-dimensional exteriors are extremely difficult to construct. Nonrealistic interiors in pre-modern plays, operas, ballets, and musical comedies sometimes employ the wing-and-drop technique.

A *backdrop* (or simply *drop*) is a large, flat expanse of cloth suspended from a wooden batten, with another batten at the bottom to hold it taut. A drop is often considerably larger than the proscenium opening in order to compensate for the angular sight lines of the spectators in the front rows. If it is painted a uniform color of white, gray, or blue to represent sky, it is a *sky drop.* If this sky drop is curved in an arc or a U-shape, it becomes a *sky cyc* (or *cloth cyc*).

Wings are books (two-folds) which have a serrated inner edge representing foliage (*wood wing*) or architectural construction (as *kitchen wing, palace wing,* etc.). A *leg drop* serves the same purpose as a wing, but hangs from a batten instead of standing on the floor.

Painted *cloth borders* of sky or foliage usually complete the wings as full-stage arches. A *ground row* is a flat with an irregular top, standing on its side on the floor to represent a distant landscape. One or more ground rows are often used in an otherwise three-dimensional exterior setting backed by a cyc in order to conceal the meeting of cyc and floor. The adjective *cutout* is often applied to a drop, a border, or a wing to indicate that it contains holes or has a serrated edge.

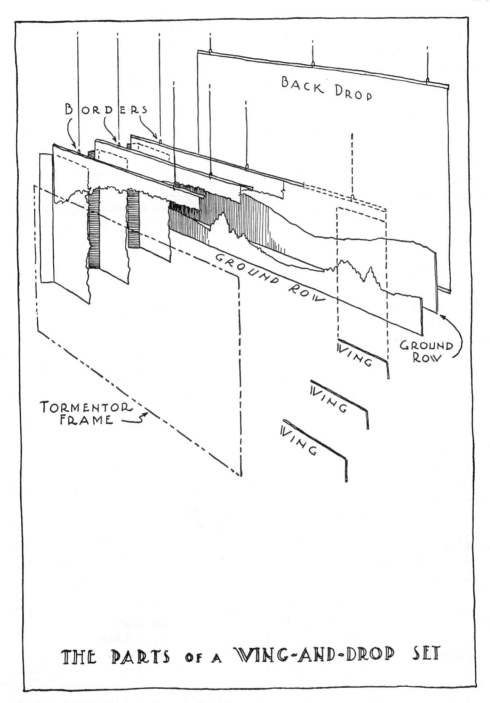

Figure 26. Wing-and-drop was the standard scenic technique of the last two centuries, and is still often used for exterior settings.

The knitted fabric *bobbinet*, and *theatrical gauze* (or *scrim*) of woven wood-pulp, are nearly transparent materials used for drops or for smaller areas when visions or ghosts are to materialize. Lighted from the front, the material reflects enough light to conceal what is behind it. But when lights are heated behind it, it becomes transparent. Scrim remains transparent even when painted with thin scene paint. These materials are also used to give haziness to painted exterior settings and skies.

To reduce the sound of footsteps, the stage floor is usually covered by a *ground cloth* of heavy canvas or duck of a neutral color. Professional productions often paint the groundcloth as a rug, a flagstone terrace, or a parquet floor as part of the design. Some substitute a neutral carpet, rug, or sheet of linoleum. In the eighteenth century it became traditional to lay a green carpet for tragedy.

Scene Painting. Scenery is painted with *dry colors*, which are the same pigment materials that are used with different solvents for easel painting, sign painting, and house painting. The pigments are minerals, earths, chemical precipitates, dyed chalk, and so on. Scene paint uses *size* (water and glue) as a solvent, and is therefore soluble in warm water and can be scrubbed off when the scenery becomes too thickly coated from repeated painting; but it does not run when merely dampened — as by rain.

Texture — the suggestion of a slightly variable surface which gives the illusion of solidity — is obtained by various methods of applying broken color (or *pointillage*). *Chiaroscuro* is the same technique used in illusional painting; light and dark colors are used to give a three-dimensional illusion. Such attempts at realism used to be almost the sole purpose of scene painting, and great technical skill was developed by the scene painters. Today chiaroscuro is more likely to be frankly decorative, except in *lining*. Lining produces a semblance of three-dimensional architectural construction by means of highlights and lowlights. The evenness of the usual stage lighting, with the elimination of cast shadows, often requires that even three-dimensional construction be lined in order to preserve its plastic nature.

Standardization of Scenery. For efficiency in the repeated use of the same scenic units, standard dimensions for the units are established by each theatre group. Not only does this permit rearrangement of existing units, but it allows a designer to plan his setting without measuring the scenery on hand. Flats are 12′, 14′, 16′, and less frequently 10′ or 18′ high. When the top of a flat is raked, unless special requirements necessitate its construction as a pure irregular, each side is one of the standard heights so that it can be used as a transitional piece between the standard-height flats.

Widths are likewise standardized as 6′, 4′, 2′, and 1′, or 6′, 4½′, 3′, and 1½′ sizes. Scenery for the professional stage is built to go easily through a 6′ door, in anticipation of its possible shipment in a railroad baggage car with a 6′ door, so its greatest width is 5′ 9″. There is no need to introduce this irregularity into scenery which never will be so transported.

Door casings, doors, windows, and arch constructions are similarly standardized to permit maximum interchange. Stage hardware is attached to flats at standard heights.

Platforms are standardized, though the systems of standardization vary widely. Uniformity in the size of parallels allows tops to be interchanged between them and so requires fewer tops to be built and stored. Ramps are designed to fit the same tops. Wagons, too, are standardized in dimensions related to those of the parallels which they frequently will carry.

Where there is a shortage of labor or

PLATE 15. **Constructivism.** This style was born of a desire to present "truth" in the theatre by hiding nothing from the audience through "theatrical trickery." Scenery is functional rather than depictive. This picture shows the final moment in Aristophanes' *The Birds:* When the King and the Queen of the Birds join the chorus on the steps, the stairs descend through the floor. (*University of Michigan: director, William P. Halstead; designer, Jack E. Bender; costumes, Phyllis Pletcher; choreography, Esther E. Pease.*)

PLATE 16. **Selective Realism.** (Above) A relatively simple interior for *The Heiress*. This unusual grouping of characters for the first meeting of Catherine and her future fiancé draws attention to every glance that passes between them, since they are silhouetted against Dr. Sloper, who dominates the scene. (*Broadway production: director, Jed Harris; designer, Raymond Sovey; costumes, Mary Percy Schenk.*) (Middle) A box set for *High Ground*, selectively simplified in arrangement and décor. (*Shreveport Little Theatre: director, John Wray Young; designer, Margaret Mary Young.*) (Below) In *Dark of the Moon*, the extreme selectivity in detail approaches the frugality of Impressionism. (*Wellesley College: director, Eldon Winkler; designer, Peter Larkin.*)

PLATE 17. **Revivals of Theatrical and Formal Staging.** (Above) Theatrical Staging used for *The Beaux' Stratagem,* including tormentor doors, footlight shields, chandeliers, wings in perspective, and shutters at the back. *(Northwestern University: director, Ramon Kessler; settings, Lee Mitchell; costumes, Berneice Prisk.) (Be-low) The Trojan Women performed outdoors in front of a neoclassical façade. (University of Michigan: director, Claribel Baird; costumes, Helen Forrest Lauterer; movement, Juana de Laban.)*

PLATE 18. **Modern Versions of Simultaneous Staging.** (Above) The Passion Play at Oberammergau, 1910. The technique used here is less obvious in more recent performances because the architectural style has been simplified and unified. (Below) Jo Mielziner's setting for *Death of a Salesman* is an extreme example of the recent revival of multi-roomed settings. In addition to rooms shown in actualistic relationship to one another, architecturally unrelated locales were placed at the front and at the sides. (*Broadway production: director, Elia Kazan; costumes, Julia Sze.*)

money, standardization can be carried one step further by painting a flexible permanent set of flats with a neutral-colored textured surface which can be varied slightly by colored light. This can be used repeatedly without repainting. With imaginative design, it can produce quite varied settings, especially when combined with panels of drapery.

REVOLTS FROM THE PATTERN

The proscenium-arch theatre here described, as developed in the eighteenth, nineteenth, and early twentieth centuries, is still by far the commonest method of organizing theatre space in the western world. Nonetheless, it is no longer the *only* method, as we shall see in Chapter 15.

Indeed, a number of challenges to the proscenium stage — and to Actualism itself, with which the proscenium is so closely and so naturally associated — have been offered in the present century. As early as 1913, for example, Adolphe Appia mounted *The Tidings Brought to Mary* in a hall at Hellerau without benefit of proscenium arch. A few years later, Jacques Copeau — whose Théâtre du Vieux Colombier has been called the first presentational playhouse of the modern world — placed his actors in a semi-permanent setting, on a stage without a proscenium arch, in a small theatre with stage-lighting units hanging frankly from the ceiling of the auditorium. Noticeable features of the stage arrangement were the absence of footlights and the presence of steps leading from the stage to the forestage and from there to the audience level. The only curtain, which failed to mask the forestage, fell at the point where the walls of the auditorium became the walls of the stage. Among the permanent units in the setting were a balcony, a back wall with a center arch, and side walls allowing the actors to get offstage unseen. The principal changes in setting

were accomplished by changing the width of the pseudo-arch or the line at the top of the balcony, by adding doors, steps at one side, or railings, and particularly by using significant properties or screens. (See Plate 14.)

The Copeau experiments are perhaps of special interest to Americans because Copeau and Louis Jouvet brought their company (and in a sense their theatre structure) to New York at the end of World War I. It should be noted, however, that Copeau's project was not an isolated phenomenon; he was but one of a number of artists seeking to challenge what they considered the tyranny of the proscenium arch. Max Reinhardt, for example, built a long tongue-like forestage in the Grosses Schauspielhaus, staged many of his scenes there in the midst of the audience, and suggested to the spectators that they were participating in the action. In *Julius Caesar* and *Danton,* he seated actors among the spectators. In the well-known *Miracle* in New York (to be discussed in the following chapter), he transformed the auditorium of a theatre into the nave of a cathedral, played the early scenes as though they were taking place in a cathedral, and had processions of worshipers enter through the theatre aisles.

Inspired by these experiments as well as by other influences, Frederick Kiesler, Hermann Rosse, Norman Bel Geddes, and Frank Lloyd Wright have designed a variety of experimental theatre forms. Some of them merely provide ingenious methods of scene changing and are thus adaptable to any scenic style, but most of them abandon the proscenium arch and install stage and auditorium under a common roof.

It is possible to think of Copeau's stage (and others of a similar nature) as "architectural." Meyerhold's *constructivist* stage in Russia, again just after World War I, shared the anti-illusionistic philosophy of the architectural stage but carried it a step further in insisting that it be anti-decorative as well.

Constructivism abjures all scenic illusion. It assembles stairs, platforms, ramps, slides, firemen's poles, and the like, as needed for violent stage action in three dimensions. Machines, lighting equipment, and the stage walls are frankly revealed. Its aim is to eliminate all the "false" and artificial elements of a proscenium production so that what takes place will have the impact of truth. In its pure, anti-decorative form, constructivism had a temporary popularity in Europe but little acceptance in America. (See Plate 15.) It is still seen occasionally in a pure form, but more often it is modified, in the sense that its non-representational structure is somewhat decorative, unified, and balanced.

In Russia after the revolution, and throughout most of Europe, experiment flourished, and a host of other "isms" grew up. *Impressionism* (based on self-conscious frugality in suggestion) was a passing example. *Expressionism,* a dramaturgical as well as scenic pattern of considerable influence both here and abroad, attempted to objectify inner and subjective experience. The entire drama and its décor were conceived of and seen through the imagination — usually distorted — of one or more of the characters. There were other intentionally eccentric styles and patterns, copied almost directly from contemporary trends in graphic art. (See Plate 14.)

The Brechtian "Epic Theatre" is a special production method, usually of necessity practiced in a proscenium theatre and characterized by little or no attempt to create illusion. The purpose of the production is "edification" or "clarification," and all possible devices are used to convince and persuade the audience of the social context and intellectual import of the play. The playwright deliberately avoids continuity of action by using many short scenes, sometimes without continuity of cast. Sometimes he interrupts longer scenes by narration, by direct address of actors to audience, or by a motion picture sequence illustrating a parallel action. These breaks in illusion are intended to contribute to the "alienation effect" desired by Brecht in opposition to an empathic effect.

Various types of nonrealistic scenery are used, including signs stating locales and scenic elements. The actor does not attempt to induce belief in his performance in the usual sense, but instead suggests that he is a person with a mind of his own performing a role for its use in the play, at the same time commenting upon the character and the action. The "Living Newspapers" produced by the Federal Theatre used some of Brecht's techniques; Erwin Piscator directed a few productions in modified Epic mode at the Dramatic Workshop (first associated with the New School for Social Research but later independent of it). In recent years there has been an increasing number of Brechtian productions, particularly in colleges and universities.

In a larger sense, most if not all of the proposals here described were — as has already been suggested — directed not solely at the proscenium arch, but at the extremes of Actualism with which the arch had come to be associated. That is to say, the anti-proscenium experiments derived generally from a growing tendency, dating from the very beginning of the century, to challenge Actualism, per se. The first frontal attack was spearheaded by Adolphe Appia and Gordon Craig.

Appia's *Die Musik und die Inscenierung*[26] appeared in 1899, followed by several books in French. He took the position that the essence of drama is conveyed by the living body of the actor, that it is the function of

[26] Translated by Robert W. Corrigan and Mary Douglas Dirks as *Music and the Art of the Theatre* (University of Miami Press, 1962). Also available in English is Appia's *L'Oeuvre d'Art Vivant,* translated by H. D. Albright as *The Work of Living Art* (University of Miami Press, 1960).

scenery to support the actor, and that scenery has no independent function of its own. He therefore rejected the two-dimensional painted scenery of the nineties as a background for three-dimensional actors but not a true environment, and in particular he rejected the contemporary flat and even lighting, which tended to reduce the actor to two dimensions. He proposed to surround the actor with plastic forms which would be "expressional" rather than meaningful or representative. They were to be almost unrelieved planes, because they would best give dramatic meaning to the curved lines of the human body by opposing them. The forms were to appear solid and static to contrast with the movement of the actor's body. Appia lighted both actor and scenery to emphasize their plasticity and at the same time to allow the mobility of the light itself to reinforce mood and dramatic action. The simplicity of his scene and the almost geometrical forms on which it was based are particularly evident in his later designs, but even the earliest show the basic trends. To many readers, the validity of Appia's concepts was better demonstrated by his drawings than by his complex writing style. (See Plate 13.)

Gordon Craig wrote in English, and as a result he was more immediately effective than Appia in England and America. With publications from 1905 onward,[27] he popularized the concepts he shared with Appia, as well as some original ones. Craig emphasized the need for organic unity in each production and believed that the surest way to achieve it was to put the production in the hands of a master designer-director. He, like Appia, designed screen-like settings which

gave an impression of solidity but were frankly theatrical because of their suggestive simplicity. (See Plate 13.)

The simplified and suggestive settings designed by Craig and Appia, with an expressional rather than representational goal, have had a profound influence on both professional and amateur designers. As late as 1932, Lee Simonson[28] acknowledged that the basic aesthetic principles of modern stage design were elucidated by Appia in 1899. Such simplicity and expressiveness have become the hallmarks of twentieth-century stage setting. Designers and directors everywhere have recognized the inherent faults of extreme realism: at the least, realistic scenery is expensive and cumbersome to shift and store; more important, it is aesthetically unsound, as well as distracting and inexpressive. Theatre artists have discarded the unwieldy and aesthetically unsatisfying paraphernalia of the Actualistic stage for the "three S's" of modern scene design: Simplification, Suggestion, Synthesis. To use often-quoted examples, a section of a hedge might represent a garden, a corner of a house might suggest a street, and a carefully-designed window or set of columns might indicate a cathedral. Stage scenery needs no longer to be wholly or fully representational; if it is expressive or evocative, if it is organically unified, if it is conceived in three dimensions and tied together by ambient light, it belongs to the new stagecraft of the twentieth century.

As these trends have developed and intensified, the proscenium itself has been bypassed on more than a few occasions. The succeeding chapter will describe and justify those occasions, as it presents the "open" stage.

---

[27] E.g., *On the Art of the Theatre* (London: William Heinemann, 1912).

[28] *The Stage Is Set,* p. 352.

15 | The Open Theatre

*The Open Stage • Origins • Influence of the
Shakespearean Festivals • The Thrust Stage
Open Theatres • Some Open Theatres of
Modest Dimensions • Virtues and Disadvan-
tages • Some Combinations*

When any art form or style has flourished long enough for its practitioners to approach the limits of perfection possible within the familiar conventions, a current of restlessness and dissatisfaction develops among the artists who have mastered the conventions as well as those who are still learning them. It is as if the familiar form had by its mere presence intensified the general awareness of its inherent shortcomings. The result is a revolt against the familiar conventions accompanied by a groping for newer and fresher forms. As a rule, the insurgents join in opposing the older style, although their opposition may take varied forms. In time one of the innovations predominates and becomes an accepted "new" style. Once this new style is accepted, an increasing number of artists experiment with it to bring it to its perfection, and this in turn precipitates another revolution.

At the present time, the new form is the open theatre and the new style of staging is that engendered by the open stage. Both stand in opposition to the form and style of the proscenium theatre, which is old and familiar.

The actors and audiences who occupied the proscenium theatre often suffered from its restrictions. The actor, separated from his auditors by the gulf of the orchestra pit, the psychological barrier of the curtain line, and the darkness of the auditorium, felt handicapped in his efforts to gain their attention and sympathy. Spectators in seats far from the stage complained of the oppressive tunnel-like feeling forced on them by the narrow auditorium, the impossibility of seeing facial expression from the gallery or the rear of the auditorium, and the difficulty of hearing caused by the built-in echoes and reverberations which plague most proscenium theatres seating more than a few hundred persons.

Over the years a succession of noteworthy productions overcame the separation of actor and audience by bringing the performers in through the auditorium instead of the wings, by extending the acting area out over the orchestra pit, or by masking the proscenium frame with elements of the stage setting. As early as 1896, William Poel, attempting to counteract the ponderous historical-picture mounting of Shakespearean plays by Henry Irving and others, presented Elizabethan plays on a platform stage without act curtains or interruptions for scene changing and attracted praise from no less a critic than Bernard Shaw:

Kit Marlowe . . . did not bore me at St. George's hall as he has always bored me when I have tried to read him without skipping. The more I see of these performances by the Elizabethan Stage Society, the more I am convinced that their method of presenting an Elizabethan play is not only the right method for that particular sort of play but that any play performed on a platform amidst the audience gets closer home to its hearers than when it is presented as a picture framed by a proscenium. Also, that we are less conscious of the artificiality of the stage when a few well-understood conventions, adroitly handled, are substituted for attempts at an impossible scenic verisimilitude.[1]

Soon after World War I, Max Reinhardt in Germany began to experiment with various kinds of open stages. One was the vast "circus theatre" of the Grosses Schauspielhaus in Berlin, in which a semicircular seating slope surrounded a forward-thrust stage. Here he put on notable productions of classics such as *Oedipus the King, Lysistrata,* and *Faust.* Another was his Redoutensaal in Vienna, in which audience and actors shared a handsome imperial ballroom under crystal chandeliers which remained lighted throughout the performance, the play being performed on a platform at one end of the room in front of decorative screens in the same style as the décor of the ballroom.

In 1924, the American, Norman Bel Geddes, designed a phenomenally successful production of Max Reinhardt's extravaganza, *The Miracle;* the whole theatre, both stage and auditorium, was transformed into one vast acting area with aisles, apron, and even boxes used freely in the action. The production was first given in the large Century Theatre in New York, then toured the larger cities across the country. In each city one of the largest theatres was remodeled to accommodate the novel staging.

For a long time, the experiments of Reinhardt and others bore little fruit in the form of theatre buildings constructed specifically to accommodate open staging. One reason

was that very few theatre buildings of any kind were being built, for in 1929, the worldwide depression brought to a halt all kinds of venturesome building. Then came World War II, turning the energies of builders in other directions. Not until the war ended and the current of change regained its momentum could the newer concepts of theatre take tangible form.

THE OPEN STAGE

Today the number of open theatres is impressive and is increasing steadily. Furthermore, enough open theatres have now been in operation long enough — three seasons or more — to reveal the significant features of the development and to indicate the probable direction of future growth. Five or six features are beginning to show up in nearly every new theatre built with an open stage, and it will be worthwhile to examine them in some detail.

If the actor is to perform among his audience instead of in front of it, he must have the audience on his right and left as well as facing him. How completely the spectators should surround him — whether they should be all around him or only on three sides — is less important than that he should not be facing them all at the same time. In a typical arena theatre the audience completely surrounds the performer, while in certain other very popular arrangements the seating area barely exceeds a semicircle. In a few theatres the acting area juts out into an auditorium whose walls diverge at an angle of only 90°. Most directors and actors who work regularly in the open theatre prefer a wider spread, with the seats occupying at least 180°, or half a circle, in an auditorium which extends some degrees beyond a semicircle.

Wherever the circle of seats approaches 180°, the slope of the seating area tends to be steeper. The result is a bowl-like audi-

[1] *Saturday Review,* July 11, 1896, and reprinted in Bernard Shaw's *Our Theatres in the Nineties* (Constable, 1942), II, 184.

torium in which the audience looks down on the action. In general, this slope, if 20° or more, is agreeable to both actor and spectator. Looking down requires less effort from the spectator. It also makes the performer seem closer and the action more intimate.

The most successful shape for the stage appears to be oblong, or oblong with the corners cut off, the longest dimension corresponding to the central axis of the auditorium. Round or elliptical stages are generally avoided because actors complain that it is difficult to orient their actions consistently without some corners to help them get their bearings.

Open stages, when surrounded by steps, make it possible for the players to approach from every direction. Surrounding the acting area with steps which descend outward from it results in a declivity between the stage and the first row of seats which has come to be called "the ditch." Players not centrally involved in the action retire to this ditch and hence to the periphery of the scene. Here wait minor members of the crowds and armies, the pages and lesser courtiers, not out of sight, but out of the sight lines and quite out of mind for the time being.

When the stage projects far out into the auditorium it is no longer practicable to have all the performers enter from the side away from the audience, for the distance is considerable and the approach, being limited to the single forward direction, is certain to become monotonous after the first two or three entrances. Some other means must be provided for getting performers on and off quickly from the outer perimeter of the stage and from the ditch around it. For this purpose open theatres are often built with two or more vomitories rising from the seating slope and debouching upon the forward perimeter of the acting area. With only two of these vomitories, if they are large enough,

sizable crowds can enter swiftly and as boldly or unobtrusively as the scene may require.

When the stage is not completely surrounded by the seating slope, one end is usually joined to one wall of the auditorium, forming a façade capable of providing such conveniences as door-entrances and upper levels which can be used for scenes requiring balconies and city walls. This façade is not, strictly speaking, a background to the action, because no more than a small proportion of the spectators can ever see it in that relationship to the players. To most of the audience it will appear to be on one side of the acting area. Nevertheless, the façade adds a much-needed vertical dimension to the visual scheme.

The façade is usually convex in shape. Sometimes it has as many as three stories, the uppermost being used for musicians or for the appearance of deities or supernatural characters. Sometimes the façade is constructed on a turntable or within an opening of variable height and width to permit considerable change in general shape, height, and depth.

ORIGINS OF THE OPEN STAGE

Until a theatre building of major importance was erected featuring an open instead of a proscenium stage, the open theatre remained experimental and theoretical. The building of theatres was inhibited by the depression, World War II, and the unsettled times which followed, so that it was not until the middle 1950's that plans for theatres with open stages began to take shape in any significant numbers. During the interval, however, a number of minor theatres had been experimenting with the various actor-audience relationships which could be attained without the proscenium frame. These experiments gradually defined the possibilities.

Theatres then began to come into being with stages and seating arrangements of novel design, based on one or another of about three distinct plans. All these theatres were of modest cost and seating capacity. Most began as adaptations of spaces originally intended for nontheatrical use. A few began as temporary structures erected for some special occasion but continued in use when their existence filled some community need of more than temporary nature.

The three kinds of open arrangements take their names from the distinctive shapes of their stages. They are the "wrap-around" stage, the "arena" stage, and the "thrust" stage. (See page 177.)

The wrap-around stage was the first to take definite form. Its principal characteristic was an acting area extending around three sides of the auditorium, with side stages and entrances from the sides as well as from within the central stage area. The proscenium opening was often retained but redesigned to eliminate its framing effect and instead to blend acting area with auditorium. In its basic structure the wrap-around stage appeared at first to be merely a variation of the proscenium theatre with the same two enclosures, auditorium and backstage, joined by an opening between them, the only significant addition being the extension of the acting area along the sides of the auditorium. The effect, however, upon a person seated within such an auditorium is quite different from that of the typical proscenium theatre. The effect is distinctly one of openness and of occupying the same room as the performers. One of the oldest wrap-around stages is used as a second performance place by the Cleveland Playhouse. It was developed by remodeling a church building when expanding subscription audiences made a second theatre necessary. A similar reconstruction provided a wrap-around theatre for Wayne State University in Detroit. Others have been built at the University of Oregon, the University of Oklahoma, the University of California at Los Angeles, and Trinity University at San Antonio. Some very interesting plans for wrap-around stages have been developed by James Hull Miller, and others have been built by organizations for whom he acted as consultant.

The arena theatre, also called "theatre-in-the-round" and "circus theatre," employs a central acting area entirely surrounded by spectators. Four aisles at the corners of the stage are used for entrances and exits. In some instances the stage is raised, but in others the playing space is level with the first row of seats and the rearward rows elevated rather steeply.

The arena theatre first made its appearance in this country in the early 1930's as various kinds of rooms were converted into small, intimate theatres. One of the earliest was Gilmore Brown's Playbox Theatre, which began as an adjunct to the Pasadena Playhouse, of which Brown was director. The Playbox seated less than a hundred persons in comfortable armchairs which could be grouped around the open center of the room or turned to face any wall or corner. Doors, windows, and staircases already in being were used as the requirements of the particular play dictated. A few years later at the University of Washington, Glenn Hughes moved his Studio Theatre into the penthouse atop the Hotel Meany a few steps from the campus. The penthouse was a small but exceedingly attractive room surrounded by a promenade which afforded a magnificent view of Seattle, with Mount Rainier in the distance. Like the Playbox, the room could accommodate only a small audience and the most intimate performances. It quickly became popular. Presently, with the help of a Federal grant, Hughes built on the campus the first true arena theatre in America. It seats 172 persons in three rows around an elliptical acting area. It is still called The Penthouse Theatre.

Hughes's theatre attracted a great deal of interest. Arena productions began to be given in gymnasiums and church halls throughout the country. Not until after the end of World War II, however, was another theatre built specifically for arena production; then, in quick succession a number were built or adapted, most of which are in operation today. Among them was Margo Jones's Theatre '47 in Dallas, noteworthy for the number of first productions it provided for plays which afterward became commercial successes; the Ring Theatre at the University of Miami; the Pavilion at Pennsylvania State University; the Carousel Theatre at the University of Tennessee; the Arena Stage in Washington, D.C.; the Drury Lane Theatre in Evergreen Park, Illinois; and the Golf-Mill Theatre in Morton Grove, Illinois. What had begun as an expedient capable of accommodating only intimate plays and tiny audiences eventually gave rise to the construction of specialized structures seating audiences of a thousand or more and costing millions to build.

One of the most interesting sidelights of the arena development is the way it has been put to use by summer musical theatres, in many instances under large circular tents or circular structures designed to resemble tents. The circular form seems to encourage a carnival atmosphere which makes theatre-going much more of a lark and favors the lighter and more colorful forms of entertainment, including musical comedy and concerts by popular musicians. There are now almost more of these summer musical-arena theatres than one can count. Every metropolis has at least one on its outskirts. They make a welcome addition to the summer season and one which might never have come into being had it not been for the economies possible through arena production.

INFLUENCE OF THE SHAKESPEAREAN FESTIVALS

Since the turn of the century, when William Poel delighted his contemporaries with revivals of Shakespearean plays on circumstantially reconstructed Elizabethan stages, this mode of production has continued to attract both amateurs and professionals. At first it was simply a dependable way of putting the elaborately costumed and many-scened Shakespearean plays before audiences with a minimum of expense and time-consuming scene changes. These advantages soon made possible the production of Shakespearean festivals featuring three or more plays in repertory, with a different offering each evening during a summer season lasting from three weeks to five months.

The festivals were seasonal affairs. They came into being each June and closed each September. When they reopened the following summer, the company, the stage directors, and the staff were often substantially changed. The size, shape, and details of the stage might change also. But the basic apron stage without scenery or scene changes was usually carried over from season to season, so that in time a large number of actors and directors became accustomed to presentational staging and the techniques which make for an effective production on an open stage.

The first festival of this kind in America was produced by B. Iden Payne, a disciple of Poel's, and T. W. Stevens at the Century of Progress fair in Chicago in 1934. Presenting four ninety-minute abridgements of Shakespeare's plays each day, the company played to packed houses throughout the summer. The next season Payne and Stevens repeated the experiment with equal success at the San Diego World's Fair. The San Diego Festival is still in operation under the direction of Craig Noel, one of Payne's students. The success of these experiments encouraged others to follow suit. Soon there were the Oregon Shakespeare Festival, the Colorado Shakespeare Festival, the Vermont Shakespeare Festival, and many more, all playing to good audiences, all playing on open stages based on Payne's reconstruction.

In 1953, two festivals were launched, more ambitious than anything heretofore, which were to exert a lasting effect upon the physique of the American theatre: the Stratford Shakespearean Festival, in a huge tent at Stratford, Ontario, and the Antioch Shakespeare Festival, on an outdoor stage on the campus of Antioch College at Yellow Springs, Ohio. The Stratford theatre will be given detailed consideration further on; for the moment we need only note that its design was both original and extraordinarily successful. Of the Antioch venture the following comment by Brooks Atkinson, drama critic of the *New York Times,* is significant:

> The whole theory of the proscenium stage that has dominated the English-speaking stage since the Restoration has begun to crumble. Not only Shakespeare but modern playwriting needs the poetic freedom of some sort of platform stage. And anyone who now builds a theatre that is tied permanently to a proscenium stage is likely to find himself with a mausoleum on his hands before he has amortized the mortgage.[2]

THE THRUST STAGE

About the time arena staging was approaching the peak of its popularity, a variation came into being which made certain of the problems inherent in the form somewhat less acute. It consisted simply of placing the acting area not in the exact center of the enclosure — auditorium, ballroom, tent, or gymnasium — but touching one side of the

room. This arrangement provided at least one entrance where the performers would not have to be visible to the audience throughout the time it took them to cover the distance from the point of entrance to the edge of the acting area. What emerged at first was a sort of three-quarter arena. This was the form used successfully for many years by the Circle-in-the-Square in New York and also, although for shorter periods of time, by the Playwrights' Theatre in Chicago and the University Theater at the University of California at Los Angeles.

Action on the thrust stage, three-quarters surrounded by spectators, seemed to call for some device to define the acting area and to mark the division between actor and audience. In only a few instances were the performers to be found on the same level as the first row of spectators with no barrier of any kind between them. In most cases the stage was raised enough to set it off unmistakably as a stage. In others, as at U.C.L.A., a barrier of wainscoting or baseboard was introduced, nominally to suggest the location of the imaginary walls of the room in which the action was taking place, but actually to keep the spectators from feeling crowded in on the performance space.

Such were the origins of the open theatre: arena theatres improvised from ballrooms, living rooms, gymnasia, and warehouses; thrust stages shoe-horned into the ends and corners of rooms; wrap-around stages fitted into structures originally planned as churches or lecture halls; platform stages designed for the circumstantial revival of Elizabethan plays. All were expedients, occasional or temporary. Not until a major theatre building was designed and constructed with the specific intention of accommodating performers and audience within a single enclosure would the open theatre as we know it today come into being. By 1956 the time was ripe.

[2] *New York Times,* Aug. 23, 1953.

BUILDINGS ERECTED AS OPEN THEATRES

The designing of theatre buildings housing actors and audience in the same room entailed a radical departure from the architectural conventions which had governed theatre planning for over a century. During the hundred years preceding the Depression, the typical form of the proscenium theatre had gradually crystalized. The proportions and shape of the proscenium opening, the dimensions of the backstage area, the sight lines, slope of main floor, pitch of balcony, and proportionate size of lobby had all been reduced to workable formulae and codified by city ordinances governing construction, wiring, and fire prevention. Ordinances such as the one requiring an automatic fire curtain between actors and audience were based on the assumption that theatres built for use by living actors would always have prosceniums. The laws made it unlikely that the first open theatres would be built in New York or Chicago, or in fact in any metropolis subscribing to the New York Building Code.[3]

The first fully developed permanent structure designed as an open theatre was inaugurated at Stratford, Ontario, in 1957. Since 1953, the Stratford Shakespearean Festival had been playing to near-capacity audiences in a tent. After four seasons it became apparent that the success of the Festival warranted the construction of a permanent theatre; furthermore, the box office income could obviously go a long way toward paying off the mortgage.

The core of the building was already in existence: a 220° seating bowl, a thrust stage backed by a three-level façade, and the main backstage and under-stage areas, all of which

had proved eminently workable during four years of elaborate and varied productions. The building which rose on the site therefore began as a shell covering stage and seating slope, with extensions for offices, shops, and storage. The final structure retained the peaked tent-like roof and with it something of the original festival spirit. The result was a most unusual and attractive piece of architecture. Because it has proved functionally effective to a high degree, it has been widely imitated. (See page 167.)

In its original form the Festival Theatre was intended primarily for Shakespeare's plays. Accordingly, it emphasized those features which would facilitate the production of Shakespearean repertory: a forward-thrust apron stage with a central "grave" trap, side entrances, and an upper level for use as a balcony or as city walls. The stage resembled the one recommended by William Poel for the circumstantial revival of Elizabethan dramas, but it improved on its model in several ways. Tanya Moiseiwitsch, who designed the stage, had been experimenting with unit settings of this kind at Stratford-upon-Avon in England. Now she struck out with a bolder and more original scheme than any of the earlier experimenters had ever attempted. Her most adventurous innovation was extending the seating slope beyond the semi-circle to 220°. This placed such a large proportion of the spectators at the far sides that henceforth all the directors would be obliged to center their main actions well forward on the apron and balcony and away from those portions of the façade which any of the audience could not see. Her other additions were a center entrance underneath the balcony, steps coming down to the main acting area from either side of the balcony façade, and two vomitories in either side of the seating slope from which performers could enter and exit quickly from the outer corners of the stage.

---

[3] Even today, the Vivian Beaumont Theater in Lincoln Center, although built as an open theatre, is obliged to use an incongruous convex steel fire curtain to cover its thrust stage before and after every performance.

After ten seasons Miss Moiseiwitsch redesigned the stage in order to smooth out certain difficulties which had affected the movement, especially of crowds, on the stage. The basic features remained unchanged — the forward-thrust stage and balcony, the 220° seating curve, and the vomitory entrances. But the side entrances were moved apart to make possible entrances from opposite directions without necessarily bringing the performers face to face. Two of the columns supporting the upper level were removed to allow more space under the balcony. A number of improvements were made in the spacing of minor elements at the top and sides of the façade, but to the average spectator these would scarcely be noticed. The overall effect of the new design was to leave the stage looking the same as before but with a better proportion and distribution of performance spaces.

The most radical innovations in this theatre — the extended seating curve, the thrust stage, and the absence of provision for pictorial effects — seem to have caused little difficulty to directors and actors. Not all directors, of course, have been equally adept at solving the problems of this stage or of exploiting its virtues to maximum effect, but few have complained that it restricted them and some have developed extremely ingenious devices to meet the needs of the occasional plays not originally written for this kind of stage.

Ever since the second season at Stratford, when Sophocles' *Oedipus the King* was included in the repertory, plays from periods other than the Elizabethan have been a regular part of the season; over the years such classics as *Cyrano de Bergerac, The Cherry Orchard, The Government Inspector,* and *The Country Wife* have been staged, along with original works like *The Canvas Barricade.* A few of the familiar details of *Cyrano* and *The Cherry Orchard* have been unattainable

on the open stage, but none has been missed seriously. *Cyrano* in particular, in spite of having been originally intended as a spectacle for the proscenium theatre, proved one of the most successful productions ever mounted at Stratford. It demonstrated that plays written for the proscenium theatre could be staged with equal success on the thrust stage, two-thirds surrounded by spectators, and it encouraged abandonment of the widely held belief that the open stage was suitable only for Shakespearean revivals.

Although the Stratford Festival Theatre proved functionally effective for many kinds of plays besides those for which it was originally planned, its design was far from perfect; those who worked in it year in and year out became acutely conscious of certain shortcomings which could not be eliminated and could be overcome only through the most heroic expedients.

The gravest defect is that no provision was made for hoisting performers or properties from the central acting area. Nor is there any way in which hoists can be installed, for the peak of the ceiling directly above the stage is filled with ventilating equipment. Shakespeare's plays have many scenes which require apparitions to ascend or descend and supernatural creatures to fly. Without hoists these requirements cannot be met except through less impressive makeshifts. In *The Tempest* Ariel cannot descend in the guise of a harpy. In *Macbeth* the apparition of the armed head cannot rise from the witches' cauldron to confront Macbeth with the prefiguration of his fate. In *Cymbeline* Jupiter cannot descend on his eagle to reassure Leonatus in his prison cell.

Less important to the spectacle but much more important to the flow of action is the design of the vomitories. The slope has proved dangerously steep and the head room uncomfortably low for the innumerable fast entrances and exits of flag-and-spear-carrying armies. This difficulty is intensified by the hairpin turns in both vomitory passageways, just out of sight of the audience; the concrete walls have to be padded in order to prevent the actors from bruising themselves.

Underneath the stage is a room where a rig is placed to raise and lower the traps and to lift into view those who must ascend by this means. Into this room converge the two tunnelways coming from the vomitories — with the result that when armies, processions, and trap-raising apparitions come close together in the scene sequence, the crowding and confusion in the understage space is something which might have been imagined by Dante.

Other difficulties arise from the fact that the stage manager in control of the lighting and cueing systems is difficult to "hide" on an open stage, in any position where he can readily follow the action. Still others arise from the inaccessibility of the ceiling spotlights for relamping and refocusing. In any open theatre, spotlight positions must be provided at a great many places in the ceiling of the auditorium. It is easy to overlook the fact that every spotlight has to be accessible for service and adjustment, and that the technician has to be able to see his target while focusing a spotlight.

From the point of view of the spectator, the greatest shortcoming of the Festival Theatre is not apparent at once and often not during one performance. However, since the plays are offered in repertory, most visitors spend several days in Stratford and see three or four plays in succession. By the end of the second evening, one begins to feel the oppressive sameness of the setting. By the time one reaches the end of the fourth play, he cannot escape the sense of visual monotony. The permanent setting appears to have been conceived to provide an unobtrusive background for the performers. It is of unornamented wood stained a grayish brown.

A number of ingenious decorative devices such as false floors and façades have been used from time to time with considerable success. But the dominant visual impression after seeing four plays in succession is one of drab sameness.

Feeling the need for variety, both in kinds of plays and range of styles in setting, the Festival Foundation acquired another theatre, the Avon, which had seen good days both as a stock and a cinema house, and spent a fortune turning it into what is now one of the handsomest small proscenium theatres on the continent. With this second more conventional theatre, the Festival can now produce practically any kind of play in any style, thus providing for a variety which was lacking as long as every production had to be fitted to the stage of the Festival Theatre.

After five or six seasons, it became apparent that the Stratford Festival had attained two things sought by every theatrical venture: permanence and financial security. Soon other organizations of similar character began to appear. One of the most interesting was the Chichester Festival Theatre, founded in England in 1962. The company was headed by Sir Laurence Olivier and included a number of the best actors on the English-speaking stage. The Chichester Festival differs from the Ontario Festival in basing its repertory not on Shakespeare but on classics from all periods and cultures.

Because of the rather conventional requirements of the majority of the plays in its repertory, the Chichester Festival Theatre might be expected to have a more conventional auditorium and stage. Instead, its interior goes far beyond Stratford's in the direction of functionalism. Performers and audience are enclosed together in an octagonal, high-ceilinged, barn-bare room with unconcealed spotlights hung from the rafters. There is a stage thrusting forward almost to the center of the auditorium and an upper level with an iron railing behind the stage continuing halfway around each side wall to join finally with the spectators' balcony. The dominant impression is of a machine for the presentation of plays — a bare, wide-open acting area where the actor is close to his audience, free to move in any direction with a minimum of encumbrance from visual trappings. Perhaps with actors as able as Olivier, Richardson, Scofield, and Quayle nothing more is needed.

In 1963, this country saw its first fully developed open theatre, the Tyrone Guthrie Theatre in Minneapolis. Seeking to duplicate the success of the Stratford venture, Guthrie, with the encouragement of two New York producers and the support of the Minneapolis-St. Paul community, established a repertory company in a theatre built especially for the purpose. (See page 171.)

Once again Tanya Moiseiwitsch provided the design. She repeated the features which had proved most effective at Stratford, and — since the repertory was to embrace plays of all kinds and not only those of Shakespeare — she aimed for much greater variety.

The basic actor-audience relationship was the same as at Stratford, with the seating arranged on a 20° slope encircling the stage in a curve extending beyond the half-circle. As at Stratford, the stage was oblong, its longer dimension perpendicular to a façade, with steps going down from its edge to the surrounding "ditch" and two vomitories converging upon the corners. The stage itself was somewhat larger than the one at Stratford.

The most striking difference between the Tyrone Guthrie stage and the one at Stratford is in the design of the façade. In the Guthrie Theatre the whole wall can be made to open or close to any size and to accommodate walls, doors, balconies, and wagons which might be rolled into place to provide the physical elements of the setting for any play. Hoists were also made available as they had not been at Stratford.

Another interesting novelty is the asymmetrical plan of the stage and auditorium. Whether there is any advantage to be gained from having a balcony on one side of the auditorium and a straight slope of seats on the other is open to question, just as one might question the effectiveness of a thrust stage of irregular outline. But the plan did attract a great deal of attention and make people want to see this unusual theatre.

The Tyrone Guthrie Theatre was built all at once, so to speak, instead of growing gradually as the Stratford theatre had done. Inevitably there were problems. For example, the slow corralling of funds forced the builders to abridge their plans in order to meet opening-date deadlines. This resulted in a building which, while attractive in exterior appearance, encloses a smaller, more informal (and less profitable) auditorium lacking both in its interior design and its siting the impressive majesty of its prototype.

The most ambitious open theatre of all is the Vivian Beaumont Theater, designed to house the Lincoln Center Repertory Company in New York. This building is one of four in a complex which includes the new Metropolitan Opera House, Philharmonic Hall, and the New York State Theater for ballet and musical shows.

With ample funds and the aid of the most experienced consultants, every effort was made to achieve a model American theatre plant comparable to the great state theatres of Europe. Careful planning over a long period of time produced a handsome structure, impressively sited and attractively furnished. The auditorium seats 1,140. It is semicircular, with a steep seating slope and a shallow balcony. The semicircular thrust stage can be converted into additional seating space when the proscenium arrangement replaces the thrust stage.[4] From under the

[4] This particular feature of the Beaumont will be discussed further at the end of this chapter.

seating slope two small vomitories debouch upon the outer corners of the acting area. Facing the audience is a façade which can be opened to provide a proscenium of any desired height or width, with a backstage cyclorama, revolving stage, and hoists. An intricate combination of hydraulic elevators and sliding platforms makes it possible to change the shape of the acting area to an open stage, a proscenium stage, or any combination of the two. Into the façade can be fitted enough doorways, balconies, stairways, and upper levels to meet the requirements of any play of any period. (See page 170.)

With this flexible façade and an acting area capable of taking many shapes, it should be possible for the Vivian Beaumont to escape the visual monotony which tends to afflict the open theatre when used for repertory. Up to now, however, the Lincoln Center company has not attempted repertory, offering instead a series of plays in succession in what is in effect a "stock" season. True repertory makes much greater demands upon the theatre plant than does stock. The fact that costumes, properties, lights, and set decorations must be cleared away after each performance and the elements of the new production put into immediate readiness means that everything must work with a high degree of efficiency. In repertory, difficulties such as inaccessible spotlights, recalcitrant traps, and balky hoists assume greatly increased importance. At the Beaumont, the plays are changed only four times a year instead of every performance; stage facilities consequently are not heavily taxed, so that their shortcomings are much slower in coming to light. It may be some years before it will be possible to appraise the Vivian Beaumont Theater in as great detail as was possible at Stratford after the first summer of its operation.

Situated in New York among the most active commercial theatres in the country, the most sophisticated theatregoing audiences, and the most demanding critics, the Vivian Beaumont Theater has been subjected to detailed and wide-ranging criticism of a kind it would not have had if it had been built in Minneapolis or Stratford. Consequently, all the shortcomings of its design have been widely advertised. One is the scheme which combines lobby, lounge, and foyer into one large room, with the box office tucked away in a corner of the lower lobby underneath the main entrance and therefore invisible from the outside. Another complaint comes from those who work in the theatre: that it lacks rehearsal and storage space, so plays in preparation often have to rehearse in the theatre on the stage set up for the current production. This also complicates the problem of keeping two or more plays in rehearsal at the same time. Inadequate storage space increases the cost of operation (in New York already the highest in the country) by making it necessary to dispose of many items which might otherwise have been preserved against the certainty of being used again. Complaints about the backstage traffic pattern have not been numerous, but one cannot help wondering whether the vomitories, much smaller than the ones at Stratford, might not be even more difficult to use. Also, an open stage without side entrances must at times be difficult to use for Elizabethan revivals.

SOME OPEN THEATRES OF MODEST DIMENSIONS

All the theatres described above were major developments representing the investment of millions of dollars. Not all open theatres have been so costly. Several very modest structures have proved quite effective as playhouses as well as architecturally attractive. Three of these merit attention.

The earliest of the three was constructed

almost ten years ago on the campus of the University of Waterloo, Ontario, as a facility for drama and small musical groups. Seating only four hundred, its plan and general appearance are strongly reminiscent of the Stratford Festival Theatre a few miles away. Being smaller, it has eliminated the vomitories, the under-stage rooms, and the Elizabethan two-story façade. In place of the façade is a pair of sliding panels which can be opened to provide a modified proscenium with an inner stage backed by a cyclorama. Sight lines and acoustics are good. The theatre has elicited enthusiastic praise from musicians and actors who have performed in it.

Of comparable size is the building which houses the community theatre of Western Springs, Illinois. This theatre combines the wrap-around with the thrust stage in an auditorium having a 90° spread instead of the more familiar semicircle. The 20° seating slope yields good sight lines and a pleasant airy feeling. The stage is spacious, with a screen behind it which can be used as a sky backing or upon which scenery can be projected. There is no gridiron or loft and no division between stage and seating area, but the ceiling supports a number of catwalks from which all the overhead spotlights can be reached. The overhead girders, masked from the view of the audience by a number of panels, provide unlimited places where hoists can be attached. (See page 168.)

The third modest theatre, the ANTA-Washington Square Theatre in New York, was originally a temporary structure to house the Lincoln Center Repertory Company while the Vivian Beaumont was being completed. It proved effective as a performance place, and as it was inexpensive to operate, it continued to be in demand for commercial use after the Lincoln Center company moved out. Functionally, the theatre is very like the Vivian Beaumont, with the same actor-audience relationship resulting from similarly shaped seating slope and thrust stage. It lacks the flexible façade and mechanized forestage of the Beaumont, but its design provides for a wide variety of arrangements nevertheless. Temporary entrances, steps, and balconies are easily accommodated.

The future of the ANTA-Washington Square Theatre has been difficult to predict. Had it become a permanent, fulltime playhouse, it would have required extensive adapting and remodeling. But despite a good deal of active support for just such a course, it is now scheduled for demolition.

VIRTUES AND DISADVANTAGES OF THE OPEN THEATRE

The millions lavished on the construction of open theatres during the past decade would never have been spent had this new form not supplied something that theatregoers liked and theatre workers needed. Nor would the ingenuity of architects and engineers have been so zealously applied to the technical problems had this form not promised to be more efficient and economical than forms of theatre already in being. Not every characteristic of this new kind of theatre offers advantages over the older and more familiar proscenium theatre. Any new form is bound to have shortcomings and to raise at times almost as many problems as it solves. But discussion of the difficulties of the form can wait. First let us examine the virtues which have been responsible for its acceptance and growth.

The dominant impression one receives on entering the auditorium of an open theatre is of its spaciousness. Whether it seats 172 as in the Penthouse Theatre or 2,258 as in the Stratford Festival Theatre, the feeling of the interior is airy and roomy. This is largely due to the bowl-like curve of the seating slope; curves in an interior, especially those which bend away from the eye, give this feeling to an enclosure.

Seeing and hearing have always been the first necessities for the enjoyment of drama, although they have not always been guaranteed by the various kinds of buildings erected to house plays. In many a fine theatre built during the eighteenth century, only the occupants of the royal box in the center of the auditorium were able to enjoy a perfect view of the stage. In many theatres built after steel construction came in around the turn of the century, poor acoustics were so common that even today any proscenium theatre having good acoustics attracts comment.

In an open theatre sight lines and acoustics are so invariably good that they generally escape comment completely. This is due to the shape of the auditorium which, with its deeply curved rows of seats, provides no parallel surfaces for the development of echoes which blur the sound of speech and make perception difficult; to the steep slope which raises the sight line of each row above that of the row in front; and to the fact that no spectator, even in the largest theatre, is farther than sixty feet from the center of the stage. In the smaller theatres of this kind, the farthest seats are even closer.

The other virtues are economic. The scaling down of scenery saves construction costs, reduces the number of stagehands needed, and also eliminates much of the time normally spent on perfecting shifts in the dress rehearsals. The elimination of the big fly loft over the stage saves costly cubage and simplifies heating and air conditioning. Finally, the fact that the open stage remains pretty much the same size and shape from season to season and production to production eases the work of the stage director and makes rehearsals less fatiguing to the actors. With these advantages, it is possible to attain finer and more finished productions in relation to the amount of time and money spent in preparation.

The disadvantages of the open theatre are much less obvious than its virtues, but they are the causes of thorny problems and are responsible for the failure of many a production from which much had been expected. An appreciation of them is therefore indispensable to an understanding of the open stage.

Perhaps the greatest difficulty of all is the shortage of directors who know how to use the open stage to advantage. One might reasonably expect that a form which has flourished for over a decade would have attracted a considerable number of practitioners intent on exploiting the advantages of the new form, but this has not been the case. A few, such as Tyrone Guthrie and Michael Langham, have understood the form and used it effectively. Most others appear to be trying to apply the same principles of picturization, grouping, and movement which served them in the proscenium theatre. The result is that many productions which ought to have been interesting have been tedious, muddled, and tastelessly overelaborated. In all open theatres at present it is possible to see productions in which principal characters cover one another, blackouts interrupt the progression, and attempts at novelty yield unendurable coyness.

The investment in costumes and properties needs to be much greater in an open theatre. Because the spectator is closer to the stage, he can easily detect sleazy fabric and shoddy workmanship. This means that a generous budget must be provided for excellent materials and highly skilled labor.

The lighting of a play on an open stage is difficult to plot because the spotlights must converge upon the acting areas from all directions and still not shine in the eyes of the audience. It is also less interesting: the open theatre does not usually have a cyclorama

PLATE 19. **Modern Productions of Greek Dramas.** (Above) Euripides' *Ion*. (Northwestern University: director, Lee Mitchell; settings, Delbert Unruh; costumes, Linda Rogers; lighting, Douglas McCullough.) (Below) Sophocles' *Oedipus Rex*. (University of Hawaii: director, Earle Ernst; designer, Richard Mason.)

PLATE 20. **Modern Arena Productions.** (Above) Three-sided arena for a pro-
duction of *Papa Is All*. Notice the complete scenic enclosure of the acting area.
(*University of California at Los Angeles: director, Edward Hearn; designer, John H.
Jones; lighting, Melvyn Helstien.*) (Below) Pre-Broadway production of *Southern
Exposure* in a complete arena. (*Theatre '50, Dallas: director, Margo Jones; costumes,
Dhu Wray; lighting, Marshall Yokelson.*)

PLATE 21.   **The Thrust Stage Adapted to Chekhov and Gogol.** (Above) *The Cherry Orchard. (The Minnesota Theatre Company: director, Tyrone Guthrie; designer, Tanya Moiseiwitsch.) (Below) The Government Inspector. (Stratford Shakespearean Festival: director, Michael Langham; designer, Leslie Hurry; music, Raymond Pannell.)*

PLATE 22. **Two Treatments of Macbeth.** (Above, Wayne State University: director and designer, Richard D. Spear; costumes, Robert Pusilo; lighting, Gary M. Witt. Below, *Indiana University:* director, William E. Kinzer; designer, Gene Parola.)

and scenery clamoring to be imaginatively lighted, and costumes and properties require more even and less colorful lighting. In fact, some of the best open-stage designers insist upon white light throughout so that the rich details of clothing and furniture will be visible without distortion.

For the designer, the greatest difficulty of the open theatre is that without background scenery most of the means of keeping interest alive throughout a repertory, or even during one play, are not available to him. He may start the play off well with interesting floor coverings, set decorations, costumes, and props, but it is extremely difficult to devise a good temporal progression which will grow in interest and bring the play to an end with some delightful surprise. (See Chapter 18.)

The disadvantage of the open theatre most often talked about is that a production tailored to an open stage is not easily transferable to another open stage or to a proscenium theatre; a company cannot tour easily with a repertory of plays originally staged on an open stage. Up to now only a few companies have attempted to tour such a repertory. But since all have played theatres quite different from one another without any unusual amount of extra rehearsal, the disadvantage in touring may be negligible or non-existent.

THEATRES COMBINING OPEN AND PROSCENIUM STAGES

A number of organizations have been attracted by the virtues of the open stage but, reluctant to abandon completely the familiar proscenium, have attempted to combine the two forms in one theatre building. Among them are the American Shakespeare Festival Theatre at Stratford, Connecticut, the Loeb Drama Center at Harvard University, the Hopkins Center Theatre at Dartmouth College, the Loretto-Hilton Theatre at Webster College, and the already mentioned Vivian Beaumont Theater in Lincoln Center. So far, none of these has been entirely successful. The combination is difficult to achieve because the two basic actor-audience relationships have little in common.

The least successful attempt is embodied in the American Shakespeare Festival Theatre. A proscenium theatre was adapted for presentational staging by the addition of a large apron and steps permitting the actors to enter from what had been the orchestra pit. These steps are very steep and face a concrete wall at the bottom, and performers find them awkward to negotiate. Much of the strength of the apron is lost because the horseshoe shape of the auditorium makes it impossible for the actor to play among his audience instead of merely in front of them.

Both the Loeb Drama Center and the Hopkins Center Theatre are modified by the laborious shifting of platforms, seats, and side screens. Eventually, the form most favored by the principal tenants of both theatres will probably remain in place most of the time, and the variations in form will be infrequently used. What will result will not be a flexible theatre but a theatre of one dominant form possessing a number of possible but rarely used variations.

Since its opening in October of 1965, the Vivian Beaumont Theater has not used its proscenium setup. Consequently, there is no way of determining whether the structure works as well as a proscenium theatre as it does as an open theatre. As far as we know, no one has succeeded in building a theatre which can be used as both a proscenium and an open theatre and still satisfy the major aesthetic and functional requirements of both forms. But this does not mean that the combination is impossible. Sooner or later someone is certain to find the key. For the virtues of the open theatre are overwhelmingly appealing to actors and directors who have been hemmed in by the limitations of the proscenium form. At the same time, the proscenium theatre is going to enjoy the advantages of familiarity and the fact that all theatre workers know and can use the secrets of its effectiveness. Finally, how many organizations are likely to construct two distinct theatre buildings in order to achieve two different actor-audience relationships, no matter how incompatible the physical demands of the two may seem to be?

Section Four

Design

16 | The Nature and Function of Design

A Definition of Design · The Nature of Design · The Function of Design

A DEFINITION OF DESIGN

To theatre people the word "design" possesses a special meaning. In this respect it resembles many another term which is used in one way by the layman while the professional, particularly when speaking of his work, employs it in a more specific and limited sense. Thus, if one goes to the dictionary and looks up the word "design," one finds it synonymized with "plan," "scheme," or "project." Among theatre people, however, the word is narrower in its meaning, being applied not to the whole scheme of the production but to only one aspect of that scheme: the visual aspect. It is not the best word for this purpose because when speaking to laymen one must continually qualify its meaning. Unfortunately, there is in our language no other word which is any better for the purpose of naming theatre design. We have, for example, no term as apt as the French term, *mise-en-scène,* nor any as unmistakable in its meaning as the German *inscenierung.* When speaking of theatrical production, therefore, we will have to use the word "design" as it is customarily employed by theatre workers. The following definition is recommended. *Design is the visual scheme of the production, including scenery, costumes, properties, and stage lighting.* "Design" therefore consists of all the inanimate things which contribute to the visual effect of the performance.

THE NATURE OF DESIGN

The visual scheme of the production is developed simultaneously in both time and space. Scenery, costumes, and properties exist in space, and either separately or together they make their primary appeal to the eye. At any given moment during the performance the arrangements and the effects of which they are capable respond to principles which govern the spatial arts. The same principles of scale, balance, and proportion which make works of architecture, sculpture, and painting pleasing to the eye apply with equal value to the composition of the scene.

But the design of a play is also a temporal thing in that it exists in time, like music. And in this respect it differs from the other spatial arts. A painting or a piece of sculpture has a degree of permanence which the stage design does not have; once completed, its composition is stable, and it is capable of retaining its form for an indefinite period. The performance of drama, on the other

225

hand, like the performance of music, occupies a comparatively brief time, and although the script of a drama may be performed many times, each performance is a complete work of art. It is, moreover, impossible to duplicate the work exactly. Some performances are much better than the average; others are worse; no two are identical at all points. What is true of the performance as a whole is necessarily true of each of its parts. The visual scheme of the production is as temporal as the performance of which it is a part.

Along with the performance, the design moves forward in time, and as it moves forward each visual effect impresses the spectator in relation to the visual effects which came earlier in the performance. Each effect adds to the cumulative impression of the whole design. Each composition of costumes, scenery, and light is part of an active sequence, changing continually and piling effect upon effect until the total design is completed and the performance is concluded. The design of a play is, like the design of a parade, a series of visual evolutionary phases to be seen in a certain sequence, each phase to produce a certain effect and the entire series to produce a satisfying sense of completeness.

The infinite possibilities of successive variation, contrast, surprise, and repetition are inseparable from the design. Temporal factors similar to those which prevail in music apply to the design. Many of the strongest effects are limited in duration, for the attention of the spectator can be concentrated only so long at a time. When an effect is kept before the eyes of the spectator for a longer time, greater variety and subtlety of design are necessary. Most of the pioneering in stage machinery has as its object greater fluidity of design and more perfect control of the desirable changes of scenery and lights. To the designer the ideal stage is the completely flexible stage capable of accommodating infinite variety of movement by the actors — as well as changes of scene and of light — with a minimum of effort.

In summary, the nature of the design may be described as being both spatial and temporal. This bilateral nature distinguishes it from other similar arts. It resembles architecture, sculpture, and painting in its organization of visual appeals, but differs from them in that it is active while they are static. It resembles music in that both exist within a comparatively short period of time during performance, and both consist of sequential cumulative changes. It differs from music in that music appeals primarily to the ear while design appeals primarily to the eye.

THE FUNCTION OF DESIGN

Stated in the broadest possible way, the function of the design is to assist the spectator's perception of the performance. It does this through various appeals to the eye calculated to strengthen both the intellectual and the emotional content of the performance. Where the design is faulty the totality of effect suffers, emotional impact is lessened, and meaning is blurred. For convenience of examination this general function will be divided into three interrelated functions. These are: to clarify; to intensify; to identify.

The First Function: Clarification

During the course of a performance each significant action must be made clear while it is happening; each important idea must be made to register as it is being presented; each emotional appeal must be made to take hold at once. The spectator cannot go back and review the scene whose meaning he missed. He has no time to ponder over the idea which he did not understand. For the performance marches forward in time and new ideas and new actions are claiming his attention. Immediate clarity is therefore essential to both understanding and response.

To clarify the action is a continual necessity. The audience must see and know what is happening. It must see each important action clearly and grasp its significance on the instant. In some dramas this is not particularly difficult to achieve. In others the problem is acute. In Greek dramas the problem scarcely exists, because of the custom of having but three characters visible, of having certain characters enter from certain entrances, and of having a minimum of physical activity. But in Elizabethan plays the problem is extremely difficult because of the great amount of action and the fact that frequent shifts from one plot to another are in danger of leaving the audience a jump behind the developments. The problem is further complicated by the fondness of Elizabethan playwrights for the "bipolar" scene, in which two or more character groups simultaneously carry on divergent activities. An example of this is the ball scene in *Romeo and Juliet* (I, v) where the meeting of the lovers, Tybalt's recognition of Romeo, and the festivities of the evening all take place at the same time. The problem is to keep each action clear, and there have been as many solutions as there have been productions of this play. Dividing levels, framing arches, contrasting colors, and many other means have been employed.

Similarly, Molière's plays, with their paired characters, abrupt entrances, and sudden exits are readily subject to loss of clarity unless the various lines of action can be kept distinct by means of entrances, steps, causeways, or similar devices. In the later dramas of Ibsen and Chekhov clarity of action depends upon design to an even greater extent. One room described by Ibsen in *The Wild Duck* requires four doors, a double door, and a skylight, all distinct and all equally visible to the spectators. Each entrance is identified with certain characters and certain actions. In spite of the implausibility of having this number of doors in any one

room, the reduction of the number is certain to confuse the spectator. Chekhov, unlike Ibsen, is not in the habit of describing the scene in terms of action requirements, but the action which he presents is exceedingly complex because of the number of individuals pursuing different aims. The visual scheme of a Chekhov play must be managed in such a way as to keep these various lines of action separate and to keep one from impinging on and obscuring others. The curiously vague and pointless effect in performance of much of Chekhov's work is often traceable to failure of the design in regard to the function of clarification of action.

The problem of keeping clear the relationships of characters varies according to several factors: the number of characters; the number of times each character appears; and the number of scenes in the play. The greater the number in each case, the greater the problem. A particularly good instance of this is *Antony and Cleopatra*. Here there are three different character groups: Egyptians, Antonian Romans, and Octavian Romans. In the recent production of this play by Katharine Cornell, John Boyt, the costume designer, achieved an imaginative solution to the problem by translating the basic differences into differences of hue, putting the Antonian Romans in warm colors, the Octavian Romans in cool colors, and the Egyptians in neutral tones. Within each group the leading characters were distinguished from the lesser ones by differences in brilliance. Thus, of all the Antonians, Antony himself appeared in the lightest and brightest of the warm colors, while the lesser characters of his group followed a descending scale of brilliance to a kind of dull maroon for the supernumeraries. A similar scheme prevailed within each of the other groups.

Costume is only one means by which character relationships can be made clear. In cases in which the ascendance or decline of one character or group must be shown, the setting plays an important part, providing steps, platforms, and ramps which elevate the ascendant characters above the neutral floor. The commonest example of this is seen in the tendency to elevate a character such as a king or a judge beyond the height required by visibility or verisimilitude.

As conceived by the author, the theme of the play — a third element in clarification — varies in its importance to the total effect. As a general rule, one might say that in serious drama the theme is likely to be of greater importance while in lighter drama it is likely to be of less. Also, in poetic drama the theme is usually more apparent than in prose drama, for the latter, being composed within a less exacting form, is usually less explicit. Clarification of the theme by visual means, therefore, depends primarily upon the clarity with which the author has stated his theme and secondarily upon the importance of the theme to the total effect of the performance. For the time being it will be necessary to avoid the question of whether it is possible to clarify the theme to a greater degree than the author intended.

Where the theme is dominant, it is a function of the design to make that theme clear to the spectator. A number of productions within the past generation afford brilliant examples of this function. Perhaps two instances from the work of Robert Edmond Jones will suffice at this point. One of these was his design for the opening scene of *The Sea Gull,* where the bleak orange sunset and dark tree trunks like imprisoning bars expressed the idea of confinement and ennui with tremendous effect. Another was his design for the production of *Lute Song.* In this play he heightened the basic idea of the pressure of wealth and power upon the poorer classes by means of a violent contrast of hue and texture. The story concerns a man who leaves his parents and his wife in order to enter royal service, intending all the while to return and rescue them from the poverty into which his departure has thrust them. But as time passes he finds it more and more difficult to return to his home. Before he finally succeeds both of his parents perish of starvation and his wife is forced into beggary. The play is composed of scenes at court alternating with scenes in the parents' home. Jones emphasized the contrast between the two locales by putting the court scenes in reds accented with gold and the home scenes in unaccented grays. As the son rose in power and his parents grew poorer, the contrast increased. Scene by scene the reds and golds of the court became brighter while the grays of the home grew darker and colder.

The Second Function: Intensification

Being a temporal art, the performed drama moves forward in time, creating expectation, disappointment, surprise, and numerous other temporal effects. It is essential to the art that each successive action be most impressive at the time that it is performed. Much of the art of the theatre consists of creating mood, sharpening interest, or heightening emotional impact in such a way as to deepen the impression of the moment. Much of what we call "dramatic" is this very intensification of some temporal quality which makes a passing impression vivid and memorable. And it is this same intensification which often accounts for the difference between a brilliant performance and a tedious one.

It is at this point that the design of a production makes its most telling contribution. For while the temporal values originate for the most part in the script or in the acting of the script, the final intensification of them is a function of the visual scheme, and when the performance is over the memory of what was seen is likely to persist long after the memory of sound and timing has faded.

The first problem here is one of *mood.* The state of mind in which the audience experiences the drama is always important; occasionally it is of paramount importance to the success of the work. The feeling of danger in *The Emperor Jones*, the air of melancholy in *The Cherry Orchard*, the lusty opulence of *Volpone*, the restlessness of *Winterset* — each is a mood, or a state of mind, which must be established before the performance can register its full effect.

All of the arts of the theatre figure in the establishment of an appropriate mood, and design is one with the other arts in this respect. Its most significant contribution, however, is not only toward the creation of mood, but the intensification of mood by visual means. It is when the mood is dramatized by being raised to its highest pitch that it counts most, and one of the functions of design is to contribute to this heightening.

The opulent mood of *Volpone* requires light colors, elaborate ornament, and an abundance of detail. The restless mood of *Winterset*, as designed by Jo Mielziner, was perfectly expressed by a design which gave the setting the effect of being an exposed unsheltered place — not a place where one could rest or feel at home. It had an impersonal public-place look about it, and though majestic in its dimensions, seemed to say: "There is no shelter here." Jones's opening scene for *The Sea Gull* clinched the melancholy mood of that play by means of bleak autumnal coloring, an austerity in the simplification of the foliage lines, and a suppression of detail.

But the thing which distinguished each of these, and which always distinguishes superior design in this function, was the degree to which each designer had succeeded in intensifying the mood prescribed by the playwright and established by the behavior of the performers. Each design acted upon the spectators in such a way as not only to produce a favorable state of mind but to raise that state of mind to its highest point of receptivity.

Secondly, there is the problem of *impact*. Each drama contains moments when the significance of the action is revealed in a striking speech or a flash of physical activity. Script, acting, and design combine to give each such moment the greatest possible impact on the beholder. Often it is around these high points of the play that the visual scheme is developed, keying the design to the moment of greatest impact and subordinating the rest of the scheme in proportion to its value as compared with these moments.

Instances of this kind abound in drama of every age and kind. Many a drama contains several such moments. The following instances, therefore, represent not the only great moments, but one of several in each of the plays named. There is one in *Oedipus the King* at the moment when Oedipus realizes the truth of his origin. In Molière's *Imaginary Invalid* there is one when Argan finally recognizes Beline's hypocrisy. In *Macbeth* there is one at the point of Macbeth's receipt of the news of Lady Macbeth's death and his subsequent realization of the futility of his ambition. In *The Tempest* it is Ariel's appearance as purgator of Alonso. In *Winterset* it is Mio's first glimpse of Miriamne. In Sartre's *The Flies* it is Zeus's revelation of the planetary system which he controls and which exemplifies his power.

The designer, from among his resources, chooses an appropriate device for heightening each of these. One of Mielziner's designs for *Winterset* was composed entirely in cold colors. The scenery was slate gray, the sky a steely blue, the lighting without warmth. Within this chilly environment moved people dressed in black, gray, or grayish shades only. Miriamne sat inconspicuously wrapped in a dark coat while the action flowed about her. But as Mio's eye first fell upon her, she loosened her coat so that it fell open a little, revealing the bright red dress which she wore beneath it. That sudden red among the cold tones of the design was like a fire lighted in an icy room and her magnetism for Mio became a vivid and meaningful thing.

Finally, the design can intensify *interest*. Among all the things which a spectator might see in the performance, there is at any one instant only one thing upon which his attention can concentrate. It is the business of director, actor, and designer alike to be sure that the thing which he does see is the thing which carries the play forward. This one thing may be a person or a property or a part of the setting, but it must be the thing which matters most as far as his apprehension of the play is concerned. One function of the design is continually to attract, hold, and intensify the spectator's interest in the significant thing. "What compels attention determines response" is an old saying. It is nowhere truer than in the theatre.

It is in the intensification of interest that design contributes most; in the fixing of the spectator's eye upon the significant object and holding it there until the desired response is aroused. In Cornell's *Antony and Cleopatra* the spectator's interest in Antony was intensified by the fact that Antony was costumed in the brightest colors of any character. His interest in Cleopatra was intensified by the fact that she was costumed always in darker shades than those who surrounded her. In the Tyler production of *Macbeth*, Gordon Craig sharpened interest in Macbeth on his first appearance by putting under his feet an arching causeway which raised him high above the other characters. In the Theatre Guild *Liliom*, Simonson fixed attention on Liliom in the final scene by causing a number of sloping roof lines to decline toward the spot where Liliom sat, so that wherever the eye wandered the pointing lines brought it back to the significant figure.

Often the play requires that the interest

of the spectator be fixed upon a listening character while the spoken lines fall in the periphery of attention. This happens in the final scene of *Tartuffe*, when Tartuffe himself stands silent during his unmasking by M. Exempt. In *Oedipus the King* it is Jocasta, as she listens and finally grasps the meaning of the colloquy between her young husband and the Corinthian. In *Antigone* it is Eurydice, as she listens to the Messenger's description of her son's suicide. In *Payment Deferred* it is the wife, as she enters unseen by her husband and finds him in the arms of another woman.

The Third Function: Identification

The function of design in identifying locale and character is the one which customarily receives first attention in discussions of theatre art. Perhaps this is because of all the functions it is the one which is most readily apparent. Certainly among the more familiar modern dramas, identification of locale is usually necessary. But viewing drama as a whole and including plays of all periods along with the modern ones, one can see that identification of locale by visual means is far from being uniformly desirable. In modern productions of older plays it figures mainly as a concession to recently established conventions of theatrical production.

Turning to the identification of *character*, one finds the reverse to be true. The older the play the more positive must the identification be, for among the customs and manners of unfamiliar times characters are easily overlooked or misinterpreted. The marks of rank, occupation, and nationality which were once well known are now no longer easily recognized, and their incorporation into the visual scheme acquires the nature of a special problem. The two hours more or less which a drama occupies in performance is very little indeed when an action of great size or great complexity is to be presented. The time limit makes no allowance for misunderstanding on the part of the spectator. Each mistake in recognition is a dead loss to the play.

The first and most important thing about a character is his position in relation to the plot. The characters whose personalities and actions determine the course of the plot must be identified to the eye and made readily recognizable each time they appear. There can be no chance allowed that one of the dominant characters might become even momentarily confused with one of lesser importance. The necessity for ready identification is particularly acute in plays whose structure is episodic and in those which have unusually large casts with many minor characters appearing infrequently. David Ffoulkes showed an admirable awareness of this necessity in his design for *Richard of Bordeaux* when he kept Bolingbroke in strong reds throughout a series of arrangements consisting mostly of weaker hues.

The necessity for identifying the principal characters is fairly obvious to any observer. Another necessity which is not so apparent and which is therefore frequently overlooked is that of singling out a lesser character who momentarily dominates the scene and alters its course. We may call this character the *significant odd man.* On numerous occasions his appearance at a critical moment or his comment aptly placed is one of high dramatic significance, and capable of giving a tremendous lift to the scene. Such a character is the silent blood-stained Banquo among the elegant banqueters in *Macbeth.* Others, less vivid but equally significant, are Surly in Ben Jonson's *Alchemist,* Thersites in *Troilus and Cressida,* and the old shepherd in *Oedipus the King.*

Other aspects of character which occasionally require identification are those having to do with social station, occupation, nationality, and historical period. With these, however, the function of acting overlaps that of the design to a considerable degree.[1]

The number of characters, both principal and minor, whom the designer is able to identify to the audience bears a distinct relationship to the total effect of the performance. As a general rule, the minor characters tend to lose identity in a play where there are many speaking roles, and the spectator may fail to recognize or remember any but those who are continually before him. Well planned, the design may identify many who might otherwise be lost track of. The greater the number of characters who can be established as individuals within the limit of the two hours' performance time, the richer the feeling of experience and profit which the play can be made to yield.

A second factor here is identification of *locale.* Playwrights vary in the importance which they attach to the localization of action. In the plays of most of the Greek dramatists the locale seems somewhat conventionalized to take advantage of the outdoor theatre and the natural scenery visible beyond the playing area. Shakespeare more often than not omits any reference to the place of action. In the works of Molière locale is indicated only in the most general terms. Among eighteenth-century playwrights locale is usually standardized as one or another of about a dozen places: "A Hall"; "An Inn"; "A Promenade"; "A Hovel"; and so on. Modern playwrights, by contrast, are usually rather explicit as to the place of action, and often preface their plays with detailed descriptions of locale, giving clues to the nature and habits of their characters through these descriptions.

The custom of localizing each scene of a play is only about two hundred and fifty years old. At first there was no close relationship between locale and action. The

---

[1] Refer, in this connection, to Chapter 11.

place was named, but not described: "Scene — A Gallery in Lady Bountiful's House"; "Another part of the garden"; "Scene — An old-fashioned House." Succeeding generations, aided by some remarkable scene painting, inclined to greater and greater detail in the representation of locale. Kean, in 1856, was able to offer *A Winter's Tale,* "reproducing a classical era, and placing before the eyes of the spectators . . . the private and public life of the ancient Greeks, at a time when the arts flourished to a perfection, the scattered vestiges of which still delight and instruct the world." Kean was only slightly dismayed to discover that "chronological contradictions abound . . . inasmuch as reference is made to the Delphic oracle, Christian burial, an Emperor of Russia, and an Italian painter of the sixteenth century." All this for a play whose author paid almost no attention to localization!

By about the beginning of the present century, identification of locale had become something of a fetish. Not only were historical plays mounted with scrupulous regard for archeological accuracy, but an equal verisimilitude was accorded the most commonplace locale, and a certain delight was produced among spectators by the fidelity with which familiar places were represented on the stage: libraries with real books, kitchens with real faucets, middle-class living rooms with the "lived-in" look about them. At the present time such detailed identification of locale is still more nearly the rule than the exception.

But verisimilitude in the representation of the commonplace eventually loses its appeal, and the most inspired accuracy is not capable of avoiding dullness after indefinite repetition. In a long succession of typical hotel rooms, "lived-in" living rooms, and practical kitchens, each representation comes nearer to being no more interesting on the stage than it would be in actuality. Archeo-logically-inspired cathedrals and palaces, on the other hand, gradually emerge as piece-meal representations of things which are considerably more interesting in their entirety and hence progressively less interesting on the stage.

Thus, while the custom of identifying the locale survives, the mode of identification changes. The current tendency seems to be in the direction of according detailed representation mainly to those locales which are somewhat novel, quaint, or at least unfamiliar to the majority of the spectators, and to employ suggestion rather than depiction for those which are well known, giving a few significant details only and allowing the spectator to supply the remainder of the locale from his imagination. In designing *Mister Roberts,* Jo Mielziner, required to localize the action aboard a certain kind of naval vessel which none but a few of the audience could have known well, represented the ship's forecastle with great accuracy and a wealth of detail. But Thornton Wilder, in composing *Our Town* with a locale intended to be familiar to all, chose rather to show a bare stage and let the audience picture the place from the characters' descriptions.

Playwrights of the modern period consistently specify the locale, but emphasize different qualities of the place of action. Some attach importance to the place, some to the stage setting, and some to the atmosphere. Some emphasize all three equally. Bernard Shaw is one who describes the setting, and his descriptions are notoriously exacting, as every designer who has tried to vary them has probably discovered. Shaw's furniture and doorways are described and located in such a way that alteration of their relative positions is all but impossible. The habit of Ibsen is different, for he describes, not the stage setting as viewed by the spectator, but the place, from the point of view of one in the place. Many of the details of locale are such as might be present, but without regard primarily for the exigencies of stage action or design. A number of Ibsen's scene descriptions require doors and items of furniture such as were in the study where he did his writing, things at which he looked as he wrote. It is often quite difficult to crowd all the required things into one setting and still have a plausible looking stage room. Chekhov differs from both Shaw and Ibsen in that he describes locale mainly in terms of the atmosphere or feeling of a place, without much attention to physical details. Since atmosphere is more readily translatable into color and line than are the physical specifications for doors and furniture, Chekhov's plays have yielded many notable designs.

Audiences of today have been conditioned to accept depiction or suggestion with equal enthusiasm, providing only that the locale is clearly made known. Detailed verisimilitude is no longer the measure by which the design is judged. In this respect, the determining factor is the intent of the playwright, and since this allows a maximum of latitude in the mode of identification, this is, it would seem, as it should be.

17 | Aesthetic Factors in the Design

*The Appropriateness of the Design to the
Script · The Appropriateness of the Design
to the Director's Interpretation · The Need
for Individuality · Visual Unity*

We have already noted a number of resemblances between theatre art and other arts which appeal primarily to the eye. All exist in space. All involve some ordered arrangement of line, light and shade, or color. But theatre art is different from most other arts in that it really exists only for the brief space of time during which the play is being performed. Thus, design in the theatre is a temporal art in addition to being a visual one.

As we turn from the consideration of design in a general way to the examination of the individual design, another striking difference becomes apparent. This arises from the fact that the scene design is a work of interpretative art. It is interpretative because it helps bring into being something — the performance — for which a master plan — the script — already exists. Apart from the play for which it is created, the design has no independent existence of its own. Empty costumes and uninhabited settings do not comprise the design, for the design lives only during the performance of the play.

Because the design has no independent existence, its conception is necessarily influenced by a number of considerations, and by a greater variety of considerations than in

any comparable art. The fact that it is an interpretative creation means that its appropriateness to the play, or the general way in which the play is being presented, assumes importance. The fact that it is part of a temporal work means that freshness and originality of treatment are vital to its fullest effect. These two facts figure among the aesthetic considerations. In addition to these there are many practical considerations springing from the conditions of the performance, such as the amount and kind of action, the number of different scenes in the play, and the physical nature of the theatre. Thus, there are two kinds of influences: the aesthetic and the physical; and all of the factors conditioning the conception of the design fall into one or another of these two categories.

Appropriateness, individuality, and *unity* constitute the aesthetic requirements of the design. The interpretative aspect of the design, the fact that it is inseparably allied to the overall task of giving life to the play, gives appropriateness the place of first importance. Appropriateness is the first standard by which the quality of the design is judged. The best design gives visual substance to the same emotions and ideas as are revealed in the course of the performance. The worst design is that which in one or another of many possible ways is out of keeping with the nature and style of the performance. The design impairs the performance when it causes the spectator to expect a different kind of play from that which is unfolded.

The temporal nature of theatre art requires that each production of a play be distinguished from other productions of similar plays, and especially from other productions of the same play. The peculiar appeal of theatre art springs mainly from two things: one of these is its power to make a vivid impression at the time of performance; the other is its power to create impressions which persist beyond the performance. Both of these depend to a great degree upon the individuality of the visual presentation, for visual impressions are most vivid when most novel. Repetition of effect operates under a law of diminishing returns. What resembles earlier impressions, especially in drama, not only registers with lessened force, but invites the danger of confusion between one production and another of like substance. That which is best known may be, as Dr. Johnson avers, that which is best loved, but in the theatre it is also that which needs the freshest treatment if its significance is to continue to register regardless of age and familiarity.

The necessity for visual unity is common to all space arts. In the theatre the need is more acute because of the fact that the design is not seen all at once, so that if a singular impression is to be made upon the mind, the sense of completeness must be firmly established by the way in which the earlier parts of the design are related to the final ones. In the theatre, moreover, because of the sequential relationship of the various parts of the design, extraneous details of any kind are capable of misleading and confusing the spectator to a greater degree than is possible in the static arts.

THE APPROPRIATENESS OF THE DESIGN TO THE SCRIPT

The first essential is to know what kind of a design the author had in mind when he imagined the performance of his play. Did he, like Sophocles, visualize a performance predominantly formal in its manner of presentation, conventionalized in action and setting, and depending heavily upon the familiarity of the audience with the legend being enacted? Or did he, like Chekhov, imagine a performance designed to give an impression of actual daily life, replete with detail of daily living? Or perhaps, like Maeterlinck, he envisaged a performance in which the things seen and heard are charged with symbolic meanings that transcend immediate appearances. There is also the possibility that the author has conceived the play as wholly fantastic, intending its performance to solicit no conviction of life, but to appeal only to the eye and the ear, and only for the moment. This is what Dekker does in *Old Fortunatus.*

The preceding paragraph notes four intentionally different modes of presentation: formalized, actualistic, symbolic, and fantastic. This is not a classification, for there are many more than these four, and no two persons agree upon the number or the names that should be given them. The reason for this is that the dramatist in developing his script often strives for a mode of presentation different from those usually seen, or else combines several existing ones. Eugene O'Neill, for example, is a frequent experimenter in the unusual; many of his works definitely resist classification according to any system of labels. Yet, in his own terms, his intentions are clearly developed in each instance. Other dramatists combine modes, as Hauptmann combines the symbolic with the fantastic in *The Sunken Bell,* and the actualistic with the fantastic in *Hannele.*

In any case, the author's intention is usually determinable. The responsibility of the designer is to define it, not classify it. He is also responsible for seeing that the visual scheme does not violate the dramatist's conception. To clothe *Pelléas and Mélisande* in actualistic costumes or *The Cherry Orchard* in fantastic ones would make the performance artificial and confuse its appearance. No doubt there are many tragedies which, if designed in dainty tints and fragile lines, would seem absurd rather than profound, and there are farces which, in massive settings and deep-colored robes would be no longer amusing but only dull; and this would be so, not because of any appropriateness of particular colors to certain kinds of drama, but because the authors did not see them in that way.

The author's intention, then, if not classifiable, is nevertheless determinable. It is often much easier to determine what kind of design he intended by first ruling out those qualities which he clearly did not include in his visualization of the performance. By this process the predominant kind or combination of kinds of design is arrived at, and it is this predominant intention upon which the design is developed.

THE APPROPRIATENESS OF THE DESIGN TO THE DIRECTOR'S INTERPRETATION

The author's intention is the first factor influencing the conception of the design. But it is only the first factor, for between script and performance lie many steps, which condition the interpretation accorded the script. A particular interpretation is seldom at variance with the author's thought; it is mainly a matter of emphasis, a question of which of several values in the script shall receive the greatest emphasis in production. The design must be appropriate both to the script and to its performance. And so the director's interpretation be-

comes the second factor affecting the conception of the design.

For example, in Sophocles' *Antigone* the script as written clearly indicates Creon as the central figure of the tragedy. It is Creon to whom the tragedy, in the classical sense, occurs. Antigone suffers, but she suffers nothing that she had not already counted on, and she goes to her death substantially unchanged. Creon appears in every scene but one. Antigone appears only three times, and the actor who played her part in the original production would have had to double in at least two other roles according to the Greek limitation of three actors. But a producer [1] today, with a great actress on contract, might require that his director place the emphasis on Antigone, building up her role to star proportions and diminishing Creon to the position of a foil for her characterization. With the emphasis thus changed, the whole production, including the design, would have to be planned in such a way as to secure the new interpretation and bring it through with maximum impact.

Productions featuring symbolism allow the widest latitude of interpretation, since the symbols are usually only suggested by the script, leaving the way open for the director to develop the suggestions through a variety of different emphases. Georg Kaiser's *From Morn to Midnight*, an allegory containing a high proportion of symbolism, has had nearly as many forms in performance as there have been directors to stage it. The same is true of Elmer Rice's *Adding Machine* and of Leonid Andreyev's *The Life of Man*. In fact, each of these allows so much freedom to the director that the design problem is likely to become one not only of appropriateness but also of making

[1] In this country the "producer" is responsible for the financing and the general supervision of a dramatic production; in England the "producer" is the production's director.

the various scenes look as if they belonged to the same play.

There is also the possibility that an entirely original interpretation may be applied to the lines and situations of the script. For example, one might take *The Trojan Women* and treat it as a present-day sermon against war, and, working with that emphasis in mind, costume the captured noblewomen in modern dress and set the action against the ruins of a modern metropolis. It was an original interpretation of this kind which led Orson Welles to costume his *Julius Caesar* in modern dress and Fascist uniforms and to cast for Caesar's role an actor who bore a striking resemblance to Benito Mussolini. The result was as powerful a performance as has been seen of this play in our generation, although it made no pretense of giving us Shakespeare's intention. Such a radical interpretation poses the difficult question of whether the design can achieve appropriateness to both script and interpretation when the two diverge. Further treatment of these points will appear in a later section.

The possibilities of interpretation, whether according to the emphasis of elements inherent in the script or according to those original with the director, are, as these examples may indicate, practically limitless. The important thing is that the particular interpretation be clearly thought out before the process of visualizing the design begins. Otherwise a confused, or at best unimaginative, design is apt to result. Confusion between interpretation and design will leave the audience bewildered, with the net result that its reception of the work will be somewhat less enthusiastic than might have been hoped for.

THE NEED FOR INDIVIDUALITY

People do not go to the theatre to see the same things as are visible from their office windows or their kitchen doors. There may be at times a certain delight in their recognition of the familiar, but this delight is of extremely brief duration, and it turns quickly into boredom. Robert Edmond Jones describes the desirable effect of the design as one which causes the spectator to think: "It is evident that this play . . . is no common play. It is evident that these men and women . . . are no common mummers."[2] And not only must this impression be created at the rise of the curtain, but it must be re-created at intervals throughout the performance. For the design must live, not at first glimpse only, but also — perhaps more so — at the final curtain.

Freshness of design is commoner in short plays than in long ones, in new plays than in revivals, and in plays concerning strange people in faraway places than in those showing familiar people in everyday places.

Brilliance of design is easiest to achieve in bizarre productions. Leon Bakst and Alexandre Benois were favored in their designs for the Ballet Russe by the fact that many of the ballets involved barbarian legends, Russian folklore, or fairy tales, most of which were unfamiliar to Western audiences. The original designers of our own contemporary folk dramas, such as *I Remember Mama,* or *A Streetcar Named Desire,* are favored by the strangeness of Swedish San Francisco and the New Orleans Latin Quarter, both unfamiliar to the vast majority of the playgoing class. Both possess the appeal of the bizarre. Quaint customs, quaint dress, quaint places encourage the thought: "It is evident that this . . . is no common play."

The plays most likely to suffer undistinguished design are those presenting the most typical characters in the most familiar places. The middle-class family in its "lived-in" living room, back yard, or kitchen; the politician or businessman in his "hotel room in any large city of the present day"; the

[2] *Drawings for the Theatre* (Theatre Arts, 1925), p. 16.

stage-struck girls in their walk-up flat or run-down boardinghouse; the contesting lawyers in the typical courtroom; these lend themselves least to individuality of design. It is, therefore, only by the touch of genius that such a play is made visually enthralling. Jo Mielziner succeeded in his design for *Death of a Salesman* by stripping the design to its bare essentials and outlining the house with a skeleton framework which concentrated interest without copying many familiar details. Norman Bel Geddes achieved a comparable freshness in his design for *Dead End* by the opposite process of multiplying detail until that drab melodrama teemed with lifelike trivia. These are the two extremes of inspiration by which the familiar may be vitalized. Of these two, the elaboration of typical detail is the usual procedure; and it is usually the less successful for the reason that nothing less than genius can prevent satiety when the design is composed of sights with which the spectator has already been satiated before entering the theatre. Suggestion, of the sort employed by Mielziner, is more likely to succeed because very little is needed to bring to mind sights already well known. But it takes genius to select and suggest those details which will encourage recall. Between the two peaks of selection and suggestion lies a vast gulf of mediocrity, even more deadly familiar than the plays which it habitually enshrouds.

Individuality of design in a play which is not new, whether it be the amateur production of a commercial hit or the revival of a classic, is a different kind of achievement. It is an achievement in combining two different things: the avoidance of imitation of the work of previous genius, and the penetration to new depths of the author's intention.

The first of these, avoidance of imitation, sounds like a negative achievement, and it is, but it is a very important one, neverthe-less. Theatre art is fundamentally an imitative art in that it imitates or represents human life on the stage. But the theatre artist often imitates other theatre artists as readily as he imitates life; frequently he fails to distinguish the one from the other. The result is that a brilliant design such as Simonson's *Peer Gynt* or Jones's *Hamlet* tends to be reproduced endlessly by less original artists, with a considerable loss of effect on each repetition. Also, certain characteristics tend to reappear beyond all possibility of effect. Of these, John Gielgud's complaint about the "hopeful furs" with which certain Shakespearean productions are draped is typical. But the hopeful furs nevertheless reappear with monotonous regularity nearly every time these plays are done.

It may be that a design is sometimes unoriginal through ignorance of what has been done before, so that the design duplicates some earlier work, with consequent loss of effect upon the beholder who has seen both. But it is far more likely that the unoriginality is rooted in unconscious repetition of effective forms and colors seen in designs for the same or similar scripts. Various designs for *Hamlet, Lear,* and *Macbeth,* though widely separated by time and place of performance, often show marked resemblances. Different designs for Greek tragedies frequently look very much alike. In each instance one of the designs might, at one time, have had individuality. But with duplication the individuality diminishes into stereotypes no longer capable of stirring interest.

A design may avoid this kind of imitation and achieve originality and yet fail by reason of its shallowness. Scripts that merit production over a space of several generations or several centuries do so because they possess more than temporary appeal; probably they do so because they contain some truth which transcends fashions of thought, changes of taste, or regional mores. The sources of their appeal are exhausted by neither frequent performance nor frequent production. But each production must plumb these sources deeper and yield more meaning, and each design must throw more light upon the subject. Intensive study, thorough analysis, and original thought are all requisites to the design of a theatre classic, and from these things each designer must develop his own production project as a fresh revelation of certain basic truths.

The ultimate achievement in individuality is the design which retains its freshness throughout the two or three hours' performance. Many a design seems to have individuality when first seen, but loses this quality during the course of the performance through insufficient variation or from the fact that no visual refreshment is introduced after the initial display. The result is that the first impression of individuality is lost; the design which seemed original at first acquaintance becomes familiar and finally tiresome, and the spectator leaves the theatre without any feeling of having witnessed a fresh treatment of the play. The longer a play is, the more difficult it is to prevent this feeling. A shorter play allows a more definite visual impression because its duration is brief, and the impression which is created during its first moments does not have as much time to lose effect.

VISUAL UNITY

Last among the aesthetic factors is the need for a sound unity in the visual scheme. This unity is most simply defined as *oneness*. In the production which possesses it, all the various parts of the design seem to belong together and to contribute to some central plan or idea. A perfectly unified design is one in which nothing is absent which could add to the total effect and in which nothing is present which does not strengthen the whole.

In performance the unity of the design is not apparent at the outset, but comes into being gradually as the play progresses. It is not something which exists, final and complete, at any one time during the performance. Rather, it is a thing which evolves by degrees, developing and growing as the performance progresses. It consists of successive additions — additional changes of setting, costumes, and lights — which, bit by bit, add up to produce a sum which is complete when the performance is concluded.

This cumulative addition works in two ways, causing two effects, one of which is apparent during the performance, and the other of which emerges only upon conclusion of the performance. The first of these occurs when some effect is introduced which fits notably well into the visual scheme so far established. The opportunity for such an effect is apparent in the *Agamemnon* of Aeschylus, when the color of the crimson carpet upon which the King has walked into the palace to his death is echoed by the bloodstained costume of his murderous Queen, reappearing in the very doorway through which he has passed. Another occurs in Lope de Vega's *The Sheep Well*. In this play there is a scene in which the victorious Commander, with all the panoply of the conqueror, enters and is greeted by the peasantry. Several scenes later, during the celebration of a peasant wedding, he appears again, but this time in defeat, with few followers and no ceremony. The picture established in the first instance is reversed in the second instance, so that two opposite effects emerge as parts of a balanced whole. In each case the addition of the second effect not only falls with considerable impact upon the beholder but contributes to a sense of order and design which is aesthetically pleasing.

The other effect is that of completeness, achieved when the performance is over. The feeling here is one of having witnessed a complete presentation in which each thing seen was clearly a part of some larger and more significant effect. This feeling of completeness is in itself satisfying. It is satisfying not only upon conclusion of the performance but often for some time afterward as well. Unity is one quality in temporal art which continues to please in retrospect.

In any design, two aspects of unity are discernible. It is seldom that both are perfectly satisfying; nevertheless, both always exist in some degree. These two aspects are: unity of style and unity of form.

Unity of Style

Unity of style is a consequence of the artist's consistency in his treatment of the problems at hand. When present in a marked degree, it gives the spectator a definite sense of witnessing a work created all by the same hand.

This impression is most difficult to create in productions in which the script shifts from one style to another. *Liliom* is such a play. Part of the action is lifelike and realistic, but another part is unearthly and fantastic. The problem of accomplishing a design which can encompass such widely different patterns and make them seem to belong together has at some time or other plagued every designer who has attempted to mount this play. A similar problem occurs in *The Winter's Tale.* In this case the difficulties are caused by the wide differences between the somber first half and the lighter second half, and the problem becomes one of making two plays look like two parts of a whole.

Unity of style in costume is rare in a production which calls for characters to appear in the dress of widely dissimilar times or places. Fantasies which require characters in both ancient and modern dress are of this kind, as are plays which bridge such a wide space of time as to require scenes set in different historical periods. The tendency of

designers in such cases is to capitalize on the possibilities for variety of treatment, with the result that nothing remains to show that the characters all belong in the same production.

An episodic play, because of the fact that its composition often lacks unity, is likely to suffer imperfect unity of design. This danger increases in rough proportion to the number of scenes. Extreme variation in the duration or mood of the scenes multiplies the hazard. An instance of this is the Auden and Isherwood *Ascent of F.6,* which, although providing many opportunities for brilliant design, tends to resist singularity of visual treatment because of its jerky scene sequence and contrasting moods. Sidney Howard's *Paths of Glory* failed in its initial production because of the designer's inability to bring unity of appearance out of an episodic and quickly changing plot. The failure was rectified in subsequent productions by providing the play with a single unlocalized setting, and the play went on to become a signal success in the noncommercial theatre until certain shifts of public opinion rendered its plot unattractive. The use of a single unlocalized or only partly localized setting which rescued *Paths of Glory* is the customary method of establishing visual unity for a disjointed script, and is likely to be seen whenever this problem occurs. In recent years, some form of "unit" setting, recognizable by the use of set elements which serve with minor modifications throughout the scene sequence, has become the standard solution to the problems of the episodic play.

This solution has not always been as successful as could be wished, however, and designers are continually experimenting with means of varying the unit treatment of the episodic play. One difficulty is that while the unit setting does very well during the earlier scenes, it becomes less interesting as the play progresses and often becomes downright monotonous before the play has reached its end. The designer of such a play is hamstrung between the need for some visualization which will hold the play together and the equally urgent need for cumulative variety. Forty-odd scenes (as in *Antony and Cleopatra*) can exhaust the possibilities of even the most versatile setting. Hardly less trying are the demands of contemporary episodic works such as *Death of a Salesman* and the musical *Allegro*. In these last two the designer, Mielziner, by almost heroic ingenuity, employed varied levels, scrims, and projected lights, thus maintaining a visual variety throughout the play. Yet in spite of his resourcefulness, both productions declined in visual interest as they approached their final and most dramatic scenes.

Unity of Form

In this discussion we will use "unity of form" as a general term referring to only the physical substance of the design — the color, the texture, the bulk, and the line of the design. "Unity of form," then, will mean unity of substance and of the sense-impressions created by substances. This will help to establish unity of form as a quality of the design distinct from unity of style, which has been previously defined as consistency in the treatment of the general problems of the design sequence.

Unity of form becomes apparent during the performance as homogeneity of the substances of which the design is composed. The total effect desired is one of relationship of color to color, of texture to texture, and so on. A design possessing a pronounced unity of form is likely to give one a distinct feeling that the successive sensations belong together. One may often have seen the same colors or textures before without gaining any particular sense of their relationship. In a superior design the discovery of such relationships often comes as a very agreeable surprise.

Some years ago a production of Molière's *The Would-Be Gentleman* at Yale displayed just such a unity of form. The revelation in this instance was really brilliant. Many of the spectators, although they had witnessed performances of this script before, felt as if they were seeing it all for the first time. Of many unifying devices employed, the most conspicuous consisted of the use of the same fabric in all the costumes. Another was in the costume colors, all of which were achieved by means of combining two basic hues (one a sort of rust red and the other a kind of forest green) with each other and with white. At first the spectator was not aware of anything unusual, but as more and more characters appeared the similarity of color and textures became apparent, and after this came an infinite number of variations on the basic relationship, produced by modifications of the lighting. Castillo's costumes for the Judith Anderson *Medea* developed, in the first half of the performance, a comparable unity of texture, color, and line. The fabrics were of soft nubby stuff, accented with trimmings of metal. The colors were all related by a common quality of grayness, with the minor characters in the grayest tones and the principals in the more colorful ones. All the costumes were made with plenty of material, full-draped and arranged so as to yield long graceful lines with each movement. However, after about the middle of the performance no further changes were made, and as the lighting added nothing to the costumes, the design lost most of its power long before the play came to a close.

In the setting, unity of form is likely to appear as the continuation or repetition of some dominant impression of dimension, color, or line. Adolphe Appia's sketches for the Wagnerian *Ring* have long held the imagination of theatre folk largely because of their powerful and singular appearance of great depth and weight. The designs for each opera are related primarily by this quality of simple massiveness. Lee Simonson employed a similar unity to relate the sequence of scenes which he designed for the Guild *Peer Gynt*. A few years later, for *Marco Millions,* Simonson unified the many scenes of that work by another means, using a linear triple-frame structure to enclose all locales but one. This one, which occurred at the beginning of the performance, was an exterior consisting of a tree painted flatly on a drop, and it bore no strong relationship to the succeeding scenes. Its effect at the outset led one to expect a somewhat different unity than emerged as the sequence developed. But fortunately, being first, it was soon forgotten as the performance progressed. An outstanding unity of form was achieved by Jones in his design for the Barrymore *Hamlet,* by backing up the acting area with a Romanesque arch of prodigious size and bulk. This dominant form held the scene sequence firmly together throughout the play, while variations of drapery, gate grilles, and directional light kept the design alive in spite of a performance which lasted four hours.

Unity of form is rare in productions requiring detailed localization of action among any combination of architectural, terrestial, or marine settings. One reason for this is that these various locales generally call for differing textures and colors as well as strikingly different treatments of line and mass, so that it is extremely difficult to harmonize the irregular lines and textures of natural forms with the more regular ones of man-made creations, especially architectural interiors. Another reason doubtless lies in the inability of most designers to deal equally well with all kinds of locales. The average designer does best with architectural settings, noticeably less well with natural settings, and rather poorly with marine settings. Lacking the mastery over natural forms which he has over man-made ones, his conception of the former is generally inferior, and the result is that the two go ill together. Many a designer, moreover, seems able to represent only a few favorite species of trees or rocks, so that when he attempts to unify the style of a production which is partly natural and partly architectural, the architectural locales are necessarily distorted in order to harmonize with his limitations in regard to the others, and this distortion often mars the unity of the total effect.

18 | Physical Factors in the Design

1: Setting and Lighting

The Kinds of Stage Action • The Place of Performance • The Technical Demands of the Script

Up to now our main concern has been with the aesthetics of the design — with those qualities of appropriateness, individuality, and unity which determine its artistic value. This is the theoretical side of the art. On the other side are the practical considerations which affect the physical nature of the design: its dimensions, its weight, and its efficiency in operation. At this point the design is best understood if its main elements of setting and costume are considered, for the time being, apart from each other. This is logical, for the physical nature of the setting is conditioned more by the requirements of stage action and of stage space and by the number of scenes required, while that of the costume group is likely to be conditioned by certain requirements as to historical period, possible effects in the grouping of the costumes, and the bodily action necessary to each role.

By "setting" we mean the acting area of whatever shape and location, with the scenery and properties, however related to it. By "lighting" we mean the illumination which gives to the setting its characteristic highlight and shadow and its dominant hues. The stage setting possesses no intrinsic form.

It exists for only a few hours at a time when lighted in a certain way and inhabited by actors. At the end of that time, when the actors are gone home and the lights are turned off, it is often meaningless and even unrecognizable as a setting. In this respect it is unlike a painting or a piece of sculpture, which exists at all times with no fundamental change. It is more like a piece of music which has been played, and which, when the final note has died away, ceases to exist except in the memory of the listener. For this reason scenery, lighting, and the actions of the performers must be considered together; separately no one of them is complete.

THE KINDS OF STAGE ACTION

The settings serve primarily to accommodate and enhance the activities of the performers, so that the kind of setting is closely related to the kind of activity which takes place within it. The total amount of activity is one part of this, the tempo of activity is another, and the plan or pattern of action is another. Let us consider the plan of action first.

243

Some directors call this plan the action plot. It is the scheme of activity, a plan of who goes where and when, where they pause, when they sit or stand, and so on. While there are a great many varieties of action plots — probably at least as many as there are stage directors — all the various kinds that there are can be identified as one or the other of two main species: *pictorial* or *dimensional*. Other names for this dichotomy are: pictorial or sculptural; and representational or presentational.[1] The pictorial is what we see when the performers maintain an imaginary or actual separation between themselves and the audience and pretend to be unaware of the presence of spectators. The dimensional is what we see when the performers are surrounded either entirely or partly by spectators. The actors move toward and among the audience, and there is a strong inclination to recognize the presence of the audience and even address it directly. The script usually dictates clearly and intrinsically which kind of action plot the director and actors are to follow. The two species of action plots are seldom employed within one production except for especially novel effects such as occur in *Our Town,* where the Stage Manager addresses the audience directly while the other performers ignore its presence.

In pictorial staging the action is thought of as occurring within some definite limits of space — such as a room, a forest clearing, or a ship's deck — and is usually contained within the proscenium if the performance takes place indoors. The visual qualities of the action thus contained are established in terms of the relationship of the characters one to another or to some element of the setting such as a doorway, a piece of furniture or a flight of steps. This pictorial staging is of course most commonly seen in contemporary "slice-of-life" or "realistic" drama. The fundamental illusion for the spectator is that of watching in action characters who are unaware of being watched. This illusion is essential to much of the finest of modern drama, a fact which makes this kind of staging indispensable. The effect of pictorial action upon the dimensions of the setting is easily perceived, for in order for the action to be seen from all points in the theatre the acting area is necessarily rather wide and comparatively shallow.

The dimensional action plot is based primarily upon the relationship of the performers to the audience rather than to one another and is usually mandatory with scripts in which asides and soliloquies make ease of contact between actor and audience desirable. With this kind of action the acting area is apt to be much less clearly defined and the division, if any, between spectator and performer naturally vague. One would expect that the shape of the acting area and the form of the setting would be radically different from that preferred in pictorial staging, and this is exactly the case. The acting area is likely to be as deep as it is wide, or even deeper, and instead of being framed by the proscenium, to project forward among the spectators.

The amount of activity which the setting must accommodate is the next most influential factor affecting the physical nature of the setting — the amount of activity as gauged by the number of performers, and the complexity of the actions which have to be followed and understood by the spectator. A work such as *The Heiress,* in which the acting area is occupied by no more than three or four characters at any one time, makes few demands of the setting. But *Macbeth,* with its large cast, its banqueting, its witchcraft, and its battles, taxes the facilities of almost any setting which can be imagined. A play like *Volpone,* or like *The Cherry Orchard,* in which distinct actions occur almost simultaneously in different parts of the stage, requires great care to provide the appropriate effect of juxtaposition without the risk of confusion. In such a case, division by height,

[1] In this connection, see Chapter 12.

PLATE 23. **Two Treatments of Brecht.** Groupings from *The Caucasian Chalk Circle* (above) and from *The Threepenny Opera.* (Above, Carnegie Institute of Technology: director, Lawrence Carra; designer, Donald Beaman. Below, Cornell University: director, Richard Shank; designer, Anne Gibson; costumes, Kathy Kresh.

PLATE 24. **Recent Productions of Gilbert and Sullivan.** Group scenes from *H. M. S. Pinafore* (above) and *The Pirates of Penzance*. (Above, *University of Illinois:* director, Clara Behringer; designer, Sanford Syse. Below, *University of Denver:* director, Edwin Levy; designer, Terry Rodefer.)

PICTORIAL AND SCULPTURAL ACTION

Figure 27. In pictorial staging, the stage functions like a framed picture; in dimensional staging, like a pedestaled sculpture.

or by some sort of partitioning, is likely. More recent use of this effect in *Death of a Salesman* resulted in a setting with five different levels and nine exits. As a rule the greater the total amount of activity, the more complex the action plot. This springs from the necessity of preventing various characters or lines of action from becoming confused one with another.

Closely related to the amount of activity is the tempo of movement. The faster the tempo the more complicated the problem becomes. For example, *The Cherry Orchard* and *Volpone* are alike in that both require about the same number of characters and the same kind of bipolar action to be perceived without confusion. But the tempo of *Volpone* is at times much faster than any in *The Cherry Orchard*, with the result that the setting is necessarily more fluid, with wider entrances, more ample offstage space, and provision generally for greater freedom of movement.

We may now sum up the main kinds of activity and their effect on the physical nature of the setting. (1) Pictorial action tends to produce an acting area contained within the limits of the stage, separated from the audience, and generally much wider than deep, while dimensional action tends to produce an acting area of opposite shape, at least as deep as wide, and generally projecting into the space occupied by the audience. (2) The greater the amount of activity during the performance the more varied the acting area is likely to be as to height and as to provision for entrances and exits. (3) The faster the tempo of the stage action the larger the entrances and the greater the offstage space required for ease of movement.

THE PLACE OF PERFORMANCE
The Auditorium

Whether the play is performed in a building constructed for theatrical use or on a grassy slope in a park, the place of performance conditions the design of the production by the fact of its being less adaptable than the performance which it accommodates. To a very considerable degree the relationship between performers and spectators is fixed by the plan of the theatre and is usually capable of but very slight variation. No one place of performance is likely to be equally effective for all kinds of stage action. The theatre which best accommodates pictorial staging is generally much less useful for action conceived dimensionally, and the reverse is also true — for with the former, the spectators tend to prefer seats along the center line of the auditorium and facing the stage, while with the latter, proximity to the acting area regardless of frontality takes precedence over all other considerations.

A wide auditorium favors dimensional staging, especially when the actor can be brought forward of the proscenium — as is possible where there is an apron or when the orchestra pit can be platformed over to provide a projecting acting area. But the same width of the sight line, when pictorial action is mandatory, makes necessary a rather shallow setting, and usually a rather wide one if the action is to be fully visible from all seats.

Most auditorium floors slope more or less, rising in height as the distance from the acting area increases. The steepness of this slope has a definite effect on the appearance of the stage and on the kind of elements which may be employed in the design. As a rule, the more nearly flat the seating area the more effective are those elements of setting which vary the height of the acting area. Steps, for example, and platforms and ramps, are most striking when the spectator looks up at them, and the elevation which the actor gains as he ascends from the stage floor to higher planes enhances the dramatic value of his action. The converse is true when the auditorium floor slopes steeply away from the stage, for the spectator then looks down on the stage and is thus less conscious of variations in the height of the acting area; although the actor may ascend four or five feet above the stage floor, the spectator may still be looking down on him so that the effect of the higher position is lessened. The result of this is that as the slope of the auditorium floor increases, the effectiveness of levels and steps is reduced. And of course, to the spectator in the balcony or upper gallery height variations contribute little or nothing to the appearance of the design.

In theatres having balconies, the height and steepness of the balcony has a considerable effect upon the appearance of the design from the upper seating areas. If the balcony is a high one, the height of the proscenium opening and the height of the scenery within it ought to be increased in order that all may see. If the balcony projects very far forward, or if it slopes rather gently, the area forward of the proscenium is likely to be invisible to many spectators. Most modern designers seem to ignore the fact of the existence of the balcony, with the result that while their settings look good from the main floor seats in almost every position, considerable areas of the stage are obscured to the balcony patron. In the balcony scene of *Romeo and Juliet*, Juliet, as often as not, is visible only from the waist down to those who sit in the upper balconies. In *Death of a Salesman* a slight apron which was built out over the orchestra pit made for most effective action as seen from the main floor of the theatre, but was invisible to the upper balcony in many theatres which had been constructed solely for visibility of the stage area behind the proscenium line. All this reduces the value of the design, for the best design is that which appears most nearly the same to all spectators.

Effects of weight, such as are gained by the use of deep thicknesses on arches or pylons, are strongest when closest to the spectator. As the distance between spectator and stage increases, the illusion of weight achievable by actual dimension is greatly decreased. At a distance of fifty feet or more it is usually impossible to discriminate between the appearance of weight caused by the play of light and shade and that caused by clever painting. Robert Edmond Jones took advantage of this fact in his design of *Mourning Becomes Electra* by employing flat pieces painted to represent fluted columns of the Mannon house; and it was quite impossible for some minutes after the curtain went up for one to discover whether the columns were flat or really as round and heavy as they seemed to be.

Nearly as important to the design as the shape of the auditorium is its size. The larger the auditorium, the bolder the design must be if it is to register in the eye of the spectator seated far from the acting area. This means stronger colors, sharper focus of attention, and less subtlety of detail. The larger the theatre, the more distinct must be the differences in costuming between one character and another, for otherwise confusion is invited. A common fault of the design of road shows duplicating New York successes is that, having been designed for the comparatively small theatres of Broadway, they lose power when placed in the larger theatres which are sometimes found outside New York. An opposite error of crudeness and coarse detail is often made by designers who, having been used to designing for large theatres, attempt to repeat their successes in smaller theatres.

There is one more way in which the architecture of the auditorium affects the appearance of the design, and this is in the illumination of the acting area. The possibilities of lighting the stage from the front are conditioned to a great extent by the opportunities afforded for the hanging of spotlights in the auditorium and by the angles and lengths of throw made necessary by the peculiarities of its plan and ornamentation. The incandescent spotlight is a comparatively recent development. Many of the older theatres make no provision for its use except from the projection booth. Often the construction of the auditorium ceiling is such that good positions for spotlights are hard to find. Rarely does the auditorium contain enough outlets of sufficient amperage to accommodate the great number of spotlights which must be placed in the auditorium if forestage and apron are to be adequately illuminated. The likely result is that either the downstage areas are dimly lighted or else that the angles of illumination are such that definite highlights and shadows are difficult to achieve.

In the commercial theatre the difficulty is partly overcome by fastening spotlights to the forward edge of the balcony or by using the side boxes as spotlight booths. But in an auditorium which has no balcony or boxes — as do few theatres built since 1930 — the designer is forced to forego many effects of dimension which he would have employed had proper illumination been possible.

In the more recently built noncommercial theatres provision for spotlighting is made by means of ports in the ceiling of the auditorium, and somewhat less often, by openings in the side walls. However, neither sufficiently varied angles of illumination nor sufficiently numerous outlets are usually provided. It remains, therefore, for the designer to accommodate his mounting of the production to the facilities available to him. The measure of his success will be his ability to achieve an effective design regardless of theatre or equipment.

The Proscenium Stage

Turning from the auditorium to the stage, we find that only one aspect of the backstage directly affects the appearance of the design. All other aspects relate principally to the mechanics of assembling and operating the production.

The single feature of importance, visually speaking, is the depth of the space between the proscenium and the back wall of the stage. The greater this depth in relation to the width of the proscenium opening, the more impressive and the more varied are the illusions of space and distance which can be placed before the spectator. As the stage becomes shallower, the possible illusions of spaciousness become fewer in number and necessarily simpler. On the shallowest stages the proximity of the performers to the deeper portions of the setting allows the use of almost no module or measure of scale other than the actor's own figure.

The easiest stages to design for are those in which the depth is equal to or greater than the width of the proscenium opening. Few plays require the actor to work at any great distance away from the audience or very far upstage of the curtain line. Fifteen or twenty feet is the likely maximum; in most plays the average depth of the action is much less than that. Thus, if the proscenium is, for example, thirty-five feet across — a proportionable width for an auditorium seating less than a thousand persons — and the stage is of equal depth, sufficient space remains between the deepest action and the back wall to allow a fair number of illusive devices of linear and aerial perspective without immediate comparison with the dimensions of the actor and without the danger that his shadow, falling upon scenic elements in the upstage area, will reveal false textures or distances.

The other features of the backstage — the amount of space at the sides of the acting area, the height of the fly loft, the number and position of floor traps, the position and capacity of switchboard and pinrail — bear more closely on the mechanics of setting up and changing scenery, on the traffic plan of backstage movement, and on the ease or difficulty with which the production is operated than upon the appearance of the design from the audience. For visual effectiveness

SAME SETTING AS SEEN FROM ORCHESTRA
AND FROM BALCONY SEATS

Figure 28. Designers often fail to remember that no two spectators see exactly the same setting.

is a matter of originality of design, of appropriateness to the play, of pleasing proportions, and of colors soothing or striking as the scene requires. It springs from thorough understanding of the script and careful calculation of visual impact. The roomiest stage and the finest stage equipment cannot, by themselves, bring a good design into being; they can only make it easier of achievement.

In general, the design of a production, in so far as it is related to the stage space and equipment, is largely a matter of making the best of what is at hand, capitalizing on the advantages provided and circumventing whatever obstacles are caused by the peculiarities of the stage plan and machinery. No stage is perfect for all purposes. And since the production is a temporal creation of much greater adaptability than the building which houses it, the practical side of the designer's problem is principally one of making his setting fit, for better or worse, into a given stage. For the time being, it will suffice to note the commonest limitations existing among theatres already built.[2]

Inadequate Wing Space. In theatres in which the space at the sides of the acting area is less than half the width of the proscenium opening, no great reliance may be placed upon the use of large rolling units as a means of swift changing of setting. Some other means must be found, either of dividing the rolling units into smaller pieces for clearing out of sight, or of folding flat pieces so as to stack them in the limited cubic space provided. This often means that the weight and complexity of the setting must be reduced in order to get it on and off stage quickly, or some other means must be found for clearing the setting out of the acting area. Inexperienced designers habitually overload the side stage regardless of the limitations

[2] This unit, which focuses on limitations which especially affect the designer, should be read in connection with Chapter 14.

present, with the result that the changes are cumbersome and often much slower than they ought to be.

Inadequate Loft Space. In theatres in which the height of the loft over the stage is less than twice the height of the proscenium opening, no great amount of scenery can be cleared by lifting it out of sight. There are, it is true, many ingenious devices for clearing pieces into a limited loft, but every such device reduces the total number of pieces which can be cleared by such means. With a low loft, reliance must be placed upon some other means of changing scenery, or else the amount of scenery must be reduced in the interest of efficient handling.

Inadequate Loft Capacity. It often happens that a loft, although of sufficient height, lacks the capacity to support much weight. This means that the weight of each piece lifed out of sight must be carefully computed so that the total of such pieces does not add up to such weight as to invite the danger of the grid collapsing. The result of inadequate capacity, therefore, is substantially the same as that of inadequate height: limits are placed upon the quantity of scenery removed by this means, so that either some other means of clearing must be devised or the total amount of scenery must be reduced.

Poorly Located Controls. The controls for the lights, the curtain, the rigging, the signal system, and whatever else is provided as part of the stage equipment, are usually built into the theatre and not capable of change in position for the benefit of a single production. It is therefore necessary to simplify the design to what can be controlled and operated efficiently. For example, if the switchboard is so placed that the operator is unable to see the acting area, the number of light cues and subtlety of each are necessarily less than when the operator can see what he is doing and adjust his controls accordingly. If the controls for the lights are on one side of the stage and those for the curtain and rigging on the opposite side, the designer would not ordinarily plan for a succession of closely co-ordinated light-and-curtain cues. As a rule, therefore, the more decentralized the various controls and the lesser the view of the stage from each, the simpler must be the cueing dependent upon their intercommunication.

The Open Theatre

It is only within the last decade that the open theatre has been housed in buildings planned to accommodate it, so the principles governing the design of productions for the open stage are just beginning to take shape. It is already apparent, however, that while many principles of design are the same for both open and proscenium theatres, certain others useful in the proscenium theatre cannot be applied to problems arising in the open theatre; also, several new principles are applicable only to design for the open stage.

The general principles governing appropriateness, individuality, and unity are applicable regardless of the form of the stage or the shape of the auditorium. Principles governing temporal compositions are also applicable to both kinds of theatres. In the uses of color and light the principles are the same although their applications differ from one theatre to another. In the matter of composition, however, especially in the uses of line and pattern to control attention, the open theatre is a new and different world.

In designing for the open theatre, the most significant factor is the wide and varying view of the stage from the audience. Not only do the spectators see the action from many different points of view, but they also see it from opposite directions: what is on the left of one spectator is often on the right of another; what moves toward one spectator is at the same time moving away from another. On the open stage, the composition that catches the eye and controls attention is not so much pictorial as dynamic, for it exists mainly in the movements of the performers rather than in their relationships to the background. Only occasionally, in some quieter moments, does it concern the way the characters are grouped. The term "sculptural" is sometimes used to distinguish this kind of composition from the more familiar pictorial composition of the proscenium theatre, but the term is misleading because it suggests that grouping is static when in fact it is full of purposeful movement. In any case, composition becomes one of the arts of the director rather than of the designer, while the design of the production becomes more a matter of visual style, ornamentation, and accentuation.

It is often difficult for a designer brought up in the pictorial tradition of the proscenium theatre not to attempt to apply pictorial principles to an open-stage production. But in a theatre built specifically for open staging the attempt at pictorialization is almost always unsuccessful. Most of the audience feel forced to view the setting from an awkward position. They seem to resent attempts to provide any indication of locale beyond the barest suggestions, although the reasons for this resentment are different from person to person and often difficult to articulate. When the Lincoln Center Repertory Company produced *The Caucasian Chalk Circle*, a conscientious attempt was made to picture the various places along Grusche's journey and to develop the spectacular possibilities of the scene where Grusche crosses the mountain bridge. But the critics complained that the production was spoiled by being treated too realistically, that the design lacked imagination, and that it would have been better if there had been more suggestion and less depiction of locale.

Why should a play on an open stage be more interesting when the stage is sparsely furnished and more tedious when the stage is filled with atmospheric detail? No one has yet attempted to answer this question. It is evident, however, that the most successful designs in the open theatre are not developed from compositional principles carried over from proscenium staging. Fully developed open theatres have been in continual operation for over a decade, and several hundred productions have now been completed, clothed in designs by the finest theatre artists of our time. Many of the productions have been acclaimed for brilliance of style, richness of detail, and ingenuity of machinery and scene changes. By reviewing the salient features of the designs which are generally agreed to have been outstanding, we should be able to devise some principles which can in the future be applied with some certainty to the open stage.

In open theatres the seating slopes are usually rather steep, so that the average spectator looks down on a good deal of the stage floor. The design of the floor cloth thus becomes one of the most reliable means of identifying the play through distinctive colors, patterns, and textures. Most open theatres have a different floor for every production. Some use several floors for various scenes in a single play. In the Lincoln Center *Tartuffe* the floor was made up of tiles, each about two feet square, in two shades of gray-green. The tiles were laid diagonally and drew the eye toward various important actions by seeming to converge at the point toward which attention had already been attracted by some other means. In the Stratford, Ontario, *King Lear* the acting area was covered with a false floor of rough, seemingly hand-hewn boards which suited the barbaric costumes and properties admirably. In the Tyrone Guthrie Theatre's *As You Like It* the acting area appeared to have sprouted grass and small flowers.

Accentuation through lighting is not peculiar to the open stage but it is more effective there if only because the means of accentuation are fewer. A great many more spotlights are needed in the open theatre than in the proscenium theatre because footlights, borderlights, and floodlights — all means for *general* illumination — are useless. Accentuation is usually accomplished by marking the area where the principals will stand during some important scene, then raising the level of light in that area when that scene approaches. Isolation spotting in the usual sense is seldom used because the isolation effect depends mainly upon lighting a character so that he stands out in strong contrast to the background; it is seldom possible to achieve a dark enough background on an open stage. Occasionally, however, using the façade as a traditional background provides a memorable isolation effect. In the Stratford, Ontario, *Measure for Measure*, Angelo, sitting on the extreme forward corner of the stage balcony, was spotted for his soliloquy while all the rest of the theatre remained dark. The effect was highly dramatic. Angelo seemed suspended between heaven and earth and yet so close one felt one could almost have touched him.

Many designers who work with open stages prefer white light and hence use no gelatines for tinting. They reason that without extensive background scenery there is no need for tinting or blending; that there are no effects of night or sunset or firelight which are not attainable on an open stage just as well through dimming light as through tinting it; that the consistent use of white light makes it easier to go from one light plot to another as the plays change in repertory; and finally, that the color and detail in costumes and properties can be developed better if they do not have to be subjected to colored light.

Plotting lights for the open stage is quite different from plotting for the proscenium stage. Because the actors are seen from three or four sides of the stage, they must be lighted from that many directions if they are to be equally visible to all spectators. Thus a rather complex and dimensional light plot replaces the familiar proscenium light plot based on two-dimensional cross-spotlighting.

It is in costuming that designers for the open stage have made their greatest contribution. Since scenery is sparse, groupings are three-dimensional, and characters are constantly in motion, designers have found it desirable, if not mandatory, to use extravagant quantities of material to give the robes of regal characters voluminous folds and trains of prodigious length and spread and to introduce white or other extremely bright hues generally avoided on the proscenium stage. Ornament of every kind is elaborated to make a king taller, a warrior more fearsome, or a maid more dainty. Fine costume details such as embroidery, braid, ruffles, and piping — which might escape notice on a proscenium stage — are easily seen and appreciated. Shadows are airbrushed to deepen the folds of a robe, highlights are added to give metal ornaments sheen, a patterned surface is outlined to strengthen weight and boldness. The authenticity and artistry of detail in accessories — purses, belts, badges, prayer beads, parasols, daggers, swords, and chains of office — are heightened to near-perfection.

The same reasons which lead costume designers to accentuate ornament and pattern for the open stage also lead the set designer to enrich the stage properties. On the open stage properties show up to especial advantage: they are seen at extremely close range and are not in competition with elaborate scenery. Handled with full flair and freedom, they join with costumes in bringing about that breath-taking richness which is one of the chief delights of the open stage. Take food, for example. At Stratford, Ontario, the pastry shop scene in *Cyrano de Bergerac* was given not only the pastries and roasts specifically called for by the script but also trays heaped high with exquisite delicacies of every imaginable kind. Similarly, the contraband food which Roxanne smuggles to the starving cadets: there were giant hampers of clove-studded hams, whole dressed salmon, huge crisp loaves, round cheeses, shining apples, oranges, bananas, pineapples, and at least one green bottle of Burgundy for each cadet.

Furniture on the open stage can and should be finer and more detailed in its woodworking and richer in its upholstery than furniture for the proscenium stage. Weapons can be inlaid with gold, damascened, engraved, and finished with handsome tassels, martingales, baldricks, and scabbards. Croziers, banners, ewers, and all the thousand items carried on should not be skimped. On the open stage banners can be bigger and halberds longer than on more conventional stages where overhead hangings limit their heights.

The façade which backs the acting area of a thrust stage usually needs some decorative treatment to forestall visual monotony and also to differentiate successive plays. Sometimes the decoration takes the form of constructions such as the ship superstructure used for the *S. S. Glencairn* at the Tyrone Guthrie Theatre or the gallery-and-gate structure used in *The Alchemist* at Lincoln Center. At other times decorative pieces are added to the façade. For *The Country Wife* at the Canadian Stratford, the permanent façade was covered with another of identical shape but different period style. This false front furthermore carried fittings to which could be fastened doors, windows, shop fronts, and various other accessories to liven the action. For both *As You Like It* and *The Miser* at the Tyrone Guthrie, elaborate background pieces helped to establish the individual style of the production. For *As You Like It*, grass mats, tree trunks with

Spanish moss, and a little foot bridge over the "ditch" gave the stage a distinctly "deep South" feeling. For *The Miser,* a tent-like backing piece with a scattering of trunks, musical instruments, and old costumes made the stage seem like the quarters of some itinerant theatrical troupe. On the other hand, in both *As You Like It* and *The Miser,* the decoration of the background inclined more toward localization than an open stage can sustain, with the result that both plays grew somewhat tiresome visually before the final scenes were reached.

Novelties, especially those which move, are particularly effective in the open theatre. Thus we see all kinds of vehicles. Sometimes they are specified by the script, such as the coach in *Cyrano de Bergerac,* the taxi in *Pygmalion,* or the touring car in *Man and Superman,* but more often they are added to vary the action or heighten some particular effect. Tyrone Guthrie had a cannon rolled on for the siege of Harfleur in *Henry V,* to fill the stage with smoke and provide an elevation from which the king could harangue his soldiers. In *The Taming of the Shrew* at Stratford in 1962, the players made their first entrance and their final exit pulling a cart upon which their costumes and properties were heaped. In the Minnesota *Volpone,* the mountebanks brought in a wagon hung about with their quack drugs and remedies; it provided a ladder which Volpone used to climb to the level of Celia's balcony and from which, when surprised by her husband, he fell into the arms of his henchmen below. Vehicles are never easy to manage on an open stage. Usually they have to be hauled up steep ramps and manhandled through narrow passageways and around sharp bends. But they always delight the spectators.

At the Stratford, Ontario, theatre there seem to be no prohibitions against the use of open flame on the stage; designers frequently gain novel effects with real torches, candles, candelabra, and fires. Fire possesses

a powerful dramatic appeal and it is intensified on the open stage. Unfortunately, the ordinances of most cities prohibit the use of open flame in theatres. However, except for flaming torches, all fire effects can be simulated, and it is undoubtedly safer to handle them in this way.

Scene changes on the open stage consist mainly of the changing of properties, lighting, and floor covering, but they are often complex and require planning of an entirely different kind than that used for the proscenium stage. The difference springs from the fact that the open stage is approached from four directions instead of only two. This means that the change must be planned so that pieces are removed outward away from the acting area while those brought in converge on the stage from different directions. Because of this diverging and converging movement, changes can always be accomplished speedily, but the possibility of error is increased because at no time can the stage manager see all the workers or all the pieces being moved.

In most open theatres the properties are carried on and off by actors rather than stagehands. Sometimes the change is accomplished by the same liveried actor-servants who wait on the principals in the play — Sampson and Gregory, for example, in *Romeo and Juliet,* and the housemaids in *The Sea Gull.* In *S.S. Glencairn* at the Tyrone Guthrie, the sailors moved the various properties into position by means of the booms which were part of the set.

When all the properties have to be carried on and off by performers, the designer is obliged to give more thought to ease of handling. Actors are not chosen for strength or manual dexterity and their costumes often must be guarded against soiling or rough use. Furniture to be moved by actors must therefore be light in weight — much lighter than if stagehands were to move it. Handholds must be designed for each piece so that it can be comfortably carried and easily balanced. Furthermore, the clearances of vomitories and entranceways must be considered, whether the piece has to be carried past other pieces moving in the opposite direction, and whether it has to be maneuvered around sharp corners. If some pieces are going to be rolled on and off, ramps must be planned to cover the steps.

One of the most interesting phenomena about the open theatre is the ease with which audiences accept the mimetic representation of things which in the proscenium theatre have to be fully depicted. In the first scene of *The Tempest* at Stratford, Ontario, the storm at sea was vividly rendered by four green silk banners which were waved and rippled over the acting area while lightning flashed and thunder rolled and frantic sailors ran this way and that. The effect of engulfing waves was remarkable and quite believable.

The Theatre Outdoors

The outdoor theatre in fine weather affords an agreeable environment for relaxation and the enjoyment of the play. The site of the theatre has usually been chosen for its scenic value, so that the spectator waiting for the play to begin looks out over green hills or the lights of a city or into a glade of some beauty. The park atmosphere is carefully nurtured. Elaborate landscaping and abundant greenery usually improve on the natural advantages of the site.

The principal problem of design for the outdoor theatre is providing settings which will harmonize with the site and seem well placed against the foliage and the open sky. Certain kinds of settings commonly seen in indoor theatres tend to seem out of place here. In particular, successful settings of interiors with any feeling of confinement are difficult to achieve. Detailed three-wall interiors which depend for their effect upon

the proscenium frame and the act curtain present special problems of adaptation which can be met only by developing some kind of architectural treatment of side areas to set them off against the natural elements of the setting provided by the site itself. Other kinds of settings, which the restrictions of the indoor performance severely limit, are often extremely effective in the outdoor situation. First of these is, of course, the natural exterior requiring trees and rocks. The absence of the problem of masking top and sides makes this one of the easiest of locales to set. Next are architectural exteriors of substantial size and weight. Perhaps they are so successful outdoors because the spectator is accustomed to seeing architecture enhanced by foliage. Lastly there are the marine and ship settings. One would think that foliage in juxtaposition with marine or nautical elements would seem absurd, but it does not. Possibly this is because one associates such things with the open sky which, in the outdoor theatre, is always present.

The whole design of the outdoor production is greatly assisted by the fact that outdoor theatres usually have very good sight lines and but one seating slope. The absence of the balcony frees the designer from the necessity of having to contrive a setting which will look equally well to both the spectators looking up at it from the main floor and those looking down on it from the balcony above. Thus the audience as a whole is likely to see more nearly the same design no matter what arrangement of elements is placed on the stage before it.

Auditoriums of outdoor theatres generally average several times the capacity of the larger indoor theatres. A seating capacity of 10,000 is not at all unusual. This great size inhibits the employment of much fine detail but allows great freedom in the use of bold combinations of color, strong and highly varied arrangements of set elements, and units of great apparent weight and massive proportions. The most effective designs, therefore, are likely to be much larger, brighter, and heavier than would be possible on an indoor stage.

Because of the great distance from which the design is seen, brightness of illumination is more important than direction or color. Subtleties of shading or of coloring of light are easily lost on the average outdoor spectator and so are seldom employed. Nor are they needed. References to time of day, whether noon or midnight, are easy to accept in an outdoor performance, even when the acting area is lighted the same for both.

Naturally, in an outdoor theatre there is always the hazard of the weather. Scenery must be built to withstand air pressure and provisions must be made for anchoring settings which would otherwise disintegrate in a thirty-mile wind. Protection must be provided for furniture and properties against evening dews, dampness, and flash showers. And painted scenery must be made proof against drenching rains.

The paucity of floor space which characterizes most indoor theatres is seldom encountered in open air theatres where stage depth and side stage space is often equal to several times the proscenium width. Of course there is no loft, and no way of hoisting scenery. But the amount of floor space available for rolling units more than makes up for the lack of a loft.

THE TECHNICAL DEMANDS OF THE SCRIPT

In many productions the design is conditioned by certain basic requirements of a technical nature which, having been conceived as part of the whole, cannot be omitted or slighted without impoverishing the play. The imagination of a playwright will sometimes cause him to write into the play effects, often very good ones, which bear no relation to stage or equipment, and seemingly not even to human capabilities. Yet the designer must provide the required effects somehow; the more successful designers have again and again demonstrated phenomenal ingenuity in providing such effects. Nothing is impossible of achievement in the theatre. There is nothing a playwright can imagine, but some designer can provide for it, and often accommodate it brilliantly to the whole visual scheme of the production. Ships that float, trees that are climbed or cut down, fires that blaze, factories that hum with life, objects or persons that materialize from nowhere or vanish into the air — none of these is impossible in the theatre; all of these and many more have been seen at one time or another.

The technical problems which occur, or may occur, are practically unlimited in their variety. Some are caused by the fact of the script requiring a multiplicity of acting areas to be contained in one setting, some by the diversity of the design elements necessary in one production, others by the great number of locales to be shown or by the speed of change from one to another. For purposes of discussion the commoner problems will be grouped, according to their causes, into six headings: (1) Elements required by the play; (2) Diversity of elements; (3) Multiplicity of details; (4) Spectacle and legerdemain; (5) Multiplicity of scenes; (6) Speed of scene change.

Elements Required by the Play

One of the commonest technical problems is that which occurs when the script requires that two or more distinct areas of action be shown simultaneously with the attention of the spectator either divided between them or shifted quickly from one to the other. The problem which arises from this requirement is partly one of composition — of effecting a successful balance of interest — and partly one of controlling and directing attention as the double action develops. It is most likely to be seen in plays requiring simultaneous action inside and outside a house, in scenes featuring balconies, and in interior scenes requiring simultaneously either upstairs and downstairs action or forestage and inner stage action.

Both Ibsen and Chekhov are fond of interior scenes which require some small action to take place close to the spectator while something else goes on a bit farther away, usually in a room visible through an archway or other opening upstage of the main acting area. Chekhov calls for this sort of scene several times, the purpose being perhaps to give an effect of lifelike confusion through dispersion of interest. The opening scene for *The Three Sisters*, for example, requires a living room with a dining room visible beyond. While action takes place nearer the audience, in the living room, the dinner party in the farther room progresses with laughter and eating. A similar division is basic to the third scene of *The Cherry Orchard*. In this a dance is in progress, glimpsed through a large opening upstage, while nearer, in the downstage area, a series of more intimate scenes proceed. Ibsen specifies an almost identical division of action in the opening scene of *The Wild Duck*. Once again festivities are in progress, partially glimpsed, while the downstage area is occupied with less lively action. In Ibsen's *Hedda Gabler* an inner room is visible through an arch across which curtains are sometimes drawn, but through which, when the curtains are open, one can see certain actions and at the very end glimpse the dead Hedda. The problem of sight lines is acute in each of these. Any device which will put the upstage action within view of the majority of spectators is likely to make the inner room seem unrealistically shallow.

The balcony scene is another form of the bipolar scene, usually simpler in composition, but no less perplexing because of the fact that the balcony, to be convincing as such, generally has to be high enough to be out of reach, or nearly out of reach, of one standing on the main acting area. Some famous balcony scenes are the ones in *Romeo and Juliet* and *Cyrano de Bergerac*. The latter requires, in addition to the verbal love-making, that the hero climb up vines to reach the heroine. In Ben Jonson's *Volpone* a similar requirement is made when Volpone, disguised as a mountebank, entices the beautiful Celia to her window and gives her a twist of paper supposed to contain a magical drug. In Calderón's *Mayor of Zalamea* an upper level, called a "garret" by the characters, but necessarily open to the audience, is seen first as a sort of balcony and then becomes the main area of action of eight characters. In all of these, and in most other balcony scenes, there exists the difficulty of making both areas equally visible along with that of placing the balcony in such a position that both the performers above and those on the floor are equally favored.

Scenes requiring simultaneous action both upstairs and downstairs are somewhat easier to compose, but often quite difficult to construct. The composition is easier because, as a rule, there is no communication between the two levels, so that the problem of sharing the scene between two characters does not have to be considered. The construction is difficult because the upstairs quite often must hold as many persons as the main floor area, and it is especially difficult if the scene has to be changed quickly. Probably the most difficult scene of this kind occurs in Barrie's *Peter Pan*. Above is a forest in which a number of strange things happen, among them a battle between Pirates and Indians, while below is a rather commodious hovel with a fireplace and sleeping accommodations for eleven children. *Romeo and Juliet* contains a scene — seldom performed today — in which the preparations for the wedding of Juliet and Paris proceed on the floor area while in the chamber above the Nurse is trying to waken the drugged Juliet. A similar division occurs in *Death of a Salesman,* in which action develops concurrently in the kitchen at stage level and in the bedroom above it.

Of all the varieties of the bipolar scene, the most difficult to design is the one in which action must be visible simultaneously both inside and outside a house or other enclosure. O'Neill's plays require this in several instances, of which the most notable is *Desire under the Elms,* where bedroom, kitchen, and garden must all be seen at once. Most of the plays of Tennessee Williams contain this requirement. In his *Summer and Smoke,* interiors of two dwellings must be seen at the same time as the street between them. In both *The Glass Menagerie* and *A Streetcar Named Desire* a portion of the exterior is required along with a view of two rooms inside. In his *You Touched Me!* the old captain's den is seen at the same time as the living room beyond, but with a wall separating them. Jo Mielziner's designs for the first three of Williams' plays have provided a novel and extremely successful solution to the inside-outside problem and one which could no doubt be applied in numerous other cases where this problem is found. In order to ease the difficulty of making all areas visible from all angles Mielziner used walls of gauze which could be made transparent or opaque according to the needs of the moment. When action in the street had to be seen, the light in that area was brightened while that in the interior was dimmed so that the walls seemed to dissolve; when the interior only was to be seen, the lights of the street dimmed and the walls appeared opaque and solid. When both areas had to be seen at once, both areas were illuminated and became visible with the partially transparent walls suggesting the division between them but without obstructing the view of either.

In Auden and Isherwood's verse play, *The Ascent of F.6,* the script requires that a team of mountaineers be seen attempting to scale a peak in the Himalayas while folks at home in their kitchens and living rooms follow the progress of the venture through newspaper and radio reports. The design of this play is difficult because the mountain side needs to be given an appearance of great size and majesty. This is hard to effect when no more than three-fourths of the stage is available for it. Ben Jonson's *The Alchemist* requires at one point that a crowd be seen gathering outside the door of Lovewit's house at the same time that the rogues within are hustling their loot into trunks in preparation for departure. The door in this case must be heavy enough to withstand several poundings and one attempt to break it down, and must also have a practical lock and a peephole. Yet the interior must be spacious enough to accommodate an unusual amount of varied activity, especially in the scenes immediately preceding and following the inside-outside action.

Graves, particularly those which must be dug within sight of the audience, are problematical. The best known of these appears in *Hamlet* where, during the course of one scene, a grave is dug and Ophelia is buried in it. A similar requirement appears in the old morality play, *Everyman,* in which, toward the end of the play, Everyman descends into his grave and shortly afterward ascends from it to heaven. Technically, the unearthing of buried treasure poses the same problem as the grave scene, for both necessitate digging and some activity below the line of the main acting area. Action of this sort occurs in *Treasure Island,* in Martin Flavin's *Brains,* and in some versions of *Tom Sawyer.* All of these are most easily managed, of course, on stages of which the floor is trapped so that an opening can be made at a spot easily seen by all spectators. When no traps are provided, or when those that are there are poorly located, the common solution is to platform over part of the acting area so that a trap can be made in the platform lid. This does not give as deep a trap as one might like, but it usually serves for the basic action.

Gallows on which a character can be hanged are needed in Holberg's *Jeppe of the Hill,* Kyd's *Spanish Tragedy,* and the musicals, *Knickerbocker Holiday* and *The Vagabond King.* In the first three of these the character is actually suspended — in *Jeppe* he plays a whole scene hanging — so that the designer is confronted with the double problem of providing a frame strong enough to support the weight of a man along with a rig capable of producing the illusion of hanging without injuring the performer or interfering with his speech. Trees which can be climbed create much the same problem as do gallows. There is one of these in *On Borrowed Time,* an apple tree which must support the weight of a man in it during a large part of the time it is in view. Two musicals, *Finian's Rainbow* and *Brigadoon,* demand similar tree action. In the latter the tree has to be large enough to conceal a man and strong enough that he can leap from it to the floor of the stage.

Heavy machinery, especially machinery which must be operative during the course of the scene, is surprisingly scarce when one considers the great number of scenes in modern drama requiring localization in shops or factories. The commonest heavy machinery is that of the derrick, crane, or cargo net, and this is by no means new to our time, for a scene in Aristophanes' *Peace* requires the same device. More recent works in which characters are swung aloft are Heggen and Logan's *Mister Roberts* and Maxwell Anderson's *High Tor,* the former employing a cargo net and the latter a bucket crane. In each the purpose of the device is comic. An odd mechanism is the adding machine, in Elmer Rice's play of that name, described as being of such size that the hero climbs across its keyboard from column to column, using his whole body to depress each key. Ernst Toller's play, *The Machine Wreckers,* culminates in a factory scene in which the stage is occupied by a spinning jenny with running crankshafts and driving belts and a lever which starts and stops its motion. During the course of the action, the engineer goes mad and darts across catwalks and moving wheels until he is finally caught in a moving belt and his body is carried to the top of the setting.

Something in the nature of the machine scenes described is the scene requiring a practical automobile. Shaw calls for two of these, one in *Man and Superman* and another in *Pygmalion.* A moving auto is also necessary to the first scene of Jules Romains's *Doctor Knock.* As the scene progresses, the vehicle, an ancient two-cylinder Panhard, struggles up a mountain road with much spitting and backfiring and finally stalls. Scenes of this type present no great difficulty other than the obvious one of offstage storage space. The vehicles are generally faked to save weight in handling, and since the distance traveled is never great, propulsion by hand-wound wire is much more efficient than the auto's own engine would be — if it had one.

Fires as part of the scene are less common today than they were fifty years ago when the possibilities of electric light were still being discovered. A good many melodramas of the last century, now unperformed and generally unknown, require forest fires, burning bridges, and flaming buildings. Perhaps the best known of these today is Dion Boucicault's *The Poor of New York.* In this work a fire is seen, first from a distance, as firemen gird themselves for action. Then follows a full stage scene in which the heroine is rescued from the burning building while smoke pours from the windows, beams fall, and a flickering red light dances across the smoke. Several Greek tragedies, originally written for outdoor performance, require fires of some magnitude. In Euripides' *The Suppliants* a funeral pyre is kindled for the six kings killed in the attack upon Thebes; and Evadne, the wife of one of them, crazed with grief, flings herself into the flames which are consuming her husband's body. In *The Trojan Women* the climax of the play is marked by the burning of Troy. As the cries of the captive women, accompanying the mounting flames, reach a crescendo, the burning walls crumble and come crashing down until the embers are level with the plain. Today the full effect is usually suggested with a bit of red lighting. We have no way of knowing what the Greeks actually showed in this scene, but there is no question but that the effect is a moving one and worth attempting in its entirety.

Water, with ships or boats afloat upon it, occurs in plays of every age. One of the most recent is Irwin Shaw's *The Gentle People* in which some very effective action takes place in a rowboat. Barrie's *Peter Pan* contains one scene of a lagoon with an island in it. Mermaids sun on the island and sport in the water about it, a skiff is rowed in and moored to the island, and a hat floats by with a bird nesting in it. In some versions of *Treasure Island* there is a scene in which the schooner "Hispaniola," cut loose from her moorings, drifts seaward as the boy Jim and the pirate Israel Hands maneuver for control of the helm. James A. Herne's old favorite, *Shore Acres,* has a similar scene in which the packet, "Liddy Ann," awash in a storm with a rock coast to leeward, is saved from destruction by the timely appearance of a light in the nearby lighthouse. Most of the scenes above are achieved with a lightweight floor cloth rippled for waves, confetti for spray, directional lighting, and a scrim to obscure all but the essential details of the vessel. Real water is seldom used, though at least one instance of its use is known in recent times. This was in a production of *Roar China*, designed by Lee Simonson. The play required a quay, a battleship, and a number of sampans. Simonson replaced the stage of the Martin Beck Theatre with a large tank filled with water and floated the sampans on it. The battleship, an impressive hybrid of naval architecture and armament, towered above pier and sampans and at the end of the play moved toward the audience with guns ablaze.

Diversity of Elements

The more diverse the elements of the design required by the playwright, the more acute are the problems, both mechanical and visual, which the designer must solve. And since novelty and variety are among the principal sources of visual delight to the spectator, it is to be expected that an unlimited diversity will be found. The problem is most conspicuous when the sequence of scenes is arranged in such a way as to require sharp juxtaposition of unlike locales — such as a palace being succeeded by a hovel and a cave by a hilltop; or of divergent scenic forms — such as a dungeon replaced by an ocean liner's deck.

Within the general problem caused by such diversity, two factors in particular affect the designer's concept of the production. One of these is the degree of difference between the elements of a given scene and those of the scenes immediately following or preceding it. The other is the total range of diversity within the whole production. Let us consider the immediate degree of difference first.

The commonest change employed to introduce variety in the scene sequence is the change from interior to exterior. The effect is that of opening up and expanding action which has been confined within often narrow limits and thus giving a feeling of refreshment to the sequence. The difference required between the two is often extreme. As a rule, the more intense and confined the interior has been, the more airy the exterior

PLATE 25. **Minimal Detail for Designs with Varying Requirements.** Relatively simple décor for two plays of divergent style and form—the Shavian *Shewing Up of Blanco Posnet* (above) and Ibsen's *Lady from the Sea.* (Above, *San Jose State College:* director, Hal J. Todd; settings, Donald Beaman; costumes, Nancy Johnson; lighting, Weldon Durham. Below, *University of Texas:* director, Francis Hodge; settings, Clayton Karkosh; costumes, Paul Reinhardt; lighting, David Nancarrow.)

PLATE 26. **Maximum Environment with Minimal Means.** Simplified scenic detail for large-cast productions—*Lysistrata* (above) and *West Side Story*. (Above, University of Hawaii: director, Joel Trapido; settings, Jack Dreier. Below, University of Kansas: staging director, Lewin Goff; musical director, Bob Baustian; settings, Jim Harrington; costumes, Chez Haehl.)

is likely to need to be. For example, in *The Cherry Orchard,* a rather long scene in the room "which used to be a nursery" is followed by a scene in the park requiring a considerable vista and a definite spaciousness. In Hauptmann's *Hannele* the action begins in a poorhouse and continues there through most of the first half of the play. Then the walls of the poorhouse evaporate and the scene expands into an airy nowhere with a stairway to heaven glittering in the background while angels sing in choir. In this instance the two locales are interrelated. The more confined the poorhouse, the better is the heaven effect when it comes, and the greater the difference between the murk and oppression of the first scene and the light and spaciousness of the second, the more exhilarating the change.

The reverse change is employed with equal frequency and for opposite purpose. In this case the intention is to achieve an effect of narrowing action. That which has begun capaciously, out of doors, is confined and narrowed down — a kind of funneling effect. This is what happens in *The Madwoman of Chaillot* when, after the first half of the play has taken place in the street in front of a Parisian cafe, the second half is removed to a cellar some distance underground. The speculators and confidence men whom we met in the first part come down into the cellar and are done away with there. The action of the first part is diffuse, while that of the second is increasingly purposeful so that the total effect is like that of a whirlpool which sucks in the worldly, the hypocritical, and the mercenary and draws them down to their final destruction.

Sometimes the enclosure-expansion effect works both ways, with the scene sequence composed so as to permit an alternation. The exterior is followed by a confining interior which in its turn is succeeded by the same or another exterior, so that the effects of confinement and expansion succeed one another.

Such an alternation is employed in *The Sea Gull,* which opens with a park scene — followed by an interior which in turn is followed by another exterior — and ends with an interior. *Winterset* employs a similar sequence. In it the towering bridge-pier scene is followed by an extremely confined cellar scene, then by a second pier scene and a second cellar scene, and finally the scene with which the play began. Shakespeare composes many such alternations. In *Julius Caesar* the large "forum" scene of the funeral orations is followed shortly by the small scene between Antony, Octavius, and Lepidus; and the night scene in Brutus' tent is followed by an outdoor scene in which the contesting generals and their armies come face to face in parley. In *Macbeth* the scene of Lady Macduff's murder, an interior, is followed by a scene between Macduff, Malcolm, and Ross in what seems to be an exterior. This in its turn is followed by the somewhat confined night scene showing Lady Macbeth's somnambulism, succeeded by the direction "Drum and Colours," signaling the approach of the Scottish lords and their retainers.

The technical problem of the change from interior to exterior or the other way around is not an especially difficult one and is usually solved by placing the smaller setting inside of the larger one and either lifting it out or rolling it offstage intact through an opening at the side of the larger setting. The problem of space is sometimes complicated by the fact that as many actors must be crowded into the smaller of the two settings as into the larger one. The problem can also be complicated by an overhead space insufficient to lift the smaller set combined with offstage space inadequate for a whole rolling unit, in which case the designer is taxed to find some means of clearing which does not require space in any direction.

It now remains to consider the problem of the total diversity of elements within the whole play, for the wider the range the more difficult becomes the conception of the whole production. Alternation from interior to exterior and back is not much of a problem; but when the progression of scenes includes no return to earlier scenes but proceeds from one odd locale to another, the greatest ingenuity is severely taxed to design the sequence so that it possesses some unity and yet moves smoothly forward. Ibsen's *Peer Gynt* is a prize piece in this respect, although the diversity of its requirements seems not to have deterred anyone from producing it, and some very fine designs have in fact been developed for it. Its sequence requires a mountain mill, a village square, a troll's cave, a bedchamber, a body of water, a beach, a Bedouin camp, a lunatic asylum, a mountain side, and a mountain hut. When so great a diversity of elements is required, the commonest solution is to neutralize a large part of the setting by means of wings or draperies and to suggest the various locales in each instance with a rather simple arrangement of the indispensables.

Multiplicity of Detail

The number of indispensable details which the playwright may prescribe is practically unlimited and bears no relation to the number of elements or to the diversity of elements which constitute the whole design. As a general rule, the greater the number of scenes in a sequence, the less the quantity of detail required by each, but there are many exceptions. Practically speaking, the only limit to the number of details which the playwright may require lies in the capacity of the spectator to see and remember, and even this limit is not always observed. David Belasco, whose productions were famous for their abundance of realistic detail, coined the phrase "the importance of trivia" to describe his attitude in the matter. The phrase represents a contradiction in terms, and perhaps a confusion in purposes as well, but

his attitude toward detail is still highly regarded by many writers for the theatre.

Details indispensable to the design may originate in the necessity for providing certain objects referred to in the lines and employed in the action, or in the author's specifications for "local color." Details thus incorporated into the script become part of the play as a whole and therefore indispensable to its performance if the whole intention of the playwright is to be realized.

Oddly enough, many details fully described by the characters but not used by them can be omitted from the design without having spectators aware of their absence. For it is a curious fact that audiences habitually accept what they hear in direct contradiction to the testimony of their eyes. Romeo's reference to "the moon that silvers all these fruit-tree tops" is acceptable as a description of the lighting and the orchard, even though neither is represented in the design. Pelléas' description of the seaside cavern, with its great stalagmites and salt-encrusted arches is as effective when these details are not seen as when they are — possibly even more so. In both instances the imagination of the audience sets the stage, and it will probably do so in any scene in which the details are not functional.

But it is much more likely that the details referred to by the characters will also figure in the action of the piece. This is because the playwright making use of details in the action of his work usually takes care that the speech of his characters makes the audience aware of these details in advance of their employment in the action. Thus, in *Kind Lady* the various *objets d'art,* the Whistler and El Greco paintings and the Ming horse, provide the motivation for the thieves who take her captive and pilfer her house. The portraits and the screen in *The School for Scandal* are integral to the action and for that reason are commented on at some length. This is also the case with the various details of the setting of the pastry shop in *Cyrano* — fowl roasting on spits in the fireplace, paper bags on which poems are written, great trays of pies, and a lyre of puff-paste. Rageneau fences with the spit and reads the poems, and his hungry friends devour the pies and the puff-paste.

The author's specifications for details of local color are most significant, of course, when the locale in question is somewhat unfamiliar to the majority of spectators. A classic description of this kind is the one which is given in preface to the first act of Tom Robertson's *Caste*. It describes a shabby room with peeling paper, actors' things strewn about, a teakettle on the hob in the fireplace (not lighted), and doors with practical knobs and locks. The description is famous mainly because at the time the play was written settings did not ordinarily have practical fireplaces and practical doors but were made up for the most part of stock wings and backdrops with the details painted on them, so that the setting specified was something of a novelty. The shabby everyday interior has long since ceased to be a novelty. Playwrights, however, have not yet ceased to specify it in the hope of convincing the spectator that the characters are as lifelike as the place represented, although their chance of doing so grows less with each passing season.

For more unusual locales, the descriptions given by O'Neill for the barge deck in *Anna Christie* and by Dubose Heyward for the courtyard in *Porgy* are especially fine, and the beginning designer would do well to study them as models. Each is rich with the feeling of the particular place: the barge "Simeon Winthrop," heavily laden, riding easily at its moorings in Provincetown harbor at night, with the great coils of cable on its deck and the lights of its cabin dimly visible beyond, the creaking of the hawser, the lapping of the waves against the hull, the clanging of an unseen buoy, and the various

harbor sounds coming clear through the haze; the courtyard of what was once one of the finest residences in Charleston, with its flagged paving and walls varicolored from innumerable washes of differing tints, its great gateway crowned with a beautiful arch of Italian ironwork, and visible beyond the arch an ancient gas street lamp and the harbor with masts and spars of the fishing boats there, and over it all the many sounds of the awakening day.

Spectacle and Legerdemain

Spectacle and legerdemain are considered together here because they are, in actuality, but two sides of the problem arising from the attempt to startle or impress the audience in order to make memorable some important moment of the play. The idea of spectacle calls to mind effects of some magnitude while that of legerdemain suggests the magical. Between these two one may find as basic requirements of the play every conceivable illusion and among them many famous effects in which generations of theatre craftsmen have taken especial pride.

A few of the best known of these will bear description. Among them is the flying in *Peter Pan*. Peter flies, then teaches Wendy, John, and Michael how. Presently the air is full of children flying, gleefully testing their new accomplishment, and when all are sufficiently air-borne the four of them fly out the nursery window with Peter in the lead. Another is the great cauldron scene in *Macbeth*. After an elaborate conjuration the witches raise from their magic cauldron the decapitated head of a warrior, who speaks a warning. Then the head dematerializes and in its place appears the figure of a newborn infant which speaks encouragement to the hero. The infant then vanishes, to be replaced in its turn by a child in royal robes, crowned with the crown of Scotland. The child speaks additional encouragement and also disappears. Nor is this all, for next the witches conjure up the images of eight future rulers of the realm and then themselves vanish. Nearly as well known is the table scene in *The Tempest*. In this the shipwrecked King of Naples and his party hear solemn music and are suddenly confronted with a troop of monsters who carry in a table heaped with mouth-watering viands. The monsters graciously invite the starving men to eat, but as the King begins to taste the feast it vanishes, leaving an empty table which the monsters presently carry away. Some other effects, familiar because of their recency, are the bedevilled furnishings in *Blithe Spirit;* the dwarf in *Rumpelstiltskin,* whose intense anger causes him to explode; and the Southern Senator in *Finian's Rainbow,* whose complexion changes unexpectedly from Caucasian to Negroid.

Many of these effects require special skill and knowledge. Those of Shakespeare are problems as much for the magician as the designer. *Peter Pan,* when recently produced in New York, required the importation from England of a specialist in aerial devices. But whether the effects are contrived by specialists or by the designer, the best of them are of such prominence in the play and so well known that it is often necessary to plan the production around them.

Multiplicity of Scenes

Above and beyond the demands of diversity, detail, and trickery, the sheer number of scenes is one of the most frequent factors in the concept of the design. Since Elizabethan times, plays of panoramic scope or multiple plot have tended toward multiplicity of scenes. Within the past thirty years this tendency has been encouraged by the example of cinema and radio drama, where the sequence of action moves freely through locales unlimited in number. In earlier times the fact that the performance took place in a theatre in which locale was either not depicted at all or else represented upon painted flat surfaces rather easily moved made the number of scenes in a play of slight consequence technically. But the more recent taste for three-dimensional effects and more patently practical settings has made many a multiple-scene play a real technical problem, and often a problem of such difficulty as to condition the whole concept of the design.

A good example of this problem is Galsworthy's *Escape*. The scene sequence requires ten settings: Hyde Park at night; Dartmoor in a fog, by day and by night; a bedroom in an inn; an open space by the river; an open space on the moor; another open space on the moor; a gravel pit; a parlor in a cottage; the vestry of a village church. Each of these requires a measure of verisimilitude; none is capable of very imaginative treatment. But the sheer weight of numbers against the inevitable limitations of space and manpower demand some very ingenious scheme of production if the play is to be acceptably mounted.

Sidney Howard's *Paths of Glory,* as originally adapted from the novel of that name, contained some twenty episodes, each in a different locale, among which were a roadside cafe, a general's office, a barracks, a roadway, a trench, a dugout, an officers' quarters, and a barn. After witnessing the New York production of the play, which represented each of these rather drab locales rather faithfully, Howard, in his preface to the published play, suggested that the whole action might more effectively be performed against some neutral background such as that of the monumental tomb of the unknown soldier in Munich. His suggestion was put into practice in a number of amateur productions afterward, and with considerable success.

Dark of the Moon, a folk fantasy of the Smoky Mountains, requires some thirteen scenes, including a mountain ridge, a village square, a poor cabin, a general store, and a backwoods church. The original production of this play presented the locales in fragmentary settings, each quite detailed but small in area and doing considerably more to suggest the various places than to show them as completely as probably would have been done had the piece been produced twenty years earlier. The solution to the multiple-scene problem in this instance was prophetic, for it has since been applied to a number of similar scene sequences with marked success. The idea of fragmentary settings was not a new one — it had been explained and illustrated by Samuel Selden in the book, *Stage Scenery and Lighting,* many years before. It consists simply of a paring away of the neutral elements of the more commonplace locales, thus putting the multiple-scene sequence within the capabilities of the small theatre.

Fast Changes

Audiences accustomed to cinema, where the scene changes frequently and instantly, have come to expect the same continuity in stage productions. Except for those changes made during intermissions, the shorter the wait between scenes the smoother the performance is likely to seem. Also, the greater the number of scenes, the faster the changes need to be. For regardless of the number of scenes in the sequence or the diversity between them which makes change more difficult, there is a definite limit to the amount of time which an audience will spend looking at the act curtain and that limit is much less than it was when cinema was unknown. When the number of scenes is unusually large — as in *Antony and Cleopatra,* which contains more than forty changes — even the momentary dimming of lights between scenes eventually becomes tiresome.

Occasionally one encounters plays in which fast changes are made necessary by the fact that actions occurring in sequence in the script are supposed to be taking place simultaneously. This happens in the first act of *Green Grow the Lilacs,* where the scene in Aunt Eller's house ends with her hearing a shot and running out into the yard. The scene immediately following, in the smokehouse, shows the actions leading up to the shot. The same sort of thing occurs in *She Stoops to Conquer,* toward the end of the play. In this case the locale changes from the interior of the house to the back garden and returns again to the house without interval between, the actions inside and outside the house being represented as overlapping in time. Both of these are examples of the intercut or overlapping sequence — borrowing the descriptive terms from cinema — and the more nearly instantaneous the change from one scene to another, the better it plays.

Another kind of change is the "dissolve," which requires the locale to change while action continues uninterrupted by either dim-out or curtain. These have become quite common in recent years. *Death of a Salesman* contains a number of them, as Willy Loman's imagination shifts from present to past. *Anne of the Thousand Days* has several, as the focus of interest shifts from the characters' activities to their thoughts. In *Green Pastures* there is one as the Lawd walks the earth while forests and fields and houses go past him on the stage. Plays beginning in dentists' offices and operating rooms often employ this change to show the character's mind wandering under the influence of anaesthetic. In fact, this device is so common that one wonders what our playwrights would have done had anaesthesia been invented a hundred years later than it was.

A third is the "breakaway" change, in which one scene opens up to reveal a second and usually larger one. One of these occurs in Sartre's *The Flies,* when Zeus causes the temple walls to fade as he reveals to Orestes the universe with its myriad planets turning in their orbits. In *The Insect Comedy* the tramp studies the insects among the grass roots with his magnifying glass and as their voices become audible the wood around him disappears and in its place are the roots, highly magnified, with insects the size of human beings hustling among them. *The Prince and the Pauper* begins with a scene outside the palace gates. Then the gates are opened, and as the characters pass through, the royal chamber materializes and the gates disappear.

The technical problems in all of these changes, whether occasioned by intercutting, dissolve, or breakaway, are much the same. Fundamentally it is a question of achieving the maximum speed compatible with smooth operation. If dialogue continues through the change there is the additional problem of quietness. The commonest solution at present is to place the scenic units on casters and roll them on or off the stage by hand. The noise of the rolling is reduced by the use of rubber-tired casters together with linoleum-covered floors. As is always the case when rolling units are employed, insufficient offstage space is the worst part of the problem; assembling and moving the rolling units themselves is comparatively simple. Revolving platforms and the so-called "sliding stages" are but different applications of the rolling-platform principle.

Changes made in view of the spectators are usually made by rolling if possible, because the appearance of objects in motion horizontally is more pleasing. However, when the change is concealed by the act curtain or obscured by blacking out lights, the units may be either hoisted or rolled. Instantaneous changes are generally planned so as to be made entirely by one means or the other, in order to avoid the hazards of imperfect co-ordination which are present wherever two different means are combined.

19 | Physical Factors in the Design

2: Costume

Style · Mobility
The Costume and the Actor

The importance of costuming as an element of the design varies in proportion to the prominence of the actor in the visual scheme. In plays requiring dimensional staging, with a high degree of kinesthetic action and continual rapport between actor and audience, costume often assumes first place in the design, with the setting considerably subordinated. This is particularly evident in productions of Greek drama, of Shakespeare when done on a platform stage, and of Molière however done. The extreme of this is seen in arena productions, in which no scenery at all is used and the visual scheme is entirely a matter of dress, with whatever assistance the lighting can provide.

In more pictorial staging the costume scheme becomes part of the whole design, with the setting more nearly on parity and with the two necessarily related in color and texture. In the best designs the two are calculated to complement and set off one another, although the costume, since the actor wears it and moves and speaks in it, is the more continually within the attention of the spectator.

The following discussion is intended to treat costume as the setting has been treated — as a series of problems of design; the his-tory of costume and the techniques of costume making are dealt with only as they relate to the whole design, and not in detail.[1] In particular there are three aspects of costume which are indigenous to the concept of the whole design and which need to be considered before we will be in a position to discuss the problems of stage composition. They are: (1) style; (2) action; and (3) the actor.

STYLE

The style of costume in any production is the externalization of the spirit of the play — the sobriety or flippancy of its attitude toward life and the dignity or triviality of its theme, and, on occasion, the period of its composition. Style is expressed in certain qualities of costume: in silhouette; in texture; in accent; and finally in the relationship of individual costumes one to another within the ensemble.

Silhouette

The silhouette is the basic outline of the costume and is the quality most closely re-

[1] See, however, the additional treatment of costuming which appears in Appendix B.

267

lated to its general concept. We speak of silhouette as the whole outline, but it is in fact a combination of two things: the silhouette of the body and the silhouette of the head.

The characteristic body silhouette of a well-designed costume is fairly constant whether the costume is viewed from the front or the side. There are two main kinds of silhouettes, and a third kind which represents a variety of combinations of these two.

The first main kind of silhouette is that of the *draped* costume. Its outstanding feature is an abundance of material falling in full folds and attached to the figure at few points — usually the shoulders and sometimes the waist also. The outline of the body beneath it is not very clear, for it is the material and the way it falls that is of primary visual interest. The best effects are generally gained with a "natural" drape, that is, with the material hung from some clasp or girdle and either wound about the figure or allowed to fall in its own folds. Such a drape is difficult to keep in place and almost impossible to arrange in identical folds at successive drapings. For this reason the folds are sometimes stitched down to tapes or partial foundations in order to hold them in place after a good drape has been worked out. The French are particularly deft at this and the style of their draped costumes is usually superior to that of most others.

Draped or partially draped costumes seem to recur with some regularity throughout history. The Greek *chiton* and the Roman *toga*, the draped costumes which most of us know best, are followed, in various periods, by a variety of capes, trains, cassocks, and cloaks.

The second principal body silhouette is that of the *fitted* costume. Its characteristic is that the material is cut so as to encase the body, with the seams coinciding rather closely with the body's joints — shoulder, waist, hip, knee, and elbow. The fitted cos-

tume reveals the outline of the body in varying degrees depending on the closeness of the fit. Men's clothing today, for example, is fitted clothing, and although the fit is not now as close as it has been at various times within the past fifty years, the outline of the body and its main divisions of torso and legs are clearly apparent, and certainly much more apparent than in a Roman toga. In this kind of costume the fit is somewhat more important to the whole effect than is the material, and this is more true as the distance from which the costume is viewed increases.

Fitted clothing generally alternates in fashion with looser and more draped clothing. The tight doublet and hose of the Elizabethan is followed by the cavalier's loose breeches and draped cassock, and the loose Directoire gown by corseted bodice and hoop skirt. Of course, men's and women's costumes are not always alike as to drape or fit in any given period; and although they occasionally coincide, as in classical and Elizabethan times, it also happens that women are wearing draped clothing when men are wearing fitted things, and the other way around.

The third kind of silhouette is found when drapped and fitted elements are combined in one costume, and some of these are extremely handsome. Thus one may find fitted torsos combined with draped skirts or trousers, or fitted small clothes with voluminous cloaks or caped greatcoats. But whatever the combination, it is usually the torso or bodice to which the closer fitting is done, however the legs and arms may be treated.

The art of fitting is the art of cutting material to coincide with the body's joints, for the areas between joints, such as the chest and thigh, do not change their shape. It is possible by accurate placing of seams very nearly to cover the body with unwrinkled cloth. The bullfighter's costume is a good example of this.

DRAPED

FITTED

DRAPING AND FITTING COMBINED

DRAPED AND FITTED COSTUMES

Figure 29. The fitted costume directs attention to the physique of its wearer; the draped costume to the wearer's movements.

The art of draping is the art of securing abundant folds and graceful gathers by the way the cloth is hung about the figure. When draping and fitting are combined in one costume, the division between the two, usually the waist, is clearly marked so that the difference in treatment between one area of the costume contrasts clearly with that of the other.

The draped costume looks best on the firm and somewhat spare figure. If firmness is lacking, a foundational garment is provided. Women, whose figures are naturally soft, usually look best in draped costumes when underneath they wear leotards or lastex swim suits. Without such firming, the feminine figure, especially, is in danger of appearing sack-like.

The fitted costume shows up the best on the shapely and not too angular figure. Tights, for example, the commonest item of fitted costume, are pleasing on shapely, well-proportioned legs and unsightly on more angular ones. Because the fitted costume is more revealing of the figure, good posture is essential to its best effect and is likely to be assured, when necessary, by means of braces and corsets.

In order to maintain the quality of the silhouette from every angle a variety of devices are employed. Among these are weights in the hems of draped pieces to keep the folds falling right; canvas linings in doublets and in skirted coats to stiffen and smooth the outline; hoops and petticoats under full skirts; and paddings to fill out hollows or irregularities of the figure which impair the outline.

Plate armor, required in many plays set in the years between 1350 and 1650, is probably the extreme of fitted costume, since the metal is cut and rounded very close to the outlines of the body and when finally fitted holds its silhouette perfectly. German designers are particularly good at plate armor and achieve impressive silhouettes in their his-torical plays wherever armor is required. American and British designers generally lack this ability and tend either to employ leather or papier-mâché — both of which produce a totally different effect than metal — or else to substitute some sort of silvered knitted stuff. The result is that the warrior often appears in something that looks as if it were made out of old gray sweaters, and the silhouette sadly lacks style. There is no excuse for this lack. With the proper shears, sheet iron is as easy to cut as heavy paper, and riveting is no more difficult than the sewing on of overcoat buttons.[2]

The silhouette of the head completes the effect begun in the treatment of the body and consists of collar and shoulder line, hairdo, and headgear. Collar, ruff, and jabot are best conceived in relation to the head. As in everyday life, the neckwear is less a part of the body silhouette than a frame for the face. Certain harmonies between head and body are also essential. For example, the draped body usually requires a treatment of hair and hat which makes some sort of transition between the two, as in the Psyche knot; the horse's tail depending from the back of the Greek warrior's helmet; and the cavalier's broad sweeping hat, which joins the shoulder line of his cassock. The reverse is true of the fitted garment. Here the hair is more likely to be swept upward, clear of the neck, and the hat to perch high on the head. The result is a head silhouette which stands

---

[2] A new material, Celastic, recently come into the market, has proved useful for armor. The material replaces both papier-mâché and buckram for this purpose. It has the advantages of drying faster than either and of producing a surprisingly durable and lightweight form. If any good metal armor is available it can be easily copied in Celastic by using the real armor as a model and moulding the Celastic duplicate over it. Helmets can also be copied quite easily with this substance. The maintenance on Celastic armor should be easier, as the material does not rust. Chief disadvantage at present is that Celastic costs more than most sheet metals (aluminum, black iron). It is also more difficult to get a good metallic patina on it.

clear of the body with the firm lines of one silhouette repeated in the other.

Texture

It is common knowledge that textiles look very different at a distance under stage lights than they do on the yard-goods counter of the store. Some, which at close hand seem cheap and unattractive, appear of rich and appealing quality when made into costumes. Some that are expensive look like sleazy imitations of themselves. The appearance of a fabric is determined by its texture — its bulk, density of weave, and surface; its behavior under stage lights; and its relationship to the design of which it is a part.

Bulk in a fabric usually makes it look heavy because in daily life we associate thickness of clothing with weight. The bulk is determined by the size of the thread, the complexity of the weave, and the depth of the nap if any. Monk's cloth, terry cloth, and velour are bulky materials widely used in costuming where the effects of weight and richness are needed. Fabrics lacking in bulk because of their thinner thread and simpler weave are cotton voiles, canton flannel, and cheesecloth. These are used where the effect of lightness and thinness is desired.

The density of a fabric is determined by the tightness of its weave and the stiffness of the thread. A very dense fabric such as canvas has a stiffness which makes it appropriate to fitted garments, linings, and foundations, but inappropriate to draped garments which require softer and more loosely woven stuffs. Some materials, such as satin and velvet, are rather closely woven; but because the thread is of flexible silk, they seem less dense than muslins or challis of comparable thread count. The effect of starching a material is the same as that of a tighter weave.

The principal surface characteristics of cloth are smoothness or roughness, sheen, and pattern. Uneven or rough surfaces such as those caused by variations in thickness of thread or in tightness of weave look heavier than smooth ones. Terry cloth and monk's cloth look heavier, as much because of their roughness as their bulk. Sheen emphasizes detail in a costume because of the way the glossy surface reflects light. Flounces and gathers as well as draped folds and skin-fitted bodices all gain interest when made up of high-sheen material. But because fabrics of high sheen always look flimsier under stage lights, the tendency is to employ them rather sparingly and to depend mainly upon duller surfaces for richness. Pattern in a textile interrupts the dominant surface characteristic and often gives it a pleasing variety. When spotlights were still a novelty many designers preferred unpatterned stuffs, believing that the lights destroyed the quality of the pattern, but this belief has had its day. Self-patterned materials such as are used in upholstery are often extremely effective. Lucy Barton used these in her costumes for the Globe Shakespeare Company in 1934, and their effectiveness was much remarked at the time.

Stage lights usually strike the costume from many directions. This has two results. One is that the fabric with a sheen picks up many highlights, causing it to appear both shinier and thinner than it really is. This excess of highlight is what often makes expensive satins seem thin and cheap. The other is that light coming from several directions fills in the shadows of the folds in draped garments, making them seem skimpier and less bulky, so that in order to achieve an effect of weight and fullness the costume must contain more material than it would need in daylight.

Costume groups are more pleasing when a degree of homogeneity is observed in the choice of textures. Where very pronounced contrasts exist, the materials of greater bulk and duller surface make the others look sleazy and skimpy. The reverse is true regarding the relationship of costume to setting, for here the contrasts of texture always favor the costume. A matte-surfaced setting goes well with costumes having some sheen, and a setting with high surfaces, such as those of polished floor or waxed woodwork, gives increased richness to costumes of rougher texture and duller sheen.

Accent

An accent is a detail which sets off the silhouette or texture of a garment. Often a costume which seems to lack distinction in spite of good silhouette, texture, or color may gain just what it needs from an accent tastefully conceived and cleverly placed. (See Figure 30.)

Accentuation of the silhouette usually takes the form of some sort of emphasis of the figure, particularly of the points of its articulation. Typical examples of this are the girdle marking the waistline, a buckle or rosette the instep, a necklace the collar line, and a garter the curve of a shapely leg.

Accentuation of texture is generally achieved by providing some small item sharply contrasting with the principal fabric of the costume, such as metal braid against velvet, soft plumes on a helmet, silk facings for a broadcloth coat, or trimming of tulle with a satin bodice.

Where need for accent is indicated, it is likely to be supplied by the addition of one or another of three things: trimming, jewelry, or accessories. Trimming is accent applied to the costume and made part of it. Jewelry, however, may as easily go with the wearer as with the costume, and the same jewelry is sometimes used as accent on all the costumes worn by one person. An accessory is an article of utility or decoration which accompanies the costume without being an integral part of it.

Among the commoner trimmings are ruffles, lace, embroidery, appliqué, braid, pipings, facings, buttons, tassels, fringe, and feathers or plumes. Costumes of various periods and nationalities have their characteristic trimmings, such as the crimson border on a Roman senator's toga, the wrist lace of an eighteenth-century gentleman's coat, the ruffle of a rumba skirt, and the wool embroidery of a Tyrolean jacket.

Pieces of jewelry most likely to be seen on the stage include brooches, medals, bracelets, and the large neck-chains or "orders" of nobility. Neck-chains are a conventional mark of certain societies such as the Order of the Golden Fleece, as well as of mayoralty in many European countries. The smaller kinds of jewelry such as earrings, finger rings, and lockets, although favored by actors, are often too small to be seen from a distance or to give any kind of accent to a costume.

Accessories are extremely varied, but among them belts and purses are probably commonest, with canes and swords making a close third. Beyond these lies an infinity of sashes, scarves, prayer-beads, spurs, garters, cockades, wimples, fans, riding crops, watch fobs, and parasols. (See Figure 31.)

Nearly every costume needs some accent. None needs very many. Few need more than one of each kind. A common fault in costume design is overaccentuation which, instead of giving the costume distinction, turns it into a freak. The better designer uses few accents, but to telling effect. Sometimes the attempt is made to indicate a character's poor taste by tasteless accents, but this ends up with a costume which merely offends the eye. Characterization in a costume ought to go deeper than its ornament.

Relationships

The impression of style is necessarily related to the total costume ensemble. In any group the costume having the more marked treatment is likely to seem the best styled. In a Greek tragedy where all are garbed in draperies the costume with the fullest

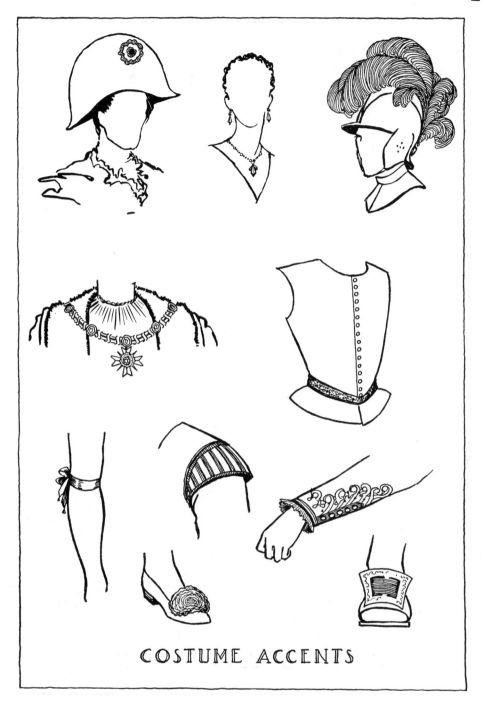

COSTUME ACCENTS

Figure 30. A costume may gain just what it needs from an accent or two tastefully conceived and cleverly placed.

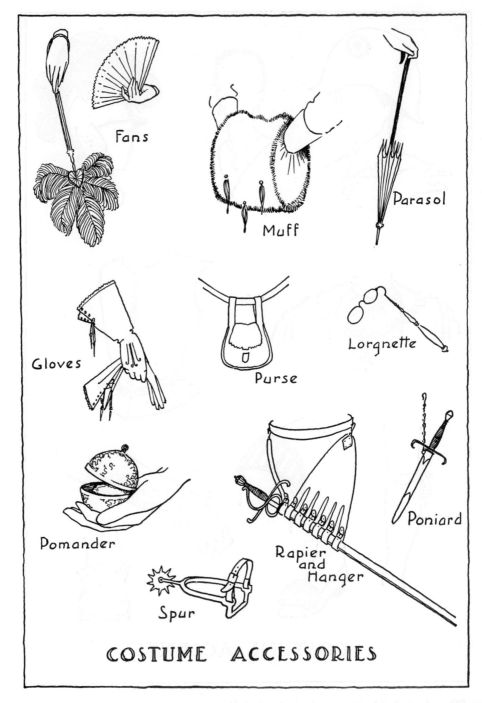

Figure 31.   A costume is practically never complete until it has been supplied with appropriate accessories.

drape and most graceful folds will look the best of the group. In an Elizabethan drama in which the group is clad in closely fitted things the costume with the finest fit is likely to enjoy a comparable eminence.

It is useful to know this, because in every scheme certain costumes must stand out and certain distinctions of rank and occupation must be established. The principal characters must stand out from the group. The nobleman must be distinguished easily from the merchant, the officer from the soldier, the squire from the peasant, the king from his subjects, and the heroine from her hand-maidens.

Boldness of accent and strength of coloring will not of themselves insure this effect, for although they may at first glance make the principles recognizable, they may also make them tiresome to look at after a time. The best costume is one which describes relationships, is easy to recognize, and easy to watch without tiring.

MOBILITY

Costume is a living thing, if only for the duration of the performance in which it appears. But during the performance it is in continual motion from the breathing and movement of the actor who inhabits it. From time to time certain costumes may be seen in repose, but in any performance it is the quality of the costumes' movement and the way they look in motion which is the final measure of their effectiveness. Mobility of costume is therefore a factor of some importance. Dressing a doll or draping a manne-quin is fun. But creating a costume whose movement perpetually surprises and delights the eye — this is a work of art.

There are two aspects to the subject of mobility. One, of course, is the necessity for accommodating the activity of the performer — dancing, fighting, kneeling, sitting. The other is the necessity of providing a costume

which will not only enhance essential action but at the same time please the eye with its own movement. Let us consider the question of activity first.

Accommodating Activities of the Performer

The activities required of the performer are many and various, and practically all of them affect his costume. Clearly the best costume in this respect is that which most readily accommodates his actions. He may be required, like Géronte in Molière's *Scapin*, to crawl into a sack — wig, skirted coat, and all; or to change outfits as fast as one of Ben Jonson's rogues; or to dance a lively jig. The possible actions are limited only by the playwright's powers of invention.

Violent activities, such as fights, duels, and morris dancing, require carefully fitted garments. The faster and more staccato the action, the less practicable are draperies. Entirely draped costumes are usually out of the question. Capes and skirts, if used, need to be roomy, firmly attached to the body, and to offer no impediment to the legs or arms. Spirited dances demand especial freedom of the feet and legs. Fabrics with some elasticity, such as jersey or satin lastex, serve well. Where the use of these is undesirable, materials cut on the bias are often employed.

Footwear is nearly as important to action as garment. Nimble footwork needs light, flexible, snug-fitting shoes. Extreme activity further necessitates nonskid soles of rubber or rosined leather. Heavy soles slow down and regularize movement. High heels shorten the stride and limit movement to fairly even surfaces. Clogs, mules, and loose-fitting sandals make it difficult to lift the foot in walking and also induce a distinctive shuffling gait.

Fast changes of dress are the rule in the theatre. Even when costumes are changed during intermissions, the allowed time is seldom more than a fraction of the time one would take elsewhere. But most acute are the changes which are allowed no more than a few lines. Toinette in Molière's *Imaginary Invalid* changes from her regular dress into the gown and hat of a doctor and back again several times so fast as to make Argan think he sees both her and the doctor side by side. In *The Alchemist* both Face and Subtle make a number of changes, appearing several times each in three different outfits during the course of the play. Volpone appears as himself, as an invalid, as a mountebank, and as a police officer, and in the end is disrobed in full view of those whom he has deceived. Macbeth calls for his armor, puts it on while giving orders to his soldiers and conversing with the Doctor, then orders it removed and walks out without it, all in the space of fourteen lines. Such fast changes require special attention to fastenings, combinations of items of dress which would ordinarily be separate, and designing which provides for various garments to be slipped on over each other.

Masks need to be designed with particular reference to action. The masked mountebanks in *Volpone* must sing and dance, both difficult accomplishments since the masks tend to affect hearing as well as to limit the vision. The monsters in *The Tempest* do not sing, but they must dance, and their dance is in danger of appearing a bit aimless if they are unable to see where they are going. The mask of the ass's head which Bottom wears in *A Midsummer Night's Dream* presents a similar difficulty, one which has been experienced from time to time by the ape in *The Hairy Ape*, the lion in *Androcles and the Lion*, and the dog, Nana, in *Peter Pan*. This effect of a mask can be controlled if the design allows for the need for seeing. In large masks such as those for Bottom and the lion an opening large enough to see through is made in the mouth or throat of the mask and concealed with gauze. The rest is a matter of anchoring the headpiece so that the actor's movements cannot dislodge it and cause the opening to shift out of line with his eyes.

Costume in Motion

Balletomanes for two generations have decried the *tutu* — that short bouffant skirt of the ballerina — because of its ugly bobbing and general lack of grace in motion. The complaint is based upon comparison both with the longer skirt which preceded it and with other styles of dress. Neither the origin of the *tutu* nor the reasons for its persistence need concern us here. Mention of it is merely intended to remind us that in a costume grace of motion is a quality not always determined by the grace of its wearer.

Certain styles and textures possess grace in motion. Others enhance the motion of the wearer. Still others transfer interest to the physique of the wearer in such a way as to emphasize whatever individualities his movement may possess.

Draperies are most likely, of themselves, to be pleasing in motion. In this respect there are two kinds of draperies, according to weight, and the behavior of each is distinctive. Each, accordingly, is employed to different purpose as part of the whole effect.

The characteristic motion of heavier draperies is a following motion. This is caused by the combination of two things: the movement of the wearer, and the inertia of the material. A drapery hanging free from arm or shoulder moves somewhat more slowly than the part of the body from which it hangs. It is more pleasing when the line connecting the two is curved and when it is continuous through all movements. The bullfighter's cape, when properly managed, affords an example of this. Its motion originates in the wrists of its manipulator and flows in unbroken curves from wrist to hem with each pass and sometimes through a series of "linked" passes. The same trait marks the behavior of all pendant draperies. In repose they hang in vertical folds. But in motion the verticals change to curves. It is in these curves that the movement of a costume is pleasing to the eye.

Trailing draperies, such as robes and trains which touch the floor, produce a different kind of continuum by connecting the moving figure with the plane on which it moves. The curves are longer here, and increase in length as there is more material in contact with the floor. The effect becomes increasingly pleasurable as the quantity of the material is increased, thus multiplying the folds and the number of curving lines. An infinite variety of curves is possible by relating the drapery to the surfaces over which it moves: steps, ramps, and balustrades. With certain actions such as turning, sitting, and reclining the long curves are replaced by a greater number of smaller ones which, although less striking, introduce many welcome variations.

The characteristic motion of light drapery is a floating motion. Although the motion is usually initiated by activity of the wearer, the pressure of the air through which the material moves affects the follow-through to such an extent that the fabric seems endowed with life of its own.

The possible varieties of motion are much greater with light draperies than with heavy ones. In general the denser the material in proportion to its weight, the more readily it floats. The shape of the drapery will also affect its behavior. A cape of silk tissue will bell out like a sail. Streamers and narrow pieces will seem rather to ripple as they move and the slightest current of air will agitate them even when the figure is still. As a rule, the larger the area of the piece the more air it catches and the wider it floats.

Light draperies, because of their liveliness, are often employed to add mobility and life to heavier garments. A floating veil goes well with a velvet gown. Scarves and handkerchiefs of gauzy stuffs are common accenting accessories for stiff fabrics.

Closely fitted garments such as tights, doublets, and bodices do not of themselves possess much individuality in motion. Their coincidence with the lines of the figure tend rather to shift interest to the actor so that the mobile character of the costume is that of the figure which it fits and often no more than that.

Costumes which enhance the motion of the figure are those which combine drapery and fitting in such a way that interest is guided to certain motions of the figure, supplemented by the motion of the costume. Costumes of such combined effect are commoner than those embodying the extremes of either drape or fit. Such a costume is achieved when fitted bodice is combined with full skirt, or tights with ballet shirt. Increased control of motion is gained by a variety of means among which are hoops, paniers, farthingales, weighted hems, and boning of free-swinging folds.

Length of drape increases in importance in costumes combining drape and fit. When the drape of skirt, tunic, sleeve, or cape is short, the effect is better when the hem is curved and when its highest point comes either just below or just above the nearest joint. For example, a skirt whose hem coincides with the bend of the knee is decidedly less attractive than one which comes several inches below it, and the same is true regarding coincidence with the ankle. Draped sleeves move more gracefully when their hems come either just below or just above the elbow. Short capes are better when terminated just above the knee, below the hip, or above the waist. The reason for this is that the angular action of the joint in motion is exaggerated by any horizontally moving hem to the degree that the whole motion appears ungainly. Thus either the angle must be covered by the drapery or, if uncovered, provided with a hem at such distance as to share interest as it moves.

Trimmings accentuate motion. Lace,

DRAPERY IN MOTION

Figure 32. Grace is often as much a matter of proper costume design as of graceful movement by the actor.

ruffle, or braid around the bottom of a full skirt emphasizes the swing of the hem line. The nodding plumes on a helmet make movement of the head both more conspicuous and more graceful. Wristbands and wrist laces emphasize the movement of the hands. The facings of coats and the linings of capes accentuate in the one case the movement of the neck and in the other the movement of shoulders and torso.

Motion is also affected by the sheen of the fabric and the play of light on its surface as it moves. The higher the sheen the more emphatic the motion becomes. Extremely high-surfaced materials can give a definite feeling of restlessness to a garment. This is an effect which is occasionally desirable and somewhat more often to be avoided.

Finally, there is the relationship of the mobility of the costume to the general style of movement which marks the play as a whole. The action of *Lute Song* was worked out in such a way that the characters moved always in curves and with curving gestures. Jones's design accordingly placed them all in draped costumes of heavy silks of definite sheen, so that the swing and curve of the costumes as the actors moved about was a thing of great beauty. As the play progressed, in order to sustain interest, he introduced a number of varying highlights from gold threads woven into the fabrics. The predominant movement in *Murder in the Cathedral* is slow and dignified, with the result that the play does best in heavily draped costumes. A variation in the general tone of the movement occurs with the appearance of the knights who murder Thomas. For these sharper accents, higher surfaces and more closely fitted costumes are desirable; boots, belts, glittering helmets (without plumes, of course), and glossy tabards give the appropriate quality of restlessness to their movement which contrasts so strongly with that of their self-possessed victim. In the musical, *Oklahoma!,* the movement is lively, vigorous, and staccato. Tight-fitting costumes with accents of floating neckerchiefs and flounces on the skirts heighten the movements of all the younger and livelier characters. Even if the production were not costumed in cowboy clothes, comparable closeness of fit and sharpness of accent would be desirable. This can be seen by comparing *Oklahoma!* with its progenitor, *Green Grow the Lilacs,* in which the plot and characters were the same but the movement considerably less vigorous. In *Green Grow* the cowboys were more loosely garbed, most of them with high-heeled boots and some with chaps. The women's costumes were much less pronounced as to fit and few of them had flounces.

THE COSTUME AND THE ACTOR

It is impossible, except by chance, to create the best costume for a role without knowing the actor who will wear the costume. Character as expressed in carriage and posture is principally the business of the performer; his costume assists him in this by accommodating his movement and by accentuating his manner and bearing. A well-designed costume will, moreover, help to make him easy to see and interesting to watch, and it should give him confidence in his appearance.

Each actor is an individual problem. His natural appearance may or may not contribute to the solution of the problem. But it cannot be blamed if it does not contribute. The effectiveness of an actor in performance springs primarily from personality, projection, and technique. Costume must enhance the performance visually. The design of the costume must correct or conceal physical deficiencies of the actor which threaten to interfere with his appearing as he ought.

It is as important that the actor have confidence in his costume as that he actually be comfortable in it. He will be confident if he believes that he looks as he ought even though certain elements of his outfit constrict his torso and pinch his toes. One sees ample evidence of this fact in everyday dress. Neither a woman's girdle nor a man's dress shirt can be called comfortable, yet people wear them with confidence. And the number of women who endure undersized shoes for the sake of appearance must be very great indeed. To the actor, looking as he ought usually means looking better than he would out of costume. In most cases this is as it should be; the human beings we see on the stage are for the most part more acceptable if somewhat shapelier and more graceful than those in the life around us.

The problem of accommodating costume to actor has several facets. One of these has to do with the visibility of his features. Others are concerned with enhancing his face, figure, and movement. Then there is a variety of special problems, some of which occur in nearly every production. Let us turn first to the matter of visibility.

Visibility of Features

Costumes ought to be designed so as to make the actor's face easily seen. Elements of costume which obstruct the view of his features give the spectators a feeling of frustration and annoyance. Hoods, wide-brimmed hats, and helmets are constantly in danger of producing this unhappy effect. In a well-designed costume the headgear is shaped to leave the face unobscured and unshadowed from all points of view except when such obscurity is an intentional part of the staging. Ruffs, especially the wide and elaborate ones, cause similar difficulties by treacherously hiding the face they ought to frame. The fault in this case is likely to be insufficiently stiff starching or inadequate boning.

Long-haired wigs, unless carefully dressed and hairpinned in place, interfere with the view of the face from the side and give the performer a stuffy look. Renaissance page-boy wigs and the full-bottomed wigs of Molière's time are the most troublesome of these, so that a good deal of attention needs to be given to their effect in profile. Failure to consider the side views of headgear, ruffs, or wigs is certain to invite unpleasant consequences.

The character's complexion is another item in costuming which needs attention. The darker it is, the more difficult his face is to see. Othello is a case in point. The many arguments over the precise shade of this gentleman's "black" coloring are academic beside the fact that any very dark make-up puts him at a disadvantage in comparison with the minor characters by making his features harder to see. The same problem exists in regard to all roles which require Othello's complexion. Since suntanned skins became fashionable a generation ago, actors have inclined toward darker make-ups with the result that the Othello problem has become general. Our audiences have become accustomed to seeing men in any drawing-room play several shades darker of complexion than the women to the point that a foreigner not familiar with our fondness for suntanned men might think the two sexes to be of two different races.

In order to overcome the disadvantages of Othello's dark features, the framing elements of ruff, beard, and headwear need thoughtful designing. Contrast of beard and wig with more definitely modeled features will also help. Supporting these a careful treatment of the lines of his neckwear and his helmet, hat, or turban is required. The low visibility of our own leisure-class modern complexion is fortunately less of a problem, and a lighter base make-up is usually all that is needed.

Beards ought to be planned to increase visibility of the features. If the beard is dark, attention to the lines of the mouth and cheeks and avoidance of overly sharp contrasts between beard and complexion may achieve this. If the beard is light or grayed, emphasis is shifted to the modeling of the face and the problem of visibility is less acute. Bushy beards, luckily, are rarely required. When they are, the greater mass of the beard should, if possible, be shaped away from the face so as not to obscure its lines.

Improving Face and Figure

Once visibility is assured, the appearance of the face is largely a matter of proportion between face, beard, hairdo, and hat. A head which is shapely from all points of view and well proportioned to the features is pleasing to see and will make the actor seem handsome even though his features be undistinguished in the extreme.

When a hat is part of the costume, its shape is conditioned somewhat by the size of the actor's face. Large hats seldom look right on the small-featured person, nor do small hats go well with the large face. Sharp contrasts between the lines of the hat and the modeling of the face should be avoided except for comic effect. In general, the linear character of the face should be continued in the hat and subtly modified for the better. Angular features, for example, will seem less sharp if the hat is of slightly soft lines. Very bland features need headgear of somewhat crisper character.

What is true of headgear is also true of the hairdo. Both are capable of considerably improving the shape and character of the head. In addition to this, the hair is capable of being changed in texture to suit various roles. It can be curled, frizzed, or straightened, and dulled with powder or made glossy with hairdresser's lacquer. Its color can be heightened temporarily or changed completely with the washable powders prepared for this purpose. Since hair color is one of the readiest means of identifying characters, a wide range of colors is desirable in nearly every production.

The features often need modification to harmonize with the costume. Dignified draperies, for instance, go best with aquiline features. It is possible with nose putty to increase the symmetry of the features, sharpen prominence, fill in receding foreheads and chins, and improve the shape of the nose. Turned-up noses can very easily be remodeled into Greek or Roman ones. But putty is useless in treating features already overdeveloped, and something else must be provided to balance a large nose or to mask a too pronounced chin. With men beards are helpful here, and careful designing of beard and mustache can go far to balance a large nose, mask either a large chin or a weak one, and correct an ill-proportioned mouth. With women or unbearded men the solution must, of course, be sought elsewhere, providing accents in hairdo, collar, or hat which will compete for interest with the faulty feature and thus divide the attention of the spectator so as to make him less aware of the fault.

The torso is easily improved either by padding or corseting as the case requires. Men's chests and shoulders often gain from a bit of filling out. Also, in most men's figures the right shoulder is usually an inch or so lower than the left one and needs padding in order to present a symmetrical outline. Since nine out of ten men are somewhat flatter of chest than the ideal, a bit of padding across the pectoral muscles is sure to give vest or doublet a better shape. Women's busts, which used to be a problem, have been greatly improved by Hollywood in recent years; and since the various devices invented there are now everywhere available, there is no longer an excuse for any but the most perfect bustline.

When portions of the body are bared, powdering the skin softens both outline and texture. Greasing the skin, because of the highlights it adds, makes the body appear both slimmer and more muscular.

Arms and legs should as a rule be exposed only when naturally shapely. When tights must be worn, it is possible by bandaging to add shape to thin legs, but the process requires such skill that it is usually only a last resort. Even then it is not always dependable if the role requires much violent movement. It is better to plan on concealing angular or unshapely limbs. Fortunately, few roles really demand completely bare arms or legs. Boots, which are appropriate to almost any costume of which tights are an integral part, are the most dependable means of overcoming leg problems. The boots can be as high as the case requires — thigh-high for poor legs or knee-high for those who have good thighs but poor calves or knees. Jones in his *Mary of Scotland* put all his men in boots, and their appearance was most impressive. None but a tyro would design an ensemble requiring bare legs or tights for all characters except possibly in ballet where the dancers' legs are often uniformly well shaped.

Feet are less of a problem on stage than in life because costume shoes are worn for no more than a few hours at a time and hence can fit more snugly than everyday footwear. Feet can be made to appear smaller by being put into shoes a bit darker than the hose or trousers or skirt. Polished leathers and fabrics of some sheen also reduce the apparent size of the foot. In addition to darker shade and higher sheen, the use of accenting buckles and rosettes rather low on the instep will shorten the foot. Heels of contrasting color serve the same purpose.

The apparent height of a character is largely relative to those around him. Persons of only average height will seem tall in a group of undersized ones. Thus the design problem becomes one of making some actors taller and others shorter. When the impression of height must be changed, it is usually the footwear which does it. Heels, and lifts inside the shoe, are capable of adding as much as three inches to an actor's stature.

Heelless pumps, especially under long skirts, are capable of making a woman seem much shorter.

Problems of figure proportion include the short neck, the high waistline, the thick waist, and disproportionately long arms. The short neck calls for an avoidance of bulky material between the collarbone and the ear. Ruffs and collars need to be thin and of lightweight material, and if possible to be turned down. If turned up, they are best high and filmy. Fur, except the thinnest and sleekest, needs to be avoided. The high waistline is best without pronounced pleats or bustles to accentuate it. Paniers should be placed low and sloped somewhat. The thick waist demands first of all a tight corset and after that a contrast, if possible, between tight bodice and full skirt. Accents in the form of belts and girdles look best on the thick waist when affixed so as to curve or slant; in no case should they be horizontal. The reduction of the long arm is a matter of using contrasting textures between sleeve and hand plus careful calculation of the position of the sleeve hem.

Improving Movement

The quality of movement springs partly from the design of the footwear and partly from that of the upper garments. The footwear corrects the gait and modifies the stride. The upper garments mostly conceal or mitigate faults.

The design of the heel of a boot or shoe has the most to do with the posture. The higher the heel, the further forward the body is thrust in repose and the shorter the stride in walking. Beveling the heel slightly helps to correct a tendency to toe in while walking. The smooth heel-and-toe glide appropriate to hoopskirts requires a heelless or nearly heelless shoe.

A heavy sole makes a heavy gait. The walk of a character in boots is often improved by increasing the thickness of the sole or weighting it or by both. Increased thickness of sole makes little change in the character of the walk unless weight is increased too, and then it slows it. Jones used cork soles several inches thick on his men in *Lute Song* and although they gained in height there was little change in their stride or their ease of movement. In *Oklahoma!*, by contrast, where the dancing required great agility, the cowboys' boots were made, not like those of life, but lighter and softer and without the high heels of the horseman.

Long skirts are a godsend to actresses whose walk is ungainly, as are trailing capes for men. With both of these the design is largely a matter of concealing what cannot be changed. The same principle applies to angular movements of the arms. The device is simply one of masking the offending joints.

In cases where defects of movement cannot be concealed, it becomes necessary to provide some accent or line which takes attention away from the movement. Thus a sword, a cane, or a scarf swinging counter to the line of movement distracts the eye and turns an awkward motion into an unnoticed one.

Special Problems

Special problems of the relation of costume to actor occur in every production; their number and variety are infinite. But certain special problems are encountered so frequently that recognition of them is imperative. These are the problems (1) of anachronism in historical dress, (2) of simulating corpulence, (3) of women disguised as men, and (4) of making the appearance comic.

Anachronism in Historical Dress. The actor's idea of his own best appearance is often influenced by the fashion of his time. If broad shoulders are in vogue, he is inclined to favor a broad-shouldered silhouette regardless of the period of his costume. If the current Hollywood bust is high and pointed,

the actress tends to prefer such a bustline whether playing Cleopatra, Mary Stuart, or Josephine Bonaparte. Nor is the actor alone to blame. Sometimes the designer, in an attempt at style, uses the silhouette of his own era and grafts to it details from the period of the play. The costume which emerges as a result of this process becomes a popularized version of the original, but without lasting value. It will look absurd twenty years hence, and students looking at photographs of it will wonder how the performance could ever have been as good as their parents said it was. Today we look at pictures of Sarah Bernhardt as Cleopatra, with her corseted hourglass figure, and it is impossible to believe that her representation of that queen could ever have been called "divine." Joyce Redman as Anne Boleyn in *Anne of the Thousand Days* will look equally absurd twenty years hence with a bust which, although fascinating in itself, is alien to anything seen in England in 1535. When definite period style is aimed at, the silhouette of the period must be attained if the design is to have anything more than transitory value.

Romans and Greeks do not have pronounced waistlines. Elizabethan bodices show no bustline whatever. Elizabethan men have sloping shoulders and broad hips. Eighteenth-century men have protuberant torsos and natural shoulder lines. Nineteenth-century women have tiny waists and ample hips. These and other characteristics are the externalization of the times to which they belong. Every age has its own. It is the business of the designer to discover them and to use them to intended effect.

Simulating Corpulence. The world's great dramas have many parts for fat men; many more than there are fat actors, for the actor's life does not encourage corpulence. Thus one is faced with the problem of suiting a thin actor to a fat part.

The solution to the problem is more than

a matter of padding. Ordinary padding can add a little bulk but it cannot make a thin man into a fat one without making him uncomfortably warm and weighting him beyond endurance. Sponge rubber, punched through with air holes, is useful where the increase in bulk is no more than an inch or two. For greater bulk a structure of rattan or light wire is better. Beyond this the thickening effect is largely a matter of proportion. Fat men are fat in the back, belly and buttocks, not in the shoulders. The neck is thickened by reversing the devices ordinarily used to correct the short neck. Rough-surfaced fabrics, horizontal accents, and colors a shade lighter than those of the others' costumes complete the illusion.

Women Disguised as Men. Drama of the sixteenth and seventeenth centuries is full of situations depending upon a woman's assuming man's clothing so successfully as to deceive parents, lover, and even husband into accepting her as a male. In *As You Like It* Rosalind is mistaken for a youth by her lover through most of the play. Viola in *Twelfth Night* dresses as a boy with the consequence that the Countess Olivia falls in love with her and Sir Andrew challenges her to a duel. Portia in the trial scene of *The Merchant of Venice* is able to pass as a barrister and Nerissa as a page in spite of both their lovers being present. Chispa in *The Mayor of Zalamea* and Toinette in *The Imaginary Invalid* deceive their friends in like manner and with equal ease.

It is difficult for an actress with shapely legs not to display them when the opportunity is afforded by men's tights and trunk hose. It is also impossible for a performer to be at the same time both femininely attractive and plausibly masculine. This being the case, it seems logical that plausibility should take first place and that some other kind of play should be chosen for the display of the actress' physical assets.

The dress of the period makes disguise of sex easy if the costume is properly designed. The stiff doublet, belled breeches, and boots of man's clothing readily conceal the bust, hips, and legs which give a woman away, and the hats are such that the hair is easily covered. Toinette and Portia have the further advantage of doctors' gowns, which if furred and of sufficient fullness give them the same silhouettes as the real doctors in each play. The costume for Helen Hayes' Viola was extremely well designed and went far toward making hers the most convincing *Twelfth Night* of recent memory. It consisted of a close straight doublet and rather full breeches of knee length. Her hair was short and atop it she wore a boyish cap, fez-shaped, with a feather.

Making the Appearance Comic. Comical appearance in costume is principally lack of dignity. There is no need for the silhouette to violate the general style of the design, for the colors to offend the eye, or for the texture to clash with that of the other costumes in the group. The comical effect is gained simply by reversing one or two of the principles which apply to the improving of appearance. For example, a small face when topped by a large hat is likely to become amusing, just as a large face will with a small one. An element of incongruity is introduced into the appearance when the lines and textures used to set off the features are the opposite of what one would expect, as in an angular face and figure set off with soft and frilly things.

The emphasis of ungainly movement is comic. The hems of capes and coats instead of mitigating peculiarities of movement can be cut so as to emphasize them. A rolling walk is set off with some element of costume which swings with the motion of the body instead of contrary to it. Angular movements of the arms are intensified by the treatment of the elbow and wrist.

Oddities of figure are emphasized. Flat chests are flattened further. Bony bodies are skimpily covered and pudgy ones are clothed so as to make pudginess fully apparent. Spindly legs are left unbooted. Disproportionate costume elements are invoked, such as a short cape for a tall man and a long full cape for a short one.

In women's dress the cut of the neckline to set off face and shoulders to disadvantage is usually effective, as is the cut of the sleeve to emphasize the worst qualities of the arms. And of course the skirt hem can coincide with ankle or knee, sometimes with a ruffle or other trimming for additional emphasis.

Red wigs, bald pates, whitened eyelids, and patches on the breeches ought not to be necessary. Such devices are appropriate enough to the burlesque hall and the circus tent. But the comedian who needs them in legitimate drama is probably already beyond the help of the designer.

20 | Principles of Spatial Composition

Line · Light and Shade · Color

Order is the essence of all art. It makes colors and sounds pleasing instead of painful. It gives meaning to impressions which were otherwise chaotic and confusing. In visual arts this order is the consequence of selection and arrangement, the selection of lines and colors and the arrangement of them into coherent wholes. In some arts — painting for example — the terms "arrangement" and "composition" are practically synonymous. In music, however, "arrangement" usually stands for one sort of thing and "composition" for another quite different. Since theatrical design resembles in certain respects both painting and music, we will have to settle on one term or the other in order to avoid confusion in our discussion. In the visual scheme of the production there is nothing exactly corresponding to arrangement in music. On the other hand there is a great deal of similarity between the composition of the design and the composition both of the painting and of the piece of music. For this reason we will employ the term "composition" in our discussion.

A good design is composed so as to produce a definite sense of order. It reveals relationships, reconciles conflicting impressions, supplies transitions, and ultimately leaves the spectator with a satisfying feeling of balance. The well-composed design produces this effect whether it be static, as in sculpture, or temporal, as in music.

The design of a play is both static and temporal. It is static at any given moment, so that the principles of composition which produce a pleasing statue or painting will give similar pleasure to the perception of a moment in drama. But the design of a play also moves forward in time as music does, so that the successive sensations must add up to something if the sequence is to be meaningful. This dual nature of the design makes it desirable for us to consider its composition in relation to principles of temporal as well as spatial composition. Spatial composition, being the simpler of the two, will be considered first.

Any composition in space, whether it be a painting, a sculpture, a work of architecture, or a theatrical design, represents a combination of three visual properties: line, light and shade, and color. These three are always unavoidably present, although varying in importance. In a charcoal drawing color may be negligible, being present only in the tone of the paper and the light falling upon it. In a building or a piece of sculpture the properties of light and shade may greatly outweigh those of both line and color. In a stage design all three are usually present in marked degree.

Where line, light and shade, and color are employed together, line is the foundation of the composition as the plan is of a building. It is the property which most nearly determines the form of the whole and which holds the parts of the whole together.

LINE

A good deal of the art of scene design is the art of focusing attention, of making the spectator see what he is supposed to see. The lines of the setting guide his attention to the character or action at that moment most indispensable to his comprehension of the whole.

There are two principal means by which lines can be made to focus the attention. One of these is by the *convergence* of lines toward the center of interest. The other is by *enclosure* of the center of interest with a curve or a rectangle. Almost all the settings which one can call to mind feature one or the other of these devices.

Convergence

Convergence is the most direct and by far the most forceful means of controlling attention. The lines of the setting may converge either upward or downward. In either case the result is the same — the eye is forced to move toward the center at which the lines converge. Downward convergence is most commonly seen in settings where the lines of the background forms descend or recede toward an apex. Perspective, especially in exterior settings, often serves to provide the convergence, since receding horizontals meet at eye level and thus fall naturally behind the head of the actor. The convergence of rising lines is most likely to be seen where ramps, steps, and levels vary the plane of the acting area so that the highest-placed actor stands at the apex of an upright tri-

angle composed by the lines of the setting or of the group about him. (See Figure 33.)

Because of its strength convergence must be used sparingly, for such compelling composition tires the eye quickly. This being the case, it is best held in reserve for climactic moments of the play, or, in a sequence of scenes, for the shorter and more irregular ones where the use of it will not wear out the attention by forcing it too strongly for too long a time.

Enclosure

Enclosure is a less compelling means of gaining and holding attention and consequently better suited to scenes of lower dramatic intensity or greater duration. It is certainly one of the most dependable devices known. Based upon the optical principle that the eye always travels to the axis of an arc, it draws attention always to its center. On stage it may be seen most often in the use of the arch enclosing and framing a character. Its general action is such that the experienced performer can seldom forego using it when making an entrance of any kind through a large opening in the setting. Its intensity may be increased indefinitely by increasing the number of arcs concentric upon the single axis of interest. (See Figure 34.)

The logarithmic spiral is really only a variation of the device of enclosure, and its general effect is the same, carrying the eye toward the axis of the curve. It is generally less effective except in scenes of little activity where its focusing action can be brought to bear fully. If a character moves across its axis, its focusing action ceases to function.

Intersection and Opposition

This leaves us with two distinctly less forceful means of directing attention: intersection and opposition. Intersection of the object of attention by a line crossing the vision seems most effective when the line

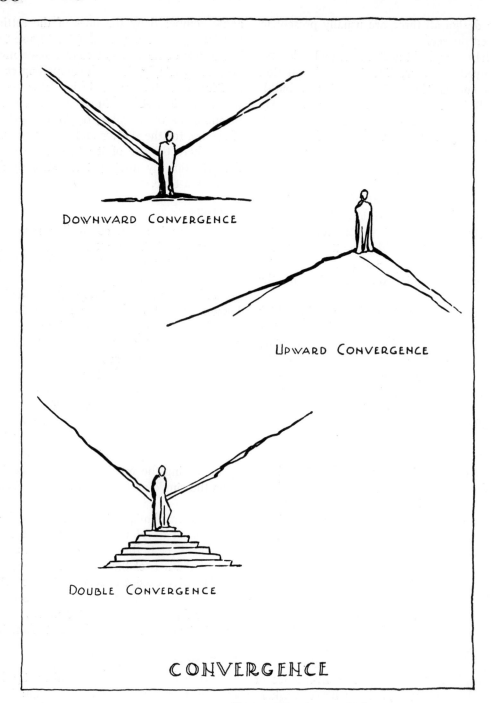

DOWNWARD CONVERGENCE

UPWARD CONVERGENCE

DOUBLE CONVERGENCE

CONVERGENCE

Figure 33. Lines which converge upon a center of interest constitute one of the most forceful means of compelling attention.

ENCLOSURE

Figure 34. The attention-attracting power of enclosure is based upon the tendency of the eye to move toward the axis of a curve.

in question declines from left to right. This is generally believed to be due to the reading habit which has given to the Western eye a direction tendency of that kind. Seemingly the attention is caught by an object which interrupts the direction of the line. (See Figure 35.)

Opposition is believed to be gained by declining lines in one direction opposed to a movement of the actor predominantly in the opposite direction. But so much depends upon the movement of the actor that it would be foolish to say that opposition operates definitely in one direction or another.

Symmetrical and Asymmetrical Balance

After focus of attention, the next most important quality of the linear composition is balance. Whatever the design, its parts should weigh equally against one another, as on a fulcrum. This usually means that the heavier elements of greatest interest should be nearest the center of the composition with the lesser ones further out, and that where interest is shared, the elements should be roughly equidistant from the center of the composition.

There are but two ways in which a design may be balanced. It may be symmetrical, or it may be asymmetrical. A symmetrical composition is the same on both sides. An asymmetrical composition has differing sides balancing each other upon some imaginary center. The most striking designs in the theatre are usually symmetrical for the reason that this is the kind of balance most apt to be used for the most dramatic scenes, in which attention is sharply focused upon one character, as it is focused upon Orgon during the table scene in *Tartuffe.* Asymmetrical balance will be found as a rule in scenes requiring several centers of interest and in scenes which must last for such a length of time that the eye would be wearied by the simpler and more intense balance of symmetry. (See Figure 36.)

Transition, Repetition, Progression, and Dominance

Some other principles of linear composition are those of transition, repetition, progression, and dominance. The first of these is brought into use as a means of lightening an arrangement of lines which in its first form seems too bold and stark. It is the linking of lines so as to ease the movement of the eye from one to another. For example, between two lines meeting at a right angle a transition might be produced by joining them with a third line at a gentler angle or by placing in the corner some different form, say a circle. Either of these will form a sort of bridge across the juncture of the lines, permitting the eye to make the change in direction with a minimum of effort.

On a large scale, repetition of the basic lines of the composition may be used to reinforce their effect. On a smaller scale, repetition of lines at variance with those of the main composition — such as the repetition of curves within a composition of straight lines — may be used to give variety and added interest to the whole composition. This use of repetition is most often seen in the ornament of a setting. Devices such as the Greek wave or the bead-and-reel possess considerable charm because of their regularity and also by virtue of the fact that any motif which is repeated more than twice tends to establish its own effect of rhythm.

In regard to repetition, the ancient saying that "the eye counts to five" is based on the knowledge that beyond that number the identity of separate units of a sequence is apt to be lost and only the sense of a rhythmic sequence retained. Hence if an impression other than that of uniformity is desired some change must be made in the sequence. The recourse in this case will be to one or the other of the devices of dominance or progression. The uniformity of identical forms in sequence can be broken up by mak-

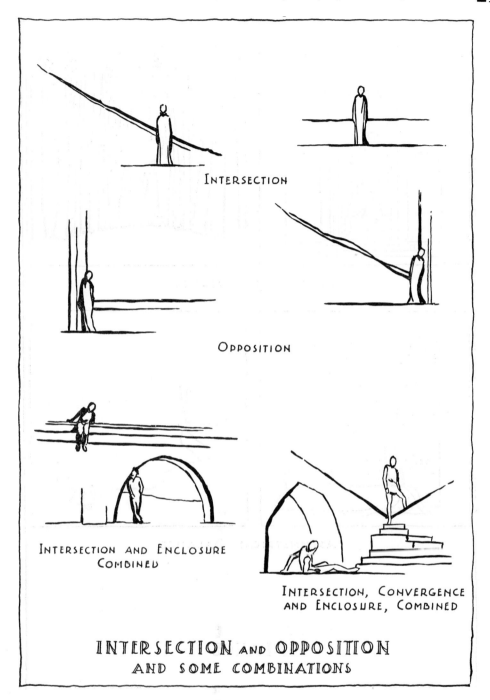

INTERSECTION

OPPOSITION

INTERSECTION AND ENCLOSURE COMBINED

INTERSECTION, CONVERGENCE AND ENCLOSURE, COMBINED

INTERSECTION AND OPPOSITION
AND SOME COMBINATIONS

Figure 35. Intersection and opposition most definitely guide attention when the object of interest is in motion.

SYMMETRICAL BALANCE

ASYMMETRICAL BALANCE

BALANCE

Figure 36. In any pictorial composition, balance is one of the essentials for a satisfying aesthetic effect.

ing one of them either larger or smaller. Or the uniformity may be broken but the sequence and rhythm retained by giving the units a progressive change of scale. (See Figure 37.) The progression of similar forms seems to possess some fascination for the eye which compels it to follow the change. For this reason progression has always been very popular and has been used for all sorts of optical tricks under various names, of which dynamic symmetry and arithmetical progression are but two. The reader who would like to follow the subject further will find some extremely interesting illustrations of it in Claude Bragdon's book, *The Frozen Fountain.*

LIGHT AND SHADE

If only the setting could be conceived as a pure linear composition, scene design would be the simplest of arts. As it is, the presence of the actor and the depth of the acting area make it impossible to think of it as other than three-dimensional. As in sculpture and architecture, the dimensional quality of the setting makes light and shade of utmost importance for it is by highlight and shadow that its shape and seeming weight are perceived.

There is in English no one word which describes the property of light and shade as accurately as the Italian *chiaroscuro* or the Japanese *noton.* The commonly used terms, "value," "mass," "volume," and "tone" are each more restricted in meaning as well as being somewhat confusing because of their frequent use in relation to color. For the purposes of this discussion, therefore, we will do better to stick to the phrase "light and shade," using it as if it were one word covering all the properties of light, highlight, and shadow.

In the stage setting four properties of light and shade must be taken into consideration. These are: *value,* the general level of brightness of the scene; the *quality* of the prevailing illumination; the predominant *direction* of illumination; and the *degree of concentration* of light. Each of these has a strong bearing on the appearance of the setting as well as upon the mood of the scene.

Value

The chief contributor to the mood of the scene is the value or general brightness of the scene. There is an immense range here between the lowest and the highest values perceptible to the spectator. A setting might be dark in color, dimly lighted, and inhabited by somber figures, or it might be done in delicate tints, brilliantly illuminated and used to support the appearance of gay characters. Each setting would be seen with nearly equal ease. It is generally true that more serious drama tends to require lower values while lighter drama calls for the reverse. The mood of the scene as it lies between these two extremes of darkness and brightness may be largely influenced by the level of value given it. Once in a while an inexperienced playwright will turn out a play calling for comic action to take place in moonlight — a thing which is almost impossible to stage, since the very nature of the scene militates against the proposed setting of it. But such things are bound to occur and it is up to the designer to effect the necessary adjustment.

While values appropriate to tragedy and comedy are generally agreed upon, there are a few other principles which may be applied to other kinds of drama. Melodrama, which is usually made up of a number of fast and abrupt actions, requires high values, for the swift staccato action must be comprehended by the spectator more readily than is possible at low levels of illumination. If the mood of the melodrama is somber, it has to be established by the first impression conveyed to the audience and adjusted thereafter to the requirements of the action.

Farce, which is quite similar to melodrama in its action requirements, differs only in its initial impression of mood.

Quality

The quality of light and shade depends on the degree of differentiation between values of light and dark in the setting. The particular quality of the moment may be any one of innumerable variations lying between extremely soft, diffused illumination and the corresponding extremity of hardness produced by direct light with its accompanying shadows. The latter of these is the more intense of the two and possesses the heaviest shadows; as a result it is the best suited to scenes of a more serious nature. Conversely, the softer quality is more appropriate to scenes of a lighter sort such as occur most often in comedies and romances. Between the two extremes of softness and hardness lies that quality of light which yields the highest visibility. This quality is most likely to figure in designs which must support a considerable variety of complex actions and rapid movements. Good visibility is obviously necessary to make possible the utmost comprehension of such a scene. Under a very soft quality of light and shade the spectator has difficulty in distinguishing details of form or subtleties of expression, since the delineation of these is not clearly marked by highlight and shadow. An extremely harsh light, on the other hand, makes discrimination difficult by reason of its lack of intermediate values. The perfect medium so far as visibility is concerned lies midway between the two extremes at the point where the different forms and the various textures — smooth, rough, hard, soft — are most easily distinguished. How close the designer is able to come to perfect visibility depends on his ability to reconcile the necessities of mood of the piece with the demands of illumination made according to the speed and amount of movement in the scene.

Direction

The third property of light and shade, the direction or angle of illumination, is of utmost importance, in relation to both the mood of the piece and the visibility of its performers. Architects and sculptors, in planning their respective works, always take into consideration the predominant direction of the light by which the finished work must be viewed. In architecture the 45° angle of light, falling from the upper left toward the lower right, is conventional and appears in nearly every architectural sketch or rendering. In scene design, however, the direction from which the light falls upon performer and setting is at once both variable and subject to control. Again the question is one of appropriateness to the scene of the moment.

Imagine a scene in which the rise of the curtain reveals two characters seated at a small table near the center of the stage, with a single shaft of light falling almost perpendicularly upon them from some unseen source high above. The characters are heavily cloaked and hooded so that nothing of their facial expression is perceived. What would your first reaction be to this setting? Would it not suggest conspiracy or some such evil at work? Certainly gaiety or humor or fantasy would be the last thing one would think of on viewing such a design.

The direction from which the light strikes the center of interest is of significance not only as it influences the appearance of the object by the highlights and shadows which it produces but also as it affects the mood of the observer. If we think for the moment of the central performer as this object, there are 180 degrees in every direction from which he can theoretically be illuminated. Of course the same is true of the setting and any part of it. While it is neither necessary nor desirable to codify all the various effects produced by light from all these angles, a

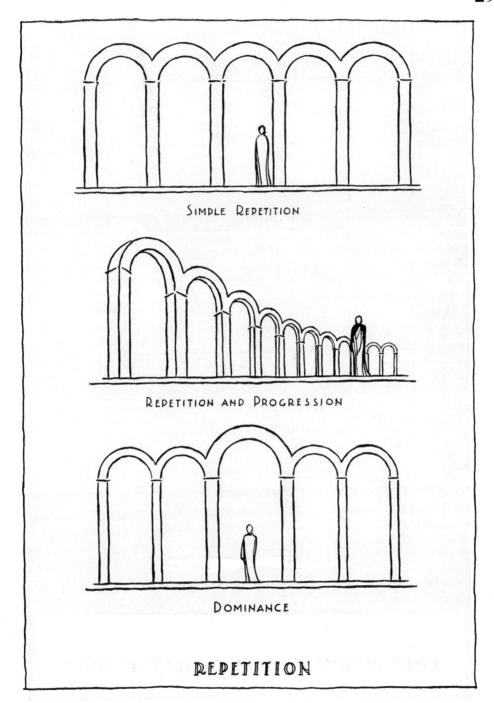

SIMPLE REPETITION

REPETITION AND PROGRESSION

DOMINANCE

REPETITION

Figure 37. In linear composition, the uses of repetition are based on the rule that "the eye counts to five."

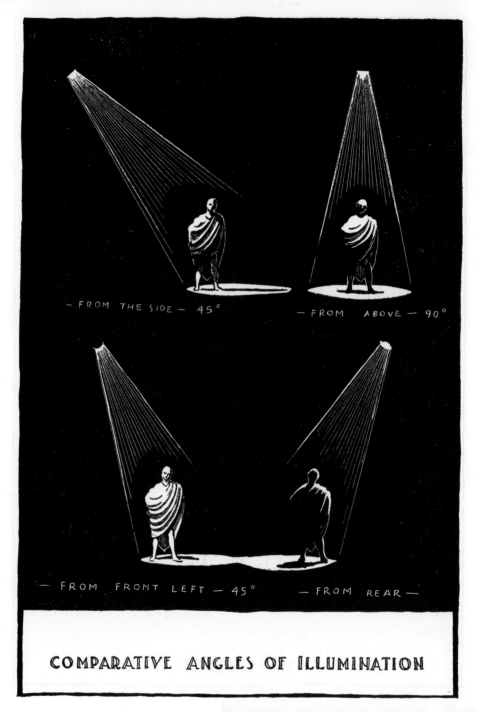

Figure 38. The angle from which the figure is lighted is capable of causing great variation in its appearance.

few general principles may be noted as well as a few "effects" which are not entirely governed by principle. (See Figure 38.)

First, visibility is best — that is to say form is most completely and accurately revealed — by light striking an object at about 45° to the horizon and about 45° to the line of vision. Light approaching an object from a higher angle, say 60° to 70°, intensifies the appearance of form somewhat at the expense of visibility and with some distortion of appearance. Likewise, as the direction of the light swings around to a more nearly obtuse angle to the line of vision, the plasticity increases as the visibility decreases, until when the light is directly behind the object with the figure intercepting the rays passing from the source of the light to the eye of the spectator — as is the case in silhouette or back-lighting — only the outline of the object is perceptible, with practically no detail of surface. This device of either silhouetting a figure against a lighter background, or back-lighting it so that the details are subordinated and the whole shape outlined, is a favorite device on the stage as it is in photography. It catches the attention of the spectator by contrasts of value but directs it to the general form rather than to parts of that form. As a result it is one of the commonest means of emphasizing particular performers or parts of the setting.

As the direction of the light approaches the horizontal and swings around more nearly parallel to the line of vision, shadows are shortened and the sense of plasticity of the object as a whole is greatly diminished. The human face is so constructed, with its deep eye sockets and rather receding planes below the cheek, that when much of the face and its expression must be seen, the angle of illumination which is employed is nearer 30° than 45° — the 45° employed to reveal general form. With the setting, on the other hand, which usually possesses more regular planes, a somewhat higher angle of forward illumination is likely to reveal its best shape. It is common practice in scene design to light the actor from a lower angle than the setting and to gain the impression of weight in a setting by emphasizing its most plastic element by means of rather narrowly controlled highlights.

Scenes of much action and swift movement are best when illuminated by light from an angle very nearly in line with the line of vision. The play of light and shade is thus minimized, but the attention is controlled by other devices of line and color rather than lighting.

Generally speaking, as the direction of illumination approaches the line of vision the appearance of plasticity of the center of interest is decreased and with it the dramatic intensity of the scene as a whole. Conversely, as the predominant direction of light moves further away from the sight line the plasticity and dramatic intensity of the scene increases, accompanied by a corresponding decrease in the perception of detail. Finally, as the angle of light approaches a direction opposite that of the sight line, outline sharpens, plasticity is reduced, and when the center of interest stands in silhouette the composition to all intents is without weight.

Deserving separate consideration is the case of light and shade coming from below and in front of the center of interest, such as is produced by footlights, firelight, or spotlights placed in the footlight trough. The dramatic power of such a direction of light is remarkable although the reason for its power is difficult to give. It may be that the associations built around firelight are more dramatic. The sheer difference of this direction of light from that in which objects are usually seen may account for its effect. Whatever the cause, it cannot be denied that this direction of illumination is intrinsically dramatic and is to be used as such, though sparingly, like all dependable and powerful effects.

Concentration

The fourth property of light and shade is that dependent upon the degree of concentration of the light falling upon the center of interest, together with the value of the transitions between the light and dark areas. The concentration of light upon performer or setting is determined by the amount of emphasis required. In a group of objects otherwise equal the eye goes naturally to the one most brightly lighted. Thus this becomes an additional means of focusing the spectator's attention.

The dramatic intensity of the scene determines the sharpness of the concentration of light. It is apparent that the more acute the concentration the more intense will be the appearance of the composition. Hence, sharp concentration of light may be employed with fullest effect only in scenes of relatively high dramatic intensity and rather brief duration. If the scene is protracted, visual fatigue and consequent weakening of interest is bound to result.

Between such intensity and absolutely even illumination possessing no emphasis whatever there are innumerable degrees of concentration possible, according to the nature and temper of the scene. For it is not only the inclusiveness of the illumination but the degree of transition or gradation of values between the center of interest and the lesser elements of the composition which regulates the spectator's attention. In composing the setting it is well to imagine the most dramatic moment of the scene with the concentration and gradation of light appropriate to it, and to work outward from there.

The action of these four properties of value, quality, direction, and concentration may be clarified with a few examples. For the first one, imagine the fourth scene of Molière's *Tartuffe* in an interpretation emphasizing the romantic elements of the script, conceived in the spirit not so much of the original as of a stylistic re-presentation of the baroque. Since the mood of the scene is light, its value or brightness level would be high. The swift action requires a fairly hard quality of light, a low angle of front illumination, and slight concentration. Altogether one could sum up the light and shade of the scene as bright, clear, and widely distributed. For contrast to this, one might choose the opening scene of *The Trojan Women*, where a somber scene in low value, with diffused light falling from nearly directly overhead and strongly concentrated upon the weary body of the captive Queen. The first scene of *Hamlet* is still different in the properties of light required. This scene is dark according to the time of day and the nature of the impending tragedy. Yet the characters must be clearly seen and readily identified, and later in the scene a ghost appears. This would seem to suggest a general low value of illumination in the neighborhood of 45° front, and a narrow concentration of light which could include the human beings but exclude the ghost.

COLOR

Color is perhaps the most powerful means which the designer possesses for influencing the emotional response of the spectator. The emotional appeal of color is generally believed to be rooted in the reaction tendencies of an individual resulting from various associations with different colors which have figured in his past experience. This is but one explanation. It is widely accepted, and no doubt partly true, but it fails to explain the pleasure produced by occasional harmonies of color unrelated to any other recognizable forms. One does not know the source of the acute discomfort produced by the juxtaposition of pure green and pure orange, nor why pure blue and pure violet when placed side by side are so irritating to the average spectator. No one really knows why black and bright green or violet are so seldom seen together, except that the combination is not as popular as some others.

Fortunately, much more is known, and much more definitely, about those combinations of color which do appeal to the average observer, for they have formed the basis of most of our use of color for many generations. Because these combinations are pleasing and because they evoke a sense of completeness, they have come to be called *harmonies.* It is with these that our discussion will be chiefly concerned. Whatever the scene, however composed, a harmony must be produced — harmony between the colors themselves as satisfying as the harmony between the colors and the other elements of the design — if the whole production is to have that completeness which signalizes a work of art.

While the possible number of harmonies is probably infinite, upon the spectator the effects of no two of them are alike. This is a fact of considerable significance. For of the host of different harmonies available to the designer, some are bound to be better than others, a few will be particularly suitable to the scene, and perhaps one will be imperative. All the others will be inappropriate in varying degrees, and some will be utterly impossible. This is due to the natures of the harmonies themselves, based as they are upon either the opposition of colors or their appearance of similarity to one another. Contributing to this distinction are the properties of certain groups of colors and their ability to evoke an impression of warmth or coldness, lightness or darkness, or brilliance. It is with these properties that the discussion of color logically begins.

It is generally agreed that the phenomenon of color is the result of the difference in the wave lengths of light perceptible within the limits of human vision. The longest rays produce a sensation of redness while the shortest ones have the appearance of what we have

come to call violet. Beyond these extremes at either end of the visible colors are the infrared and ultraviolet waves, which are ordinarily invisible. In between the two lie all the sensations to which the eye is capable of responding. It is the reflection of these varied wave lengths from different surfaces which produces our principal impressions of color. (See Figure 39.)

Three Attributes of Color: Hue, Purity, and Value

Every color visible to the eye possesses three attributes: hue, purity, and value.

Hue is the factor which causes us to see red as red and green as green and enables us to distinguish between them. It is the characteristic sensation of redness or greenness accompanying the perception of a certain wave length of light. For example, forest green and emerald green, although differing in other respects are both green because their wave lengths are essentially the same. One is definitely darker than the other, but there is small likelihood that normal vision will confuse either with the very different hue of yellow.

The *purity* of a color is its saturation or depth of hue. It is determined by the position of the color in relation to the neutral, gray. An olive green and a chartreuse green are similar in hue but different in purity, the olive green being less pure, less saturated, and hence duller and grayer. A beige and an orange belong to the same hue area, but the beige is more neutral than the orange. Colors such as beige and olive green are usually referred to as neutrals because the impression which they make on the eye approaches grayness as much or more than hue. A color of high purity is neutralized by adding to it a bit of some other very different color, for this weakens its hue and grays it, making the sensation of color much less pronounced. The attribute of purity, unlike that of hue, has many synonyms among which

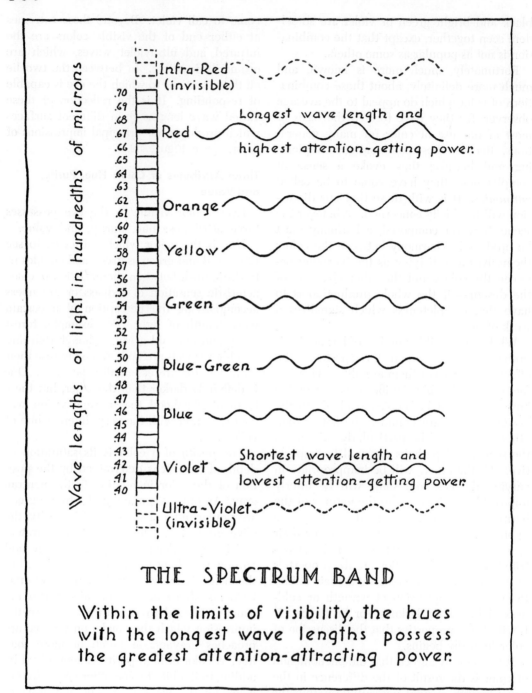

THE SPECTRUM BAND

Within the limits of visibility, the hues with the longest wave lengths possess the greatest attention-attracting power.

Figure 39. The spectrum band of visible hues, as shown here, underlies all theory about color.

those of "saturation," "depth," "density," and "chroma" are most commonly seen.

Both hue and purity are relative sensations and vary according to the conditions under which the color is perceived — the number of colors within the field of vision, and the color sensations which have immediately preceded the perception.

The *value* of a color is its relative lightness or darkness as determined by its power to reflect light. This is also called "brightness" and "brilliance." High values or tints are the lighter variations of hues, as pink is a tint of red. Low values, called shades, are the darker equivalents. Thus maroon is a shade of red, as is navy of blue. The number of shades and tints which can be developed from any one hue is variable. Whether this is due to the behavior of dyes and pigments or the limitations of human vision is hard to say. Thus red and green each have many shades and many tints, but violet and yellow, which each have many tints, have few shades. Dark yellow and dark violet are rarely seen, and when they are one can seldom distinguish them from neutrals.

The impression of value is the result of three things: the brightness of the light in which the color is seen, the quality of the surface reflecting the light, and the distance from which it is viewed. Colors have higher value in sunlight and on a brightly lighted stage than when the light is dim. Thus an increase of illumination heightens all colors visible at the time. Shiny surfaces such as those of satin and polished metal reflect their colors in higher value than matte surfaces of identical hue. If a piece of velvet and a piece of satin are dyed with the same dye and to the same depth, the satin will emerge with the greater brilliance. The same pigment mixed in two batches of paint, one flat and the other glossy, will seem brighter on the surface to which the glossy paint is applied. As distance between the eye and the colored object increases, the value of the color lessens. In part this is due to the increase in the number of color sensations within the field of vision and the decrease in the area of the object. Where distances are great, as looking across a landscape, the haze usually present in the atmosphere interposes between the eye and the object a translucent curtain which cuts down brilliance of color.

Visibility of Color

The visibility of a color varies according to its wave length. Those at the extreme ends of the visible spectrum are less easily seen than those in the middle of the band. The hue most easily seen of all is a yellowish green of medium wave length, about equidistant from the two extremes of red and violet which mark the limits of vision. In this hue it is also possible for normal vision to distinguish more variations than are possible in any other. Colors lying to either side of this mid-point become gradually less visible as they approach the ends of the spectrum band (and fewer variations are discernible), until finally nothing at all is visible as the waves pass from red to infrared and violet to ultraviolet. Colors lying close to the ends of the band — the purest reds and violets — often possess a fuzzy appearance which blurs outlines, confuses details, and makes judgment of distances difficult. (See Figure 40.) In this respect color may be compared to sound. The shrillest and the deepest sounds — those lying nearest to the limits of audibility — are more difficult to hear and allow less discrimination than sounds nearer the middle of the range. The sounds which are easiest to hear are those lying well within the limits of audibility, and it is among these that the normal ear is capable of distinguishing the greatest number of variations.

Attention-Attracting Power of Color

One might think that the color of highest visibility would also be the one with the

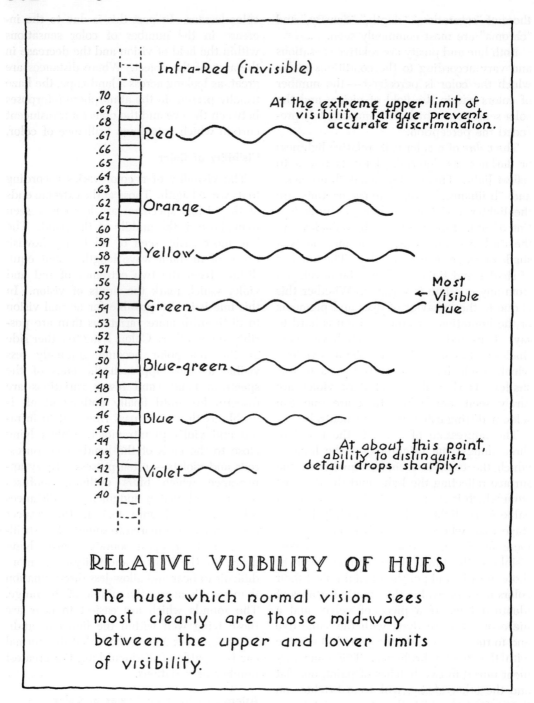

Infra-Red (invisible)

.70
.69
.68
.67 Red
.66
.65
.64
.63
.62 Orange
.61
.60
.59
.58 Yellow
.57
.56
.55
.54 Green
.53
.52
.51
.50 Blue-green
.49
.48
.47
.46 Blue
.45
.44
.43
.42 Violet
.41
.40

At the extreme upper limit of
visibility fatigue prevents
accurate discrimination.

← Most
  Visible
  Hue

At about this point,
ability to distinguish
detail drops sharply.

RELATIVE VISIBILITY OF HUES

The hues which normal vision sees
most clearly are those mid-way
between the upper and lower limits
of visibility.

Figure 40. Some colors are much easier to see than
others; some attract attention, yet are hard to see.

greatest power of attracting attention, but this is not the case. The colors which most strongly attract the eye are those of longest wave length: the reds. From the top of the spectrum band the attention-getting power of color seems to diminish as the wave length grows shorter until at the bottom of the band it reaches violet, whose power in this respect is least of all. If we compare color with sound, the reds of long wave length may be likened to notes of high pitch whose shrillness compels attention more readily than those of lower pitch, all the way down to the lowest audible notes, which possess in themselves no attention-attracting power of any consequence.

It is a curious fact that colors of high attention-attracting power seem nearer to the eye than those of lesser power, just as shrill sounds seem closer to the ear. Of two costumes, one red and one violet, the red one will — all other things being equal — seem closer and the violet one will seem to recede. In a combination of orange and blue the orange will make the stronger bid for attention. This quality is called *proximity.* It is more or less pronounced accordingly as the wave length of the hue is greater or less than others within the field of vision. It is this impression of relative proximity which makes possible many of the most striking effects in stage design. It is also the basis for numerous optical illusions.

Warm and Cool Colors

Certain colors — principally yellow, orange, and red — seem warm. Quite probably this is because of their association with sunlight, fire, and other sensations of high temperature. Of these, red-orange, in the middle of the group, is certainly the warmest. At the other end of the spectrum are the colors which give an impression of coolness. This may be due to their association with ice, steel, deep water, and other things which are usually cold. Of this group, blue-green seems

the coldest. (See Figure 41.) Altogether, much of the emotional significance of color is probably tied in with its habitual association with various tactile sensations of temperature.

The emotional effect of warm and cold groupings of color is often likened to that of the major and minor scales in music. In this comparison the warm combinations are seen to resemble the major scale which is generally lively and cheerful, while the cool combinations are viewed as paralleling in feeling the somewhat more saddening minor scale.

Color Harmony

As indicated earlier, an arrangement of color which is especially pleasing to the eye is a harmony; it is the result of good proportion between colors of differing strengths and the areas occupied by them. There is no practical limit to the number of hues or values which may be employed within a given harmony if the areas are proportionate to their varying powers. A useful rule of thumb is the old axiom, "the brightest color in the smallest space," and while this rule need not be religiously followed it does provide a dependable guide by which good proportion may always be assured. There are two principal schemes for composing harmonies of color. One is called harmony of *contrast;* the other, harmony of *similarity.*

In the harmony of contrast, colors of distinctly different temperature or attention-attracting power are juxtaposed, with the weaker colors occupying the larger areas. For example, when yellow and blue are used together, the blue usually occupies the larger area and yellow the smaller one. Or red and green are placed side by side with the red in the smaller space. Often one strong hue is opposed to two or more weaker ones. Thus green and blue may be used to balance the stronger red, in which case the opposition to the red is divided between the blue and the green and the areas proportioned accordingly.

Hues of striking difference in strength when placed side by side are more pleasing if one of them — usually the weaker — is dulled, lightened, or darkened a bit. For example, orange and green of equal purity if placed together in any proportion are decidedly unpleasant to see, but if the green is darkened, the combination becomes more endurable. If the orange is lightened to a tint or dulled toward brown, a rather agreeable balance becomes possible.

The other harmony is built upon a sequence of similar tones such as might be gained by a grouping of predominantly warm or cool colors, of colors all marked by a similar grayness, or of hues whose positions at the ends of the spectrum give them the same indistinctness.

In a sequence of warm colors the grouping might include yellow, orange, and red, with some additional modification of value so as to result in a sequence either of dark red, orange-brown, and yellow or of dull yellow, orange-gray, and bright red. This arrangement is called a sequence because of the tendency of the eye to move toward the purest hue in the group, with the intermediate tones assisting the movement.

In a sequence of cool colors a variety of comparable groupings are possible, and because of the lower attention-attracting nature of cool colors, a somewhat greater degree of subtlety is possible. Green, yellow-green, and yellow usually yield a pleasing harmony. Violet, blue-violet, and green, with the intermediate blue omitted so that the eye jumps, as it were, from blue-violet to green, is also agreeable. In each sequence the eye seems to move toward the hue of greatest wave length.

With tones which are definitely grayed, lightened, or darkened, the effects of hue difference are greatly diminished. The similarity upon which their relationship is based then becomes one of neutrality, of tints, or of shades. Even between colors of widely differing hue the element of contrast is reduced to the point where — if the modification is sufficiently pronounced — almost any grouping becomes possible. Very light green and very light orange become pleasant together if their areas are well proportioned, even though the juxtaposition of these hues in their pure state is unendurable. Lavender and pink, lavender and pale yellow, pale blue and light blue-green — all are equally acceptable to the eye. Lemuel Ayers employed such a harmony in his design for *Oklahoma!,* using every hue of the spectrum with all of them lightened to tints, and the effect was very agreeable.

Sometimes a grouping of colors is tied together by mixing one hue with each other color present, so that a predominant yellowness or greenness or blueness overlays the hue differences and gives all tones a family relationship. This is a favorite harmony of seventeenth-century painters, with a yellow or amber color used to produce the similarity. Rembrandt's "golden tone" is this kind of harmony.

Arrangements of hues from opposite ends of the spectrum are tricky and hard to develop to best effect, and for this reason are rarely seen. However, when the composition of such colors is successful the result is most dramatic. Stewart Chaney used such a sequence in his costume ensemble for the Leslie Howard *Hamlet.* Violet, purple, and red were his hues, harmonized in several costumes and repeated in certain elements of the setting, with very moving results. Leon Bakst, who designed a number of the more memorable productions of Diaghilev's Ballet Russe, was fond of the violet-purple-red harmony and employed it frequently to stunning effect.

The violet-and-red combination is difficult, because the difference between the attention-getting powers of the two principal

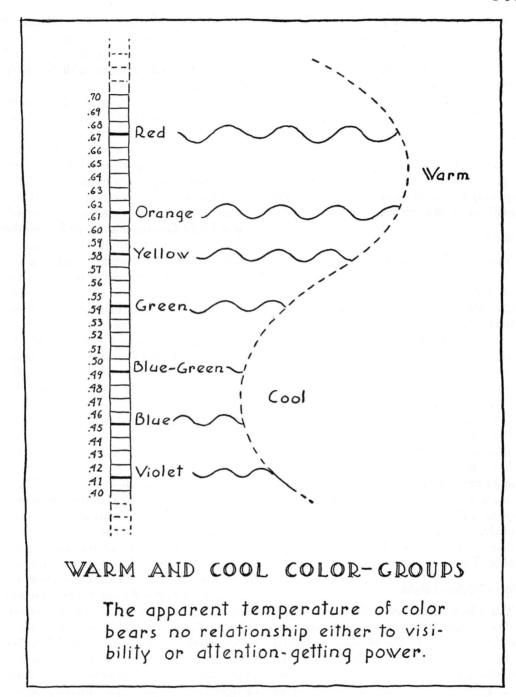

.70
.69
.68
.67 — Red
.66
.65
.64
.63
.62
.61 — Orange
.60
.59
.58 — Yellow
.57
.56
.55
.54 — Green
.53
.52
.51
.50
.49 — Blue-Green
.48
.47
.46
.45 — Blue
.44
.43
.42 — Violet
.41
.40

Warm

Cool

WARM AND COOL COLOR-GROUPS

The apparent temperature of color bears no relationship either to visibility or attention-getting power.

Figure 41. Impressions of warmth and coolness in color are probably caused by association of certain hues with certain tactile sensations.

hues are extreme. Only their peculiar vibrance or fuzziness of outline relates them. The harmony is effected by introducing a third color, red-violet, properly called "purple," into the combination to form a sort of bridge between the two extremes. This purple in its purest state is a peculiar hybrid of a color which seems to reflect to some degree both the short waves of the violet and the long waves of the red and to possess the fuzziness of both. The colors popularly called "magenta" and "cerise" are variations of this purple.

Color Accents

Small touches of strong color are often used to liven a harmony. The areas of color used for this purpose are best when only large enough to be visible and too small to attract or hold the eye in competition with the major colors in the arrangement. These touches do not alter the basic harmony of whatever kind although they do increase its general vitality. For the most part the accents are hues which oppose the major tones of the composition. Thus a green costume will be accented with a braid or piping of red, a blue-shadowed area of the setting will be touched here and there with red-orange or yellow. When a combination of colors emerges with less life than had been expected, discreet accentuation is often the remedy. The work of many a skillful designer is distinguished by his tasteful and telling placement of accents.

Effect of Colored Light

The effect of colored light upon setting and costume is a matter of prime importance, for the final impression of color conveyed to the spectator is always the sum of the illumination and the light reflected to the eye. Fortunately the initial impression of the design under colored light is of less consequence than its true coloring, for while it is difficult to revise a color scheme involv-

ing costumes and scenery the readjustment of colors of light is comparatively easy. Sources of light may be brightened, dimmed down, or given new filters with relatively little effort.

The appearance of colored objects under light is explained by the phenomenon of selective reflection. When light falls upon a colored surface only a part of the light is reflected. Thus if a white light falls upon a red surface only the wave lengths related to red are reflected back to the eye. Theoretically the other wave lengths are absorbed. If a red light falls upon a red surface all the light rays are reflected and the appearance of the surface is unchanged. But if a red light is directed upon a green surface, the surface, which is capable of reflecting only green rays, reflects no light, and hence appears much darker than it would under white light. The same is true of any surface. It can reflect only the wave lengths of its own hue; if a particular tint of the light reduces the number of those rays falling upon it, it reflects less and looks darker.

If the same red light is focused upon a composition containing both red and green, the red will appear unchanged, but the green will be reduced virtually to blackness. Each color of light behaves in precisely the same fashion: it makes no change in its own hue but it darkens and dulls all others. The stronger the contrast between the color of light and the colors of the surface, the darker those colors will seem. When colored light falls upon a composition containing a variety of colors it will make the least change in those colors which are most nearly identical with its own and the greatest in those which most directly oppose it; all other colors in the composition will be modified in proportion to their opposition to the color of light and always in the direction of decreasing value.

Generally speaking, the action of selective reflection is such that any combination of

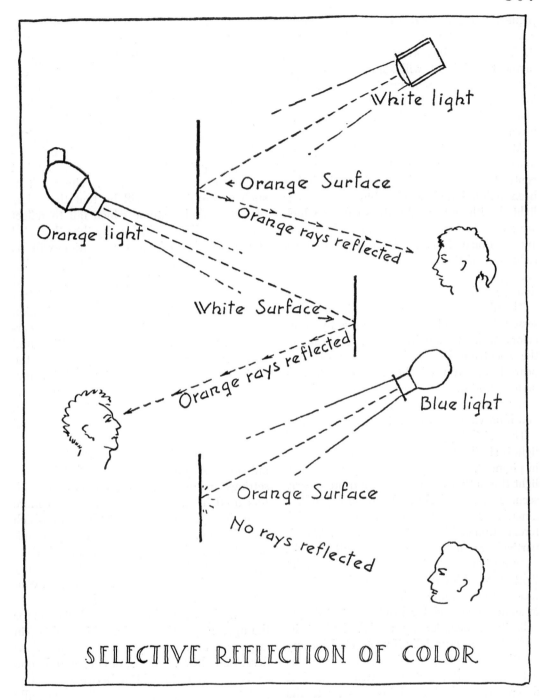

White light

← Orange Surface

Orange rays reflected →

Orange light

White Surface →

Orange rays reflected

Blue light

Orange Surface

No rays reflected

SELECTIVE REFLECTION OF COLOR

Figure 42. Most color is perceived as light reflected from the surface of a wide variety of materials.

pigments or dyes tends to be toned down by any very definitely colored light falling upon it. While certain correspondences between pigment and light will sometimes seem to intensify one pigment by darkening its fellows, the range of colors in the composition, considered as a whole, will always be lessened.

At the same time, by darkening opposing tones, the colored light induces a stronger contrast of values. If a setting which has been painted amber with blue shadows is lighted with amber light, the shadows which are incapable of reflecting amber light will appear much darker. The result will be a reduction of the colorfulness of the setting, accompanied by an increase in its apparent dimensionality.

The ability to neutralize opposition is possessed in a much greater degree by some colors of light than by others. In terms of the spectrum band, those colors of light nearest the top of the scale — red, red-orange, and orange — are the most positive, while those at the other extreme — violet and blue-violet — are least positive of all.

The visibility of objects under colored light is similar to the visibility of certain hues in pigment. Under yellow and yellow-green light the outlines of objects are quite clearly seen. But violet light and red light produce a marked fuzziness in outline and in the differentiation of highlight and shadow. This is particularly noticeable when either falls upon a pigment of similar hue. A blue-violet light upon a blue surface will make that surface seem to vibrate as if it were alive. Used in small areas and for brief effects this peculiarity is occasionally useful. But at its highest point, especially if protracted for any length of time, it is as offensive to the eye as is the extended vibration of two similar but differently pitched wind instruments to the ear. It is obviously wise to avoid it.

Much of the complexity of light and pigment combinations is mitigated by a practice in stage lighting known as *cross coloring*. In this the main sources of colored light are opposed to each other. Either the general illumination of the scene is of one color, such as blue, while the spotlighting is of another, such as amber; or else the opposition will be effected by using opposite colors in the converging spotlights, such as blue against amber or pink against green. The result of such a combination will be that the colors of setting and costume which fail to reflect one light will be picked up by the other, and the total effect of the composition will be similar to that under white light. (See Figure 43.) Often a triangular combination of lights is employed, such as orange-red, blue-green, and violet. With such a combination it becomes possible to control the appearance of various compositions of setting and costume by regulating the brightness of the various colors of light. In this way it is sometimes possible to produce a more perfect harmony of all the visible colors in the design than would be possible with pigments and dyes alone.

In order to reduce the number of unpleasant surprises produced by colored light upon settings and costumes, the colors of the filters used in the lights are usually no more than the lightest tints of the hues to which they belong. Thus whatever the predominant tone of the light, the amount of white light present is still very high so that every surface on the stage is able to reflect a considerable amount of its native hue.

As we have noted elsewhere, designers for the open stage often prefer white light — in large part because of the very complications described above. This is, of course, only one of the variations in lighting between the open and the proscenium stage. (See especially the unit on the open theatre in Chapter 18.)

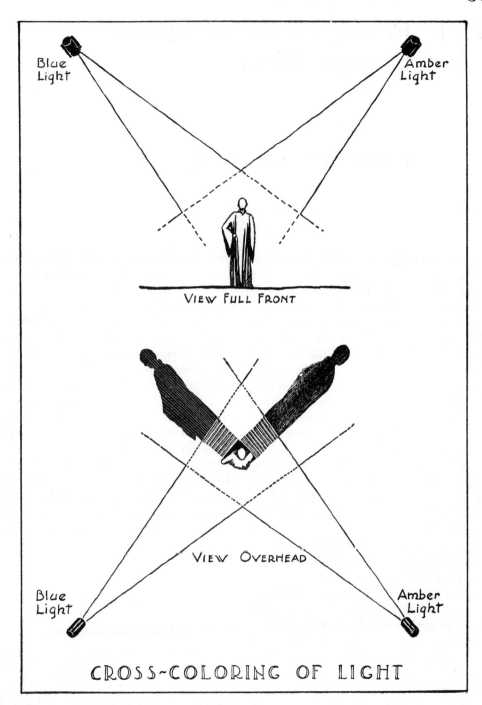

Blue
Light

Amber
Light

VIEW FULL FRONT

VIEW OVERHEAD

Blue
Light

Amber
Light

CROSS-COLORING OF LIGHT

Figure 43. The practice of crossing one color
with its complementary is basic to most modern
stage lighting.

21 | Principles of Temporal Composition

Duration · Variation · Accumulation

A person newly encountering a great painting or an architectural creation catches first the general organization of the work and then grasps one by one the subordinate elements of the composition down to the fine details, gradually perceiving how each confirms and enriches the whole. The spectator experiencing the design of a play cannot do this. He is forced by the temporal nature of the piece to proceed from the perception of the parts to the comprehension of the whole, building his impression piecemeal with the details as given him, unaware of the full import of the design until at the conclusion of the performance its total character stands revealed. If the design is a good one, his interest will be sustained throughout the two hours that this construction continues. When the performance is concluded, he will have the feeling that all he has seen "adds up" to something.

The design of any given moment of the play, no matter how striking, is but one of a series of related compositions adding up to the whole design of the production. The various compositions must be presented to the spectator in right order so that their relationship to earlier ones is clear. The total number of impressions must not exceed the capacity of his memory if all connections from beginning to end are to be made. Nor

must the stimulation of his visual sense be so great or so protracted as to exhaust his responses and cause him to lose some necessary link in the developing chain.

It is sometimes facetiously said that the art of the cinema is the art of cutting and splicing film. But there is some truth in the statement, for in this editing process the relationship of the duration of a picture to the intensity of its composition is determined, while at the same time the continuity of shots and their cumulative effect is settled, for better or worse.

The same temporal factors which govern the effect of the cinema apply equally to the visual effect of a play. *Duration, variation,* and *accumulation* are their names. And this is the order in which we will examine them.

DURATION

The Principle of Diminishing Effect

All visual sensation operates according to what may be designated as the principle of diminishing effect. For example, when confronted with a composition of very low value, such as might be encountered in a dimly lighted stage setting, the eye gradually ad-

310

justs itself, and details which were at first imperceptible are seen with increasing clearness, until eventually the impression of darkness disappears altogether. Similarly, passing from a sunlit street into a dark theatre, one at first sees almost nothing. But gradually, as the eye becomes accustomed to the lower values of the place, one is able to see the aisle, locate an empty seat, and discern the other spectators. If he returns outdoors, the process is reversed; the sunlight is dazzling for some minutes, until the eye readjusts to the higher level of values.

A similar adaptation affects the perception of color. When the attention is concentrated upon an area of singular hue, the sensation of color undergoes a comparable attrition as the protracted stimulus exhausts the capacity of the nerves to respond to that particular hue. This can be demonstrated by closing one eye and focusing the attention sharply upon some convenient surface of solid color. If, after gazing at this surface for some minutes, the observer then opens his eye, the area will suddenly brighten. This is because the color response of the other eye was exhausted while that of the closed eye was unstimulated, thus retaining its ability to respond more completely. By winking the eyes alternately in rapid succession, one can make the surface change from its right color to a grayer tone of that color and back again; and this illusion will continue for some seconds until the response of tho fatigued eye has caught up with that of its fellow.

Prolonged concentration not only exhausts a person's sensations of value and color but also lessens his ability to control his attention. Eventually, unless change is provided, either his attention wanders or he falls asleep. Sophomores call this phenomenon *schola lethargica,* because the necessity for concentration in the classroom so frequently exhausts interest and induces drowsiness there. A composition of compelling line and strong color, if maintained too long, produces an identical result in the theatre. Fortunately, the scene designer has at his disposal more means than the teacher for frustrating this undesirable somnolence, and it is his business to make use of them. There is no excuse for the design of a production causing either fatigue or boredom. Both are the result of defective proportion between intensity and duration.

In relation to scene design, the principle of diminishing effect can be stated very simply: the simpler and more intense the design, the more quickly it exhausts interest. And the corollary of this is that the more complex and subtle the design, the longer it sustains interest.

There is, however, a limit to the complexity of the design imposed by the length of the play and the nature of the audience. The organization of visual sensations must be simple enough to be grasped within the limits of attention. Too much color can be crowded into two hours' performance time, and when this happens some necessary elements are likely to be overlooked by the spectator. With some audiences, particularly children — whose attention-span is shorter than that of adults — the design must be much bolder and more frequently varied. In this case, subtleties and transitions become less important than numerous attention-attracting devices continuously employed.

Intensity of Scene

Having seen that intense interest is capable of being sustained but a short time and that protracted intensity exhausts interest, producing inattention and tedium, let us now turn to the factors which are already present in the individual scene and to which the composition must be adjusted.

There are two things which condition the intensity of the composition: the duration of the scene or episode as conceived by the playwright, and the amount of activity given it by the director.[1]

The briefer the scene, the more powerful its composition may be, compelling the attention toward the center of interest by vivid coloring and strong converging or enclosing lines. The more dramatic the scene, the more appropriate strong composition will be. But as a scene increases in length, less forceful composition, with subtler coloring, more detail, and less obvious controlling lines, becomes desirable. Either that, or else some means must be devised for varying the impression by changes of light or the introduction of new color.

The amount of activity within the scene allows some modification of this principle because the amount and speed of actor movement is in itself a varying factor. The amount of activity has little effect on the strength of the linear or light-and-shade composition, but great activity does make possible more vivid coloring than would be agreeable were the scene more static. In some cases, contrasts of color may make movement more easily followed. Bakst's designs, which were noted for their bizarre coloring and daring harmonies, have never been successfully imitated in drama. For Bakst designed ballets whose large casts, elaborate choreography, and vigorous performance left him no problem of holding attention; his main problems were to identify his principal characters, prevent confusion between characters, and then surround them with as vivid a setting as possible.

Complexity in the Production Design

The principle of relative duration and intensity which governs the strength of the individual composition applies with equal validity to the design of the whole production. The production as a whole, being of much greater duration than any of its episodes, naturally requires more varied treat-

[1] See, in this connection, Chapter 23.

ment and successive compositions of greater total complexity. If the design as it evolves is too easily grasped, the interest of the spectator will not go along with it. It should therefore not be so simple that its course is evident from the outset.

Simplicity in a production is best complemented by a relatively complex design. A play of singular plot, few characters, and slight activity, as is seen in Greek or neoclassic tragedy, requires a design which, while clear in its main outlines, has some depth of subtlety in its ornament, color harmonies, and arrangement of light and shade. Such a production comes close to the static nature of architecture or pictorial art in that the confirming details are successively perceived. The nature of the details, therefore, should be such that complete comprehension is not attainable within much less time than is occupied by the whole performance.

Plays of complex plot, numerous characters, and great activity, such as those of the Elizabethans and seventeenth-century Spaniards, require an opposite handling of the visual scheme. Characters must be identified, their relationships must be clear, and confusion of identities must be prevented. Because the complex-plot play usually moves forward in many short episodes, detail and subtlety of design are less developed, being less needed. Composition of the production as a whole is likely to be in the direction of simplification of visual stimuli in order to give the play an augmented coherence.

VARIATION

If the design is to remain alive and interesting, variation must be provided many times during the course of the performance, and in every episode before the span of attention is exceeded. Any change, whether of costume, light, or scene, is refreshing.

Furthermore, it heightens the sense of movement of the play and gives the spectator the feeling that the production is "going somewhere."

Variation of Episode

The variation of episode is accomplished mainly by the introduction of new or varied costume and by changes of light. Let us consider the device of variation by costume first.

By Change of Costume. The appearance of a new character or the re-entrance of one already familiar always provides an opportunity to freshen the design, even though the change may amount to no more than the turning back of a cape to reveal a lining of different color. With new characters, differences of color, style, or texture of costume are often already provided for in the script. But the designer must judge the possibility of variety afforded by the new costume in relation to those already seen, and treat it accordingly. The interest of the audience tends to liven in any case with the entrance of a new character; it is only appropriate that this interest be capitalized to enhance the design.

Re-entrance of a character already known to the audience is capable of equally freshening effect, because the combination of recognition with some change in appearance is pleasing both to the eye and the mind. One masterful effect of this kind has already been described as part of the first Mio-Miriamne scene in Mielziner's design for *Winterset.* A somewhat similar one is written into Robert Sherwood's *Road to Rome,* where the heroine, upon hearing of Hannibal's approach, slips out of sight, then reappears in a stunning gown of green silk and hurries off toward the Carthaginian camp, leaving her elderly husband quite puzzled. In Maxwell Anderson's *Joan of Lorraine,* which begins with actors supposedly rehearsing in street dress, interest is increased by successive entrances of the principals, each time with an added garment or two from the fifteenth-century costumes they are to wear in performance.

By Change of Light. Variation of light is the readiest means of refreshing a scene because of the ease with which value, quality, direction, and color can be controlled from the switchboard. In a strongly illusionistic production, changes of light are plausible with the passage of any part of the day or night — the fading of twilight, the lighting or extinguishing of lamps, and the poking-up of hearth fires. A fading light is often very useful for both variety and the sharpening of interest, since the decreasing visibility makes necessary closer attention in somewhat the same way that a speaker's lowering of his voice to a whisper causes his auditors to prick up their ears. There are many splendid effects of this kind, some in the script and some added by designer or director. Two very fine ones are those in the final scenes of Rostand's *Cyrano* and Martínez Sierra's *Two Shepherds.* In *Cyrano* the autumn light in the convent garden wanes as the old hero at the point of death challenges his invisible adversary. In *The Two Shepherds* there is a very moving scene as the aged priest, deprived of his parish, takes leave of his church and his few friends as the sun sinks, immersing the garden in shadow. An opposite of these is the daybreak in one of the scenes in *Porgy,* with the light increasing as the courtyard gradually wakens and comes to life, with the sounds of opening shutters, children laughing, cart wheels creaking, and hucksters calling, all rising to a crescendo.

Variations of Continuity

Variations of continuity may be based on a progression of line, light, or color, or upon a succession of alternations of basic qualities of composition, or upon some combination of the two devices.

Progression. A progression is established when the sequence of compositions moves forward according to a clearly perceived scheme. In *The Trojan Women* the play begins in the dusk just before sunrise and ends with the coming of night so that the successive episodes move through a cycle of dawn, morning, noon, afternoon, and sunset. This allows a different lighting of each episode, but with all effects fitting plausibly into the cycle of the day. Shakespeare, although he wrote for the inflexible lighting of afternoon outdoor or candlelit indoor stages, habitually designates time of day, so that practically all of his plays afford cyclical progression of lighting. In *The Tempest* the play begins about one o'clock in the afternoon of a stormy day and ends before six, the skies in the meantime clearing, the sun coming out, and a beautiful rainbow crowning the lovers' pre-nuptial masque. In *Julius Caesar* the episodes of the final sequence move through the night in Brutus' tent to the morning parley of the opposing generals, the subsequent battle, the renewed attack at three o'clock in the afternoon, the battle lost "ere night," and the retreat of the beaten Brutus by twilight.

Occasionally a progression of linear compositions is developed. Jones did this in his design for the Barrymore *Macbeth*, employing a group of angular arches which seemed to wilt and collapse as the hero approached his end. Gordon Craig devised a similar progression for the same sequence in his design for the Tyler *Macbeth*. The ramparts and grilles of the initially formidable castle setting reappeared each time more broken until in the final scene the wreck of the structure stood silhouetted against the horizon.

In Andreyev's *The Life of Man* a series of episodes, representing birth, youth, wealth, old age, and death, lends itself admirably to progressive variation of all the elements of composition. (See Figure 44.)

Sometimes the sequence is so constructed as to permit progressive acceleration by means of increasingly strong compositions and sharpening contrasts. This opportunity is most often afforded by the plays of the Elizabethan era, where the accelerating episode-sequence is an established feature of the dramaturgy.

Alternation. The multiple-scene sequence is most commonly varied by alternating between some two major factors of composition. Thus a light scene is followed by a darker one, a harmony of warm colors by a harmony of cool ones, a harmony of contrast by one of similarity, a symmetrical balance by an asymmetrical one, a concentrated arrangement by a diffuse one, or a concentration through convergence by a concentration through enclosure. Such alternation of visual effect refreshes the eye with each change of scene and helps to sustain interest throughout the continuum.

In many plays the scene sequence as given favors such alternation. Witness Shakespeare's sequences of alternating indoor and outdoor locales. But even when the necessity for visual change is not recognized by the playwright, the resources of design are so many that alternation of appeals is easily developed. In any case, it is best to have no two scenes in the sequence exactly alike in line, light and shade, or coloring, even when the locale of the action remains the same.

Cecil Beaton's famous design for *Lady Windermere's Fan* in the season of 1947-48 encompassed the most remarkable alternation of color and texture. The first scene was given a harmony of very slightly cool colors in which a light yellow-green dominated. Touches of pink and light orange were included in the arrangement but bound into

Figure 44. In a good temporal progression, each
scene is clearly related to the sequence of which
it is a part. (See page 314.)

the cool harmony by a predominantly yellow-green tone of light. The second scene was warm in feeling, with pinkish lighting and a good deal of lavender, pink, and gold in the scenery. The third scene was cool again, for although the general tone of light was amber, the scenery was a pleasant gray-green set off with green leather furniture. For the fourth scene he returned to the second setting, instead of to the first as specified by the playwright, thus balancing his scheme of alternate warmth and coolness of color. Then he capped the warm tones of the setting by putting Mrs. Erlynne into a coral red gown, so that her entrance brought the whole scheme into harmony.

We have already noted Jones's alternation of warm and cool colors in *Lute Song*, where the reds of the court scenes were alternated with the blue-grays of the famine scenes. But it is interesting now to recall this design and to notice the way in which he increased the force of the alternation and progression conjointly by having the successive cool scenes grow colder and darker while the successive warm scenes climbed to progressively higher peaks of both value and temperature.

ACCUMULATION

The sequence of impressions which the spectator receives must be more than merely varied and interesting from moment to moment and scene to scene.[2] They must add up to something; they must constitute an aesthetically satisfying whole in which there is sense of neither superfluity nor lack. This necessity is served by three aspects of the cumulative process: *accretion, repetition,* and *completion.* The three are strongly present in the temporal compositions of both

[2] Note, in this connection, the actor's concern with continuity and growth, discussed in Chapter 12.

drama and music — witness the conventional repetition of the measure in music — although the drama, because of the variety of its stimuli, is probably the more complex of the two.

Accretion

The accretion of visual impressions throughout the performance may be compared to the experience of watching a parade or of making a trip through unfamiliar terrain. As the parade passes, the banners, floats, and marchers come into view in a certain order, the lesser units interposed between the more elaborate ones for the sake of variety, with the more spectacular displays toward the end of the sequence and some recognizable terminus such as a calliope bringing up the rear. Sometimes the terminal unit repeats the form and color of the leading element, thereby rounding out and completing the sequence. A trip through unfamiliar country or by a novel route provides a similar chain of impressions. If the trip is purposeful and the destination known, impressions of various sorts accrue, with the more relevant ones standing out: the landmarks, the important turnings, and of course the beginning and the ending.

The design of a production gives significance to a similar piling up of impressions by marking direction of movement and distance traveled, if not toward some known terminus at least away from the starting point. Some plays end where they began, coming full circle, as it were. Others end up far from home base. *The Green Pastures* is one of the latter. The opening scenes are carefree and light in mood. But as the Lawd becomes more deeply involved in the destinies of mankind the seriousness of mood increases. Jones's design for the play was marked by an increasing use of shadow, a lowering of value, and a gradual deepening of color. By the time the Hezdrel scene was reached the spectators knew they had been brought a long way from the pink and blue heaven in which the play began.

Along the course which the plot takes it is also necessary that the landmarks stand out and that the turning points be unmistakably marked. To this end two means are employed. One is called *proportional emphasis.* The other is *impact.*

Proportional Emphasis. The designing of a production starts out, not with its first scene, but with its most important one. The question of which moment of the play is of greatest significance to the whole is necessarily pre-figured by the author in his composition of the script. Sometimes his stage directions answer the question. But more often the director must settle the point. It is not usually the business of the designer to decide it — although he may help — for the question involves much more than the visual scheme. But once the question is settled, it is his business to make sure that the peak moment passes no eye without being recognized. With this assured, the process of design moves outward to the subordinate climaxes, relating each to the principal peak, giving each appropriate emphasis in proportion to its importance. This proportion must be correct. There must be no possibility that the spectator will mistake a lesser climax for the greater one. Improper emphasis will mislead the spectator and confuse his apprehension.

Impact. The sudden disclosure of hitherto unknown relationships, between characters, between actions, or between action and consequence, is fundamental to the art of the drama. The disclosure of relationships increases significance, while the suddenness with which it is accomplished heightens its impact. Sometimes the revelation is startling both to the characters involved and to the audience. Sometimes it is anticipated by the audience, whose interest is then held in

suspense until the expected discovery is made by the characters in the play. In either case the revelation marks a turning point in the progress of the plot. As such it must be a well-marked point in the visual scheme and it is best if carefully planned so as to deliver its effect with the greatest possible impact.

Instances of such disclosures embrace many a famous *coup de théâtre.* One of the greatest is the moment in the Sophocles *Electra* when Aegisthus, having been told that his enemy, Orestes, is dead, insists upon seeing the corpse. The body is carried out on a bier, covered from head to foot. Aegisthus triumphantly flings aside the cloth, to find himself looking, not at Orestes' body, but at that of his own wife. With this he realizes that his enemies are still alive and that he has been trapped by them. In *Macbeth,* the hero, although cautioned to beware Macduff, is led on by the Witches' prophecy that no man of woman born can harm him. Believing himself invincible, he is attacked by Macduff whom he repels, boasting of his invulnerability. This leads Macduff to reveal himself as a being who has been delivered into the world by Caesarean section and not "born" in the ordinary sense. Macbeth is thus confronted both by the one whom he had been warned particularly to avoid and by the only man against whom he is vulnerable. In *Tartuffe,* Orgon and his family, finding themselves betrayed by one to whom they have given shelter, make plans to leave Paris, but are stopped by the appearance of Tartuffe with an officer and men to arrest them. But as they are about to be led off to prison the officer intervenes and arrests Tartuffe instead, revealing that the betrayal had been known to the authorities, who had temporarily assisted the wrongdoer in disclosing himself.

Each of these disclosures as well as most others like them gains from sudden intensification of the design at the moment of disclosure. A beam of bright light or a focusing of lines into which a character steps, the revelation of a startling new color theme and innumerable other devices can be brought into play. In the *Electra* the background is usually dark, so that the black-draped bier and its background are similar until the uncovering of the corpse gowned in red produces a startling contrast.

The sudden intensification by any such means reminds one of the sound effect used in cinema and radio drama to mark a turning point. Called the "stab," it consists of a sudden penetrating chord struck at the moment that the disclosure is made. A comparable "stab" in visual composition is produced when to a stable arrangement of similar colors the sudden addition of contrasting hue replaces the harmony of similarity with a more vital harmony of contrasts.

Repetition

The repetition of an effect is frequently used as a means of relating an incident to some preceding one or of relating characters to others seen earlier in the play.

Repetition of visual impression is only effective when it acts to increase the significance of the current composition. Otherwise it falls a victim to the law of diminishing effect and the second impression is less vivid than the first of its kind.

Repetition of costume colors or styles is useful to describe the relationship of characters, particularly when the second member of the family appears without introduction. Ida Mae Goe used this device in the design of the costumes for her *Macbeth*. Macbeth and his men were in reds while all the others were in cooler tones. When Lady Macbeth appeared unannounced but gowned in a color which repeated that of Macbeth's costume, her relationship to him was immediately clear. Similarly, Lady Macduff and her son, who also appear without introduction, were dressed in a green which repeated the hue seen earlier on Macduff so that one

knew at once without being told whose wife and child they were.

Sometimes repetition doubles the impact of a significant action. The spectacle of Macbeth's severed head, for example, is twice as impressive at the end of the play because of its having been seen before as one of the apparitions conjured up from the Witches' cauldron. In most cases this is a matter of reinforcing by visual means some parallel already present in the plot. In Ibsen's *Ghosts* the destruction of the orphanage and the ultimate disintegration of Oswald are paralleled so that the final scene undoubtedly gains if its composition is made to recall that of the earlier episode. Ibsen had provided for such an effect by specifying the light of the burning orphanage for one and the light of the rising sun for the other. In *The Green Pastures* the parallel scenes between the Lawd and Adam, then Moses, and finally Hezdrel, suggest repetition of design. In *King Lear* the relationship of Lear and his daughters, paralleling that of Gloucester and his sons, is capable of gaining significance from repetition of compositional scheme.

Completion

Whether the play concludes with a return to its starting point, as in *Marco Millions, Street Scene, Peter Pan,* and many another example one could recall, or comes to a stop at some far distant terminus, a sense of completeness is necessary. The accumulation of diverse compositions should in its final moments reach an acceptable balance. The end of the performance should be recognizable as such and aesthetically satisfying.

The commonest means of relating the end to the beginning is by repeating the composition with which the sequence began. The prologue-epilogue frame, which occurs so frequently in pre-modern drama, is a great help in this. The obvious thing is to repeat in the epilogue the composition of the prologue. When possible, this is an invariably satisfying device to employ in the design of a Greek tragedy. It is usually acceptable in any play. Raymond Sovey in his design for the Cowl *Twelfth Night* used a huge picture book which Feste opened at the beginning of the play, turning the pages as the sequence moved from one locale to another, and finally closing its cover when the final scene was concluded.

Another scheme is the cyclic sequence, not necessarily returning to the first composition but to some comparable terminus. Of these, the dawn-to-dusk or sunset-to-sunrise cycle is a favorite. One instance of this, from *The Trojan Women*, has already been cited. The device is effective in any play in which the action is nearly continuous within one day or one night or within the span of twenty-four hours. *From Morn to Midnight*, as the title indicates, is one of these, with the first half of the play taking place by day and the second half by night. Jo Mielziner managed a very effective cycle in his design for *Death of a Salesman*

by duplicating in the last scene the lighting of the first. Since the play has an epilogue but no prologue to balance it, he then tied in the epilogue by repeating in it a leaf-pattern lighting effect which he had used in the scene immediately following the opening.

In other plays, in which neither repetition nor cycle is possible, a more occult fore-and-aft balance is necessary. In *The Winter's Tale*, for example, the second half of the play is contrasted in mood with the first so that the second half balances the first. This would seem to indicate a differing treatment of the two halves, employing contrasting elements of color, line, and value designed to effect a balance at the moment of conclusion. Sometimes an alternating sequence of contrasting compositions can be developed by following each device with its opposite until an even number of opposite compositions is achieved, with each one balancing some earlier one until all the pairings are completed.

Section Five

Direction

22 | The Function of the Director

The Director as Administrator
The Director as Leader
The Director as Interpreter

The proper goal of every dramatic production is to project a complete and accurate theatrical effect to an audience. Such an effect is a composite pattern of visual and auditory stimuli which produces an intellectual or emotional response on the part of the spectators; it is the direct translation of the form and purpose of a play into the expressional mode of the stage. The script initiates the production;[1] actors, assisted by all the aspects of design, are the medium for creating the effect.

These elements alone — script, actors, design, plus a theatre and an audience — have on occasion resulted in effective theatre production. At times a playwright, a theatre manager, a patron, an actor, or perhaps a "prompter" has acted as the co-ordinator of the production, and has performed some of the functions which we now assign to a director. By reason of the individual skills of the artists themselves, it is possible today as in the past for a superior company to give an effective performance without the guidance of a director.

However, by the end of the nineteenth century, theatre workers began to recognize that a single individual with the function of patterning and co-ordinating all the elements of a production could give it unity and proportion, and could assist each artist to make his maximum contribution to the play. The theory of Gordon Craig and Adolphe Appia, and the practice of the Duke of Saxe-Meiningen, Max Reinhardt, Constantin Stanislavski, Harley Granville-Barker, André Antoine, David Belasco, and other celebrated directors and producers demonstrated the merits of co-ordination. As a result, a distinct art of direction has arisen in this century.

The primary function of the director, then, is to pattern and co-ordinate the work of his associates in a manner which will result in an exact theatrical effect. In carrying out this function, he works in various ways and from various points of view. He interprets the script and plans the auditory and visual stimuli which constitute the performance. He serves as critic or super-spectator: appraises, as if he were a member of the potential audience, every phase of the preparations; and strives, with his associates — actors, designers, technicians, and perhaps the playwright — to heighten the effectiveness of the whole and of each part.

He has acquired some administrative and

---

[1] It may be the script as originally written by a playwright, or it may be a script radically altered in some manner, as will be discussed in Chapter 27.

leadership duties. Today he is usually respon-sible for every feature of the production except the business management — and in some theatres, for that also.

The conductor of a symphony orchestra is a partial counterpart to the theatre direc-tor, and the analogy is valuable in identifying differences as well as similarities. The con-ductor, like the director, ordinarily selects the work to be performed; chooses the per-formers; determines the visual effects; re-hearses the performers in co-ordination after they have studied and practiced their parts; and attempts by patterning tempo, volume, rhythm, balance, and progression (which the musician calls "phrasing" or "develop-ment"), to mold the performance into a meaningful whole which creates the effect intended by the composer. It is the con-ductor who is at fault if the tempi are wrong, if the composition has less unity than other conductors have obtained from the score, and if the mood is not transmitted to the au-dience. Just so, the theatre director is respon-sible for the tempo, mood, rhythm, balance, progression, and unity of impression of a play.

The visual setting of a symphony con-cert is of relatively minor importance: the arrangement of the instrumental sections, the design of the music racks and the con-ductor's podium, the dress of the musicians, the manner in which the conductor and orchestra enter, acknowledge applause, and exit, and the actions of the conductor him-self. The audience gives little direct atten-tion to these things, except, possibly, the visual performance of the conductor. But the theatre director must pattern the visual stimuli as thoroughly as the auditory ones.

Music is written much more explicitly than dialogue, for the score gives not only the pitch and relative duration of each sound, the tempo, and the rhythmic patterns, but also, through conventional symbols and words, instructions as to mood, style, and relative volume. The conductor is given license on certain sustained notes and pauses between movements, and on some matters of tempo. Similarly, balance, emphasis, and tone qual-ity are controlled only partially by the score; and in the interpretation of the score he is allowed to vary from strict accuracy within certain narrow limits. His skill as a conduc-tor shows itself in this interpretation, and when he varies appreciably from the score, he is likely to be criticized for inaccuracy.

The actor and the director find in the script only the words, a few instructions for action, and meager and vague indications of motivation. All the rest they must obtain from an imaginative interpretation of the dialogue. The director, by delving into this internal evidence, discovers clues to melody, tempo, volume, and style, but these are never as explicit as in a piece of music, and since he finds them by subjective interpretation, they may be strongly influenced by his own personality.

But the greatest difference between the theatre director and the conductor is that the latter leads the orchestra during the per-formance. In fidelity to the score, he gives the tempi, he can cue in the instruments, he can signal to raise or lower the volume of the orchestra or of a single instrument, and he can by his presence communicate to the orchestra his enthusiasm or any other emo-tion. In contrast, the theatre workers must so rehearse the production that they will perform at their peak ability without the immediate guidance of the director. He can give advice and encouragement backstage during the performance, but he has no way to signal an actor who becomes overemo-tional, overtensed, inexpressive, or inaudible.

THE DIRECTOR AS ADMINISTRATOR

The director's administrative duties fall to him as the responsible head of the co-opera-tive effort. These duties will be discussed in detail in Chapters 27 and 28, and therefore need only be indicated here.

Unless the casting is done by the producer, the director selects from available talent the actors who he believes will best interpret the script as he understands it. In the commercial theatre, the star often is engaged ahead of the director, while the remainder of the cast is chosen by him. The director calls rehearsals and conducts them.

Unless there is a distinct producer or art director, during the preparatory period the director keeps an eye on all phases of the production to make sure that satisfactory progress is being made. He sees to it that the artists concerned are informed of all alterations made by himself or by the designers.

The director conducts dress rehearsals, and in those his administrative ability meets its greatest test in the complex problem of apportioning rehearsal time to different phases of the production.

THE DIRECTOR AS LEADER

In most theatre organizations, the director provides leadership for the producing group, and maintains its morale. Other individuals, such as the producer, the playwright, or a leading actor, can help with morale, but the director is primarily responsible for the group spirit. This is of great importance in the noncommercial theatre, where the interest of the actors and technicians is avocational or extracurricular rather than professional, and where other activities have to be curtailed by the demands of rehearsal. Even professional actors, if they are to do their best work, need to be kept optimistic and enthusiastic about the potentialities of the play and about their own performances.

This task begins before the rehearsals. In the announcement of the play, at tryouts, and at early rehearsals the director shows clearly his confidence in the script and in the success of the production which can be developed from it. The actors must be convinced that the play is within their capacities, but must be impressed with the fact that its successful performance will require concentrated effort on their part. In a light modern comedy, for example, the actors may be overconfident and may slight their preliminary study. They need to be convinced that, while the motivations may be easily within their comprehension, the play requires unusually complete characterizations or great skill in comedy techniques such as timing. A difficult classic may frighten the actors; they will need to be shown that, except for a possibly unfamiliar style, and some special study necessary in order to understand obsolete language and outmoded social points of view, the motivation and expression is to be approached in the same manner as for a contemporary play.

The director endeavors to convince each actor of the importance of his role, and of the value to himself and to the play of casting him in it. It is more convincing to the actors given small parts if the director makes clear to the entire cast, as a part of his initial analysis of the play, the exact contribution of each part, than if he explains it in private interviews, a procedure which is suggestive of afterthought and apology. The theatre axiom, "There are no small parts, only small actors," is valid and effective when one talks in generalities, but such a broad statement will not satisfy an actor playing a butler who enters only once to serve tea, and it can be said in such a way as actually to offend him. The actor himself and the entire cast must recognize that this butler, as much as anyone in the play, can convey by his manner the social status of his employer. Likewise, the cast needs to be shown that each walk-on in *Street Scene* must establish an accurately drawn and completely believable characterization in order to make Elmer Rice's naturalistic method effective. Each actor must discover from his study of people the traits and mannerisms that will give reality and individuality to his role. The director then manifests his continuing interest in the small parts by serious if not prolonged attention to them at later rehearsals and critiques.

A director can increase loyalty to the production by consideration of the cast in calling rehearsals. In early rehearsals when continuity of action is less important, the scenes involving bit parts and mob scenes can be called just often enough to keep the actors interested.

Actors make their best progress if they receive a judicious mixture of praise and blame. They differ in their development under these techniques, and so the director adjusts his critical method to the temperament of his actors. Ideally the director at each rehearsal gives an honest appraisal of the work of each actor. But he is careful that his criticisms are not too discouraging; and to avoid this, he may withhold some necessary corrections until the progress of the actor in other phases of his work gives him confidence.

The degree of assurance engendered at the final rehearsals and at dress rehearsals vitally affects the performance. The director wants the cast and crew to leave these rehearsals with the belief that they and the production will be successful, and yet with a realization that by doing their best work with the audience present, all can further improve the performance.

THE DIRECTOR AS INTERPRETER

The primary purpose of the director is to communicate to an audience as completely and perfectly as possible his interpretation — that is to say, his understanding — of the logical and emotional content of a playscript. This content can be distorted deliberately, either by revising the words in the dialogue or by modifying their expressive intent. But such distortion produces a new production script, and the interpretative process thereafter is the same as for an author's unaltered script. (See Chapter 27 for a discussion of the ethics involved in a revision of this magnitude.)

Interpretation has three phases: *impression,* understanding the script through study; *expression,* preparing the vocal and physical means by which to convey this understanding to an audience; and *criticism,* evaluating this expression in order to perfect it. In performing these steps, the director takes successively the roles of student, artist or creator, and critic.

The Director as Student

At the moment that a director decides to produce a specific play, he has a strongly favorable response to it. If he immediately writes out his reactions to the script — his general impression of it, his understanding of its meaning, what he especially likes about it, and what he believes to be the most effective and least effective scenes — he may find these useful for later reference. Rehearsals may change his opinions, and he may find his later judgments better than his initial ones, but such notes can serve to revive his enthusiasm and to remind him of strengths, weaknesses, and implications which he has lost sight of during rehearsals.

Directors vary as to the intensity and the method of their study of a script and its backgrounds, and they vary in these from play to play. The general process is to obtain a clear general understanding of the play and its meaning, to study the particulars discussed below, and then to work back to the overall thought and intent of the script, now deepened and sharpened by the detailed study.[2]

[2] The several elements making up the playscript have already been discussed, from other points of view, in Section I on Drama and Section II on Acting.

Dramatic Structure. The director analyzes the play from the standpoint of dramatic as well as literary structure. Ordinarily the literary structure is emphasized. However, the turning point of a play, important from a literary standpoint, may not be a dramatic climax. In a mystery play, the turning point may be some minor slip made by the criminal early in the play which receives no attention at the time, while the dramatic climax may be postponed until near the final curtain. In *The Perfect Alibi* (called *The Fourth Wall* in England), the turning point is in the second act when one of the criminals claims that he saw, through his field glasses, the other conspirator looking at his watch. At the time he speaks, this seems a perfectly valid part of the tissue of lies by which the two murderers fake alibis for each other. The dramatic climaxes, however, are in the third act when the hero discovers the fatal discrepancy, and the heroine inveigles the murderer into an admission of his guilt. The director will not want to put emphasis upon this turning point lest it anticipate the playwright's purpose and encourage some members of the audience to find the solution too soon, but the line must be clearly communicated so that all members of the audience hear it and will be able to recall it at the denouement.

Ordinarily, the director accepts the dramatic climax, subclimaxes, and the important and subordinate actions of the script; and tries to express faithfully this dramatic pattern. He intensifies the climaxes and stresses the important scenes; he makes the subordinate actions as interesting as possible, but at the same time indicates clearly to the audience that they are of lesser importance to the plot. Comedy scenes, in particular, can assume an unwarranted importance, as can irrelevant philosophical passages, public speeches, and other scenes in which a character expresses some social or political point of view with fervor. The stronger the writing in such passages, the more dangerous are they as false leads. If, for example, too much emphasis is given to the "Hence! home, you idle creatures . . . " scene of Flavius and Marullus with which *Julius Caesar* begins, the audience may accept them as leading characters, and keep expecting them to reappear prominently in the action. Lillian Hellman as playwright and director of *Another Part of the Forest* made this mistake in arousing our interest in the lover of the young Regina Hubbard, and then keeping him offstage except for one other short scene. The ghosts of the Dutch seamen introduced in the second scene of *High Tor* can be distracting if the scene is acted with too much verve.

Plot. The plot itself seldom provides a problem for the director, though the major motivations sometimes do so in plays from former or foreign cultures. For example, the religious importance of human burial to the Greeks is essential to an understanding of any play dealing with Antigone.

Since conflict is usually a key element in drama, the director seeks the major and minor conflicts of the play, and identifies for each such conflict the protagonist, the antagonist, and those related to each of them. He ferrets out every other kind of conflict which he can emphasize to give interest and vitality to the play.

Occasionally the director sees the need to indicate to the audience the key plot characters. *Once in a Lifetime* introduces and establishes only the three key characters in the opening scene. Thereafter extraneous distracting characters and incidents can be introduced without confusion. In other diffuse plays like *Street Scene, Two on an Island, The Weavers,* and *Strife,* the director may need to use position, grouping, or costuming to enable the audience to recognize the main thread of the plot as quickly as possible.

The relative importance of subplots is studied to see if the early episodes in them need extra stress or subordination. The plot concerning Gloucester in *King Lear,* almost as important as the primary one, may be established early by the seriousness with which it is played. Moreover, everything possible needs to be done to make the audience aware of Edgar so that it will recognize him in his various disguises. In *Command Decision* care must be taken that Major General Kane is acted with more sympathy than is indicated in the script so that his explanation of the difficult decisions he has to make seems in character. Incompletely dramatized episodes occasionally appear in plots, and these need to be searched out and staged for greater effectiveness.

Since the main plot usually is self-evident in meaning, the director's principal attention is focused on the author's attitude toward it. Partly from internal evidence, and partly from supplementary study, the director interprets the attitude of the playwright toward his primary plot — whether he takes it seriously and seems to be emotional with regard to it; whether he presents it realistically and unemotionally as a set of circumstances; whether he treats it frivolously; or whether, while he tells one story, he expects the audience to be reminded constantly of an analogy, such as a contemporary political event.

Tragedy, comedy, and farce have typical attitudes toward plot, but there is considerable variation within these forms which stems from the personality of the playwright. Whatever the attitude, it is part of the total effect of the script, and the director wants to preserve it in the production.

Arthur Miller and Tennessee Williams seem to have such great sympathy for the desperate and confused characters they draw in *All My Sons, Death of a Salesman, The Glass Menagerie, A Streetcar Named Desire,* and *The Rose Tattoo,* that they approach identification with their characters, and tend to induce this same identification in the minds of the spectators. Such writers sometimes are said to be autobiographical because the particular nature of the speech and the thought — and the "real" quality of the incidents — suggest that if the plays do not record personal experience, at least they are based on events of real life which the authors have observed directly.

Lillian Hellman and Sidney Kingsley, on the other hand, usually are more detached commentators. Miss Hellman doubtless abhors the Hubbards of *The Little Foxes,* yet she seems unimpassioned about it, and holds them up to intellectual rather than emotional scorn.

Some playwrights vary in this detachment from play to play. Maxwell Anderson seems much more emotionally concerned with Mio in *Winterset* than with any of the royal figures of whom he has written in other dramas. While he has sympathy for Elizabeth, Mary, and Anne, and attempts to gain audience sympathy for them, and while he often allows them to express his personal philosophy, in *Winterset* he seems to say that Mio's intellectual and emotional problem is similar, to a greater or lesser extent, to that which he and many of us have faced, and seems to protest personally against what he regards as the inevitable defeat of the honest person by the lawless and ruthless elements of society.

Moss Hart, Noel Coward, and George S. Kaufman seem to say to the audience, "Let's see all the funny things that could happen if we start with this absurdity." If an audience fails to adopt this point of view, it will be annoyed by the lapses from logic.

Many satiric scripts from *The Clouds* to *Marco Millions* say by means of plot and character, "Aren't we silly when we behave this way?" Sometimes these plays contain general social satire, as in *The Birds, Tartuffe,* and *Amphitryon 38.* But, just as Aristophanes included direct burlesque of contemporary individuals, so Maxwell Anderson in *Knickerbocker Holiday* wanted his audience to think of the President, Franklin D. Roosevelt, although he wrote about Peter Stuyvesant. Kaufman and Ryskind in *Of Thee I Sing* similarly wanted the audience to think of Herbert Hoover when they presented the character of Vice-President Alexander Throttlebottom. Later, American playwrights became freer in their burlesque, and Kaufman and Hart made President Roosevelt and other contemporary officials leading characters in *I'd Rather Be Right.*

Satires can be serious as well as frivolous. It is said that the popularity of Anouilh's *Antigone* during the Occupation of France was due to the analogy which it offers with the conflict between the individual citizen and the totalitarian state. Productions of the Lewis Galantière translation in the United States, however, have tended to give an unfortunate degree of sympathy to Creon, the tyrant.

The Time of Your Life and *You Can't Take It with You* have a surface similarity. Each has a bare thread of plot, numerous incongruous characters doing amusingly unconventional things, a setting which permits them to pop in and out of attention to produce absurd contrasts, and a sentimental and joyous attitude toward life. It would be possible to direct *The Time of Your Life* as a wild farce; it would be possible to direct *You Can't Take It with You* sentimentally and make it preach a definite philosophy of life; neither performance would be as effective as one faithful to the intent of the author, though it might still be amusing.

In any case, the author's attitude toward each episode is examined by the director. Usually this attitude is related closely to his overall point of view. However, a playwright sometimes writes what he considers to be scenes of "comic relief" which have a contrasting mood. *The Green Pastures* cleverly alternates the pathetic and the farcical. The art factory scene of *Beggar on Horseback* has a much deeper sense of social protest than the broad and obvious satire contained in other scenes. The writing style shifts considerably from scene to scene in *The Hairy Ape.* The last act of *The Merchant of Venice* is almost a separate play. In *A Midsummer Night's Dream,* Shakespeare integrates the early clown scenes with the rest of the script, but near the end interrupts the action and gives the comics free rein. Sometimes these shifts of attitude and style are part of the deliberate plan of the script, and need to be emphasized in performance. Sometimes they appear to be lapses on the part of the playwright, and the director then does what he can to restore unity.

The director studies each bit of dramatic action, or episode, separately and in its relation to all the others. In English drama, a new scene is indicated only when there is a change of locale or time. In French drama, a new scene is indicated when there is a change in the character group because of the entrance or exit of a plot character, the perfunctory entrances of servants usually being ignored. When this device is used in English, these are spoken of as "French scenes." This division into dramatic units is useful for study and rehearsal, though the division need not be mechanical and rule bound. A change in the character group nearly always marks the end of one dramatic episode and the beginning of another, though it is possible to have more than one episode in a French scene, and sometimes two or more of them may conjoin to make a single episode. Dividing the script into French scenes may permit the director to call his rehearsals economically in early sessions, rehearsing together bits from different acts that contain the same characters.

Whether or not the episodes are numbered as French scenes, the director studies each one individually. An episode usually has a beginning, one or more climaxes, and an ending. It should have meaning and interest in itself, and also make a contribution to the overall structure of the play. Usually one character wants something, others oppose this actively or passively, and the protagonist succeeds, fails, or is interrupted. There is frequently a change of attention, of emphasis, of tempo, or of atmosphere at the beginning of a new incident, and the action will be clarified if these shifts are emphasized. Aware of the exact points of transition, the director often is encouraged to strengthen contrasts, thereby diversifying the sequences. Indication of French scenes also may help the actor to envision the structure of the play and may lead him to form minor dramatic entities within the play.

The director wants to understand just what led the playwright to decide on his succession of episodes, for knowledge of this may help him to recognize relationships and contrasts which he might otherwise overlook. Sometimes, for example, a playwright introduces a scene almost solely for suspense — to postpone his climax as long as he dares, and thereby to increase the anticipation of the audience and intensify the climax. This explains the length of the tipsy Shriner scene in *Light Up the Sky*. In *A Doll's House*, Nora's dancing of the tarantella to delay Torvald's finding the incriminating letter in the mailbox similarly serves to heighten the suspense.

Character. Both actor and director analyze a character to learn his physical, intellectual, and emotional characteristics, and the influence of his past life and of his present environment. The director can content himself with what the playwright has stated about the character, whereas the actor, in order to give an individualized characterization, must fill in imaginatively what has been left nebulous by the author.

In contrast, the director is more concerned than is the actor with the relation of the characters to one another and to the structure and meaning of the play. He needs to identify the protagonist and those associated with him, the antagonist and his associates, and the other individuals and groups who have subordinate functions with relation to the main plot. Occasionally a play has a double plot, as has *King Lear;* and the complex relation of the characters to each plot needs to be very clear to the director so that he can clarify it to the audience. In *Uncle Vanya* and *Three Sisters* there are a great many interrelated plot sequences, each with a definite plot line of its own. Here, especially, it is important to analyze character relationships, both personal and dramatic.

The director needs to know the contribution each character should make to the play, so that he can insure this effect, and guard against extraneous effects. For example, comic or eccentric character parts may be highly amusing, but may arouse independent interest and fail to relate themselves correctly to the scheme of the play. The drunken Porter in *Macbeth* and the First Grave-digger in *Hamlet* are familiar examples of comedy roles which can either interrupt the flow of the story, or can take their intrinsic place in the play's structure. The Reinhardt motion picture of *A Midsummer Night's Dream,* which shifted the emphasis to the fairy sequence, and secondarily to the comic sequence of Bottom and his cohorts, obscured the central plot involving Hermia, Helena, Demetrius, and Lysander, and failed thereby to produce any feeling of unity and completeness. In this play the scenes of the quartet of lovers must be played with great effectiveness if the correct balance and proportion are to be maintained between them and the comedy and fantasy elements.

The director determines the desirable audience reaction to each character — sympathy, antagonism, amusement, or scorn. He needs especially to recognize the characters to whom the audience must give its sympathy. This factor is important in casting, since the meaning of a play will be distorted if sympathy is won by the wrong character, or if the main attention and interest becomes focused on an effective actor in a minor role who disappears midway in the story.

Language. Since the director tries to communicate to the audience the ideas of the playwright, obviously he must understand precisely the words of the author. He must understand not only the ordinary dictionary definition of the words — their denotation — but also their intellectual and emotional connotation. *Traitor* means different things in the U.S.A. and the U.S.S.R. The meaning of *loyalty* varies widely even within the United States. The strength of various swear words varies widely in different countries, communities, and social environments. These are merely simple examples of the myriad subtle differences in the meaning of words.

The director needs to know the customary usage of words so as to know when the author is employing them according to custom, and when he is deliberately violating ordinary usage for an effect. When a character says, "Dwight Eisenhower, Winston Churchill, and others of their ilk . . . ," this is not ordinary speech; some comment is being made on the character who speaks the line. He may be a leftist, he may be an individualist with an embittered distrust of all government leaders, or he may be merely a satirist amused by tricks of speech. In any case, the word will help the director to understand the character. Similarly, when one character describes another who is overweight, his choice among the words *big, heavy, fat, stout, stocky, gross,* and *plump* characterizes both the person described and the person who speaks.

Some playwrights choose words which will most easily and clearly tell their story and its episodes without embellishments.

Lillian Hellman, George S. Kaufman, and John van Druten seem to find language merely utilitarian, and use it to make their dramatic or comic points with the same sort of precision a lawyer uses. Their interest is in the ideas rather than the words. Other playwrights consciously use language for characterization. Examples include William Saroyan in *The Time of Your Life* and other plays, Garson Kanin in *Born Yesterday,* and Elmer Rice in *Street Scene, Dream Girl,* and other plays. Still others use it for humor in addition to characterization. Clifford Odets in *Awake and Sing!* and *Golden Boy* demonstrates his fascination with pungent and unexpected words and expressions. Arthur Miller follows this tradition. Other playwrights are equally fascinated by the humor and expressiveness of the unusual word order and unusual analogies which they hear in speech which is influenced by a foreign culture. Such expression is a major ornament of *Papa Is All, I Remember Mama, The Happy Time,* many of the Irish plays, and most of the plays about Jewish life. The director, as well as the actors, must appreciate the humor and pathos of such language, and endeavor to convey it to the audience. Further, in these plays the director must be aware of the rhythm which the playwright has achieved by word order and he must help his actors to acquire this rhythm. By so doing, the actor will be aided in establishing the national aspects of the character, since the rhythms of language, maintained by inflection and phrasing, are more significant in the speech of a race or nation than is the dialectal pronunciation of particular sounds.

Christopher Fry is representative of the writers who use words themselves for entertainment. He deliberately chooses the bizarre and unusual word, phrase, and analogy for the sheer pleasure of novelty. This can also serve the utilitarian purpose of underscoring ideas by the attention value of the words in which they are clothed. *The*

Lady's not for Burning has the same plot as *Man and Superman,* but Shaw's hero tries to defend himself against women by brilliant and startling ideas, while Fry's defends himself, equally unsuccessfully, by words alone. Both are examples of language used as an ornament to drama.

Writers like T. S. Eliot use words for the memories which they arouse. A familiar phrase from another piece of literature is woven into a sentence in order to obtain support from the previous writer, to suggest a larger application of the idea, or to make an ironic comment upon the idea or upon the author who is quoted. In *The Admirable Bashville,* Shaw satirizes the cult of blank verse writing by interlarding phrases quoted directly from Shakespeare, others which are alterations of Shakespeare, others which are pure Shaw but sound as though they must have been written by Shakespeare, and pure burlesque lines.

The director needs to be aware of all these special uses of language, in order to help to underscore effects, and to avoid the loss of any major one.

Verse requires special study on the part of the director in order to decide how much emphasis is to be given to it. Should the actors deliberately conceal the verse form as much as possible by reading against the rhythm whenever they can; should they read purely for sense but with a sustained level of volume and a regularity of tempo which permits the underlying rhythm to exert its effect; or should they underscore the rhythm by an even greater regularity of tempo, by slightly lengthening words or pauses at the ends of lines, and by inflectional patterns planned to emphasize the verse?

To be effective, any treatment requires a harmonious approach, even though this may include some planned variations between scenes and characters. The individual actors would instinctively take differing approaches. Therefore a decision is made by the director. It is made in terms of his understanding of the playwright's intent. Eliot surely does not want the audience to be conscious of hearing verse in *The Cocktail Party;* but Fry does expect an awareness of verse at some times in *Venus Observed.* To conceal the rhythm or to speak against it in the plays of Synge would be to ignore one of the chief elements of their aesthetic pattern — whether it be his verse plays or *Riders to the Sea,* in which the simple speech of the Aran Islanders is made poetic.

Directors sometimes feel justified in varying from the intent of the author when they produce pre-modern verse plays. They believe that they obtain better audience appreciation for the play by adapting to the greater familiarity with prose drama. Directors have, for example, typed plays by Shakespeare in prose form, believing that the actors then make a more direct attack upon meaning than they do if they are confused by evenly-printed lines.

Thought. As a result of his initial study of the overall effect of the script, and of his study of it in detail, the director obtains his understanding of the thought or meaning of the play.

Some scripts have a definitely apparent theme — a logical pattern of meaning which the author wishes the audience to recognize. *Macbeth* says that ruthless ambition may ruin a man. *Oedipus the King* says that a man cannot escape his predestined fate. *Tartuffe* says that a hypocrite may be found in any walk of life, and also that a hypocrite usually will be exposed. *Death of a Salesman* says that the American go-getter's standard of values is unsatisfying and therefore false. *What Every Woman Knows* and *To the Ladies* say that a wife often contributes more to her husband's success than he himself does, but that she must not let him know it. *State of the Union* says that there are so many corrupting influences in politics that a man cannot retain his integrity if he runs for national office.

In many comedies and farces, however, such a statement of purpose is artificial and misleading from the standpoint of direction, for it is patent that the author's sole purpose is to hold audience attention for two hours, give the spectator a feeling of satisfaction, and make money for all concerned. This commercial point of view seems no handicap to contemporary success, though the history of drama indicates that such plays have short lives.

An audience sometimes sees a meaning or theme in a play which the author did not have in mind. It is doubtful if Anne Nichols intended *Abie's Irish Rose* to preach racial tolerance, yet many individuals so interpreted it, and, strangely, a motion picture adaptation of it aroused exactly the opposite response. Sometimes the director finds it difficult to determine whether a possible theme is intended by the author and is therefore to be stressed, or whether it is part of his own imaginative interpretation and should have no emphasis.

Even though the playwright has no conscious serious purpose, the choice of plot, episode, character, language, and style indicates his habitual logical and emotional attitudes toward life, and his particular attitude at the time of writing — all of which are part of the play's meaning. Theatre artists, in order to impart this underlying meaning, do not need to adopt it as a personal attitude, but they need such complete understanding of it and such complete sympathy with it that they present the play in a manner which permits the spectators to evaluate the attitude for themselves.

The meaning of a script may, of course, be misinterpreted. Noncommercial directors sometimes are accused of this; and each year we learn of shifts of directors of commercial productions during the rehearsal period which indicate disagreement on interpreta-

tion. Deliberate alteration of plays is discussed in detail in Chapter 26, but a few examples will indicate its possibilities. George M. Cohan's burlesque treatment of *The Tavern* is famous. George Jean Nathan states that *The Firebrand* was altered from romance to comedy during a tryout tour. John Barrymore completely overrode the script of *My Dear Children* by his constant ribald asides. Revisions and the personality of Charles Boyer seriously altered the effect of the Sartre play known in America as *Red Gloves.*

A famous or notorious personality in the cast has been exploited to secure success for a play, and has nearly always corrupted the intent of the script. More often in a musical production than in a straight play, an actor in a small part is so effective with the audience that the part is expanded tremendously during a tryout tour. A notable example of a mere incident's affecting the success of a play is Clyde Fitch's potboiler *Sapho,* which became a notorious success because of the furor created by the first act curtain when, at the end of a love scene, the hero took Olga Nethersole in his arms and carried her up a flight of stairs.

Some plays, like *The Moon Is Blue, The Man Who Came to Dinner, My Three Angels,* and *The Youngest,* are, of course, written solely for immediate pleasure, and have no meaning beyond this.

Background. The director can — by reading other writings of the playwright and writings about him — supplement the information about the play and the playwright he gets from a study of the script itself. Personal conversations with the author, when he is available, about the play and even on general subjects, help the director to understand the script and its motivation. It is commonly said that all writing is autobiographical in that the author inevitably reveals his attitudes toward every subject he mentions.

An author's preface is vitally important. George Bernard Shaw is the most expansive preface writer, often using more words here than for his dialogue. His preface sometimes directly explains aspects of the play it introduces, but more often it is comment on a related subject. The two types are of almost equal value, for the latter records the personal attitudes of Shaw at the time he wrote the script, and often constitutes his motivation for writing it. The preface helps to indicate when he is speaking from personal conviction, and when he is writing transitional or plot material.

There is a wealth of critical writings to tell the director how the classics and standard works have been interpreted by scholars. They vary from casual references to certain plays to the hundreds of volumes of critical studies of Shakespeare and of his individual dramas, climaxed by *A New Variorum Edition of Shakespeare* edited by the Furnesses (usually referred to simply as "The Variorum"). Much of this is purely literary criticism; but recent criticism is more theatre-conscious than the older writings. The two volumes of *Prefaces to Shakespeare* by Harley Granville-Barker are of especial value. *Shakespeare and the Actors,* by Arthur Colby Sprague, often suggests useful stage business.

Newspaper and magazine criticisms are available both for modern plays and for revivals of older plays. Since 1939 the *New York Theatre Critics' Reviews* has assembled the criticisms appearing in the major daily papers. Most of the larger libraries maintain a permanent file of at least one New York daily newspaper. *Theatre Arts,* old and new, *Theatre Time, Dramatics, Players Magazine, Educational Theatre Journal, Saturday Review, The New Yorker, The Nation, Time, The New Republic, Stage Pictorial* (English), and other magazines review plays regularly, as did the defunct *Stage, Theatre,* and *Theatre Guild Magazine.* The annual *Dramatic Index* serves as a guide to some of these. George Jean Nathan publishes a yearbook of criticism; other critics publish selections from their criticism. These reviews are useful both for a general evaluation of the script, and for an indication of some of the danger spots. Occasionally they contain constructive comments on interpretation. The annual volume of Burns Mantle's *Best Plays* (which has had several editors since the death of Mantle) contains condensations of ten plays, and the descriptive and summary passages of omitted sections sometimes clarify the effect conveyed by these scenes in their Broadway production.

If the action of a play takes place in the past, and particularly if it is biographical, the director can obtain valuable background information from histories of the time, biographies of the characters, and contemporary fiction and nonfiction. He uses this to aid him in interpreting the play — not to make important additions to it. The playwright adopts a viewpoint toward each of his characters, and toward the period and locale of the play. In doing so, he may deliberately or unconsciously falsify the character, the locale, the period, or all of them — the director follows the author. The playwright may distort or simplify a character by emphasizing certain characteristics and omitting others. Maxwell Anderson makes his two portraits of Elizabeth so different that they hardly seem to be one woman in two sets of circumstances. Anderson probably does not intend to synthesize them. The dramas are fictionalized biography, and he draws his second portrait of Elizabeth in the manner most useful in telling a story of Mary Stuart.

Design. Design is a distinct phase of the production process, and is fully discussed in an earlier section of this book. While designers usually supply the initial plans for all visual elements except the actors, the director also analyzes the visual needs, for he is as much concerned with them as are the designers, and he will want to appraise the designers' plans from his own point of view.

The aspects of design which most concern the director in planning and in early rehearsals are the floor plans of the settings; the size and possible uses of furniture and other properties; the general form and line of each costume; limitation or restriction upon action caused by costumes or any other part of the design; and color — especially color relationships among costumes, and color relationships between the costumes, the settings, and other visual elements.

The floor plans are of such immediate concern to him that in many instances he makes the first draft. Theoretically, if director and designer have complete understanding of the script, and both are perfect theatre technicians, they will arrive at identical floor plans, because both will desire to provide acting areas and backgrounds which will best clarify and intensify the dramatic action. In practice, however, both the director and the designer have individual preferences, prejudices, and habitual visual responses based more upon their own past experiences than upon logical analysis. A director may "see" a door in a certain area, and the designer may "feel" it in another. The designer knows from his training in design that an odd number of steps is more artistically decorative when the number is five or less; the director knows that steps which descend parallel to the curtain line permit a more graceful descent by an actor if they are even in number so that both his first step and his last step can be taken with the upstage foot. And there may be radical differences in the way the director and designer would plan the dramatic action. Often from these differences of opinion, with the thorough analysis which is forced upon both, the two collaborators evolve floor plans which are superior to the first ideas of either one.

The Director as Creator

The expressional function of the director is to design the total dramatic production. However, the unmodified word *design* has come to have restricted meaning in the theatre, where it is limited to the visual aspects of the production minus the acting. In consequence *director's design* or *design of the production* is used when it is applied to direction. It means the creation of atmosphere, style, proportion, balance, and unity, as in any other art.

The painter thinks in terms of design, but he creates visual stimuli by applying color with brush strokes. These stimuli cause sensory responses in the viewer of his work; they may set off associative responses — made possible by the viewer's past experience — which give the entire pattern a specific or general meaning, and this meaning may give pleasure. The meaning may be the same as that of the painter, or it may not be, depending upon the past experience of the two persons involved. The writer — who may be a playwright — thinks of character, plot, and mood, but writes black marks which have symbolic meanings as letters of the alphabet. The composer also thinks in terms of composition or design, but puts on paper musical notes and other symbols which will direct the musician to produce certain sounds which serve as auditory stimuli. In each case, the artist's skill lies in his imaginative and creative conception, and in his success in selecting and patterning the various stimuli so that they arouse the response he desires.

The performing musician turns the symbols of the composer into the appropriate vocal or instrumental sounds. But after he has mastered the mechanical phase, he turns his attention to an effort to re-create the overall effect and design, and his skill is evaluated in terms of his successful interpretation of these. In a performance requiring collaboration by a number of musicians, a leader or conductor co-ordinates their efforts and participates in the re-creation of the composition.

Just so, the actor speaks the words and performs the actions of the playwright. He is bound to reproduce these effects set down by the author, but there are many factors left uncontrolled by the playwright, and in these matters the actor becomes an almost free creative artist. In the modern theatre he is guided by a director, who assists him in perfecting his individual work, and also has creative responsibility in producing the total interpretative effect through scenery, costumes, make-up, lighting, music, dance, and the composite patterns produced by the acting group. But, in recognition of the limits placed on their creation by the playwright, some refer to the work of actor and director — like that of the musician and conductor — as re-creative rather than creative.

The director has as his media both auditory and visual stimuli; and his skill lies in his interpretation of the script, and in his success in patterning these auditory and visual stimuli so that they cause the audience to respond to his wishes. Details of this patterning are discussed in the remaining chapters of this section.

If a director approaches his work with the actors methodically (and especially if he is a novice), he may plan in great detail the expressive means by which he can clarify and intensify each speech and episode and thus produce the overall pattern by which he can communicate atmosphere, style, proportion — i.e., complete meaning. A danger of overmechanical direction is that the director may become so enamored of these plans that he judges the rehearsal results by mere accuracy of execution of his instructions, overlooks his critical function, and so fails to judge correctly whether the plans produce the effect he intended.

Occasionally there is a successful director in the commercial or noncommercial field who has had no formal training in the expressional phase of direction, and so depends upon his "intuition." If he has a strong interpretative understanding of a script, and a high degree of sensitivity to the vocal and bodily expression used spontaneously in conversational speech, he can apply them to the appreciation and criticism of representational acting. The less aware he is initially of the technique of expression, and of the picturization opportunities offered by the proscenium-arch stage, the more does he have to rely upon the competence of his fellow-artists, using his critical sense to evaluate their efforts, rather than guiding them in method. The intuitive director is likely to overlook some expressional opportunities, particularly in presentational productions — e.g., of pre-modern plays.

Most experienced directors employ a preparation and rehearsal method which combines the intuitive and methodical approaches. They plan in advance the techniques for some effects, plan the major action patterns sufficiently to draw floor plans, and then improvise the remainder of the scheme during rehearsals.

The Director as Critic

The ultimate function of the director is that of critic, or super-spectator, judging everything on the stage in terms of the meaning which it conveys to him personally and hence, presumably, to future spectators. If he finds that visual and auditory expression is ineffectual or wrong, he analyzes for his associates the specific factors which are responsible. In considering the director as artist it was observed that keenness of critical ability can compensate to a large measure for incomplete knowledge of principles of expression.

The critical function depends partly on a layman's viewpoint, in that a layman knows the meaning conveyed to him by the expression. But the analytical aspect of criticism requires knowledge of the art either as a practitioner or as a student, and a keenness of perception as to the relative contribution to the effect by each phase of the expression.

This position of critic does not imply that the director is inherently superior to his colleagues as an artist or that his judgment is infallible. In practical situations, the opposite may be the case, and the director may receive more help from the designer and the actors than he gives them in return. Actors may help each other, and there may be other interchanges of assistance and criticism. But, however useful, this is unofficial and gratuitous, whereas it is a specific duty of the director as critic to point out ineffectual or erroneous expression. An extension of this makes it his duty to find solutions of difficulties for his co-workers when they fail to discover them.

Complete and perfect communication is the director's goal; and he measures his success by this goal. Partial communication is partial failure; communication which distorts the intent of the script must be condemned. Yet true perfection seldom is achieved in any art, and in many circumstances partial success is recognized as being artistically valid. In judging partial success, some allowance is made for the height of the aim. Unless we recognize this in the theatre, we might content ourselves perpetually with cheap and easy plays because we can expect to attain a higher degree of success with them than when we attempt a more difficult and complex one, which often has more artistic merit. So, if a production partially communicates to the audience and thereby arouses a response which gives pleasure and a feeling of wholeness and completeness, it will be to some extent successful and justified.

Probably no production of *Hamlet* or *The Trojan Women* or *Peer Gynt* communicates all the meaning and implications which can be found in the play. T. S. Eliot puts so many layers of meaning in his verse plays, like *Murder in the Cathedral, Family Reunion, The Cocktail Party,* and *The Confidential Clerk,* that full understanding can be achieved only by reflection and rereading. Yet the audience may receive satisfaction from that part of the meaning which is imparted to it in a performance.

A production may successfully communicate to only part of the audience. This may be true especially with production of certain classics, experimental plays, and closet dramas which may appeal to groups which have an esoteric point of view. The satisfaction of the director and his associates depends upon their intent and upon their relative respect for the two parts of the audience. While this esoteric point of view is popular in some arts, theatre workers seldom adopt it, though there are occasional productions of *Four Saints in Three Acts, Sweeney Agonistes, The Poetaster, The Cenci,* and the like.

The director of an educational theatre seldom has sufficiently skilled and experienced students to impart *Oedipus the King, The School for Scandal,* and *Winterset* as completely as they can *Dear Ruth, Kiss and Tell,* and *Arsenic and Old Lace.* Yet if the audience receives from one of these difficult plays more pleasure and more meaning than they obtain from reading the play, the production serves an educational purpose by increasing the appreciation of literature. Not only may it increase the appreciation of the individual play; but seeing a play which seemed dull in reading take on meaning and excitement on the stage may stimulate the theatrical imagination of the students so that they read other drama with more understanding and appreciation. The educational theatre director keeps before him the goal of perfection, and tries to approach it as nearly as he can, but he and his audience usually feel that partial success is justified by the general educational benefits.

Similarly, in the educational theatre the audience is asked to tolerate as conventions some unavoidable limitations such as the youth and inexperience of the actors, and those limitations imposed by low budgets. But to have self-respect in his work, the director has to feel that the play imparts its essential meaning, that there is educational as well as entertainment value in the play chosen, and that his audience is aesthetically satisfied.

The theatre is sometimes used for didactic purposes; and the intent of some plays by Ibsen, Shaw, Hauptmann, Brecht, and Odets is to impregnate the mind of the spectator with social or political ideas to which these authors are partial, regardless of the pleasure they give. The production is then a success from a utilitarian standpoint if it stimulates the thoughts and emotions the playwright wishes, even though the audience may dislike the play.

It is to be seen from this analysis that the director has highly complicated duties. As interpreter, he analyzes the script for the intent of the whole and of the parts. He conducts the rehearsals, and makes various other preparations. He supplies leadership for the group in order to inspire the best effort of each associate. He so patterns the auditory and visual stimuli that the full intent of the script is imparted to the audience. And as an objective critic, he evaluates the work of all of his associates and, if need be, coaches them in those phases of their efforts that fall short of successful expression. In consequence, he is responsible for the total effect of the production.

23 | The Visual Stimuli

Stimuli Provided by the Actor • Stimuli Provided by the Influence of Design on the Actor

Numerous books and articles on direction contain valuable suggestions on the general viewpoint of the director, on his attitudes and goals, and on technical phases of his work. But in their haste to give practical advice to the fledgling director who often has to help some of his associates with their problems of expression, these treatments often mix this advice on coaching with their analysis of the function of direction. They thus give the impression that the director personally creates every detail of the production through automaton actors and designers who merely execute his orders. Though the director as critic is responsible for the entire production, much of the creative work is done independently by his colleagues.

The confusion arises because direction overlaps both acting and design, which supply the auditory and visual stimuli which the director patterns. And actors and designers, in addition to their creative work in their individual activities, do much of the organizing for themselves.

There is danger of being overmeticulous in making minute distinctions between the things the director can and must do because he is the director, and the things which he does when he finds that the actor, designer, and stage manager fail to make what he believes to be their proper interpretative con-

tribution to the production. But this danger is risked here in order to differentiate clearly the creative function of the director from his other activities. It is not suggested that the director be restricted thus in actual practice, for out of his supplementary function as critic grows the necessity to provide this coaching. Chapter 26 discusses his practical working relations with his associates in that respect.

Another reason for making the present distinction is that sometimes a director devotes so much attention to coaching the actors and to purely technical matters, that he gives scant attention to his primary function, and a scene or the whole play may prove ineffectual even though the individual work of the other artists is good. A beginning director easily falls into this error, for often he is more familiar with acting and technical work, and finds attention to them easier and more immediately rewarding than striving to develop the overall pattern of the production.

Accordingly, in this chapter and in the next two, attention will be restricted to the expressional aspect of direction. For this purpose, impossibly ideal conditions are assumed to exist — a perfect script, a theatre structure completely suitable for the play, every actor ideally cast and highly competent, the designers all perfect technicians

339

and artists, and the crews faultless in their skill and in their sensitivity to the timing of cues. And most important of all, and most extraordinary of all, the director and all of his colleagues have in mind exactly the same interpretation of the play. The director, therefore, can on this assumption forget his critical function, and work exclusively at his primary task of patterning the visual and auditory stimuli.

STIMULI PROVIDED BY THE ACTOR

The single, crucial stimulus of any given effect can often be identified, described, and discussed independently of all others. But it is nevertheless part of a complex pattern, and most of its meaning is in relation to the stimuli accompanying and preceding it. Even a sudden flash of light or an offstage pistol shot takes most of its meaning from association with other stimuli. For example, an actor sits down. What that conveys to the audience depends not only upon his appearance, the exact manner in which he takes his seat, and the physical attitude which he assumes, but also upon his previous pose, the position of the chair on the stage, its previous use, the physical appearance of the chair, its relation to the scenery, the grouping and movement of other actors, his character relationship with them, which of them are standing and which seated, the lighting of the stage, his costume and that of the other actors, the words and other sounds which accompany the movement, the episodes which immediately precede it, and many other factors. (Figures 1 and 6, pages 85 and 97, suggest the contribution of some of these related elements.)

Because so many variable factors are involved, and because variation of any one stimulus will permit or demand change in others, few precise rules can be set down for expression or for direction. Books on the Delsarte and other systems of pantomimic expression, and detailed analysis of some phases of direction as in *Fundamentals of Play Directing* by Alexander Dean, supply valuable theoretical guides for many details of expression, but these rules are always modified by the other details of expression which attend and precede them, sometimes to the point of complete reversal.

This book does not attempt to lay down rules or to describe all the minutiae of expression, but only to identify its elements and to demonstrate some of the ways in which a director uses them. Before analyzing the types of stimuli which he can employ, it will be helpful to examine a few instances of their ultimate patterning.

The ceremony of raising the curtain, for example, is planned to produce anticipation and to secure complete attention. Unless the theatre has a traditional procedure for it, the director and the designer devise the exact sequence and timing of the steps involved, including the correlation of curtain signals in the lobbies, the raising of the fire curtain, the dimming of the house lights, bringing up the footlights and other front lighting, and possibly co-ordination with an orchestra or with backstage sound effects. If their initial pattern fails to produce silent attention as the curtain rises, they adjust the sequence or the timing until it does so at subsequent performances.

An important speech may open the play. The setting may completely depict the locale, suggest the mood, and emphasize the actor; the lighting may perfectly support the setting and give proper prominence to the actor for his speech. Yet, if the actor begins his speech at the moment the curtain rises, some of its meaning is lost while the spectators explore the design of setting, lighting, properties, and costumes. The director, from his seat in the auditorium, can judge the necessary delay better than the actor on the stage, and business is devised to justify the delay. In reverse of this, most playwrights recognize the distraction of the design, and write opening lines which do not require close audience attention; in such cases the actor needs to begin speaking at once. In still other cases, particularly in pre-modern plays, the opening lines are sufficiently arresting to be spoken immediately.

For a long important speech with many characters listening, the actor plans his own attitude, gestures, and vocal expression, but the director decides the actor's location for the speech; and both participate in planning his movements. The director may even prepare carefully for this moment and design the floor plan to give an exact position-emphasis to the speech. He arranges the listeners in a composition which gives the speaker his proper prominence. He decides how much minor action the listeners make, and the moments which receive emphasis through responsive or antagonistic action and sound among them. He decides whether the lighting is to be altered to give the speaker a special brightness-emphasis. The colors of the costumes of the speaker and of the entire cast may be designed for their visual effect at this moment; if not, the director composes the group with the colors in mind.

An instance of careful patterning of stimuli is the Broadway production of *The Jest*. (See Plate 27.) The opening episodes establish the importance of Giannetto, and reach a climax at his entrance. Because he is weak and frightened through most of the action, it is vital that he make a striking and impressive entrance so that audience interest is centered on him throughout. In the production starring Lionel and John Barrymore, with Arthur Hopkins as producer and director and Robert Edmond Jones as designer, the problem was aggravated because John, who played Giannetto, was short and very slight in contrast to Lionel and the other actors. Hopkins and Jones met the problem by hanging enormous doors in the back wall

at the head of a flight of stairs, closed and unused until the entrance of Giannetto. There was a verbal preparation for the entrance, then a silence. The doors opened to reveal a brilliant blue sky behind Giannetto, who stood in a bright light in a long white cape which billowed out on the floor around his feet. Behind him stood a hunchbacked servant shorter than he. All on the stage turned to look up at him. He stood for a moment absorbing stature and importance from the height lines of the doorway and of the stairs, from the whiteness and mass of the huge cloak and its contrast with the sky behind him, from the majesty and immobility of his own posture, from the attitudes of the actors turning toward him, and from their upward gaze. Then, slowly and majestically he descended the stairs, immediately discarding the cloak — and attention was focused upon him for the entire play.

An obviously contrived device such as this runs the risk of being recognized as a mechanical trick, of calling attention to itself, and of producing an opposite effect to that intended. In this instance the device was accepted and so was effective, but the thin line separating it from the ludicrous was shown later in the same season, when the incident was burlesqued by that extravagant comedian, Marie Dressler, and her company. In a skit called "The Barrymores at Home" climaxing in a song entitled "Lionel, Ethel, AND John," every character entered through such a door wearing such a white cloak, which he immediately gave to an attendant at the foot of the stairs to be passed on to the next character to enter. Though few members of the vaudeville audience had seen *The Jest*, they laughed at the first of the entrances because the action was given that little additional pomposity which made it ridiculous, and they were convulsed at every succeeding entrance.

Without intruding upon the creativeness

of the actors, then, the director does plan the way in which attitude, position, movement, and gesture of each actor relates itself to the general pattern of stimulation.

Attitude

Attitude, used here in the dancer's sense of the word, refers to any arrangement of the parts of an actor's body which is held long enough to communicate to the audience an effect other than that of motion; and it includes those parts of his body which remain in relatively fixed relationships during movement or gesture, though it excludes movement and gesture themselves. "Posture" is sometimes used as a synonym for attitude, but has for most people the limited meaning of the habitual carriage of head, shoulders, torso, and legs; moreover, it excludes the positions of lying, squatting, kneeling, etc., and it excludes an arm extended and held for a few seconds, as well as such positions as leaning with an elbow on a mantel. The painter's term, "pose," is a synonym for this meaning of attitude.

Posture, in its limited sense of habitual manner of standing, sitting, and moving, arises from characterization, and is controlled almost exclusively by the actor. The attitude at any moment is the result of the actor's specific motivation in addition to his basic characterization, and also is the responsibility of the actor. However, the slightest gradation of motivation by the actor can produce a completely different pose, and supply a different line and silhouette. Many such gradations can be made by the actor without injury to his motivation and characterization. Therefore, much of the detailed control of this attitude can be assumed by the director.

Director and actor are equally concerned with what the attitude tells of the character's relation to other onstage characters, and of his interest in the immediate incident. His degree of dominance or subordination is the concern of the director.

The attitude, gesture, and movement of the actor who is speaking, or is otherwise active, is dictated to a large extent by his motivation, so little alteration of these is feasible. He would find it difficult to change from a sitting to a standing position, for example, but a passive actor may feel that, even though he is speaking, the casualness of his interest in the scene and conversation can be suggested by sitting with relaxed posture and crossed legs. If he crosses his legs toward his partner in the scene, even though he does not look at him, he gives the scene a feeling of compactness, and helps the other actor to get attention; while if he crosses his legs in the opposite direction, he contributes to a diffuseness of impression. The director can choose which effect he wants without disturbing the actor's motivation. An actor speaking to a group usually can adjust his gaze so as either to look at, or away from, any other actor at a particular moment.

The silent and less active participants in a scene are much less controlled by the script than the speaker, and find it easier to adjust their attitudes. In listening, one usually alternates between several patterns of thought — concentration on the speaker, evaluation of what he is saying, effort to fathom his motivation, preparation for a reply. Each produces a distinct pose. So the listening actor can plan the succession and the relative dominance of these thoughts to produce at a given moment the type of physical attitude which the director wants.

A character who is not immediately concerned in the dialogue may, for example, stand relaxed, looking at the speaker. He can stand facing the audience with his head turned to the speaker, he can turn his body in profile and look straight forward at the speaker, or he can turn his back to the audience and look at the speaker over his shoulder. The first draws more attention to himself than the profile or back position. Attitude with profile or back to the audience have about equal attention value; a back-to-the-audience position will cause less interest in the listener, but he will have twice the mass-attention value and may also have novelty and variety value. (See Figure 10.) He probably can sit as easily as stand if a motivation is found for the act of sitting.

The director's concern with style also may require that he set an overall pattern of attitudes in order to suggest an historical period, or to produce a generally light or heavy posture pattern for the actors as a group, out of which grow their individual attitudes, gestures, and movements. In the highly mannered drama of the seventeenth and eighteenth centuries, for example, the director wants his actors to carry themselves erect and high, and to stand most of the time. They face front and three-quarters front more frequently than they do in a realistic drama. (See Figure 3, page 91.)

The director also is concerned with attitude for its contribution to composition, particularly on a conventional stage. An actor lying on the floor or on furniture, squatting or kneeling, seated in a relaxed pose, seated but alert, leaning on furniture or against a wall while standing, standing erect and in open space — each contributes a line which has its distinct meaning to the observer. Each pose can be used singly or in a group pattern to suggest mood, style, emphasis and proportion.

Moreover, the director wants variety in attitude. Ordinarily, standing or sitting in profile or three-quarters front will be the predominant poses. But to avoid monotonous uniformity, characters out of the immediate scene can be faced full or three-quarters back to the audience. For a striking effect, even the speaking character, surrounded by enemies on all sides, can turn his back to the audience near the footlights to face the entire group. Other positions can be used and may be striking because they are a break with convention. John Buckmaster, playing St. John Hotchkiss in *Getting Married*, sat on a table far upstage center with his back to the audience and carried on a conversation with characters downstage on each side. This gained him fine attention, for in addition to the novelty of the position, he had to twist about with his face three-quarters front to speak to the others.

Actors occasionally deliver speeches lying on the floor or on a table. Romeo lies "there on the ground" through much of Act III, Scene iii, of *Romeo and Juliet*. Gertrude Lawrence played a long scene in *Skylark* lying on the floor with a scrapbook. Maria Jeritza used to sing the "Seguidilla" in *Carmen* lying on her back on a kitchen table, and she addressed the Queen of Heaven in *La Tosca* lying flat on her face.

Jed Harris designed a striking bit of business for *The Heiress*. In one scene of this play, Catherine first meets her future fiancé, Morris Townsend, while others carry on a light and relatively unimportant social conversation. So Harris grouped the actors at the back of the stage behind a low settee with the dominant figure of Dr. Sloper standing center back and full-front, and with Catherine and Morris seated on chairs whose backs were toward the divan and the audience, but silhouetted in front of the dialogue scene. These striking back-to-the-audience attitudes drew attention to every look which passed between them. But the novelty of any such unusual attitude may draw too much attention to the action itself and distract from its meaning. (See Plate 16.)

The principles underlying the use of attitude on a proscenium stage — like those for position, gesture, and movement — are in many cases transferable to open staging; in other cases they are not. Some of the distinctions and differences involved are treated elsewhere in this volume, particularly in Chapters 18 and 26.

In any case, attitudes sometimes are used to communicate meaning by symbols. Many plays which have religious meaning use a crucifixion pose or a blessing pose to emphasize a parallel between Jesus and a character in the play. Similarly, parallels have been attempted with the Statue of Liberty, the Thinker, The Last Supper, The Man with the Hoe, and other famous works of art. Such poses must be exact in order to be recognizable, and therefore deliberately planned, since the actor does not fall into them through motivation alone.

Position

The term "position" refers to the actor's location on the stage in three dimensions — width, depth, and height. Traditionally the first two of the dimensions are roughly indicated in five lateral divisions of the stage: right, right-center, center, left-center, and left; and by three divisions in depth from the curtain line to the back wall: downstage, upstage, and center (usually undesignated). Right and left are those of the actor facing the audience. In a shallow setting the downstage area is omitted from the designations. Apron may be added as a fourth depth designation when the actors play in front of the curtain line.

This produces a graph of the stage in approximately six-foot squares. Initial letters are commonly used in acting editions of plays to indicate these approximate positions. The fifteen or twenty areas can then be diagrammed as follows:

UR	URC	UC	ULC	UL
R	RC	C	LC	L
DR	DRC	DC	DLC	DL
	C u r t a i n L i n e			
AR	ARC	AC	ALC	AL

B for back is sometimes substituted for U in the upstage row.

Doors used to be similarly designated; R1 for the downstage right door or the opening between wings, with R2 and R3 for those further upstage. CD stood for the center door in the back wall and BR and BL for the two side doors in the back wall. Realis-

tic box settings have reduced the number of openings and reduced the need for these symbols.

Height symbols seldom are needed, since the actor has no choice but to stand on any elevation which he finds at his designated position. Large platforms are ordinarily referred to as first level, second level, etc., starting at the front of the stage. An actor is said to be *above* a piece of furniture when he is upstage of it, *below* when he is in front of it.

The positions of actors are usually planned by the director in relation to another actor, to furniture, to architectural features, or to a very exact compositional pattern, and only secondarily with reference to these diagrammatic areas; and so the vague area designations described above are of little use to him, for they do not indicate the reasons for the positions or the relation to other actors and objects on the stage. More often a rough diagram of the setting is used by the director. The designation by initials is still used in many printed acting editions of plays, and is of general use to indicate the direction a movement is to take.

Other things being equal, which they seldom are, the actor at center is in a more favorable position to obtain audience attention than one at the side of the stage, for the seats in most auditoriums are arranged in curves which tend to fix the relaxed gaze of a spectator upon center stage.[1]

The actor facing the audience in what is known as open position, as distinguished from closed position (see Figure 9), can obtain audience attention more easily than one standing three-quarters front or in profile, for not only does he have more mass — and is able to communicate his motivations more completely — facing front, but this position draws special attention through its

[1] Refer in this connection to the treatment of "strong" and "weak" areas on page 100, in the section on Acting.

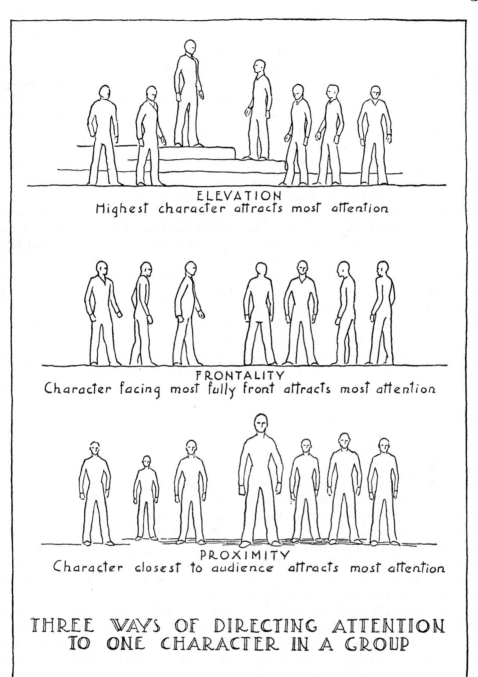

ELEVATION
Highest character attracts most attention

FRONTALITY
Character facing most fully front attracts most attention

PROXIMITY
Character closest to audience attracts most attention

THREE WAYS OF DIRECTING ATTENTION
TO ONE CHARACTER IN A GROUP

Figure 45. On a conventional stage, modes of emphasis can reinforce each other, but may be opposed — e.g., proximity in opposition to frontality or to elevation.

suggestion of direct address to the audience.

The actor who has height advantage will find it easier to attract attention. A tall actor, one standing among seated figures, and one standing on an elevation, all receive this advantage.

The actor nearer the front of the stage is in the more favorable position to obtain audience attention, since he is closer and optically larger, and thus can be better seen. For the most part, however, if the actor speaks to others on the stage, then this is reversed, for the advantage of an open position is greater than that of proximity. In consequence, the actor in the upstage position facing more nearly full-front finds it easier to get attention than the downstage actor who has to turn to profile or even into a closed position away from the audience in order to speak to the one upstage. "He upstaged me" has come into popular use to describe the stealing of attention from another person who should have it. Inconsiderate actors deliberately take positions which give them this attention advantage even when they are unimportant in the immediate action, and thereby injure themselves by attracting attention at moments when they are passive and least interesting. Unskilled actors often upstage others unwittingly; some even think they are being modest in forcing others into more prominent positions by "keeping themselves in the background."

Dominance by position not only helps in the impression of dominance itself, but also gives an actor a more open position. In the last attic scene of *I Remember Mama,* there are complex alternations of emphasis between Katrin and Mama.[2] Katrin sits at a table as she writes her diary and talks to the audience. When Mama enters, Katrin jumps up and steps below her chair. Mama sits on a trunk which gives her the open upstage position for her early speeches. Katrin's dis-

[2] The action here described is diagrammed in Figure 46.

couragement about her writing can be used to get her behind the chair facing Mama with her downstage hand on it, so that when she moves to Mama in her amazement at the visit with the "lady novelist," it seems natural for her to cross above the chair and desk. This brings her to an open position above Mama for her scornful speeches about teachers of writing. As Mama reports what the novelist had to say, Katrin, humbled and embarrassed, moves around below the desk again, giving Mama the upstage position, but keeping her profile to the audience so that it can observe her reactions. A further movement away in embarrassment lets her put her upstage hand on the back of her chair as she faces away, so that when she turns back to Mama, she inevitably turns toward the hand and takes a position behind the chair. From this position it seems natural after Mama's exit for her to move further upstage of the chair and occupy a good position for the soliloquy in which she decides to write about Mama. Meanwhile, Mama moves toward the door, and, by turning her head back toward Katrin, is opened to the audience for her touching speech about Papa. Though this is deliberately calculated by actor and director to give the best possible position for each speech, it has naturalistic motivation which makes it seem unplanned.

In contrast, there is the story of the tour in 1927 of the all-star cast of *Trelawney of the "Wells,"* when Otto Kruger found himself constantly upstaged in one of his important scenes by another member of the company. He kept moving back with the other actor until they stood near the back wall. Finally, one night, Kruger in exasperation threw open the double doors at the back of the setting, walked six feet upstage of the other actor, and delivered his important speech from there. Thereafter his partner humbly took his proper downstage position for this scene.

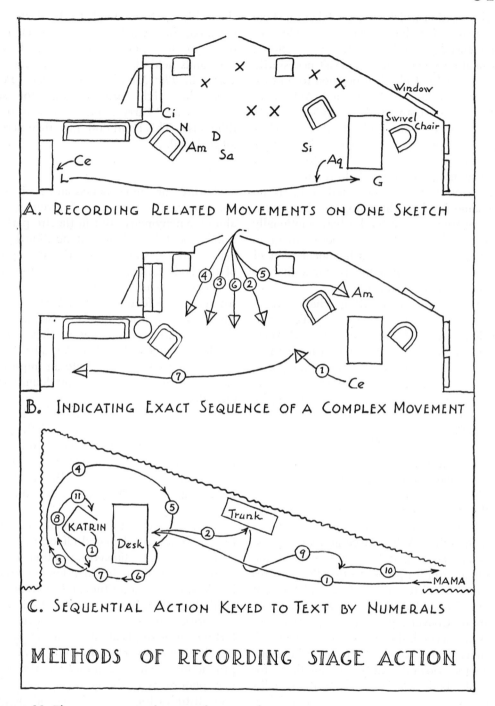

A. RECORDING RELATED MOVEMENTS ON ONE SKETCH

B. INDICATING EXACT SEQUENCE OF A COMPLEX MOVEMENT

C. SEQUENTIAL ACTION KEYED TO TEXT BY NUMERALS

METHODS OF RECORDING STAGE ACTION

Figure 46. There are many shortcuts for recording stage action, e.g., for use in a prompt book. Adaptations of the above are needed for open staging.

The position which an actor takes on stage is a matter for the director to decide. An experienced actor knows when he should dominate a scene, but he doesn't necessarily need the help of physical position to do this. In the orations of Brutus and Antony in *Julius Caesar,* both speakers attain complete domination over the mob of citizens. They will be helped by being elevated and thus able to speak "down" to the citizens. At the beginning, however, Antony's method of persuasion is better suggested if he is on the same level as the mob, and his ascent to a rostrum only after he has emotionally ensnared the populace will better diagram for the audience the psychological plan of his speech. The dialogue requires that he descend again for the climax.

A weak character often challenges a stronger character, as does Mary Turner in the first act of *Within the Law* and Mary Stuart in her final scene with Elizabeth in *Mary of Scotland.* The usual technique is to place a threatening character upstage, and on an elevation if possible, so that he can dominate the scene physically as well as emotionally. But on occasion the revolt of an underdog may be better pictured by letting such a character fight with auditory means alone against an antagonist in a more dominant position.

The dominant hand of an actor, usually his right, is stronger and more expressive than the other. When large and strong gestures are needed, it helps the actor if the dominant arm is upstage so that the gestures do not "cover" the actor's face and body; if he is right-handed, this suggests a left-stage position. Conversely, if small restricted gestures are needed, the right-handed actor will be more expressive on the right. When one character violently upbraids another, for example, both attacker and inarticulate listener are helped if the attacker is on the left. In the balcony scene of *Romeo and Juliet,* Romeo will be more effective on left stage

since his gestures tend to be large and elevated, Juliet will be more effective on the right since her gestures are small, with her hands held close to the body. Similarly, Portia in *The Merchant of Venice* (IV, i) needs her right arm upstage for such speeches as, "Tarry a little; there is something else. This bond doth give thee here no jot of blood. . . . "

Gesture

Gestures are movements, and so in ordinary usage "gesture" and "movement" are almost synonymous. But in theatre parlance a movement is a change of position by the actor, and a gesture is an action of any part of the body which does not alter the stage position. Gestures include movements of the head, the features ("facial expression"), the shoulders, arms, hands, torso, and also the legs and feet so long as they do not result in change of location. A gesture which is held long enough to create an impression of arrested motion becomes by definition an attitude.

Gestures are almost exclusively the concern of the actor, arising out of the characterization and motivation of his role. Our belief in the evidence of our eyes in preference to that of our ears usually makes gestures dominant over speech when they are contradictory.

However, a director occasionally uses gesture to create a calculated effect, though in such cases the climactic position of the gesture is usually maintained long enough to be classified as an attitude. He may want a symbolic echoing of a gesture to indicate similarities, or to point up a reversal of fortune by a duplication of an action with the characters reversed. In an expressionistic production, such as *Man and the Masses,* he may plan many of the gestures, movements, and attitudes for visual effects independent of the immediate motivation of the characters. In *R.U.R.* the director sets the pattern of movement and gesture for the mechanical robots. In *The Insect Comedy* (also called *The World We Live In*) he may set special patterns for the butterflies, the beetles, and the ants. To establish a period style, he may establish a pattern to which the actors adjust their gestures. In mob scenes, he often prescribes a pattern for the gestures. In *Julius Caesar*, for example, he may restrict gestures during Brutus' speech to those below shoulder level, allow the hands gradually to become fists at head level during the early part of Antony's speech, and withhold the gesture of arms fully extended over the head for the climactic moment.

Gestures also may be expository. It is often necessary to forewarn the spectators about a property, an architectural feature, or a trick of costume. They may be shown the place where a pistol is kept. In *The Madwoman of Chaillot* the Sewer-Man is introduced in order to call attention to a trapdoor and thus foreshadow its use by Countess Aurelia to entice the villains of the world to their destruction. *Charley's Aunt* uses extensive exposition to prepare the audience for the dress worn by Charley. In *Justice*, in preparation for a suicide leap, the audience must know that the room seen on the stage is on an upper floor, and so the director has his actors find opportunities to look downward from the windows of the setting.

Ordinarily the playwright supplies the means for such foreshadowing, but the director makes sure that it is treated adequately both in the dialogue and in the execution of the business. The familiar pistol in the pocket or in the top drawer is not only discussed, it is taken out and handled as much as possible in order to "plant" it clearly. Later an actor, if he feints to use it, opens the drawer and puts his hand on it, rather than merely touching the drawer. If the script forewarns by pantomime and not by dialogue, the director makes sure that this pantomime is emphasized. He may further plant it by additional pantomime not called for by the author; on rare occasions he forewarns the audience of matters which the author has not demanded. A modern audience may not be aware that Renaissance gallants often wore a dagger in addition to a sword. A British audience at an American gangster play may not be aware that a gangster or policeman habitually carries a gun strapped under the left arm. The director may have other characters kiss casually in the ball scene of *Romeo and Juliet* so that Romeo's kissing of Juliet at their first meeting is recognized as conventional period behavior.

Gestures can be used to clarify a complex scene. With a large cast onstage, it is sometimes necessary to draw attention to a speaker when he has been out of the conversation for a few moments. In *Command Decision* an actor playing the newspaper correspondent, seated far to the side of the stage, and only occasionally throwing in sarcastic comments and questions, found useful devices for obtaining attention just before he spoke — in a wide sweep of his swivel chair, a casual toss of a correspondence file, and a lighting of a cigarette interrupted by his speech, with the flaming match serving as a beacon. A warning needs to be given once more against overdoing such devices. A professional actor with a similar problem in a production of *Here Come the Clowns* began to get snickers the fifth time he noisily set down his highball glass to attract attention for a line.

Movement

An actor can change his onstage position by movements of crawling, creeping, or sliding as well as of walking. Since movements are frequently specified in acting editions, and are recorded in their production scripts by the director and stage manager, symbols for them have been developed, *X* for *cross* being virtually the only purely conventional sign of wide use. The others are initials and abbreviations, so that *X URC* means cross to up right-center, *X D of sofa* (or *X below sofa*) indicates cross to downstage of sofa, and *X Dor.* tells the actor to cross in front of the character named Dorothy. Individuals devise additional symbols of their own.

A director who records movements in the margin of the script more often uses an initial for each character on the stage, and an arrow-ending line for each movement. He may draw a rough floor plan of the setting and locate all the characters present, and then draw a line with an arrow from the initial of the moving character to his new position. Or he may note only the character who moves, the ones he crosses, and any others to whom the movement is related. Furniture may be included in either method. Some directors plan the movements on a scale model of the setting with pins, checkers, or other movable symbols, and then record them. Others use exact scale floor plans in duplicate, record a number of movements on one plan, and cross-reference them to the text by numerals. Figure 46 shows samples of various techniques used in such diagrams.

The movements incident to characterization and motivation are basically created by the actor, and, when the director assists the actor with them, he becomes coach. The actor knows whether his movement should be flamboyant, foreboding, threatening, or hesitant; whether a cross should be long or short, straight or curved, strong or casual; and whether the tempo is fast or slow, constant or progressive. Actor and director agree upon these movements if they concur in their interpretation of the play, the scene, and the character.

Movements toward a character or an object are determined by motivation, though the nearness of approach may be variable. But the details of a movement away in rejection, scorn, or indifference are little influenced by motivation, and the director may

suggest its length, direction, and path. It may be used to create an immediate effect, or to locate the actor for later action. If a character scornfully withdraws from a scene down right, he can cross to far left and take up a position out of the immediate attention of the audience, or one which relates him to others who share his attitude. Instead, he can stroll to center and then upstage, ready to turn back in fury on a new motivation and rush back to center to dominate the scene. Or he can start toward left and halt suddenly as a new motivation comes to him from introspection, with attention focused on him because of the sudden interruption of the rhythm of his walk. Similarly, in a very crowded setting, such as the various tiny tenement rooms in . . . *one third of a nation* . . . , it is necessary to calculate movements in such a way as to prepare for subsequent ones and clear a path for them.

Some guiding principles for movement can be set down if it is remembered that the complexity of interacting stimuli prevents rigid rules.[3]

Movement secures attention; purposive movement holds it; but movement made in reaction to a speaker can be made to direct attention to the speaker, and seemingly casual movement can be made to repel attention, though it may distract for a moment. Actors used to be taught "Never move while another character is speaking." Because any such movement is distracting, the rule has merit as a guide, but it is frequently violated legitimately. "Cross in front of another character if you are speaking, cross behind him if he is speaking" has similar validity and similar exceptions. Ordinarily, crosses behind other actors are avoided because the movement seems apologetic, but servants often cross upstage of other characters. "Move simultaneously with another actor only if you are moving on the same motivation" is another valuable guide. In repre-

[3] See also pages 103–110.

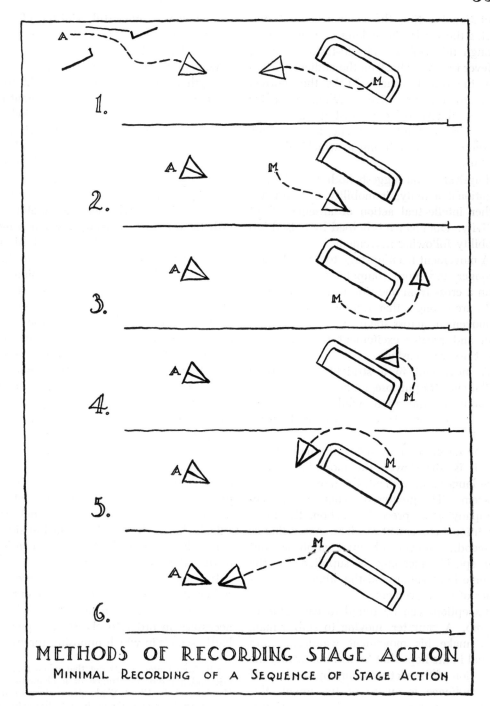

METHODS OF RECORDING STAGE ACTION
MINIMAL RECORDING OF A SEQUENCE OF STAGE ACTION

Figure 47. Sequential action usually requires additional diagraming. (Compare Figure 46.)

sentational acting the actor usually "completes the circle" in making any turn, even though this violates the old-fashioned rule, "Never turn your back on the audience!" Today the rule is usually "Take the shortest path to the objective." When an actor moves almost directly upstage and then must turn back into the scene, the principle of the circle will tell him in which direction to turn.

Physical action suggests both dramatic and emotional activity; immobility may suggest either intellectual action or absence of all activity. Dominance is helped by poised immobility following movement.

A movement from upstage to downstage is stronger and more compelling of attention than a cross from one side to the other, and both are stronger than a movement upstage. A movement across stage suggests more motion and greater excitement than a movement up or downstage.

A movement in a straight line implies definiteness of purpose, an arc suggests poise without determination, while a wandering movement suggests casualness and disinterest.

The faster the movement, the more exciting it is; the slower, the more impressive. The longer a movement, the more important it seems. The greater the contrast with accompanying or preceding action, the more attention a movement receives. Ascending or descending movement gives emphasis, but the specific meaning is supplied by the change in elevation and the other characteristics of the movement.

Exceptions can be found to each rule of thumb. A gangster, moving to stab a man, may make his movement wandering and casual in the hope that he will not attract the attention of the victim or any bystanders. If the audience is aware of his intent, this broken movement may build and prolong suspense far more excitingly than a direct movement toward the object. Immobility

can convey a powerful, sinister effect, as Sidney Greenstreet and Peter Lorre constantly demonstrate.

Directors disagree about the relative strength of a movement from right to left as compared with the same movement from left to right. They argue about the influence of the habit of reading from left to right, and about the relatively stronger empathic response aroused in a spectator by the sympathetic action of his dominant arm and shoulder. These arguments are complicated by consideration of whether a spectator's kinesthetic response is stronger when a movement is made in the direction of his own greater strength or in opposition to it. In the face of the contradictory opinions, and absence of any thorough scientific study of the subject, this remains a moot question.

In representational settings the use of doorways is dictated by an attempt to be "natural." In unlocalized settings, such as are often used for Shakespearean plays, the choice of entranceways sometimes is made for purely visual effect; sometimes each entranceway is treated as if it is a specific building or locale; and sometimes it follows a purely theatrical pattern according to which each character re-enters through the same opening as that of his previous exit. The opposite of this can be even more theatrically effective on an unlocalized stage such as the Elizabethan — to re-enter from the side opposite the exit in order to suggest continuity of directional movement.[4]

In some cases, the direction of crosses — rather than their relationship to entranceways — can be given meaning. This is often necessary in order to clarify a sequence of battle scenes in which opposing forces alter-

[4] B. Iden Payne points out that when there is an exit and a rapid re-entrance of a character, as of Hamlet and the Ghost, Shakespeare always provides four to six lines of dialogue to give the actors time to cross backstage. Payne is preparing a book on the staging of Shakespeare in "modified" Elizabethan style.

nately cross the stage, as in *Macbeth, Henry V*, and *Henry VI*, Part 1. The psychological meaning of many of the entrances and exits in *King Lear*, as well as the physical relation between the numerous locales, can be clarified if one cross indicates moving away from security, as represented by throne, shelter, and protection, and the other implies movement toward it.

Transitions in the script between French scenes are often emphasized by movements.

The basic rhythm of a play can be conveyed in part by the general pattern and amount of movement, but within this scheme, variety in type and tempo of movement is desirable. (Note in particular Figures 51, 52, and 53.) As in all phases of direction, contrast gives emphasis. In *The Green Pastures*, the seated Moses becomes the center of attention in contrast to the movement of the mass of the Children of Israel as they enter the Promised Land and leave him behind. A hard-hitting melodrama like *The Front Page* has fast cross-stage and vertical movements in straight lines, with sudden physical transitions, many surprises, and many entrances and exits.

A drawing room comedy such as *The First Mrs. Fraser, The Constant Wife,* or *Design for Living* uses unhurried, smoothly curved crosses and relatively few and unvaried movements. *Candida, Pygmalion,* or *Mr. Pim Passes By* can be played with the actors seated much of the time, with the entrances and exits practically the only movements. The director decides whether to accept the inherent physical inactivity of the script and concentrate attention on the words and ideas, or to attempt to insert physical action at every opportunity in order to underscore the dramatic action. A few years ago there was a tendency to load all plays with movement. Laurence Olivier, in one of his first engagements on Broadway, playing Gaylord Esterbrook in *No Time for Comedy*, gained tremendous publicity, including a picture spread in *Life* magazine, by the constant flow of novel gestures and movements with which he concealed the weakness of his part and "stole the show" from Katharine Cornell. Though this was praised at the time, more recently Broadway critics tend to complain of such superfluous activity. While movement can help to clarify action, too much of it can obscure the dialogue and the dramatic action.

Comedies and farces of family life often have erratic, jerky, and complexly curved movements, as do *Juno and the Paycock* and *Dear Ruth*. They often employ much novel naturalistic business, and the character tempi are likely to be highly varied. *George Washington Slept Here* makes notable use of this variety of pace. Many modern farces and farce-comedies call for a good deal of action. But the direction can increase or reduce its effect by the arrangement of the furniture and the architectural features, thereby shortening or lengthening the crosses. The predominant characteristic of a farce like *Three Men on a Horse* is contrast — alternation between very rapid and unnaturally slow movement and alternation between straight and extremely curved movement, with very sharp transitions. The typical movement in farce is a strong, swaggering, straight-line cross culminating in a shock transition which sends the character scuttling back in a huge circle. Bobby Clark, Danny Kaye, and the Marx Brothers use this technique constantly; Bert Lahr's use of it is masterful.

Tragedy of the Greek and French classic periods tends to have slow, grand movements in straight lines or smooth curves, with some violent and rapid movements in contrast, chiefly by messengers. Romantic drama including Shakespeare has a faster, stronger, more varied, and more violent action pattern, and often contrasts straight-line actions with curved movements; all contrasts are strong. Both types of tragedy demand little movement, but permit considerable; and the director determines whether the essence of the play is better communicated by limiting action or by taking advantage of every opportunity for it.

The mannered periods incline toward slower, self-conscious action, and predominantly curved movements, with a great deal of emphasis upon the small gestures of the head, arms, and shoulders, which can be rapid. *Love for Love, The Beaux' Stratagem,* and *The Importance of Being Earnest* are examples. Contemporary mannered plays, such as *Private Lives* and *The Play's the Thing,* adopt actions with these characteristics, though they are less accurate and less graceful than in the plays from the periods of greater style and manner.

In plays using an exaggerated style, either period or expressionistic, it is often expedient to emphasize movements. It is appropriate to the plays, and the expression of style in large movements can be learned by inexperienced actors more easily than in gestures and in vocal expression. In such cases, the actors can convey a sense of style when they move, which they might fail to do if they remained stationary for long. In *The Doctor in Spite of Himself* and *The Gardener's Dog* movement can be constant and almost as precise as a dance pattern.

Dance is related to other movement in the play. It is required in a surprising number of nonmusical plays: e.g., *The House of Connelly, Salome, Burlesque, Broadway, A Doll's House, Herod and Miriamne, Lute Song, Idiot's Delight,* and in most of the comedies of Molière and Shakespeare. But dance is beyond the scope of this book except to note that the dances need to be designed for dramatic effectiveness rather than as independent creations, and that they need to be designed in relation to the setting in which they will be performed.

STIMULI PROVIDED BY THE INFLUENCE OF DESIGN ON THE ACTOR

Design and direction are inseparable, because the designer works for exactly the same clarification and intensification of the dramatic action as does the director, and the designer and director have identical points of view in planning the décor and the floor plan. Since these interrelationships are treated in detail in the section on Design, the following discussion is limited to the influence of design on the actor.

Openings

The entranceways to a setting control the larger movements. They are placed where they produce the action patterns which best picturize [5] action, atmosphere, and style.

An upstage opening near center provides the most conspicuous and impressive entrance, particularly if the actor can pause for a moment and be framed by the opening. (See Figure 34.) If the entrance is violent and hasty, an opening at the side or at one of the upstage corners is more effective because it gives the actor a longer cross in taking his position in the scene. If the appearance of the character is to provide a shock as he is discovered on the stage, an entrance from the side is more desirable. Since all members of the audience must receive the surprise at the same instant, the setting must be planned with this in mind. With poor sight lines, this side entranceway may have to be jogged in. It may even be necessary to push a doorway far enough onstage by means of an irregularly shaped setting to provide an "inconspicuous entrance downstage center," as one director requested for Elizabeth's first appearance in *Elizabeth the Queen* so that she could slip in suddenly but unostentatiously and dominate the stage without moving.

An actor entering up center finds it easy

[5] See Picturization unit in Chapter 25.

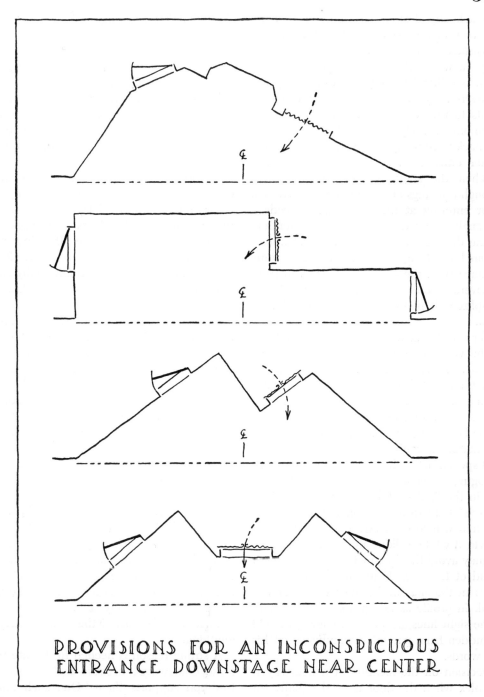

PROVISIONS FOR AN INCONSPICUOUS
ENTRANCE DOWNSTAGE NEAR CENTER

Figure 48. Three plans allowing Elizabeth to slip in suddenly and unostentatiously and yet dominate the stage without moving. (Discussed in an accompanying section, under "Openings.")

to reach any desired position, for then he can veer toward right or left as he comes downstage. This is more satisfactory for plays in which the action is played seated, for it is difficult to keep such entranceways uncovered by standing actors, and movements to uncover it for entrances soon become obvious. Openings well to the side at the back have many of the advantages of the center entrance, and fewer disadvantages.

When the stage is crowded, entrances through openings at the side are difficult. An actor entering at the side usually needs a reasonably long cross to gain full attention, so the director sees to it that the character whom he is to approach is placed at some distance from the opening. A cross in front of several actors to face another requires a complex S-shaped cross which can look artificial.

For exits the advantages and disadvantages of the various entranceways are almost the reverse. It is difficult to exit effectively through any back-wall opening. Older plays often provide dialogue for such exits. The actor's motivation for the exit is in his next to the last speech; he moves to the door during another's reply, and then turns for a final speech before he leaves. Contemporary dialogue, in contrast, often motivates the exit in the final speech, and the actor times his speech to disappear on the final word. His line will lose effectiveness if he has to deliver it while walking upstage. The director may avoid this by moving him to the exit ahead of the line. Exits are easier through doors in the side walls, since the actor can speak in profile as he approaches the door. If the sight lines are poor, of course, he will be hidden from part of the audience on his exit words.

Decision on the location of a doorway is complex when the door is used equally for entrance and exit, and the director has to decide which use is the more important. Sometimes, however, even though entrances through a door are important, the door serves as a passage rather than a frame, and a side entrance, or a compromise of a side entrance jogged into the room, will serve equally well for both entrance and exit.

In the light of these advantages and disadvantages, when realism does not prevent it, a director frequently brings his actors in at back entrances, and sends them out by side doors.

An interruption of a cross and an exit in order to open a door confuses the exit; such an opening similarly delays an entrance if the door must be closed again. An open arch or door frame is preferable. If a door must be used, the direction of its swing is vital to the action. Exterior doors traditionally swing into the building except when fire laws require the reverse. Except for these exterior ones, stage doors in the side wall are hinged to swing offstage and upstage; doors in the back wall, to swing backstage and toward center. An up-center door is hinged on the side opposite to the direction of the path the actors take after the door is closed. An onstage swing requires that the exiting actor grasp the knob, take a few steps backward, and then exit. This backing motion may create a visual effect that is contrary to his motivation. Also, the departing actor then remains in view while he closes the door. Since the audience assumes that he hears the dialogue during these moments, the delay in his disappearance may cause a needless pause before the remaining actors can continue the dialogue. The movement of closing the door is inherently an awkward one, and requires especially skillful co-ordination to make it with grace if the actor is carrying anything.

A strong reason is needed to deviate from these doorswings, because logic as well as tradition supports them. One such reason is the need to have a character eavesdrop through a half-open door. In *Berkeley Square* the downstage right door is hinged to swing onstage and downstage. This is planned so that the two Peter Standishes, on their entrances at the curtain moments of the two first scenes, are hidden from the audience while the onstage characters pretend to see them. When possible elsewhere in this play, the door is left open against the wall, but it still results in some awkward entrances and exits at other points throughout. This same doorswing is sometimes used when a trapdoor is not available for the last scene of *Elizabeth the Queen* in order to achieve the impressiveness and suspense of Essex' entrance and exit.

If characters look out of windows or other openings in the setting and report what they see, as in the long speech by Chu-Yin in *Marco Millions* (describing Marco's politician's pose as he approaches the palace and addresses the crowd while his hand rests upon — and pats — the head of the celestial bronze dragon), they are placed in the side wall so that the character can remain in profile or slightly more open. Windows through which characters suddenly see something while they speak need to be located in direct relation to the action.

Elevations

Levels, ramps, and stairs can give variety and emphasis to stage movements and pictures. They permit the director to use his third dimension of composition, height. In recent decades both noncommercial and commercial design have used these devices increasingly, though there seldom is as imaginative use of them as by Max Reinhardt and Leopold Jessner early in this century, and in the productions of Norman Bel Geddes and Robert Edmond Jones in the twenties.

Use of elevation is one of the easiest ways in which to establish dominance for a figure, even if the level is only six inches. The advantage in attention and dominance varies almost directly with the height.

An ascending or descending movement receives tremendous emphasis because the action is less familiar visually than a movement on a single level, and so is attention compelling. Whether the desired effect is majesty, stealth, despair, joy, excitement, physical strength, or physical weakness, the actor communicates it more effectively because his movement in doing so is relatively novel.

The architectural structure of buildings, and therefore of stage settings, is such that levels, ramps, and stairs increase in height as they approach doorways. Therefore, in both interiors and exteriors, they are usually found around the perimeter of the setting. Because of this, the descent of stairs usually is associated with strong movements, for an entering actor moves downstage or onstage as he descends. He usually has a strong motivation when he moves to these positions of greater prominence. Also, audience attention naturally goes to a new figure, both because it provides novelty, and because it is moving, so for an instant at least the character has almost undivided attention. The descent of stairs helps him to use this attention to full advantage in establishing his motivation and, if this is his first entrance, in projecting his characterization as well.

Ascent of stairs can have almost as much meaning as descent, but it is less frequently used to create an important effect because of the inevitable location of stairs on the stage. The actor ordinarily has to face back or in profile when he is ascending stairs, and move upstage or to the side. There is a psychological contradiction in an actor moving backstage and ascending at the same time. The backward movement tends to suggest retreat and weakness, partially offsetting the strength and dominance of the ascent.

Highly effective ascents have been made with the back to the audience. Lavinia Mannon's proud back is very affecting as she turns at the end of *Mourning Becomes Electra* and walks up the front steps to shut herself up forever in her New England mansion. A weak and beaten figure climbing stairs on hands and knees can be effective.

Great psychological value, as well as novelty value, is obtained by having important entrances made up a flight of stairs toward the audience through a trap, as in the ball scene of *An Ideal Husband*. The Katharine Cornell production of *Antony and Cleopatra*, with settings by Leo Kerz, used concentric revolving rings. Two-thirds of each ring was covered by a low platform with steps at the ends. In some positions this provided ascents toward the audience, and gave considerable variety to the movement patterns.

A stairway which starts in an upstage corner and rises to approximately center back permits effective ascents, such as Horace's crawling upstairs to reach his medicine and Regina's final tense ascent in *The Little Foxes*, and Teddy's dash up the stairs shouting "Charge!" in *Arsenic and Old Lace*.

Almost any of these effects can be reversed by overbalancing them by other factors. In *Angel Street* (called *Gaslight* in England and in the motion picture version),[6] Mr. Manningham, from floor level at right stage, successfully dominates his wife in one scene while she stands well above him at the head of a flight of stairs at center stage. Every effective device of attitude, posture, and vocal expression must be used in order to achieve this reversal.

A great rectangular doorway at the head of a flight of stairs can be used to give importance to an entering character, as it did in the production of *The Jest* cited earlier. But a shy, timid little man can use the same doorway to dwarf himself, the straight lines of the arch contrasting with his curved back, bent knees and head, and timid cramped

---

[6] See Plate 30. The elevation in the New York production was higher than that in the photograph reproduced here.

movements and gestures, while he stares up at the arch to contrast his height with it, and peers at the stairs apprehensively while he descends as if they were opposition instead of support.

The familiar scheme in the educational theatre for uninterrupted productions of Shakespearean plays — that of covering most of the stage with a level raised two or three steps above a forestage — has to combat the handicap that an actor must make a weakening upstage movement in order to ascend to the level and obtain visual dominance over those on the forestage.

A stage cut by a diagonal level has the same difficulty. An actor near the front of the stage has to move away from center in order to ascend the level. As in the more traditional arrangement, a character who enters on the level can use it with ease to secure and maintain dominance. Another problem which this diagonal scheme presents illustrates the way in which motivations are sometimes altered in order to move actors into new positions. Ordinarily an actor who wishes to subordinate himself can initiate a movement from a definite motivation, and then continue it casually until he reaches a position on the fringe of the action. But in this setting, when moving toward the side which has the level, he has to have a sufficiently strong motivation to make him ascend steps after he is well out of the immediate action. An alternative device is to get the character to the level by giving unnecessary emphasis to some earlier motivation, and leaving him in an undesirably prominent position for a few speeches in order to have him already on the level when he needs to withdraw.

A level which extends to downstage center in a sharp or blunt point has advantages over both of these schemes. An actor moving to center usually has motivation strong enough to carry him up the two or three steps, and the two directions of movement supplement

A SETTING PROVIDING THREE PLAYING
LEVELS AND THREE PLAYING DEPTHS

Figure 49. A conventional arrangement of
several levels such as those shown here permits
continuous action in a Shakespearean play.

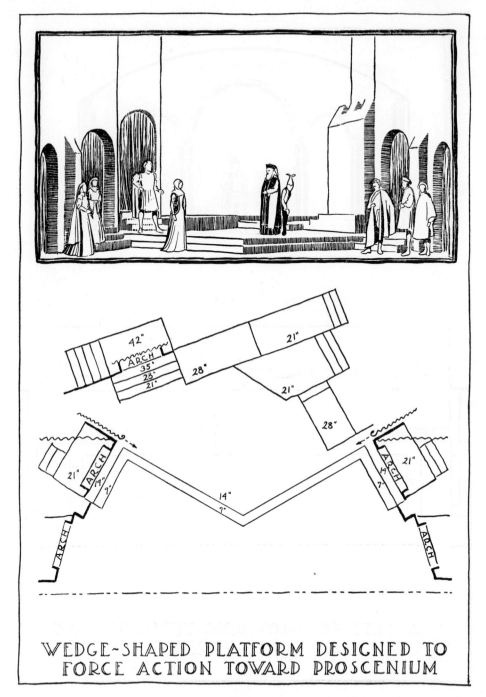

WEDGE~SHAPED PLATFORM DESIGNED TO
FORCE ACTION TOWARD PROSCENIUM

Figure 50. A platform which extends down-stage center permits the actor to ascend at the same time that he moves toward center stage.

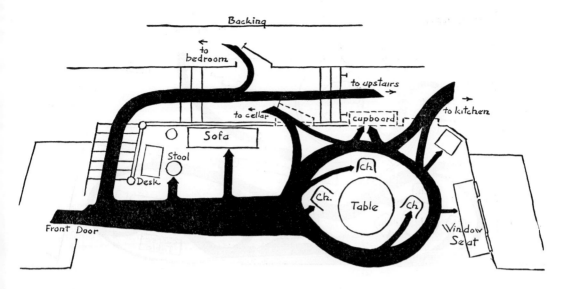

STAGE MOVEMENT

Schematic diagram of stage movement in acting edition of ARSENIC AND OLD LACE. Floor plan opens stage for free movement and forces long straight crosses for this farcical melodrama.

Figure 51. This setting encourages straight and smoothly-curved movements in contrast to the intricate curves of those in Figure 52.

and reinforce each other; the actor moves up and to center, or he moves down and away from center. Shifts of dominance are easily made visual.

Furniture and Background

Furniture determines the details of the action patterns, as entranceways control the major actions. It provides the traffic paths which are encouraged, offers additional paths which are possible but less inviting, and blocks some paths. Trees, shrubs, fences, and rocks do the same in nonarchitectural exteriors. The influence of furniture was discussed partially in connection with Movement.

In contemporary plays the items of furniture required by the dialogue, either directly or by inference, are so multitudinous that

the noncommercial director and designer often find it difficult to group these within the stage space provided by a thirty-foot proscenium or narrower as against the thirty-six- to forty-foot openings used on Broadway.

Arsenic and Old Lace calls for the prominence of the following successive acting areas across the stage: the front door and foot of the stairs, a desk with a telephone, a sofa, a cellar door that must not be covered by any other object, a dining table surrounded by chairs, passage space beyond the table, a window seat capable of holding a body, and French windows raked so they can be seen by everyone. It is desirable, but not necessary, that the sideboard be in full sight. The dialogue is so carefully adjusted to this floor plan that it is difficult even to alter the order

361

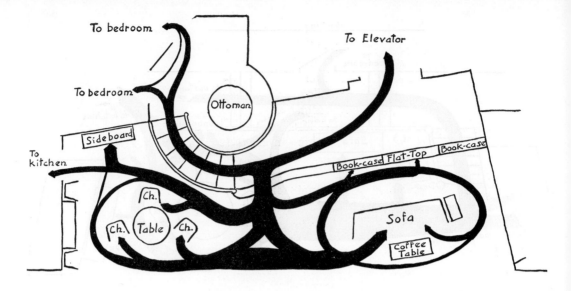

STAGE MOVEMENT

Schematic diagram of stage movement in acting edition of BORN YESTERDAY. Floor plan invites movement and channels it into curves for this satiric farce.

Figure 52. Long straight crosses are possible in this setting only at the curtain line and on diagonal lines in the upstage area.

of these areas. Still, with all this furniture, straight-line action can be obtained by a careful arrangement of the furniture. *Arsenic and Old Lace* does so by keeping the furniture well back of the curtain line, and opening a passageway across the front of the stage. (See Figure 51.) To encourage long crosses, the front door, the stairs, and the telephone are placed at one extreme side, and the table, the window, the window seat, and the kitchen door at the other, and little encouragement is offered the actors to stop at center stage for any length of time. The long flight of stairs provides similar long crosses in the upstage area. The floor plan also permits the director, when he so wishes, to emphasize long curved continuous movement from the cellar door or any of the left stage areas up the flight of stairs, or the

reverse; and it is relatively easy to find motivation to circle left and downstage of the dining table, and then swing toward center.

In the floor plan for *Born Yesterday* (based on Donald Oenslager's Broadway setting), the only opportunities for long straight crosses are the discouragingly shallow strip across the front, and the path behind furniture from front door to service door. (See Figure 52.) A relatively smooth long curve can be made from the front door up the stairs to the bedrooms. But the stage is cluttered with so much furniture, and provides such circuitous paths to the doorways, that the action has to consist of short crosses and complex curves. These patterns help this nervous and contrasty farce-comedy, and the action suggests the confused state of mind

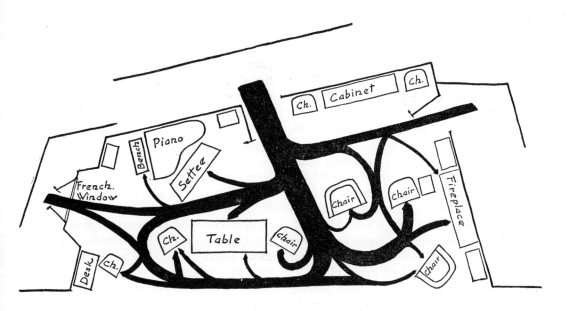

STAGE MOVEMENT

Schematic diagram of stage movement in acting edition of THE WINSLOW BOY. Floor plan encourages naturalistic movement by scattering the furniture, yet keeps the movement in relatively straight lines.

Figure 53. A floor plan producing short straight crosses and smooth curves is typical of settings for most realistic interiors.

of most of the characters. In the direction, Paul Verrall, the one straight-thinking character, moves in the easiest curves which the setting permits, and remains seated in one position most of the time he is on stage.

The Winslow Boy floor plan provides the familiar plan of a center-back door with furniture grouped at the sides. This produces relatively straight-line action with short crosses, either up and down or cross stage between the two furniture groups. (See Figure 53.) It induces a feeling of straightforward action, but avoids the melodramatic effect of long crosses. Passageway on the extreme sides permits casual curved movements for variety. *The Late George Apley* uses much the same floor plan, but the stage

directions make much more use of the curved movements, and place a great many of its scenes off-center.

Acting areas are planned for the action patterns. Center stage is usually the most important acting area, for this is the area to which it is easiest to draw attention. Not all important scenes are played there, but many are, and it is generally the most frequently used. The nature of the scenes played there determines the basic plan of the furniture for the setting. In almost all melodramas and other plays with an emphasis on action or violent passion, center scenes are played standing, and the central area is left relatively free of furniture. Settings for many other types of plays provide this open area at

363

center. Comedies, problem plays, and restrained representational dramas which emphasize thought and dialogue may call for important scenes to be played seated, at or near center.

The stage directions of *The Heiress* (following the Jed Harris production) place a low settee in center stage on a different basis. It is used by Dr. Sloper, the father of the heiress; his fatal heart attack takes place at a desk behind the settee, and the identification of the prominent settee with him preserves his influence in the room even after his death. The settee is seldom used in other scenes, a fact which forces many climactic scenes to right stage. The daughter, playing her final scene well off-center, has to make greater effort to obtain dominance, but if she succeeds, she picturizes a victory of the weak over the strong. (See Plate 16.)

The most important scenes may be between a seated figure and a standing one in opposition. In *The Silver Cord*, Mrs. Phelps sits on a sofa reveling in the picture she makes of a loving and self-sacrificing mother, while her daughter-in-law, Christina, stands facing her, denouncing Mrs. Phelps' cunning and selfishness, and fighting for her husband. In this scene the weight of the argument shifts back and forth between the two women, with only minor movements by Christina to change the physical balance. Other scenes of the play require similar balance. Here the furniture is placed so as to allow the seated Mrs. Phelps to balance the standing woman. She need not be able to dominate Christina physically, for she fights by indirection, but she needs a good stage position for this long scene and for the previous scenes in which she establishes the sofa as her throne.

Another familiar arrangement is chairs at center facing each other in opposition, perhaps across a table. Such different plays as *Anna Christie, The Road to Rome, Member of the Wedding, Journey's End,* and the Elizabeth scenes of *Mary of Scotland* all employ this grouping. With furniture at center, the director decides whether he wants it well downstage, or far enough back to permit playing in front of it.

Supplementary acting areas are planned upstage and at the sides. Except for upstage center when it is unblocked, the rear areas have limited use as playing areas; but standing scenes can be played behind low furniture. In large-cast scenes, furniture placed upstage can help to group the actors standing in those areas. The furniture arrangement usually provides a playing area at each side, whether or not there is a furniture group at center. The furniture is chosen to help picturize the scenes played in the area, with attention given to variety in grouping, to variety between areas, and to the design of the entire furniture arrangement in a scheme which has some "natural" justification. A furniture group on one side may extend to center or even past it with an open area slightly off-center for standing scenes. Slanting and other irregular groupings are possible, especially if the floor plan of the setting also avoids a rectangle. A "fourth wall" theory is held by some directors, and they plan an arrangement which would be feasible if the wall were actually present. Others feel that the picture-frame stage by convention permits the furniture to be angled with reference to the proscenium.

The furniture of each acting area is composed so as to give a sense of unity and isolation to a scene played within it, and to permit variety of grouping within it. The action of a scene need not be restricted to a single area, though the advantages of such a scheme will be discussed later. When there are two or three groups of furniture, any one may be used alone, with standing figures on one side of it, with figures standing on both sides, or with actors using two or more areas at once. A new area may be made by using the furniture on the adjacent ends of

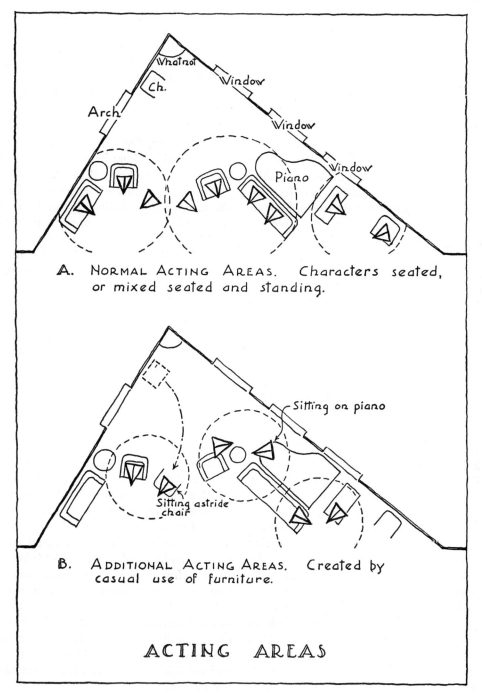

A. NORMAL ACTING AREAS. Characters seated, or mixed seated and standing.

B. ADDITIONAL ACTING AREAS. Created by casual use of furniture.

ACTING AREAS

Figure 54. The director creates new acting areas when characters relate themselves to furniture at proximate ends of other acting areas.

two groups. Seemingly isolated furniture can become related to an area, as when a chair is placed to face a desk against a wall but is later turned around to become part of a nearby area, or when an actor sits astride such a chair facing its back.

The director is not limited by the initial position of the furniture. In *Berkeley Square*, the furniture is rearranged for the ball scene of the second act. The acting edition of *The Perfect Alibi* tells the stage manager to shift the centrally placed furniture two feet toward downstage right for the second act in order to improve the location of a table for a long scene played around it. The dining table in *Arsenic and Old Lace* can be moved toward center for the second act.

In real life, people move furniture to adjust it to the conversational grouping and for other purposes; this can be done just as readily on the stage, and it supplies interesting "natural" movement. In most of the furniture arrangements for *Both Your Houses*, Sol needs to move a chair to a prominent open position when he sits to tell of his struggle with his good angel; and movement of the furniture by actors is inevitable in the third act of this play. In the Maurice Evans production of *Man and Superman*, it was fascinating to watch the peregrinations of one little straight chair, as Evans and the others moved it about to one and then another relationship with the other furniture.

Instead of providing means for letting actors come together for various scenes, the director sometimes wants to keep them apart; so he puts a table, a desk, or a davenport where it separates them. *Temper the Wind* supplies two examples. An American colonel of the Occupation Army meets again a German woman who ten years before wrote to him to break her engagement to him in order to marry a Nazi. The colonel still loves her and his impulse is to sit close to her. The visualization of their relationship, however, is best picturized if they sit apart at an un-comfortable distance, so the director avoids a davenport in the setting, and plans her movements so that it seems natural for her to sit in a chair where there is no nearby furniture, and the colonel has to sit ten feet away. In the other episode, her husband throws wine in the colonel's face. To give the other characters time to intervene and prevent a fight between them, the wine is thrown across a table, and the others have time to interpose before the colonel can circle it.

Furniture, naturally, is chosen for the effect of each individual piece, its relation to other furniture in the area, its mass effect in stage balance, and its ability to reveal or conceal action by its height, width, and shape. One extreme example is the use of oversize furniture when children's parts are taken by adults, in order to reduce the actors' apparent size, as in the opening bedroom scene of *Peter Pan* and in many other children's plays. Perhaps the most striking example was the early motion picture version of *Brewster's Millions* which starred "Fatty" Arbuckle. Cherubic faced, 250-pound Arbuckle impersonated Brewster as a two-year-old, a five-year-old, then as an adult; and, for the final scene, appeared as Brewster's infant son playing in an enormous baby-buggy. All were made convincing by the relative size of furniture and scenery.

Furniture placed in front of doors lessens their importance and weakens entrances made through the doors, so such an arrangement is avoided unless that effect is intended. In *The Male Animal* a maid makes many unimportant crosses from the kitchen door in a side wall to answer doorbells and to serve food. A davenport downstage of the kitchen door, parallel to the curtain line, conceals the lower half of her body when she enters, and considerably reduces the distraction of her crosses.

A related technique can be used when a director has to use a rectangular setting with bad sight lines, and wants to avoid hiding actors from part of the audience when they make side entrances. Furniture immediately downstage of the doorway forces the actors to pass this before they pause, for the furniture has the psychological effect of extending the entranceway, and neither the actor nor the spectator feels that an entrance has been completed until the actor clears the furniture.

Occasionally a character is onstage for a long scene in which he takes no active part, as are Cecily and Gwendolyn in the last act of *The Importance of Being Earnest.* Even when the actor listens intently to the scene, he produces some distraction. It is seldom feasible to hide the actor, but he can be concealed psychologically by relating his attitude to the line and mass of the scenery or furniture. Seated in a chair, especially if it is massive; standing behind a chair so as to extend the line of its back; leaning against a fireplace with the body and arms carrying out its lines; standing in front of draperies; leaning against a door frame, a column, a cupboard, a window frame, or just an angle of the setting — all these will relate the actor to the lines of the furniture and architecture and divert attention from him. At the same time, they make his figure and his pose a unified part of the design and avoid disturbing its balance. If this need for concealment is recognized early, the designers can plan the costume, the furniture, and the scenery so that the colors help in this psychological concealment.

Furniture or an architectural feature can serve as an excuse to draw an actor to a position which is desirable, either for immediate pictorial effect or as preparation for subsequent movements. The motivation which moves him away may be strong enough to carry him only a step, but if his eye focuses on a mantel while he is moving, this attention can carry him clear across the stage to put an elbow on it. An object can similarly guide him to a specific position.

A movement seems less arbitrary if he halts at an architectural feature or a piece of furniture than if he stands in the clear, for then he could have taken one more or one fewer step with the same motivation.

When an author uses for his setting a room or a location that he knows or imagines vividly, he ties the dialogue, incident, and action to it in detail, and thus makes the setting an integral part of the play. In much the same way, the director relates physical action to the setting in order to establish the "reality" of the room and to connect it with the play and with the characters. The director tries to have the actors use every item of furniture and every architectural detail in order to lend conviction and a feeling of unity to the action by making the setting seem "lived in." He encourages them to touch walls, look out windows, lean against door frames, mantels, and other architectural features; to sit on steps, windowsills, radiators, and the floor; and to handle the furniture and properties with ease, and, if they live or work in the room, with a sense of familiarity. A comedy example is the young boy who tosses his hat on a peg without looking. A character may sit in a familiar chair in the ordinary manner, may use it sideways, or may even turn it around to straddle it, with his elbows on its back. He can sit on one foot, sit cross-legged as a tailor does, or sit with one or both legs over an arm of the chair. He can sit on stools and benches in a comparable variety of ways. Tables and chests are inviting places to sit. Such actions are not limited to a modern play, for the same poses are seen in Hogarth engravings and in the genre painting of almost every period.

Furthermore, actors can seem at ease and comfortable — both as actors and as characters — in a formalized setting of steps and levels to the extent that they use the setting. An actor can stand with both feet on one step, or with each foot on a different step;

he can lie on them or he can sit on them squarely, longitudinally, or sideways with his thighs resting on one step and his feet stretched forward or tucked under him and resting on a lower one.[7] He can stand on a low level, sit on its edge, or stand with one foot on it; he can descend from it by walking down the steps, or by jumping. He can lean against a higher level as well as stand on it, and can sit on it with his feet dangling. He is encouraged, similarly, to use every projection from the walls in as many ways as possible.

When the play is of a distinct time or locale, the period, national, or provincial customs can govern the use of furniture and architectural elements. Paintings, engravings, manuscript illustrations, and photographs all depict these customs.

An exception to this easy use of furniture is a character who is out of place or ill at ease, such as one introduced into a level of society to which he is not accustomed. In *Kind Lady* the leader of the crooks has sufficient poise to make himself at ease in the house they invade, but his cohorts are uncomfortable and sit awkwardly on the edge of chairs and avoid touching the other furniture.

The furniture as well as the background scenery is designed in part to intensify the dramatic action, as has been explained in the section on Design. The design can give particular emphasis to one or two positions on the stage, so that a character occupying one of them receives emphasis beyond what would ordinarily be the case. Frequently the design also supplies areas of secondary emphasis, either planned, or incidental to the decoration of the setting. The director is constantly aware of all these emphatic positions in order to use them for certain effects, and to avoid a distraction by their accidental use when emphasis is not desired. It has already been suggested that the director

[7] Note in particular the varied attitudes in Figure 55.

is aware also of the positions in which an actor receives emphasis through the mass, form, line, and color of the scenery, augmented by the mass, line, and distribution of the other actors; where he seems more important by virtue of the support given him by architectural backgrounds; where he can be dwarfed by such elements, and where he can best be subordinated.

In all these matters of design, the addition of a large group of actors or of numerous brightly colored costumes can considerably alter the basic design, as well as the emphatic positions.

In the section on Design, a number of suggestions are made for the intensification and clarification of action. The director is aware of these opportunities as he plans other phases of the production so that the fullest possible use is made of them. Special problems in designing, constructing, and shifting scenery and costumes for the open stage are treated in Chapter 15 on the development of the open stage, in Chapter 18 on design, in Chapter 26 on directing for the open stage, and in Appendix C on make-up. A unit on open-stage lighting — intended to complement and supplement the material which appears below — is on pages 252–253.

Lighting

Lighting is used to support the actors in the matter of emphasis and dominance, or in subordination. It is an especially important tool of the director because it can be changed during the action, and thus can shift the emphasis from one area to another; can alter the dominance of characters even while they stand still; can give prominence to furniture or architectural elements at the exact moment they are important; can change the mood, the design, and even the locale of a setting; and can give specific information to the audience as to the time of day, the state of the weather, and the season of the year.

Lighting can be used in a purely arbitrary

manner to produce effects which are impossible in nature; but, if it is desired, a "natural" excuse can be found for many changes of lighting. A change in the apparent source of light, such as opening or closing a door or window draperies, lighting a lamp, or the approach of a storm or twilight, is accepted by the audience as justification for almost any alteration of lighting. Modern playwrights often cue natural phenomena into their dialogue to help create mood. Shakespeare and other pre-Mazda playwrights did this frequently, though we presume that they relied on the imagination of the spectator and did not expect corresponding changes in the sunlight in which their plays were performed. Directors often justify a change in lighting by inserting motivated business not mentioned in the dialogue, such as the closing of curtains and the lighting of lamps.

Few playwrights have been as explicit in explaining light changes as John Balderston in *Berkeley Square*. Approaching twilight, or rain, thunder, and wind prepare the audience for the dimming of lights. The electricity fails during a storm in the second scene, and a few candles hurriedly found justify the eerie lighting at the time the modern and the long-dead Peter Standishes exchange bodies across a hundred and fifty years. Balderston's cleverest device is having a maid start to extinguish candles in wall brackets, but be frightened away after putting out half of them, and thus justify a concentration of light at stage right for the climactic love scene.

Comedy and farce are conventionally played in bright light, and tragedy in heavy shadow. This convention has some validity, because the highly subtle use of words and facial expressions in comedy demands that the audience see every expression and all the actor's articulatory movements in order to help it catch the rapid flow of his speech, whereas tragedy often deals with more elemental emotions which can be projected less subtly. But this statement is oversimpli-

fication, for tragedies and serious plays may demand similar appreciation of subtleties, as in some of Hamlet's soliloquies, and in the tent scene, the first half of the trial scene, and the epilogue of *Saint Joan*. Moreover, shadows are produced by bright light with a directional beam, not by the excessively dim lighting which sometimes is mistakenly given to tragedy. Shadows are visually effective only when they fall on upright scenery. The shadows cast by actors lighted from overhead merely fall on the floor invisibly, and produce little effect in return for the obscuring of actors' features which accompanies strong overhead lighting. In any case, the director judges each play and each episode for its individual lighting requirement, rather than using some undependable rule of thumb.

Change of the color of lighting can be as effective as change of intensity. The color of the sky can be changed for mood or symbolic effects, either justified by natural phenomena, or used arbitrarily. Scenery and costume colors can be altered by colored light; they may appear brilliant in one color, but dull and drab in another. If an inconspicuous character must become prominent during the course of a scene, he can be dressed, for example, in a blue-green costume and lighted in saturated amber to gray it. When green and blue are added to the lighting of the whole stage or of his area alone, the true vividness of the color is revealed, and he may assume complete dominance of the stage even while he sits still.

Lighting instruments and control devices are approaching such perfection that light can theoretically do anything that is desired, including lighting an actor without spilling onto the scenery six inches away from him. Practically, such feats are limited by the amount and type of the equipment available to the electrician. Therefore, in a single production, the director can ask for few such special effects, and he must adjust the acting positions accordingly. If, for example, the director wants Ariel in *The Tempest* or Grimm in *The Return of Peter Grimm* to play always in a green light, and if a follow spot is impossible, the director and the electrician plan the two, three, or four positions on the stage where green spotlights can be focused, and the actor shifts between them. Similarly, there is a limit to the number of "pools of light" which can be supplied, and the director often needs to use a few such areas repeatedly rather than demand a multitude of them. If the "shadows of tragedy" are being used in the acting area, the director learns before rehearsals the main source of light so that he can face the actors into it when their faces need to be well lighted.

Costume

Costume affects the attitude, movement, and gesture of the actor. In extreme cases, it restricts the stage positions he can take. Both actor and director therefore consider this factor constantly in rehearsals; costume accessories and "rehearsal costumes" (hoops, underskirts, garments from the wardrobe, and occasionally the actual costumes) are often requested by the director for some of the earlier rehearsals of an historical play in order to accustom the actors to the garments they will wear.

Hoops, farthingales, paniers, trains, bustles, and headdresses complicate the life of the actress, as cloaks, gowns, loose-hanging sleeves, swords, and canes do the actor's. These, and the cut of the armholes and the fit of other parts of the garments, restrict the actions of the players, though designers, with a variety of style in each historical period, can usually choose a design which permits any necessary physical action. These are essentially problems of the costumer and the actor; and the director is concerned chiefly to help the actor learn the correct use of costumes and properties. The director is aware of the basic function of costumes, co-ordinating with other aspects of design, to intensify, clarify, and locate the action; and likewise of the influence on his planning of the line, mass, color, and form of the costumes. And he is aware, of course, of the space requirements of the costumes both when the actors stand and sit, and of the increase in attention value a character receives through the mass value offered by a bouffant skirt, a high headdress, or a long train.

The manipulation of a train is the director's chief problem arising from costume. In costumes of certain periods a woman loses poise when she touches her train. In consequence, her movements are planned in circles as much as possible, and each movement is calculated in anticipation of the next one so that the train will lie out of the way.

Occasionally, instead of treating costumes seriously and in period, the director asks the actors to exaggerate the influence of costumes on manners, or to satirize some aspect of the style of the period portrayed. Some revivals of nineteenth-century melodrama do this, making fun of bustles or of hoop skirts worn for housework. In the Maurice Evans production of *Man and Superman* the costumes were exaggerated; the leading actress accented this by deliberately adopting bad positions for her short train so that at nearly every move she had to kick it out of her way with a graceful flip of her ankle. Productions of *The Critic; The Tragedie of Tragedies, or, The Life and Death of Tom Thumb the Great;* and other satires on acting often use a good deal of cape-swishing and unnecessary sword-rattling in addition to exaggerated costumes.

In *Elizabeth the Queen,* an awkward costume was used for serious dramatic effect. For her collapse at the end of the play, Lynn Fontanne wore a very stiff farthingale and a rigidly corseted bodice so that she crumpled on the throne like a marionette, with her torso remaining stiff while her head and arms drooped, thus suggesting her tragic defeat as a result of the conflict between will and love.

Rigid theoretical distinctions have been made between the expressional function of the director and the work of other theatre artists in order to emphasize his essential responsibility to pattern the visual stimuli, plus the auditory stimuli to be discussed in the next chapter. Each individual stimulus affects the audience as a fragment of a complex pattern from which the fragment acquires its meaning, whether or not the audience is conscious of the relation. Attitude, movement, and gesture arise from characterization and motivation, and so are largely the concern of the actor. However, attitude and movement can be adjusted within the motivation in order to fit the larger pattern of the director; the possibility of adjustment is often slight with the active characters, but extensive with the passive characters. The position and the arrangement of the actors for picturization are within the domain of the director. The action of the characters is determined to a considerable degree by the design. Entranceways control the large patterns of action, and the furniture controls many phases of the movement by providing the traffic paths and acting areas. Elevations give variety and emphasis to the action. Background, lighting, and costume emphasize and clarify it.

24 | The Auditory Stimuli

Characteristics of Voice and Speech
Other Auditory Stimuli Provided by the
Actor • Stimuli Supplied by Other Media

Every sound has certain characteristics which can be measured by laboratory instruments. When the sound is produced by the human voice, these characteristics are called volume, pitch, duration, quality, and articulation. When vocal sounds are uttered in sequence, additional characteristics of the combination are called rate, rhythm, accent, pause, pronunciation, inflection, and key. Other terms are applied to special combinations of sounds, and alternative terms often are used. Every spoken phrase, and almost every monosyllable, has all of these characteristics. They are interactive in conveying meaning in the same way that visual stimuli are interrelated. When visual and auditory stimuli occur together, they also influence each other. Therefore, while a single characteristic can be isolated for analytical study, it is never heard independently. Further, the accompanying stimuli may completely alter the effect of such characteristics. Speech at a rapid rate, for example, suggests great urgency to get information conveyed as quickly as possible. It can also suggest the completely meaningless chatter of a nitwit. A loud voice can suggest a dominant personality accustomed to giving orders, or the assumed manner of one who is insecure.

A distinction is sometimes made between the characteristics of *voice* (volume, pitch, and quality), and those concerned with *speech* (articulation, pronunciation, and duration). However, it is impossible to make a sharp distinction. For example, the same muscles act in essentially the same way in producing voice quality and in the articulation and pronunciation of vowel sounds. Similarly, accent can be achieved either by voice or speech characteristics, or by a combination; and while the pause might be classified as an element of speech rather than voice, the muscles most directly concerned are those which produce volume and pitch. Such classification would serve no purpose and would be needlessly confusing here.

Unless we consciously control them, the muscles of the body contract in response to mental action. Muscles tend to tense and relax in sympathy with one another; it is almost impossible to tense the biceps or to tighten the jaw without tensing other muscles. Since speech is a production of muscular activity, it naturally tends to reflect, and to be indicative of, the muscular movements and tensions of the entire body. When we listen to a radio speaker, we form impressions of his posture and gestures. Similarly, when we overhear people talking in another room, or children at play, we hear a great many clues to their postures and their bodily actions.

So if one speaks while the muscles of the body are tensed in vigorous movement, or while antagonistic muscles are tensed in equilibrium in preparation for movement, the sympathetic tension of the abdominal muscles tends to increase the volume of the voice; tension in the vocal folds raises the pitch level; tension in the walls of the oral and pharyngeal cavities amplifies the higher pitched overtones and so produces a quality which is variously described as harsh, thin, bright, or "white"; and the rate and accuracy of articulation tends to increase because of the greater readiness for action of the muscles of lips, tongue, jaw, and palate.

In relaxation, the vocal muscles tend to produce sounds which are less loud, lower and less varied in pitch, less sharply articulated, and slower in rate, resulting in voice qualities which are described as full, hollow, orotund, broad, tired, or sepulchral.

In special circumstances, the voice can be controlled independently of the main pattern of thought, and independently of the muscular tensions of the body; and the vocal characteristics can be controlled separately. One does this when one acts and when one tells a lie — when one "hides his thoughts" or "covers up his feelings." Little inconsistencies between the vocal characteristics sometimes can be detected in this artificial expression. "Forced gaiety," "oratorical manner," "preacher's cadence," "tea-party chattering," and "ham acting" describe partial failure to achieve the attempted expression; and they produce the effect of insincerity because the listener perceives that the speaker is consciously controlling his expression. On the other hand, it is considered commendable when the mind controls the emotions, even when it is not completely successful, as in "controlled anger" or "controlled grief." Insincerity is consciously used for satire in "ironic manner" and "mock seriousness."

The actor uses this willful control in terms of characterization and motivation of his role, and he wants the spectators to be aware of it to the same extent that they would be in real life. However, in addition, the actor employs, as a part of his acting skill, certain controls which he wants the audience to ignore because they are unrelated to character and motivation. He slightly exaggerates all phases of his visual and vocal expression so that they are seen and heard throughout the auditorium, but he tries to exaggerate everything in proportion in order that the audience is unaware of the exaggeration — or is aware of it only for the first few moments of the play. Also, while he increases his volume and makes his articulation more accurate, he may slow down his overall rate and consciously add to the richness of his voice; he accomplishes these without the normally concomitant rise in pitch, and maintains the degree of flexibility and variety in all the characteristics which the ordinary person has in lively but relaxed conversation, but which ordinarily would be lost at the level of volume which he is using.

The vocal characteristics here described ordinarily arise directly from the actor's response to the script, and are the outward expression of his characterization, motivation, and stage energy. But when one is told some very bad news and replies "No!" in sudden shock, surprise, apprehension, and disbelief, one can produce an infinite variety of patterns of expression, depending upon which reaction is dominant. Introspective apprehension may be emphasized and may result in an almost inarticulate exclamation. Alternatively, it can produce a sharp, shrill, uncompleted exclamation, which indicates an instinctive and unreasoned denial, stopped short by apprehension as the character realizes that the news is true. Or it can produce a vehement refusal to believe, spoken in a loud insistent voice. The fine actor, completely characterizing and motivating, instinctively selects the appropriate motivation and the clearest expression of it. It would seem that this expression cannot be changed. Yet each person in real life, and each character in a play, responds under the influence of the environment — the emotions and thoughts which immediately precede this particular reaction, and his state of mind and of energy at the moment. Therefore, if the motivation of the actor does not produce the vocal expression desired in the scene, the director can, without damage to the pattern of the motivation, ask the actor to alter the motivation slightly so as to produce some other auditory pattern; or he can change some of the attendant circumstances and thus cause the actor to alter his expression in the manner desired. For example, a character reacts differently when standing and when sitting. Whether the character is or is not looking at the bearer of the bad news as he speaks produces a tremendous difference in the vocal reaction, and in the physical reaction which is reflected in the voice. Few plays are written with such exactness of motivation that the script directs where the actor is to be looking at every instant.

The director, of course, disastrously intrudes upon the actor's prerogative if he requires the actor to do something which is out of key with his role. In recognition of this fact, the director, rather than speaking the lines himself and asking the actor to reproduce the expression, usually suggests an altered motivation, or he asks the actor to find one which produces a certain type of vocal expression. The director may not obtain in this way the exact vocal effect he has in mind, but he probably gets an expression which produces the type of auditory effect he wants and one which has more justification in terms of characterization than the director's reading, for, after the first few rehearsals, the experienced actor often knows better than the director the characterization and motivation of the part.

Pitch level, inflection, duration, volume, articulation, and pronunciation are especially susceptible to minor alterations without affecting the basic motivation and characterization of roles.

As a background to the discussion of individual characteristics of vocal expression, a few examples can demonstrate the way in which the director uses them to produce meaningful effects. A mob scene permits the director to manipulate the vocal effects in considerable detail, for there is then less concern with the individual characterizations, and so less chance of falsifying characterization or motivation. Further, a mob scene is usually written for a very definite emotional impact, and the intention can be seen more clearly and precisely than in a complex conversational scene. The intuitive director, without an awareness of the techniques employed, may — as explained in an earlier chapter — achieve an exciting mob scene by inspiring the actors to produce the emotional effects he wants. But technical knowledge saves time by permitting a direct attack on the problem instead of the fumbling trial-and-error method, and insures that the desired effect is reproduced at each performance. Instead of saying to the actors, "The mob scene didn't come off tonight. Now, tomorrow night let's try to make it better," he knows that the fault lies in failure to reach the desired maximum of pitch, rate, or volume; in failure to maintain sufficient variety of attack; or in failure to prepare for a climax by de-emphasizing — during passages of descending action — some of these factors after their use at maximum effectiveness for previous climaxes. He recognizes also that one or more of the factors may have reached so intense a climax earlier in the scene that the intended final climax cannot top it. In any case, he can take steps to correct the fault. The technical training of the actors forming the mob determines whether or not the director discusses these matters with them in technical terms. But if he knows the technical characteristics himself, he can make the corrections by clarifying the motivations, and suggesting indirectly that the actors decrease or increase tempo, raise or lower the pitch, increase or decrease the volume, or vary motivations among the mob in order to produce greater variety.

Also, knowledge of techniques permits the director to secure varied effects, and thus enables him to produce a series of climaxes which top each other in intensity though each seems at the time to produce a maximum effect. In the orations scene of *Julius Caesar,* as an example of this, the director reserves the greatest climax for the end of the scene when Antony sends the mob off to kill and burn. Just as it was suggested in the previous chapter that the gestures be kept low until this moment, so he may keep the pitch of the actors' voices low in the early parts of the scene, and then send the mob off screaming and yelling. A distinct vocal effect may be used for each of the four prior climaxes. Some of the available techniques are lowering the pitch of the voices to threatening rumblings, increasing the rate of speech, increasing its volume, increasing the harshness of the voice quality, extending the length and speed of the inflections, shortening the length of the phrases, and increasing the strength of the accent.

The planning of vocal effects, especially the pitch and volume levels, is more obvious in mob scenes, but can be used in any scene of a play. In fact, the expression of the actors creates these patterns whether or not the director consciously uses them for that purpose.

In *Both Your Houses,* for another example, the newly elected Representative Alan McClean is shocked when he discovers the extent of logrolling in the Congress. When he finds that as a member of the Appropriations Committee he cannot reduce the grants in a pork-barrel bill, he decides to overload it with such excessive appropriations that it is an obvious treasury steal and so can be defeated on the floor. Since Simeon Gray, through his power as committee chairman, has trimmed from the bill a pet project of every member of the committee, McClean proposes in committee meeting that all the items ever proposed for the bill be restored. Gray, after years of scrupulous personal incorruptibility while presiding over the distribution of "pork," has succumbed and put into this bill a provision benefiting his home district. McClean makes a veiled threat to reveal this fact, and thinks this will frighten Gray into silent consent.

Gray, instead, demands that the committee take his more experienced judgment on what is politically expedient, and send the measure to the House as it stands. His dignity, courage, and power impress the other committee members, and they fall silent. The audience believes that Gray has won through the strength of his personality. After a long pause, one member asks apologetically, slowly, and in a low-pitched voice, if Gray has a personal interest in one of the items. Gray calmly replies that he has. After a shorter pause, another member asks if that provision is to stay in the bill. The chairman replies that it is. A third member, in a slightly higher pitch and louder tone, asks why other items cannot also go in. Gray insists that it is impossible. The member replies in a higher pitch yet, and then they all pounce upon Gray, insisting that they "get theirs" if he "gets his." Their voices gradually increase in pitch, rate, and accent until the scene is brought back to the same degree of tension and excitement it had before Gray calmed them. Of course this analyzes merely an obvious mechanical phase of the scene, which can enhance its dramatic tension but cannot substitute for the inner tension of the actors' motivations.

CHARACTERISTICS OF VOICE AND SPEECH

Volume

Volume [1] is measured roughly in terms of the amplitude of the vibrations of a sound wave, and is appreciated by the ear as degrees of loudness. One is inclined to speak more and more loudly as he becomes increasingly excited; hence, volume and excitement normally vary together. Directors can use volume directly to produce the impression of action and emotion — though, like all expressive devices, it can be overused and thus defeat its purpose. Greatly subdued volume, accompanied by manifestations of tension in other vocal characteristics, also can be exciting.

For purposes of direction, the general level of volume can be used in a play as it is employed by an effective speaker, to give emphasis to some points and to subordinate others. Volume can be used directly to support the script, or can add clarity to the play. Inexperienced playwrights often fail to indicate in their writing the relative importance of the episodes to the plot. One recognizes this in reading a play, when he discovers that a character or an incident almost ignored in reading is later found to be of crucial importance; and when, on the other hand, excitingly written episodes, introduced by the author out of his own personal interest in a subject or viewpoint, turn out to be red herrings which have no connection with the plot. This fault may appear in a play which is otherwise excellent. Shakespeare, in spite of his transcendent instinct for the dramatic, often introduces a theme or a speech which foreshadows action that never takes place. Either he changed his mind and forgot to remove the misleading lines, or a scene has been lost in the mutilated versions we have of his plays. While speeches of this

kind must be spoken believably, their importance must be reduced in order to prevent the audience from anticipating any special development from them. Decreased volume is one method of subordinating such speeches.

An overall variation in volume makes its impression upon an audience. In melodramas and most romantic dramas, for example, there is an extreme range from whispered conspiracies to loud quarrels. This is true in modern plays such as *Deep Are the Roots* and *Anne of the Thousand Days* as well as in *Macbeth* and *Henry V*. In classic tragedies there is apt to be less variation, since the violence of the emotion is more evenly sustained, as in *All for Love, Phaedra,* and Sophocles' *Electra*. Modern serious plays written under the influence of "naturalism" tend to keep the volume down, as in *Watch on the Rhine, The Children's Hour, Hedda Gabler,* and *A Doll's House.*

Volume is strong in farces in all periods, with some softly spoken scenes for contrast, as in *Lysistrata, Ralph Roister Doister,* and *Boy Meets Girl.* Drawing-room comedies like *The Way of the World, Lady Windermere's Fan,* and *Paris Bound* usually have moderate volume, evenly sustained, since the characters in drawing-room comedies are practiced at maintaining their composure in all situations. Other forms of comedy vary considerably in their use of volume — from the noisiness of the near-farce *Born Yesterday* to the quietness of *The Cradle Song* and *The Cherry Orchard*, with plays like *Life with Father* and *Golden Boy,* containing wide contrasts as to volume, in between. Occasionally plays provide volume contrasts between plot sequences, as in *A Midsummer Night's Dream, Yellow Jack,* and *Dinner at Eight.*

Though these requirements related to volume are inherent in the scripts, the director, by being aware of the objective, can emphasize either the consistency or the contrast

---

[1] Volume and other vocal characteristics are treated also in Section II, from the standpoint of the actor.

in the script, or even strive for greater consistency or greater variety than the script itself requires.

Volume contrast can be used as a part of characterization, the most obvious instances being when one character speaks louder than the others. George Bernard Shaw enjoys introducing overloud characters into his drawing rooms, such as Mrs. George in *Getting Married,* the father in *Pygmalion,* and almost the same father again in *Candida. The Time of Your Life* uses both Blick and Kit Carson in the same way. Similarly, there is Harry Brock in *Born Yesterday,* another ill-mannered father in Clyde Fitch's *The Truth,* and the Squire in *The Corn Is Green.* Many Restoration and Georgian plays contain such incongruous characters. Sir Anthony Absolute in his quarrel scenes with his son in *The Rivals* is one; others are Mr. James Formal in *The Gentleman Dancing Master,* and Tony Lumpkin in *She Stoops to Conquer.* In recent plays the effectiveness of a woman for this purpose has been rediscovered, and we have Mme. Arcati in *Blithe Spirit,* and the raucous mother of a prominent actress in both *Light Up the Sky* and *Merrily We Roll Along.*

A conspicuously soft-spoken character provides an equally effective contrast in volume. In *Three Men on a Horse* the meek little greeting-card poet is contrasted with the violent group of gamblers. Other examples are Mr. Pim in *Mr. Pim Passes By,* the Dauphin in *Saint Joan,* Miss Preen in *The Man Who Came to Dinner,* and Mrs. Midget in *Outward Bound.* A gradual increase in volume as the outward sign of the growing strength and freedom of a character is a familiar device which appears in *Captain Applejack, Happy Birthday,* and *Once in a Lifetime,* and in Ensign Pulver in *Mister Roberts.*

Scenes between excited characters and very calm and soft-spoken ones are much used in both farce and comedy. Serious plays occasionally employ it, though a strong contrast is apt to be comic. Examples include Abby in the quarrel in the last act of *The Late Christopher Bean;* almost all the scenes between Mother and Father in *Life with Father;* and many scenes in *Teahouse of the August Moon.* A number of the scenes in Goldoni's *The Servant of Two Masters* contrast Truffaldino's imperturbability with the excitement of other characters.[2] A serious use of contrast is the calmness and despondency of Lincoln in the excited election-night scene in *Abe Lincoln in Illinois.* In tragedy there is the title role of Euripides' *Iphigenia in Aulis,* and the same part in Robert Turney's version called *Daughters of Atreus;* and in the role of Othello in the first act of the play.

One exciting figure surrounded by calm ones is used for comedy in the case of Sganarelle at the end of *The School for Husbands.* Sir Giles Overreach in *A New Way to Pay Old Debts* provides a pathetic effect of the same kind. Similarly in *I Remember Mama,* the youngest daughter, Dagmar, returns from the hospital in great eagerness to see her cat again, and the rest of the family stand around helplessly unable to tell her that the cat is dying.

Since volume of voice is associated with excitement, the climaxes of many plays use loudness for part of the effect. However,

2 Probably the most successful use ever made of calmness of manner for the purpose of contrast is the curtain line of the second act of *The Torchbearers.* The scene is behind the stage setting at an amateur performance by a little theatre group. A long series of comic mishaps is climaxed by the breaking of the rope on the front curtain in the midst of the bows of the cast just before the directress is to appear for her bow. Cast, crew, and the directress are in a frenzy, running about wildly trying to discover what went wrong, trying to get the curtain fixed, chattering about the horrors of the situation, and arguing as to what to do. After a full minute of this pandemonium, when the confusion is at its height, the imperturbable leading lady opens one of the doors from the setting and whispers helpfully to the directress, "There's something the matter with the curtain."

emphasis by volume is so commonly used, and actors fall into it so easily, that the director guards against undue loudness early in the play in order to insure that when the climaxes come they are not anticlimactic because the peak of volume has been previously reached.

Pitch

The rate of vibration of the fundamental or "base" tone of a sound is its pitch, and it is perceived in terms of high or low. The general pitch level of the acting company has an effect upon the audience. If the actors speak at a high level of pitch, then tension and excitement are suggested, partly because increased pitch is the result of increased muscle tension in the vocal folds. If this is carried to an extreme, it is distinctly unpleasant; frequently this is true of performances of *Stage Door* in the scenes containing fifteen chattering ingenues.

Voices tend to become lower when the body is relaxed, so predominantly low pitch is normal in quiet unemotional conversations. The early episodes in plays by Ibsen, Galsworthy, Kingsley, and Rice, and in many of the "well-made" plays, for example, are likely to be low pitched. Just as body movements are likely to become slower when brought under conscious control of the mind, so the voice tends to drop in pitch. Therefore low pitch also tends to predominate in scenes of deep passion, such as those in classic and romantic tragedy in which there is tremendous muscle tension in the body, but the mature characters, with their strong wills and their seriousness of thought and purpose, avoid hysteria and control their minds, bodies, and voices. Warnings often are given in low pitch because the threatener wants to impress upon his listeners the seriousness of the mental state which prompts them. Low-pitched speaking voices generally are more pleasant than high-pitched ones, so as many opportunities as possible are

sought to use them. Moreover, low pitch is further useful in acting because it permits more opportunities for pitch emphasis.

Predominantly high pitch suggests strong, uncontrolled emotion of any type — gaiety, anger, fear, sorrow, hysteria. Actors tend to make use of it for any strong emotion. It helps to create excitement and to induce sympathetic tension on the part of the audience. But at the same time it suggests lack of emotional control and poise, and consequent shallowness of character. For that reason it is a dangerous technique, and its use is carefully restricted.

Directors ordinarily cast their actors so as to secure pitch contrasts between them, particularly between those who have scenes together. A quarrel scene, for example, is much more exciting when alternate speeches strike the ear at distinctly different pitch levels than when it is played between two men with bass rumbles or two women with coloratura squeals. On the other hand, too great a contrast may be ridiculous, such as would be a quarrel between Pinza and Pons. So, ordinarily a cast contains a variety of voices from bass through baritone to tenor, and from contralto through the soprano ranges to coloratura.

Limits on pitch are set for certain plays. Greek tragedy, for example, is usually cast with deep voices. A high tenor or soprano is apt to be distracting and to sound weak in contrast with the customarily richer quality of lower voices. On the other hand, the director may want a high pitch for Helen's voice in *The Trojan Women* to contrast with those of the suffering women of Troy, and thus to suggest her trivial nature. Tenors with full voices can be effective as the messengers in Greek plays; high voices can be used effectively for some of the gods and goddesses.

Low pitches predominate in Chekhov's plays except for a few contrasting characters and for some hysterical episodes, since these plays contain few emotional scenes between excited characters. Lillian Hellman's plays call for low pitches in most of the scenes, but often have a number of emotional peaks at which all the actors raise their pitch together, or, more frequently, have climaxes in which some of the characters use high pitches while a dominant figure secures contrast by maintaining a low pitch. Regina and her husband, Horace, in *The Little Foxes* provide such a contrast when she deliberately taunts him in order to excite him and bring on a heart attack, and then ignores his pleas for medicine. For the final scene, when Alexandra defies her mother, the director almost certainly plans a reversal of the pitch levels, with Alexandra dropping from the high pitch of youth to a determined low one, and Regina's level rising as her nervousness increases.

When Anna Christie desperately pours out her resentment of all men, she is emotionally excited, but has an iron grip on herself in most of the scene because of her prolonged brooding and the earnestness of her desire to revenge herself upon the male sex by torturing Mat and Chris with the revolting story of her life. The men are amazed and horrified, and have no compensating emotions by which to provide control of themselves. Anna is likely to use an insistent, harsh, low pitch for most of the scene, with high-pitched protestations from the men. Anna may use a pitch which is actually lower than that of the men, but this is not essential, for the low pitches of a woman's voice give the psychological impression of being lower than the upper range of a man's.

Ibsen often writes dialogue embodying tremendous tension and emotion arising unexpectedly from a conversation which starts casually. The pitch level may rise in some of these dialogues; in others it is curbed by the inhibitions of the social discipline of the characters. In *Ghosts*, for example, most of the dialogue is pitched at the level of casual, relaxed conversation. Mrs. Alving, in a number of episodes, is emotionally stirred as she thinks of distressing aspects of her life with her late husband, but she has practiced emotional control (including control of her voice) so long that it has become habitual. This low pitch level which she ordinarily maintains throws into enormously effective contrast the two or three moments in which she loses control of herself and approaches hysteria. The pitch used for Oswald after he goes insane, for "The sun — the sun — Mother, give me the sun," can be determined by the director only at a late rehearsal. And this can be decided by the director, inasmuch as paresis — at least as Ibsen has written of it unscientifically — can produce any pitch level at the moment of attack, and has little relation to Oswald's previous characterization. Mrs. Alving is likely to speak in a tense, almost inaudible, high-pitched scream, alternating with a low, determined pitch. Not until her exact pattern is established will it be clear whether the emotional impact of the episode is most helped if Oswald speaks in a childish treble or in a slow, mumbled, guttural tone to contrast with Mrs. Alving's high-pitched, smothered screams.

Inflection. When two or more pitches occur in succession, they produce a pitch pattern called inflection or intonation. Since the voice almost without exception rises or falls in pitch in speaking each syllable, even a spoken monosyllable is inflected. The gross inflectional patterns are described as falling, rising, circumflex, etc. These terms signify only the very largest aspects of inflection; the subtleties defy description, though they can be recorded visually by laboratory instruments. The term *melody* often is applied to the pitch changes over a series of inflections; but this term also takes into account duration, accent, and other characteristics as well as pitch change, and it suggests the sustained tones of singing rather than the constantly varying ones of speech. However, the relative duration of sounds also influences inflection.

Inflection is the chief factor in conveying intellectual meaning, and it is the intricacies of the inflections which produce subtle meanings over and above those of the mere sense-meaning of the actual words spoken. Some of the factors which impart these subtleties of meaning are the general pitch level; the presence of small internal circumflex inflections; sustained tones held for a fraction of a second; the speed of the rise or fall, its relative length, and the relative speed of its various parts. And, of course, the impression made by inflectional patterns is influenced by all the other vocal factors accompanying them.

Inflections arise from characterization, motivation, and stage energy, and so are controlled almost exclusively by the actors. Coaching by the director often concentrates on inflection or melody.

Rarely does a director make calculated use of melody in his patterning except as it clarifies meaning, but occasionally by its use he gives an overall effect to a play, a scene, or an episode. Motivation can be found in dialogue, for example, which dictates for almost every sentence a rising inflection, a sustained final note, or a falling inflection which still stops short of what is called in music the tonic note — the note which gives the impression of conclusion. These inflections recurring time and again produce an effect of suspended indecisive action. Some of Maeterlinck's plays can make such use of inflection, particularly *The Blind, The Intruder,* and some episodes of *Pelléas and Mélisande.* Much of the dialogue of *The Iceman Cometh* can be spoken with this indecisive quality. At the opposite extreme, a director may want to emphasize the decisiveness and definiteness of a play or a scene by stressing falling inflections and tonic notes. This is required by *Waiting for Lefty, Command Decision,* and *Sun-Up.* Actors often adopt a lyrical mode of speaking for all poetry and need to be encouraged to use such falling inflections and tonic notes in poetic plays by Shakespeare, Anderson, and others. Most mannered plays, both period and contemporary, call for an extreme use of circumflex inflection, because these plays tend to toy with words, to make fine distinctions of thought, and to coin epigrams and paradoxes. This quality of such dramas can be exaggerated by the actors in order to increase the self-conscious, mannered effect, and they may need to be encouraged to appear to savor the words and phrases and to be amused by them.

Occasionally a playwright gives a character the same line repeatedly, or indicates an identical inflection for a variety of speeches. In *Lady Windermere's Fan,* Lady Agatha Carlisle's complete part consists of saying, "Yes, Mama," thirteen times with the same inflection, after which her mother refers to her as "my little chatterbox." Comedians and radio programs demonstrate the effectiveness of the repetition of key phrases. W. C. Fields for years reiterated, "It ain't a fit night out for man nor beast"; the radio character of Baron Munchhausen popularized, "Vas you dere, Sharlie?"; Henry Aldrich's "Coming, Mother" and the Lone Ranger's "Hi-yo, Silver" have become household expressions. Less frequently a playwright has several characters speak the same line in similar circumstances, usually for comic effect. *Hay Fever* supplies an example of a repeated inflection used for comedy. The four uninhibited members of a family have each invited a week-end guest to their country home. Those invited by the father and the daughter arrive together, are left in the living room, and "make" social conversation which finally simmers down to shallow reminiscences of travel. When the conversation lags one starts it off again with "Spain is very beautiful," or "France is beautiful in the Spring." Finally the hostess is heard approaching; she enters chattering to her own guest, nods to the others, and exits to the garden. The two stranded guests look at each other, sit simultaneously, and the girl begins again, "Russia used to be a wonderful country before the war." These tricks of repetition ordinarily are supplied by the author, but a director can sometimes point up the reversal of a situation by employing repetition of a distinctive melody pattern, either with identical or varying language.

Key. Key is a specialized type of overall inflectional pattern. In music it denotes the particular scale upon which the composition is based, as C, C♯, D, D♯. Keys in music are approximately half a note apart. Pianos are tuned so that the twelve half-notes of the scale are exactly equidistant; thus, the instrument can be played equally well in any key, the keys differing only in pitch. On a true scale, as used for stringed instruments, however, half-notes are not quite equidistant, and so in the different keys there are subtle differences of relationship between the notes. Each key produces its own distinctive mood, and composers set their compositions accordingly in the key most appropriate to them. A keen musical ear can identify any key it hears. With the flowing variations in the pitch of human speech — as opposed to the step variations of music — such subtleties cannot be controlled directly in acting.

Related effects, however, such as the difference between a major and a minor key in music can be reproduced in speech. A musical composition written in a major key is one which emphasizes the usual or "easy" intervals — the third, the fifth, and the octave; while a minor key emphasizes the minor third (or second), a half-note lower than the major third, and thereby gives a plaintive or wistful mood to a composition. While a speaker does not control his speech with the same degree of accuracy, he can create a similar psychological effect. Inflections which rise and fall freely give the impression of a major key, while those which are short, tentative, and lacking in definiteness give the impression of a minor key. It is possible that in spoken dialogue some approximation is made to the major and minor intervals of music, for when one speaks indecisively or wistfully, the inflections give the impression of being uncompleted, just as do minor intervals.

It may be that this impression is almost exclusively a matter of the tonic note, with which a composition usually ends. At times the first note is the same as this final note, but the composition may begin at an interval above or below it. Strong definite speech gives the impression of beginning and ending a sentence on this tonic note. When the final falling inflection of a sentence stops short of the tonic note, it gives the impression of weakness and of indecisiveness.

This matter of a minor or major key, and of the tonic or atonic close, can be used by a director to give a desired mood to a scene or an entire play, but it requires a technical control of voice by the actors which few possess or can be taught to use without betraying self-consciousness. Therefore, key is normally left to the actor's instinct. If the director wishes to control it, he does so by casting an actor who uses the key he wants, or he coaches it indirectly through characterization or motivation. Roles which call for a minor key include the wife in *Ethan Frome,* most of the characters in *The Iceman Cometh,* Lennie in *Of Mice and Men,* and many characters in the plays of Chekhov and Maeterlinck. Conspicuously major and tonic speech is used by Sheridan Whiteside in *The Man Who Came to Dinner,* Father in *Life with Father,* most of the characters in *Holiday,* and most characters in melodramas. In *The Barretts of Wimpole Street,* Elizabeth, in minor key, contrasts with her father and Robert Browning in major key. The opposite effect is obtained in *Dodsworth,* where the main character, by speaking in a major key in contrast to the minor key of his wife and her sycophants, is shown to be out of place in artificial society.

Quality

A perfect tuning fork produces a single note; almost all other sounds are made up of a fundamental pitch plus as many as a hundred associated notes, many of them being the successive octaves above it. These associated notes vary greatly in their relative loudness, and it is this variable, composite, chord-like sound which is appreciated as quality. The ear identifies — by these differences in quality — sounds made mechanically, as by a hammer; those made by musical instruments; and those made by animals, including man. Quality also helps to distinguish between different human voices. Differences between the vowel and liquid consonant sounds are merely differences of quality. In man, the overtones are created, and then selectively amplified and dampened, by the shape of the vocal cavities, by the degree of tension of the walls of the cavities, and by the proportion of the breath which escapes through mouth and nose. The phrase "good placement of the voice" is used to describe a certain quality produced by an emphasis on the higher pitched overtones induced by enlarging the opening at the front part of the mouth cavity at the expense of the pharyngeal cavity. Such selectivity becomes habitual and then determines the typical voice quality of the individual, though physical condition, social environment, and motivation produce meaningful variations in it. Tone color is a term applied to the special qualities resulting from these variations, and from the influence upon quality of specific motivations and characterizations.

Present-day actors, with meager technical voice training in keeping with the philosophy of anti-"elocutionary" naturalness in the current teaching of speech, have little facility in varying their voice quality except through characterization, so the director is usually restricted to suggestions on characterization in securing changes in the quality of the actors' voices. His decisions on casting are materially influenced by his judgment of voice quality. He may be aware only of the need for securing variety in the voice qualities; but he thinks at tryouts, "His voice doesn't sound right," or "She seems to suggest this character to me." While other factors influence him to some extent, voice quality often is the major factor in such impressions.

Voice quality occasionally is put to calculated use by both actor and director. Ghosts on the stage usually speak in sepulchral tones which are designated as of *pectoral* quality. *Aspirate* quality is used in stage whispers, and often in intensely quiet conversations even when the actors do not actually whisper.

Normal well-placed tone quality is designated *oral* quality. The *orotund* quality, which we hear as rich or full, has emphasis upon the lower overtones. In fullness of resonance, it is the most beautiful tone which can be produced by the speaking voice, but it may call attention to itself by its beauty, and if the audience thinks that the actor betrays self-consciousness in forcing roundness into his voice, it intrudes between him and the listeners. Actors of the past, particularly when playing in romantic and classic drama, used the orotund quality more freely than do contemporary actors: some employed it naturally, but others were self-conscious. It is from the period of transition between romantic and "natural" acting that we have the saying, "Beautiful voices have ruined more actors than whiskey." Yet, the orotund remains the most beautiful of all vocal tones, and is appropriate to the rhetoric of the romantic and classic drama. It is the rich cello tone as compared with the thinner violin tone of ordinary speech. When it is produced without affectation we admire it in actors, preachers, politicians, radio announcers, and radio commentators. It is produced by moderate or stronger volume, fully opened mouth to obtain maximum amplification, lengthened vowel sounds, and corresponding sharpened consonant articulations like the singer's, instead of the lengthened frictional and liquid consonants of conversational speech.

One fairly common quality effect is when the hero, a pure-toned speaker, is in opposition to a group having harsh or guttural voices — for example, an honest man opposing a group of gangsters.

Part of the effectiveness of *The Kingdom of God* is the contrast of voices between Sister Gracia and the other characters: her lilting young voice of the first act contrasting with the mature and eccentric voices of the inmates of the old men's home and of her parents; her calm, melodious, self-controlled voice of the second act contrasting with those of the heterogeneous group of women with many extreme characterizations; and in the third act, her rich baritone quality of strong-willed old age contrasting with the light, excited children's voices of the orphanage. Not only do the deliberately calculated contrasts in the voice of Sister Gracia serve to highlight her vocal development, but they also supply the outward manifestations of the development of her character.

Articulation, Pronunciation, and Dialect

Articulation is the name given to the production of recognizable vowel and consonant sounds. Vowels, like the various phases of quality, are produced by the shape of the vocal cavities, by the tension of the cavity walls, and by the proportion of the breath which escapes through the mouth and nose.

Consonant sounds are the explosions, frictions, and stops produced by the movements of the tongue, the lips, the soft palate, the pharynx, and the vocal folds in beginning and ending syllables. Liquids are produced by constrictions which do not quite cause friction. The combination of sound waves so produced are appreciated by the listener as vowel and consonant sounds. The singer's terms *attack* and *release* are sometimes applied to speech, and then refer to the degree of sharpness with which a sound is begun or stopped.

The director is seldom immediately concerned with articulation except as it affects intelligibility.

Plays which depend for their effect upon intricacies of language and upon the precision with which it is handled, such as high comedies from the Restoration period to those of today, are assisted by meticulous articulation without too much exaggeration, since conscious perfection and nicety of style are implicit in the scripts. The director of such plays may insist upon accuracy and care in articulation which would seem artificial in romantic, classic, or realistic drama. On the other hand, he wants to eliminate all awareness of articulation in strongly representational drama, as well as in broad earthy farce and comedy from Aristophanes to Kaufman. The New York cast of *The Cocktail Party* (as can be heard in the recordings) used an exceptional distinctness of articulation, unusual in a contemporary play, which contrasted markedly with the usually inferior articulation heard on Broadway from stars and supporting players alike. British actors in general are notably superior in articulation to their American peers, though they are no better at projection.

Articulation per se can be put to use for characterization. In *Berkeley Square*, for example, comparative characterization is aided by having Kate, Lady Anne, and other fastidious eighteenth-century characters speak accurately without contractions; by letting Tom make the sloppy drunken contractions fitted to his role; and by allowing Helen and the present-day people to make the usual contemporary contractions such as "don't," "can't," and "haven't." While this intrudes upon the actors' field of choice, the necessity for co-ordination among the actors justifies directorial guidance in such cases.

Articulation is the manner in which sounds are formed; *pronunciation* is the choice of the sounds to be articulated. A speaker has options in vowel sounds, in syllabic accentuation, and occasionally in consonant sounds. Sometimes the choice is between equally acceptable pronunciations, and sometimes between that of good speech as recorded in the dictionaries, and that which is colloquial. One has a free choice, according to the dictionary, to accent either the second or third syllable of *gladiolus,* to pronounce *Elizabethan* with a long *e* or a short *e* for the vowel of the fourth syllable, to pronounce *blouse* with an *s* or a *z*. These are matters of individual preference or of regional custom. The dictionary requires one to omit the *p* in pronouncing *corps,* to accent *extraordinary* on the second syllable, and to pronounce *err* to rhyme with *cur,* not *air.* In order to suggest colloquial speech, however, an actor may use the alternative pronunciations for some words.

Pronunciation in most cases is the actors' concern. In plays laid in a particular locale, however, the director decides the degree of the sectional *dialect* to be used. This applies to the regional accents of the United States as well as to the strikingly distinctive brogues of Cockney, Scottish, and Irish. This directorial choice also embraces what speech is to be used in a classic. Until recent years "stage speech" was used widely — a slightly variable dialect which was roughly equivalent to the speech of Southern England minus the British colloquial inflectional pattern. There

was sufficient uniformity in this when spoken by trained British and American actors to make it acceptable both in the United States and in England as unlocalized conventional speech. Since this was spoken universally by actors at the beginning of this century, newcomers had to learn it in order to obtain engagements.

In recent decades the increase in plays dealing with provincial American life has made it possible for an actor to secure engagements when speaking only his own regional dialect, so it now is difficult in the professional theatre to employ a company with consistently unlocalized speech. Radio has exaggerated the difficulty, for Midwesterners persist in their notion that the dialect of Easterners is "affected," and radio announcers from the East have had to learn a dialect which would pass for "General American."

When stage speech had uniformity, teachers of interpretation and of acting throughout America taught it to their students, and an attempt was made to have amateurs use it in acting in order to be trained for the professional stage. With the greatly lessened employment opportunities on Broadway and the emphasis on General American dialect on the radio and in motion pictures, stage speech has lost its popularity. Most directors today are willing to have classics and unlocalized plays spoken in any dialect which the cast can use consistently and which is accepted by the audience as unlocalized. High school and community theatre directors have comparatively little trouble in adopting this point of view, for their casts and audiences ordinarily come from a single dialect area. To college and university directors it is more serious, for their student actors come from all parts of the country, and thus have a variety of dialects. It obviously is impossible to assemble as members of a stage family a mother from Alabama, a father from Indiana, and children from Vermont, Texas, and Iowa, without requiring them to adopt nearly uniform speech. Few students are able to learn a dialect fully during the usual rehearsal period. An audience may not recognize inaccuracies in the speech of a distant region, but it is disturbed by the slightest imperfection in its own. Therefore, the instructors have to consider making all the students available for casting by training them in a consistent dialect. If a student goes to college in Ohio but expects either to go to New York or return to Alabama, it is a serious pedagogical problem whether he should be taught the good speech of Alabama, of Ohio, or of the New York stage. No solution is completely satisfactory.

In producing plays which require a distinct regional dialect or a foreign accent, such as *Riders to the Sea, What Every Woman Knows, Green Grow the Lilacs, Papa Is All, They Knew What They Wanted,* or *Blithe Spirit,* the director decides how much accuracy of dialect the cast must use. He may ask fidelity to the accent indicated by the script, he may decide to make no attempt at accent, or he may decide upon a compromise — using the dialect inflection and a few distinctive phonemes, but accepting the local accent in the other sounds. He knows that in this he completely satisfies no one; nevertheless, he may avoid the worst strictures of both the dialectal purists and the provincial patriots. To the nonspecialist, the distinctive inflectional pattern of a region often gives a better suggestion of the dialect than the specific eccentricities of the pronunciation of vowels and consonants, and a compromise based on this often is adopted.

Consistency is the safeguard in any decision which the director makes. If, in Louisiana, he performs a Noel Coward play in a uniform New Orleans accent, few members of the local audience object strongly, but if there is one actor with a true British accent in the cast, there is a jarring note — attention is called to both the British and the New Orleans accents, and the audience is forced to decide upon its preference.

Duration

Duration is concerned with the length of a speech sound. "Rate" and "tempo" are the terms used more often to refer to the speed of connected discourse. Rate signifies the speed with which the actor speaks. It is the number of syllables which he would articulate per minute if he were to maintain the same speed for a given period. It is perceived by the audience as gradations from fast to slow. Tempo is almost synonymous, but it is a more subjective term, and indicates the seeming rate, which may be different from the actual one; it also applies to the variations in speed which occur even within a single sentence.

Rhythm is often associated with rate and tempo because variation in rate is the most conspicuous and the most easily identifiable element in rhythm. But rhythm is a complex matter, and it is produced by other recurrent factors of vocal or visual patterning as well as by rate. Therefore, it is discussed later as one of the organizing patterns of the director.

A fast rate of speech gives an impression of action and excitement almost as effectively as does loudness. It can suggest gaiety and good spirits. Extreme examples appear in comedy, as in the chattering of the woman who recovers her speech in *The Man Who Married a Dumb Wife,* in the character of the hostess in *Dinner at Eight,* and as a mannerism of Billie Burke in any part. A slow rate may suggest calmness, sadness, age, dignity, physical exhaustion. Most tragedies require this rate. In *Harvey* it suggests the calmness and imperturability of Elwood P. Dowd as long as he is accompanied by his six-foot-two rabbit friend. In *Arsenic and Old Lace* the excitability of the nephew is contrasted with the tranquil explanations of his homicidal aunts. In *Of Mice and Men,* the slow easy-going conversations between Lennie and George suggest the former's strength of body and slowness of mind. In *Ethan Frome* the slowness of speech suggests the repressed introspective faculty of restrained New Englanders. Regularity of rate suggests control, while irregularity or jerkiness may suggest uneasiness, nervousness, or hysteria. *Family Portrait, Abe Lincoln in Illinois,* and *Victoria Regina* represent the one, and *Dream Girl, Margin for Error,* and *Oh, Men! Oh, Women!,* the other. *Tovarich* gets fine comedy contrast from the slowness and evenness of tempo used by the Russian prince and grand duchess employed as house servants, and the jerkiness and erratic tempi of their bourgeois French employers. *Pigeons and People,* similarly, contrasts the slow-speaking, pigeon-feeding, unknown man with the excitability of the other characters when they are irritated by his frank statement of the truth about everything but his own identity. A great deal of the fun of *The Play's the Thing* is the imperturability of the character of the playwright in the midst of emotional upheavals.

Alternation and variety of rate produce effects over and above rate itself. Any rate maintained for a period of time becomes customary and habitual and its effect diminishes rapidly, so a changing rate has more effect upon an audience than one which is sustained.

While the rate of speech basically is the actor's concern, he can adjust it quite freely in response to the tempo of the episode as a whole. Therefore the director can work with comparative freedom in adjusting the tempo of episodes and in creating contrasts between them. Within the general tempo the actor finds the right ones for his individual speeches. The impression of speed and tempo is more influenced by the speed with which cues are picked up than by the actual rate. An actor need speak no faster than the rate at which he can articulate well and can

impart full meaning. Picking up cues instantly gives an equally good sense of haste.

In the thirties George Abbott had the reputation of breakneck speed in directing farces and melodrama like *Broadway, Three Men on a Horse, Room Service,* and *Brother Rat.* In an interview [3] Abbott explained that, while some scenes of these plays were acted faster than the general practice, the impression of speed was gained by contrast between fast and slow scenes, and all other contrasts he could devise, much more than by the actual rate of speech. If the cast of one of his plays had maintained the tempo at which they seemed to play, not only would the tempo have lost its effect, but the audience as well as the actors would have been exhausted.

Contrast of rate can create other such psychological effects. A scene is weightier and more impressive when played slowly between fast-moving scenes. Constantly increasing rate produces the impression of mounting tension, and is used for that purpose in many mystery melodramas. The opposite effect is created if a play starts at a fast tempo, and the pace then slackens as the characters become more and more tired and exhausted. This is the acting technique for the character of Lear, since he is a virile and excitable old man at the beginning of the play, and becomes physically and mentally weakened by the emotional blows he receives. However, in the last acts the play itself cannot have this pattern, for Shakespeare telescopes the action more and more as he nears the end, making the subplots move faster and faster toward their climaxes, often providing barely enough lines to present the action. Retarding the tempo is a dangerous technique in any case, for the audience is used to mounting tension as a play progresses, and this reversal of tempo suggests that the play is subsiding into unin-

[3] "The Director Takes Command," Morton Eustis, *Theatre Arts,* XX (February, 1936), 120–123.

teresting inaction. It is used successfully, however, in *Old English,* where the long next-to-the-last scene consists of the almost wordless serving and eating of a dinner by which the leading character violates all his doctor's orders about food and drink and thereby commits suicide; and the final scene contains only a few speeches as his body is discovered.

OTHER AUDITORY STIMULI PROVIDED BY THE ACTOR

The Pause

Closely related to the tempo of speech is the use of pauses. Pauses can give overall variety to a play as well as variety to rate and tempo, for there is no greater contrast to a continuous flow of dialogue and action than its cessation. This, however, is chiefly an actor's concern, for the interest of the audience must be sustained through the pause, and this interest is nearly always in sympathy with the thoughts of an actor. A pause dictated by direction is likely to be a "dead wait," making so great a contrast that it injures continuity.

The effectiveness of a speech is tremendously increased if it is delivered after a pause to make a decision. The impressiveness of an entrance is sometimes heightened by a pause — the audience is prepared for it, starts to wonder what the character is like, and then the entrance is withheld for an instant to allow the curiosity to increase. The 1950 revival of Shaw's three-hour-long one-act play *Getting Married* announced the arrival of the fabulous Mrs. George about whom everyone had been talking — and then took an intermission before she entered. However, a delay is disastrous if the audience does not anticipate the entrance. The reversal of this is often comic, as in the farce, the revue, and the musical comedy, when the entering figure is insignificant, is the wrong character, enters from the wrong doorway, or is otherwise a letdown.[4]

A pause cannot be a mere interruption and wait. Usually it is made meaningful by thoughtful silence on the part of the actor which the audience comprehends and follows with suspense, as when a character has to make a difficult decision before he can reply to a question, such as that of the parson in the last scene of *Escape* who must decide whether or not to lie about the presence of the escaped convict. The exact thoughts do not have to be pantomimed if the conflicting motivations have been foreshadowed. Occasionally an audience itself supplies the thoughts for a pause without relying on the actor for them. In a murder melodrama, for example, when all lights are turned out and the audience is in suspense, unable to see anything, wondering who will enter the scene, a stage can be left empty for many seconds. The last act of *The Bat* opens with several minutes of action on a stage so dimly lighted that it is impossible for the audience to see what is being done and who is doing it.

In order to create mood, Maeterlinck indicates a number of pauses in *The Blind, The Intruder,* and *The Death of Tintagiles. Macbeth* can afford long pauses, such as during the scene of the murder of Duncan. *King Lear* has a dead wait written in, because *Lear's* "Who stirs?" in the first scene undoubtedly means that the court is so shocked by the actions of Lear that no one dares to

[4] A famous old vaudeville act opened on a stage backed by beautiful brocade curtains, the orchestra played an impressive introduction, a few beautiful coloratura cadenzas floated in from the wings, and a tramp clown named Milo entered singing in falsetto. In one of the Weber and Fields musical comedies, elaborate preparation was made for the entrance of Peter Dailey, there was prolonged applause from the offstage room where he had been making a speech, a long-delayed entrance, and Dailey entered ostentatiously waving thanks to the cheering crowd offstage. Then he turned to the audience and remarked, "Jolly dogs, those stagehands."

move in response to his first order. The scene at the court of the Dauphin in *Saint Joan* is usually played with chatter at Joan's entrance, which is hushed as she walks to the center, identifies "Bluebeard" standing in for the Dauphin, and hunts for the Dauphin himself among the courtiers. Announcements on the stage by a doctor or a nurse that a patient has died are almost always played with a suspense pause preceding them, and audiences still respond to this emotionally, though their thoughts leap ahead of the dialogue.

Effective as good pauses are, nothing damages the tempo of a play more than the meaningless and empty pauses while actors wait for one of the characters to complete his exit so that they can talk about him, or the fifth-of-a-second pauses between speeches with which many inexperienced actors punctuate their dialogue. Some actors, having learned the value of the pause before an important reply, use it on every speech, with the result that when they come to a line where it is appropriate, its effectiveness is dissipated. Occasionally ponderous tempo is required in a scene. The pause for thought before speeches produces this effect more convincingly and subtly than perhaps any other technique. The director's more usual practical problem is to eliminate meaningless pauses from the dialogue.

Accentuation

Accentuation is a matter of emphasis given to a syllable, a word, or a phrase. Within a word, volume and pitch tend to accent certain syllables. The most important word in the body of a sentence is usually stressed by means of a peak in both pitch and volume; while the final important word of a sentence receives emphasis through a strongly falling inflection.

Words, phrases, and sentences also can receive emphasis through a distinctive tone quality, usually a relatively fuller tone produced by a more open mouth; or through more careful articulation, often accompanied by a decrease in the rate of speech so that each sound is given more duration than is customary. In rare cases, accentuation is secured by a more rapid rate; by a slow rate; by pauses preceding, following, or separating the important words; or by an exaggeration of any phase of the melody pattern. These exaggerations of inflection include lengthening the rise, the fall, or the circumflex; speeding or slowing them; and sustaining a pitch for an appreciable time. Any such technique grafted onto a sentence without being motivated from within risks the usual danger that it will be recognized as mechanical and therefore artificial.

These factors belong almost exclusively to the actors' techniques, and the director becomes a coach when he points out to them the opportunities for obtaining accent which varies from the more obvious techniques of loudness and high pitch. However, the director frequently asks, without dictating the method, that certain key lines or phrases be stressed in order to insure that they are heard and remembered.

Unison Patterns of Speech

The discussion thus far has dealt with vocal effects produced by a single speaker or by speakers following one another in sequence. In mob scenes, in choral speech, and in some other instances, two or more actors speak simultaneously. When they do so, the author and director usually want an effect of summation — not distinct word patterns. Everything said previously about solo speech applies to simultaneous speech; and, in addition, opportunities are provided for harmonic and inharmonic combinations of the voices.

When chorus speakers use the same words, a harmonic effect is usually desired. They may speak in perfect unison on the same pitch; they may use the same melody pattern but speak on different, but harmonic, pitch levels; or they may use the same basic melody pattern, but freely vary both the pitch level and the length of the inflections so that all voices rise together, but the low pitched voices rise much less than those of higher pitch. It is possible to have actors speak identical words with different inflectional patterns, but this seldom is feasible unless they are speaking with different motivations — some using a straightforward motivation, and some speaking ironically, or some reporting an event with sorrow and others with joy. Although conventionally the chorus of a Greek play reacts as an abstract entity, it is possible to characterize individually each member of the chorus and to have each one react in terms of character. The same is true of *Murder in the Cathedral.* However, since a large portion of the meaning of speech is conveyed by the inflections, it is difficult to make such speaking intelligible, because the listener is unable to follow a single inflectional pattern. It is possible to use a lead voice with a free-speaking chorus, with a good deal of the communication being made by the single voice at a different pitch level and at greater volume than that of the supporting chorus. Other variations include a lead group which speaks continuously, with the rest joining at times, but remaining silent during important exposition; and a distribution of the chorus lines to individual members.

When voices of a mob speak different words simultaneously, the intent usually is a total effect, and the emphasis is upon the emotion projected by the group rather than upon the spoken words. Individual speeches can be communicated either by strong projection and a contrasting pitch level, or by reducing the volume of the rest of the group during the speech. This effect of general comment with a few recognizable speeches to clarify the motivation is that wanted for the mobs in *Julius Caesar* and most other plays. Occasionally a play contains a mob scene which contrasts two different reactions. The early parts of the oration scene in *Caesar* can have contrasting opinions in the mob. The vocal effects need careful control and definite planning. Usually, every possible factor of contrast is used — pitch, melody, rate, quality, and key, as well as visual factors. Usually, too, the vocal patterns are used antiphonally rather than simultaneously, i.e., following one another in alternation to make the contrast clearer. This kind of contrast is employed even more frequently between a single voice and a chorus.

Independent conversations spoken in different areas of the stage are occasionally employed, usually for an effect of random chatter. More often several such conversations are carried on in pantomime, and then each is fully vocalized in succession. Gilmor Brown and Alice Garwood [5] call attention to the injury to illusion, however, when the audience hears the words of actors in a certain area at one moment, but sees them moving their lips without being able to hear them an instant later. The director, if he can, shifts the figures as they change from audibility to pantomime or the reverse.

In plays with divided settings, scenes are sometimes played in two rooms simultaneously. They are usually played by overlapping the ends of sentences, instead of in simultaneous speech, and the dialogue is written so that the important words are in the middle of the sentences where they are heard without interference. This is the method of *Anna Christie, The World We Make,* and *She Loves Me Not.* Telephone conversations are often carried on in half-voice while another dialogue demands major attention. Among the tricks in *Beggar on Horseback* is a double conversation — a man and his fiancée converse on one side of the stage while her family chatter on the other side — with the audience expected to hear

[5] *General Principles of Play Direction* (Samuel French, 1936), p. 61.

both. If the dialogue is spoken with about the same volume but at different pitch levels, a spectator can hear either of the two conversations to which he directs his visual attention (and thereby sees the articulatory movements involved). This conversation is long-winded and repetitive on the assumption that the spectator will listen part of the time to one conversation and then to the other and that any short passage of either one he hears supplies adequate exposition. A comparable scene occurs in Act III of *Pygmalion.*

Comic Exaggeration

Most of the previous discussion has been concerned with the serious uses of the vocal elements mentioned. All of them can be turned to comic uses by an exaggeration in the effect itself, by its inconsistency with associated stimuli, or by unexpectedly sudden or unexpectedly delayed timing. Much of the skill of the broad comedian who depends upon his own performance rather than upon gag material for his effects, lies in his exaggeration of vocal or visual expression. This is the technique of Bobby Clark, Danny Kaye, the Marx Brothers, Betty Hutton, Abbott and Costello, Bert Lahr, Ray Bolger, and Carol Channing. Victor Moore, Fred Astaire, Bing Crosby, and sometimes Bob Hope and Ed Wynn produce a similar comic inconsistency by extreme underplaying. Charles Butterworth made a revue and motion picture career for himself by the single trick of a gesture made after the appropriate verbal moment for it had passed. Zasu Pitts makes stereotyped use of a vague, pointless flipping of her hands to express confusion. Charlie Chaplin mixes overplaying and underplaying, thus providing his own contrasts.

Farce employs the technique of exaggeration consistently; the broader the farce, the more extreme it can be. The dramatic form which permits greatest latitude is the burlesque of acting style, like *A Midsummer Night's Dream,* the Duke of Buckingham's *The Rehearsal, The Critic, Tom Thumb, The Admirable Bashville, The Torchbearers,* and *The Potboiler.* In them, all vocal and visual acting devices can be burlesqued.

Contrast

Any pattern of sound, whether it be of pitch, rate, volume, inflection, quality, or articulation, loses its effect after a few seconds. Contrast to other patterns within a single vocal factor — such as varying the level of volume — extends its effectiveness for a longer period, though regular alternation also soon loses its effect. Consequently, in addition to the variations within a vocal factor, the director strives for constant variety by the use of different vocal factors — obtaining emphasis, for example, by rate, pitch, articulation, and pause, in alternation with volume. Each factor is made more effective by the variety. Most of these contrasts arise naturally out of the motivation of the actors, but the actors may be guided to make use of a greater variety of attacks, and, in special cases, to use a specific effect.

STIMULI SUPPLIED BY OTHER MEDIA

Music

Music is another auditory element which the director co-ordinates with the dialogue and action. In an opera, where all the lines are sung, the music, though in many respects fixed by the composer, is interpreted by the actor and the director in the same manner as are vocal patterns of speech. For their dramatic effectiveness and their emotional meaning, the actor and director can exert control over rate, volume, voice quality, accent, articulation, pronunciation, the melodic line, and the contrasts between them.

A musical comedy or a revue presents more complex problems, for here the director has to interrelate sung and spoken passages. When the script has been previously produced, most of the integration has been effected, at least for one production and one audience. In the premiere of a musical production, the correlation of music, speech, dance, and spectacle requires much more experimentation than is necessary in the first performance of a new drama. Straight plays often "open cold" on Broadway after a few previews, but musical shows plan a tryout tour of from four to ten weeks. Musical comedies used arbitrarily to interrupt the action every five or ten minutes in order to insert a musical number introduced by a bit of contrived dialogue, having little relation to the plot. Integrated musicals of the type of *Oklahoma!, Carousel, Brigadoon, Finian's Rainbow, South Pacific,* and *The King and I,* and their predecessors such as *Show Boat,* introduce the musical numbers more naturally, and the songs and ballets form an integral part of the script. In revivals of older scripts the attempt often is made to adapt them to the contemporary style of production; sometimes this is successful, but often it results in a confusion of styles.

Incidental musical numbers in plays are ordinarily employed naturalistically, with dialogue introducing the musician or singer as an entertainer. The chief directorial problem in these cases is to coach the entertainer to take an actor's attitude toward his performance rather than his more accustomed concert-stage manner.

A constantly recurring problem met by a director is the co-ordination of background music and spoken dialogue. In nineteenth-century plays, musical support often was given to dramatic scenes. The memory of "Hearts and Flowers" as a support for many sad scenes now provokes a smile. During the period of its acceptance as a convention, such musical accompaniment was an effective additional stimulant to the emotions of the audience. In recent years motion pictures have restored its acceptability. They use especially composed scores rather than familiar music, but the effect is identical. Recent Broadway productions have adopted

it: *A Streetcar Named Desire, Death of a Salesman,* and a number of Shakespearean productions. Musical support remains a dangerous technique if the audience becomes aware of it, but is an extremely effective one if it gains acceptance from an audience early in the performance.

The same considerations which govern the composition of the auditory patterns of speech apply to the music, except pronunciation and perhaps articulation. In this case, the director's planning can be less restricted, for no individual motivation is involved. In patterning the auditory stimuli, he is concerned with the choice of the musical instruments for quality, style, and volume; and with the melody, volume, accent, rhythm, key, and attack (equivalent to articulation) of the composition and of the playing. Furthermore, he considers the harmony or disharmony of the instruments with the speaking voices they accompany, to be sure that the combination produces the desired effect, that the tonal effects of the instruments do not interfere with hearing by too great similarity to the voice quality, or overpower the voice by volume or sharpness of attack.

The director decides how aware of the accompaniment the audience should be. Music is used obviously in *Death of a Salesman,* and so can begin with a sharp attack. In *A Streetcar Named Desire, The Glass Menagerie,* and most motion pictures, the music steals in under the speech and slowly rises in volume, often subtly growing out of the melody and emphasis of the speeches, so that it supports the scene without the audience being aware of when or how the music began. Many plays justify the musical accompaniment realistically: an actor turns on a radio or a phonograph, the dialogue explains that the music comes from a musician or a radio in a nearby room; and the audience accepts the coincidence that the music underscores the dramatic action.

For a representational play, the musicians

are usually hidden backstage, or in a concealed orchestra pit, or even in a room under the stage; and heard then by means of a public-address system. In presentational performances, however, the musicians may be purposely and conspicuously visible, and the audience may be asked to accept them and forget them. In nineteenth-century melodrama, when the audience is invited to laugh at the artificiality of this convention, the music starts with a sharp attack to call immediate attention to the musicians. In performances of Shakespeare, Congreve, Molière, Goldoni, and Sheridan, the musicians may be costumed in the style of the period and become part of the visual as well as the auditory performance. But it does not seem to disturb an audience attending such plays, or even Greek dramas, if a visible orchestra is dressed in modern clothes.[6]

Recorded music is judged for its effect in the same way as is live music. Careful calculation is made of the way in which such music, used for an overture or to introduce or conclude a scene, blends into the action or stops climactically just as the action begins. The integration of the music with the lights, the curtain, and the acting requires considerable rehearsal, and the director usually tries to co-ordinate as many as possible of these elements before dress rehearsals.

Sound Effects

Sound effects, like music, can be used either representationally or conventionally. Doorbells, telephone bells, buzzers, rain,

[6] Where the actors elsewhere in the play break through the proscenium line with asides to the audience, it is often amusing to have the actors directly acknowledge the musicians, cuing them when to start, frowning at them in order to transfer to them the blame when a singer flats a note, making eye contact with them in connection with some stage horseplay. In *The Servant of Two Masters*, when Truffaldino sets his pudding on the footlights while he goes to wait on his masters, it is amusing and completely in keeping with the style of the play for him to pantomime a warning to the musicians: "Keep fiddling and don't touch the pudding, or I'll paste you!"

wind, thunder, hail, automobile and airplane noises, doorslams, cricket chirpings, and birdcalls are ordinarily employed actualistically, and every effort is made to have the audience accept them as real. It takes skill and prolonged rehearsal to reproduce these sounds credibly, whether they are operated manually or are obtained with phonograph records and a public-address system, because they usually have to be produced much louder than in nature, a fact which adds an element of artificiality difficult to overcome. Also a public-address system has its own artificiality of tone quality. Outdoor sounds, perfect or not, usually remind the audience that it is seated in a theatre; therefore, many directors, whenever possible, eliminate sound effects altogether. They even omit some of those which seem imperative, believing that it is less disturbing to audience illusion to be unable to hear a sound which an actor claims to hear, than to hear a poor imitation of it. Sound effects, however, can be used as an integral part of the play. *The Royal Family* sets the tone of the household by the opening obligato of doorbells, telephone bells, and buzzers, with servants hurrying to answer them. The rumble of the subway in *Subway Express*, the blasting underfoot in *My Sister Eileen*, the experimental explosions of fireworks in *You Can't Take It with You*, and the thump of the well-digging apparatus in *George Washington Slept Here*, all produce hilarious moments.

Occasionally sound effects are used in a presentational manner. John Gielgud's production of *The Importance of Being Earnest* used birdcalls as a presentational and obvious comment on speeches in the play, and they have been used similarly elsewhere. *The Love of Four Colonels* obtains comedy from an offstage gunshot which coincides exactly with the onstage pretense of shooting, to the utter confusion of the character who does the pantomime. Productions of *Androcles and the Lion* vary in using offstage roars of lions realistically, or conventionally for humor. The scene in which Truffaldino serves the two dinners in *The Servant of Two Masters* can be spiced by putting screen-door slams on the doors of the setting, slamming these doors at every entrance and exit, and increasing their number by separating the movements of the two waiters. The Marx Brothers stage production of *The Cocoanuts* used the same device in a farcical hotel bedroom scene.

Sound effects, whether representational or presentational, have almost the same characteristic factors as human speech, being restricted only partially by the nature of the actual sounds they imitate.

A great many sound effect devices have delayed action, whether mechanically or manually operated, and they must be initiated an exact fraction of a second before the cue in order to produce sufficient sound when the cue occurs. Such timing requires a great deal of rehearsal no matter how skillful the operator, and so, just as with music, the timing, when possible, must be rehearsed by the director before the dress rehearsals. Sound effects produced by actors just preceding their entrances, such as approaching footsteps or knocks on a door, also need rehearsal, for even actors who strive for complete credibility in playing seem unaware of the fact that stamping and shuffling their feet on the floor does not produce a true effect of approaching footsteps, and the crew needs to be reminded that a special wood surface is required on which an actor can simulate knocking on a door, since neither the batten of a flat nor the floor itself gives a surface on which the sound can be made convincingly.

A speech sound has volume, pitch (including inflection and key), quality, duration, and articulation. Combinations of sounds may have the additional factors of accentuation, pronunciation, and pause. These individual stimuli interact among themselves and with the accompanying visual stimuli to convey meaning, and the meaning of a specific stimulus is determined largely by the associated stimuli. The muscles of the body, including those involved in speech, tend to respond in habitual ways under the influence of the mind, and all the muscles tend to tense and relax sympathetically. Thus, when the other muscles tense under some form of excitement — in strong movement or in equilibrium in anticipation of movement — speech tends to become louder, higher in pitch, shriller in quality, faster, and more sharply articulated. Relaxation of the body produces the opposite effect.

A reversal can be obtained by conscious control, for the muscles which produce speech, or which produce any single factor of it, can, within limits, be controlled consciously and independently of the main pattern of thought and action. Vocal stimuli are produced by the actor out of his motivation, characterization, and stage energy, and while the director can control any factor in order to create an effect, he ordinarily exerts less control over them than he does over the visual stimuli, except in coaching. Their use varies widely between plays and between episodes of a single play. Because actors can seldom control vocal effects under direction and keep them believable, the director usually achieves his patterning by helping the actor to alter his motivation rather than by direct control of the voice. Inflection, rate, volume, articulation, and pronunciation are the factors most susceptible to variation at the wish of the director. Usually his greatest attention is given to securing variety in the vocal stimuli. A mob or chorus scene is the chief instance in which the director patterns the vocal stimuli in detail. Music and sound effects have essentially the same sound characteristics as speech, but can be governed by the director much more specifically.

25 | Patterning the Visual and Auditory Stimuli

Emphasis and Subordination · Style · Atmosphere · Picturization · Balance · Proportion Unity · Progression · Rhythm

It is necessary to organize or to pattern stimuli in order to make them meaningful. Seven or eight are the maximum number which can ordinarily be comprehended when presented together without organization. Many more, however, can be comprehended when they are organized in a recognizable pattern. A large number of stimuli can be perceived and understood when they are arranged in successively more complex patterns, as long as the elements at each pattern level are not more than seven or eight.

Ten half-inch red diamonds scattered over a card make a jumble. Concentration is required to count them. But the pips on the ten of diamonds of a deck of playing cards are organized; the two columns of four, and the one column of two are immediately comprehended as a total of ten. The point is demonstrated in the illustrations appearing on pages 396 and 398. Experience with playing cards soon teaches one the traditional patterns of the fives, sixes, sevens, eights, nines, and tens, and they are immediately recognizable without an intermediate step of mentally grouping the pips into columns. Most players find it difficult to evaluate an unarranged bridge hand of thirteen cards, yet a hand arranged in suits, and in sequence within suits, can be readily comprehended.

When stimuli are organized in successively larger patterns, one can have immediate recognition of the total pattern without analysis of its components. "Man" can be analyzed into "head," "torso," "legs," and "arms," and each of these can be analyzed into successively smaller patterns almost down to the individual stimulus which energizes a rod or cone in the retina of the eye. But one recognizes a man without any such analysis either in life or in the representation of a man in an art form. Forty men can be placed in rows of chairs with one man facing them from behind a desk, and be recognized as a "class." A painting can picture hundreds of men and still receive immediate comprehension, provided the figures are presented in some organized manner. The same is true of auditory patterns — of a simple one like an auto horn, or a complex one like "The Star-Spangled Banner."

Applying these considerations to a play, we can note that each spoken word is composed of many stimuli — the vowel and consonant sounds, its volume, pitch, quality, duration, etc. The eight to twelve words of the average sentence are assembled into a unit meaning by their inflection. All the characteristics of voice and speech — volume, pitch, quality, rate, and articulation —

394

are appreciated together as "meaning" without analysis into these components of the pattern. The separate sentences of a speech, a paragraph, or a dialogue are organized into a larger unit by their emotional or logical connection. The visual actions which accompany the vocal expression are perceived and comprehended as a part of the same meaning. Larger and larger patterns of stimuli may be formed which make the whole organization of a play comprehensible.

If the pattern fails to organize the stimuli so that their interrelation is perceived, the play seems a collection of disconnected bits, and lacks unity. It is the function of direction to organize all phases of the performance so that it produces a single total impression. All the stimuli must be made part of comprehensible units, having completeness within themselves, and being in turn parts of larger and larger syntheses until the entire play takes on a single recognizable pattern.

The major patterns which direction can use for organization are discussed in this chapter. Most of the arts have developed over the centuries a distinctive set of terms for expressing technical meanings. Since the separate function of direction is a relatively new conscious skill, its terminology has been partly borrowed from other arts and there still is indiscriminate use of almost synonymous terms from different arts, and an overlapping of terms expressing slight differences of viewpoint.

A performance must first gain the attention of the audience, and the attention must then be maintained and focused in sequence on the stimuli which establish the pattern. At any given moment in a performance many stimuli are available. If attention is allowed to wander at will among them, the result cannot be a single impression. Some such wandering can be tolerated in the case of a painting. In a purely spatial art, the eye can examine the details, and then return to the

larger patterns which organize the elements into a total impression, though even here the artist tries to guide the spectator through his stimuli in a sequential order. The performance of a play, being a temporal art as well as a spatial one, allows no opportunity for return, and the director must make each phase of the temporal pattern — such as speech and action — comprehensible at the brief instant of its occurrence.

Other patterns which the director uses to relate stimuli to each other meaningfully are variety, style, atmosphere, picturization, and progression. Variety is not given separate treatment here, but is discussed in connection with other patterning devices. Balance, proportion, unity, and rhythm can be employed creatively, but usually they are used as standards for evaluating the whole production; and the director looks for violations, rather than deliberately patterning with these elements in mind.

EMPHASIS AND SUBORDINATION

That which gains and holds attention tends to be accepted both at the time and subsequently in memory. The spectators ordinarily give undivided attention as the performance begins, since they come to the theatre to do so. Complete attention may be forestalled by extra-theatrical distractions such as noisy latecomers, the arrival of a notable person, or the raising of the curtain without adequate warning. *Our Town* (which begins with the casual entrance of the Stage Manager) and some presentational productions of pre-modern plays (which have a costumed stagehand light the footlights with a taper) do not gain complete control at the very outset; but such actions are part of the ceremony of opening the play, and they are designed to secure full attention by the time the play actually begins. The obligation of direction is then to maintain this attention as much as possible during the rest of the performance.

How many heads are here?
How long did it take you to
count them?

Now turn the page and
count the heads in the next
illustration.

But attention begins to wane as soon as it becomes fixed. In the theatre, the director seldom asks an audience to attend to a single stimulus for a protracted length of time, as the psychologist does in an experiment. An actor is usually made the focus of attention, and his physical appearance presents numerous visual stimuli. His gestures and movements supply additional ones. His speech provides auditory stimuli as well as further visual ones (i.e., through articulatory movements). When two or more actors carry on a conversation, a greater variety is offered, for the eye moves to each speaker in turn, and the ear adjusts itself to the alternations of voice. Broad physical action holds the attention readily, and for relatively longer periods.

Even with extreme variety of activity, the audience ultimately tires of keeping its eyes on the stage area, and of hearing sounds from that area of the same general type and intensity; and for relief and still greater variety, it then stops looking, stops listening, and turns its attention elsewhere, perhaps to introspection. Spasmodic inattention does little damage if direction holds it to a minimum. However, individual spectators are ordinarily inattentive at different times; and when the attention of a considerable part of the audience leaves the performance at the same moment, the performance is at fault.

As has been indicated, emphasis and variety are the two chief means of recovering and refocusing attention; subordination supplements them by reducing the possible distracting elements. The director tries not only to hold attention to the stage, but also to direct it in succession toward particular actors and stage areas. Many techniques have been discussed previously by which an actor can be emphasized by vocal and visual means, and only special problems need consideration here.

Emphasis on the Speaker

Attention is ordinarily focused on the actor who is speaking. His voice itself commands attention. The other actors customarily look at the speaker; if a spectator glances at them, his gaze almost automatically follows that of these actors and shifts back to the speaker. The poses of the listeners on the stage usually provide leading lines toward the speaker. An actor often gestures or moves during his speech. All these factors shift and direct the attention of the audience in the desired manner, so that the director need give little attention to the matter if the actors do adopt the logical course and do not create distractions. On the other hand, not all the listeners on the stage have to look directly and fixedly at the speaker, for this is unnatural. Further, the gesture of an actor turning to look at the speaker supplies more guidance for the attention of the spectator than a continuous stare. During a long speech by one character, the listeners give him better support if they find opportunities to communicate their reactions to each other, and then look once more at the speaker as he continues. This allows the audience its moment of relief from continuous staring, and then refocuses its attention on the speaker more strongly than ever because of the short period of rest.

The director can compose stage pictures so as to emphasize a single figure or a group of figures. The grouping of actors and of leading lines produced by their bodies follow the same principles as those used in other types of design. (See Jo Mielziner's setting for *Jeb,* Plate 30.) A director can learn a great many technical means for producing emphasis through composition by a study of the theory of linear composition and of its exemplification in individual paintings. Examples include: the emphatic figure placed at the balanced center of the group, preferably isolated from it; one placed at the apex of a triangular formation; one backed by a mass of supporting figures; or one isolated in balance with an oppositional mass of figures. Alexander Dean's *Fundamentals of Play Directing* contains an extensive analysis of such methods of securing emphasis and support.

If an individual member of the audience hears seventy per cent of most stage conversations, he can follow the plot completely, and understand most aspects of it. But certain lines or actions must be heard or seen in order for him to understand some vital phase of the plot. Immediately preceding such a key speech or action, the attention of all distracted spectators must be recaptured and focused on the key character. Obvious devices for recapturing attention include a loud and sudden noise, either a mechanical one like a doorbell or a doorslam, or a loud exclamation, laugh, or cough by an actor; a sustained pause which gives a moment of quiet; a broad or a sudden movement; or any other sudden change in the level of the auditory or visual stimulation. Because some spectators are attentive, such an effect must be motivated, and must be fully justified within the style of the production. This limits the use of the most obvious and effective devices. But some directors plan strong stimuli such as these periodically in the performance to recover the attention of spectators who have become distracted. To make certain that all spectators see the bloody arm as it reaches through the broken pane of glass to unlock the French doors in *The Bat,* the acting edition of the play has a speaking character cross in front of the door. As the gaze of the spectator follows the moving figure, it is led to the arm.

The Perfect Alibi has been cited as concealing its structural turning point within one of a series of seemingly casual lies by

Note how organization
speeds comprehension.

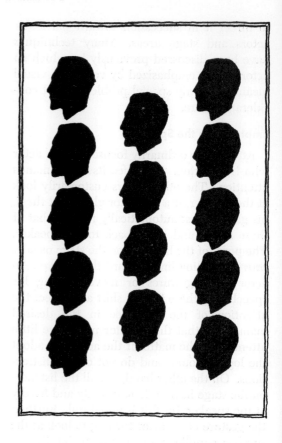

which a murderer attempts to establish an alibi for himself and his confederate. Every member of the audience must hear this particular lie and be able to recall the very slight error. Yet the audience must attach no importance to it when it is spoken. Naturally, the author highlights the episode, but he cannot emphasize the crucial speech too strongly without destroying suspense. The director can underscore it inconspicuously, and certainly must avoid any distraction from it. The most effective means of accomplishing this is to focus the attention on the villain just before he speaks, with no additional emphasis on him during the line or afterward. The attention of any distracted spectator is recaptured thirty seconds before the important speech. The actor makes some

extraneous but "natural" movement such as crossing his legs, shifting his position, or lighting a cigarette. The other actors in the scene adopt poses which cause the lines of their bodies to lead the eye toward him. Several of the other actors may look away during the preceding dialogue, so that they can turn to the speaker just before he speaks the vital line and thus transfer to him the attention of any spectator whose eyes have wandered to them. Another actor may cross the stage and sit; for ordinarily the gaze of a spectator follows a moving figure, watches him seat himself, and then looks elsewhere when the actor relaxes to indicate that his movement is completed. If he looks at the criminal at the exact moment he relaxes, the eyes of the spectator tend to follow his gaze.

If, on the contrary, the other characters inadvertently supply leading lines to the detective, and if at this moment he picks up and moves the telephone, which also was involved in the murder, some members of the audience might give attention to that action and later have difficulty recalling the key speech.

The inherent action and speech of the script, then, usually serve to direct attention correctly. The director sometimes finds it wise to underscore these, and to find effective devices to guide the attention.

Emphasis on a Silent Actor or an Inanimate Object

Direction has to use every possible means of emphasis if it is necessary for the attention of the audience to be focused on a silent actor or an inanimate object; on an inactive actor; or on a seated one or one placed in a weak stage position. In a presentational production, such mechanical devices as spotlighting can be used. In a play conceived representationally, contrast is probably the most effective device for the purpose. In the opening act of *Cyrano de Bergerac,* for example, Cyrano warns an actor to stop the speech of prologue he is delivering on an inner stage, and the mob exhorts the actor to continue. Cyrano sits calmly on a stool while the members of the mob turn their backs to him and to the audience in order to face the actor on the inner stage. These mob actors speak and move violently. Audience attention is frequently drawn to the excited group, but it inevitably reverts to the contrasting immobile figure of Cyrano. This attitude would be ineffectual, however, if others remained seated or inactive.

Attention is often focused on a doorway in anticipation of an entrance there. Design and the grouping and the attitudes of actors can form a composition which is complete only when the entering actor steps into its focal point. This gives the spectator a feeling of completion and satisfaction which adds emphasis to this actor.

Selective lighting and other similar devices may obscure the complete design of the setting until a key moment, and reveal it suddenly for some special effect. Plays like *The Man in the Bowler Hat* and *Cock Robin* reveal halfway through a scene that the action is a rehearsal of a play or a motion picture; the action of *Outward Bound* is well under way before the audience learns that all the characters are dead. One of the most effective scenes in *Cavalcade* is the honeymoon episode at the rail of an ocean liner which ends as the couple moves away and allows the spectators to read "S.S. Titanic" on a life preserver, and thus to surmise that the couple will drown the next day. *The Terrible Meek* begins in darkness, and the audience guesses from the peasant speech of the woman and the Cockney speech of the soldiers that the action is contemporary. It is not until the dawn reveals three crosses, at the end of the play, that the audience realizes the scene is Calvary.

Emphasis on Groups

An episode played downstage seems more important than one played at the back; one played at center seems more important than one played at the side. However, the "strength" and "weakness" of areas is relative. Dialogue spoken close to any wall, at the side or at the back, produces an apologetic or surreptitious impression. An episode played at unusual depth seems unimportant. But there is little difference in effect between playing slightly downstage of center as against slightly upstage, or between playing at center or playing just right or left of center. The elevation of an area increases its strength, and furniture in it may strengthen or weaken it. A long episode played at the side is weakened for those in the front-row seats because the muscles of

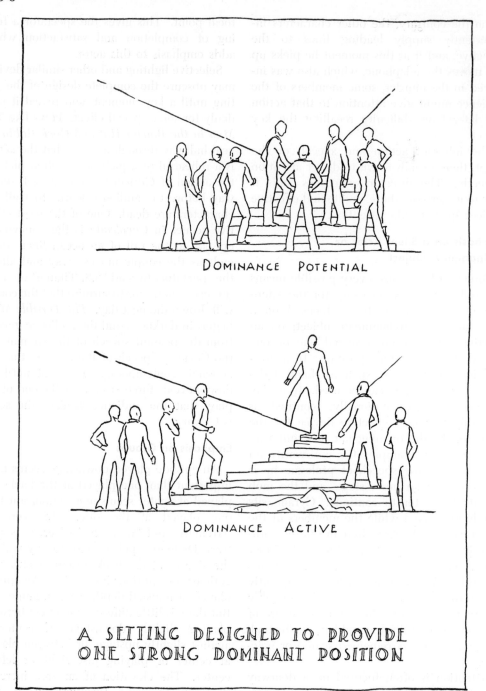

DOMINANCE   POTENTIAL

DOMINANCE   ACTIVE

A SETTING DESIGNED TO PROVIDE
ONE STRONG DOMINANT POSITION

Figure 55. In a setting designed to focus on one crucial position, the character who first takes the position receives tremendous emphasis.

eye and neck tire and they tend to revert to a relaxed, comfortable position focused on center.

Upstage side areas are seldom used for an episode unless they contain elevations, for in addition to being weak, they are frequently blocked by furniture. Occasionally they are used for actions which the director wishes to conceal partially, as when Oscar slaps Birdie in *The Little Foxes.* A double purpose is served in this scene by the use of the side area, for Oscar's blow can be faked there more readily, and the emotional shock of its surprise overshadows the physical action.

The director need not invariably place the important conversations at downstage center, and the least important ones in the weakest areas. Rather, he can afford to put effective dialogues at the side or upstage, and can depend upon the episodes themselves to command attention. He may put them right or left of center deliberately in order to prevent a preliminary climax overshadowing a major one which is approaching. He may bring the episodes which are least theatrically effective to the strongest areas in order to increase their impact. In *The Little Foxes,* the episode of Horace's heart attack is strong enough to be played at the side, but that in which Ben and Oscar persuade Leo to steal the bonds needs every help that position can give it.

If center stage is used repeatedly, an episode played at the side or back may obtain extra attention through variety. On the other hand, decreasing importance is suggested when a group of characters moves from center to one side. In anticipation of such a shift, the director may during the preceding dialogue move a key character to the side position so that the others make strongly motivated movements to join him there, and thus conceal the shift of focus from a strong to a weaker area.

Variety, so important in all phases of direction, can be obtained by irregular alterna-tion between the use of the full stage and of the restricted areas, and between the different small areas. For maximum variety in stage position, all actors in an episode played in a restricted area are kept within it, because spreading actors into other nearby areas reduces their value in terms of variety when they are used for subsequent episodes. This consideration does not apply to the upstage side areas because they are so seldom used for dialogue that any use of them contributes to variety. Nor does this prevent the use of a limited space which includes the proximate ends of two basic areas, for this in itself provides variety (illustrated in Figure 54). John van Druten's direction of *The Voice of the Turtle* maintained vitality and interest through its long dialogues by notable variety in playing positions and the way in which various areas were combined and overlapped. Undoubtedly the variety of areas provided by an Elizabethan stage compensated for the monotony of the permanent setting. A modern director similarly finds the many scenes in plays of this period helpful in securing variety of playing positions for the numerous episodes. He may need to employ benches or other furniture at the sides to counteract the natural impulse of experienced actors to move to the optical center of an open area.

The design of a setting containing two or more rooms is related to this matter of the placement of scenes. Ordinarily it is poor design to have the dividing wall at center, for that prevents the use of stage center as a playing area, and it provides a continuous strain on the spectators by making them keep their heads turned to one side or the other. Well-designed split stages can be seen in photographs of *The Voice of the Turtle, The World We Make, Awake and Sing, She Loves Me Not,* and Robert Edmond Jones's setting for *The Iceman Cometh,* which was shifted from side to side for the different acts in order to allow each room in turn to fill two-thirds of the stage, and so to allow use of center stage in all acts. Less successful was his setting for *Anna Christie,* and the settings for many noncommercial productions of the plays mentioned.

Subordination

The director sometimes wants to reduce the importance of a character, a speech, or an episode. Examples of speeches which need to be subordinated were cited in the discussion on volume. Elsewhere, devices by which actors can be psychologically concealed — e.g., by relating them to setting and furniture — have been suggested.

In discussing the director's analysis of the play, it was pointed out that the playwright occasionally gives undue emphasis to an episode. Some of these episodes can be subordinated by playing them in a weak area. Some can be de-emphasized by playing them as introspective musings, and so removing from them any sense of immediacy or necessary connection with the plot. Some can be weakened in effect by the nature of the transition with which they terminate. If, at the end of a strongly played episode, the characters, or all the characters except the protagonist of the episode, make complete physical transitions, and turn their attention to something else, this is notice to the audience that the dialogue has made no lasting impression on these characters and suggests that the reaction of the audience should be the same.

Subordination of a character is ordinarily accomplished by directing attention elsewhere. It is the same technique as that of the stage "magician" who uses his words, his gaze, and his pose to hold the attention of the audience on his right hand, ostentatiously turning it back and forth to show that nothing is concealed in his palm or on the back, while his seemingly relaxed, and unnoticed, left hand slips from his pocket the ball or card which will miraculously materialize in his right hand as soon as he can transfer it there under cover of some other distracting ruse.

An almost identical technique has been used in the laundry scene of *The World We Make* to reduce the number of stage properties. A large cast of extras ironed and folded towels, sheets, and clothing, accenting by purposeful movements the active pantomime of folding and ironing; and then, casually, smoothly, and without emphasis, unfolded the pieces and started again.

Margaret Webster prided herself on not cutting a line in the production of the full-length *Hamlet,* but feared a laugh on "Something is rotten in the state of Denmark," which she says "audiences think is the funniest line in the whole of Shakespeare." Since she did not want to omit it, she smothered it in a roll of drums offstage.

Strong and weak positions are constantly used for emphasis and subordination. The second proposal scene in *Abe Lincoln in Illinois* uses a pattern similar to the one in *I Remember Mama* previously mentioned, alternately emphasizing and subordinating the two characters involved. At the beginning of the scene, audience interest is focused about equally on learning the purpose of Abe's visit and on Mary Todd's reaction to him — i.e., at their first meeting since he deserted her a few hours before their wedding. So the director places them on a line midstage, with Abe humble and apologetic, and Mary excited but steeling herself to appear calm. Abe's intention is soon clear to both Mary and the audience, and interest then is concentrated on Mary, whose reactions the audience should see as fully as possible. Mary, wanting to hide her emotions from Abe, uses a casual speech as a pretext to turn and walk away. This allows her to move slowly downstage in deep thought. She gets almost sole attention from her nearly open position and by her downstage movement. Lincoln is almost forgotten

SUBORDINATION OF MINOR CHARACTERS

Figure 56. In order to emphasize one character at a key moment on a proscenium stage, the others can be subordinated most easily by having them turn upstage.

SUBORDINATION OF MINOR CHARACTERS

Figure 57. Emphasis and subordination on the conventional stage can be achieved in a great variety of ways.

during this movement, though he continues to speak. (See Figure 47, page 351.)

Emphasis should then be thrown back to him during the inner struggle while he frames the new proposal of marriage. Mary times her movement so that she subordinates herself at this moment by turning her back three-quarters to the audience as she circles the downstage end of a settee. She rests her upstage hand on the back of the settee to prepare for an upstage turn on her next motivation. This position (facing slightly upstage), far from limiting her expressiveness, takes the attention off her face, which Mary has learned to keep impassive; and focuses it on the pose of her head and shoulders lifted in triumph as she hears the proposal. When Abe suggests that it may humiliate her to take him back after his desertion, she swings around in a sharp, attention-catching movement and contradicts him across the settee. Then as she demands assurances of his political intentions, the settee, set at a slant, forces her forward-motivated movements to guide her upstage, so that she is well upstage and in a highly open position for her final question and her acceptance. Abe meanwhile is subordinated as he more and more faces upstage. Mary makes a strong diagonal movement downstage to clasp him in her arms for her final speech: "Whatever becomes of the two of us, I'll die loving you!" Only then does Lincoln regain attention as he turns to profile while he awkwardly puts his arms around her.

STYLE

In the theatre, style is apparent in scenery, costume, make-up, and all other parts of the visual environment, and is evidenced in all phases of the visual and auditory patterns of acting. Among the auditory characteristics, articulation, pronunciation, tempo, inflection, accentuation, quality, and key are the ones most amenable to the influence of style. When all these factors are in the same style, the play gives a uniform and distinctive impression.

Every object and every action has style in the broadest meaning of the word. One usually pays attention to the style of an object or an action, however, only when it is of a recognizable mode or fashion. Since one does not think of utilitarian objects or of accustomed actions in such terms, one is oblivious to their style. Yet they all have "utilitarian" or "contemporary naturalistic" style. All the participants give attention to it when a play is produced in a distinctive style such as expressionism or the relatively unfamiliar style of an historical period; the director watches and listens closely in order to call the attention of the actors to any contemporary gestures, movements, and inflectional patterns which are inconsistent with it. The most obvious example, perhaps, is that no "lady" crossed her legs prior to 1917, whereas today she may cross them and still keep her place in society.

A director, however, sometimes attempts to "avoid any style," and the production is a hodgepodge, without the audience or the theatre staff knowing quite why. That which is thought to be without style actually contains a considerable range of style. Each year, for example, even women's house dresses or coverall aprons have distinctive lines which are related to the contemporary fashion silhouette. Some of the details of dressmaking which change year by year are the neck and collar lines; the length of the bodice, the skirt, and the sleeve; the way in which the sleeve is set in; the amount of fullness at the bust, the hips, and the hemline; the texture, the pattern, and the color of the material; and the decoration. There is a range of choice for the costume period of *I Remember Mama, The Playboy of the Western World,* or *The Great Big Doorstep,* but to dress the characters in mere "old clothes" is likely to produce as bad a motley as the mixing of clothes of several historical periods. Instead, the clothes must be selected and altered carefully for consistency, or for meaningful inconsistency.

Consistent kitchen furniture for *Our Town* is no more simple to gather than consistent costumes, for all furniture has style, usually an imitation or modification of a period style. Any one of a variety of such styles can be used for *Our Town,* but a heterogeneous collection is not satisfactory.

Just as with costumes and furniture, styles in gesture vary also, and are controlled partly by the clothing and partly by the general spirit of the time. For example, women's clothes of the late twenties made the ugliest combination of lines which has so far been conceived by the fashion experts. The joints of the human body have grace and beauty only when a reasonable amount of the contiguous parts of the body can be seen, giving them a utilitarian significance. A joint is ugly when seen alone; half a joint is uglier than a whole joint. The styles of the twenties exposed half a knee joint, half a shoulder joint, and half of the articulation of the neck with the torso, unrelieved by even a ruffle or other decoration. The waistline was dropped so low that it became a tight band at mid-thigh with the hips bulging above it, the natural waist producing an unfashionable break in the theoretically straight line from shoulder to thigh. With this awkwardness inherent in the dress, unity of style was achieved only by cultivating a corresponding awkwardness of gesture and posture, emphasizing elbows, knees, hips, and shoulders by jutting them out asymmetrically.

The manner of that period is typified by a John Held drawing of a flapper with a hip protruding on one side and a shoulder and knee on the other, manipulating a cocktail shaker from side to side instead of up and down so as to extend the elbows as far as possible from the body. This style was re-produced for comic effect in the revue *Lend an Ear,* while *Gentlemen Prefer Blondes* "prettified" it by compromising with the contemporary mode. This period is nearer to caricature than any other of recent years, yet it indicates the way in which gesture and posture styles change even within a few years, for it was followed immediately by one of graceful style. In 1954, the fashion of larger hips, and decorative fullness to emphasize them, encouraged an asymmetrical posture of the hips which would have been awkward and unstylish in the slim-hip styles which preceded it. When large hats are stylish, women's posture improves through the need to hold the hats at the proper angle. Men's styles change less conspicuously, but the extensive shoulder padding worn after World War II made men aware of the contrast to their natural shoulder width when they wore unpadded sports clothes, and tended to make them throw their shoulders back and out. Thus, the fashion of the clothes of any period has a strong influence upon gesture, movement, and pose, and in a pre-modern period these often can be deduced from the clothes.

Vocal factors also are subject to period style. Soft, well-modulated, "refined" voices were admired in conservative periods such as the nineties and the early years of this century as opposed to the more blatant twenties. The mannered and self-conscious literary style of the Restoration and the eighteenth century must have been reflected in a similar mannered preciseness of articulation and of inflection.

Any type of vocal or visual stimulus can be styled consciously in a production if the actors and the director give their attention to it. Once alerted to it, the actors find opportunities provided by the script for its use.

Therefore, the director does not attempt to produce a play with "no style," but rather selects a specific style, even if it is merely the simplest contemporary, utilitarian style.

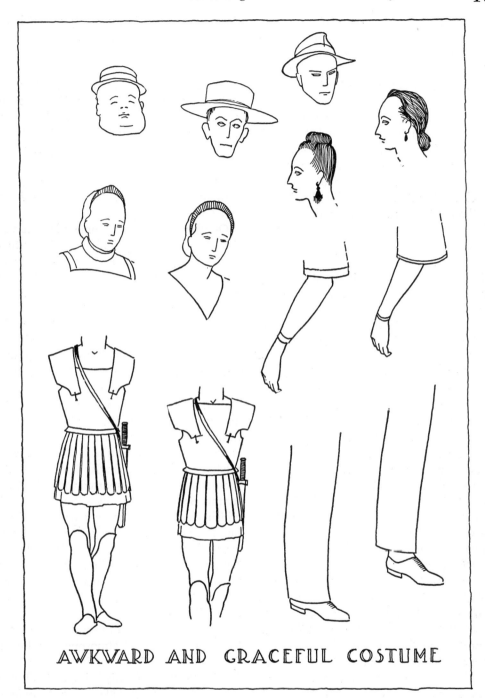

AWKWARD AND GRACEFUL COSTUME

Figure 58. Joints are attractive only when we see enough of the contiguous parts of the body to appreciate their utilitarian function.

He may find it expedient to say to a cast, "We'll use no particular style in this production," because that is clearer than to say, "We'll play this in a contemporary naturalistic style." The latter might produce self-conscious and even forced attempts to "be natural," for it may be as surprising to the cast to learn that their normal behavior is "naturalistic," as it was to the *bourgeois gentilhomme* of Molière's play to discover that he spoke "prose" spontaneously.

A deliberate mixture of styles also is possible, though it requires extreme definiteness on the part of the actors in order to demonstrate to the audience that it is intentional and not accidental. The sentimental and the sophisticated scenes of eighteenth-century plays can be played in contrasting acting styles. The comic plots in Shakespeare's plays often are acted in a much broader style than the romantic plots. Directors often ask for serious playing of some scenes in nineteenth-century melodramas and burlesque treatment of others. Occasionally voice and action are contrasted, as in a Restoration play in which the dialogue may be spoken with great delicacy, while the vulgarity of the action is emphasized. Scenery and acting may be seemingly inconsistent. Very broad farce such as *Boy Meets Girl* is often given representational settings to emphasize the absurdities by contrast. Thornton Wilder has shown in *Our Town* and *The Happy Journey to Camden and Trenton* that the conventionalized absence of scenery does not interfere with "natural" acting. The musicals *A Connecticut Yankee* and *DuBarry Was a Lady* contrast genuine period style with the eccentric behavior of a modern man transported to a former age.

Every script has an inherent and distinctive style, and one of the tasks of study and rehearsal by actor, director, and designer is to appreciate this essential style and to realize it in performance. Yet certain generalizations can be made about style which can serve as a starting point for study.

Locale

Locale is one of the factors which influence style. Many plays of family life calling for representational playing can be laid in almost any community in the United States, and can be played in contemporary dress despite an earlier date of authorship. A few of these are *The Family Upstairs, Junior Miss, The First Year, Three-Cornered Moon,* and *Craig's Wife.*

On the other hand, some plays have a definite locale or period, and, in spite of universality of meaning, any change in the time or place produces inconsistencies. *Our Town* is laid in Vermont in 1901. The New England environment is vital to the play. The two mothers are characterized within the stereotype of the cold, reserved New Englander who is averse to showing affection, even toward her own children. Their sharpness in speaking to the children, their embarrassment at even a hint of affection, and particularly Mrs. Webb's inability to talk intimately with Emily when she asks if she is pretty, are amusing yet affecting when related to the New England mores. But if these women are transported to the Midwest, to the South, or to any other community which traditionally has a more affectionate family atmosphere, they lose sympathy because they seem to be more irritable than the average mother, while some of their repressions border on the neurotic. Similarly, the courting, wedding, and graveyard scenes are indigenous to New England.

The director therefore establishes as positive a New England atmosphere as he can. Sectional accent is the easiest device to use for this purpose. If this is impractical, more reliance has to be placed on other techniques. He asks the actors to exaggerate straightness and firmness of posture, economy of gestures, and even stiffness and awkwardness. He asks that the costumes be plainer and the colors duller than if the cast were able to speak with a Vermont accent.

Some plays must be laid in a specific town or locality because of vital topical references or conditions peculiar to the locale, as in *Tobacco Road, Mamba's Daughters, The Philadelphia Story, Tovarich,* and . . . *one third of a nation.* . . .

Except for these specifically localized plays, the importance of establishing locale varies with the play. The Southern roots of most of the plays by Tennessee Williams explain special traits of some of his characters. Similarly, in *The Little Foxes,* Birdie Hubbard must be recognized as a Southerner, but it is less important with the other characters because their motivations are similar to those found in people of other sections of the country. Lillian Hellman chose the locale chiefly because industrial development occurred more recently in the South than elsewhere. Her *Another Part of the Forest,* using the same characters, is more innately Southern.

Awake and Sing, Golden Boy, Having Wonderful Time, and *The Gentle People* require that most of the characters speak one of the borough dialects of New York City. Other plays which — by the circumstances of the play or the attitude of the characters — are laid in New York or in some other metropolis include *The Women, Paris Bound, Biography, John Loves Mary,* and *Accent on Youth.* However, the characterizations and motivations are so unlocalized that it does not disturb an audience to have them played in the dialect of the community in which the play is performed.

The characters in *The Male Animal* are Midwestern in their mental attitudes, and so would seem out of place in New England, New York, or parts of the South. Similarly, *Seventeen, Alien Corn, The Star-Wagon,* and

Lightnin' require a small-town Western or Midwestern setting. *The Late Christopher Bean, Ethan Frome, Icebound,* and *Alison's House* require New England atmosphere. Most British plays need thorough revision of the dialogue if they are to be transferred to an American locale.

On the other hand, casual references to exact locales are sometimes almost accidental. *Ah, Wilderness!, Craig's Wife, On Borrowed Time, One Sunday Afternoon,* and *Ladies of the Jury* can be laid in a small town in any section of the country. Since he can do so without damage to the spirit of the play, the director may elect to substitute fictitious place names for the specific ones in the script in order to avoid dialectal inconsistency between them and the local accent.

What has been said here of dialect is equally applicable to other vocal and visual habits.

Period

An impression of period is the usual goal of directorial attention given to style. The designers assume the responsibility for this in so far as the scenic environment and the costumes are concerned. The actor is responsible for the style of his performance, but, unless the director has an extraordinarily learned cast, he needs to assist the actors in the matter of style. In any case, he decides how accurately the period manner is to be reproduced, and whether it is to be treated seriously, is to be treated flippantly and satirically, or is to be burlesqued.

Period costumes are not necessarily attractive or convincing when worn on a modern figure. If, for example, an actress puts on a 1900 gored skirt, a stiff shirtwaist, and a man's hard straw hat, without adjusting her posture to them, she looks the height of dowdiness. Yet photographs taken in that period show by the pose and carriage of the women that they thought themselves beautiful and knew themselves to be dressed in the acme of fashion. While that style may not be attractive to modern eyes, it does entail a skillful display of the human body without distorting it unduly, an achievement which is one of the goals of fashion. When the actress learns to stand extremely erect, to throw her hips back, and to arch her chest, she and the costume acquire the style of the period and become visually related.

Our knowledge of period gesture, movement, and vocal expression is based upon conjecture from dependable evidence. Paintings, drawings, etchings, and many artifacts such as china, pottery, and decorative metal pieces picture the costumes and poses of the various historical periods. The clothes indicate the actions and gestures which the wearers could and could not make, and the poses in the paintings give a good picture of the habitual attitude and posture of the people of the period. Their gestures and movements can be conjectured, for the muscle tensions of the body reveal which gestures are climactic and which are not.

Types of vocal expression are associated with types of gesture, movement, and attitude. This is a valid assumption, because the muscles of the body tend to tense sympathetically. Strong gestures and movements are accompanied almost inevitably by strong vocal expression, and small, self-conscious gestures are likely to be accompanied by equally self-conscious and mannered vocal expression.

Certain conclusions, then, can be formed about the manners of a period, but they cannot be exact. If each actor forms his own opinion, there is likely to be a wide divergence of style among the cast. So the director makes the choice, and selects the basic qualities of style to be used by the company as a whole, but permits individual variations stemming from characterization.

Decision on style is particularly important when the date of authorship of the play is more recent than the date of the action, because historical perspective often produces special viewpoints. The same historical figures from the court of Henry VIII must be played with widely different manners when they appear in *Anne of the Thousand Days, Master of the Revels,* the motion picture of *The Private Life of Henry VIII,* and Shakespeare's play about the same Henry. Even more strikingly different are the Cleopatras of Shakespeare, Dryden, and Shaw, and the Joan of Arcs of Shakespeare, Schiller, and Shaw.

Historical acting style used in modern productions is usually modified to make it more readily acceptable to a modern audience. The most distinctive period style which can be viewed now in a pure, unmodified form is that developed by the actors in silent motion pictures. To modern eyes, that kind of acting seems overobvious and the actors overexplicit. This was thoroughly acceptable to audiences habituated to the silent films, and was accepted as a conventional substitution of visual stimuli for the missing auditory stimuli. It seems comically exaggerated now when a different set of conventions has been adopted for the talking pictures.

Type of Play

Style used in a production is influenced also by the type of play. The grander, the more self-conscious, and the more cultivated styles of pose, gesture, movement, vocal quality, and inflection are employed in the classic tragedies and high comedies of a period, while the simpler style of the common people of the day is used in melodramas and farces. Though all eighteenth-century style has basic similarity, that used in *The School for Scandal* is much more extreme than that for *The Rivals,* and the same author's *The Critic* introduces an additional element of burlesque of acting style. This is equally true of the varying types of plays in any period, including the modern.

Though the visual stimuli are influenced by the type of play, this has an even greater influence upon the voice and speech characteristics. Articulation and pronunciation vary widely, from meticulous accuracy in high comedies such as *The Way of the World, The Relapse, Private Lives,* and *Ring Round the Moon,* to the inconspicuous articulation of the actualistic problem play. Eccentric speech is used for characterization in farce, both modern and pre-modern. "Stage speech" is often used for high comedy laid in any period, because it seems a self-conscious speech to many American ears, and so suggests the artificiality of manner found in many of these comedies. High comedy and farce are alike in using strong contrasts in tempo; serious drama is more likely to use a consistent one. Accentuation is strongest and most abrupt in farce and melodrama; romantic and classic tragedy use a strong accent, but one which is more smoothly modulated. High comedy, being intellectual, makes its accents almost exclusively by inflection.

Most acting today employs oral voice quality, with some use of other qualities for characterization. Even romantic and classic tragedies and melodramas are often played with this voice quality, though some productions attempt the orotund quality. The most conspicuous uses of minor key for purposes of style are in the dreamy plays of Maeterlinck, in the strongly illusionistic plays of Chekhov and Gorki, and in the dramas of other playwrights who have been influenced by a representational technique.

Inflection is the most useful vocal factor for creating style. All forms of drama, except those in a representational style, tend to use extreme inflectional patterns. High comedies are distinguished from other forms of drama by a preponderance of the circumflex and other intricate inflectional patterns with which the characters treat words and phrases playfully. Few other general dicta can be given on the use of melody, but distinctive inflectional patterns are found in every play as the actors rehearse the language of the play. They are inherent in the text by reason of the choice and the order of the words employed. So actors cannot avoid these patterns, though they have the choice of restricting or extending them. The patterns can be appreciated most immediately in dialect plays like *I Remember Mama, Papa Is All, Juno and the Paycock,* and *Abie's Irish Rose,* but rehearsals soon reveal it in *Golden Boy, The Glass Menagerie, The Lady's not for Burning, All My Sons,* and *Bernardine.*

ATMOSPHERE

Atmosphere can be defined as the emotional tone of a performance. The spectator receives from it an impression which produces a corresponding mood in him. Atmospheres, and their corresponding moods, are identified verbally by the prevailing emotion evoked, as "gay," "sad," "morose," "ominous," "tragic." A play has an overall atmosphere, though in a good play it is distinctive and complex and cannot be stereotyped by one of these easy adjectives. Each of its episodes has an atmosphere. This ordinarily is a variation within the general one of the play, but it can be in contrast to the general atmosphere. Shakespeare uses low comedy scenes in this way, such as those of the Gravedigger, Osric, and sometimes Polonius in *Hamlet;* the Nurse in *Romeo and Juliet;* and Oswald in *King Lear* — just as he uses broad farce for contrast with light comedy in *Twelfth Night, The Two Gentlemen of Verona,* and *Much Ado About Nothing.* Episodes sometimes reinforce the main atmosphere by ironic contrast. Ibsen used gay moments in this way in *A Doll's House, The Wild Duck,* and *John Gabriel Borkman.* Shakespeare in *The Merchant of Venice* alternates serious scenes involving Shylock with light scenes concerning the choice of the caskets and low comedy ones involving Launcelot Gobbo, and then adopts an entirely new atmosphere in the idyllic last act.

All the types of visual and auditory stimuli can be patterned to reinforce a particular emotional tone. Ordinarily the director plans considerable variety within the range permitted by the general atmosphere, but sometimes he seeks consistency, as in the short Maeterlinck plays in which an emotional tone is the chief factor of interest. A few thorough examples can best illustrate this point.

For example, to suggest lighthearted gaiety, as typified by parts of *As You Like It*, *Lysistrata*, *The Importance of Being Earnest*, and *Peter Pan*, the director may attempt within the limits of feasibility to make every type of stimulus contribute to that effect. The actors adopt light and elevated poses, with all emphasis placed at the top of the figure. The visible support of the body is minimized, either by raising one leg to remove it from support, or by placing one leg behind the other to give the impression of a single one. When feasible, the actors stand on their toes rather than on the full foot. They sit on tables, on chair backs, or on other elevations rather than on chairs or on the floor. They are distributed over the entire stage area and kept as far from one another as the action permits. Full, graceful gestures are employed, but with no hint of strain. They are made at shoulder height or above, and, when possible, are sustained as poses. Representational gestures, and other reminders of familiar movements and objects, are avoided. The actors use many light, quick movements, with fast physical transitions. In ascending movements on levels, they emphasize both the upward movements and the height of the level.

Openings in the setting are made as large as possible; they are placed high, and widened at the top. Many levels are used, and are so arranged that the actors can make swooping ascents and remain poised at the top of their flights. The movements back to the floor level are made inconspicuously, or with the effect of floating. The floor plan allows complete freedom of movement. Furniture is reduced to the minimum, and is delicate in design. The background carries out this feeling of lightness and height.[1] The emphasis of the design is kept off the floor. Suspended objects are highly effective, the ultimate device of this kind being the flying actors of *Peter Pan*. Occult balance, or unbalance, sometimes suggests a gayer effect than symmetrical balance, though the latter is restful and disclaims tension.

Colors are gay, preferably in pure tints. Lighting is bright, and highly colored, with few shadows — plasticity being obtained by color contrasts rather than by light and shadow. Draped costumes are of light, thin material. Fitted costumes are as tight as possible to reveal an unrestricted body. Long skirts are thin and very full, or are so bouffant that they seem to float in the air; they are lifted or kicked as much as possible. Feathers, ribbons, veils, and scarves are used for their floating quality. The emphasis of the costume is placed high, with the chief decoration at the shoulder or in the headdress.

The actors use relatively low volume, but sufficient so that the listeners do not have to strain to hear; higher pitches than the average, with wide and rapid inflections; the lighter voice qualities; accurate but unstrained articulations and pronunciations; a major key; a rapid rate, but with variety of tempo; few pauses; little emphasis upon ar-

[1] Transparent scenery, or skeleton scenery, is ideal. Two-dimensional scenery stresses lightness and unreality; cutout scenery, standing or hanging, is preferable to flat backdrops.

ticulation; and many contrasts. Music and sound effects are used liberally.

Exaggeration suggests lightheartedness and the satiric spirit, so exaggeration of vocal expression, gestures, movements, costume, scenery, lighting, and make-up are employed generally. Transitions of all kinds are rapid.

Otherwise similar plays like *The Way of the World, The Play's the Thing, Three-Cornered Moon,* and *Arms and the Man* are handicapped by requiring actualistic scenery, stiff period costumes, or acting in a "natural" style. In these cases, the director uses as many of the techniques as the script permits, and either minimizes the inconsistent features, or uses them for comic contrast. The contrast may even increase the effectiveness of the techniques which are used. The lovers and fairies of *A Midsummer Night's Dream,* for example, take on added piquancy when they must sleep on the ground in Elizabethan farthingales and padded hose, provided they learn to handle them gracefully.

To use an extreme contrast as a second example, a director may want an atmosphere of gloom and depression for a play or an episode, preparing the audience for tragedy or catastrophe. Plays which require this mood, in varying degrees or in some episodes, include *The Lower Depths, Riders to the Sea, John Gabriel Borkman, Winterset, Here Come the Clowns, The Dybbuk, In Abraham's Bosom, The Weavers,* and *Ethan Frome.* Within the limitations of the script, the director uses various combinations of the following techniques.

Shoulders and chests are drooped; the head is carried low and forward to reduce the height, in addition to giving a sagging line; and eyes stare at the floor hopelessly. When an actor is standing, the feet are separated with the weight distributed on both. The characters preferably sit or lie. The seats of the chairs are low, but the characters sit, when they can, on doorsteps, curbs, and other still lower objects. Postures are fixed and unvarying whether the actor is standing or sitting, as though the bodies had ossified. The actors are grouped compactly like cattle huddling together in a storm, unless dispersed positions as a sign of their emotional isolation better suggest the atmosphere. Episodes are played in restricted areas. Characters are related to furniture and to scenic elements so that they seem to blend with them and become inanimate likewise.

Movements are held to a minimum, are made with apparent effort, and are in economical, straight lines, unless the character is wandering. They are slow, heavy, and suggestive of weight, exhaustion, and desperation. Feet are dragged as though there is insufficient strength to lift them. Gestures are made chiefly below the waist level, and emphasis is placed upon their downward phase. For example, an actor sits slowly and with concentrated attention on the action, and continues the movement until he becomes relaxed into seeming immobility. He rises either as inconspicuously as possible, or accomplishes it with great physical effort, using his arms to lift his body. If levels are used, emphasis is on the descending movements, or on the physical effort required for an ascent.

Doors are few, and are so low that the characters have to duck their heads when they pass through. Windows are small, and are either low or placed high in the walls to suggest that the room is partly underground. Few elevations are used, except for long flights of steep, narrow stairs. Furniture is heavy, large, and uncomfortable; either bareness or overcrowding is emphasized. All scenic elements are kept low, broad, and thick. In outdoor settings, foliage hangs comparably low, and the branches of trees are low and twisted. Other twisted and tortured lines are employed. Unless the drama has classic balance, the stage is not balanced formally, and may be unbalanced deliberately to suggest lack of plan. Lighting is spotty and highly directional, so as to throw shadows on the setting, and so that part of the actor's body remains in shadow even when he faces the source of the light. There is little color in the lighting, and the color is in the cool range, except when a few streaks of bright sunlight are used for contrast. Scenery and costumes are dark in value and dull in color.

The costumes emphasize shortness and heaviness in the figures. The materials are coarse, heavy, and voluminous. Clothes hang rather than fit; men's coats are unbuttoned, their shirts hang outside the trousers; women wear aprons and shawls to give additional downward lines. Garments have narrow shoulders and the head coverings are tight — shawls for the women worn over low tight hairdresses, and caps rather than hats for the men. These combine to produce the effect of a wedge standing on its broad base instead of on its point as in the example of gaiety. Make-ups emphasize the downward lines and sagging flesh; they are dark in color and use dull rather than bright lining colors.

The volume of the speech is low. Low pitches predominate in almost uninflected monotones. The key is minor. The voices emphasize harsh and rumbling qualities, with some variety obtained by aspirate tones and nasal whines. Articulation is slighted, and dialectal pronunciation is adopted. The rate of speech is consistently slow, interrupted by long pauses. Accentuation is kept to the minimum, except when it is hysterical. All vocal contrasts are kept at a minimum. Music and sound effects are as dissonant, discordant, and harsh as can be justified.

Lest the audience dismiss so depressing an effect as unnatural and exaggerated, every element of unreality — in characterization, speech, and action, as well as in scenery, properties, and costumes — must be rigorously excluded. In any case, such unmiti-gated gloom is seldom employed on the stage, because the interest of the audience can be held on such a depressing atmosphere for only a few minutes, and it requires brilliant playwriting and fine acting to make an effective impression. Even in *The Lower Depths,* Gorki varies the mood with character comedy to prevent monotony. Hauptmann's *The Weavers* uses a revolutionary figure and constant change of setting to relieve the extreme gloom established in some of the episodes.

Furthermore, gloom is not the consistent atmosphere of tragedy. The prevailing mood at the beginning of a tragedy is often one of vitality — even gaiety. Sometimes the hero is a participant in the gaiety, with no foreshadowing of the fate in store for him; sometimes he is a figure apart, and the gaiety is contrasted with his gloom. The first court scene of *Hamlet* uses the latter mode, though the audience has been prepared for tragedy by the ominous opening scene on the platform. *King Lear* starts with pompous splendor as Lear happily distributes the responsibilities of his kingdom and prepares to retire to a jovial life with his favorite daughter. During the scene he banishes Kent and Cordelia in the growing irascibility of a stubborn and proud old man. The root of the tragedy is here, but there is little hint of its violence, and at Lear's next entrance he is still the virile, active, boisterous octogenarian roaring good-naturedly for his dinner and his court jester after a day spent on horseback.

Greek tragedies seldom present this atmosphere of gloom, for they are raised above, and set apart from, life by many presentational elements, including verse, a speaking chorus, and expositional rather than dramatic action. If the protagonist dies, he meets death courageously and not cravenly. Ibsen's dramas usually begin on a light note. Modern serious plays such as those of Anderson, Hellman, Rice, and Williams seldom open with a depressing episode.

The possible atmospheres of plays and of episodes are innumerable, particularly when the protagonist or a group of characters is contrasted with others. The director finds a different pattern of atmosphere in each play, ordinarily one less radical than either of the extremes discussed above. But the same principles apply in all cases. He seldom plans as analytically as these examples suggest; but, with a keen impression, nevertheless, of the flavor of the exact mood he desires from his performance, he may "intuitively" work out a pattern equally precise.

PICTURIZATION

Picturization in the theatre is the sum of the individual stimuli supplied at each moment by the actors and the design, whether they are static or in motion; but the audience ordinarily responds to the summation without analyzing it into specific contributing stimuli. This is most obvious in mob scenes, but it is equally true when the actors are individualized. Much of the tea scene of *First Lady,* and several episodes of *Stage Door,* are planned for a general effect, rather than for attention to the separate factors.

The director plans the combination of visual stimuli for each moment of the play — he arranges the actors in meaningful relation to one another and to the design, and has the actors adjust their poses, gestures, and movements to make the combination dramatically meaningful. These group arrangements are called "stage pictures." Alexander Dean's term, "picturization," is better because it suggests movements as well as static groupings, and includes design. Most of the photographs reproduced in this volume were chosen for their meaningful picturization.

Among the more obvious uses of picturization are the grouping of characters to show their sympathies and oppositions, to show their dominance or subordination, to indicate their strength or weakness, and to dramatize

alterations of these by changes of position. Many examples of picturization have been discussed in other connections: the changes in relative dominance between Abe Lincoln and Mary Todd in the second proposal scene; the oration scene of *Julius Caesar;* the use of the sofa to maintain the psychological influence of Dr. Sloper in *The Heiress* after his death; the sofa "throne" of Mrs. Phelps in *The Silver Cord;* and the selection of backgrounds against which to play the scenes of *Dead End.*

The director strives for the unattainable ideal of picturizing the motivations, character relationships, and actions so clearly as to make them understandable to a deaf person or to one who does not understand the language. This can become overly self-conscious and a source of distraction, as the mode of acting and direction of silent motion pictures seems to a modern audience.

In nonrealistic plays, the director uses picturization frankly as a convention, and thus invites audience attention to it. In the actualistic play, the director composes his action with equal care, but he conceals the technique, and obtains his effects through less obvious stimuli. "Natural" motivation is sought for each position, move, gesture, and pose. This handicaps the director in some ways, but the director of such a play has available other conventional techniques for manipulating his actors into desired positions with almost as much freedom as in more presentational plays. The audience has been habituated by the stage and screen to the acceptance of superfluous illusionistic business "to fill out the action." Without breaking the illusion for a modern audience, an actor can move clear across the stage to get a cigarette or a match, to light another's cigarette, to drop a cigarette in an ashtray or a fireplace, to put down a teacup, to mix a drink, or to get a handkerchief from a handbag left far across the stage in complete defiance of natural action. Gertrude Lawrence, in playing *Susan and God,* spent her first fifteen minutes on stage in perpetual animation. The movement was "motivated" by her adjustments of a trailing orange chiffon scarf, and by conveying accessories to and from a purse which she left on a piano as she entered in order to be able to return to that upstage center position whenever she pleased. Though the audience was aware of the hectic movement, her skill as an actress allowed her to seem impromptu in her general pattern of movement, and still give explicit picturization to each line.

Unless special attention is drawn to stage pictures, the audience responds to their meaning without being aware of them except for a few times during the play. It sees the opening picture as the curtain rises. The final grouping is fixed in its memory by the interruption of a blackout or a curtain, and it may become aware of the picture when a new figure enters the action, or as a figure leaves the stage with a dramatic movement. The audience is likely to be aware of the picture also during any moment of suspended action. A sharp accentuation by some sudden visual or auditory stimulus, like an off-stage pistol shot, the opening of huge doors, or an abrupt reversal of the direction of an actor's movement may fix the visual pattern in consciousness whether or not the action stops. A spectator whose attention wanders from the immediate action may at any moment give his attention to the stage picture before him as a whole or in detail, so any picture may by chance be noted as such by any spectator. Movement, as well as static pose, has picturization meaning.

Casting is frequently influenced by the director's sense of picturization. Audiences tend to feel protectively sympathetic toward the innocent little girl and the naive young man. The sympathy increases if the girl is beautiful and the man handsome. In general, the larger the girl, and the stronger and more self-possessed the man, the less protective the audience feels, though admiration and respect may replace it, and sympathy may continue. This trait of audiences accounts for the casting of tiny Helen Hayes to play the extremely tall Mary Stuart [2] in *Mary of Scotland* instead of assigning the part to a taller actress like Katharine Cornell or Blanche Yurka. Maxwell Anderson portrays Mary as a woman of dignity and queenliness, who fights a losing battle against opposition and against her own emotions. An audience feels sorry for a small, weak woman who is unequal to a political struggle, and who is led by her emotions into wrong decisions; but it expects a large, strong woman to be able to take care of herself and to control her emotions.

"Mr. Money-Bags," an enormously fat, paunchy man, is the accepted cartoon symbol for capitalism. Playwrights often use this symbol. Directors add symbolization of their own by casting an actor with such physical characteristics for nonsymbolic parts; or they avoid the type in order to prevent the audience from attaching wrong symbolic meaning to the character. Before the motion pictures typed Sydney Greenstreet as a villain, his physical resemblance to the capitalistic stereotype caused momentary confusion when he played Uncle Waldemar, the organist, in *There Shall Be No Night* and the experimental biologist in *Idiot's Delight.* Once the audience recognized that he was not playing the stereotype, his figure and mannerisms added interest to the characterizations.

"Traditional stage business" is a phase of picturization which refers to actions which have been invented by actors to illustrate certain lines in the standard and classic repertory and which have become associated with the line through repeated use. A few

---

[2] Brooks Atkinson in his initial review of the play refers to her as six feet tall. The writer has been unable to find proof of the exact height, but has found much confirmation of her exceptional height.

examples illustrate the type of picturization which the director can invent to clarify and intensify the action.

Launcelot Gobbo, in dramatizing the argument between his conscience and "the fiend" in *The Merchant of Venice*, traditionally personifies them by his feet, though actors experiment with other devices — Romney Brent in the George Arliss production used two water jugs. In *A Midsummer Night's Dream* Quince puts red paint on Thisbe's mantle in preparation for Pyramus' line, "What? Stained with blood?" In the same play, Pyramus' sword refuses to come out of the scabbard when he is to kill himself, and he finally stabs himself with the scabbard. He lies on the sword when he dies, causing Thisbe to run around the stage looking for it and calling, "Come, blade," when her turn comes for suicide, and Pyramus has to hand her the sword. This time, to the amazement of all, the sword comes out of the scabbard easily. When Dogberry and Verges are offered wine in *Much Ado About Nothing*, Dogberry takes both glasses with the intention of passing one to Verges, but his gesture to hand it to Verges turns into one illustrating his speech, and after several feints of this kind, he forgets that it was for Verges and drinks it himself.

Serious plays have similar traditional business. Hamlet draws his sword in the scene with his father's ghost and holds it before him to serve as a cross to protect himself in case the ghost is an evil spirit. To clarify Hamlet's relation with Ophelia in the "Get thee to a nunnery" scene, Hamlet often indicates by pantomime that he is aware that Polonius and Claudius are listening; he often feints to stroke Ophelia's head in the midst of the calumny which he heaps upon her. Margaret Webster, in her direction of the full-length *Hamlet*, admirably picturized the comic, platitudinous motivation she wanted for Polonius' advice to his son by having Laertes and Ophelia roll their eyes upward and sit down in resignation to indicate that they knew exactly what was coming when their father began, "And these few precepts. . . ." Other actors have read the precepts from a book. The poisoning of Regan by Goneril in the last scene of *King Lear* can be made clearer to the audience by letting Goneril hand Regan a goblet of wine during the scene; the actual poisoning of the wine can be shown, but the opportunity to do so is all that is needed. The Fool in *Lear*, so prominent in the first three acts, disappears at the end of the scene in the farmhouse, and no explanation is given. Scholars postulate his death as a result of his exposure in the storm. His imminent death can be picturized by his slow collapse beside Lear's straw pallet in the farmhouse on his last speech of the play, "And I'll go to bed at noon."

It is said that when Mme. Janauschek starred in *Macbeth*, she sought to increase the relative importance of Lady Macbeth without damaging the play. Attention is ordinarily on Macbeth at the end of the banquet scene, but she transferred it to herself by symbolic picturization. Near the end of the scene she sank down on the steps of the throne in emotional exhaustion, and gradually reclined on the top step. This dislodged the gold band which she wore as a crown, and it rolled away. At the final line of the scene, she stretched out her hand to retrieve the crown, but found it just beyond her reach.

Directors use such picturization in all plays. It is the most obvious aspect of direction, and the one most likely to be noticed by the audience.

BALANCE

Balance is that element in the composition of a work of art which produces the impression of equilibrium. Some point or line of a spatial composition, or some moment of a temporal one, is perceived as its axis. This may coincide with a detail of the composition, or it may only be imagined. The impression of balance or unbalance depends upon the "weight" of the details of the halves formed by this axis. The composition may have symmetrical balance in which one half is the exact reversal of the other; it may have occult balance in which the two have a different arrangement of elements, but are felt to be approximately equal in weight; or it may be an unbalanced composition with the two parts perceived as distinctly unequal.

The concept of balance is familiar in the spatial arts like painting, sculpture, or architecture. Balance exists, but is less obvious, in the halves of a temporal composition such as music, a piece of literature, a play, or a dance. The same visual elements of dimension, line, and color, plus all phases of movement, constitute the weight of the visual details of the parts created by the temporal axis. The volume, pitch, melody, key, quality, rate, and accent of the sounds gives them weight in the balance between the divisions created by the axis. Almost perfect auditory balance results from the sound of an airplane passing overhead. The sound crescendos to an axis or climax as the plane approaches, and, as it leaves, diminishes in approximately the same length of time.

Visual balance has been discussed under the subject of Design, and the addition of actors to the design does not change these principles. For beauty of visual balance, the director designs a stage picture just as does a graphic artist. He can arrange his figures in three dimensions within the setting — breadth, height, and depth. He has free and full use of the breadth dimension. He is limited in design of the height dimension unless the setting contains a great many stairs and levels; in a setting with an unrelieved flat floor, the opportunity for height composition is restricted to the difference in height between actors, and the differences in their standing and sitting heights. However, since the height dimension is thus fixed and stable on a flat stage, when a figure does rise above the customary level, as by standing on a step, on a level, or on a chair, the effect is magnified out of all proportion to a similar height in a graphic art like painting. The effectiveness of full use of the height dimension on the stage is shown in the frequently reproduced photographs from Norman Bel Geddes' *A Project for a Theatrical Production of the Divine Comedy*.

So far as depth is concerned, the compositional effect of perspective is far less on the stage than in the graphic fields. Looking down on the stage from an angle, spectators in the balconies have some appreciation of the depth dimension, though the actual effect is more a height than a depth dimension. (Review Figures 27 and 28, pages 245 and 249.) A psychological equivalent to the depth dimension is achieved by decreasing the intensity of the light at the back of the stage, or by other uses of light "zoning," and thus substituting brightness perspective for distance perspective. The director thus has full use of the breadth dimension; can obtain a fair substitute for depth by a brightness variation; and can make limited use of height, but can expect even slight variations in height to have considerable effect.

When an actor is alone in a stage picture, he usually provides its axis, even though he may be well to one side. The symmetry of his body balances the composition. This effect cannot be achieved, of course, if the design is so prominent that it distracts attention. A grouping of actors in a restricted area at the side of the stage is similarly appreciated on the basis of the internal balance of the group. However, when the eye and neck muscles of the spectators tire of the tension of looking to the side, their gaze returns to center, the axis is established there, and the stage picture becomes unbalanced.

While attention can be held within a

limited area and internal balance can be produced there for a short time, the use of the side areas calls for overall occult balance. The play seems visually unbalanced if a preponderance of the action takes place on one side. *Arsenic and Old Lace* has many episodes played on the left side because of their necessary relation to the table and the window seat. Tying the actor who plays the drama critic to a chair on stage right, rather than to a more logical one on stage left, helps to restore balance by requiring that the episodes of his intended murder, and the policeman's narration of the plot of his play, be played on stage right.

Since interest, including meaning, is the strongest factor in the balance of an object, the protagonist can balance many other actors if he is sufficiently active and challenges the group. A character may balance a good many others at his first entrance; if his importance has been established in advance, he can balance an even larger group. Whenever the interest focuses on a single character, he may balance a large group in whom the interest of the audience is passive. For the nose speech in the second act of *Cyrano de Bergerac*, Cyrano and Christian often balance twenty other Gascoynes. Because all members of the audience had heard about Geiger counters, but few had seen one, the one in *The Traitor* balanced a large group of active figures — in fact, for its first few minutes on the stage, it produced unbalance by receiving the sole attention of the audience. An object or person being discussed by other actors acquires considerable interest weight. A closed door behind which the villain lurks with a revolver assumes tremendous interest weight.

Vocal balance is usually a relatively minor problem for the director. He makes sure that the actors have reserve powers for emphasis when they reach the climax, and that they have not exhausted their variety of auditory stimuli in the first half of the play. The

climax must seem the most important moment of the play, and usually the most exciting. Vocal stimuli rather than visual ones are more likely to be the chief contributors to climax. The vocal factors which are to be used to achieve climax — volume, pitch, rate, a pause, etc. — must be conserved against previous overuse which decreases their effectiveness. If climax is to be secured by a combination of the maximum effectiveness of several vocal factors, then the individual factors can be used earlier at their maximum strengths.

The director is aware of the balance embodied in the script, or of the need for improving it; for balance gives a play the impression of poise, of a carefully planned work of art, and produces a sense of completeness and satisfaction when the play is ended.

Vocal expression arises so directly from the actors' response to the dialogue and the dramatic situation that if the auditory stimuli have more interest in the first half of the play the fault usually lies in the playwriting. The director, however, may remedy this by encouraging the actors to seek opportunities for variety and vividness of expression in the latter part. Volume, pitch, and rate are the most impressive of the vocal factors, and so can be most readily used for this purpose. But they are also the most conspicuous when the expression overshoots the content. To improve the balance, the director may increase the vividness of an episode, or add entertaining eccentricities to a characterization. Sometimes he can substitute visual for auditory stimuli by inventing interesting and novel business. He may add an otherwise unnecessary change of setting, or revolve a single setting so as to show different walls. He may introduce costume changes which are otherwise unnecessary. As a last resort, and a distressful one, he may reduce some of the interest factors in the early part of the play, either to transfer them to the last half, or just to equalize the interest of the two parts.

The third act of *The Children's Hour* is far less engrossing than the first two acts. To overcome this difficulty, the director can increase the intensity of the confession which leads to the suicide, and can cast the finest available emotional actress in the part of the grandmother in order to increase the emotional impact of her anguish and humiliation.[3] In *Murder in the Cathedral*, the speeches of the knights, and the final episode, must be played brilliantly to prevent the play seeming anticlimactic after the assassination of Archbishop Becket.

Shaw tends to labor his basic theme at such length that audience interest is exhausted before the end of some of his plays. Other plays which make direction difficult by allowing interest to run down in the last act, but which have sufficient other merits to make them popular, include *Lady Windermere's Fan, Doctor Knock, Topaze, Accent on Youth, Alison's House, Peter Pan, Craig's Wife, John Gabriel Borkman,* and *What Every Woman Knows.*

Most of Shakespeare's chronicle plays are unbalanced in that some episodes have greater interest than others, and, being treated independently and in sequence, they give no sense of balance in interest on the two sides of a climax. *Henry V* achieves more balance than some of the others by having a more unified plot. To prepare for and balance the charming, halting love scene between Henry and the French princess, Shakespeare inserts the similarly paced English lesson of the princess. Though the plots of *Henry VIII* are cumulative in interest, the three successive plots are relatively independent, concerning the Duke of Buckingham, Queen Katharine, and Cardinal Wolsey, and the play concludes with the pageantry of

the baptism of the infant Elizabeth. Shakespeare's best dramas are intrinsically evenly balanced, with the climax shortly after the temporal center, and with interest maintained evenly in both parts.

The impression of balance is often increased by some form of repetition of stimuli or echoing. A prologue paired with an epilogue is one such device. The visual echo of the breakfast on the veranda served to Marcus Hubbard in the first act, and to Ben Hubbard in the last act, of *Another Part of the Forest* helps to symbolize Ben's usurpation of his father's place. Margaret Webster added a similar echoing device to the American Repertory Theatre production of *Henry VIII*. The coronation of Anne Bullen (Boleyn) in Westminster Abbey was seen through a scrim as the Gentleman described it to Katharine. Later the same setting, now empty, was dimly seen during Katharine's vision of her own coronation. Contrast was employed at the same time, in Miss Webster's words, "trying to emphasize that Anne's coronation had been full of temporal pomp, while Katharine's was materially lonely, but a spiritual crowning all the same."[4]

Lady Macbeth's gestures and movements in the sleep-walking scene can arise from memories of those which she uses earlier in the play, and now almost exactly duplicates. This repetition, in addition to assisting balance, ties the scene to the previous action, and helps the actress to find exact motivations for some of the lines which paraphrase previous ones.

PROPORTION

Proportion is concerned with the relation between parts of a whole. In a fine playscript, the proportion is perfect or nearly so, and the director's effort is to maintain that proportion in his performance. If the director detects a disproportion between the parts

---

[3] Some such direction must have been given to the 1952 Broadway revival, because this criticism was not made of that production.

[4] Letter to the writer, October 27, 1950.

of the play by insufficient emphasis upon the main plot and upon the climax, or by undue stress upon some minor part at the expense of others, he may try to better the proportion by re-emphasis through direction. Various devices for emphasis have been discussed in earlier sections.

Proportion also requires that the dimensions of a work of art in time and space be appropriate to the content. A two-foot-square frame used to mount a dime is disproportionate; so is a frame one inch by twelve inches; and so is a tiny three-quarter-inch-square frame which crowds the coin.

The overall length and elaborateness of a play is a matter of proportion. It sometimes is said that a play is overwritten and should be reduced to a single act because the situation and theme are insufficiently dramatic to warrant a full-length script. The good one-act play *Overtones* is weak in its full-length expansion. Eugene O'Neill has sufficient content in *Strange Interlude* and *Mourning Becomes Electra* for the four-hour performances required by them, but in *The Iceman Cometh,* though the individual episodes are not overwritten, the multiplicity of illustration is unnecessary, and enough case history of the derelicts could be deleted to reduce the play to normal length.

Present-day productions of Shakespeare's plays are usually reduced in playing time. Some of them omit episodes and subplots, while others pare the dialogue while leaving the structure intact. Many scholars prefer the latter technique, though crowding the action may result in disproportion. The full action of *Hamlet,* for example, cannot be presented in two hours, and a director has to choose between presenting part of *Hamlet* adequately, or presenting a skeletal *Hamlet* unadorned and therefore dull.

Objects and effects are proportionate when they seem to be in the same scale, and seem related to one another in the impression which they make. Lack of proportion exists when the associated visual elements have too great a contrast in dimension, line, color, or interest. Lack of proportion in the auditory field exists when sounds vary too greatly in volume, pitch, and rate so that they seem unrelated to one another. Lack of proportion in composition exists when there is too great contrast between episodes in length, style, mood, or rhythm.

Disproportion may occur between the visual, auditory, and compositional phases of a production. If a play like *Ring Round the Moon* is played as essentially "real" and thus allows the audience to become emotionally concerned with the plot, the composition and auditory stimuli are out of proportion. If *The Doctor in Spite of Himself* is designed delicately in tints, in thin materials, and a piquant nonactualistic style, but is played with strong, positive voices, the auditory phases are out of proportion with the design. In reverse, if *The Importance of Being Earnest* is spoken in a frivolous style, but designed with heavy, actualistic 1895 scenery and costumes, the design is out of proportion with the acting and the script.

Proportion is faulty when the actors seem to "play in different keys." This may be owing to differences in volume, or in the strength and expressiveness of their gestures and movements, or it may be because of a difference in their acting styles, including their mental attitudes toward acting.[5]

As a phase of proportion, the director sees

---

[5] Sometimes a star is criticized for insisting upon toning down the performance of a minor role which "steals the show." While stars sometimes abuse their privileges, many such requests by them for subordination of minor characters are artistically right and show discernment. Playwrights often write showy minor roles without realizing the damage they do to the overall structure of the play. A small part can often be made sensational by a clever and unusual characterization. In either of these cases, if the character receives more audience interest and sympathy than the lead, it throws the play out of proportion. Either the secondary character must be subordinated, or the play must be rewritten with a new leading role.

to it that the actors maintain their own character patterns and do not unconsciously pick up those of some especially dominant actor in the group. They are particularly apt to copy from the dominant character his tempo or rhythm but may imitate other of his voice and gesture patterns. This results in an overuse of a particular type of stimulus, and damages proportion. The 1950 all-star production of *Getting Married* filled the stage with a big timber table specified by Shaw, with the result that the only position in the setting which offered any physical dominance was a six-inch-high hearth in front of a fireplace at stage left. There the actor had the advantage not only of the elevation, but also of the visual emphasis provided by the frame of the fireplace as a background. The director had every actor step onto the hearth as he propounded a major thesis in the ten-sided intellectual debate on marriage. This was excellent picturization, for a man standing with his back to a fireplace verbally settling the problems of the world is a familiar stereotype. But overuse of it produced snickers as each new actor approached the rostrum. The director may have wanted to emphasize the polemic nature of the play, but the repeated pattern defeated his purpose.

An audience tends to sympathize with the underdog. It tends to do so with any nonconformist, though it does not necessarily admire the character with whom it sympathizes. It is likely to respond to a poor person, a sick or dying character, a hunted criminal, a dope addict, a drunk, a "fallen woman," a "heel," or a wisecracking character. But sympathy extended to such characters over too long a time throws the play out of proportion.[6]

[6] The Production Code of the Motion Picture Producers and Distributors of America requires that there be no sympathy with a criminal act, though sympathy may be invited for a criminal. Often this is obeyed mechanically without conformity to the spirit of the rule. The punishment or retribution

Proportion, as well as balance, is disturbed when a play has less interest in its second half. *Julius Caesar* presents a problem of this type for the director. The primary interest of the audience must be focused on Brutus rather than on Caesar in the first half of the play. If the audience's primary sympathy inadvertently falls to Caesar, the story finishes with his assassination at the beginning of the third act, and the rest becomes overlong exposition of the denouement. The director, then, emphasizes the early Brutus scenes and subordinates those between Caesar and Calpurnia without having them played any less well.

Macbeth is slightly unbalanced, for the most effective and active Macbeth scenes occur in the first half; the Macbeth and Lady Macbeth scenes after the banquet scene are predominantly passive and introspective; and Macduff and his lady are insufficiently established in the first half to make their fine scenes as proportionately effective as they might be. Direction can prepare for these scenes by having Macduff and Lady Macduff appear in early scenes, by associating Macduff with Duncan at every opportunity in the first act, and by emphasizing the few Macduff scenes.

The title character of *Cyrano de Bergerac* needs to be played with great skill and variety to create proportionate interest in the long dialogue about the trip to the moon, and the long final episode leading to Cyrano's death. *The Torchbearers* is an extreme example of disproportion. The second act is so hilarious that the audience leaves the theatre dissatisfied with the play because of the anticlimactic third act. This act might be acceptable if it did not follow the backstage scene. George Kelly further throws the final act out of proportion by switching

episode seems a hasty and unconvincing afterthought, and it fails to have the proper proportion to the picture because of its brevity and its undramatic quality.

from farce and burlesque to relatively high comedy. The comic, though extraneous, rehearsal scene in *The Play's the Thing* prevents the otherwise dull last act from seeming anticlimactic.

Many comedies can lose proportion if the broad comedy sequences are overplayed or underplayed. Dekker's *The Shoemaker's Holiday* is easily thrown out of proportion in favor of the farcical journeymen led by Firk. *High Tor* suffers from an inherent disproportionate interest in the low comedy episodes of the real estate speculators and the ghostly love story. This cannot be corrected, for subordination of the comedy to the dull level of the love story removes all interest from the play.

To subordinate scenes in order to retain proportion, the characters, as either speakers or listeners, can treat the dialogue casually, and in this manner tell the audience that the scenes are unimportant. The dialogue between Touchstone and Corin in *As You Like It* has lost most of its humor for a modern audience, but part of it is needed to indicate a step in the alteration of Touchstone's character. One production suggested its unimportance, and at the same time added an extraneous amusement to the scene, by letting Corin and Touchstone sit on the footlight trough with their feet dangling in the pit, with poles in their hands, pretending to fish among the orchestra. In the first scene of this play, Charles the wrestler has a long exposition about his coming wrestling match. It disturbs credence to curtail this dialogue materially, yet only a few of the facts need to be impressed upon the audience. Oliver can provide a substitute interest by walking away during the exposition and thus attract attention to his own malicious thoughts, which are more important than the exposition.

The famous set-pieces of rhetoric in Shakespeare can receive too much dramatic emphasis. The attention of the audience is drawn to them by its recognition of the opening words; so the director needs to warn the audience when the speeches are irrelevant. This partly accounts for the casual manner in which modern productions treat the "Seven Ages" speech of Jaques and the "Queen Mab" speech of Mercutio. Hamlet's "Advice to the Players" is a directorial problem. Casual treatment of it is one solution. The more frequent method is to have it spoken impressively, and subordinate it by having the players listen to it disinterestedly, and immediately ignore it in the bustle and chatter of their exit. The audience need not be denied the pleasure of good readings of these and similar speeches, but it needs to understand that they are incidental entertainments, extraneous to the plot, like interpolated songs. To illustrate the potential danger in such speeches, it would be possible for Hamlet to read the "Advice to the Players" with such immediacy and importance that members of the audience who are seeing the play for the first time would expect a dramatic moment subsequently in which Hamlet and the players clash about the acting.

Modern plays, particularly those of some young leftist playwrights, often contain similar dramatically irrelevant episodes and speeches in which the author expounds his social theories through a character. These are more dangerous as false leads than the rhetorical set-pieces, because the characterization and motivation usually require that these speeches be spoken with conviction and vehemence. Their irrelevance usually has to be indicated by the reaction of the other characters — by the casualness of their attention, and by the speed and completeness of their mental and physical transitions following the speech.

In contrast, Shakespeare sometimes writes an important plot scene in very few words. Unless actors and director are aware of the importance of such a scene, it is passed over without sufficient emphasis. In *King Lear,* he uses many long scenes for the quarrels of Lear with his two thankless daughters, and for the villainy of Edmund when he betrays his father and half-brother. But in the last half of the play he rushes through the scenes establishing the competition of Goneril and Regan for the love of Edmund, and those establishing their mutual hatred, which culminate in Goneril's murder of Regan and her own suicide. The speed with which this subplot develops and climaxes gives it intensity, and the scenes are long enough to establish the motivations, but the director needs to devote special attention to them to insure that they are not slighted because of their brevity. The accidental quarantine of Friar John, which brings about the tragic ending of *Romeo and Juliet,* is explained in a slightly obscure thirty-line scene.

UNITY

Unity resembles both balance and proportion, because all three are criteria for evaluating the plan of a work of art. They designate three distinct concepts of perfection, but distinctions between them are sometimes difficult because violation of one of the criteria is usually accompanied by concomitant violation of the other two. If the last act of a play is dull, for example, the play is overbalanced and disproportioned toward the first part, and it probably lacks unity.

The basic purpose of the director being to communicate a complete and accurate theatrical effect, one of the essential qualities to be sought is unity of impact upon the audience. Though unity is a positive quality which can be appreciated in a work of art, the artist works in a largely negative manner to secure it — that is, he achieves unity by rejecting the inappropriate and irrelevant details which occur to him. Occasionally, however, he does work positively by adding an element which welds together

what otherwise might be unrelated materials. An obvious example in visual art is the frame of arches which is used to tie together the scenes of a set of murals or the series of illustrations in an illuminated manuscript.

In the section on Design, examples are cited of methods for achieving visual unity by background and costumes, particularly by using for the purpose some permanent elements in the scenery and dominant colors in costumes and scenery. All the phases of patterning discussed in this chapter are directorial devices which contribute to unity.

Margaret Webster, in the American Repertory Theatre production of *Henry VIII,* added a unifying element to this episodic play by having Phillip Bourneuf in the role of First Chronicler read periodically from the Holinshed *Chronicles* to supply exposition of some matters deleted in this production as well as matters not treated in Shakespeare's play because they were familiar to the Elizabethan audience. To secure additional unity in a production of *Romeo and Juliet,* the final speech of the Prince was treated as a formal epilogue echoing the staging of the prologue. The Prince materialized out of a void to speak the prologue, with the full scene slowly becoming visible about him; for his final speech in the tomb, he took the same stage position facing the audience and the scene dimmed out around him in exact reversal of the technique at the opening of the play. This technique of dimming out the rest of the stage for a final speech is used in many productions of Shakespeare, and has become a traditional practice for the final speech of *Saint Joan.*

There are many examples of insufficient unity in plays performed on Broadway, as well as in plays in the amateur theatre. Critics praised Bobby Clark's extravagant performance in *The Would-Be Gentleman,* but pointed out that the other members of the cast did not play in the same style — the run was short. The highly emotional acting style of the celebrated European actor, Fritz Kortner, was completely out of key with that of Katharine Cornell and the other members of the cast of *Herod and Miriamne* — the production did not reach Broadway. Though Cyril Ritchard gave a remarkable performance of the fop in *The Relapse*, it only threw into contrast the less stylized acting of the rest of the company — again the run was brief. The famous Arthur Hopkins–Lionel Barrymore–Robert Edmond Jones production of *Macbeth* was a phenomenal failure because of the lack of unity between the comparatively restrained acting style and the vividly expressionistic scenery. The argument still arises sporadically as to which was at fault. However, few critics objected to a caricature performance in the role of Clive Mortimer, the American, in *I Am a Camera*. Examples of successful inconsistency could be multiplied indefinitely without changing the fact that it is usually objectionable and confusing to an audience.

To many people, a mixture of styles of settings disturbs unity. The Jo Mielziner settings for Katharine Cornell's *Romeo and Juliet* pleased some spectators and critics, but annoyed others with their mixture of two-dimensional painted drops, three-dimensional full-stage settings, and a tiny three-dimensional cell of Friar Laurence treated in space staging technique. There was also some objection to Rolf Gerard's settings for *That Lady* which similarly mixed a heavily realistic main setting, a bedroom of drapes, and a tiny realistic setting on a wagon. This type of mixture occurs frequently in the professional and amateur theatre, and is acceptable to many.[7]

[7] The criterion of unity does not preclude variety in every phase of the production; but the variety must be within the limits set by the fundamental meaning of the script. In extreme cases, the director deliberately plans seeming inconsistencies as the clearest way to interpret the play. The motion picture *A Royal Scandal* contrasted gorgeous regal settings and costumes with an amusingly vulgar

Walter Kerr's acting edition of Aristophanes' *The Birds* [8] is an example of deliberate mixture of styles and periods. Retaining the ancient Greek setting and story and a traditional translation of the choruses, he has modernized the other dialogue so that it sounds contemporary and becomes immediately meaningful to a modern audience. Though Kerr's initial production based on this acting edition also retained Greek dress and a relatively "real" setting, other directors have found it consistent with the spirit of the script to abandon such scenery and to mix costumes of different periods selected for their association with the stereotypes being satirized.

In one production, for example, Euelpides, Hercules, and the Messengers remained Greek in costume; but Pithetaerus, the other explorer, became an Elizabethan; and the cast included an Italian Renaissance poet, a Persian prophet, a modern businessman as the real estate promoter, an eighteenth-century British redcoat as the tax collector, a villain from a nineteenth-century melodrama as Prometheus, and a Directoire belle as Iris. This production also, to provide more parts for women, altered Neptune to a stiff-backed, turn-of-the-century Juno. Since a modern audience is unlikely to remember that Neptune was the uncle of Hercules, substitution of Hercules' foster mother helped to clarify for the audience the episode in which Hercules learns that he is illegitimate. But this raises a grave question of the latitude of the director in altering a play. Some, like the director of this production, maintain that this type of alteration is permissible when it preserves the spirit of the script. Others maintain that there can be no justification for it.

Catherine the Great played by Tallulah Bankhead. Mae West's play about the same queen, *Catherine Was Great*, missed this satiric opportunity by using settings as intentionally vulgar and tasteless as the character she played.

[8] (Catholic University Press, 1952.)

Unity, then, is more frequently a concern of the director in his function as critic (i.e., in making sure that nothing violates unity) than in his function as a creative artist (i.e., in deliberately planning unifying devices). Every factor of the production is considered and evaluated for its contribution to the total effect. This includes the theatre itself and its adaptation to the particular performance, the script, the visual and auditory stimuli supplied by the actors, the music, the scenery, costumes, make-up, sound effects, and stage management. The director adjusts these elements in order to make each contribute actively to the interpretation of the play; any of them which distracts from the desired overall effect is minimized as much as possible. Since unity is in the final analysis a subjective criterion, it becomes essentially a demonstration of the taste of the director.

PROGRESSION

Progression is concerned with the impression which the audience receives that a plot sequence has a beginning, a development, and an ending. It is related to unity, but in unity the emphasis is upon the inclusion of relevant material and the exclusion of all that is irrelevant, while the emphasis of progression is upon dramatic development and continuity. It is the counterpart in performance to the evolution of the plot in the script — a factor discussed in an earlier section. The progression of the major plot encompasses the whole play; and every phase of acting, design, and direction contributes to it. As a vital phase of progression, the director sees to it that the main plot sequence — or atmosphere or theme in other types of plays — receives proper attention and emphasis; that it moves with a sense of immediacy and development; and that it reaches a conclusion which gives satisfaction. These last four criteria are interrelated,

because the satisfaction in the conclusion **is** augmented by the sense of balance and unity so achieved. The sense of proper progression contributes to proportion.

Since it is given major attention by all theatre artists, consistent progression of the main plot is not likely to be neglected. But sometimes so much attention is claimed by the internal interest of individual episodes that they make independent impressions upon an audience, and thus do not contribute to a sense of continuity. This is especially likely to occur in diffuse plays like *The Three Sisters, Porgy, Stage Door, Outward Bound, The Wild Duck, Ladies of the Jury, Two on an Island,* and *Alison's House;* and in episodic plays like *Johnny Johnson, Escape, Doctor Knock, The Kingdom of God,* and *Milestones.*[9]

In many episodic plays the element insuring progression as well as unity is the intellectual or emotional development of the leading character. Concentration of interest on a single character helps to give a feeling of progression to other types of plays, but this technique is not always applicable. The essence of a play like *The Three Sisters* or *Uncle Vanya* is the web of interaction between the characters, and no one character can be stressed at the expense of the others. The development of a theme or mood is the essential factor in other plays like *Waiting for Lefty, The Blind,* and . . . *one third of a nation.* . . . The individual scenes depict different facets of this theme and have interest within themselves. It is difficult in

[9] The motion picture of *The Blue Bird* starring Shirley Temple has this fault. Each episode acquires an independent interest like a skit or production number of a revue. This danger is inherent in the play because of the spectacular features of the individual scenes and their autonomous unity. Nevertheless, the plot line can be maintained if — for example — the acting and direction emphasize the seriousness of the search for the blue bird of happiness at the beginning and end of each scene, and if Tyltyl and Mytyl at the end of the scenes emphasize their disappointment at their failure to find it.

such cases to maintain the feeling of progression. To achieve it, the director may have to request the use of what seems to be overemphasis of the speeches which develop the theme, more than the usual emphasis on rhythm, and the deliberate utilization of every possible phase of visual and auditory stimulus to produce a sense of mounting tension.

Productions more frequently fail to secure progression in the subordinate plots. The director gives attention to the clarity with which each subplot is initiated; to the way in which its succeeding episodes are related to each other vocally and visually; to the clarity of the dramatic progress in the scene; and to the definiteness with which the subplot is concluded. Shakespeare's concern with the resolution of his subplots accounts for the protracted exposition in the last scenes of his comedies. If the modern director abridges this exposition, he has to be sure that an adequate conclusion remains, or that he substitutes a visual conclusion for the verbal one in the script. Many of the comedies near the end have some such speech as, "And you, brides and bridegrooms all . . . to the measures fall." If dialogue is omitted which pairs some of the lovers, a pantomimic succession of embraces or hand clasps at this moment under the direction of the speaker may be an adequate substitute for it. The Katharine Hepburn production of *As You Like It* had each couple present themselves for the blessing of the Duke.

In some modern plays, such expositional pantomime, particularly when performed during a silence, can similarly clarify subplot conclusions. It is the failure to resolve minor plots which results in the complaint at the end of certain plays that "many things were left up in the air." Naturally, a director does not add a conclusion to a plot which the author intentionally leaves in suspense. In *Ghosts,* it will be remembered, Ibsen purposely conceals the decision of Mrs. Alving on poisoning her insensate son. Mrs. Patrick Campbell as Mrs. Alving usurped Ibsen's prerogative and threw away the vial of morphine; Nazimova, in an otherwise brilliant performance, indicated by her final movement that she would give the son the tablets.

RHYTHM

Rhythm can be defined as the seeming recurrence of any stimulus which produces a conscious or subconscious feeling of organization and progression. The stimulus actually may recur with regularity, or it may be a purely subjective patterning of the stimuli in more or less regular form by the receiver. Rhythm can be produced by the recurrence of a single stimulus like a phoneme, a vocal emphasis, a color, a line; or it may be a tremendous pattern like the parallelism in the double plot of *King Lear,* or the return to the nursery setting in the next-to-the-last scene of *Peter Pan.*

In music, the measure, with its fixed pattern of accentuation, supplies the basic rhythm. Increasingly large rhythmic patterns include the musical phrase; the verses of a song with repetition of melody; the chorus of a song with its repetition of both melody and words; the movements of a long musical composition; the repetition of themes either exactly or in the form of variations; or any other internal repetition, near repetition, or progression. A symphony balances many musical factors, uses some for rhythmic repetition, but usually employs a volume crescendo — progressive rhythm — for its conclusion.

The most familiar feature of rhythm in language is the recurrent accentuation of the foot pattern of verse. A larger pattern of rhythm is the line, which tends to produce a rhythmic beat of its own in spite of caesura and run-on lines. Iambic pentameter is the verse form which has been most successful in English. This conforms satisfactorily to the habitual length of English sentences and phrases in formal speech. Formal prose tends to take this same pattern — many passages of prose, particularly of oratory, can be scanned as irregular iambic pentameter. This kind of line produces a moderately fast rhythm, adaptable to varied purposes.

The popular French dramatic verse form is the Alexandrine. While this has a syllable count, and is rimed, the French language rimes so much more easily than the English that the rime is less conspicuous, and the major effect is the division of the line into two nearly equal parts with one major accent in each half. It produces a slightly longer line than iambic pentameter, and it can give an impression of greater dignity and formalism than usually can be achieved with the popular English line. Greek verse, too, probably was more concerned with major emphases than with the details of long and short syllables. Maxwell Anderson's poetic prose usually employs this pattern of major accents rather than regularity of foot pattern. In all such lines, the longer time between strongly accented syllables produces an impression of slower tempo, and hence of greater impressiveness. In consequence, it runs the danger of becoming ludicrous if the content is not as elevated as the style. William Poel and B. Iden Payne insist that Shakespearean verse be read similarly, with only one or two accents to the line, and consequently less stress on other strong syllables.

The ends of lines can be emphasized by rime, but this is so conspicuous in English that it is seldom used in serious dramatic verse. Satires like *Aria da Capo* and *The Dark Lady of the Sonnets* use it, and Arthur Guiterman and Lawrence Langner made it an additional factor of entertainment in their adaptation of *The School for Husbands*. Shakespeare used it chiefly in couplets to mark the ends of scenes.

Alliteration, which is the repetition of consonant sounds or accented vowels, particu-

larly of initial sounds, is another device for producing rhythm. Anglo-Saxon poetry employed it instead of rime, but it now is used primarily as an additional ornament of verse, without the regularity of rime.

Good prose also is rhythmic, though its pattern is more intricate and less pronounced, and hence harder to identify. The rhythmic regularity of formal oratorical prose has been mentioned. Much modern prose, conforming to the journalistic style of written expression, has shorter lines and highly irregular phrase length. This produces a fast tempo, as in the plays of Saroyan, Odets, and Coward, for example. In between the two styles are varying levels of regularity.

Time magazine [10] gives an illustration of the kind of example Robert Frost has used to demonstrate rhythm. The prosaic sentences:

> The cat is in the house.
> I will put the cat out.
> She will come back.

are turned into:

> There's that cat got in.
> Out you go, you cat.
> What's the use? She'll be right back.

The next larger unit of rhythm is the poetic stanza, which varies from the regularity of the quatrain form to the irregular long canto form of *The Divine Comedy* and *The Faerie Queene*. The paragraph is the prose parallel to the stanza, and is highly irregular, determined more by content than by form. Yet, in good writing, the paragraphs have internal unity of form as well as content and end with a sense of completeness, to such an extent that they can be recognized as units when read aloud. The oral reader, aware of the printed paragraphs, is likely to under-

[10] LVI (October 9, 1950), 79. In a letter to the writer Mr. Frost gives the different last line used here.

PLATE 27. **Ingenious Solutions of Difficult Problems.** (Above) Every possible device is here used to establish the importance of Giannetto at the moment of his entrance in *The Jest,* and to exaggerate the physical stature of slight John Barrymore, who played the part. (See page 341.) *(Broadway production: director, Arthur Hopkins; designer, Robert Edmond Jones.)* (Below) On a stage less than twenty-one feet wide, the three-room apartment of *The Voice of the Turtle* is organized as a duplex. *(Erie [Pa.] Playhouse: director and designer, Newell Tarrant; costumes, Dorothy Nies.)*

PLATE 28. **Shakespeare at the Stratford (Ontario) Festival.** A grouping from *Henry V*, showing various aspects and levels of Stratford's thrust stage. Another treatment of *Henry V* appears in Plate 29. (Director, Michael Langham; designer, Desmond Heeley; music, John Cook.)

PLATE 29. **Two Treatments of Shakespeare on an Open Stage.** *Coriolanus* (above) and *Henry V* at the University of Michigan. (Above: *director, William P. Halstead; designer, Alan Billings; costume designer, Zelma H. Weisfeld; director of battle sequence, Robert E. McGill. Below: director, William P. Halstead; designer, Vern Stillwell; costume designer, Zelma H. Weisfeld; lighting designer, J. Shelton Murphy; music, Paul Miller.)*

PLATE 30. **Exceptions to the "Rules" of Emphasis.** (Above) In *Angel Street*, the advantages of centrality, height, and upstage position emphasize Mrs. Manningham, but the characterizations, motivations, and physical attitudes of both actors successfully transfer dominance to her husband in a "weak" position. (*University of Michigan: director, Claribel Baird; designer, Dean Currie; costumes, Lucy Barton.*) (Below) Leading lines in the scenery and attitudes in the actors here focus attention on a "weak" area at stage left. For this set for *Jeb*, Jo Mielziner uses only properties, two cut-down flats, two partially transparent borders, and a backdrop. (*Broadway production: director, Herman Shumlin; costumes, Patricia Montgomery.*)

score them by vocal means. Long speeches in plays, however, are not printed in paragraphs, though the paragraphic organization is present, and the actor speaking the lines must find and clarify this organization.

The largest forms of rhythm, appreciable in good novels as chapters, parts, "books," and even the separate novels of such works as Galsworthy's trilogies, are often more apparent in the drama than they are in other forms of literature since dramas are written to be heard at a single sitting, and since the audience thus is more immediately aware of rhythmic form than in the novel read with interruptions. These larger units in plays are the episodes, each with a sense of completeness and unity; scenes and acts when marked by intermissions; and the overall sense of unity produced by an ascending action, a climax, and a descending action which wholly or partially restores equilibrium.

Rhythm is appreciated by the sense of vision as well as the sense of hearing. We recognize rhythm in the systematic arrangement of a row of trees, bushes, or flowers, and in the more elaborate pattern of an orchard where the trees are lined up in three or more directions. The landscaping of formal or informal gardens employs a more intricate pattern — obtaining variety, but with carefully planned repetitions of species and colors and shapes of the beds to give the scheme unity. Visual artists use rhythm as one of the pleasure-giving qualities of their compositions. As a utilitarian example, wallpaper and printed dress and drapery material have a regular rhythm in their all-over design, either repeating a single pattern, superimposing patterns, or obtaining still greater and greater variety within repetitive pattern by increasing the number of individual elements which are applied in alternation.

Architecture uses highly regular rhythm, with parallel lines indicating the foundation, the floor levels, and the roof, with doors and columns in horizontal rows, and with windows in both horizontal and vertical rows. In rooms, doors are usually of the same height and width; the windows are of the same height and width, and their dimensions are usually related to those of the doors. The architect avoids any slight variations from a standard which would look accidental rather than intentional; when any single feature is of a different size than related features, he makes it so distinctively different that it becomes definitely either a dominant or a subordinate feature.

The painter uses rhythmic repetition of line, of form, of color, of texture, and of mass to achieve balance and proportion. This is discussed at length under the subject of Design. The choreographer similarly seeks rhythms in his grouping of figures, and in their movements, gestures, and poses, to parallel the rhythms of the musical accompaniment. He uses repetition. The co-ordination of the visual and the auditory stimuli also creates a rhythmic impression. The multitude of illustration from other arts has been supplied because they are more familiar and so are more easily appreciated than those which occur in the complex structure of the performance of a drama. Many of the devices, however, can be applied directly to the stage.

In the production of a play, any recurring pattern of stimulus which makes an impression on an audience contributes to rhythm. It gives to the play its overall effect of organization. Though it is seldom appreciated consciously, it makes a major contribution to the feeling of satisfaction which the audience experiences. When a spectator says that a performance seems jerky and disconnected, that it gives the impression of uncertainty or of being underrehearsed, or, on the contrary, that it seems smooth, appears to flow, and has unity, he is responding to the rhythm. The basic rhythm is provided by the script, but the director can improve or damage it, and can add factors of his own which help or hinder it. He strives for an effect of continuously flowing action, but with variety not only in the factors which contribute to rhythm, but in the rhythm itself.

Rhythm is provided by alternation between forestage and full-stage scenes in Shakespeare's dramas, both in the Elizabethan type of theatre and in a production elsewhere which uses this alternation pattern. This depth rhythm is usually underscored by the brevity of the forestage scenes as compared to those played in full stage. A related sense of visual rhythm is produced by the staging of vaudeville, revues, and musical comedies where there is continuous action and rapid scene change. Scenes "in one" [11] alternate with those using greater depth. In vaudeville, the stellar act often makes use of the deepest stage area even for a vocal soloist, a large visible area of the stage tending to emphasize the climactic nature of the act. Both vaudeville and the revue tend to alternate comedy routines and musical numbers or vocal and dance numbers. It is from such rhythmic devices that one perceives some unity even in a revue or a vaudeville program.

If the episodes, scenes, and acts, and the major action of the play, produce an impression of regularity of form and structural unity, they give to the play an overall effect of symmetry, unity, and rhythm. By their regularity, they produce "psychological beats," which create the impression of inevitability of form. The final beat gives a sense of conclusion and repose which produces satisfaction. This type of ending is used more frequently in tragedy and melodrama than in comedy and farce.

[11] I.e., in the space downstage of the first set of wings and their accompanying drop; "in two" includes the space downstage of the second set, and so forth.

Problem plays often end with the problem posed but unsolved, forcing the audience to supply a conclusion of its own. The author hopes that this conclusion thereby makes a more lasting association pattern in the mind of the audience. Such is the ending of *Ghosts*, with the spectator forced to choose between euthanasia and horror, rather than being allowed to dismiss the problem by learning the choice made by Mrs. Alving. Farce, with its turbulent action, often achieves a sense of finality just before the ending, and then for a fillip, throws everything off balance again at the curtain. *Dear Ruth* ends with an unknown sailor inquiring for Ruth in almost the same words as the aviator of the first act. *My Sister Eileen* ends as a workman for the new subway finally blasts his way through the floor of the basement apartment. *Arsenic and Old Lace* ends with the homicidal sisters giving a glass of lethal wine to the official who has come to take them to an asylum.

Voice patterns also contribute to rhythm. An individual actor may use a repetition of one or more vocal factors to establish his characterization. The speech of the entire cast may be planned for its rhythmic effect — either a uniform pattern to create an overall atmosphere, or distinctly contrasting rhythms to produce tension and excitement.

Attention to any phase of rhythm gives it emphasis. Once actors are asked to stress or subordinate a type of rhythm, they find for themselves the opportunities to do so. Maxwell Anderson has his poetic prose printed in the form of blank verse. This makes the reader aware of the rhythm, and produces from most actors a more consciously rhythmic reading of the lines than if they were printed as prose. In contrast, directors often have Shakespearean verse typed in prose form in the belief that the actors approach the motivation more directly than they do when they are visually aware of the poetry, and particularly that they read

Shakespeare's run-on lines more meaningfully when they are unaware of the line division.

The Guiterman-Langner adaptation of *The School for Husbands* often uses rimes amusingly in the middle of sentences, as is done by Cole Porter, Irving Berlin, and other modern lyric writers. These can be so subordinated that the audience misses them. If the actors are conscious of the rimes, and are amused by them, they communicate them to the audience for their full value.

In much the same way, the director decides, in doing a Shakespearean drama which contains a number of rimed couplets, whether they are to be emphasized or concealed. Emphasis usually results in a slightly lengthened duration for the rimed syllables, with a fraction-of-a-second pause following them. Emphasis on the uniform length of the poetic line usually is achieved by a similar emphasis on the last syllable, and by using falling inflections at the end of the lines. Such techniques are too subtle for most actors to handle mechanically, and so, when such emphasis is desired, it is usually obtained by the indirect means of motivation.

Other auditory and visual elements which can contribute to rhythm by meaningful alternations include: light and dark lighting of scenes; bright and dull colors; shades and tints; elaborate and simple scenery and costumes; loudly and softly spoken scenes; high-pitched and low-pitched dialogue; slow and fast dialogue; dialogue spoken in major and minor keys; serious and comic episodes; scenes underlined by music and those without accompaniment; relatively "real" and "unreal" acting style. However, some of these factors, such as simple and elaborate scenery, and variations in acting style, can be so antithetical that they clash and so are likely to destroy the unity of the production.

Rhythm can be produced otherwise than by contrast. Cumulative progression and retrogression is rhythmic. This pattern often appears in the main plot, and in the internal structure of individual episodes. There is a secondary rhythmic element in the organization of a vaudeville bill or a revue, since acts and numbers are usually presented in the order of their cumulative interest value. One climax is the closing number of the first part; the performance starts again after intermission at a reduced interest level, and builds up again to the major climax — in vaudeville terminology, "next to closing." Vaudeville usually closes on a lower note, which traditionally is acrobats or an animal act. The revue usually has a scenically spectacular closing number, but the point of highest entertainment value is just before it.

The chief effect of a play may be a change of rhythm. The main interest in *The Silver Whistle* is in the change in the mental attitude, and hence, the rhythm of speech and movement, of the inmates of an old people's home. The same device is used in *Joint Owners in Spain*. The tragedy of *The Iceman Cometh* is the failure of Hickey to change permanently the mental outlook of the other characters. This is made apparent by their return to their initial rhythm of speech and gesture.

Maurya in *Riders to the Sea* uses a slow, exhausted rhythm in both voice and movement. Early in the play this rhythm contrasts markedly with that of the other characters, but as her last son is carried in drowned, all the characters adopt her rhythm. *Harvey* contrasts the easygoing, unaccented speech and movement of Elwood P. Dowd and his invisible friend Harvey, the six-foot one-and-a-half-inch rabbit (two inches taller in the motion picture so as to top James Stewart), with the excited, jerky, and highly accented speech and movements of the other characters.

Rhythm can create an effect in its own right. Emily White has composed a dance-pantomime entitled "Political Meeting" which depends solely upon it. The musical accompaniment is by three percussion instruments, all played at the same tempo — a woodblock accenting three-quarter time, a tom-tom accenting four-quarter, and a drum beating a count of twelve, accenting both these patterns of rhythm. This produces a resultant rhythm of a very strong, simultaneous beat of all three instruments on 1, strong supplementary accent on the woodblock on 4, 7, and 10, strong supplementary accent by the tom-tom on 5 and 9, and no accent at all on 2, 3, 6, 8, 11, and 12. This can be represented graphically in the manner indicated at the bottom of the page.

The scene of the dance-pantomime is an open forum in a park. Many dancers are used and each one is individually characterized. They wear varied actualistic costumes and intermingle casually, pantomiming various activities. Each adopts for his actions either the three-quarter or four-quarter time. Within this rhythm, however, he may move in any variation of the rhythmic time; a dancer in four-quarter time may move only on the accented beat, he may make two movements to the measure, or four, or even

eight. The other dancers follow a similar scheme. One metric beat represents those of one political party, and the other, an opposing party. A political speaker mounts a rostrum and makes a pantomimic speech in the resultant rhythm, with the 1, 4, 5, 7, 9, 10 accentuation pattern becoming increasingly vehement. As the onlookers pay more and more attention to him, they begin to add to their original movements the additional beats which he uses, and which belong to the other political party. Thus all eventually are using the same syncopated rhythm. The dance reaches a climax as the crowd takes the speaker on its shoulders and marches out gesticulating wildly in the resultant rhythm.

These examples suggest the more obvious phases of rhythm. The inherent rhythms of the script and the production include the intricacies of the alternation of ascending action with descending action; the increasing intensity of motivation and concentration of the actors as they approach an intellectual or an emotional conflict; and the slightly decreased energy which they use as they move away from climaxes and settle into a new alignment of forces. These often are called the "beats" of a play. These attitudes

4/4 time 1 2 3 4 1 2 3 4 1 2 3 4 1 2 3 4 1 2 3 4 1 2 3 4 1

3/4 time 1 2 3 1 2 3 1 2 3 1 2 3 1 2 3 1 2 3 1 2 3 1 2 3 1

Resultant Rhythm 1 2 3 4 5 6 7 8 9 10 11 12 1 2 3 4 5 6 7 8 9 10 11 12 1 of the actors produce slight variations in all the visual and auditory stimuli, which are too subtle for analysis but which the audience subconsciously appreciates because of its conditioning to such faint stimuli by past experience. They are even more effective in communicating the meaning of a script than the more obvious phases of rhythm. A superior director controls them directly and still does not overdo them to the extent that they become obvious, call attention to themselves as technique, and so defeat their purpose.

It is such subtleties which warn an audience that the climax is near and which tell them almost infallibly when the curtain is about to fall. *The Play's the Thing* satirizes this anticipation of the curtain by having it descend halfway three times as different characters humorously attempt to supply a good curtain line.

Rhythm has been discussed primarily as though it were a pattern of repetition — a consistent alternation of stimuli. But the recurrence need only be sufficiently regular to be recognized, and some of the strongest dramatic effects are produced by a shift from regular recurrent patterns, such as an unexpected lag in the action which heightens anticipation. Shakespeare, for example, usually places the climax of a tragedy shortly after the middle of the play — about three-fifths of the way through the dialogue. But in *Othello* he delays the turning point until late in the third act — thereby emphasizing Othello's resistance to jealousy under the goading of Iago. The "detective play" delays its climax as long as possible, the ideal being the nearly impossible one of revealing the solution, and thereby placing the climax, in the final line.

The Front Page, though a different type of melodrama, achieves this effect with its final line. It concerns the struggle of Hildy Johnson, a topnotch crime reporter, to get away for his honeymoon and a new job in spite of the breaking of important news stories and the effort of his sadistic managing editor, Walter Burns, to keep him on the job without the encumbrance of a wife. After delaying him repeatedly, with Hildy's fiancée more and more exasperated, Burns finally surrenders, gives Hildy his watch as a token of his appreciation of his services, wishes him well, and sends him off on his honeymoon. As Hildy leaves the room, Burns picks up the phone and asks the railroad-station police to arrest Hildy, explaining, "The son of a bitch stole my watch!"

A seemingly erratic repetition of any stimulus produces a disjointed, and possibly disturbing, sense of rhythm. A complete absence of such repetition may have an effect like that of dissonant and unresolved music, giving an impression of irregularity and lack of poise. It dismisses an audience with a sense of confusion from having witnessed a jumble. But that may be a playwright's intention. Odets obtains an erratic effect in *Waiting for Lefty* with his varying tempi and rhythms, but his pattern of alternate direct speech and flash backs maintains rhythm, and a final unity is produced by the vote for a strike.

Auditory rhythm can be more easily studied in a musical composition than in a play, because the score records more directions for its performance than does the play-script, and so it is possible to identify the devices of the composer, and then experience their auditory effect. The symphony or the sonata is the art form which uses a temporal rhythmic pattern most similar to that of a play. But the best study of rhythm is by means of a fine performance of a fine play. One way to undertake this study is to pay repeated visits to a play, studying the script between visits and experimenting with alternate actions, tempi, emphases, and readings of lines until one becomes aware of the exact techniques being used and understands the reasons for the director's choices. One also learns by these visits the way in which rhythm varies from performance to performance and thereby materially changes the impression of each one. Skillful actors permit little variation in the mechanical details of their performances, for those they can control regardless of their personal mental and emotional states. But mental and emotional states of actors do influence their personal rhythms, and hence the rhythm of their acting, in ways which are beyond their conscious control. These have important effects upon the impact of the play. While the director, to a large extent, establishes the rhythm, the final control of it in performance passes to the actors. The acting method of Stanislavski attempts to teach the actor to control his subconscious emotions and their expression, including rhythm.

Another method for learning to appreciate rhythm in a performance is to study, either as an actor or an observer, the rehearsals conducted by a good director. Reasonably early in a rehearsal period, characterizations and the acting performances seem to approach completeness, and few important changes are to be anticipated in the remaining weeks of rehearsal. Yet the play obviously is not ready for performance. It hasn't yet "jelled." As the rehearsals continue, the episodes take on more and more meaning, and acquire a total impression which is greater than the sum of the parts, although the acting seems to remain the same. The additional element is rhythm. The well-acted isolated bits become integrated into larger and larger units. If a successful integration is finally made, and all units become part of a perfected whole, a superb performance results. Much of this integration is accomplished by the actors, but much of it also stems from the skill of direction. In studying the rehearsals, the student should concentrate his attention on the little changes made in the last few rehearsals, for these are likely to be made to improve faulty rhythm — the director suddenly discovers, as the rhythm becomes perfected, that some action or vocal expression, though seemingly satisfactory in itself, disturbs the rhythm. The observer has to discover for himself what is wrong, and why the change is for the better. The director often knows this only intuitively, and does not take time to analyze it himself during the rush of final rehearsals. Naturally, the observer can only hope to identify it if he has studied the play intently over the full rehearsal period — very little except trivial mechanical "pointers" can be learned at a dress rehearsal, for example, unless one has seen a minimum of ten previous rehearsals.

There are a few elementary and obvious rules for the initial steps in establishing rhythm. But beyond these, the director's work with rhythm is apt to be intuitive rather than analytical. Once he has set a rhythmic pattern, it can be analyzed. But, while based upon experience, the creation is a direct and intuitive emotional response to the script and to the effects of rehearsal performances. This is true of any art; exercises can be performed in accordance with analyses and rules, but a work of art is created only when rules and techniques have become habitual and subconscious and the artist is free to work directly and "intuitively." A creditable performance of a play can be prepared by careful analysis, but the final effect depends upon the cultivated sensitivity of the director.

The eye, the ear, and the mind are limited in the number of independent stimuli which can be perceived at one time. Organization of the stimuli into patterns of increasing complexity increases enormously the number which can be appreciated at one time, provided the stimuli or groups of stimuli are kept to a simple number at each level of organization. This chapter discusses nine high-level patterns by which the director can give meaningful organization (particularly on a proscenium stage) to the multitudinous details presented in a play. To these should be added a tenth, variety, which — though it has not been accorded independent treatment here — has been discussed at length in connection with individual types of stimuli and with other patterns of organization.

Attention of the audience is secured and guided by emphasis and subordination. Variety assists in holding this attention, and in addition provides an aesthetic pleasure in itself. Style and atmosphere can assist organization by increasing the consistency of impression or by providing meaningful variety. Picturization clarifies the meaning. Balance, proportion, and unity are compositional patterns which give an overall effect of symmetry, equilibrium, and plan. Balance is concerned with equilibrium on the two sides of an axis or climax; proportion, with the appropriate relation of the details one with another and between the form and content; and unity, with the appropriateness of the selection of the particulars. Progression stresses the impression of movement and development of the plot from a beginning to a conclusion. Rhythm is the impression created, and appreciated consciously or subconsciously, of the recurrence of similar stimuli with a recognizable degree of regularity or progression. All of these patterns contribute a sense of plan and of inevitability to the mass of stimuli of the play — and produce a sense of organization which increases the satisfaction of the audience.

In applying such patterns to the open stage, a number of adaptations are ordinarily required; these are the subject of the next chapter.

26 | Directing for the Open Stage

*Directing the Movement • Other Directorial
Principles • Inherent Advantages and Difficulties*

The staging of plays in the open theatre is based on clear-cut principles, many of which are the same as for the proscenium theatre but some of which are strikingly different. For example, the principles governing control of the auditory stimuli are generally the same in both kinds of theatres, but those which apply to the visual stimuli are often not only different but diametrically opposed. In addition, there are certain principles — governing continuity, traffic flow, furniture arrangement, and localization of action — which spring from the shape of the open stage or the proximity of the audience to the performers and which have no counterparts in the proscenium playhouse. Since the principles of proscenium staging have already been covered in detail, this chapter will be devoted to those principles which are peculiar to directing for the open stage.

DIRECTING THE MOVEMENT

The first and most important principle is that movement (rather than pictorial composition) is the key to both control of attention and aesthetic effect. This is not to say that groupings are not useful, for there are times when a static arrangement is desirable as a rest or to punctuate the progression. But movement assumes major significance in open staging, while attitude and grouping become decidedly secondary.

Among the most effective movements are those involving large numbers — processional entrances, promenading, and armies parading with drums beating and flags waving. Thus the entrance of a king, as in *The Winter's Tale,* the return of travelers, as in *The Cherry Orchard,* or the return of the victorious army, as in *Much Ado About Nothing,* becomes an occasion for elaborate theatricalism.

Entrances and exits on an open stage do not depend for effectiveness upon either suddenness of approach or the pictorial emphasis gained from a framing enclosure such as a door or archway. For one thing, all points of entrance are too far from the center of action, and for another, no point of entrance is usually visible to all the spectators. The entering character therefore comes well out toward the center of the acting area before he can command the attention of all. His movement from the place of entrance is given no special focus, but as he steps into the center of the platform the opening up of the others, the turning of eyes toward him, and the brightening of the light upon him all combine to fix the attention of the audience.

436

At this point an actor on the proscenium stage would probably hold for a moment, but the actor on an open stage will instead enter and turn, executing an unobtrusive curve which will allow the whole audience to see his face soon after he enters the circle of attention. A properly executed entrance of this kind opens the scene up to all observers without many of them being conscious of the means. For the sake of variety, successive entrances are usually made from different points of the compass. The typical open stage has four entrances onto the acting area from four opposed quadrants of the auditorium, plus whatever central, upper-level, and trap entrances can be added for novelty and surprise. Using the greatest possible number of different directions keeps the movement interesting to watch.

"Enter and turn" — the term most commonly heard in rehearsals — is a key to the secret of successful open-stage blocking: practically all movements are curved, turning outward toward the audience in a wide variety of arcs, spirals, compound curves, and half turns. Such movement is not motivated at all, in the usual sense. Its *raison d'être* arises from the practical necessity for actors to be seen by all and from the imposed aesthetic principle of movement attracting attention, not from the psychological motivation of the character. A character will usually move slightly quite a few times during a long speech so that all spectators can see his face during some part of the speech. When an audience member can see the actor's face even part of the time (instead of his back all the time), the feeling of being left out because the actor's back is turned is likely to disappear.

An actor usually delivers soliloquies on the open stage directly to his audience, describing his thoughts and feelings or explaining the plot as the case may be. In order to make his address natural, the actor delivers it on a "tour of the apron" like a public speaker, appealing first to one quarter of the audience, then to another, until all have been reached.

The "tour of the apron" and the "enter and turn" are two of the most highly developed movements, having originated with William Poel and been perfected subsequently in the productions of T. W. Stevens and B. Iden Payne. The tour of the apron is often used as a terminal flourish for processions, such as the entry of the King and Queen to the play scene in *Hamlet* and also in *Midsummer Night's Dream*, of the doctors to the convocation in *The Imaginary Invalid*, and of the mountebanks in *Volpone*.

Ghosts and supernatural characters are often introduced as moving figures passing in silhouette between the spectators and the characters occupying the center of the stage. The silhouette makes it possible to recognize the ghost without having to see much detail. Proximity makes the figure seem larger and more impressive. Motion makes it seem transparent. The device was first employed by B. Iden Payne and has since been used by many others for such supernatural figures as the ghost of Hamlet's father, the ghost of Julius Caesar, the ghost of Banquo, and the ghost of Brachiano in *The White Devil*.

Long scenes involving large numbers, such as the final scenes of most pre-modern dramas and the climactic scenes of many modern ones, are easier to direct on a thrust or apron stage because there are many more places where the minor characters can be put: the perimeter of the acting area, the "ditch," and the upper level. Also, the fact that the audience usually looks down from a fairly steep seating slope makes the problem of covering less acute. The longer scenes demand, however, that the grouping be rearranged from time to time. This regrouping usually coincides with the entrance of a new character or with some climactic development, when a flurry of activity is appropriate. Otherwise, the group can be rearranged during a pause in the action, the general movement then being used like a pause separating the parts of a concerto.

There seems to be no specific direction of movement on the open stage that can truly be called strong or weak. This is due, no doubt, to the fact that the apparent direction varies according to the part of the auditorium from which it is seen. The seeming strength of a character's movement is determined therefore by its manner and force rather than by its direction.

OTHER DIRECTORIAL PRINCIPLES

The second principle of directing for the open stage is that the speaking character must always be specifically identified, usually by movement. Only a portion of the audience is in a position to see the face of the speaking character at any given time. The spectators facing his back may find it difficult to tell who is speaking unless he is pinpointed in some other way. Gestures or gross bodily movement are the most common devices used to attract the eye of the spectator to the speaker. After a few weeks of work on the open stage, the actor becomes so accustomed to accompanying speech with some sort of movement that he rarely needs reminding from the director. Other ways of making sure the audience knows which character is speaking are having other characters look at the speaker and setting him off with space between him and the others in some variation of the "odd-man" grouping.

The third principle applies to grouping. With the audience surrounding or nearly surrounding the action, groupings must be developed which are effective from all points of view. This is sometimes called "sculptural" grouping in the effort to distinguish it from the pictorially-conceived grouping characteristic of proscenium staging. Since in most open theatres the audience looks down on the acting area, sculptural groupings are relatively easy to achieve. The most typical grouping to which the principle applies is a large throng dominated by one character. On the proscenium stage the dominant character is usually upstage at the apex of a triangle, with minor characters on either side and downstage of him. His position is strenghtened by putting him on steps, a platform, a throne, or a similar elevation, and possibly also framing him with an arch, a baldachin, or a pair of columns. On the open stage he is more likely to be placed at the center of an arc with the minor characters surrounding him. Levels do not add much to the scene because they cannot be visually differentiated by an audience looking down on it. Furniture, such as a throne, is desirable only when required by the action. Anything overhead, such as a baldachin or archway, only interferes with the high sight lines.

The grouping of three or more characters on the open stage is most often convex, the convexity changing from time to time to swing toward different quarters of the audience. On the proscenium stage, similar groupings incline toward concavity, with the main characters upstage and away from the audience. On the open stage, the strongest position in a group with much interplay is the position closest to the audience. Consequently, the main characters are usually placed nearest the spectators and the lesser ones farther away. The covering of one character by another is minimized by frequent movement and rearrangement, radical or slight depending on the play.

The fourth principle is that of unbroken continuity. The open theatre provides no curtain which can be raised to reveal applause-getting stage pictures and dropped to conceal scene changes or to cut off the progression at some suspenseful moment. Attempts to achieve comparable effects through the use of black-outs or dim-ups usually end rather lamely and undramatically. The open theatre's diverging exits do provide a means of maintaining without interruption a smooth, continuous flow of action from scene to scene which, implemented through a variety of ingenious devices, has become its distinguishing feature and chief delight.

The most widely used technique for strengthening continuity is the linking of cues so that the line which terminates a scene (the "curtain" line in much proscenium staging) functions both as exit line and as cue for the entrance of the characters in the following scene, who are already speaking. The old characters disappear as the new ones enter, attention shifts to the new ones, and the plot continues to unroll without interruption.

In its simplest form this cue-line link is effected by directional movement, with the entering character coming in from the side opposite the exiting characters. When this is done several times in succession, a seemingly continuous flow of movement is established. Sometimes two or more continuous lines of movement are maintained for conflicting groups. For example, the army of Coriolanus will enter, parade, and exit on one diagonal while the army of Volscians will cross the stage on the opposite diagonal. This crossing of lines of movement neatly symbolizes the opposition of the two forces and the impending conflict. With a thrust stage backed by a multilevel façade, it is also possible to start a new scene in another area, such as the upper level, while the characters from the old scene are leaving the stage.

The fifth principle governs furniture arrangements and the distribution of minor characters in crowd scenes. It recognizes that the open stage is fundamentally centripetal: when an acting area is wholly or nearly surrounded by audience, the action tends to focus inward toward the center of the playing area. This tendency stands in sharp contrast to that of the proscenium stage, which opens outward to make action visible to the narrower sight lines. The more naturalistic the drama the more pronounced this centripetal tendency becomes. In plays like *The Three Sisters* at the Tyrone Guthrie or *The Cherry Orchard* in Ontario, the center of the supposed room is the middle of the stage. Furniture is arranged as it would be in an actual room with pieces normally placed against the wall, such as buffets, tables, and settees, set around the perimeter of the acting area with their backs to the audience. Such arrangements make possible patterns of movement for the characters like those of real people in real rooms. The five stipulated entrances in *The Wild Duck*, for example, can be distributed realistically around the four sides of a platform stage instead of having to be crowded implausibly into the three walls of a box set on a proscenium stage.

In less realistic plays the centripetal tendency encourages the use of the edge of the acting area for inward-facing thrones, benches, and beds, and for scenes such as the closet and duelling scenes in *Hamlet*, where the focus of interest falls primarily on the active characters in the center of the stage. The outer edges are also used for large and awkward properties such as Iachimo's chest in *Cymbeline* or Volpone's couch.

Around the periphery of the acting area the space is generally neutral, with no identity beyond that given to some element such as door or step by mention in the lines of the play. The "ditch" may serve temporarily as a river bank, the vomitory as the mouth of a dungeon, one of the doors as a gate into a castle, or the upper level as a mountain peak. But such localization of action is sporadic and transitory. As soon as the scene is over, the locale evaporates. The "ditch" which had been a river in *Saint Joan* becomes again merely a neutral space in which subordinate characters can stand while they are part of a scene, and yet remain out of the sight lines and out of the way of the principals in the scene.

The sixth and last principle can be simply stated: "Watch out for the safety of the audience." With spectators all around the acting area, many actions required by the script are fraught with danger for the unsuspecting audience member. Duels and battle scenes are especially tricky because a weapon can easily be knocked out of the hands of the actor and into the seating area. The disarming of Laertes in *Hamlet*, for example, has to be staged so that the weapon is struck downward, not up into the air, for it might fall on someone in one of the front rows. Throwing dishes, as in *The Taming of the Shrew*, has to be done so that the platters are not thrown toward the audience. The firing of the revolver in *Uncle Vanya*, the pistols in *The White Devil*, and the muskets in *Cyrano de Bergerac* has to be planned so that the weapons are not pointed toward any section of the audience, because the fragments of burnt powder and wadding in blank cartridges are often discharged eight or ten feet.

INHERENT ADVANTAGES AND DIFFICULTIES

Certain items long in use in many kinds of theatres have proved especially delightful in the open theatre because the average audience member is close enough to appreciate details not visible on proscenium stages; the wise director makes careful plans to make full use of them. As we have seen earlier, among the sources of this delight are lavish and beautifully made properties in great profusion. Properties central to the action, such as the caskets in *The Merchant of Venice* and the banquet in *The Tempest*, can be very rich and colorful, and the scene can withstand and indeed be enhanced by beautiful things above and beyond those essential to action: candles for the banquet table in the last scene of the *Shrew*, banners for the retinue of the king in *Macbeth*, cannon in *Henry V*, and the chariot in *The Winter's Tale*. Similar in appeal are elaborately detailed street scenes in *The Country Wife*, *Lute Song*, *The Canvas Barricade*, and *Volpone*, with vendors everywhere and heaps of bizarre and interesting wares on every hand.

Clever and ingenious construction of properties contributes to the production and helps to compensate for the absence of spectacular scenery. The settee, desk, and gaboon in the first scene of *Man and Superman*, recombined in the second scene to make an auto, then rearranged in the third to make a Moorish patio and fountain, are good instances of this kind of ingenuity. The huckster's wagon in *Volpone* which serves as the siege tower with which Volpone storms Celia's balcony is another. The curio shop in *The Canvas Barricade*, which unfolds out of a window seat at the side of the stage until it covers half the acting area, then folds up again into the same place, is still another.

Magical property changes always delight an audience. One moment there is a stage full of properties and the next minute a bare stage without either people or properties. The bigger the property, the more elaborate in shape and varied in color and texture, the better the effect. Changes are always better when they occur as part of the scene or at least as part of the pattern of movement beginning and ending the scene. They are much less effective when made during intervals between scenes because all the various means of effecting the scene changes in view of the audience through the use of costumed servants and such have been grossly overworked during the past decade.

Because of the high sight line from which

the average spectator views the scene, the ingenious use of forestage traps is highly entertaining. Surprise is the source of delight here. The rabble pouring out of the trap in *Measure for Measure* and the fortuitous rising of the pawnshop in *The Canvas Barricade*, both at Stratford, Ontario, are good instances.

Such are some of the special possibilities available to the open-stage director. On the other hand, a few problems of technique and organization are peculiar to the open theatre. There is, for example, the problem of prompting actors on an open platform some distance from any position where a prompter can be concealed. This is complicated by the fact that in most open theatres the actors are playing three or more different plays in succession and often have to master several roles at one time. Similar to the prompting problem is the problem of co-ordinating cues which involve several actors and technicians stationed at different points of the façade, under the stage, backstage, in the vomitories, and in the lighting control booth in the back of the auditorium. This is mainly a problem of organization, but it is nevertheless many times more difficult than any comparable problem in the proscenium theatre.

The problem of staging scenes which will be equally effective from three or four sides requires that the director continually check the appearance of the scene from various places in the auditorium—close up, far away, and on all sides. The familiar image of the director esconced in a comfortable chair in the middle of the center aisle can never apply to the director in an open theatre. If he sits still very long his staging is certain to suffer, and the spectator who had the misfortune to secure a seat somewhere in one of the far corners of the auditorium would have been better off at home with his television set.

27 | The Director's Relationship with His Associates

The Director's Relationship with the Playwright • with the Audience • with the Actor • with the Designer and Production Heads The Other Side of the Picture

In the four preceding chapters it has been assumed that the director and his collaborators are infallible, that a script has such finality of form that only one interpretation is possible, and that this interpretation and its perfect expression in the eventual performance are recognized by everyone concerned. Having used this assumption in order to analyze the exact task of the director, we must abandon this theoretically ideal situation, and consider the practical compromises which are necessary in actual production.

THE DIRECTOR'S RELATIONSHIP WITH THE PLAYWRIGHT

The script used for the production of a play is not necessarily the original draft supplied by the playwright. It may be altered by the director, deliberately or by accident of misinterpretation. The adaptations made then become an integral part of the script used for the production, and it is this adapted script instead of the original to which the director gives expression. The artistic judgment shown in such adaptation is criticized on the basis of coauthorship, and not strictly on that of direction.

The extremes of slavish acceptance *versus*

adaptation are diametrically opposed, but the intermediate types of alteration shade imperceptibly into one another. At one extreme is the director who accepts the script as a completed entity and bends every effort to express it faithfully in theatre terms. At the other extreme is the one who makes use of the script only in order to create a theatric effect of his own or to communicate values or meanings totally different from those intended by the author.

Only the most unimaginative director accepts a new, untried script as a perfected work. He does accept the basic form and thought of a script, and then works with the author to improve the theatrical craftsmanship of it.

Under the Dramatists' Guild contract with producers, a script cannot be altered without the approval of the playwright, but most authors welcome criticism from a director in whom they have confidence. Those who write of their work in readying a script for professional production [1] say that they read the play again and again, clarifying their reactions to its intended effects and to its

[1] Examples: Worthington Miner in *Producing the Play* (The Dryden Press, 1953), ed. by John Gassner, pp. 211 ff.; Melville Burke, Bertram Harrison, and Priestly Morrison in *Our Theatre Today* (Samuel French, 1936), ed. by Herschel Bricker, pp. 199 ff.

442

strong and weak portions. They try to grasp the intent of the play, and to judge whether it fully produces this effect. They make sure that the progress of the plot is clear, and that it maintains interest and excitement. They look for incidents which may be eliminated in order to reduce confusion, and, on the other hand, for places where relief or variety is needed. They watch for repetition and unnecessary obviousness. They look for every superfluous word. They make sure that climaxes are sufficiently established, and that curtains are effective. They consider whether the play needs shortening or lengthening. They study each character in detail to make sure that it is consistent, and that it contributes to the intended effect of the play. This is not mere presumption, for discrepancies and shortcomings that one would seldom notice when reading a script as a literary work become apparent when a script is studied for translation into theatre form.

With the shorter time usually available for the noncommercial director's study of a script, and no tryout tour, new scripts produced in college and community theatres are usually closer to the author's original script than those used in the professional theatre.

When a director produces a modern or an older script in the absence of the author, he ordinarily uses a script which has been tested by performance, so it is less likely to need revision. Most directors feel that they are morally bound to limit themselves to the words of the author. However, many feel that they are privileged to make cuts in order to shorten the play, and to adapt it to the attitudes of the local audience, especially with respect to profanity and other aspects of local mores. They avoid cuts that would alter its essential spirit, but believe, for example, that in one community "damn" or "Hell" spoken from the stage is equally as profane as much stronger language spoken in another locality, and that these stronger

words would repel their particular audience. This type of cutting is frequent in school productions, for some audiences object to hearing words spoken by a student to which they do not object when spoken by a professional actor or an older person. Changing social mores make it almost obligatory to delete for modern audiences a few words of Shakespeare and other writers of past centuries.

When a director uses stage business different from that of the production in which the script was originally perfected for acting, he often finds that speeches which correlate with action, such as exits, entrances, and the serving of food, are too short or too long. Some directors, knowing that these speeches are frequently altered in an initial production to fit the action, feel justified in condensing or expanding them to match the movements in the new production. Similarly, many directors reassign an uncharacterized expository speech like, "Here he comes now," to the character who can most readily see through the stage opening, rather than move another character into an undesirable stage position merely because he spoke it in the initial production.

The problems of cutting are more extreme in the plays of Shakespeare and other classics. Even with uninterrupted action, few modern companies can play these in "the two hours traffic of our stage" which Shakespeare seems to claim for them. It is difficult to reduce any play of Shakespeare to two hours without making some changes in the emphasis. Thus most contemporary productions do him at least that injustice. The modern audience is accustomed to approximately two hours of playing time, and becomes conscious of the length as the performance runs beyond this. Fatigue, and the heightened critical attitude produced by it, require that a long performance be better than one of customary length. But the longer the script, the less rehearsal and dress rehearsal time each portion can receive, and therefore the less effective the performance is likely to be.

There are variant wordings and variant passages in the different Shakespeare quartos and folios. Over the centuries scholarly conjecture has been employed to guess at the correct words behind the errors in the printed texts. The director has to make choices between these variants, usually with the help of the Furness *Variorum* and the Granville-Barker *Prefaces to Shakespeare.*

A word used by Shakespeare may have changed in meaning since his time, and may now provoke a laugh, as does the "base football player" in *King Lear.* In the last scene of *King Lear* the line "And my poor fool is hang'd" is an affectionate reference to Cordelia, but it is considered comic by some spectators. It is too vital to the scene to be omitted, and is too well known by Shakespeare students to permit substitution. One solution is for the actor of Lear to speak the phrase in almost a whisper, and to articulate "fool" without vocalizing it. Thus it is recognized visually by those who know it and who therefore understand it, but it is not heard by those who are unfamiliar with it.

Many obsolete and semi-obsolete words in Shakespeare are made clear by the context, and need not be altered. A modern synonym is sometimes substituted for one which is not so explained. Many object to this practice if they are aware of it, and prefer to clarify the meaning by unusually explicit expression, even though this destroys the intended rhythm of the line. In *Much Ado About Nothing* (I, i) and elsewhere "presently" is used in the sense of "immediately." One can maintain the original rhythm by altering it to read, "In practice let us put it instantly," or can change the rhythm and say: "In practice let us put it. Presently!" Which does more damage to the line is a matter of taste. Such "interpretation" of

Shakespeare by changes in punctuation is employed in connection with many of his lines. Scholars as well as directors employ it. Because Shakespeare punctuated dramatically rather than grammatically (the punctuation found in modern editions being supplied by an editor), the director of a play by Shakespeare can find helpful hints in a study of a facsimile of the First Folio.

Some directors shorten plays by omitting subplots, believing that it also strengthens the plot line. For example, the murder of Lady Macduff is not often played in *Macbeth,* and the reports of Falstaff's illness and death in *Henry V* (II, i and ii) are frequently omitted. Other directors feel that this practice hurts the balance of the play, and prefer to make piecemeal cuts.

Shakespeare in his rapid composition was occasionally careless; he is sometimes inconsistent, and he often forecasts a development which does not eventuate. The scene of the Duchess of Gloucester in *Richard II* (I, ii) foreshadows a conflict which is not contained in the play, and establishes an impressive character who never reappears. Some directors omit the scene. And some directors change the order of Shakespeare's scenes and assemble noncontinuous matter, as in the forest scenes of *As You Like It* and the first and third scenes of *Richard II.* Scholars usually object to this more than to internal cuts with the material kept in its original sequence.

Few directors feel justified in making additions to a script, but in translating and adapting Molière's *The School for Husbands,* Arthur Guiterman and Lawrence Langner included some scenes from *The School for Wives* by the same author, as well as the ballet sequence from his *The Forced Marriage.* A speech of Richard from *Henry VI,* Part 3 (III, ii, 124 ff., in the *Oxford Shakespeare*) is sometimes used as an additional prologue for *Richard III.* When they did *Henry IV,* Part 1, Maurice Evans and

Margaret Webster were not widely criticized for including the Falstaff scenes from Part 2. Bound by the five-act tradition of the seventeenth century, Wycherley in *The Gentleman Dancing Master* has the pretended dancing master pay four visits to his sweetheart, with much repetitious exposition. A faculty acting group in a university reassembled the lines so as to reduce the visits to three but retain all of the best of the double-meaning dialogue. The director regretted that they had not been reduced to two.

The number of settings is often reduced to save expense, to adapt a play to an inadequate stage, or, by combining several acts of a four- or five-act play, to reduce the number of intermissions. *The Youngest* has been done in a single setting. The fourth act of *You Never Can Tell* can be played in the setting for the third act. Such changes often reduce exposition, but they sacrifice what the author felt he gained by the visual interest of an additional setting.

Either as a matter of interpretation, or as an additional comment which he wishes to make, a director may want the spectators to be aware during the performance of certain analogies which the author either did not intend, or wished the audience to recognize only in retrospect. Several noncommercial productions of plays by Shaw have made up one of the characters as a portrait of Shaw; and Shaw assisted an actor to imitate him in a play by another author. A Harvard production of Sheridan's *The Critic* was given in modern dress with portrait make-ups of contemporary critics. The three servants of the Old Queen in *The Death of Tintagiles* are sometimes made up as skeletons in order to suggest to the audience that the Queen is Death.

More frequently the director does the opposite and reduces the emphasis on the political and social overtones. In a problem play like *A Doll's House,* an audience can

still be interested in the personal story of Nora and Torvald, even although feminism is no longer a public issue; and the modern director is likely to avoid any suggestion of generalization. In producing *Knickerbocker Holiday* today, it is good taste to treat this musical play as generalized satire rather than an immediate political satire on the late Franklin D. Roosevelt.

Outdated topical references are often omitted or changed, unless the play is done in period costume. The latter is an equally drastic change, however, for it may add a satiric element extraneous to the author's intent.

A director sometimes attempts to establish a modern analogy in order to give an older play a more immediate and contemporary meaning — often as a substitute for the contemporary meaning of its day of which a modern audience would be unaware. Euripides expected the Greeks to recognize a contemporary analogy in *The Trojan Women.* This play usually succeeds in suggesting modern analogies, but a director may feel that it needs to be produced in modern dress to heighten this effect. On the other hand, modern analogies can sometimes be made more pointed by dressing the actors in period costumes. Giraudoux and Sartre have used traditional Greek plots and dress in writing plays of modern social satire in order to clarify the themes. But Anouilh, in his adaptation of *Antigone,* by using formal evening dress for the men and near-modern clothes for the women, managed to isolate the essential conflict between individualism and authoritarianism, with its special significance during the German occupation of France in World War II.

A familiar play is often reinterpreted deliberately in order to give it fresh values which its surprise and suspense no longer supply. *Hamlet* is probably the play most frequently given new "interpretation" because, while most important actors desire to

Direction

play the role, they fear the familiarity of the play. The most obvious aspect of these variations is in the costuming — Leslie Howard played in eleventh-century costumes, John Gielgud's American production was costumed in the Stuart period, Maurice Evans used Elizabethan costumes for his full-length production and mid-Victorian ones for his "G.I." *Hamlet,* while Laurence Olivier's motion picture production used the medieval period.[2]

Reinterpretation inevitably creeps into many productions because of the past experience of the director and actors. Out of that experience they see and understand certain characteristics of a role, and fail to see others. Or, if they see all the characteristics, certain ones are more meaningful and more important to them than others. The same is true of the thought embodied in the play. Acting and directing, as well as writing, are subconsciously autobiographical, not in the sense that they objectively reveal patterns of personal behavior, but in that they show what most interests the artist, and disclose his judgment of relative values. In playing Lady Macbeth, for example, Florence Reed emphasized her sensuality, Flora Robson her wifely qualities, and Judith Anderson her resolution. Lady Macbeth has all these qualities; ideally all of them would be revealed together and in succession; but far more complexities can be discovered in the thought patterns of a character than can be revealed clearly on the stage, and there must be some selection. So, inevitably, in the

course of selection, there is interpretation; and this is tinged with reinterpretation.

Just as with characterization, the director has to choose the style in which a production is to be given. An indication of the range of choice for pre-modern plays is given in Chapter 15. Each director and spectator has a preference among these variant styles, and each defends his preference as being the most meaningful reproduction of the original style, or as a necessary consideration for the taste of a modern audience. All the modes, except possibly a modern-dress production, can be classified as interpretation rather than adaptation. Yet each creates a distinct effect.

Design can make its own interpretative comment. For *Himmel und Hölle,* Rudolph Bamberger used a tall narrow rectangle as the central element in each design. In the fifth act its meaning was revealed, for it was repeated in a guillotine.[3] In *From Morn to Midnight* a tree trunk turns into a skeleton in the sight both of the protagonist and the audience. Robert Edmond Jones's concept for *Macbeth,*[4] with the production dominated by three enormous masks of witches hanging over the stage, and with the arches of the setting becoming more and more bent and twisted as the play progresses, would seem to have been legitimate interpretation in design. The production was unsuccessful, however, either because the symbolism was overobvious and intrusive, or because the acting and other elements were not integrated with it.

Carried to the extreme, such symbolism defeats its purpose. In a well-intentioned production of *Murder in the Cathedral* performed in an Episcopalian church, at the moment the knights assassinated Archbishop Thomas à Becket, they snatched off his ecclesiastical garments and then lifted him,

[2] *Hamlet, Macbeth, The Taming of the Shrew,* and many other of Shakespeare's plays have been given in modern dress. Reference has already been made to the Orson Welles production of *Julius Caesar,* for which he cast Joseph Holland as Caesar because of that actor's striking resemblance to Benito Mussolini. Modern dress brought certain scenes, such as the beating of Cinna the Poet by a mob, to vivid and horrible life; but, since Shakespeare had treated Caesar with sympathy, Welles had to warp the interpretation and cut the play considerably in order to make it condemn Mussolini and Fascism.

[3] Reproduced in *Theatre Arts,* VI (April, 1922), 130–131.

[4] *Theatre Arts,* V (April, 1921), 103 ff.

wearing only a loin cloth, high in the air in the pose of the crucified Jesus. Simultaneously an outdoor searchlight flooded the stained glass Crucifixion window above the altar. No thought had been given to the physique of the actor so that to the bad taste was added the incongruity of a young, well-muscled body contrasted with the facial make-up for a sixty-year-old man.

Casting problems sometimes force the director to depart from the perfect interpretation of the play. Most directors, if they have no actor available who can play — and play well — a certain part exactly as written, cast a good actor and alter the characterization to fit his physique and personal style. Edmund in *King Lear,* for example, has been played as a charming, smiling villain instead of the more traditional type of villain. The justification for such a change lies in how much or how little this changes the total effect of the play.

At the extreme of reinterpretation is the director who has a personal viewpoint and adapts to it every script he handles. Sometimes it is a theatric style — he may produce everything as a spectacle, as Max Reinhardt did in later years. He may use a single type of setting. Stairs completely covering a stage are often called *Jessner treppen* because of this German director's predilection for such settings. He may produce everything in a representational style, as many directors do today even with classical scripts. He may warp every script toward sentimentality, emotionalism, expressionism, or theatricality.

Or occasionally a director may propagandize for some social, economic, or political ideology. A director of this type looks for a script by means of which he can express his individual views — or views dictated to him by an institution or government. So long as this merely results in a choice of plays with a single point of view, few object. But many do object to the type of misinterpretation employed by Meyerhold in Soviet Russia before he disappeared, by which every play was made flamboyant Soviet political propaganda. He used *Camille,* for example, to demonstrate the contemptuous attitude of the bourgeoisie toward women. He made little revision in the Russian translation, but, by means of emphasis, completely changed the intent of the play.

At the time of the abdication of Edward VIII, it would have been easy to make *The Apple Cart* a defense of the Duke of Windsor, and a demand for his return to the throne. The first Maurice Evans–Margaret Webster production of *Richard II* was shortly after this abdication and had special interest because of it, but there was no apparent attempt to change the emphasis of the play in order to stress the analogous elements.

An exaggerated style of any type is an easy device by which to add a comment. It would take little exaggeration of the inherent archness and condescension of manner to turn one of Noel Coward's sympathetic satires on contemporary manners into a bitter satire on the uselessness of the class of society which he depicts. Only a slight increase of tempo, and of sustained tempo, would be necessary to turn a George Abbott or a George S. Kaufman production into a satire on the farce technique of fast-moving action, for they now stretch this to an extreme just short of the ludicrous.

It takes but little heightening of the sentimentality of nineteenth-century melodrama to turn *After Dark, Under the Gaslights, The Streets of New York,* or *Uncle Tom's Cabin* into ridiculous displays of empty emotion, so that the spectators laugh at the grandiloquent rhetoric and the melodramatic action. When *The Drunkard* and *Ten Nights in a Bar Room* are thus distorted, they are turned from temperance propaganda into burlesques of temperance that almost become propaganda for intemperance. This is almost exactly what Meyerhold did on occasion to other types of plays.

Similarly, a director can pick out a single character to be exaggerated, and so bring ridicule, or scorn, or hatred, on that character — and through it as a symbol, on a class, a race, or a profession. And he can do exactly the reverse by directing the sympathy of the audience to some secondary character by having it played with greater sincerity and greater depth of emotion than the main characters. In *The Merchant of Venice* this technique has been employed to turn Shylock into a tragic figure, and the play into a tragedy instead of a comedy.[5]

In productions of the highly mannered plays of the seventeenth and eighteenth centuries, it is possible to satirize the play and the production methods without destroying the intended primary impression. Actors in such plays often satirize overobvious playwriting by reading such a line as "Why, here he comes now!" with a wide-eyed look of surprise at the audience. Even in Shakespeare's comic scenes such devices may be acceptable. These scenes are full of puns and other jokes which are no longer amusing, but which are necessary to retain the sequence of the dialogue. One or two of these in a production can be turned into laugh provokers by the enthusiasm with which the character speaks them or by his own uproarious laugh after he speaks them. An example is the line in *A Midsummer Night's Dream* (IV, i, 225), "It shall be called 'Bottom's Dream,' because it hath no bottom."

When the author has left a character or a motivation indefinite or undefined, it becomes necessary for actor and director to fill it out — at the risk of altering the intent of the author. The legitimacy of deliberate adaptation is judged by the taste of each spectator, and the judgment is in large part based on the frankness with which the adaptation is acknowledged. Finally, there is always the possibility that the director may misinterpret a play, and thereby introduce unconscious adaptation.

To summarize the relationship of the director to the playwright: the attitude of the director can vary from that of the considerate interpreter, who regards the script and its intent sacrosanct except as he can advise the author on improvements, to that of the ruthless adapter, who makes a play say anything he wishes regardless of the intent of the author. But to the extent that the director is humanly fallible, is limited by external factors, and finds a lack of definiteness in the script, he cannot achieve perfection in interpretation. Also, because of changing attitudes in the audience, he may adapt a play deliberately in an endeavor to make it produce on his audience the effect which the playwright desired when he wrote for a different audience. At the other extreme, the adapter seldom completely destroys the original intent, though he may add an extraneous comment. In between the extremes, there is wide divergence of opinion and practice in what forms of adaptation are permissible. Once adaptations are made and accepted, they become part of the production script for interpretation by the director. The success of the coauthorship of the interpretative director is judged by how closely he creates the effect intended by the playwright, and depends to a large extent upon the director's artistic integrity.

[5] Usually any satire upon the script itself damages the effect of the play. But there seem to be exceptions. Part of Marie Tempest's great skill in comedy was her almost direct communication to the audience of amused tolerance for the absurdity of some of the lines she had to speak. *Ring Round the Moon* is one of the rare plays in which the author as well as the actors ridicule dramatic technique and stage mechanics.

THE DIRECTOR'S RELATIONSHIP WITH THE AUDIENCE

The director's basic relation with the audience lies in his choice of a play. The tastes of the particular audience are an important consideration. Communities and the organized audiences within them have partialities and aversions, and the director justifiably is influenced by them, even though he may not feel permanently bound by them. The director of a noncommercial theatre cannot flagrantly violate local taboos. Experimental plays, left-wing plays, and "talky" plays are sometimes unpopular. An audience which expects "pure" plays, with no smoking and drinking, cannot adjust itself to an uncut production of *Volpone, Mister Roberts,* or *Love for Love.* But it may so adjust itself to a judiciously cut production of *The Guardsman, The Corn Is Green, Much Ado About Nothing,* or *The Happy Time,* that after a time it will accept only slightly censored productions of *Volpone, The Moon Is Blue,* and *Desire Under the Elms.* The tolerance of the audience can be cultivated gradually with respect to most of its prejudices.

The director in the school theatre has the obligation to his audience of students, parents, and townspeople, to demonstrate to them that theatre classics in good productions are still entertaining. In a period when professional theatre patronage is decreasing, the school theatre attempts to create a potential audience for the theatre in general, and particularly for standard and classic plays in revival. The college director especially has an obligation to the student body to demonstrate that the plays studied in the literature and language courses are not only "literature" of interest for its historical importance, but can be made "good theatre" for a modern audience. Many college theatres perform a representative drama from each major literary period during the four years in which a student has the opportunity to attend productions.

The welfare of the student actors is also to be considered in choosing a play. Since each actor is likely to spend from fifty to a hundred hours in rehearsing and performing a play, its content should repay such study. This requires that the plays chosen shall

have either high literary or theatrical merit. A play may be selected to give student actors experience related to their curricular study.

Naturally, a director doesn't attempt to change his repertory overnight from the puns of "high school plays" to *Hamlet, The Tidings Brought to Mary,* and *The Flies.* He shifts his emphasis slowly, as the audience learns to appreciate a wider variety of forms and types. And he still produces modern comedies to give variety to his production schedule.

A most important factor in the choice of a play is that it shall appeal to the director, actors, and technical staff who will work with it, and that they believe they can give it a valid production. A director seldom does a play in which he lacks confidence. There are depressing periods in the preparation of any production, and unless he has faith in the script, he cannot maintain the morale of the cast through such periods.

The budget is a vital consideration in the choice of plays. Among the items are royalty to the copyright owner; any salaries which are paid; theatre rental; scenery, costume, and furniture demands; printing and promotion expense; special requirements like music and dance; and any organizational overhead expenses which must be charged to the play. The expenses are weighed against the probable income. The current financial status of the organization may influence the choice of plays, liberality in expense being permissible at one time, but economy being necessary at other times.

Labor is often unpaid in the amateur theatre, but the supply is not inexhaustible, and its availability may vary, so this must be calculated almost as carefully as the financial budget. For example, a play with a large cast and crew may be feasible early in the course of a semester, but impossible near the examination period. The pre-Christmas period has similar restrictions in the community theatre.

Though educational and community theatre directors ordinarily avoid forming preconceptions of casting, in the hope that adequate and perhaps fresh talent will be discovered at tryouts, available acting talent is considered before deciding upon certain plays. Plays like *Medea, Abe Lincoln in Illinois, Elizabeth the Queen, The Glass Menagerie,* and *Born Yesterday* demand experienced and especially talented actors with particular characteristics of appearance, voice, or acting style for one or more of the leading roles. Other plays permit some latitude in casting the leads, but make such specific demands for secondary roles that the director finds it essential to be sure that these can be cast successfully before he chooses the plays. Examples include Uncle Stanley in *George Washington Slept Here,* Sol Fitzmaurice in *Both Your Houses,* Madame Arcati in *Blithe Spirit,* Pim in *Mr. Pim Passes By,* and Fanny Cavendish in *The Royal Family.*

Often the casting is a problem related to a group rather than individuals. Most of Shakespeare's plays demand a large cast of capable men, often of mature types. *Stage Door* and *The Young and Fair* require many good ingenues. *What a Life* requires a number of very young juveniles. A Chekhov play demands a group of fine character actors of both sexes. For *Saint Joan* a college director will more frequently have an actress capable of playing Joan than a qualified group of men for its ten demanding character roles. School theatres often give preference to plays with large casts in order to give experience and training in acting to numerous students, and especially to beginners. The proportion of male and female parts is sometimes a consideration. It is unfortunate for school productions, however, that in every period of the drama, male roles greatly outnumber female roles.

Special events or occasions influence the choice of a play. One may be chosen to commemorate a holiday or an anniversary. Sometimes the season of the year exerts a negative influence — pessimistic plays are unlikely to draw good houses just before Christmas or Easter. Many audiences composed of the parents of high school students and other well-wishers expect junior and senior class plays to be popular farces or light comedies which are appropriate to the festive occasion. But the supply of worthwhile plays of an appropriate character for this purpose is diminishing. The alternative of using trivial plays just because their spirit seems appropriate is stultifying to the director and the permanent audience.[6] The current tendency is to replace class plays by all-school plays and by plays produced by dramatic classes or clubs.

Plays also are chosen for the way in which they fit into a seasonal plan. Most school theatres want variety in their production schedule. This creates more interest and gives broader student training than a steady program of any single type, whether it be farces, serious plays, or classics. The attempt is usually made to equalize over a season the number of male and female roles. The widely publicized current or recent success of a play on Broadway may recommend that play, or it may recommend another by the same author which will gain public interest because of the current Broadway one.

In the professional theatre, the producer is primarily responsible for play selection. In the community theatre the director often assumes the task of both producer and direc-

[6] Since the object of a class play is to make money, some schools prefer to do plays on which there is no royalty. However, a modern play which can be produced without paying a royalty is likely to be shallow in plot, character, and thought; it affords little pleasure, and has little or no educational value. Some directors refuse to be bound to the conventional class play choices, and insist upon greater variety. Almost everyone who has produced *Our Town, The Cradle Song, The Rivals, A Midsummer Night's Dream, As You Like It,* or *She Stoops to Conquer* with a high school cast has been pleased by the audience response.

tor, though usually he is responsible to a board which engages him, makes major policy decisions, and approves the choice of plays, and therefore performs some of the functions of a producer. In the educational theatre the director often seems to be completely responsible for both functions. But a teacher is responsible to his superiors, and many important decisions appropriate to the producer are made with the general welfare of the school in mind by an administrator such as a school board officer, a principal, a president, a dean, a departmental chairman, or a senior instructor. Some directors chafe under this restriction; others accept it philosophically, insisting only that the administrator take public responsibility for his decisions and that they have the right of veto on the choice of plays. In *Encores on Main Street*, Talbot Pearson points out the advantage to the community theatre director of having a board take responsibility for some of these decisions.

THE DIRECTOR'S RELATIONSHIP WITH THE ACTOR

Most people work best when they are reasonably happy and comfortable, when they feel that they are being creative, and when they strive for a goal which demands their maximum effort. It is the director's responsibility to establish these conditions for the actors.

Distinctions have been made between the visual and auditory stimuli which are controlled by the director and by the actor. Because of special requirements of a play, the director may invade the field of the actor to become an acting coach. He sometimes has to coach the incompletely trained actor. Teaching is the essential function of a school, so it is inevitable that the director in a school should coach many of his actors. The director of a community theatre often has a few experienced and competent actors, but most

members of his casts are comparatively inexperienced people. Even the professional director of today does considerable coaching because of the partially trained actors whom he rehearses. Helen Hayes, Katharine Cornell, Burgess Meredith, the Lunts, and many of the experienced character actors trained under the earlier system of thorough professional training and experience in stock and repertory companies, can develop their roles with little help from the director. Nevertheless, many of them seek and gladly accept such help.[7] In particular, the director can help even the most experienced actor to be selective — to choose those vocal and visual effects which are expressive and effective and therefore should be retained, as contrasted with those which are "legitimate" but either confuse the spectator or fail to make an impression on him.

The actor is likely to need help in all phases of voice, and especially in obtaining variety of expression. When the director coaches a player in the use of vocal stimuli, he adapts his methods to the actor's individual method of working. One actor has learned conscious control of his vocal expression, so he can successfully turn a rising inflection into a falling one when this is suggested. Another can accept the coaching, but needs time to work out for himself a new motivation to produce the desired inflection spontaneously. But a third actor has no such technical proficiency, and can only artificially imitate the inflection. With him the director works on his motivation pattern, often without indicating the vocal effect desired.

Directors disagree radically on whether they should ever read a line for an actor to imitate. Some spend any amount of time explaining the meaning verbally, and refuse to supply a model. Others recognize that meaning can be communicated much more easily, quickly, and accurately by vocal ex-

[7] Morton Eustis, *Players at Work* (Theatre Arts, 1937). Hayes, p. 23; Cornell, p. 68; Meredith, p. 89.

pression than by words, and so use it to save time. Many have found that after a long unsuccessful explanation, they have only to read the line to have the actor respond instantly, "Oh, I see!" and read it himself with the full meaning. A compromise is to paraphrase the lines and exaggerate the expression. This communicates the meaning without supplying a model which can be imitated exactly. Another method is to discuss the motivation in such a way as to use the vocal pattern the director desires several times, and thus suggest it to the actor without his being aware that he has been given a model.[8]

In coaching gesture, perhaps as much as in speech, the imitative method has dangers. Mechanical imitation is as likely a result as is spontaneous re-creation. Helen Hayes[9] testifies to its crippling effect. She was unable to use an expressive gesture shown her by Gilbert Miller for *Victoria Regina* because she was self-conscious whenever she attempted it. In gesture, as in vocal expression, an extravagantly exaggerated model may avoid the danger of imitation.

The director often has to help the cast in the interpretative aspect of acting — the meaning and implication of the play, the characterization, and particularly the relation of the character to the play as a whole. While most professional and amateur actors today have a good understanding of literary structure and significance, their appreciation

of the detailed implications of the intellectual, emotional, and dramatic meaning of dialogue is practically undeveloped. They read novels and short stories more frequently than plays. These are usually explicit in their explanation of motives, and as a result the inexperienced actor reads plays with the expectation that their complete meaning lies on the surface as it does in other prose. When, for example, William Wister Haines, discouraged at the likelihood of the production of his play, *Command Decision*, prepared it for publication as a novel, he approximately doubled the length by explanations of action and motivation inserted between portions of the dialogue. Both directors and actors have to learn to read plays as they do poems, with concentrated attention to the implications of the phrasing, the choice of words, and the motivations. The director often has to guide the actor in finding the thought patterns implicit in the speeches but not explicitly stated. Obviously this is even more important in plays from previous centuries, and with characters whose background and environment are different from those of the actor. It is sometimes overlooked that this orientation is needed by young people playing mature roles, even when these characters are similar to their own parents or friends, because they previously have looked upon these people through their own — rather than through a character's — eyes.

It has been explained in previous chapters that the director sometimes adjusts the details of the performance of his actors to the overall effect of the play. To maintain the self-confidence of the actors, the director explains the purpose of any such changes he desires in at least enough instances so that they know that he has a definite plan in mind.

Indeed, the perceptive director tries constantly to understand the mind and temperament of each of his actors and to guide them

---

[8] The inexperienced actor usually needs as much guidance in posture, pose, gesture, and other bodily movements, as he does in voice. In this period of loose clothes which conceal rather than display the male body, and of an accompanying casualness in manners, the actors — especially the men — are not conscious of their poses and of the meaning which is conveyed by attitude, gesture, and movement. So considerable coaching of visual stimuli is needed even in a familiar and contemporary play. Many college directors require their students to take training in dance in order to increase this awareness of the body and its expressiveness.

[9] Eustis, *op. cit.*, p. 24.

accordingly. One player may be completely frank and honest about his vocal and physical limitations, and be anxious to discuss methods for concealing his weaknesses and emphasizing his strengths. Another becomes self-conscious and acquires an inferiority complex from discussions of this kind. Some can accept such assistance in the presence of the rest of the cast; others can accept it without self-consciousness only in private conversations. Like any other tactful person, the director gives as much of his instruction as possible as shared knowledge, rather than as a teacher giving instruction. Thus, "as you know" and its equivalents become his constant refrain.

There is a limit to the number of different things to which an actor can give attention simultaneously. Therefore the director chooses those which are immediately important, and leaves the rest for a later rehearsal when the primary matters have become habitual. At early rehearsals it is best to criticize a single aspect of an actor's performance, such as vocal or physical expression, characterization, or style, so that he can concentrate on that aspect of his role for a time rather than trying to remember numerous unrelated suggestions.

The director is careful, normally, to use both praise and blame. He is most likely to err on the negative side, of course, for a director is much more aware of shortcomings than of merits. He overcomes this by assiduously jotting down everything he notices which pleases him, giving special attention to matters which have been improved as the result of previous criticism. To balance a negative criticism artificially by such a comment as, "But you are good in spite of all that" lacks subtlety and is seldom effective. He needs to be as specific in praise as in blame.

An actor is happy only when he feels that he is able to meet the demands of a role. The director must convince him that he can.

At the opposite extreme, an actor may relax and give a weak performance if he sees that a part is easy for him and that he is ready for performance ahead of the rest of the cast. New problems are set for him, even if artificially contrived, in order to maintain his interest and to keep his performance from going stale.

To maintain his self-confidence, an actor needs to feel that he is creative. A director encourages him to think that he is contributing more than he actually is by such direction as: "I can see that you had an instinct to move there, so let's see if we can't give you some business," and "You don't seem happy about that motivation. I wonder if it is right?" Similarly, in making corrections, a director assumes more blame than necessary, for nothing is gained by letting the actor know that it is his weak execution which makes necessary a change in business. This sense of creativeness is seldom a serious problem, however, because people quickly forget the source of a suggestion, and assume that the idea is their own. Directors soon discover that actors appreciate direction in only the vaguest and most general way.

The director watches the temperamental needs of his actors. He sees when they need compliments, and when they need to be spurred into increased effort. The success of the production depends upon the cast's being in a proper emotional state to give its best efforts. This emotional preparation includes the actor's adjustment to costume, scenery, lighting, make-up, etc. While the technical staff shares this responsibility, it is ultimately the director who must see that the actor looks right and feels that he looks right, and that the costumes, scenery, lighting, and properties permit him to perform without undue discomfort. When there are compromises in some of these elements which impede the actor or which show him at a disadvantage, they are corrected; or, if that is impossible, the director takes means to convince the actor that they are all right.

The director who is also a teacher uses rehearsals as a laboratory for his classes. He explains the reasons for his instructions more fully than does the professional or community theatre director. Though it takes extra time, it increases the effectiveness of his classroom teaching, helps to train the students in play direction, and may improve the general seriousness of the actor's rehearsal attitude. Relating rehearsal criticism to class instruction often saves discussion time.

A school director has a few specialized problems in handling student actors. To guard against developing conceit and a feeling of undue competition in them, many directors in the amateur theatre omit curtain calls. They assign dressing rooms on some other basis than the importance of roles. They treat the cast equally in newspaper publicity. Some directors cast an actor alternately in leads and in small parts. An extreme example is a university production of *Once in a Lifetime* which cast the twelve Schlepkin brothers, who enter ad libbing as the first act curtain falls, exclusively from those who had played leads in previous plays.

A student sometimes thinks that he is being unduly singled out for criticism. He becomes sullen, and is not receptive to advice; and thereby brings increased criticism upon himself. When the director recognizes this situation, he ignores the student for a few days or has a private talk with him. On the other hand, some actors like attention and chafe when a director seems to ignore them. They, too, acquire complexes. So periodically a director goes around the complete cast at a critique, saying something vague and stimulating to an actor if he has nothing specific to say: "Your scene is good, but I think you could concentrate just a little bit harder." Particular attention is given to the actor who is playing a less important part than usual, and to the actor who was disappointed in not being cast for another part.

The actor who is embarrassed by criticism in the presence of the rest of the cast can be coached in private. But he also is sensitive to being ignored in the general critique! Many directors try at early rehearsals to concentrate their criticism on the more experienced actors, so that the beginners become accustomed to hearing criticism and to expecting it. This method also is efficient, for the new members of a group improve rapidly in the early rehearsals when they see the general seriousness of attitude. A difficult actor is the conceited one who is resentful of criticism. One director got a long series of good performances out of such an actor by complimenting him for doing the things that he wasn't doing. If the actor failed to see the wit in a line, the director praised him for the subtlety with which he projected the humor of it. The actor took a second look at the line to see wherein his skill lay, discovered the wit, and then gave a good reading of it without knowing that he had changed it. At other times the advice might be: "It is excellent the way you show the basic greed of the man," or "You are a fine Chekhov actor, motivating every word by inner thought."

Angela Morris [10] has reported a brilliant solution by George Pierce Baker of a difficult problem of criticism. In directing his many pageants he found that it embarrassed and antagonized the volunteer casts of inexperienced local people when he gave them too explicit instructions. So for several pageants he assigned Miss Morris, his assistant at that time, to be the rehearsal leader of each chorus group, and used her as a whipping boy. When a chorus of Puritan women entered and kneeled, he would yell, "No, Angela dear! Don't let your skirt wad up

[10] In conversations with the writer.

under your knees. Use both hands and spread it out so that we get as much color as possible!" All the local society women would then spread out their dresses, too, and feel much superior to "poor dumb Miss Morris," who had probably actually spread her dress as she kneeled!

All sorts of emotional problems of actors confront the director. He needs to be a trained psychologist to handle them well. But if he isn't so trained, he has to do the best he can with the layman's knowledge of human psychology. If he succeeds with every problem in relationship, he is a genius — and should take up psychiatry, which pays considerably better than direction.

There is another type of director than the one described here — fortunately a rare one — who believes that the finest work comes from an actor who is emotionally aroused, and that the actor's personal emotions are more easily evoked than those of the character he plays. In his coaching, he therefore deliberately uses criticism, abuse, sarcasm, ridicule, and intentionally nerve-racking repetition in order to make the actor nervous, angry, defiant, or frightened. He especially likes to provoke an actor to "the release of tears." When his victim is at a peak of emotion, he drives him back to the rehearsal of a scene and obtains, he says, a more complete emotional response because the actor is already emotionally stirred. He believes that this transferred emotion becomes a part of the permanent motivation of the scene. This is said to have been a practice of David Belasco in his long and successful career. Some educational and professional directors have used this technique without, apparently, permanently antagonizing the actors. But most teachers and directors condemn it as dangerous as well as needlessly disagreeable, and strive instead for pleasant and helpful relations with their actors.

There also is the autocratic director who dictates every phase of a performance in-cluding the minutiae of acting. This is a different problem which can be better discussed in the chapter on rehearsal methods which follows, for in other respects this type of director tries to maintain the morale of the actors.

To summarize: the director encourages the actors to prepare as much of their performance as they can. But nearly every director has to coach to make up for the inexperience and the lack of training of his actors. He is likely to have to coach his actors in voice projection and vocal variety; in pose and gesture; in characterization, when the part is outside the actor's immediate experience; in style; and in underlying motivation. In this coaching the director is tactful and considerate, recognizing that he is responsible for the morale of the cast. Like every teacher, he works as a psychologist, trying to understand the personality and attitudes of each actor in order to help him in so far as possible within his own working methods, and to set for him successive goals which will make him work to the limit of his capability. As performance approaches, he tries to strengthen the confidence of the entire cast to meet the emotional impact of opening night.

THE DIRECTOR'S RELATIONSHIP WITH THE DESIGNER AND PRODUCTION HEADS

Many professional designers have had more theatre experience than the directors with whom they work, and have demonstrated repeatedly their ability to design stimulating settings which have high interpretative value. From such a designer, a director learns much that is of value to him. In the amateur theatre, too, the designer is often highly trained in the technical and artistic aspects of his work. These designers of the amateur theatre, and some of the professional designers, may be less well trained in literary interpretation and in the analysis of a script. Even in New York one sees beautiful interiors which satisfy the superficial requirements of the play, but which tell nothing about the people who live in the room, or even mislead the audience about them. The director may need to help the designer understand the style, mood, and dramatic effect of the script. He usually has to arrange the floor plan with the designer, and he needs to designate the moments when the actors need assistance from the design to communicate dramatic meaning.

It was assumed in the early chapters on direction that there is only one possible visual interpretation of a play, but in this chapter it has been acknowledged that this assumption is not quite valid. It is most nearly so for a representational and contemporary play. Even here, a designer will not provide the same colored living room for a red-haired leading lady that he would for a blonde one.

A nonrepresentational modern play permits considerable freedom of choice in the manner of its production. *Murder in the Cathedral* can be staged in a church, in a theatre converted to resemble a church, in a strongly illusionistic setting behind a proscenium, in a formalistic setting merely suggesting a church transept, in a formal arrangement of levels used theatrically, or in an arena. The director and designer make their choice partly from preference, but chiefly from an analysis of what staging will best interpret the play to a particular audience. They consider, for example, the type of production to which this audience is accustomed, and whether the play will be better served by using a style within its range of experience or by some novel approach. There is, of course, no one answer to the problem.

A pre-modern play offers even more range of choice in this particular. Production schemes for a Greek tragedy — just as a single example — were discussed in Section III. The necessary choices include: the his-

torical period; the degree of historical accuracy, of stylization, of presentationalism; the emphasis to be given to the poetic form of the play; the emphasis on contemporary analogies; and whether the production is to be framed by a proscenium, projected onto an apron, or performed in an arena.

The designer is involved also in other relationships. During both the preparatory period and the dress rehearsals — except for the timing of curtains, sounds, and lights — the director ordinarily gives instructions to individual technical workers through the designer, the technical director, or the stage manager, depending upon the nature of the instruction. This at times seems a troublesome formality, and is often violated to save time, but its observance avoids confusion and annoyance. If a director instructs an individual property worker to change the position of a table in a setting without informing the property master, the stage manager, and the designer, then during a performance scenechange one of these supervisors may notice what he believes to be an error, and return it to its original position. A time-saving device is to give the instructions to an individual worker, but in the presence of his supervisors.

The relation of the technical crews with the director and actors can easily become strained. Ordinarily the director communicates with the crew only to make changes and corrections. At dress rehearsals he often yells these instructions at the top of his voice in order to be heard backstage, his voice taking on harsh qualities because of the strained volume. He often sounds angry when he isn't. Though the technicians understand this if they think about it, the director insures that they do by mentioning it during critiques. He goes out of his way to compliment their work during the preparation, dress rehearsals, and performance. He learns the names of crew members whom he doesn't know. He does everything possible to cultivate a group spirit of co-workers on a production instead of cast *versus* crew. The crew is included in any production party. They are included in acting critiques for at least a few minutes before they go to a technical one. In so far as newspapers can be influenced, articles which list the cast include the names of the crew or the crew heads. Actors are cautioned to bring their complaints about costumes, properties, and scenery to the director rather than to crew members or designers. The director may be able to pacify the actor by clearing up a misunderstanding or explaining the necessity for the discomfort. If a change is needed, the director is more likely to obtain it amicably if he can confer with the designer before the latter has been annoyed by an argument with the actor.

When music or dance is employed, the directors of these, like the designer, are usually highly skilled in their own arts, but may need coaching in the dramatic significance of their contributions, and the mood, style, and mode of the production. The director can save last-minute headaches by attending a preliminary rehearsal of the dance or music. And the director makes clear from the first discussion the emphasis which is to be given to these features, for it can be an unpleasant shock to an artist to learn at the last moment that his contribution is to serve as background atmosphere rather than to receive full attention.

At dress rehearsal, time is allotted to the musicians and dancers for adequate rehearsal, though they are expected to come to a dress rehearsal as well prepared as are the actors. Dancers are given an independent time in which to practice in the setting as early in the rehearsal period as possible.

If the music needs to be cued accurately to words and movements of the actors, the conductor attends an earlier rehearsal to practice the cues, using a rehearsal pianist. Offstage music is usually cued by a bookholder or assistant stage manager.

THE OTHER SIDE OF THE PICTURE

Though the director is as fallible as any other theatre worker, he is the administrative head of the joint enterprise, and tactful co-workers recognize this to the extent of making suggestions and criticisms in the least embarrassing manner.

A good director is receptive to suggestions from any co-worker, and is prepared to change his interpretation if he is convinced that he is wrong. But nothing irritates a director as much as waste of precious time in rehearsals, particularly at later ones. So the tactful actor, when he disagrees with the director on some matter, and sees that the director is trying to terminate the discussion, waits until after the rehearsal to protest. He is more likely to win the argument then. Similarly, when a director criticizes a detail of acting and suggests a substitute, the tactful actor accepts the suggestion tentatively. If he doesn't like it, he finds a third alternative and asks the director if he may try it at the next rehearsal. In the same way, when the director objects to the design for a setting or a costume, his veto is presumed to be correct, but his constructive suggestions have no such authority. It is the job of the designer to find a substitute which satisfies both the director and himself.

No argument between staff members is conducted within the hearing of the cast, crew, or other workers — particularly if they are students.

28 | The Conduct of Rehearsals

Casting · The First Reading of the Play
The Period of Analysis · Rehearsals
Performance

The ideal rehearsal method makes maximum use of the creative abilities of the actors, but patterns their inventiveness into a co-ordinated production which has unity and form. This implies compromise. Just as directors differ in their psychological relationship with their associates, so they vary in their working methods. Also, the technique of the director varies with the nature of the play, the experience of the actors, and the time available for advance preparation and rehearsal. A director's basic attitude is not always apparent from his surface technique. A few examples will show the erroneous impressions which can be received from superficial observation of his method of work.

Arthur Hopkins' productions include *The Jest, Paris Bound, Anna Christie, What Price Glory?*, the John Barrymore *Hamlet* and *Richard III*, and the Lionel Barrymore *Macbeth*. Brooks Atkinson said of him in 1935, "Of all the directors in the New York theatre Mr. Hopkins is the one who can put the solid foundation of truth beneath a decent sentiment." [1] He had the reputation of directing by what Dorothy Parker called the "absent treatment." The actors sat with him

and read and discussed the script for a week or ten days. Hopkins then gave them a rough plan of the action, and left them free to fill in the details from their own impulses. He made it a policy never to criticize an actor in the hearing of another, believing that an actor was self-conscious when others knew what he was striving for and could evaluate his success. [2] He worked so subtly and so secretively that actors often felt that they had not been directed at all. Yet Brock Pemberton [3] and Sophie Treadwell [4] insist that he knew in advance the exact effect he wanted and always obtained it even in the rare cases when an actor disagreed.

George S. Kaufman, [5] on the other hand, is meticulous, perfecting every visual and auditory stimulus by intensive drill. To force attention upon detail, he often rehearses a play backward until the final run-throughs. But he improvises and experiments with voice, action, and script during rehearsals and the tryout tour, and encourages suggestions from the actors. Thus, while his technique appears

---

[1] *New York Times*, January 13, 1935. During the ten years preceding his death in 1950, Hopkins worked chiefly in radio.

[2] Arthur Hopkins, *To a Lonely Boy* (Doubleday, Doran, 1937), p. 157.

[3] *Theatre Guild Magazine*, VI (April, 1929), 23 ff.

[4] "The Hopkins Manner," undated newspaper clipping.

[5] Morton Eustis, "The Man Who Came to Dinner with George Kaufman Directing," *Theatre Arts*, XXIII (November, 1939), 789–798.

to be arbitrary, it is at the same time highly flexible.

Max Reinhardt [6] took six months to two years to prepare a production book for a play, recording in minute detail every gesture, tone, and movement, and every nuance of expression he wanted from the actors. In rehearsals, he demonstrated these for the actors and required them to mimic him. Yet he asserted that, despite his dictatorial method, he left ample opportunity for his actors to express themselves, and that all his advance planning was subject to change during rehearsals. Mady Christians,[7] who was trained by him, states that he taught her to analyze the motivations of a role in minute detail, and believes the method is similar to that taught by Stanislavski.

Stanislavski also prepared a detailed production book before starting rehearsals.[8] Yet in his books on acting theory, he gives almost exclusive attention to the mental preparation by the actors, and in rehearsal he relied on stimulating their imagination rather than on personal demonstration.

It is probable that both Stanislavski, a fine practicing actor, and Reinhardt, who showed by his demonstrations during rehearsals that he too was a brilliant actor, responded to the script as would an actor, and so the gestures, movements, and vocal expression which they recorded in their notes would seem natural to an actor and leave him unimpeded.

David Belasco is said to have been an arbitrary director, and John Barrymore was thought by some to be impersonating him in the motion picture of *Twentieth Century,* drawing interminable chalk patterns of movement on the floor for his infuriated star to follow. Yet Belasco once said [9] that he would buy a real medieval cardinal's ring for an actor to wear if the play called for it, "because in so doing I am clothing him in reality, not pretense."

The extreme of a dictatorial director is described in the account by Thomas Wood Stevens [10] of rehearsals by William Poel for a production of Ben Jonson's *Poetaster* at Carnegie Institute of Technology:

> He would listen to the voices, giving the speech himself, line by line, and setting the pitch. The actor struggled only to reproduce. At night the books were taken up, lest the actors, reading ahead, get premature and erroneous notions of what the play was about.

He spent two and a half hours one day trying to help an actor obtain the exact "note" for Augustus Caesar's first line. There is the special justification in the case of Poel that he was the profoundest scholar of his day in Elizabethan theatre craft, and successfully popularized authentic reproductions of Elizabethan staging techniques.

These examples indicate the range of variation in method of direction. While the discussion of rehearsal techniques which follows may indicate preference among them, it should be remembered that directors have achieved excellent results by the other methods. A director's success can be judged only by the performance he gives to the theatre audience. Since the kinds of advance preparation which can be made by the director have been indicated, this discussion concerns only the translation of this preparation into a performance by means of casting, analysis, and rehearsals.

[6] Morton Eustis, "The Director Takes Command," *Theatre Arts,* XX (March, 1936), 211–215.

[7] William Lindsay Gresham, "Mama and Papa," *Theatre Arts,* XXIX (April, 1945), 215–221.

[8] *Stanislavsky Produces Othello,* translated by Helen Nowak (Geoffrey Bles, 1948), and *The Seagull Produced by Stanislavsky,* translated by David Magarshack (Theatre Arts Books, 1952).

[9] "Why I Produce Unprofitable Plays," *Theatre Magazine,* XLIX (March, 1929), 22.

[10] "Elizabethan Patriarch," *Stage Magazine,* XII (March, 1935), 52–53.

CASTING

Some roles require specific physical characteristics. However, many actors have succeeded in roles for which they seemed unsuited. Slight Maurice Evans was acceptable as Macbeth, who should be large and powerful. The frail and sickly Elizabeth Barrett was completely realized by tall and large-boned Katharine Cornell. Burbage is thought by some to have been stout when he created the part of Hamlet. Many plain actors and actresses have made the audience accept them as beautiful. Most physical characteristics, in short, can be overcome by capable actors.

Harold Clurman [11] points out that type casting may be necessary for bit parts. Actors of long roles have time on stage to develop a characterization by voice and gesture and by what the playwright has them say and do, while an actor in a short part must establish his character instantly, and is given no time in which to overcome the first impression created by his physique and manner.

The director does try to avoid ludicrous combinations of tall and short or thin and stout unless he wants a comic effect. He hopes to obtain variety within the cast in all characteristics: coloring, height, weight, voice, and temperament. He knows that children usually resemble their parents, and that the members of a family ordinarily have the same regional dialect. But in casting, he often ranks acting ability ahead of all these considerations.

The mental and emotional equipment of the actor is more important than his physical characteristics. The actor need not have the same temperament as the character, but he must understand and sympathize with the emotions of the character. Stanislavski believes that an actor can understand an emotion which he has never experienced

[11] "The Principles of Interpretation," in *Producing the Play*, ed. John Gassner, p. 272.

from the memory of an analogous emotion. But this may require more coaching than rehearsal time permits. During tryouts the director therefore makes sure that the actor or actress is capable of feeling the tremulous tenderness and the passionate hysteria of Juliet, the tremendous emotional release of Medea, the cold intellectuality of Canon Skerritt in *Shadow and Substance*, or the warmth of spirit of Mary in *Family Portrait*. Sometimes the more serious emotions can be stimulated by the director; but, just as a joke loses its humor when it is explained, it is nearly impossible to teach an actor in four or five rehearsal weeks a comedy style with which he has had no experience. So the actor must demonstrate his appreciation of the well-turned phrases and epigrams of *The Importance of Being Earnest* and *Love for Love;* of the humor of the incongruous word and action of *The Lady's not for Burning, Ring Round the Moon,* and *Private Lives;* of the satiric sentimentality of Faulkland in *The Rivals* and Silvio in *The Servant of Two Masters;* or of the roistering earthiness of Falstaff, Bottom, Dogberry, Juliet's Nurse, and Doll Tearsheet.

Potential audience response to an actor is an important consideration in casting. Vocal and physical characteristics and mannerisms call up in the mind of the audience stereotypes of such personality traits as aggressiveness, conceit, slyness, excitability, effeminacy, sophistication, shyness, graciousness, and frankness. Though the cues which arouse these audience reactions can be concealed or replaced in character parts, they are likely to be apparent in any straight part which the actor may play.

It is usually imperative that the audience respond sympathetically to the leading characters. A young man of action in the audience may in retrospect not admire Hamlet's vacillation; but to hold his interest during the play the actor of Hamlet must so attract his attention that he becomes absorbed in

Hamlet's problems and is oblivious to his own far different mental attitudes. This ability to arouse interest and sympathy often is called acting personality. It has not been successfully defined. It is the quality which tells a spectator that here is a vital and interesting person who should be watched. Some of its characteristics seem to be a definiteness which attracts attention and therefore induces empathy, a suggestion of tremendous latent physical or mental energy, and a sincerity and sense of taste which avoid any vocal or visual expression that repels a spectator by making him uncomfortable in his empathic responses.[12]

Competitive reading is the usual tryout method for nonprofessional casts, either in open sessions or ones restricted to specific groups. The director does what he can to encourage and facilitate study of the script before tryouts. But a tryout often depends on sight reading, with all the attendant risks. Few people have learned to read aloud well, so they often give inadequate indications of their acting potentialities. Many good actors have this failing, and a director casts them on the basis of his previous experience with them. Knowledge of an actor's successes and failures is the only sure way of knowing his capabilities, but directors who could cast satisfactorily without tryouts continue to hold them and approach them with an open mind because nearly every one produces a few surprises which affect the casting.

A constant problem in open tryouts is the time consumed by the weak actors who want to read every part at every session, and the better actors who have no genuine understanding of their limitations and ask to read many roles for which they are unsuited. Democracy demands that everyone be given an equal chance; expediency suggests that it wastes many hours to hear poor readers repeat the same parts.

Many heavy leading roles, for example, and some important secondary roles, require a calculated variety of expression which ordinarily is developed only by long training and experience. These roles are often cast, therefore, from the most experienced actors in the group even if they are outread in a few individual speeches by less experienced ones. But there is the rare individual whose experiences in life have made him peculiarly sensitive to nuances of writing, who has free and untrammeled talent for expression, and who therefore is ready for major roles while still inexperienced in acting. Occasionally a relatively weak actor has a special understanding of the psychology of a character which enables him to play that role better than any other. And sometimes leading roles are written so well that the script itself carries them. This type of script may require the more skilled actors in the secondary roles. Because of these circumstances, the director wants to hear the novice as well as the experienced actor. But the director knows, and wishes that the candidates also knew, that a night's sleep with no further study does not make one a brilliant interpreter of a role which one read abominably the previous day.

A device which permits volunteering but reduces the time consumption is to give each candidate one free choice of role and episode to read at each tryout, and for the director to assign all the rest of the readings. Another

---

12 Physical beauty is part of the appeal, because the spectator finds it pleasant to empathize with an actor who is handsome and is in love with someone who is physically desirable. But audiences also respond to the old and the ugly. Highly popular but homely actors include Marie Dressler, Monty Woolley, Peter Lorre, Charles Laughton, Marjorie Main, and a long list of septuagenarians who have lost their former beauty. In spite of her plainness, Maude Adams was America's most beloved actress early in this century. Helen Hayes, Katharine Cornell, and Judith Anderson, though still attractive women as they grow older, have never been beauties. Yet they were as popular as the beautiful Jane Cowl, Ina Claire, and more so than others who had beauty but no acting personality.

device which permits thorough tryout without undue time consumption is to hold one or two open sessions of tryouts, followed by a series of invitational sessions. The latter are divided by roles so that actors read only those parts for which they are being considered. Some directors announce the casting of the leading roles as soon as possible and thereby eliminate the need for further readings for them. Naturally, if the director has committed himself to any pre-casting, he announces this before tryouts.

Some theatres hold a general tryout at the beginning of a season, and prepare a complete file of available talent. For the tryout of a specific show, they call only a few candidates for each role. This is necessary when there is a large turnout and a heavy schedule. With the inexperienced acting corps of the educational theatre, however, the students may not do themselves justice at a first tryout, and the method does not take advantage of the sudden development which often takes place in a student in his first month in a theatre course unless instructors make entries in the casting file as they discover new talent in the classroom.

Memorized tryouts are preferred by some directors in the belief that an actor's ability in performance cannot be judged when he merely is reading from a script. This method also reduces volunteering at tryouts, because a candidate can establish his right to be heard in any role only by memorizing a part of it. Even memorization is considered unsatisfactory by some directors: they want to see what the candidate can do under direction. They therefore prefer to have him perform scenes from roles which he has played. The scenes are supplemented by an interview to determine the response to a particular role. This method permits individual tryouts, eliminating the self-consciousness induced by a tryout performance before a group of competitors.[13]

[13] The candidate's ability to respond to direction is of course important. Some directors listen for

Since physical movement is as important as vocal expression, most directors ask candidates to stand while trying out, and observe their posture and their walk from and to their seats. Some include improvised pantomimic assignments as part of the tryout.

When the tryout sessions are numerous, they become part of the rehearsal period, for the readers learn from each other, especially if the director openly commends good readings and facets of characterization brought out by different actors. He carefully calls attention to any reading which, while effective, is wrong in characterization or motivation, lest it be imitated. While recognizing the value of this guidance to a group of candidates, many directors hesitate to comment on individual readings because of the false hopes and the petty jealousies it may create.

Some amateur theatres double-cast or have understudies for some or all of the roles. Double-casting gives training to more actors with the same expenditure of effort and money for theatre rental, scenery, costumes, and promotion. It increases rehearsal time, however, because actors learn less when they watch their doubles rehearse than when they themselves do so. The extra time is reduced somewhat if the actors who double are both experienced, and if both need fewer rehearsals than the less experienced people with whom they play. Leading roles in musical productions are often double-cast when the voices of the individual singers cannot stand the strain of the necessarily long dress rehearsals.

Understudying can be valuable to the actor if he accepts the assignment as an opportunity to attend rehearsals from which he otherwise would be barred, and to develop himself as an actor by practice in

changes in readings which the actor makes in imitation of competitors and in response to the varied stimuli provided by different partners in the same scene. Some test the candidate directly by asking him to alter the characterization, the motivation of a scene, or some phase of the vocal expression.

imitating the performance of another. Understudies are usually given opportunities to rehearse. The actor who stands aside can profit by seeing his relation to the whole action. If he has a keen eye for them, the performance of the understudy may reveal to him some undesirable personal eccentricities which the understudy had copied along with the good qualities of his performance. Understudies are useful substitutes for absentees. An alternative is to have a few general understudies who prepare themselves to step into any one of a number of roles. They need to be versatile and relatively experienced actors. Many have an older actor understudy small children as an insurance against illness or loss of memory and as a substitute at some dress rehearsals.[14]

A possible objection to the use of understudies for nonprofessional performances is that one is practically committed to the use of a conscientious understudy as a replacement. Promising but inexperienced actors are usually chosen to understudy. They are likely to need so much coaching that they are not ideal last-minute replacements even though they know the lines and action. When there are no understudies, the most experienced available actor can be used as the replacement, with the assurance that he will fit in quickly. This difficulty is eliminated, of course, if the understudy is the original second choice for the part. Second choices for leading roles are often available, playing lesser roles in the production.

Most professional casting is based on past performances which have been seen either by the director or by a casting agent whose judgment he respects. This scheme encourages type casting and makes it difficult for the beginner to obtain a part, but Broad-way production is so expensive that producers reduce the risk of failure in every way they can. Also, sight reading is no more impressive in New York than elsewhere, and arranging to allow many actors to prepare a studied tryout for an unpublished play is difficult. The commercial theatre is aware of this difficulty and of the consequent shortage of experienced young talent. Sometimes efforts are made to provide "showcases" where agents can evaluate new talent and see established actors in varied roles.

The commercial director has one serious disadvantage. He may read an individual actor extensively, but because some directors once took advantage of "readings" to lengthen the maximum rehearsal period, Actors Equity ruled that the four-week rehearsal period begins when more than two actors read together. Thus the director has little opportunity before regular rehearsals to experiment with voice harmonies and contrasts.

THE FIRST READING OF THE PLAY

A first reading of the play by the author helps the cast to understand characterization, motivation, and overall meaning, even when he is a poor reader. A reading by the director establishes the mood, style, and playing method as well, even when he doesn't read well. A reading by a scholar specializing in the period of the play helps to demonstrate characterizations and motivations and to clarify diction and syntax. A truly good reading — by anyone — also establishes the general effect of the play and the relation of its parts.

The disadvantage of a reading is that it may be dull. A solo reader may not be able to make a group scene even as effective as when it was read during tryouts. If an actor has studied his part, he may be able to characterize and motivate it better than the reader, especially since the latter is performing as an interpreter rather than as an actor.

---

14 The writer recalls a dress rehearsal of the Kingdom of the Future in *The Blue Bird* from which the children had been excused, and in which one tiny college girl who had prepared herself to speak any line which a child forgot, performed almost the entire dialogue solo to tremendous applause from an appreciative cast.

If the director is the reader, the experience may lessen the actor's confidence in him. Many directors omit a reading for fear that actors will attempt to imitate the reader.

These objections are largely overcome if the reading is held before tryouts. The reader then is sure to know the play better than his auditors, and the actors are unlikely to remember the reading of a specific line since they do not know which role they will ultimately play. The danger of imitation is slight even after the cast has been chosen, because an actor cannot remember an earlier reading after he has heard so much read at one time. The pre-tryout reading also serves to help the whole group understand the play and the individual characters, and so enables them to read better at tryouts. It is especially valuable for a poetic classic, which is likely to be read so badly at sight that the group is discouraged about performing it. Chekhov's plays and many of Ibsen's are composed of episodes which seem dull and lacking in action until one understands their relation to the rest of the play, and until he becomes interested in the interplay of the characters. Candidates may be depressed and even frightened away if they hear these plays read with the meaning poorly brought out in a piecemeal tryout.

One disadvantage is common to all types of solo reading. Because a single reader is taking all the parts, he characterizes some roles less than they demand; he may unwittingly set the wrong pattern for a role and the results may be a less distinctive characterization for it than is desirable. Also, certain eccentric parts may be played in a variety of ways to fit the personal acting traits of the actor. To give the stamp of approval in a reading to one possible characterization may stifle the imagination of a good eccentric actor, or it may reduce his effectiveness by compromise between his own style and that of the reader.[15]

[15] A reading of the whole play to the cast is imperative when actors are using "sides." These

If the play is not read to the group, the director usually assembles the entire cast and has the actors themselves read the play, interrupting them only for major explanations and corrections. In order to let each actor sense his relation to the entire play, some directors hold such a reading before the analysis period even when the play was read in advance of the tryout.

THE PERIOD OF ANALYSIS

The purpose of the analysis period is to convey to the actors everything the director has learned about the play, and to stimulate them to learn still more about it — and about their roles — by personal study and by the mutual stimulation of reading and discussing the script together.

A written summary of their interpretation of the play is prepared by some directors. It includes a summary of the plot and the thought content, and a statement of the director's intent in style, atmosphere, mood, and general approach. This serves to codify his own ideas, and to clarify them for his colleagues. Conferences on this summary are held with the designer and other staff members; and it is discussed with the cast, for one of its important purposes is to encourage a free exchange of opinion. Few can accurately express their ideas verbally, and a discussion of the intent of the director's language provokes analysis which clarifies the thinking of all. A resulting change of wording may not indicate a change of the director's intent, but the arguments about the subtle connotation and denotation of words in proposed alterations reveal the

are booklets which contain an actor's speeches and a three-word cue for each of them. Professionals who are habituated to memorizing from sides, and amateurs who consider them "professional," have perpetuated the use of these relics of former times when handwriting and printing were the only methods of duplicating writings. They are now needless, since there are cheap and easy duplicating processes which allow every actor to have a full script at less cost than for sides.

basic agreements and disagreements. Such good-natured debate promotes unity rather than dissension, for any real disagreement is revealed early enough to be reconciled.

During early readings the director constantly interrogates the actors in order to force them to analyze the characters and their motives. "Why does he say that?" "What does he mean?" "What is he trying to do?" "What does that tell us about the character?" "How is the speech influenced by the presence of this other character?" "Why doesn't he say something else?" Such queries become the refrain of the director. He encourages the actors to ask similar questions. He may prepare in advance some brain-crackers for the group or for individuals. Obvious questions to which an actor can give a glib reply are of little value. The director is helped in provoking stimulating discussion if during his own study periods he jots down the questions which trouble him, both those for which he finds the answers and those for which he still has none. He recommends collateral readings and the study of period pictures when they are appropriate, encouraging the actors to duplicate his own analytic study. A dictionary is always at hand during the analysis.

When, through his explanation of the playscript and its complex motivation patterns, a director has shown that he knows the play and its background well, he can afford to admit incomplete knowledge of details. Young directors often feel that they must be an encyclopedia of knowledge and that if they admit ignorance of any fact, pronunciation, or motivation, they lose the confidence of the cast. This sometimes forces them into snap decisions which they regret later. Like all good teachers, they are entitled to say, "I'll find out," or "I'll study that matter and decide before the next rehearsal." Of course, they do come to the next rehearsal with the knowledge and the decision. This demonstration of conscientiousness and thoroughness may even increase respect.

Wesley Swanson of the University of Illinois and other directors — in a desire to emphasize the equal importance to a production of all actors — conduct the early analysis sessions by having the speeches read around the circle of the cast without regard to casting. All those present participate in the discussion. For study of the structure of the play and of the intellectual meaning of the lines, it is an advantage to have important speeches read weakly by inexperienced actors, because this stimulates closer analysis than if they were read by more experienced actors with such effectiveness as to conceal an incomplete understanding of their meaning. It has, Swanson believes, the further advantage of accustoming the actors of small parts to speak the language of the playwright.

Some directors ask for written character analysis of their roles from the actors. Each actor submits a detailed report containing the author's comments on the role in his stage directions; the character's own statements about his motivations and character; statements of others about him; evaluation of the relative truth of such statements; key speeches and actions which indicate particular characteristics; the character's emotional relationship with all the other characters; a list of known characteristics of action, thought, speech, and emotion; a negative list of the qualities not possessed by the character; and an imaginative filling in of the biography and characterization where the author has not been explicit. This forces a more minute analysis than any other method, but actors often react unfavorably to it, so its use is limited. Charles W. Cooper and Paul A. Camp [16] have prepared a form for a detailed character analysis.

The constant interruption during the early analysis period makes it difficult for the actor to respond emotionally to his lines. It is dangerous to force him to do so, lest he learn to simulate a generalized emotion. However,

[16] *Designing the Play* (F. S. Crofts, 1942).

actors should be encouraged to play as completely as possible in the analysis period, increasingly so as it proceeds and as interruptions decrease. The analysis period should include, if possible, a full realization by the actor of the emotions of the character, and these cannot be felt when he is detached. It is during this period, especially, that the director helps an actor to understand and feel emotions which are new to him. The director and actor may work co-operatively to find an experience in the personal life of the actor akin to that of the role, or to imagine one. The actor visualizes this imaginatively until he feels the emotion vividly, and then, out of this understanding of a similar emotion, transfers it to the role. While such matters should be the homework of the actor, the director can often speed the process by verbal assistance or by assuming a role in an acting-out of the experience. This is a practical use of the memory and transfer of emotions which Boleslavsky and Stanislavski advocate. Since there is danger that the presence of other people will inhibit the actor, this work is usually done in a private session with him. Stanislavski disciples also use acted-out improvisations of imaginary incidents in the life of the character in order to understand certain motivations fully. While these techniques may be used later, they are psychologically part of the analysis, and are employed as early as the need for them is discovered.

Though the theory of the analysis period is that of the "director and cast seated around a table studying together," this need not be a literal description of the method. Actors are permitted to stand and to move about if they prefer, so long as they do not transfer their attention to the perfection of specific business. If they use gestures and movements, they are encouraged to vary them from rehearsal to rehearsal to keep themselves flexible.

Not much analysis can be done after the initial period. When actors are learning business and lines, they necessarily pay less attention to motivation. Though the actors should strive for the illusion of the first time in order to motivate the business, most directors are lenient during this period about demanding it, and postpone further work on this until later rehearsals. The actors learn lines and business at variable rates. By the time all are secure, it is usually too late to stop for much detailed analysis, even though it would still be useful. Also, actors are annoyed by long discussions of characterization, motivation, and thought when an action rehearsal is interrupted for it. A way to avoid this irritation, of course, is to have special conferences with the actors concerned. In any case, as much time as possible is devoted to the initial analysis.

The more complex the play, and the further removed it is from the cast in time, place, and experience, the more time is needed for study. A modern comedy or farce of family life may need little work of this kind, though dramatic analysis is still desirable. With a high school cast that wants to get on its feet and "act" immediately, a director may set the business of *Junior Miss* or *A Date with Judy* after a single reading and a discussion of characterization, and then analyze the play, its meaning, dramatic structure, and the basic tempi of the scenes just before polishing rehearsals. This may make the cast more aware at the final rehearsals of the patterning needed for subordination and climax than if this discussion is held earlier.

On the other hand, long periods of analysis, discussion, and argument inevitably precede the walking rehearsals of such a play as *Saint Joan*. For here the romantic personal story of Joan is subordinate to Shaw's penetrating analysis and interpretation of her significance — i.e., as a symbol of the complex conflict between monarchy and feudalism and between Catholicism and

Protestantism in the medieval world. The characters have different temperaments and interests, so those who support the same doctrine argue among themselves on the practical implementation of it. It is hard for an actor who believes in one religion to learn to understand the ideas which result in absolute faith in another one; it is often harder for one who accepts democracy as the only political way of life to eradicate every thought of it and recognize that characters in *Saint Joan* are defending monarchy and feudalism only against each other, with no thought of a third alternative. Since the movement in this play is simple and relatively unimportant, the analysis may consume two-thirds of a long rehearsal period. However, once again, actors become nervous as performance approaches if they don't know the business. So the director may find it expedient to interrupt the analysis, set the action, and then revert to analysis.[17] Shakespeare's tragedies need similar work with most casts, though here more time is needed for developing the visual aspect.

In a third situation, it may be difficult for a modern athletically inclined girl — dressed in loafers, jeans, and sweater, slumped down in a chair so that she can sit on the base of her spine, and with one foot resting on the other knee — to read the epigrams, repartee, balanced sentences, and satirically sentimental passages of *The Way of the World* or *The School for Scandal.* So it may be expedient even in the analysis period to put her in a paniered rehearsal skirt and spike heels, give her a fan and a handkerchief, and teach her to stand with shoulders and head held

up and back, to sit on the front two inches of a chair, and to make the kind of calculated gestures and movements with which she is expected to point these lines. The men will be helped similarly by handkerchiefs, canes, muffs, snuffboxes, and some kind of head covering to suggest wigs. The business used can be that planned for the production, but not necessarily so, for this is still the analysis period and not business rehearsal. In the analysis, for example, it may be advisable to employ far more business than in performance, pointing every line with a gesture or movement, because the line once so pointed is likely to retain the inflectional pattern which it assimilates from the gesture, even when it is spoken without movement. Further, business learned after this inevitably clumsy initial period is likely to be more natural and graceful. A similar approach may be useful for Victorian melodramas, for Oriental plays, and for broad period farces like those of the *commedia dell'arte* or the pre-Shakespearean Interludes.

Some directors dictate movements and gestures during the early analysis period, and have the actors write them in their scripts so that they are prepared to execute them at the first business rehearsal. If they are beginning to memorize lines during this period, they can learn the business at the same time. On the other hand, there is a danger here: this method may encourage them during the analysis to imagine themselves in motion, and thereby divert them from the study of meaning. However, to help an actor understand the motivation of a line, a director often suggests that the actor will ultimately shrug his shoulder and move away on a given line, or will freeze and turn slowly to his antagonist on another line. But these bits of business can be given purely as motivation, and without regard to the direction of the movement or the relationship to other actors, and so are unlikely to divert the actor from study.

[17] The writer's most enjoyable and rewarding rehearsal experience was the seven weeks spent on this play. After three weeks of analysis, a week of setting business, and with all lines learned, most of the remaining time was spent in double rehearsal in which an assistant director schooled the actors in their business while the director himself worked with the actors of another scene seated around a table reading from their books, analyzing detailed motivation.

During the analysis the director often observes the actors showing instinctive tendencies to movement, or thinks of effective movements for them as he clarifies meanings. He makes notes of these in the margin of his script, and revises his planned action to accommodate those which he thinks effective.

The analysis period later blends into the regular rehearsal period, for as more is learned about the play, the less the director interrupts; and the actors then can practice continuous motivation. The cue to stop the readings and to put the actors on their feet comes when he finds that his interruptions are negligible. Guthrie McClintic [18] insists on eight days of seated rehearsals, George S. Kaufman [19] usually takes four, Arthur Hopkins [20] took a week or ten days, as did David Belasco.[21] A professional "day" of rehearsal can mean a maximum of seven hours (eight continuous hours with a one-hour interval for a meal).

Some textbooks on play production advocate a reversal of the procedure outlined here. They recommend giving the business almost at once, with special characterization and detailed motivation rehearsals later in the rehearsal schedule. These alternatives are discussed in more detail later in the present chapter, under "business rehearsals."

REHEARSALS

Scheduling

A rehearsal schedule is seldom the same for two productions. However, rehearsals are planned with certain constant but flexible principles in mind:

1. *The available time is used efficiently.* Rehearsals begin on time and end on time,

[18] Eustis, "The Director Takes Command," pp. 114–120.
[19] Eustis, "The Man Who Came to Dinner."
[20] Treadwell, "The Hopkins Manner."
[21] Sidney Sokolsky, "Meet the Governor," *Theatre Magazine*, L (October, 1929), 22 f.

with some latitude within the schedule to permit special attention to the episodes which need it.

With the inevitable delays which make a cast straggle to an early evening rehearsal, the director often begins a rehearsal with a duologue episode. He may call a series of small-cast episodes, gradually accumulating the cast for the large-cast scenes. The high school director rehearsing immediately after classes reverses this technique, rehearsing and releasing actors early and holding only a few to the end of the rehearsal period.

Episodes which need drill may be sent to a secondary rehearsal room under an assistant. If possible, the director himself again sees the scene during the same session. Drill sessions, and work with individuals, often take place outside the regular rehearsals. An assistant director serves as call boy to alert actors for successive scenes so that no time is lost between them.

2. *Actors are used efficiently.* For as many rehearsals as he can, the director calls actors by French scenes, grouping together those with similar casts. A chart helps him to identify these. He gives as much consideration as possible to each actor — calling him late, releasing him early, calling him alternate nights, or releasing him from at least one rehearsal each week.

An actor who plays a short role is called for a minimum time by grouping his scenes. Waiting for hours between scenes not only causes annoyance, but the irritation or listlessness may become part of the characterization. Actors in small roles may even be excused from early rehearsals while the bookholder walks for them. In this case, the bookholder or other substitute must motivate completely, for the sake of the other actors. To secure this complete motivation some directors themselves read for absentees. It is necessary to have these actors at a number of later rehearsals for periods out of proportion to the length of their parts; and the director has a distinct advantage in declining to excuse one of them from these rehearsals "because his part is so small," if he can remind him of previous considerate treatment. The director who supplies business from a plan prepared in advance may ask all actors to attend the first business rehearsal to record the details, and may then excuse them. The director who extemporizes business at rehearsals may be glad not to have the bit players present with their "How do I get there?" and "What do I do up here all this time?" Also, with a later start in rehearsals, they find that the others in the cast know their lines and are giving full motivation, and so are aware without being told that they must work hard and fast to avoid personal embarrassment.

It is less serious when leading actors have to wait between scenes, for they may welcome a rest between periods of intensive work, and they can review their lines during the rest periods. It is never possible to please everyone — Cleopatra may feel neglected if she is called only every other night.

In any case, it is imperative that rehearsal calls be posted well in advance, so that actors can plan the use of their free time. Duplicated rehearsal schedules can be distributed so that every actor has a copy and can make no claim of misunderstanding.

3. *Equal attention is given to all parts of the play so that one act is not perfected at the expense of others.* Less time is ordinarily required on successive acts, however, because of the transfer of characterization and the adaptation by the actors to the working methods of the director. In general, all the business should be set as fast as possible, though the giving of business can be spaced so that individual scenes are not confused with one another. The need for such spacing is not as great in a multi-set play as in one which uses a single setting. In either in-

stance, no one scene or group of scenes should be neglected. While business is set for one portion of the play, rehearsals of earlier portions continue, as well as readings of later acts.

A well-made plan of rehearsals permits business to be set, rehearsed once afterwards, and then given time for memorization. The following is a hypothetical and abbreviated rehearsal schedule for a three-act play in one setting.

1. Set Act 1 (1)
2. Act 1 (2)
3. Read Acts 2 and 3
4. Act 1 (3)
5. Set Act 2 (1)
6. Act 2 (2)
7. Act 1 (4)
8. Act 2 (3)
9. Act 1 (5); read Act 3
10. Set Act 3 (1)
11. Act 3 (2)
12. Act 1 (6); Act 2 (4)
13. Act 2 (5)
14. Act 3 (3)
15. Act 3 (4); Act 1 (7)
16. Act 3 (5); Act 2 (6)
17. Acts 1 (8), 2 (7), and 3 (6)

Thereafter alternate rehearsals of weak scenes with running rehearsals and specialized rehearsals.

Business need not be set in its natural order starting with the first scene. Directors occasionally reverse this order. Such a change assures thorough rehearsal of the climax of the play; and advocates of this order point out that action is then increasingly easy to set throughout the play, for the more intensely motivated action of the last act helps the actor to respond. Under this reverse order the actors attack the difficult opening scenes of exposition with their characterizations established, and with increased responsiveness to the character, the play, the director, and — with beginners — to acting itself.

F. Cowles Strickland of Stanford University recommends [22] that the key scene of the play be thoroughly rehearsed before any others, asserting that this makes the other action and dialogue more meaningful to the actors because they then conceive of them as a preparation for or a consequence of that scene.

4. *Excuses from rehearsals are granted only when presented far enough in advance to permit the director either to change the call or to change the rehearsal time.* A list of conflicting engagements during the rehearsal period is obtained from each actor at the first reading, and it is made clear that the actors are to be available for rehearsal at all other times. The rehearsal schedule is then laid out to avoid the conflicts. Any rehearsal in which work is done on relationships and mutual reaction must have all the key actors. Late in the rehearsal period, the bit players are equally essential.

Actors can be required to sign a "contract" in which they pledge regular attendance along with other obligations. Some high school directors ask that this contract be countersigned by a parent as well, as a protection against the parent who suddenly decides to take the student on a trip or who objects to a long dress rehearsal and tries to interfere with it. College students often consider such contracts unwarranted paternalism and resist them.

In spite of the adage that "Only death is an excuse for missing a rehearsal, and even death is no excuse for missing a performance," directors of course accept valid excuses, such as illness. Many of them, however, give consideration to the excuse only if they receive notice of a necessary absence in advance. They immediately replace the actor if there has been no notice. Because of the difficulty of reaching the director by phone, a telegram may be the actor's last refuge in such an emergency. Such notice merely gives the absentee an opportunity to present an excuse, and the decision on dismissal is based on the validity of the reason. Any such rigorous policy must be enforced equally for the entire cast. This necessity restrains some directors from applying too definite a punishment, lest it boomerang on them in the loss of a leading actor at the last minute.

5. *There are as many rehearsals as possible.* In the noncommercial theatre there are seldom as many as the director would like. There is a limit to the amount of time which his actors and he can spend on a production. Yet to accomplish their educational purpose, plays must be acted and directed as well as possible. A hasty and slipshod production does more harm than good.

College directors usually spend four to five weeks on a modern comedy, and five to eight on more difficult classics. Rehearsals are usually three-hour evening sessions for five or six nights a week. Four weeks of five three-hour sessions totals sixty hours. Eight weeks of five three-hour sessions totals 120 hours. This compares with a Broadway production with experienced professional actors where the director has at his disposal 224 rehearsal hours for such a production,[23] and expects the leading actors to study their roles prior to the first rehearsal. High school rehearsal periods are often shorter than three hours. Some high school directors correspondingly lengthen the rehearsal schedule. But others produce a play in fifteen two-hour rehearsal periods or less. Perhaps it is such productions which have popularized the compliment, "They all knew their lines!" The Secondary School Committee of the Ameri-

---

[22] "Directing Amateurs," *Theatre Arts*, XXI (July, 1937), 566.

[23] Three weeks of rehearsing seven out of eight consecutive hours seven days a week, and a final week in which he may rehearse eleven out of twelve consecutive hours.

can Educational Theatre Association [24] recommends four to six weeks of daily two-hour rehearsals.

6. *Rehearsals are spread over as long a period as is feasible, since maturation improves a performance.* The few directors whom accident has permitted to rehearse in spaced rehearsals over a long period, with no greater number of rehearsal hours than usual, are enthusiastic about the greater depth of meaning they obtained from the actors. Many directors report that, except for the ragged first rehearsal, they note improvement following a Christmas or spring vacation.

Directors who have had experience with double rehearsals, afternoon and evening, in summer schools and in stock company situations, vary in their opinions on the comparative quality of such productions. The intensive work, with the actors giving their roles almost exclusive attention, may compensate for the loss of maturation time. That would seem to be the only justification for the astonishing proposal of one school administrator that students in a high school play be excused from all classes for a week, starting the rehearsals on Monday morning and giving the play Saturday night.

Types of Rehearsal

Attention is focused in turn on each phase of acting and direction during the rehearsal period. Some directors attempt to give continuous attention to all phases at once or shift gradually from one to another without consciously deciding on what will receive attention from rehearsal to rehearsal. Others feel

[24] "Materials, Methods, and Special Projects for a Course of Study in Dramatic Arts in the Secondary School," Marion Stuart and others, *The Bulletin of the National Association of Secondary School Principals,* XXXIII (December, 1949), 100. This special issue of the *Bulletin* contains a great deal of material of value to the high school teacher. It can be purchased through the Executive Office of AETA or of NASSP.

that it stimulates the actors if they have a specified goal for nearly every rehearsal, and that each phase of the production can be more easily perfected if the director and the actors give it separate attention. The first group feel that this is an overly mechanical approach, and prefer to let their instincts tell them when the cast is ready to work on certain matters. The second group reason that their actors come better prepared psychologically to work on a special phase when it is scheduled. Under either plan, the rehearsal types overlap to some extent, for neither actor nor director can afford to concentrate so exclusively on one phase of preparation that weaknesses in others are ignored.

Many special names have been invented to identify rehearsals by function. The major ones which can be definitely differentiated are:

1. Setting business and co-ordinating lines and business.
2. Perfecting memory of lines and business.
3. Perfecting characterization.
4. Perfecting motivation.
5. Perfecting business — often called polishing.
6. Perfecting the flow of the action — often called running rehearsals.
7. Integrating the acting with other phases of the production.
8. Final co-ordination of all phases — dress rehearsals.

The first and the last are fixed in their order, but there can be considerable variation in the order of the others.

Business Rehearsals. Some directors follow Reinhardt in that they plan the business in minute detail, and dictate it at the very first rehearsal. The actors can then assimilate such details into their motivation and characterization patterns. This may seem an arbitrary procedure, but if the director plans his business with the instinct of an actor, he works out movement patterns which are acceptable to the actor. He searches for the line on which the actor can most easily motivate a desired movement. Studying alone, the director has ample time to make a reasoned decision. He also has time to plan the details by which he can achieve a pictorial effect without apparent effort.

Many actors like this kind of definite direction. Professional actors expect it. The careful advance planning demonstrates the director's workmanship and gives the cast confidence in him. The director of a stock company is compelled to work in this manner because with only ten rehearsals he has no time for experimentation and change.

The critics of this method say that it provides no opportunity for a contribution which could be made by the actor, and also that it is stultifying because when movement is dictated to an actor before he is fully motivated and characterized, he gives little further thought to it unless he finds he cannot perform it. Often this is true, but it need not be. The method requires high imaginative ability on the part of the director in creating interesting and varied business.

The recorded business in an "acting edition" of a play is sometimes accepted without question. Some directors say that they cannot hope to improve upon the direction of George S. Kaufman or Harold Clurman. Others are embarrassed to copy another director's ideas. In any event, an acting edition of a play is not always a record of the Broadway production. It may be prepared independently or in connection with some other production. Even if it is based on Clurman's direction, the acting script is not prepared by him. It consists of the notes jotted down by the stage manager working as a rehearsal secretary to Clurman, and its completeness depends upon the stage manager's care in taking notes.[25]

[25] A motivation is included in this script ordinarily only when Clurman mentions it — usually

Furthermore, Broadway settings are often thirty-six to forty feet wide. School and community theatre sets are usually about thirty feet. This decreased size, and other changes resulting from it, require careful restudy of the business. Characters may become too crowded laterally, and may need to be regrouped in depth. A cross from one piece of furniture to another may have been long enough to be impressive in the New York setting, but if the furniture is closer together in another production, the movement may have to be replanned to obtain the same effect.

When the director does dictate the business, or adopts that of an acting edition, he watches to make sure that it is comfortable and easy for the actors to perform. Little imperfections in its execution may mean that they are consciously or subconsciously unhappy with it. The director then makes them comfortable, by altering the business, by clarifying the motivation for it, or by so explaining the necessity for it that they make special efforts to adjust themselves.

Other directors use the *laisser faire* technique and refuse to set any business except entrances and exits, allowing the actors to develop the rest from their motivation and characterization. This system assumes that the actors are more alert to the demands of the script when they know that they must develop business of their own. They have more sense of personal participation and more creative control of their characterization and the accompanying business. Greater naturalness comes from instinctive action which the actor incorporates into his role only when he corrects an actor. In such cases, he is likely to overstate the motivation in order to impress it upon an actor. A stage manager is meticulous in entering business set by the director, ordinarily catches any major movements improvised by the actors at early rehearsals, but is less aware of later spontaneous changes. In entering new business he may forget to remove the old. For example, in the first scene of the acting edition of *Berkeley Square* there are three different instructions for Kate to put her sewing in the drawer of a table. Errors creep in, such as a cross in the wrong direction, or a cross by the wrong character.

than from imposed business. The many brains of the cast produce more interesting ideas of movement, and particularly of characteristic pantomime, than the one brain of the director. The unfamiliarity of inexperienced actors with theatre tradition, it is assumed, may develop interesting patterns which would not occur to the more channeled mind of the director.

When this technique is employed in its extreme form, however, a director throws away some of his most valuable tools. It is a rare cast that can, from purely "natural" motivations, find positions which give proper emphasis and shift of emphasis, or that give mood, style, and visual beauty to the whole performance. And if, in last-minute polishing, the director makes arbitrary changes in order to achieve these, the actor has to abandon habituated patterns and learn new ones in a few rehearsals. He is more disturbed than if the director had imposed the business earlier.

Moreover, as several writers on direction have pointed out, the *laisser faire* method is likely to encourage a static performance because, while a few actors have impulses to move and may race about, most amateur actors "feel like sitting down," and seldom have an impulse strong enough to cause them to rise again. Also, business which they themselves develop is likely to stem from personal habits rather than from characterization because they must invent the business before their characterization is completed.

Still other directors, perhaps because they find themselves most inventive when there are actors before them, go to the first business rehearsals with only general mental images of the crucial situations, and depend upon the inspiration produced by the actors and their instinctive movement tendencies to fill in the details. They do in rehearsal what the methodical director does at home. This method was used with great success by

Philip Moeller.[26] The improvisation of business during rehearsals has advantages if the director's imagination responds to it. Since the business grows directly out of motivation and characterizations of the actors and is tried out with them physically executing it, it is almost certain to be natural and adapted to them. There are moments of confusion and frustration when the director finds that a character who was not involved in the immediate action and so has been disregarded by him, is now needed on the other side of the stage, or when the grouping is bad with relation to an exit or entrance. This may frighten a neophyte director into reverting to planning business in advance. Valentine Windt, who uses this method with both amateurs and professionals, merely says, "I want you over here now. Don't worry about how you get there. We'll work that out later." If he finds that a scene doesn't stimulate his invention, he leaves it virtually unset, and develops a plan for it before the next rehearsal. While this method does not produce ideal picturization at the first business rehearsal, its flexibility permits the director to continue to improve the design by changes even in the late rehearsals.

Inexperienced directors often obtain their best results when they go to a first action rehearsal with definite plans and adjust them later. It gives them, as well as the actors, confidence that the production has a plan from the very beginning, though it may not be the best one. As he gains experience, a director can afford to depend more and more on improvisation.

A compromise technique which can be used by a beginner is to have a detailed plan and display it to the cast, but to say that

[26] Theresa Helburn, "Staged by Philip Moeller," *Theatre Guild Magazine*, VI (May, 1929). "The essence of Moeller's method is the immediate and brilliant reaction to the stimulus of the moment." She states that he came to the first rehearsal relatively unprepared, and even delayed revision until rehearsals.

he wants to take as much advantage as he can of their natural responses, so that they will work toward developing a pattern of their own. He especially marks in his book the details and picturizations which he considers vital, but improvises between them, always aware that he can revert to his planned business if he needs to.

Another modification is to start with planned business, with the most vital movements especially marked, but to let the actors play a few lines beyond the next planned movement each time, to see if they make a more imaginative response to the lines than that which he has recorded, or if they find it more natural to make a movement on a different line or phrase than that he has chosen. If not, the director supplies the business. An actor tends to take pride in business which he discovers, and is likely to motivate it more naturally and strongly than business which has been given to him and so has not grown spontaneously out of his motivation and natural impulses.

A third alternative — and perhaps the commonest — is to supply only general business at the first rehearsal so that the actors have a sense of working from a plan, but still have considerable freedom. These arrangements are modified and altered at subsequent rehearsals as the business is adjusted to the lines in detail. The scheme moves in a logical manner from the general and basic to the specific and the detailed. This is a common method of many directors — they supply the broad basic movements and the major groupings, hope that the actors will fill in the details, but do so themselves if the actors do not.

The type of play and of episode under consideration influences the director's choice of method. In a representational play he may plan the picturization of only the most important moments, and adjust the rest of the business to the instincts of the actor and his response at the rehearsals. But when he works with a classic, romantic, mannered, or expressionistic play, he wants more picturization, and so does more advance planning. A farce often requires careful planning of the mechanical features of the action. A complex scene with many actors and much business is almost impossible to set without meticulous advance planning of the path and the distance of crosses — and of balancing movements — in order to move actors to the right positions for subsequent action. On the other hand, some mob scenes and other complex action, such as the excited movements of the nuns after the miracle of the flowers in *Sister Beatrice,* are too complex to be planned in detail on paper, and are likely to be static if this method is attempted.

Despite all advance planning, changes in the business are inevitable. They continue through all rehearsals. Actors and director learn more and more about the play; as motivations are more fully understood, their patterns of expression alter. The other actors adjust themselves to this alteration, and thus set off a chain reaction which may include radical changes in business. As new relationships between characters are discovered, the director alters the business related to them in order to picturize them better.

Business is recorded methodically in writing by the bookholder or the director's assistant as it is set, so that no time is wasted in reconciling conflicting memories of it. Even though it is flexible and subject to change, a written record is needed of the tentative decisions.

Memory Rehearsals. Actors have pet theories about their methods of memorization. Sometimes these are valid for one individual, but more often they are mere motions which serve as excuses for unconscious laziness: "I cannot motivate while I have a script in my hand," "I can only learn lines when I know the business," and "Lines just come to me in rehearsal." The director has to decide which to accept and which to reject. Certainly no more than one such excuse can be accepted from any actor. The actor who cannot motivate until he learns his lines must learn them during the analysis period. The actor who waits for business rehearsals to learn lines must motivate satisfactorily while carrying his script and must not excuse himself because of it. If he cannot meet these requirements, then his method obviously is wrong for him, though it may be all right for someone else.[27]

Katharine Cornell[28] probably has the strangest method of memorizing. She learns her lines by rote before the first rehearsal without thought of their meaning. As long as she is studying motivation and characterization, she reads from the script in what she describes as a very stumbling manner. When she believes that she has mastered all the meaning of the role, she discards the script, relies on her dormant memory for the lines, and puts meaning and lines together automatically. In spite of her proof that this can be done successfully, it is hardly a practice to be recommended for others.

Directors vary in their demands with regard to memory. Some call the first rehearsal a week or two after casting or after the analysis, and require full memorization by that time. Scripts are usually permitted during the setting of business so that the actors can make notes of it. Other directors set memorization deadlines for each act, and permit no books after that time, with the object of embarrassing an actor who has not met the deadline. Such deadlines often need to be extended for the actors playing long roles, though they usually meet them anyway because their experience has taught them the value of freeing themselves from their books early. The length of the part is warning to them that they must work intensively. The

bit players, on the other hand, knowing that they can learn their few lines easily, are prone to try to pick them up in rehearsal without actual study. It is they who frequently disturb rehearsals by stumbling and paraphrasing. So the director may have to set deadlines for the shorter parts. An equitable rule is to require that fifty to seventy-five additional lines be learned for each rehearsal.

Some directors try to use as little compulsion as possible, and make no rigid time requirements. Instead, they compliment the actor when he learns a new scene, and remind the others without rancor that their failure to know their lines is holding back the perfecting of the scene. Using this as a self-evident reason, they may reach a mutual agreement on deadlines.

On the other hand, few directors want the actors to learn a speech before they thoroughly understand its meaning. Under these circumstances actors usually become so habituated to incorrect or partial expression that it is difficult for them to change it later. As actors characterize and motivate more completely, and particularly as they respond to the changing stimuli given by the other actors, meaning and the corresponding expression change in subtle ways. Also, it is easier to learn lines — and to learn them correctly — after they are understood thoroughly.

During the first few rehearsals after actors have discarded their scripts, they give so much attention to remembering their lines that lapses may occur in business, motivation, characterization, and concentration. Most of these blunders will be corrected automatically when the lines are secure. If he is present, the director may well shut his ears lest the uncharacterized and half-motivated reading dull his mind to the desired vividness of expression. He then hears the lines at later rehearsals with a fresh perception. At such times the director could well

[27] Specific suggestions for memorization are offered in Chapter 8, pages 88–89.
[28] Eustis, *Players at Work*, p. 68.

be elsewhere, leaving an assistant in charge, except that his presence stimulates the actors to greater effort. The director can best use this period to polish the business, for the repetition of lines which is necessary for meticulous polishing and for adjusting business to lines helps rather than hinders memorization.

The director must insist upon absolute accuracy in memorization. He may need to point out that it shows remarkable conceit to think that one can improvise an improvement upon a line which George S. Kaufman or Maxwell Anderson has labored long to perfect. Some directors instruct bookholders to make corrections during each rehearsal except the first time that books are discarded. Others find that this method interferes with rehearsal, and have the bookholder give corrections only during a critique. The bookholder uses a different colored pencil or a different kind of mark for each rehearsal so that he can distinguish the current errors from the prior ones. Retaining the full record of the errors distinguishes clearly between momentary lapses and serious habitual ones.

Characterization and Motivation Rehearsals. At least one director who has written on play production advocates special characterization rehearsals late in the schedule. Others feel that characterization underlies all motivation and business and that it must be given primary attention and studied continuously throughout the rehearsals. The writer in question apparently has in mind some special phase of the perfection of characterization or a final recheck of it. It is often advisable to make such a special check on characterization at a late rehearsal, with the actors and director watching for any uncharacterized speech or action and checking to make sure that a weak motivation, reading, or piece of business which has become habitual does not remain in the part

to betray an earlier, less complete understanding of the character.

All rehearsals, except possibly those in which business is first set, are motivation rehearsals. Some textbooks give this title to certain rehearsals late in the schedule. As with characterization, these are rehearsals in which the director and actors give their principal attention to motivation in order to locate any incompletely or incorrectly motivated lines or business, thus disclosing weak points which might have been overlooked while watching the general effect of the action in the running rehearsals. This type, like characterization rehearsals, may be useful to create a specific goal for the actors, and to give them a sense of special accomplishment.

Running Rehearsals. A complete run-through of the play is held as early in the schedule as is feasible, and at least a week before dress rehearsals. Interruptions are kept to a minimum. The director can then appraise the comparative state of preparation of the various sections of the play, and concentrate in the next few rehearsals on the weak spots he has observed. Many directors post an open call for the rehearsal immediately following — such as "To be used for the rehearsal of weak scenes." The schedule for a rehearsal of this kind is announced after the run-through. This has a salutary effect on the actors involved, and is likely to result in an especially valuable rehearsal.

The first run-through is a convenient time for the walk-ons and extras to see the production for the first time. They enter the rehearsals at about this point, and they understand their own participation better if they see the whole play. Some directors give them at this rehearsal written instructions on their actions, so that they can visualize these while watching the scenes in which they are to appear.

The first run-through gives the actors a fresh sense of urgency, for it reminds them forcefully that the performance is approaching and that there is still much preparatory work to be done. This is an important reason for scheduling it early.

Practice differs on interruptions during rehearsals. Some directors have a great many running rehearsals of individual acts and the entire play, interrupting only for adjustments which cannot be handled in a critique. This allows the actors to feel the flow of the action, and to practice concentration for long continuous periods. It is claimed that this results in a smoother production, and that better tempo and rhythm are thereby obtained. Marion Stuart of Champaign (Ill.) High School [29] uses this technique. She also dictates her comments during rehearsals to a shorthand pupil who types them for distribution to the actors at the beginning of the next rehearsal, limiting her oral critique to general matters. She points out that corrections and comments are more effective when made just before a rehearsal of a scene. Similarly, oral critiques can be held over until the start of the next rehearsal. To do this effectively, the director needs to review his scrappy rehearsal notes and amplify them so that a day later he will still know what they mean. Some directors who delay the critique until the start of the next rehearsal type some of their notes for distribution to the cast. This saves critique time; allows them to make fuller comment to the actor than they would take time for in a critique; allows them to say more intimate things to him; and gives him a pack of reminders by which he can recheck himself periodically. Other directors use typed notes only after performances, leaving them in the actors' dressing rooms.

Interrupting a rehearsal does have a compensating advantage. It saves the time necessary to identify verbally the moment in the play when there is something wrong. The

criticism is connected immediately and meaningfully to the matter which needs correction. It permits immediate rehearsal of the change. Few inexperienced actors can incorporate a change after mere verbal explanation. They must experience it physically in order to remember it. Such an objective can be accomplished by holding the critique on the stage and re-rehearsing the episode at this time. But this is a slow process because of the time consumed in assembling the cast of the episode on stage and accurately placing them for a particular moment.

Some directors feel that the interruption, with its implicit stress upon perfection, encourages the entire cast to strive for similar perfection. Also, many of the improvements which the director makes during a rehearsal are the result of the exact mental state of the director and the actors at the moment. The director is suddenly stimulated by a new shade of meaning which he catches from an actor. It may be a meaning of which the actor is hardly aware — of which he can be made conscious at this moment, but which he will have forgotten a few minutes later. The director can best communicate it to the actor while he is excited by the discovery. This mutual high stimulation often leads to similar discoveries in succeeding moments. This is equally true with respect to subtle meanings which will result in barely perceptible changes in expression, and of new movements and gestures which can clarify meanings.

While a few actors have the knack of assimilating a change into their role with a single rehearsal of it, most of them need several repetitions to break down the old habit. The repetition following the first success often fails, so that there is a standard pattern of: success, failure, sustained success. Recognizing this possibility, the director may make a habit of saying, "Yes, that's right now. Let's do it again to set it," with the expecta-

29 "Rehearsing the Play," *Dramatics*, XIX (October, 1947), 10.

tion that it will fail the second time, and have to be repeated a third time to set it finally.

At running rehearsals the director forces himself to watch for auditory and visual expression which fails to convey explicit meaning, or which communicates false ideas or suggestions. Directors are in constant danger of becoming so pleased with what they have accomplished and so hypnotized by the steady flow of words and actions, that they overlook blemishes. They sometimes use a mechanical device, such as Kaufman's method of rehearsing the play backward, episode by episode, in order to be able to rivet their attention on details through at least one full rehearsal. Hubert Heffner of Indiana University suggests [30] perfecting the action by having pantomimic rehearsals with the bookholder reading all lines. Seated rehearsals may produce similarly concentrated attention on vocal expression. Another device which realerts some directors is to invite a highly critical friend to a rehearsal. Even if the visitor makes no valuable comments, his mere presence may make the director see the play with new eyes.

Any error of line, business, or position which is constantly repeated by an actor warns the director to re-examine the action of the moment, for it may indicate that the lines or business are incompletely or illogically motivated, or that the cue itself is being motivated in a way which does not properly arouse the response that the author and director expect.

In his advance planning and in the business and memory rehearsals, the director has fixed the auditory and visual stimuli with which he hopes to obtain the larger patterns of picturization, progression, subordination and emphasis, style, atmosphere, variety, balance, proportion, and unity. But the

effectiveness of these patterns can be judged only when the play begins to run in rehearsal. The director is likely to use the middle portions of the rehearsal period coaching actors and perfecting business. Now, at the running rehearsals, he returns to the consideration of overall effects. He shifts to his collateral function of critic, and tries to look at the play from this fresh viewpoint. He judges the effectiveness of the large patterns as well as the details. He tries to recall his original impressions of the script and his goals to see whether the performance is producing the effect he desired. He rechecks particularly emphasis and progression, which can be altered imperceptibly by the weak playing of some episodes or by the especially effective playing of others. A beginning director, frustrated at early rehearsals by his sense of uncertainty about the general effects — and finding the coaching of the actors, in which he feels more at home and in which he can see immediate results, more satisfying — sometimes continues to coach until the very end of the rehearsals, and fails to refocus his attention on the true goals of direction.

Tempo and rhythm can be perfected only at running rehearsals, though some preliminary work can be done before. The director therefore gives major attention to these, and continues to do so through polishing, coordinating, and dress rehearsals.

Adequate vocal projection is demanded throughout the rehearsal period, but especially starting with running rehearsals, because if the actor is first asked at a dress rehearsal to speak louder, he merely increases the volume stress on the emphatic words, and contrasts them even more with the inaudible unemphatic ones. The easiest way to establish adequate projection is to rehearse in a theatre.

Polishing Rehearsals. This is the term usually applied to late rehearsals at which every

[30] Hubert C. Heffner, Samuel Selden, and Hunton D. Sellman, *Modern Theatre Practice,* rev. ed. (Appleton-Century-Crofts, 1959), p. 165.

reading, every piece of business, and the correlation between them is scrutinized to see that they are perfectly timed and co-ordinated, and that they convey exact meanings. The memory, motivation, and characterization rehearsals blend gradually into running rehearsals, and these into polishing rehearsals. But here again, some directors feel that it helps to designate some of them specifically as polishing rehearsals in order to concentrate their own and the actors' attention upon details. Many interruptions are to be expected at these.

An action can be correct and its motivation can be felt by the actors, yet neither may be clear to the spectator. The successive steps in the development of thought may merge or overlap, and so need to be more clearly defined. For example, when a character does not want to be found in a room, and hears someone coming, the thoughts and actions may be so telescoped and so unprojected that the spectator sees only: (1) the actor hears approaching footsteps, (2) looks about aimlessly and vaguely, thinking "inwardly" of hiding places, (3) runs to hide in a place at which he has not looked even though he may have had an introspective memory of it. This kind of vagueness may be acceptable at early rehearsals, but now the thought process must be made clear step by step to the spectator, in a pattern which might be: (1) hears footsteps, (2) realizes danger to himself, (3) decides to hide, (4) looks about for hiding places, (5) rejects one quickly, (6) gives consideration to another and perhaps moves toward it, (7) sees the error of his choice, (8) looks for others, (9) sees a possibility, (10) considers it, (11) decides upon it, (12) runs to it and hides, (13) reveals himself again to check possible flaws in it, (14) decides it is safe, (15) hides in it again. This motivation pattern can be very rapid and take very little more time than the first one, but because the steps are distinct, the thought is made clear and believable.

Particular attention is now given to the difficult timing of fights, duels, eating scenes, and similar complex action. Mob scenes, in which participants were formerly allowed free movement in order to let them find their own motivations and thus secure variety, are now made definite and exact, in a pattern based upon what the actors have thus far developed. Progression is checked, any gaps in thinking or in action are filled in, the groupings are balanced, and the movement and the ad lib speeches are timed so that they support rather than distract from the important moments.

At this point, tempo and rhythm are studied constantly, in both their subtle and their obvious phases. A play seems alive when the response of the actors is immediate; a pall of dullness results when inexperienced actors fall into fifth-of-a-second pauses between speeches. The director checks this in late rehearsals, insisting that no matter how slowly the actor may speak because of characterization and motivation, and no matter how long he may pause within his speeches, cues must be picked up instantly unless there is an intentional pause between them. Ordinarily the last syllable of one speech and the first syllable of the next are closer together than they could be articulated by a single individual; nevertheless, they do not overlap. The inflection pattern of a sentence is so much a unity that one often knows the full pattern when one has heard half of it, in which case the emotional meaning of the sentence is known well before it is completed. This phenomenon can be demonstrated by playing a recording of a good speaker or actor, and lifting the needle in the middle of a sentence. The listener nearly always knows the intent of the unfinished sentence. Similarly, in the theatre the audience may laugh before a sentence is completed because it has already divined its meaning. The last words of the sentence do make the meaning more specific, but one usually has his response ready before the final words are heard and so can respond instantly.

At this stage of rehearsal, the director adjusts his thinking. He has sought perfection in every detail. But now he knows that he will not necessarily obtain it. Consequently, at about the time of the polishing rehearsals, he examines the production carefully, and determines his future course. He decides what must still be demanded of his group at no matter what sacrifice of time, effort, and temper; what still is desirable and practicable to strive for; and what it is possible and necessary to abandon. He may, for example, have to sacrifice the exactness of timing he had hoped to obtain at certain moments, the perfection of picturization he had desired, and even absolute consistency of characterization. Occasionally he cuts an episode, though this produces psychological as well as logical problems, for the actors will be unhappy about it.

He must send his cast into the first performance with a feeling of confidence — with the belief that, while they have not attained perfection, and while they have to carry in mind some things to be improved in performance if possible, they will not discredit themselves if they do as well as they have at the late rehearsals. Only in such a state of mind can they face the audience and give as good a performance as they have been achieving in rehearsals. If, on the other hand, the director continues right up to the last rehearsal to carp on effects which they have never managed to achieve, and which they know they never will manage, they are likely to give a discouraged performance which is below the level of the rehearsals. While the director works most specifically on this psychological state at dress rehearsals, his attention to it begins earlier as he removes critical pressure and is generous with praise in a deliberate plan to instill optimism and confidence in the cast.

Integrating Rehearsals. Actors are given as complete rehearsals as are feasible at all periods of their work. Soon after the initial analysis, the integration of scenery, costumes, or properties with the acting helps subsequent rehearsals and repays the effort necessary to secure it at so early a stage. A director has trained himself to see imaginatively things which are not there, but inexperienced actors find this more difficult. It is always helpful to rehearse on the stage, on the platforms to be used, or in the setting either on stage or still in the shop. At the very least, rehearsals must be held in a space where a measured floor plan of the setting has been chalked or painted on the floor.

Costume rehearsals are especially important in some period plays. The women have to learn to stand, to move, and to sit in skirts with hoops or trains, and in tight skirts. Men need to rehearse in cloaks, capes, and kilts. When they are to wear tights, they need to overcome the feeling of strangeness in having their legs exposed while the rest of their bodies are covered, and especially to concentrate their attention on their legs so that they become aware of the need to stand and walk well, and conscious of the good and bad lines produced by different postures. Both the men and the women need to learn the ways in which clothes of a different period restrict their actions. Worn-out costumes can be efficiently used for rehearsal. Once a girl has learned to handle one large hoop skirt, her adjustment to a slightly different one is easy. If the organization has no costume stock, equivalents can be found: modern evening hoops; a sheet tied around the waist for a train or around the neck for a cloak; wrestling tights, long underwear, or swimming trunks and bare legs for tights. The last is not the best substitute, for one thing to be learned with tights is to avoid wrinkles in them.

Another advantage of wearing costumes

before dress rehearsals is the opportunity which it gives the director to teach the actors how to wear them with style. Nothing is quite as discouraging as the first sight of a cast of men in Elizabethan costumes with their tights wrinkled, their hose sagging loosely instead of being fluffed out and pulled as high as possible, their capes huddled over their shoulders like peasant women's shawls, their hats set squarely on top of their heads in a way that they would never wear even a modern hat, and their drooping expressions betraying their own discouragement. Wearing even makeshift costumes for a while, and joking about them, encourages the actors to experiment to find effective ways to wear and use them. This search can be stimulated by covering the walls of the rehearsal room with pictures from the period which glamorize the style.

Actual properties should be used as early as possible, with the bookholder or assistant director responsible for putting them in cardboard cartons for safekeeping between rehearsals. Properties and costume properties which can be used effectively in business and for characterization and motivation, or which require careful planning, are especially important. Examples are eating and cooking utensils, rocking chairs, fans, purses, hats, furs, canes, cloaks, muffs, and sewing. Even buckets substituted for suitcases, pitchers for urns, pie pans for plates, and boxes or blocks of wood of approximate size for other properties, are better than nothing.

Not only does the early use of costumes, properties, and scenery produce in the actor's mind a heightened awareness of the environment of his role, and so improve his performance, but early rehearsals with such articles reveal needed adjustments in the business or in the objects themselves. These changes can be made more easily at this early date. Use of any of these objects helps subsequent rehearsals, but the adjustment

to them is likely to injure the first rehearsal in which they are used. It is therefore advisable to introduce as many as possible at a single rehearsal, and none at others. Naturally, the addition of one more costume or property does not cause trouble.[31]

It is important to integrate all cueing with the action before dress rehearsals, because it often takes repeated rehearsals to perfect the cueing, and the time cannot be given to it at dress rehearsals. Manual and phonographic sound effects are rehearsed with the action. Music and dance are related one to the other, and to other elements of production. The bookholder or stage manager who is to give the cues for the lowering of the curtain proves his awareness of the exact second for it by saying, "Curtain," and being corrected by the director if the timing is not precise. If the electricians can be induced to do so, they attend rehearsals and show the director by hand signals their recognition of cues and the general nature of the light changes. Quick costume changes are rehearsed in the fitting room and the timing required for them is reported to the director.

Technical rehearsals sometimes precede dress rehearsals, and are devoted to the perfection of all the technical phases of the production. Though they look like dress rehearsals, they have a totally different atmosphere. The cast acts only those parts of the play which are necessary to test scenery, lighting, properties, and costumes, and those which give cues for technical work. Makeups are tested also, since they are needed to

---

[31] Even before technical rehearsals can be arranged, actors are encouraged to frequent the workshops and physically orient themselves as much as possible to scenery, properties, and costumes. They should walk up and down steps; sit, stand, and lie on ramps and walls; sit on furniture; handle properties; walk about in their costumes and experiment with gestures whenever they are being fitted. They are cautioned to avoid interfering with the shop work, to adopt a generally complimentary attitude toward the technical work, and to bring any fears or complaints to the director rather than talk about them with the technicians.

check the lighting. These rehearsals tremendously relieve the pressure at the dress rehearsals, and reduce the strain on the actor, since he is not asked to give a fully motivated performance at the same time that he is adjusting himself to numerous new elements. Technical rehearsals are possible when a theatre is used exclusively by one theatre organization. When a theatre is rented, or shared with other activities, they often must coincide with dress rehearsals, for the technical parts of the production may not be sufficiently completed and rehearsed to justify devoting a full rehearsal to them. Sometimes technical rehearsals devoted exclusively to lighting or scene shifting are held in afternoons between night dress rehearsals. The director usually attends these in order to show that he is willing to give as much time to them as he asks of the crew members. His presence is vital at lighting rehearsals.

Dress Rehearsals. There should be as many dress rehearsals as possible. While some directors call for only one, it is impossible to perfect the co-ordination of a production in a single rehearsal. Many insist upon a minimum of three or four, and, for a complicated show, prefer a full week of them in order to reduce their individual length. If there has been prior integration with the actual setting, costumes, and properties, the dress rehearsals can be reduced in number.

The handling of the dress rehearsals is an important part of the director's leadership, and is a test of his administrative ability. There is never enough dress-rehearsal time to perfect every element of the production. The director has to decide which among the many demands for attention are most important — repetition of episodes or acts to drill the actors or to adjust them to the technical phases; the setting of light, sound, and curtain cues; the adjustment of lights while the

actors are present in costume and make-up; the correction of costumes; rehearsal of the crews for quick changes and special effects; a critique of acting, properties, costumes, make-up, and lighting; and instructions by the stage manager and other members of the staff. Each element seems most important to the individuals concerned with it, and to keep harmony the director is influenced partly by tact in apportioning the time. He decides which must be taken care of immediately, which can be corrected or rehearsed in the interval between rehearsals, and which can be ignored or delayed until a later rehearsal. A prime consideration is the effect upon the actors, since it is they who must face the audience — when do they need continuity in rehearsal, and when is it more important to give them confidence in the dependability of the technical crew by interrupting to perfect cues and propping?

The director encourages his associates to perfect every phase of the production for the first dress rehearsal. His own direction of the actors should be at performance readiness, since the main purpose of these rehearsals is to co-ordinate the various elements; and the director is so concerned with this integration that he cannot give much attention to additional creative work.

Interruptions are avoided at dress rehearsals. If a technical rehearsal has preceded them, it sometimes is possible to run entire acts without interruption. Even with this preparation, however, constant interruptions may be necessary at the first dress rehearsal to make adjustments and improve co-ordination. When an actor fumbles in his adjustment to the physical elements, but finds a good correlation with them, it takes keen judgment to know whether he is aware that he has solved the problem and needs no further help, or whether he needs to repeat the action so that it becomes physically easy and natural. Interruption is necessary if the actor makes a poor adjustment. Similarly, the director has to guess when the technician is aware of an obvious error of cueing and will correct it next time, and when the co-ordination needs to be perfected immediately. It is so vital that interruptions be kept to a minimum at subsequent dress rehearsals that directors are often intentionally overmeticulous in repeats at the first one.

A rehearsal secretary or note-taker permits the director to have notes for his critique without taking his eyes off the stage. Since his attention often centers on technical matters, and since he may even confer at length with the designer or other workers, it is helpful to have an assistant director who has worked through the rehearsal period and can take notes on the acting when the director is preoccupied, or can call his attention to matters which need correction or comment. It is useful to have someone who can take messages backstage or summon people with whom the director wishes to confer. The assistant director can do this if he is not taking the notes.

In some situations, it is imperative that dress rehearsals end at a specified hour. The attitude of parents may govern the duration of the rehearsal of a high school play. In general, the energy of high school pupils runs low by eleven o'clock, and of college students and avocational community theatre actors by midnight, so an attempt is made to finish the respective rehearsals by those hours. However, in emergencies, effective work can still be accomplished at rehearsals which run later. Subtle and creative work on characterization and motivation cannot be done when the actors are tired, but the purely mechanical phases of the acting and the technical work can benefit from rehearsal far beyond these hours. Actors and crew members tire progressively through the dress-rehearsal period, so a first rehearsal can run longer than later ones. Ideally the final rehearsal is short.

Rehearsal conditions in the school and community theatres are bad at best. The actors and crew come to these after a full day's work or study, and must rise early again next day. This circumstance is aggravated at dress rehearsals, when the emotional strain is even more tiring than the necessarily long hours. Yet their other teachers often are unsympathetic toward excuses for absence, tardiness, or inattention, so student actors are cautioned against using late rehearsals as an excuse. Particularly they are asked not to exaggerate the length of the rehearsal to "make a good story."

Absolute discipline is enforced at dress rehearsals for the good of all. The rehearsal starts at the announced hour even though scenery, lighting, costumes, and make-ups are incomplete, and actors are absent. Nothing is more salutary to a tardy actor than to find that he missed a scene and the director shows no inclination to repeat it. The workers responsible for such incompleteness have it called to their attention at the critique. Dress rehearsals are usually called inconveniently early, and unless it is made clear that they positively will begin at the announced time, each individual asks himself, "Why should I strain myself when the others don't?" So actors blame the crew for lateness, and the crew blames the actors; no one is ready, and the rehearsal starts late. Nor is anyone allowed to transfer blame — it is the actor's fault, not the costumer's, if he couldn't check out his costume because he arrived during the last-minute rush. While such fixing of blame needs to be done in good temper so as not to cause resentment, a firm policy is needed to which no exceptions are permitted. It is advisable to issue instructions about dress rehearsal time, the hours at which to pick up costumes, etc., in duplicated form so that no actor or crew member can try to alibi himself with "I must have been out of the room when you announced that," or "I didn't see the notice."

The designer and technical staff keep

themselves within easy call of the director throughout dress rehearsals, and check with him before departing to learn if he has any questions or comments for them. If the crew is not held for the full critique period, the heads of the crews remain to get comments, or leave deputies to take notes for them while they attend a separate critique of the crew.

Some directors permit visitors at rehearsals. Some exclude them at all stages of rehearsal, admitting only the actors and crew members to dress rehearsals. Some directors are sensitive about being watched while at work. They realize that they often fumble for words, use words which elsewhere would be meaningless and even silly, and often communicate their ideas by grimaces and gestures alone. The other actors are as intent as the actor who is being instructed, and are used to the director's methods. But even a visitor present for the purpose of learning to direct lacks this group spirit, and to him the director may appear ludicrous. Conversely, an awareness of being watched may make the director restrain his normal expressive exaggeration for fear of seeming ridiculous, and thus reduce his effectiveness.

In the same way, the actor has worked with the other members of the cast for a long period, and has heard critiques, so he knows that if he has worked conscientiously there is no discredit attached to further constructive criticism. But when he is criticized in the hearing of an outsider, he may fear that his acting ability will be misjudged.

Some minor rehearsal accidents produce howls from the entire cast, crew, and directorial staff. Little harm is done if the actors involved see the humor of their mishaps. But when the disinterested outsider laughs also at forgotten lines, dropped properties, and clumsiness — matters which do not amuse the cast — it increases self-consciousness. Visitors also are prone to praise and criticize their friends in the cast, taking special delight in making the actors unhappy about their costumes. And they often violate rehearsal confidence by gossiping afterwards about what they have seen.[32]

A director who knows all the disadvantages of visitors may admit them anyway because he feels that they may learn a little, that refusal makes him seem unco-operative, and that it injures the morale of the whole theatre group if a regular worker is forbidden to attend rehearsals just because he is not working on the immediate production.

Some directors and actors like a small audience at the last dress rehearsal, particularly for farce and comedy. They find that it teaches them where the laughs will occur, and how to end the laughter. It undoubtedly helps actors learn to hold for laughs and how to stop them; but a small audience does not respond at the same places as a large one, and if the rehearsal audience consists of special friends of the group, their response is influenced by their previous observation of the actors, and the responses may thus be quite different from those of a performance audience. A full audience of personally disinterested people makes a more realistic tryout audience. Some theatres secure such an audience through clubs and factories. Actors sometimes get over their worst nervousness at this invitational dress rehearsal, and thus are more relaxed on opening night. Compliments on their work from friends and acquaintances may increase their confidence.

Even while giving his primary attention to co-ordination at the dress rehearsals, the director once again re-examines his own work to make sure that it has produced the effects he wished. He still looks for oppor-

[32] Much can be learned about direction by studying rehearsals. For the greatest value, the visitor needs to attend at least every other rehearsal throughout the entire period. The only independent rehearsal period which gives valuable training is the analysis period. Least of all is learned by watching a dress rehearsal. Knowing this, directors feel justified in excluding visitors unless they have shown serious interest by attending previous rehearsals.

tunities for improvement. Unexpected colors or dimensions of scenery, costumes, and properties and unanticipated effects of the lighting may seriously damage groupings which had seemed right, and also may give him inspirations for visual betterment through support from the scenery and the lighting. While theoretically the visual aspects of a production should be adjusted to the actors and the direction, actually there is not always time for much last-minute change, and it is often easier to alter the action. But the director does not accept inadequate scenery, lighting, or costumes, or design elements which were changed without his knowledge. Considerable alteration can be effected in a short time with paint, dye, and redesigned lighting. If possible, however, the director keeps abreast of all phases of the preparation of the technical elements, so that he will not be surprised at the dress rehearsal.

"A bad dress rehearsal means a good performance" is an ancient delusion with which actors and directors console themselves and each other. It is sometimes true that if the actors are tired at the last rehearsal and do not act quite as well as they have in previous rehearsals, they will still produce a good performance. They come to the opening night with nerves taut in an effort to force themselves to regain what they lost, and this counteracts weariness as the dress rehearsal atmosphere may not. A few technical errors at the last dress rehearsal similarly may make the crew alert to avoid their recurrence in the performance.

But a bad rehearsal offers no hope when it is merely the final evidence of an imperfectly prepared show. The most one then can expect is a performance in which each actor plays as well as in his best recent rehearsal, and in which the technical crews make slightly fewer errors than before. Stimulation from an audience may make an individual actor give a slightly better performance than

he has at a rehearsal. This little improvement may give just that degree of intensity which makes his performance far more effective than was to be expected. It can make a poor actor more acceptable, can turn a passable actor into a fairly good one, and a fine actor into a brilliant one. But it does not change a weak or unprepared actor into a successful one.

PERFORMANCES

Actors learn from successive performances, but there is a point at which the expenditure of time by a student or avocational actor overbalances the teaching value of additional performances. A minimum of three performances and a maximum of ten are usually considered the desirable range. The box office economy requires longer runs in some community theatres.

Starting with the last dress rehearsal, and continuing through the performances, the director's attitude is almost exclusively one of optimism, reassurance, and appreciation. Even when they do well, actors sometimes become depressed when they realize that they could have done even better. Memory of the director's confidence and satisfaction helps to console them. An exception to this policy is the actor who becomes overconfident as a result of praise he receives. The director may need to have a confidential talk with him to caution him against overplaying.

It is desirable that the actors be slightly keyed up for performances so that their minds will be active and their reactions keen. But most actors are more nervous than is desirable as they face an audience, and the director tries to alleviate this condition, rather than to stimulate it. Everything done immediately before the performance, especially on the opening night, is calculated to produce an atmosphere of confidence and calmness. Actors and crew are called at an hour which permits them to get ready without rushing, but not so early that they sit around waiting and worrying. Crew members are encouraged to work with business-like efficiency; last-minute bustle is discouraged. The director assumes an untroubled air no matter what his worries, and wanders through the dressing rooms and the greenroom joking and wishing actors well in a seemingly carefree mood.

He may call the cast to the greenroom for last-minute encouragement and caution. This reminder of the group nature of their effort can have a calming effect. He can give last-minute emphasis to a particular phase of the acting, but he is careful not to ask for any greatly increased emphasis upon any single phase, for in their efforts to comply, they may unwittingly alter other parts of the performance. The final words are reassuring, such as asking them to equal their best rehearsal, or thanking them for the quality of their work. There should be no remark which implies that they need to be better than in rehearsals.

Some fear that calling the cast together just before the curtain in itself suggests a lack of full confidence, and it may produce an impression of rush and confusion when actors who appear late in the play come partly dressed or partly made up. This situation can be avoided by announcing the call at the preceding rehearsal so that it does not suggest an emergency, and does not rob the actors of time they expected to use for make-up. If such a call is not made, the last critique at the dress rehearsal includes a similar general encouragement.

Some directors call the cast together only on the opening night. Others have such calls every night of performance so as to point out sympathetically ways in which the performance can be improved over that of the previous night. Some amateurs, and even professionals, vary from performance to performance, and seem unable to avoid it. After a successful opening night, the second performance may be weak, for the actors and the crew relax from the tremendous concentration which produced a good first performance. This results in slight losses in characterization, motivation, and timing which make it less "brilliant." The transitions lack speed and sharpness, making the effect immeasurably less exciting. On the other hand, an unresponsive first audience, adverse reviews, printed or oral, rumors of a poor sale, and other discouraging matters may make the actors apathetic, and again their performance will lack spirit. Since the director as the leader is responsible for maintaining the proper morale of the company, his duties continue throughout the performances, and he does everything he can to counteract the effect of either discouragement or overconfidence.

Many directors also call the cast on the second night so as to have an opportunity to counteract any effects produced by adverse newspaper criticism. A last-minute discussion of criticism may worry the cast, so the director prepares their attitude toward it before dress rehearsals. A valid viewpoint is that a newspaper review is the opinion of one individual, and is influenced by many factors. A review's value depends upon the qualifications of the critic. The mere fact of publication gives it only the added weight that the individual is expressing himself publicly and therefore is more likely to give a considered judgment than is the casual spectator in offhand comment. But it remains one individual's opinion. Audience response as measured by attention, laughter, and applause is a much truer index of the success of the production.

Once a show opens, suggestions and criticisms for individual actors are made to them privately, for even a suggestion for improvement has the negative implication that the public performance was not wholly satisfactory. However, even constructively phrased negative criticism is too valuable to the actor to be abandoned. When the director can point out that a laugh was lost because the actor did not quiet the previous laugh before speaking the line in question, the actor's experiments with it at subsequent performances teach him timing as rehearsals cannot. Similarly, the wastefulness of permitting a small laugh, which then kills the climactic one, can only be learned before a succession of audiences. Points of acting to which there is no audible audience response are more difficult to demonstrate convincingly, but actors ordinarily accept the word of the director on them.

There was once a widespread belief that the presence of the director backstage during a performance was beneficial. The belief is now quite general that morale is better when the director shows his confidence by leaving the actors and the crew "on their own." The director adopts an unvarying practice on this, for otherwise his choice becomes a comment. To improve his judgment of audience response, the director needs to sit where he can study it. It permits him to correct minor flaws in the performance. When he sits in the auditorium, he chooses a seat from which he can slip out unobserved and get backstage quickly in a real emergency. He avoids going backstage during the performance, however, for though he may be able to improve tempo or volume, his visit produces tension. In the greenroom during intermissions and after the show, he is as encouraging as possible without causing overconfidence.

A bookholder or prompter ordinarily sits at one of the tormentors. Though it is nearly always apparent to the audience when an actor is prompted, and though this reduces the empathic response for a few minutes, it gives most actors a sense of security when they know that if they forget lines and cannot ad lib successfully, the bookholder will save them from a long blank pause. Some directors, however, "put the actors on their

mettle" by withdrawing the prompter during performances. If this extreme course is taken, there should be no prompting at any late rehearsal, and the actors must be trained to improvise when they forget lines.

Some directors praise the individual actors extravagantly after a performance. Others give intentionally restrained compliments. Some withhold personal praise until after the last performance except as an actor needs special encouragement. Where newspaper critics are inclined to be harsh, the director may systematically give the least effective actors a special word of commendation and encouragement after the first performance to sustain them in case they read unpleasant criticism the next day. The actor is more inclined to believe this then than if it is said as obvious consolation after the appearance of the review. Each policy has advantages and disadvantages, but it needs to be consistent from show to show so that the actors anticipate and understand it. The director does, in any case, indicate that he is generally satisfied even when he delays individual comments, for by this time the actors consider his opinion the most important one. He is careful at performances as well as dress rehearsals to include praise of the crew and the heads of technical departments. Such compliments are given even when he delays praising the actors.

It is apparent, then, that the director in the school and community theatre performs his overall function as leader and teacher from the first announcement of the play until the final curtain. He seldom has anyone with whom to share the responsibility, or even to turn to for competent and sympathetic advice. The work calls for all the knowledge of the drama and of the stage which he can acquire. It requires administrative ability, initiative, inventiveness, sensitivity to dramatic effects in staging and acting, artistic showmanship, and a high order of skill in handling people. He is tactfully assertive and modestly self-confident, yet open-minded and conciliatory. Withal, his task is tremendously stimulating, for he sees more vividly than can the classroom teacher the rapid cultural and social growth of the actors as well as their pleasure as they learn to understand a character and a play. When rewarded with success, his task is extremely satisfying to him as a creative experience.

Appendices

Appendix A: *Projects and Exercises*
for the Student

Appendix B: *On the Art of Costuming*

Appendix C: *A Note on Make-up*

Appendix D: *Bibliographies*

A | Projects and Exercises for the Student

Chapter 1 · Drama as Art

1. Of the various elements which make up the dramatic performance (script, setting, acting), which varies the most from performance to performance, and which the least? Why?

2. Has it ever happened that you have gone back to see a second performance of a play which you liked very much, and found it on second experience much less impressive than it had been the first time? Can you explain why?

3. From among the plays that you have seen, cite three or four instances of ones in which the principal characters were not human beings, but animals, birds, or insects. In these plays, upon what did the mimetic effect primarily depend: upon the audience's familiarity with the originals of the creatures portrayed, upon the actors' understanding of animal life, or upon the resemblance of the creatures to human beings?

4. Prepare a report describing the finest piece of acting you have seen. Tell in detail why you consider it the finest.

5. Recount an instance in which an otherwise fine performance was marred by an obvious flaw in the synthesis of script, acting, and setting.

6. Why is it that people so often confuse the actor with the character he impersonates, remembering the actor as himself and forgetting even the name of the character he played? Is it because the actor is so much the same from one part to another? Or is it because the script is weak and inconse-

quential, while the actor is vivid and memorable? Are there other reasons which might account for this common occurrence?

7. Do you find it easier to remember the appearance of a setting or the exact words of the good "lines" of a play you have seen? Why?

8. Recount an instance in which you enjoyed a play but afterward — upon trying to tell its plot to another person — discovered that you were not entirely sure what had happened at all points during the performance. Assuming that the fault was not yours, what was wrong with the play or its staging that caused you to miss important points during the course of the performance?

9. Prepare a report enlarging upon the idea that the elements of the whole play are seen in one order of importance by the theatre worker, and in another entirely different order by the casual spectator.

Chapter 2 · The Dramatic Composition

1. Do you consider drama more effective as a means of persuasion than music, or less so? Do you believe that drama can be used more effectively than painting to put across an idea? After giving careful thought to these questions, prepare to defend your opinion, for — whether you reply "yes" or "no" — others are certain to disagree with you.

2. Among your friends, do you know persons who, if they were playwrights, would probably write nothing but comedy? Nothing but tragedy? Why?

3. Recount an instance of a performance in which the audience took seriously actions or lines which were intended to amuse them.

Was the fault, in your opinion, due to the script or to the actors? Why?

4. From your own experience, describe a performance in which the characters and their actions were interesting at the outset but became less so as the play progressed, and in the end seemed to "add up" to nothing of significance.

5. Jot down the titles of as many plays as you can which observed one or more of the classical unities. See if you can determine which employed one or more of these unities to confine and contain a plot which otherwise would have been formless.

6. In addition to the instances mentioned in the text, see how many plays you can recall in which exposition was effected by means of a prologue.

7. List as many titles as you can of plays in which the action is brought to a conclusion by the appearance of a new character bearing information which puts an end to all the difficulties.

8. Make three columns. Head one "plays of plot," another "plays of character," and the third "plays of language." Now see how many titles you can list under each heading. If you come to any titles which seem incapable of being truly classified in any of the three columns, list these separately under a question mark. Bring this list to class for discussion.

9. Draw up a chart of *Julius Caesar,* showing in parallel columns the progression of historical time as compared with dramatic time scene by scene throughout the play.

Chapter 3 · Plot

1. Is the plot of *Death of a Salesman* simple, complex, or compound? Which of these is *Abe Lincoln in Illinois? Born Yesterday? Summer and Smoke? Hedda Gabler?*

2. How many plays can you list in which the plots follow one after the other? How many can you list in which the plots occur one within another?

3. Take a short play, such as *Riders to the Sea* or *Murder in the Cathedral,* and count the number of distinct episodes. At places where you have difficulty in deciding whether or not a new episode is begun, note the difficulty and prepare to discuss the question in class.

4. Study the first act of a play by Molière to see how he employs the device of *liaison* to connect the episodes. Now look at the first act of *Our Town* and see whether you can find resemblances between Wilder's method and Molière's in this respect.

5. Name several plays in which the obligatory scene is omitted from the sequence of episodes and is described instead of acted out. Explain, in each case, why the play is constructed in this way.

6. Study the final scene of Galsworthy's *Escape* to discover the means the author has employed to heighten the priest's dilemma. Could this dilemma have been omitted without altering the form of the plot?

7. From five plays you have seen, recall the moments at which you experienced the greatest suspense. Describe the means which the author used to create this suspense.

8. Carefully review your favorite Shakespearean plays to see how many instances you can find of parallels of plot or character. Note these, and prepare to describe them in class.

Chapter 4 · Characterization

1. From some familiar play, such as *Family Portrait, Our Town, The Corn Is Green,* or *The Male Animal,* pick out the character "types" most readily recognizable. Note these and prepare to discuss them in class.

2. From plays you have seen, note five instances of character stereotypes, relating each to the true type from which it seems to have grown.

3. List a dozen instances of characters whose names are intended to describe them.

(Examples: Willy Loman — i.e., "Low-man"; Lucius O'Trigger.)

4. From any of Chekhov's plays, select several instances of characters describing themselves. Indicate whether you consider these self-descriptions to be accurate; account for any discrepancies.

5. Study several of the passages in *The Wild Duck* in which Hialmar Ekdal describes himself. Are these descriptions intended by Ibsen to be taken literally? Why?

6. In *Julius Caesar,* which of the principal characters is impelled primarily by ethical motives and which by pathetic motives?

7. Describe two instances, one comic and one serious, of the "turning worm" change. In each case prepare to discuss the foreshadowing of this change.

8. From plays you know, set down five instances of the pairing of characters by contrasting traits, such as a clever character with a stupid companion or helper, or an insincere character with a forthright helper or servant.

Chapter 5 · Language

1. Bring to class three or four examples, from plays you know, of speeches which are unusually difficult to speak rapidly or clearly.

2. Bring to class several examples of speeches which can be spoken in such a way as to convey totally different meanings from those which they would ordinarily suggest in print.

3. Look at the speeches of the Stage Manager in *Our Town,* in the wedding scene and again in the final scene, and describe the means used to gain cumulative power in the speaking of them.

4. Jot down half a dozen expressions which illustrate the use of imagery in everyday speech (such as "red herring," "brass tacks," etc.), and prepare to explain the imagery upon which their effect depends.

5. Recall and write down some especially "angry" language you have heard, then study it to see in what way its emphasis is related to rhythm. Bring these examples to class for discussion.

6. When you talk to yourself (for all human beings *do* talk to themselves), do you habitually speak to an imaginary listener? After an argument, do you continue to rehearse what you would like to have said? When you have something important to say, do you rehearse it in advance? How do these examples compare to the soliloquy in a play?

7. Just for fun — and to show how easy it is to contrive language embellishments — see how many amusing sayings you can concoct by garbling common sayings, such as, "All that bristles is not bold," or "You've buttered your bread, now you must lie in it," or "Don't change water in mid-stream."

Chapter 6 · Thought

1. In a brief oral or written report, enlarge on the idea that serious drama must be written according to some specific idea of life. Use as examples plays which you know well.

2. Describe two or three instances of plays in which the thought is serious but the playwright does not seem to have made up his mind as to the specific ideas he is trying to embody in the play.

3. Report on an instance or two of serious plays in which the action is interesting but the thought insignificant.

4. Give an instance in which the conclusion of a play is worked out, not according to what is probable, but according to what *ought* to be if life were more orderly than it is.

5. Give an instance of a play in which the conclusion left you with the feeling that certain characters had been unfairly treated.

6. Select several examples of prologues or epilogues which clearly explain the general thought of the play.

7. List a number of symbols you can recall from prose dramas, such as the tree in *All*

My Sons and the old flower-woman in *A Streetcar Named Desire.*

8. Bring to class at least one good example of a set speech which clearly voices the central idea of the play.

Chapter 7 · Drama and Audience

1. Can you recall an instance in which a poor performance was actually caused by a poor audience? Specifically, what was wrong with the audience?

2. Prepare for discussion several examples to illustrate the strikingly different ways in which a particular play can affect its audiences, especially when the audiences differ markedly as to age and education.

3. Name several plays which thrilled you when you were ten years younger, but which now seem comparatively uninteresting. Describe why.

4. What kind of comedy do you enjoy most at present? Comedy of wit? Of action? Of intrigue? Why?

5. List several plays which you liked better after you had had time to think about them and discuss them with others than you did at the time you saw them.

6. Among the plays listed in the text as having similar subjects, make as many comparisons as you can, noting first the specific similarities and afterward the most striking differences.

7. Can you call to mind a current play which seems especially timely? How do you think it will seem ten years from now? Can you name an old play which, being recently revived, has turned out to be surprisingly topical?

8. Name several plays for which you care little at present, but which you think may be more interesting when you are ten years older.

Section II · Acting

Chapter 8 · Purpose and Method in Acting

1. In a brief oral or written report, en-

large on the statement that some of the actor's relationships with fellow-actors and setting "are of course physical, some psychological; some are developed in space, some in time; some are directly prescribed by the playwright, some creatively imagined by the actor and his director or designer. . . ." (See page 79.)

2. With reference to the actors in a recent major production on your own campus or in your own community, discuss the proposition that " . . . the actor's freedom is no greater than his responsibility." (See page 79.)

3. The present chapter has listed five principles on which to base one's judgment of a good performance (pages 80–82). Apply each of these to the actor or actress playing the central role in a recent local production; a role of middle range as to difficulty or importance; a minor role.

4. Give specific instances of the relative focus proper to each level of the actor's "dual role": (*a*) in a comedy of your choice; (*b*) in a serious piece; (*c*) in an expressionistic play; (*d*) in a stylized version of a premodern drama.

5. With specific reference to actors at your own present level of training and experience, list the advantages and disadvantages of the two basic schools of opinion as to "systems" in acting, as described in this chapter.

6. Distinguish clearly between emotional identification with a role early in the rehearsal period and emotional expression during performance.

7. It is proposed by some actors and directors that the best plan of study for a role is immediate memorization of words, rather than meanings, so that the hands and eyes may be free during early rehearsals; as lines and actions are gradually co-ordinated, interpretation is then added, bit by bit, to this mechanical memorization. Contrast this plan of study and memorization with that outlined in the present chapter, suggesting possible advantages and disadvantages in each.

Chapter 9 • Movement and Gesture

1. Apply the principle that "effective stage pantomime is selective and unified" to a class demonstration of: (*a*) laying a table; (*b*) finding a telephone number and completing a call; (*c*) chasing an imaginary chicken off, on, and off the stage; or (*d*) rising from a chair as though in eighteenth-century costume, bowing (or curtsying), and returning to the chair.

2. In relation to Exercise 1, find parallel applications of the principle of selectivity in objects from the graphic or plastic arts.

3. Cite examples of "heightened and projected" pantomimic action observed in recent productions; in contemporary films.

4. In discussing the pantomimic action of early films (e.g., those available in 16 mm. from the Museum of Modern Art Film Library), try to account for the apparent level of exaggeration attempted.

5. Using the examples in the quotation from Lewes (page 98) as a basis, devise an exercise or demonstration to clarify the proposition that "the actor . . . must be typical." Supply only as much context as necessary for the purposes of your experiment.

6. Using simple rehearsal furniture, arrange the necessary properties mentioned in the Simonson quotation (pages 98–99) to serve as a locale for playing the Shaw scene as: (*a*) a "purely melodramatic" one; (*b*) "romance of the blood-and-thunder variety"; (*c*) "a comedy of rapprochement between a terrified young woman and a terrified young soldier. . . ."

7. Using playscripts familiar to your listeners, give specific examples of *inherent* and of *imposed* movement.

8. Draw up a director's plan for the second-act curtain of *Kind Lady;* for the John-Sam scene in Act I of *Milestones.* Give specific examples of "strong" and "weak" positions, gross bodily attitudes, and movements.

9. Try to recognize and explain the rationale behind the "rules" for stage behavior listed in this chapter; in the case of at least some of them, indicate possible exceptions even on the proscenium stage. Is it possible to make a list of such "rules" for open staging?

10. How would the conceptions of "strong" and "weak" have to be adjusted or adapted for the arena?

Chapter 10 • Voice and Speech

1. Prepare a brief report and demonstration on the advantages of diaphragmatic-abdominal breathing for the actor. If necessary, refer to other sources for your material, including Albright's *Working Up a Part* and Anderson's *Training the Speaking Voice.* For this exercise, and for some of those to follow, a tape recorder may be of assistance in supporting or clarifying your position.

2. By the use of contrasting examples, develop the points that "a good tone . . . is one that seems to flow easily through the throat, as if there were nothing there to interrupt it" and that "an 'open,' relaxed throat contributes to mellowness and richness of tone."

3. In a brief lecture-demonstration, show specifically how projection (as well as articulation) will not "take care of itself" on an open stage. (Page 115.)

4. From a playscript familiar to your listeners, read a speech of at least twelve lines. Decide clearly on the first and last word in each thought group, and be prepared to describe the relation which each bears to earlier and later groups. Find the contrasts, echoes, restatements, amplifications, climaxes, and the like. Do not plan to substitute mere punching or pounding on certain words for subtle and proportionate focus of attention on certain ideas.

5. Prepare to read aloud as skillfully as possible the brief selections from Joseph Auslander and from T. V. Smith (page 117), making absolutely clear the distinction between new and echoed material. Collect other paragraphs illustrating points made in

the sections on "Reading for Meaning" and "The Nature of Emphasis."

6. Using "Why leave it to me?" and "This is a first-class opportunity" (on page 119) as examples, illustrate *bridging* as a device for sharpening focus and suggesting implications. At first, speak the supporting phrases along with the basic idea, later dropping the phrases when clear and expressive readings have been achieved. Have your listeners check carefully on the distinctions you have been able to retain.

7. Choose *one* contemporary sonnet (e.g., Rupert Brooke's "Sonnet" or Archibald MacLeish's "The End of the World") and *one* sonnet from an earlier century (e.g., from Shakespeare, Milton, or Wordsworth); prepare to read both aloud, with special attention to specific attitudes and particular emotional values. In reacting vividly to individual lines or sections, do not violate the dominant, unifying mood of the whole.

8. Choose scenes from familiar playscripts, which illustrate the following principles: "If a character is asking a boon from a friend, a relative, or a debtor, he does not . . . ask it with quite the same flavor as from someone else"; "if two lovers, rivals, or enemies were to confront each other in physical circumstances which duplicated or reflected circumstances in their past relationship, the dialogue would need to take on new and added values." (See page 120.)

9. By referring to recent local productions, clarify your conception of "oral contact" and of "conversational quality," as described in Chapter 10.

Chapter 11 · Characterization

1. Some actors distinguish between characters in terms of "individuals," "types," and "shadows." Categorize the cast of an Ibsen play on this basis; a Shakespearean play; a Restoration comedy; a contemporary serious drama.

2. Under what circumstances and for what reasons could the following principle be violated: "If a competent playwright has written into his script a series of descending levels of individualized characterization, it is important that both actors and director respect these levels, modifying the relationships between them only after serious consideration." (See page 126.) Refer specifically to characters in a playscript familiar to your group.

3. Define, describe, and illustrate the following terms as used in the present chapter: plot line; theme; atmosphere.

4. Using the conception of "units of action" described on page 127, draw up a plan of structural units for *Riders to the Sea;* for the first act of *Ghosts;* for the first or second act of *The Inspector-General;* for the last act of a contemporary serious play. In at least one of these cases, indicate the purpose, flavor, and point of each unit, as contrasted with preceding and following units.

5. Using the plan for character analysis outlined on pages 129 and 130, describe in some detail a suitable basic characterization for a central role in a contemporary play; in a pre-modern play.

6. Prepare to report on at least one section of the following exercise, which appeared originally in Albright's *Working Up a Part:*

(*a*) Over a period of time, observe the gross bodily attitudes of representative mechanics, farmers, office clerks, clergymen, and others. Do you find in these groups any characteristic details that might be typical of the class rather than of the individual? List and evaluate any such details, especially in so far as they might later be used on the stage in motivated expression. Do not be satisfied with stereotypes borrowed from stage, screen, or popular magazine.

(*b*) Make similar observations of extremely old persons. Again avoiding stereotypes, can you find in head, shoulders, torso, knees—in action and at rest— tensions or stresses or weaknesses which may be typical of age? Which of them could most easily and readily be assimilated into a total characterization? Which of them would tend to project? Which are fundamentally masculine; feminine?

7. Using the discussion on pages 130–131 as a basis, prepare a list of examples to illustrate various types of adaptation required if characteristic details observed in real life are to be used in the theatre.

8. In a brief report and demonstration, with a view to clarifying the nature of basic motivations, enlarge on the principle that " . . . a generalized purpose will not suffice: an action cannot be characterized by mere activity." (See page 132.)

9. In discussing Dorimant (in *The Man of Mode*), the present chapter suggested that, although by contemporary standards he may be "artificial," he is not "unbelievable"; and that, although in our time he may be actualistically "impossible," he is aesthetically "probable." Is this a distinction without a difference? What functional importance can you ascribe to such considerations? Prepare a brief report on the subject.

10. "To *believe* in the distorted view of life which his character typifies" has been offered as one of the secrets of the successful comedian (page 134). In a brief report or demonstration, and with reference to at least two forms or styles of comedy, support this proposition.

11. Choose a love scene, a recognition scene, a quarrel, and an expository scene from contemporary dramatic literature. Comment specifically on the ways in which the playing of these units must vary according to: the total characterization of the players involved; the place and function of the scene in the play's entire dramatic action; the theme and atmosphere of the whole.

Chapter 12 · A Perspective on the Whole

1. In a brief oral or written report, enlarge on the statement that "any deception involving the spectator in the modern theatre is therefore conscious and willing self-deception"; use examples from playscripts of various periods, types, and styles. (See page 136.)

2. Using playscripts familiar to your listeners, give specific examples of highly *representational* scenes; of highly *presentational* ones. How would you classify the opening and closing scenes of *The Teahouse of the August Moon?* Key scenes in *Our Town; Waiting for Lefty; From Morn to Midnight; Six Characters in Search of an Author?*

3. Find parallel applications of "aesthetic distance" in nontheatrical arts; of "empathic" responses. Prepare to discuss these in class.

4. Cite examples of aesthetic balance observed in recent stage productions; in contemporary films.

5. With reference to a recent major production in your own community, discuss the principle of organic unity. Indicate devices used by the director and the players to assure continuity and growth during the later weeks of rehearsal.

6. If you were to be cast in a central role of a contemporary drama, how would you go about learning "to conserve as well as to build"? (See pages 141–142.) How would your problem differ in the case of a premodern drama? In what ways would the problem be essentially the same?

7. In discussing the serious actor's relations with his fellow-artists, Stanislavski offers such advice as "Never come into the theatre with mud on your feet" and "Seven will not wait for one." After reading Chapter XIV of *Building a Character* ("Toward an Ethics for the Theatre"), discuss his advice in terms of your own acting group.

8. What importance do you attach to maintaining a "performance atmosphere" in the later stages of rehearsal? (Refer to page 143.) Bring to class specific instances of this problem as it concerns both actor and director.

Section III · Theatre and Stage

Chapter 13 · Methods of Organizing the Theatre Structure

1. What are the inevitable differences between the acting of poetic drama and the acting of prose drama?

2. What examples have you seen of non-illusionistic elements in stage productions? What was your reaction to them?

3. Trace the variant meanings of the word "realism" throughout theatre history.

4. Discuss the photographs in an issue of *Theatre Arts* magazine in terms of the staging methods used. Look especially for clear examples of various types of Actualistic Staging.

5. Report on some of the dramatic elements in the dances of the American Indians. (Thomas Wood Stevens, *The Theatre from Athens to Broadway*, pp. ix–xii and 1–7 can be used as a source.)

6. Report on George Kernodle's theory as to the source of the Elizabethan stage. (*From Art to Theatre*, pp. 130–153.)

7. Report on the directional theory and practice of the Duke of Saxe-Meiningen. (A good source is Lee Simonson, *The Stage is Set*, pp. 272–307.)

8. Prepare a Messenger speech from a Greek tragedy, and make it as exciting as possible.

9. Prepare the final speech of Bottom in Scene i of Act IV of *A Midsummer Night's Dream*, with a view to maintaining *rapport* with the audience.

10. Prepare one of the famous soliloquies from *Hamlet, Macbeth,* or *Othello,* ordinarily delivered introspectively, and deliver it with direct address to the classroom audience.

11. Analyze, with a view to preparation and performance, *Noah* (from the Wakefield Cycle). Report on every opportunity you see for broad comedy.

12. For one act from a naturalistic play, draw a floor plan which includes furniture along the "fourth wall." Prepare an oral or written report on the effective opportunities you find for using such furniture, and for introducing other business in keeping with this concept of staging.

Chapter 14 · The Proscenium Theatre

1. In the light of the criteria presented in this chapter, discuss the shortcomings of the auditoriums in theatres with which you are familiar.

2. For what types of plays would you recommend using a different rigging on the front curtain than that ordinarily used by your producing group? (See pages 185–186 and Figure 21.)

3. Draw a scale floor plan of the stage used by your producing group. Prepare to discuss its good and bad features. (While exactly measured drawings are essential when they are working drawings for construction, paper ruled in quarter-inch squares is satisfactory for present purposes. A second sheet of this graph paper can be used to measure diagonal lines.)

4. What standardization of scenery is employed by your producing group? What additional standardization would improve the flexibility of the equipment?

5. Prepare a chalk talk on the floor plan of the revolving stage used in a Reinhardt production, or on Stanislavski's sketches for a revolving stage for *Othello*. (See footnotes on page 192 for some of the sources. The Reinhardt floor plans are reproduced in many additional books.)

6. Prepare a chalk talk on the revolving platforms used in *Lady in the Dark*. (See *Theatre Arts*, XXV [April, 1941], 265–275.)

7. Report on "Theatre Planning," by Lee Simonson, in *Architecture for the New Theatre* (ed. Isaacs), pp. 17–40.

8. Draw a scale floor plan of your auditorium and indicate the sight lines from the poorest seats. Also draw a cross section of the theatre and draw the sight lines from a

seat in the rear of the balcony when the teaser is hung at fourteen feet. Comment briefly on the implications of these diagrams for design and direction in your theatre.

9. On the basis suggested in pages 194–196, determine the minimum height suitable for the gridiron of your theatre.

10. Diagram the shop and storage needs for your theatre, in a plan based on the criteria discussed on pages 196–197. (If your instructor requests it, fit these theoretical needs realistically to the present shop and to the opportunities for its expansion.)

11. Report on Adolphe Appia's theories of design. (Sources include Lee Simonson, *The Stage Is Set*, pp 351–377; *Theatre Arts*, XVI [August, 1932], 615–686; H. Darkes Albright, "Appia Fifty Years After," *Quarterly Journal of Speech*, XXXV [April and October, 1949], 182–189 and 297–303.)

12. Report on Bertolt Brecht's Epic Theatre techniques. (Sources: *Theatre Arts*, and the writings of Eric Bentley. Best source, if available: Brecht's "A Little Organum for the Theatre," *Accent*, IX [Winter, 1951], 13–40.)

Chapter 15 • The Open Theatre

1. Report on Bel Geddes' designs for experimental theatres. (Sources include: Edith J. R. Isaacs [ed.], *Architecture for the New Theatre*, pp. 87–98, and Norman Bel Geddes, *Horizons*, pp. 159–181.)

2. Make a class report on Chapters IV through X in *Central and Flexible Staging*, by Walden P. Boyle.

3. Compare the illustrations in *Central and Flexible Staging* with those in Margo Jones's *Theatre in the Round;* with those in Glenn Hughes's *Penthouse Theatre.*

4. If you have visited a playhouse with a wrap-around, arena, or thrust stage, discuss your first impressions of both theatre and stage.

5. Criticize or support the proposition that "not every characteristic" of an open theatre "offers advantages over the older and more familiar proscenium theatre." (Page 219.)

6. On the basis of your knowledge and experience at this point, what in your opinion are the chances of successfully combining open and proscenium stages in the same playhouse? (Pages 221–222.)

7. Discuss the expressive values of new styles and conventions of production and design observed in photographs of contemporary European productions. (See *Theatre Arts* magazine, and *World Theatre*, the quarterly publication of the International Theatre Institute.)

8. If you were to direct a play by Molière in an arena, in what ways would the acting and directing differ from those in a proscenium production?

9. Develop a scheme for the production of a play by Shakespeare in your present theatre, using absolute continuity of action.

Section IV • Design

Chapter 16 • The Nature and Function of Design

1. Note for discussion several instances of settings which attracted applause when first revealed to the audience. How did these settings seem at the conclusion of the scene —as interesting as at the beginning, or less so? What particular details can you point out as being responsible for the increase or decrease in effectiveness?

2. Look up Maxwell Anderson's *Winterset*, Act I, Scene iii, and see if you can find the line at which Mielziner heightened Miriamne's appearance by means of the device described in the present chapter. (See pages 229–230.)

3. Prepare to discuss several instances in which you have known a play to be poor in one performance and excellent in another because of differences in lighting, costuming, or scene changing.

4. Study the first and last scenes of *The Emperor Jones;* suggest a way in which the

two scenes can be related — through design — in atmosphere.

5. Study the final scene of Ibsen's *Ghosts*, and devise ways in which the sunrise can be used to intensify the dramatic impact of Mrs. Alving's discovery that her son is insane.

6. Compare Chekhov's description of the scene at the opening of *The Sea Gull* with Ibsen's description of the scene at the beginning of *The Lady from the Sea*, noting differences in the detail and mood of the setting described by each author.

7. For an interesting experiment, take the room described by Ibsen at the beginning of *Ghosts* and see whether you can relate it to a plausible first-floor plan of the house.

8. Study the opening scene of Jules Romains' *Doctor Knock*, and prepare to discuss the following questions: Why is the scene placed in a moving auto? What does the motion of auto and scenery add to the play? Now turn to the final scene. Note several possibilities in the setting which might make it equal in interest to the novel first scene.

Chapter 17 · Aesthetic Factors in the Design

1. Can you recall a design which led you to expect a different kind of play than that which you saw? If so, jot down several reasons for this result, and prepare to discuss them in class.

2. Study the descriptions of the opening scenes of *Pelléas and Mélisande, Hannele,* and *The Cherry Orchard;* in your own words, in a sentence or two, describe the authors' apparent intention for kind and style of setting.

3. Note for discussion several instances in which settings you have seen were obviously copies of other settings for the same or other plays. The question at issue is whether the copies were as effective as the originals.

4. Recalling a play you have seen in which there were many scene changes, comment on the degree to which the settings achieved a unity of style.

5. In addition to the plays mentioned in the text, note several you have seen in which unity of design was achieved by the manner in which color was used in the settings and costumes.

6. Note three instances in which disunity of design arose from the designer's inability to correlate natural and architectural locales required by the script.

7. Prepare to discuss the best and the worst of the natural settings you have seen and to say why they differed in quality.

8. Prepare to discuss the best of the ship or marine settings you have seen and to say why they excelled. Bring photographs of each, if possible.

9. In addition to the plays mentioned in the text, bring to class further examples of the proposition that "productions featuring symbolism allow the widest latitude of interpretation." (See page 236.) Discuss and support your examples.

10. Bring also some additional examples of the proposition that "brilliance of design is easiest to achieve in bizarre productions." (See page 237.)

Chapter 18 · Physical Factors in the Design 1: Setting and Lighting

1. Roughly plan the first two scene changes in *Beyond the Horizon*, first for a stage with inadequate wing space, then for a stage with ample wing space, but no loft.

2. Choosing one of the plays mentioned on pages 235–242, show in some detail how various elements in the design for a proscenium production of the play would have to be adapted for open staging. Consider the problem in terms of composition (page 251); in terms of handling the floor cloth (page 252); in terms of lighting (pages 252–253); in terms of costumes and properties (page 253); and in terms of treatment of the façade (pages 253–254). Will the play lose or gain?

3. In addition to the plays named in the text, list others which require action taking

place simultaneously in two areas, such as inside and outside a building, upstairs and downstairs, or on balcony and in garden.

4. Make a close study of *Macbeth,* Act IV, Scene i (the Cauldron Scene), and see whether you can determine which of the details mentioned must be shown and which can safely be left to the imagination of the spectators.

5. For an interesting exercise in legerdemain, study *The Tempest,* Act III, Scene iii, and see if you can develop a scheme for making the various illusions operate.

6. Compare the scene sequence of Galsworthy's *Escape* with that of Arthur Miller's *Death of a Salesman,* and note the principal differences in the demands they make on the designer. Prepare a discussion of these differences for class.

7. If you have seen a play or two in which instantaneous "break-away" changes occurred, see whether you can recall any of the mechanisms employed.

Chapter 19 · Physical Factors in the Design 2: Costume

1. From current magazines or newspapers, clip five or six examples each of men's and women's clothing which combine fitted garments with draped ones.

2. Bring to class a swatch of each of the following: (*a*) a bulky rough-surfaced stuff; (*b*) a dense hard-woven fabric; (*c*) a thin stiff high-surfaced fabric; (*d*) a soft thin fabric. For each of these materials, suggest several uses, for particular garments and for particular historical periods.

3. Try combining the samples which you gathered for exercise 2, above, to see which seem to go well together, and which poorly. See whether you can say why in each case.

4. Look about you and study the clothing worn by your classmates. How many instances can you find of outfits which would be improved by the addition of an accent or two? Can you see any instances of trimming or jewelry which add nothing to the total effect? Do you see any outfits which appear to be overaccentuated?

5. Bring to class several pairs of shoes — one with heels, one without heels, a pair of bedroom slippers, and a pair of clogs or tennis shoes. Use these to show the class how different kinds of footwear affect your stride and bearing.

6. Clip from magazines five photographs of dancers in motion, and mount these on a sheet intended to illustrate costuming characters for vigorous physical activity.

7. Bring to class several pictures of what you consider to be the handsomest costumes you have seen, and prepare to tell why in some detail.

8. What are the three funniest stage costumes you have ever seen? Describe one of them in some detail, and account for its theatrical effect.

Chapter 20 · Principles of Spatial Composition

1. Collect several good pictorial examples each of convergence, enclosure, and intersection. These may be from either stage settings or illustrations. Explain how the linear scheme encourages the eye to move toward the center of the composition.

2. Devise a demonstration — to be presented to the class — of the saying, "The eye counts to five."

3. Choose a scene, preferably the opening scene of a play. Identify the atmosphere, and then describe what seems to you appropriate lighting for this atmosphere in terms of value, quality, and directionality.

4. Most designers like the job of lighting tragedies and serious plays much better than that of lighting comedies. Try to account for this preference.

5. Bring to class an object or a piece of fabric whose color gives it an unusually high attention-attracting power, and explain why.

6. Assemble three or four samples of painted surface or dyed fabric to illustrate

how several different materials may have the same hue but different degrees of purity.

7. Devise a demonstration to show how one color can be used to accentuate another.

8. Prepare for the class a simple demonstration to illustrate the various effects of colored light upon colored fabrics and paints.

Chapter 21 • Principles of Temporal Composition

1. Recount an instance of a performance in which you became confused as to the identity of some character or the locale of some setting because of unintentional similarities in color or design between those you were seeing and some which had come earlier in the play. Describe the incident and try to account for the confusion.

2. List two or three instances of settings which, while very interesting at the beginning of the play, became tiresome to you before the play was over. Can you tell why?

3. From your own experience, describe three or four scenes in which fading or brightening light was used to particularly good dramatic effect.

4. How many instances can you describe, from plays you have seen, of cyclic progression in the design?

5. From your favorite Shakespearean play, choose a sequence (of about five or six scenes) which looks as if it would allow for a striking alternation of various effects from scene to scene.

6. In the same scene sequence as in number 5, above, see whether you can determine which scene should have the greatest proportional emphasis and which the least.

7. Describe for the class the most dramatic scene you have witnessed in which the impact of some great moment was materially heightened by means of color and illumination; by means of a musical "stab"; by means of a shift in composition. Contrast it with a similar but misplaced or gimmicky effect.

Section V • Direction

Chapter 22 • The Function of the Director

1. Paralleling the analogy of the stage director and the orchestra conductor (pages 323–324), compare the performance circumstances of the stage director with those of the director of a university marching band at a football game. (Or substitute: a football coach, a general commanding an attacking army, or the court official who plans a ceremony such as a coronation or a royal wedding.)

2. If you have had experience with plays given elsewhere than at the institution where you are now studying, give examples of directors who provided good leadership, and of those who failed partially in their leadership function. Avoid using exact names.

3. What specific devices could the director use in the early episodes of *Street Scene* to draw attention to the leading characters? (See page 327.)

4. What is the playwright's apparent attitude toward the characters of *A Doll's House, Tartuffe, The Importance of Being Earnest, The Man Who Came to Dinner, Harvey, The Birthday Party,* or *Galileo?* (See pages 330–331.)

5. What are the satiric elements in *Mrs. McThing, My Three Angels,* or *The Knack?* (See pages 331–332.)

6. What is the basic meaning of *Medea; The Visit; After the Fall; Stop the World, I Want to Get off; Summer and Smoke; Little Mary Sunshine?* (See pages 332–333.)

7. Prepare a bibliography of the reading you would do to prepare to direct *Mary of Scotland, Richard III, Macbeth, The Trojan Women, Joan of Lorraine, Abe Lincoln in Illinois, Tovarich, Ethan Frome, Victoria Regina, The Weavers, The Pillars of Society, The Barretts of Wimpole Street,* or *Berkeley Square.* (See pages 333–334.)

8. Read twenty-five pages of a volume of

the Furness *Variorum* dealing with one of Shakespeare's plays, and report on the material found there which would be helpful in directing this play.

9. List specifically the probable points of "partial success" to be expected in a production in your school. (See pages 337–338.)

Special Problems for Students of Direction

10. Direct the drunken Shriner episode from *Light Up the Sky* as a demonstration of your opinion of the author's dramatic purpose in this dialogue.

11. Direct the opening thirty-four lines of *King Lear* in two ways (with the same cast): to lead the spectator to accept it merely as general atmosphere, and to have him remember the characters as important.

12. Direct Helena's awakening from *A Midsummer Night's Dream,* stressing the comedy. (If the seats in your classroom are movable, set up an arena arrangement and perform it in arena style.)

Chapter 23 · The Visual Stimuli

1. Prepare an oral report on Alexander Dean's theories of the mood value of stage areas, based on pages 180–183 of the Dean-Carra *Fundamentals of Play Directing.*

2. Report on examples of visual foreshadowing which you have seen in motion pictures or plays.

3. On duplicated pages from a play manuscript supplied by the instructor — preferably a short section from a play currently in rehearsal — record in the following ways the movement of a demonstration scene given in class:

(*a*) by arrows and initials, using abbreviations instead of complete words whenever possible;

(*b*) by language symbols such as could be printed in an acting version of a play;

(*c*) by means of numbered arrows on a single floor plan. (See pages 344 and 349–350, and Figures 46 and 47.)

4. Prepare a lecture-demonstration on the advantages and disadvantages of various locations for entranceways. (See pages 354–357.)

5. Prepare ten pantomimic attitudes expressing variations on a single emotion (such as joy, anger, timidity, aggressiveness, pain, revulsion, expectancy, or fear) in order to demonstrate how attendant and related circumstances dictate variations in expression. (See page 340.)

6. Walk six times across a flat floor, portraying one character with six different motivations. Repeat these, moving up or down steps, as a demonstration of the added emphasis supplied by the stairs.

7. What type of furniture group would you place at center stage for *What a Life, A Doll's House, The Little Foxes, The Time of Your Life, The Would-Be Gentleman, Papa Is All,* and the opening scene of *As You Like It?*

8. Using steps and platforms which are available, demonstrate the way in which actors in an Elizabethan play can relate themselves to architectural elements.

Special Problems for Students of Direction

9. Direct the scene from *I Remember Mama* which is described on page 346, in order to demonstrate the shift of attention by position.

10. In order to demonstrate the effectiveness of different stage positions, direct part of the balcony scene of *Romeo and Juliet;* and perform it twice, once with the balcony on left stage and once on the right. (Use right-handed actors, and raise Juliet at least to the top of a table.)

11. Direct part of Scene i of Act II of *Three Men on a Horse,* using every opportunity for contrast between the wife and her brother.

12. Prepare an extempore reconstruction of an episode from a Marx Brothers or a Danny Kaye motion picture, paying par-

ticular attention to contrasts and to rapid transitions.

Chapter 24 · The Auditory Stimuli

1. Demonstrate some of the varied ways in which one can say "No!" in response to hearing bad news. (See pages 373–374.)

2. Demonstrate "controlled emotion" (pages 372–373) by delivering a speech from a play in which the character is attempting to express one emotion while feeling another. (Examples: Antony's oration in *Julius Caesar*, Sheridan Whiteside trying to persuade Maggie to stay with him in *The Man Who Came to Dinner*, the exit of Sir Fretful Plagiary in *The Critic*, the final episode in *Of Mice and Men*, Amanda's telephone conversations in *The Glass Menagerie*, or one of many scenes from *Death of a Salesman* or *A Streetcar Named Desire*.)

3. Deliver Dr. Stockmann's speech to the crowd (from *An Enemy of the People*) in a standing position, imagining yourself addressing a large group; and again, seated, imagining yourself talking earnestly to only three or four people. Account for the differences in vocal and visual stimuli employed.

4. Cite examples from motion pictures of the effective use of pitch and pitch contrasts.

5. Prepare a key speech of Sister Gracia from each act of *The Kingdom of God* and demonstrate the effectiveness of voice quality to denote a changing characterization.

6. Listen to a recording of a speech from a play by Shakespeare and report on any particularly effective vocal techniques heard there.

7. Listen to a recording of a speech from a play by Shakespeare read by Maurice Evans, and a recording of some other actor reading the same speech. Comment on the comparative success with which the intellectual and emotional meaning is projected by the two actors.

8. Select a single word or a short phrase, and speak the identical words with ten differ-

ent motivations. Try to determine which vocal factors contribute most to the communication of the motivations.

9. Listen to an effective public speaker while he addresses a large audience without mechanical amplification, and then listen to him in conversation afterward. Record your observations of all the differences in vocal characteristics in the two situations. (A good preacher is one convenient model for the exercise, though nearly every public speaker is surrounded by questioners after a speech, and can be heard in conversational speech at that time. Recorded material available for similar study includes the convention speeches of Franklin D. Roosevelt, and his "Fireside Talks.")

10. Prepare a long, complex speech, such as that of the Chairman of the National Committee from *Of Thee I Sing* or of Socrates in *Barefoot in Athens*, or a speech of similar length from a play by Fry, Eliot, or Jeffers; and strive for maximum variety and contrast.

Special Problems for Students of Direction

11. Direct one of the scenes mentioned on pages 376–377 as a demonstration of the usefulness of contrasts in volume for characterization.

12. Demonstrate the director's opportunities for the use of pitch by directing the Helen episode from *The Trojan Women*, the heart-attack scene from *The Little Foxes*, the opening of the last act of *Another Part of the Forest*, part of the last act of *Anna Christie*, or one of the scenes mentioned from *Ghosts*.

13. Demonstrate the varied techniques available for unison speech by directing a group of four in a speech by the chorus from a Greek play.

Chapter 25 · Patterning the Visual and Auditory Stimuli

1. (Impromptu class exercise.) Let six students take up positions and attitudes of

their own choice at the front of the class-room. Then let six other students, one after another, rearrange the group to give emphasis to each one in the group in turn — but each time making as few alterations as possible.

2. (Impromptu class exercise.) Place one student in the front of the room. Ask one after another to join him, taking up a position and an attitude which will most help to emphasize the first student, and which will still maintain a composition which has unity as well as good balance and proportion.

3. (Impromptu class exercise.) Place a student in the front of the room. Ask one after another to add himself to the grouping, each finding the position and attitude which will focus attention on himself. Once a student has found his position and attitude, he may not alter it, even when "covered."

4. Discuss the ways in which steps and levels — as demonstrated in the photographs in this book — assist in picturization, in control of emphasis, and in composition generally.

5. Analyze five pictures of groups of people from the standpoint of emphasis in composition. (Sources may include newspapers, illustrated magazines, and reproductions of paintings.)

6. In order to observe the influence of an author's personal viewpoint, analyze different characterizations given to the same historical personage by different playwrights. (Usable examples include: Medea, Electra, Antigone, Oedipus, Cleopatra, Julius Caesar, Mark Antony, Elizabeth I, Mary Stuart, Henry VIII, Washington, Lincoln, Jefferson.)

7. Read the speech of the Grand Inquisitor from *Saint Joan*, the long speech of Magnus in Act I of *The Apple Cart*, or one of Hickey's long speeches from Act IV of *The Iceman Cometh*, demonstrating the structure of the speech by emphasizing its "para-graphic" organization. (See pages 428–429.)

8. Analyze the director's devices which could be used to add to the excitement or tension of the Ben-Oscar-Leo scene near the end of Act II of *The Little Foxes*.

Special Problems for Students of Direction

9. Direct Scene viii of *Abe Lincoln in Illinois*, following the pattern explained on pages 402–405.

10. Direct an episode from *The Tempest, The Comedy of Errors, A Midsummer Night's Dream*, Act V of *The Merchant of Venice, Lysistrata, The Birds, Finian's Rainbow, Oklahoma!, The School for Husbands, Love for Love, The Moon Is Blue, The Boor, The Youngest, Peter Pan, The Enchanted, The Madwoman of Chaillot, Ring Round the Moon*, or *Ondine*, using every possible auditory and visual device to emphasize light-hearted gaiety.

11. Direct one of the scenes from *Escape, The Blue Bird, Waiting for Lefty*, or . . . *one third of a nation* . . . , putting as much emphasis as possible on the element of progression.

12. Direct a scene from *Harvey*, emphasizing the contrast in rhythm of action and speech between Elwood P. Dowd and the other characters in the play.

Chapter 26 • Directing for the Open Stage

1. In a Shakespearean scene of your choice, show how a relatively static grouping may be desirable "as a rest or to punctuate the progression." (Page 436.)

2. Draw up a list of technical and other means for focusing on an important character, given open-stage conditions.

3. Discuss the proposition that "the seeming strength of a character's movement is determined therefore by the manner and force with which it is made." (Page 438.)

4. If the nature of the open stage is "fundamentally centripetal," is that of the pro-scenium stage centrifugal? To what degree? With what exceptions?

5. Give other examples than those in the text for multiple use of the ditch, the vomitories, and the upper level. (Page 439.)

6. The problem of prompting actors on an open stage is raised in the final pages of the chapter. Have you any specific suggestions for solving it, or at least lessening the difficulty?

7. On the same basis, discuss the problems of co-ordinating cues and of stage management generally in the open playhouse.

8. List some specific ways in which an open-stage director could properly avoid orientation toward any one segment of the house.

Special Problems for Students of Direction

9. On an approximation of a thrust stage, direct the entrance of the king in *The Winter's Tale,* the return of the travelers in *The Cherry Orchard,* or the return of the army in *Much Ado About Nothing.* (Page 436.)

10. Prepare a lecture-demonstration to clarify the nature and function of either "enter and turn" or "tour of the apron." Can you suggest ways in which either may normally be accomplished with subtlety and variety?

11. Make similar lecture-demonstrations with respect to other "principles" outlined in the present chapter—e.g., the cue-line link.

Chapter 27 • The Director's Relationship with His Associates

1. List ten plays which you consider well adapted to noncommercial production before your local audience. List ten other plays of various types, and explain why you believe they are not well adapted to this audience.

2. Discuss the particular preferences and aversions of the local audience, and indicate appropriate steps which can be taken to cultivate in it a more catholic taste.

3. Analyze the "reinterpretation" (pages 442–448) necessary in adapting a specific play for film use or in making a motion picture or a stage play from a novel or a short

story. Explain the apparent reason for the change of interpretation, and evaluate the artistic justification for it.

4. Give an example of major reinterpretation by an actor or a director in a production of a classic which you have seen.

5. Report on the advantages of having a community theatre board make certain decisions instead of the director, as given by Talbot Pearson in *Encores on Main Street,* p. 39.

6. Report on "Against the Illusionistic Approach to Directing," by Charles J. McGaw, *Educational Theatre Journal,* II (March, 1950), 66–71.

7. Report on "Directing the Verse Play," by B. Iden Payne, *Educational Theatre Journal,* II (October, 1950), 193–198.

8. Report on "Directing the Period Play," from Barnard Hewitt's *Art and Craft of Play Production,* pp. 283–324.

9. In order to demonstrate how even a translator stamps his personality on a playscript, analyze — from the standpoint of direction — two translations of the same scene. (Authors whose works have been translated frequently include: Aeschylus, Sophocles, Euripides, Aristophanes, Ibsen, Rostand, Molière. Particularly recommended for contrast are the William Archer and Arthur Miller translations of *An Enemy of the People,* and the Guiterman-Langner and any other translation of *The School for Husbands.*)

Special Problems for Students of Direction

10. Direct Scene iii of Act III of *Julius Caesar* as a contemporary scene.

11. Direct a scene from a pre-modern play in a period other than that of its composition, and see whether the class can identify the period in which it is staged.

12. In order to demonstrate the "adaptation" by the actor necessitated by his personal physical traits, select a large man with a broad comedy attack, and a small man who

can play wizened old men; and rehearse them both in one of the solo speeches of Launce in *The Two Gentlemen of Verona*. (Some omissions will need to be made in the dialogue to conform to current taste.) Account for the differences in characterization and motivation observed.

Chapter 28 · The Conduct of Rehearsals

1. Rehearse and prepare to perform as rapidly as possible the thought pattern given on page 479.

2. Discuss the specific advantages and disadvantages in Arthur Hopkins' technique of rehearsal criticism. (See page 458.)

3. To what extent is there validity in Belasco's belief in "clothing the actor in reality"? (See pages 459 and 164.)

4. Cite examples from your own experience in support or refutation of Clurman's theory of type-casting bit parts. (See page 460.)

5. Analyze plays with which you are familiar for special problems of casting. (See pages 460–461.)

6. What advantages and disadvantages do you see in setting business in the reverse of playing order? (See pages 469–470.)

7. What elements of a production can be integrated with the acting before a dress re-hearsal? Which ones must wait for dress rehearsal?

8. Analyze your personal habits of memorization and rehearsal, and the efficiency of these with regard to the total rehearsal process. (See pages 474–476.)

9. Prepare a written interpretation of a play such as that which a meticulous director would make before starting rehearsals. (See page 459.)

Special Problems for Students of Direction

10. Report on "*The Man Who Came to Dinner* with George Kaufman Directing," by Morton Eustis, *Theatre Arts*, XXIII, 789–798.

11. Report on Constantin Stanislavski's theory of direction as indicated in his article "Directing" in the 14th Edition of *The Encyclopaedia Britannica*. (Classified: "Theatre; Production and Direction; Direction and Acting." In the 1952 printing, it appears on pages 35–38 of Volume XXII.)

12. Report on the direction of Elia Kazan as described in "First Rehearsals," by Hermine Rich Isaacs, *Theatre Arts*, XXVIII (March, 1944), 143–150; and in "Elia Kazan," by Virginia Stevens, *Theatre* Arts, XXXI (December, 1947), 19–22.

B | On the Art of Costuming

The costuming of most nonprofessional productions involves three possibilities for accomplishment. The costumes may be rented from concerns especially established for the purpose; the costumes may be gathered from stock collections or from local persons who may own them; or the costumes may be planned and built especially for the production. Whichever possibility is appropriate, however, there must be someone connected with the production who knows and understands the special considerations which are involved in costuming for the stage.[1]

Many theatre workers have a loose and general working knowledge of the costumes of most ages and countries. Others have collected specific and detailed information about archeologically "correct" period costumes. As admirable as both extremes may be, either hazy acquaintance or too-specific knowledge can generate serious difficulties in the theatre. Few productions can rise above slipshod costuming, just as few productions can successfully stand the strictest accuracy in historical treatment. The ideal in the theatre is sound knowledge adapted to the needs of the stage.

The clothes a person wears, and the way he wears them, reflect the world and the age in which he lives, the time and specific place, his social position, and even his state of mind. Compare, for example, the clothes worn during the age of Pericles with those worn

[1] This unit should be read in connection with the sections on Design and Direction, both of which treat in somewhat extended fashion various problems concerned with the designing and wearing of stage costume, particularly on the proscenium stage. The present unit is intended to draw together some of the costume principles previously discussed, and to add pertinent and practical information for the untrained costumer.

during the Victorian era. At one extreme there is a minimum amount of graceful drapery, exposing much of the beauty of the human form and thus reflecting a specific concept of mind and spirit. At the other extreme, there is a maximum amount of fitted clothing, covering nearly all parts of the human form and reflecting a different concept of mind and spirit. In these cases, as in others like them, clothes can serve as the embodiment of the spirit of an age and a nationality.

However, "clothes" must be transformed into "costumes" for use on the stage. Clothes cannot be used, in most cases, just as they have been designed for daily living. Though a dress may be beautiful on a dressmaker's dummy in ordinary light, it must be transformed in various ways if it is to seem just as beautiful on an actress under stage lights. Careful selection and adaptation are part of the process of making clothes into costumes, and this is the essence of the art of theatrical costuming.

Such an art rests upon a set of principles which, when properly understood and carefully applied, can guide the producing unit to the preparation of finished costumes for the stage — costumes that will reflect the desired general spirit and atmosphere, but at the same time will satisfy the special demands of the theatre.

There are four basic principles in the art of costuming, the first of which is concerned with the general design of the entire production. It is a truism that the costumes must be an integral part of the whole design. They must harmonize with the particular style, mood, and atmosphere of a particular play. The costuming must be a part of the visual

508

and emotional pattern of the whole design, not an independent and attention-catching element in itself. The second principle grows out of the first, in that the costuming must be expressive of individual character as well as of the whole production. Third, the costuming must be able to project from the stage to the spectator all that it has been created to express. Finally, the costuming must be adapted to the individual conditions of a specific production.

These principles are so interrelated that the total value of any costume job depends on the degree to which all four have been considered and have been applied to the production at hand. Wispy, fluffy, and "feminine" clothes, for example, may suit a given characterization, yet may not adequately project their expressiveness in the theatre. On the contrary, they may project their femininity rather well, but may so hamper the bodily movement of the actress as to interfere with her effectiveness, or may not be adapted to the required lighting or the required setting of a specific production. Without sacrificing too much of its characteristic flavor and without seriously violating the total design, a satisfactory costume must project its meaning in theatrical terms.

In applying such principles in any given instance, and in determining the relative weight that should be assigned to each, the costume designer must be aware of a number of conditioning factors. One of the most significant of these — just as in the case of make-up — is the nature and size of the theatre plant itself. In a proscenium theatre, the costumer must be aware of the nearest and farthest spectator from the actors and actresses on the stage. Productions in unusually small theatres allow the spectator to see every detail in a costume. As the distance between the stage and the spectator increases, however, minor costuming details become indistinct and even lost. No costume should be treated so as to appear grotesquely exaggerated to persons sitting in the first row, yet at the same time it must be heightened somewhat if it is to project to the last one. The amount of expressive exaggeration necessary for dramatic effectiveness is thus partly dictated by the space relations between the actor and his audience. One can depend primarily on small and fussy detail — as in the wispy, feminine example already referred to — if it is to be used only in an intimate theatre. If on the other hand the theatre is of any size, then minor details must be eliminated in favor of larger and more expressive elements which attempt to project the same basic qualities recognized in the original costume. In general, the theatrical costumer must eliminate — or at least not rely on — delicate patterns and textures.

Within the theatre plant, whatever its size, the conditions of production of any particular play are factors of interest and concern to the person planning the costumes. All the variable design factors present in the theatre — and the individual details of setting, furniture, color, light, and make-up in a specific production — must be brought to bear upon the actual clothes the actors are intended to wear. If an actor is to be seen against an interior background, and if he is to hold the attention of an audience, his costume cannot fade into a wall or a window drapery. In exterior scenes, his costume must stand out against forest, building, or open sky. In general, the lines of his costume cannot play against similar lines in the background, the color of his costume against similar color, mass against similar mass, or texture against similar texture. Titania's fairies in *A Midsummer Night's Dream* should not be lost in a maze of forest shrubbery, Hedda Gabler in the gloom of the Tesman living room. Jeeter must stand out clearly amid the necessary accumulation of junk in his shed in *Green Grow the Lilacs*.

Similar problems face the costumer in regard to the furniture and the specific décor of a particular setting, since an actor can seem to disappear into a chair or a sofa as easily as into a wall or a window drapery. In addition, the sizes and the space relations of various scenic elements are of special concern, in that actors in costume must ordinarily move about the stage. Paniers, farthingales, and hoop skirts must be negotiated through doors and up stairways, and around and into chairs and sofas; and if a costume is to be aesthetically pleasing and effective, it must be functional as well. The size and shape of wall openings, the grouping of furniture and set-pieces, and the construction as well as the decorative treatment of levels and step-units are thus of immediate concern to the costume planner.[2]

Color on the stage — especially in relation to color in light — brings with it rather special problems and rather special opportunities for the costumer. By the judicious use of costume colors, reinforced by line and texture, a designer can project an impression of character and even of situation before a line of the play has been spoken. If Hedda Gabler's gown projects itself as rich, severe, and cold and if at the same time Mrs. Elvsted's clothing — though slightly out of fashion — is properly attractive and warm, the costumes can readily suggest the state of mind of both of the characters as well as their future relationship one to the other. Conversely, of course, the costumer can mislead, distract, or depress his audience if he has failed to plan his costumes with interpretative care.

Throughout the years, colors have taken on a psychological meaning of their own, and spectators have learned to base their impressions upon familiar interpretations. Various charts have been prepared suggesting that white denotes purity; red implies danger; green, jealousy; blue, innocence; purple, royalty — and so on through the spectrum. Since people have been conditioned to react to color in these and similar ways, a wise costumer may, without making foolish as-

sumptions and without relying on mere formulae, take advantage of such symbolic associations. In any case, a wide variety of emotional effects can be achieved through the careful selection, adaptation, and combination of harmonious yet contrasting color values.

People have also been conditioned to color prejudices; and the costume planner must be aware of current popular opinion and taste. It is often said that blue should never be seen next to green. Certainly some kinds of blue should never appear next to some kinds of green — yet, to cite but a single example, there is great beauty in the combinations of blues and greens in deep sea water, and such combinations could be both exciting and dramatically effective if they were worn by the right character in the right play. However, the costumer would do well to treat such common prejudices with reasonable care.

Through the large masses of color at his disposal, the costume designer can induce in the spectator an expectancy for a certain kind or style or flavor of presentation; and in many cases he can clarify dramatic relationships. The common device of using contrasting colors to clarify plot or situation has already been suggested in the section on Design.[3] Macbeth and his supporters, in the instance cited, were costumed in a range of reds, in contrast to the greens assigned to Macduff and his followers. If the costumes did not help to distinguish between groups in such cases, the spectator could easily lose track of both, with a marked loss in dramatic value and effect.

Various design values are then achieved by the addition of trim to these basic color masses. Ruffles, lace, embroidery, appliqué, braid, piping, buttons, tassels, fringe, feathers, and plumes may be added to a basic silhouette to strengthen the overall impression. Braid or embroidery may be added to break up a fairly large color area; ruffles may be added to differentiate between color areas;

[2] In this connection, refer to the Directing section, particularly Chapter 23.

[3] See Chapter 21.

and feathers and plumes and tassels may be added to make the costume decoratively complete, in keeping with the character conception on which it is based. In some cases, as will be apparent later on, the trim can be used to emphasize line or pattern. Just as a single instance, a costume with predominantly vertical lines can suggest dignity and stateliness, while one with mostly horizontal lines can give quite the opposite impression. Diagonal lines, not as common in costuming as vertical and horizontal ones, can, for example, be made to suggest movement and excitement. Line can also be used to emphasize or to conceal an excessively slim or an excessively heavy figure.

The final touch of completeness is often dependent on suitable jewelry or accessories — such as brooches, bracelets, or pendants, and purses, fans, or canes. Constructing, borrowing, or shopping for these is a real challenge to ingenuity as well as to thrift. The counters and shelves of the local "five-and-ten" usually offer manifold suggestions for objects of this sort that will project from the stage. Especially helpful also are current catalogues from Sears and Montgomery Ward; and if the costumer has for his own use — or can share with the property master — a file of mail-order catalogues of past years, he is fortunate indeed. Period jewelry and accessories, as well as hats, shoes, and the like, can often be adapted from inexpensive contemporary items.

The effect of colored light upon stage costumes, and its potentialities for determining their impact and their effectiveness, is worthy of special consideration. Since the matter is a complicated one, the special problems raised by the use of colored fabrics under stage lights should be held in view from the very beginning of the planning stage; and the costumer and the lighting technician should work closely together throughout the rehearsal period.

It should be recognized that the color in any fabric will not show up in its intended hue unless its corresponding color (i.e., in the light) is falling directly on it from some source on stage. Since, for example, yellow light contains no blue, yellow light thrown on a blue fabric will thus result on stage in a sort of muddy gray; to reflect blue light and therefore to appear blue, the fabric must be bathed also in light rays containing blue, such as those of white light itself. On the other hand, since magenta light does contain both blue and red, a blue costume on stage will appear blue under a magenta light.[4]

Adjustments in both light and costume are thus required from time to time if fabric colors are to remain true to their intended effect. A blue-green dress, to take an obvious example, should — despite the difficulties often raised with a garment of this particular color — remain essentially blue-green on all areas of the stage and in a sunlit exterior as well as in a lamplighted interior. If the lighting technician cannot introduce into his various installations enough light containing the blue-green demanded by the fabric, it may be necessary to modify the costume or to substitute a different one altogether.

Changes in color under artificial light can sometimes be attributed also to impurities in dye or in the color media used with the lights; and, for this reason as well as others that have been suggested, it is well to test actual color samples under various types of stage lights before counting upon their use for costumes. Again, the very texture of a fabric may have some influence on its effect as to color. If a white light is cast on a piece of scarlet velvet, the color can be seen with especial vividness, because of the sheen of the material. On the contrary, a piece of cotton flannel, dyed to exactly the same scarlet, would not show up with the same vividness or brightness of hue. As we shall see in a later discussion of substitute materials, the point here is not primarily one of

[4] Additional examples of these and related phenomena are to be found in Chapter 20.

cost. If they are properly handled and properly lighted, burlap and monk's cloth can be just as effective on the stage as expensive woolens, and rayon and cheesecloth can appear to suggest expensive silks and chiffons. Indeed, some expensive materials themselves appear on the stage to be quite cheap and sleazy.

The art of costuming and that of make-up are also closely allied. To the costumer, make-up should be considered as another color area in the entire costume silhouette; and to the make-up artist the portions of the costume surrounding the face are of similar importance, in planning as well as in execution. A fairly ruddy complexion, for example, may appear as sallow or wan if strong and vivid but cool colors are placed next to it. On the same basis, extremely warm colors in fabric may make pale complexions seem ruddy, and — in cases where color values are repeated in the make-up and in a military jacket and headdress, for example — the costume may tend to swallow up the actor's features altogether. The color, the texture, and the outline of materials placed next to the player's face should actually focus attention on the face, lest the spectator miss meaningful changes of expression. Generally, however, color masses in costume and in make-up should not contrast too vividly, unless specific dramatic reasons seem indicated in the playscript.

Extreme color contrasts within the costume itself, for that matter, should be avoided whenever possible, except as a matter of accent. In this connection, it is well to remember the phenomenon of *proximity* in color, the psychological effect of "advancing" and "receding." Very light and very warm colors seem to move forward in space, while dark and cool ones seem to move backward; and the effect is exaggerated when the color masses are in vivid contrast. A sizable yellow spot against a blue background appears to push the blue backward in space, to note but

a single example. In general, the costumer must avoid giving the impression that large color masses are advancing or receding too sharply, away from the rest of the costume. The upper part of a given silhouette must not seem to move in a different plane, as it were, from the lower portion — a potential problem in most shirt-and-tights and most blouse-and-skirt combinations.

However, a color combination which is required to have great contrast can be successfully built into a costume if the area of demarcation is broken by a "transitional" color which blends with both extremes, or if the contrast is controlled by line or texture. If the break between the contrasting masses is defined by a proportionately pleasing line (e.g., a belt, a sash, a ruffle, an insert), the apparent distance between the extremes of color can be controlled. Another means of control is to plan the contrasting colors for differently textured materials; silk or nylon blouses worn with wool skirts is a good instance, as is the usual shirt-and-trouser combination worn by men.

Apart from such general considerations, however, important though they may be, the physical characteristics of the individual actor for whom a specific costume has been designed bring additional complications into the picture. What is taken to be an expressive costume — planned in accord with the best design principles and with standard conditions of production — may have been prepared in the sewing room, but unless it is functionally adapted to the human body of a particular actor, the costumer's labor may well have been wasted. This factor alone accounts for many of the changes which a good costume usually undergoes between the time of the sketch board and the time of the completed garment.

To mention but one of the factors involved, a costume designed for its stately effect on a tallish figure necessarily loses much of that effect if it must be worn by an actor of fairly heavy build and of less than average height. No amount of changing measurements will restore quite the original effect; redesigning, based on the physical nature and proportions of the individual actor, is usually indicated. A striking example of this point, as it is manifested off the stage, is found in the wide disparity between the sketch of a dress as worn by a tall and slender model on the pages of a style magazine and the same dress as worn at home in a drawing room in size 40. On the other hand, few actors have the physical build traditionally associated with, let us say, Falstaff; and the proportions of an actor's body must be altered to fit a costume design as frequently as a costume design must be altered to suit an actor's body. One cannot imagine accepting a slender Falstaff, just as one cannot imagine accepting a Santa Claus who is immoderately tall and thin.

In practical terms, the problem is one of proportionate emphasis and concealment; and the untrained or inexperienced costume planner will have to depend in large measure on his own and his director's good taste and common sense. In making a heavy figure look slimmer, the value of dark-color masses rather than light or white ones is well known. Essentially vertical lines as opposed to horizontal ones gain a similar effect; and a loosely draped garment rather than a tight-fitting one will do much to fill out the silhouette of a slender form. Even for straight characterizations, it is well to remember that de-emphasis and concealment of extreme slenderness or extreme heaviness will present a much more acceptable and pleasing silhouette to an audience than the original figure might offer. In character roles, either serious or comic, the slender or heavy characteristics of an individual figure can and should be emphasized.

The fact that an actor's body is dynamic rather than static is a factor that will bear further examination here. In extreme instances, indeed, the costumer can make or break the characterizations of certain of the players, if he neglects to consider the functional mobility required by the costumes. The use of the wrong type of material (too heavy or too coarse a fabric, for example) in a gown for Rosalind in *As You Like It* would hamper the agile movement which is so integral a part of this characterization; no rationalization based on historical accuracy could explain away the difficulty if an unsuitable fabric were to be used. In many instances, a properly draped costume of suitable texture is intended to support or enhance the movement of the actor who is wearing it, and to "follow through" interestingly or gracefully as he pauses or comes to a stop. In others, the costume must move when the actor moves and must stop moving when the actor stops. In such cases, a skirt or coat or cape that continues to "move" after the character has come to a halt can be distracting to a spectator and disconcerting to the actor — though incidental comedic effects can be consciously achieved by this means. On the positive side, the costumer who gives capes to young actors in Elizabethan productions is providing for them a character-building tool as well as an opportunity to develop pleasing and dramatically effective possibilities for movement. Not at all incidentally, a cape can conceal a number of undesirable physical inadequacies.

Coupled with emphasis and concealment as a mode of "corrective" costuming is the element of exaggeration. Planned exaggeration can compensate for deficiences in bodily proportion, can focus on one portion of the body so that attention is directed away from another portion, and can in some cases completely change the actual body silhouette. For example, proper exaggeration in sleeve construction can seem to shorten an otherwise long arm; emphasis on the upper portion of a costume can call attention away from thin and spindly legs; and a re-designed silhouette that is built into a costume can restore an almost military bearing to an otherwise relaxed posture. Exaggerations in line, mass, color, or outline can turn ordinary clothing into costumes that are theatrically meaningful, effective, and exciting. Only too frequently a costume which is an exact duplicate of a period piece turns out to be dramatically dull and pointless. With suitable exaggeration in the right places, and with imaginative and expressive touches throughout, Titania's costume can make her seem truly the Queen of the Fairies, Hedda's make her truly a woman who could "do such things."

Thus the costumer can and must deal with the human body in a number of ways: short men may be made to appear taller, and tall men shorter; thin men may be made to appear fatter, and fat ones thinner; poor physical proportions generally may be brought closer to the necessary ideal, and the ideal may itself then be distorted for dramatic value and effect.

Finally — and sometimes in apparent opposition to otherwise standard factors in design — the costume planner must be able to deal in a practical way with the very practical concepts of economy and flexibility. Very few producing groups, professional or nonprofessional, have unlimited budgets; and substitutions for the more expensive materials must usually be made. In many cases, such substitutions turn out to be an asset rather than a liability, since costumes for the stage are functionally and interpretatively more useful when they are made of substitute materials and simulated fabrics than when they are built from the "real thing." Frequently they are lighter or sturdier or easier to store safely; and it is often easier to make them fully expressive under stage conditions. Finally, in the case of items which would otherwise have to be borrowed or rented, substitute materials bring fewer potential complications with owners or insurance agents.

Generally satisfactory substitutes such as lined sateen or percale for velvets, muslin for linens, cotton for furs, and outing flannel for wools are in common use. Experimentation with the new synthetics can provide imaginative as well as inexpensive substitutes for standard materials used in making hats, shoes, helmets, or plate armor, to name but a few examples. Uses can also be found for materials strange to the dressmaker and tailor — such as oilcloth, plastic materials, cardboard and other paper products, newspaper mats, and even plastic window screening. The cost of building costumes with simulated or substitute materials usually compares favorably with the cost of renting similar items for only one week of rehearsal and performance, although the rented garments must of course be returned to the costume house while the others can be added to the permanent wardrobe and can thus be used in later productions. No opportunity should be missed, of course, for strengthening this permanent wardrobe by means of gifts from local sources; purchases at sales or auctions; and miscellaneous acquisitions such as uniforms, caps and gowns, and other specialized costume pieces.

Whatever the substitute material may be, it must answer to the demands of flexibility as well as those of economy. Quick changes are imperative in maintaining the pace and fluidity of many plays; and, since playwrights occasionally allow only a minimal time for change of costume, some garments must be designed to allow the actor to get in and out of them with especial ease and promptness, and without undue damage to the fabric. In the last act of *As You Like It,* Rosalind must change from masculine to feminine attire within a very few minutes indeed, and the construction of both costumes must be flexible enough to allow the actress to get out of one and into the other with real dispatch. Other and similar examples have been cited in earlier sections. Plays written in a flash-back technique, and those containing dream sequences, raise special difficulties in this connection. In these, as in all others demanding fast changes, the structural design as well as the mode of fastening must be attuned to speed.

One other aspect of flexibility should be mentioned: given an appropriate basic silhouette, a costumer may plan to use the same costume, apart from the trim, for several historical periods. With minor additions and deletions in detail, a classic Greek or Roman drapery may become a gown of the Empire period, an Elizabethan dress may become a Victorian one, or a Restoration coat may become an American Colonial jacket. In each case the basic silhouette is the essential factor in suggesting the intended period, through line, color, texture, and drape; and characteristic and decorative detail may then be added both readily and inexpensively.

As earlier pages have suggested, a designer for the open stage depends even more heavily on costumes than a designer for a conventional playhouse. In the first place, the possibilities for elaboration of background scenery are limited, and the designer needs to capitalize on costumes and properties for scenic effect. In the second place, properties and costumes are open to direct and close examination, so that they not only can but must be shown off to special advantage. Open-stage costumes are therefore often more elaborately patterned, ornamented, and treated than their analogous types on the proscenium stage; they frequently are shown in purer whites and more vivid hues than proscenium lighting tends to allow. As a related factor, there are generally fewer gelatines (and lighter tints in those gelatines that are retained) in spotlights hung for open staging.

In summary, then, the clothes an actor wears on the stage can physically embody the dramatic value of a particular character and situation as well as that of a particular time and place. In its planning and its construction, a theatrical costume — as distinguished from clothing planned for daily use — is conditioned by special factors such as the nature of the theatre plant, the circumstances of a given production, and the dramatic needs of an individual actor. At its best, a stage costume should catch the attention of an audience yet not divert its attention away from the production as a whole; should, whether the actor is at rest or in motion, contribute to an interesting and attractive stage picture; should, by predetermined means, complement the mood and point of the play and its setting; and should help in positive ways to enrich the developing dramatic action.

C | A Note on Make-Up

On the eve of the first dress rehearsal of many nonprofessional performances, two pronounced schools of opinion concerning theatrical make-up suddenly manifest themselves backstage. That these opinions emerge only at this late stage in play production bears mute testimony to the fact that make-up is seldom considered until too late to consider it well. First there are those who regard make-up with mingled awe and frustration — those to whom make-up represents a form of necromancy, a mystic rite whose performance is confined to a select priesthood. Then there are those to whom make-up is a mere matter of "following the directions on the can," or copying a make-up previously observed. To such persons it is a kind of inherent reflex action, the sort of thing which any child can master in an hour. Neither attitude is likely to assist the performance.[1]

The art of stage make-up, like all other arts, rests upon a body of simple basic principles; and these, once understood and carefully applied, will eventually lead the neophyte through all the subtleties and mysteries which once appeared impenetrable. Without these principles, without a proper understanding of the purposes of make-up, of the conditions under which it is to be applied, and of the means available, no amount of uncritical copying from books or careful imitation of others will produce a convincing make-up.

Like most principles, however, these tend to overlap, to contradict one another, to demand interpretation. Every make-up situation requires a reshuffling of the order and importance which the various principles are to have, since every situation is different. We must always bear in mind that we are dealing with three *variables,* not — as some would suggest — with three constants. The first of these variables is the face of the individual actor, whose contours both in repose and in movement are unique compared with those of any other actor. The second variable is the conditions of performance (e.g., the nature of the lighting and the physical relationship of the audience to the playing area), which are never identical. And the third is the character whom the actor is to portray; here again, the pattern never precisely repeats itself. Each of these variables makes its own particular demands, serving to define and to limit the possible results. Their shifting relationships make necessary a different set of values for the principles in every case. Characterization, for example, may call for the use of "sallow old man" base color, yet Polonius on stage may look like "ruddy young man" if lighting has not been considered. It is necessary to keep the whole situation in mind at all times, and to adapt the principles of make-up as common sense directs.

The basic reasons for the use of make-up are four in number: (1) to emphasize, (2) to conceal, (3) to convince, and (4) to characterize. Since make-up is primarily a corrective, we might rephrase the first of these purposes to say that the initial function of make-up is to counteract the effects of distance.

A production in a small room before an

---

[1] This unit on make-up should be considered in connection with that on costuming, which immediately precedes it. Additional references to make-up appear also in the costuming units in the section on **Design.**

audience of fifteen or twenty people requires no special make-up. The spectators can easily see the minutest lift of an eyebrow or the subtlest curling of a lip. When spectators are fifty to a hundred feet away from the playing area, however, the very outlines of the actor's lips begin to fade and his eyes become expressionless black sockets. From a distance of two hundred feet, which is by no means the maximum range in many theatres, the only clearly identifiable feature is usually the dark line of the actor's eyebrows. As the range increases, then, the make-up must become progressively stronger to define and emphasize the significant and expressive features of an actor's face. The limiting factor is always the distance of the nearest spectator from the stage, however. Make-up must not be so strong as to make grotesque caricatures of the actors when seen from the first few rows. It is possible to scale the make-up to the size of the audience, and to be prepared to make compromises if the distance between the minimum range and the maximum range is very great.

The second function of make-up, closely allied to the first, is to conceal, or — to express this purpose in the negative — to counteract the irrelevant, the unimportant, or the undesirable. A play in production, considering the limited time which it has before the audience, must eliminate all that does not contribute to its intended overall effect or that definitely hinders this attainment. Make-up is equally bound by this rule of economy. If, for example, the eyebrows of the actor chosen for a straight role were excessively bushy, they would have to be reduced by make-up to prevent distraction of audience attention from more significant details of his face — details that have meaning for the play.

In this case we are merely eliminating the unimportant to make room for the important. In other cases, details such as this might be positively detrimental to the part, hamper-ing the actor in his efforts to produce a given effect. All the more reason, then, for concealment. By the careful use of highlight and shadow, the calculated placing of rouge, and the penciling of eyes and eyebrows, as well as by other means, thin faces may be made wide or wide faces thin, lips may be made fuller or thinner, eyes may be placed further apart or nearer together, chins may be made to disappear, or any number of minor miracles may be accomplished. On the stage, nature must be improved upon in the interest of focusing attention swiftly, accurately, and emphatically.

The third reason for using make-up is to counteract the unnaturalness of stage lighting. Two factors account primarily for the inability of stage lighting to convey a convincing impression of reality: (1) the direction of stage light, and (2) its color.

The angle or angles at which light strikes the face determine the pattern of light and shadow, the relationship of facial planes to one another, and the effect of depth and solidity which are the characteristics of the human face as we usually think of it. The sun, whose light is largely responsible for the impressions we retain of what the human face appears to be, is primarily unidirectional and comes from above. The shadows it casts are sharp and well-defined — a dark shadow under the brows, a softer one under the nose, occasionally shadows under the cheekbones, a light shadow which defines the lips, and a very dark shadow under the chin. These shadows alone, as every artist knows, even without the subtler tones which reveal the less pronounced contours of the face, are sufficient to convey the swift impression of a human face. Without them the face appears to be a distorted caricature of itself.

Perhaps you have seen a picture of a fortuneteller staring into a crystal ball with light streaming up from the crystal to light his face. He appears demoniac, unworldly; and only with the greatest difficulty can one mentally compensate for the reversed shadows to arrive at some idea of what the man actually looks like. This simple reversal of the customary light source — erasing the usual shades and shadows, the signs by which we habitually read the character behind the face, and substituting alien contours — is an extreme example of what happens on every stage lighted predominantly by footlights. Footlights shine upon the face at an angle from below, lighting the neck as brightly as the chin, and merging the two by eliminating any line of demarcation between them. The chin disappears. Light then catches the bottom of the nose, lighting it as brightly as the first half-inch of the bridge. This makes the under part of the nose seem longer and the bridge seem shorter, creating the effect of an exaggerated pug nose. The area between eye and eyebrow is brightly lit and appears swollen, while the eyebrow seems to be raised in an expression of fear or surprise.

Footlights have, of course, fallen into disfavor, in part for this very reason, and are now used only sparingly. But other types of lighting are equally troublesome. Quantities of borders, floods, and spotlights either create a shifting kaleidoscope of several sets of shadows whenever the actor changes position, or else the light, striking the face from all directions, brings every area of the face into the same plane, flattening and broadening the features. The result in any case is that there are no natural shadows on the face at all. Make-up must restore character to the features by artificially replacing the "normal" shadows which give it depth and solidity and form. This can only be done if the lighting sources are carefully considered. The strength of shadows must be just sufficient to carry through any lighting which might tend to eradicate it.

Counteracting the color of stage lighting is another of the functions of make-up devoted to restoring in the actor's face the accustomed forms through which our habits and our training have led us to interpret character and emotion. The light of the sun, the "norm" to which we all subconsciously refer our impressions of color, is white. Artificial light, however tinted, only approximates this norm; hence all artificial light is colored. That this unavoidable use of colored light upon the stage creates a major problem for the make-up artist is easily demonstrated. If a piece of red paper and a piece of white paper are placed side by side and lighted with a pure red light, it becomes impossible to tell them apart, for the red paper reflects just as much of the red light as does the white paper. If, on the other hand, these two pieces of paper are lighted with a blue-green light, the white piece appears blue-green while the red piece becomes black or dark gray. Here the white piece of paper has reflected all of the blue-green light, while the red pigment has absorbed the blue-green rays without reflecting them — the absence of reflection being called black. Color on the stage, then, subjected to a wide range of colored light, varies markedly from its hue in sunlight and seldom appears twice the same.

The generalization which we may draw from the above illustration, and one which is extremely important in all the visual aspects of theatre, is that a colored light, falling upon colored pigment, reduces the relative brightness of all colors like it and darkens the complementary colors. If, for example, a pink light is used upon the stage, much stronger rouge must be used than would be necessary in a white light. If the scene is a moonlit garden in blue or green, rouge must be used with caution, for under these conditions the rouged areas become dark hollows in the cheeks. Current theatre practice is to light the stage predominantly with "straw," "surprise pink," and other colors usually merging in a pinkish-yellow hue. The consequent washing out of red and yellow on the stage thus necessitates the use of a base color which appears excessively bright in the dressing room. Since every situation differs, however, the only generalization which may be drawn is that the make-up artist must consider carefully the light under which his work is to appear.

The fourth reason for the use of make-up, to characterize, may be expressed as the need to counteract unavoidable deficiencies in casting. No play is ever perfectly cast from the point of view of the visual impression created by the actors. Invariably, young women are called upon to play ancient crones, balding men are called upon to play youthful lovers, Englishmen are called upon to play Greek gods, and Russians are called upon to play Danes. Make-up can bridge both space and time. It is this contribution of make-up which is sometimes believed to be its chief function. It is undeniably an important function, but by no means the only one; so obvious is this point that little more need be said concerning it here.

Turning now from the reasons for the use of make-up, let us examine in greater detail some of the means of make-up and the uses to which they may be put. The most important make-up materials, and those which are adequate for all but the most elaborate facial changes, are: (1) base colors, (2) rouges, (3) colors used for highlights and lowlights, and (4) powders.

The base colors need not detain us long, for their uses are apparent — to suggest race, environment, and general physical condition. Not only can the general color differences between the white, black, red, and yellow races be indicated by the base color, but subtle gradations within races can be suggested. For example, the differences between the pale Scot and the swarthy Italian, or between the swarthy Italian and the swarthy Spaniard may be defined if the artist's eye be keen enough. Within these

general race and nationality classifications are environmental groups, such as those who live predominantly outdoors, those who live in cities, those who inhabit the seacoasts, and an infinite variety of other groups whose facial colors and textures are in part the results of immediate environment. Age and general physical condition are also reflected in the skin color. The pink, smooth robustness of early youth gradually changes to the sallow, parchment-like skin of advanced years; the clear brightness of good health gives way to the pale, dulled skin quality of illness. Subtle blending of the base colors can do much to further the desired illusion.

Rouge, aside from its use as a lowlight (a point which will be considered in a moment), can also serve to indicate age and general physical condition. The coloring which we daily observe in people's cheeks, and by which, in part, we subconsciously judge these qualities, requires some explanation. The skin of the human cheek is relatively thin, and tiny masses of veins are visible through it. In the case of young people, the face is full and round, and the area of coloration is high on the face. The brightest part is on the cheekbones, while the edges fade back toward the hairline, up to the eyebrows, forward under the eye, and downward to the level of the bottom of the nose. As one reaches thirty-five, forty, or forty-five, the face thins; the layer of fat underlying the skin disappears and the skin stretches a bit. Even in plump faces the fatty tissues tend to collect lower in the face. The forehead and temples in particular thin out, allowing the section of the skin where the blood shows through to sag noticeably. Therefore, the older one is to be, particularly if the face is really thin, the lower the rouge must be placed. Conversely, youth requires rouge high on the face. The brightness of the rouge is generally proportionate to the general health, although it must be remembered that some diseases result in abnormally bright cheeks. A florid, uneven complexion is popularly associated with dissolute living habits.

The fact that highlights (or light colors) and lowlights (or dark colors) may be used to restore the three-dimensional quality of the face under stage lighting is explained in part by an elementary principle of art: that light colors appear to advance toward and dark colors appear to recede from the eye of the observer, and that light-colored objects tend to seem larger than similar objects in darker colors. The principle is easily verified by a glance at the pattern of a rug, or of wallpaper, or of some woven fabric. Dark tones appear to "retire," while light tones appear to be raised, to be larger, to dominate the design. Make-up, then, requires dark tones on those portions of the face which must appear to recede, while light tones must highlight those portions intended to stand out.

This principle holds even in the case of rouge, a dark tone which depresses the cheeks, even though we commonly associate rouge with a prominent, full portion of the face. Substitute a light color on one side of the face for rouge next time you make up for the stage and observe how the lighter cheek seems swollen in comparison with the other. The fact is useful if we desire to change the contours of the face for any reason. A round, full face with ample cheeks may be thinned by covering a larger area with rouge, running the edge down toward the jawbone and bringing it in toward the nose and up toward the eye where there is apt to be a fold of flesh. A thin face, on the other hand, may be broadened by keeping the rouge high and well to the sides of the face. Here it may be blended back as far as the neck, but care must be taken to keep it away from the area underneath the eye and away from the mouth. Rouge may also be used over the eye. If the eyelids are heavy, dust the area lightly, using either a down powder puff or the traditional rabbit's foot. If a slight double chin is to be removed, dust rouge under the chin. To reduce a chin that is too strong, dust the jawbone with rouge. Any area too prominent may be subdued by a similiar application, if the artist's hand is light.

Other lowlight colors, usually called "liners," are gray, brown, and maroon. Black, a logical choice, unfortunately never appears as a skin color or as a shadow, even in Negro make-up, and its use, except for the finest of wrinkles scarcely visible to the audience, invariably destroys the illusion of reality. Black does appear, of course, as a hair color, and brunettes may use it for the eyebrows and for the area around the eyes, but it should not appear as a skin color. The various shades of gray, brown, and maroon (the latter being variously called "crimson lake," "lake," or "crimson-maroon" and usually lying halfway between dark red and brown) produced by the several manufacturing companies have, as regards hue, little significant difference for our purposes. Though some people prefer one color to another, or one shade within that color to another, for most purposes the colors are interchangeable; maroon or lake may possibly be put to a wider range of uses than the others. In general, perhaps, the defining line of a wrinkle or crack should be of the lining color closest to the dominant color of the base, with a grayed out or neutral tone used for blending and for smoother hollows without defining lines.

The facial highlight colors useful on the stage — those which make part of the face protrude — are white, cream, yellow, and pink. Pure white, like pure black, never actually appears as a skin color, but white used as a highlight blends easily with the base color over which it is applied and is therefore useful. Since the make-up is also usually "set" with powder which is pinkish or cream colored, and which subdues the white, another margin of safety is added. Yellow, as well as white, is a good all-purpose highlight color. Light pink is most appropriate to ruddy make-up, and cream or white most appropriate to pale colors. In general, highlight colors should be matched with the base colors more carefully than is the case with lowlight colors, for highlights are more frequently susceptible to subtle light changes.

Highlights and shadows should be placed on the face wherever time itself will eventually place them. This is by no means a completely accurate guide, of course, for characterization, racial type, and physical condition will necessitate adjustments; but fundamentally the principle is sound. Always start with the face as it is, for highlights and shadows. For example, if the lines in the actor's forehead are straight while the part calls for arched ones, draw the middle half of the lines where they naturally fall on the face and turn the ends down. The natural lines cannot be entirely ignored, for a disturbing crisscross of lines on the actor's forehead would result whenever he lifted his brows. Similarly, the line between nose and mouth should begin where the natural crease begins and then proceed wherever characterization directs. If the desired effect should happen to be the prominent, slanting cheekbone of the Oriental, start the highlight on the bone below the eye and then blend it up and back toward the top of the ear.

The natural highlights of the face fall, of course, wherever skin over a bone or over fat catches reflected light. The shadows fall wherever there are depressions or wherever features cast shadows. Consider now just one side of the face, and begin with the temple. A ridge of bone starts above the outside third of the eyebrow, and extends upward and backward from there to the hair. This is drawn as a strip of light color about one-quarter of an inch wide running right along the ridge. In a similar arc just below this light-colored band, a dark-colored strip

is placed; this is then softened until the lowlight it forms is almost a circle, dark at the top and fading out at the bottom. The highlight line is then blended into the base color above it and into the lowlight below it so that no sharp lines of demarcation remain. With age, this temple highlight becomes more pronounced, as do the horizontal wrinkles across the brow and the small vertical wrinkles between the brows. The gradual disappearance of the fatty tissue under the skin also makes the brows more prominent, and these too may be highlighted to suggest maturity, though less emphatically with women. The fat around the eyeballs also tends to disappear with age; therefore the entire socket, above and below the eye, should be lowlighted, preferably with a color approaching gray, since gray also suggests the collection of veinous blood which takes place here. The lowlight in this area should be kept strictly away from the bone surrounding the eye.

Age also frequently brings a pouch below the eye. This can be painted by applying a strong highlight to the pouch area and placing a dark line below it. The nose can be highlighted by a line down the bridge, about a quarter of an inch wide, breaking to follow the outline of the nostrils. The nose can be thinned by drawing dark lines down each side of the bridge and softening them away into the face under the eye. Being cartilage rather than bone, the nose continues to grow throughout life as other parts of the face do not; hence the longer the nose the older the face. The cheekbones may be highlighted by placing a spot of color on the knob of the cheekbone and softening it back toward the hair. Just as with the temples, a line of dark color is placed just below this and blended into the cheek, its final width being from one-half an inch to an inch.

There are various other highlight and lowlight areas in the face and neck, some depending upon individual anatomy. These we need not discuss, since they are easily discovered by reference to pictures or by study of the face in sunlight, and since they follow the general principles sketched above for other parts of the face.

Emphasis on different features will give a wide variety of expressions to the face. Bones become more prominent with age, but certain of these bony areas may appear in a young face to give it a unique, characteristic expression. Highlights and lowlights may also be used to render characteristic racial expression — expressions which are frequently the result of different skull formations. For example, the upper lip of the Oriental is usually thicker than that of the Caucasian. We can suggest it by painting the upper lip a lighter color, bringing it into prominence.

Lines or wrinkles in the face, the final touch in modeling the contours of the face, do a great deal less in suggesting age than do the highlights and lowlights. We so frequently see old faces that are smooth and unlined and young faces that are furrowed with anxiety that the association of age with wrinkles is not as strong as with other changes. The best advice that can be given concerning the placing of wrinkles is to observe in people and in photographs their actual forms and positions. A wrinkle, it will be noticed, is not a single line. It is a sharp, dark line, fading at the sides, always accompanied by at least one highlight line parallel to it, catching the light. One other point concerning wrinkles deserves mention here. Not all wrinkles need be seen by every spectator. Wrinkles will frequently have fulfilled their function if they succeed merely in breaking up the smoothiness or flatness of the cheek or forehead when age demands it.

Like costumes, discussed in the preceding unit, make-up on the open stage is subject to close scrutiny from an audience which in effect surrounds the actor and whose individual members are never very far away. The modeling (and, for example, the wigging) must be handled with extreme care, as though for a close-up photograph. Random lines or wrinkles poorly highlighted and crudely blended are sure to be distracting, at the very least. On the other hand, since open-stage lighting is so often basically white, or at most only very lightly tinted, the interrelationships between color in light and color in make-up pigment are usually simplified.

Thus far we have considered make-up primarily as a corrective for visual factors which stand in the way of the actor's art — as something physical and external, merely added to a characterization already complete within the actor. There is, however, another contribution of which make-up is capable, a positive contribution rather than a negative one. It is the ability of a well-conceived make-up to assist the actor in realizing the inner qualities of his role. Experienced actors frequently note how the beginner, by experimenting with a variety of outward facial characteristics, can arrive at a richer, deeper characterization. By visualizing himself in the role, through the mechanical means of make-up, he can further his spiritual penetration. Here is make-up at its highest level — a level that can only be reached by first understanding the general principles upon which technique rests, and then, with the aid of constant observation, careful experimentation, and assiduous practice, applying these principles with intelligence.

D | Selected Bibliographies

The following lists are not intended to be exhaustive. Under each heading one group of volumes — believed to be most helpful and most significant to users of the present volume — is listed first, with a second group of additional entries immediately following. In a few cases an especially useful reference is included under more than one heading. The entries are grouped as follows: Acting; Aesthetics in the Theatre; Drama and Dramatic Theory; Play Production and Direction; Scene Design and Theatre Architecture; Theatre History; Other Aspects of Production; Anthologies of Plays; Indexes, Bibliographies, and Works of Reference.

ACTING

Albright, H. D. *Working Up a Part*. 2nd ed. Boston: Houghton Mifflin Co., 1959.

Anderson, Virgil A. *Training the Speaking Voice*. 2nd ed. New York: Oxford University Press, 1961.

Archer, William. *Masks or Faces?* London: Longmans, Green & Co., 1888.

Boleslavsky, Richard. *Acting: The First Six Lessons*. New York: Theatre Arts, Inc., 1933.

Calvert, Louis. *Problems of the Actor*. New York: Henry Holt & Co., 1918.

Chekhov, Michael. *To the Actor*. New York: Harper & Bros., 1953.

Cole, Toby. *Acting: A Handbook of the Stanislavski Method*. New York: Lear Publishers, 1947.

——— and Helen Kritch Chinoy. *Actors on Acting*. New York: Crown Publishers, 1949.

Dolman, John, Jr. *The Art of Acting*. New York: Harper & Bros., 1949.

Duerr, Edwin. *The Length and Depth of Acting*. New York: Holt, Rinehart & Winston, Inc., 1962.

Eustis, Morton. *Players at Work*. New York: Theatre Arts, Inc., 1937.

Gillette, William. *The Illusion of the First Time in Acting*. New York: Dramatic Museum of Columbia University, 1915.

Kjerbühl-Petersen, Lorenz. *Psychology of Acting*. Trans. Sarah T. Barrows. Boston: The Expression Co., 1935.

Komisarjevsky, Theodore. *Myself and the Theatre*. London: William Heinemann, 1929.

Lewes, George Henry. *On Actors and the Art of Acting*. New York: Brentano's, n.d.

McGaw, Charles J. *Acting Is Believing*. 2nd ed. New York: Rinehart & Co., 1966.

Nichols, Wallace B. *The Speaking of Poetry*. Boston: The Expression Co., 1937.

Selden, Samuel. *First Steps in Acting*. Rev. ed. New York: F. S. Crofts & Co., 1964.

Stanislavski, Constantin. *An Actor Prepares*. Trans. Elizabeth Reynolds Hapgood. New York: Theatre Arts, Inc., 1936.

———. *Building a Character*. Trans. Elizabeth Reynolds Hapgood. New York: Theatre Arts, Inc., 1949.

Strickland, F. Cowles. *The Technique of Acting*. New York: McGraw-Hill Book Co., Inc., 1956.

Young, Stark. *Theatre Practice*. New York: Charles Scribner's Sons, 1926.

Also:

Brown, John Mason. *Letters from Greenroom Ghosts*. New York: The Viking Press, 1934.

Coquelin, Constant. *The Art of the Actor.* Trans. Elsie Fogerty. London: George Allen & Unwin, Ltd., 1932.

Gassner, John. *Producing the Play.* Rev. ed. New York: The Dryden Press, 1953.

Herman, Lewis Helmar and Marguerite Shalett Herman. *Manual of American Dialects: For Radio, Stage, Screen and Television.* Chicago: Ziff-Davis Publishing Co., 1947.

——. *Manual of Foreign Dialects.* Chicago: Ziff-Davis Publishing Co., 1943.

Jefferson, Joseph. *The Autobiography of Joseph Jefferson.* New York: The Century Co., 1897.

Lee, Charlotte I. *Oral Interpretation.* 3rd ed. Boston: Houghton Mifflin Co., 1965.

Lewis, Robert. *Method — or Madness?* New York: Samuel French, 1958.

Lutz, Florence. *The Technique of Pantomime.* Berkeley, Calif.: Sather Gate Book Shop, 1927.

Parrish, Wayland Maxfield. *Reading Aloud.* Rev. ed. New York: Ronald Press, 1953.

Redgrave, Michael. *The Actor's Ways and Means.* New York: Theatre Arts Books, 1953.

Rosenstein, Sophie, Larrae A. Haydon, and Wilbur Sparrow. *Modern Acting: A Manual.* New York: Samuel French, 1936.

Sprague, A. C. *Shakespearean Players and Performances.* Cambridge, Mass.: Harvard University Press, 1953.

Stanislavsky, Constantin. *My Life in Art.* Trans. J. J. Robbins. Boston: Little, Brown & Co., 1924.

Symonds, Arthur. *Eleanora Duse.* New York: Duffield & Co., 1927.

Talma. *Reflections on the Actor's Art.* New York: Dramatic Museum of Columbia University, 1915.

Verneuil, Louis. *Sarah Bernhardt.* Trans. Ernest Boyd. New York: Harper & Bros., 1942.

Woollcott, Alexander, ed. *Mrs. Fiske, Her Views on Actors, Acting, and the Problems of Production.* New York: The Century Co., 1917.

AESTHETICS IN THE THEATRE

Appia, Adolphe. *Music and the Art of the Theatre.* Trans. Robert W. Corrigan and Mary Douglas Dirks. Coral Gables, Fla.: University of Miami Press, 1962.

——. *The Work of Living Art.* Trans. H. D. Albright. Coral Gables, Fla.: University of Miami Press, 1960.

Bakshy, Alexander. *The Theatre Unbound.* London: Cecil Palmer, 1923.

Beardsley, Monroe. *Aesthetics: Problems in the Philosophy of Criticism.* New York: Harcourt, Brace & World, Inc., 1958.

Centeno, Augusto, ed. *The Intent of the Artist.* Princeton, N. J.: Princeton University Press, 1941.

Craig, Edward Gordon. *On the Art of the Theatre.* London: William Heinemann, 1912.

——. *The Theatre — Advancing.* Boston: Little, Brown & Co., 1919.

——. *Towards a New Theatre.* New York: E. P. Dutton & Co., 1913.

Dewey, John. *Art As Experience.* New York: Minton, Balch & Co., 1934.

Dolman, John, Jr. *The Art of Play Production.* Rev. ed. New York: Harper & Bros., 1946.

Gassner, John. *Form and Idea in Modern Theatre.* New York: Holt, Rinehart & Winston, Inc., 1956.

Gorelik, Mordecai. *New Theatres for Old.* New York: Samuel French, 1940.

Greene, Theodore M. *The Arts and the Art of Criticism.* Princeton, N. J.: Princeton University Press, 1952.

Harrison, Jane Ellen. *Ancient Art and Ritual.* New York: The Home Library of Modern Knowledge, 1913.

Jones, Robert Edmond. *The Dramatic Imagination.* New York: Duell, Sloan & Pearce, 1941.

Langer, Suzanne K. *Feeling and Form.* New York: Charles Scribner's Sons, 1956.

Langfeld, Herbert Sidney. *The Aesthetic Attitude.* New York: Harcourt, Brace & Co., 1920.

Pepper, Stephen C. *Principles of Art Appreciation.* New York: Harcourt, Brace & Co., 1949.

———. *The Basis of Criticism in the Arts.* Cambridge, Mass.: Harvard University Press, 1949.

Rader, Melvin M., ed. *A Modern Book of Esthetics.* New York: Henry Holt & Co., 1935.

Selden, Samuel. *Man in His Theatre.* Chapel Hill, N. C.: University of North Carolina Press, 1957.

———. *The Stage in Action.* New York: F. S. Crofts & Co., 1941.

Simonson, Lee. *The Stage Is Set.* New York: Harcourt, Brace & Co., 1932.

Weitz, Morris, ed. *Problems in Aesthetics.* New York: The Macmillan Co., 1959.

Also:

Bel Geddes, Norman. *Horizons.* Boston: Little, Brown & Co., 1932.

Bosanquet, Bernard. *A History of Aesthetics.* London: S. Sonnenschein, 1904.

Gardner, Helen. *Art Through the Ages.* New York: Harcourt, Brace & Co., 1936.

———. *Understanding the Arts.* New York: Harcourt, Brace & Co., 1932.

Lee, Vernon. *The Beautiful.* Cambridge, Eng.: Cambridge University Press, 1913.

Moderwell, Hiram Kelly. *The Theatre of Today.* New York: Dodd, Mead & Co., 1928.

Ogden, Robert Morris. *The Psychology of Art.* New York: Charles Scribner's Sons, 1938.

Prall, D. W. *Aesthetic Judgment.* New York:

The Thomas Y. Crowell Co., 1929.

Stanislavsky, Constantin. *Stanislavsky on the Art of the Stage.* Trans. David Magarshack. London: Faber & Faber, Ltd., 1950.

Vernon, Frank. *The Twentieth-Century Theatre.* Boston: Houghton Mifflin Co., 1924.

Whitworth, Geoffrey. *Theatre in Action.* London: The Studio, Ltd., 1938.

DRAMA AND DRAMATIC THEORY

Anderson, Maxwell. *The Essence of Tragedy and Other Footnotes and Papers.* Washington, D. C.: Anderson House, 1939.

Artaud, Antonin. *The Theatre and Its Double.* Trans. Mary Caroline Richards. New York: Grove Press, 1958.

Bentley, Eric. *In Search of Theater.* New York: Alfred A. Knopf, Inc., 1953.

———. *The Playwright as Thinker.* New York: Reynal & Hitchcock, 1946.

———. *What Is Theatre?* Boston: Beacon Press, Inc., 1956.

Bergson, Henri. *Laughter.* Trans. Cloudesley Brereton and Fred Rothwell. New York: The Macmillan Co., 1911.

Bogard, Travis and William I. Oliver, eds. *Modern Drama: Essays in Criticism.* New York: Oxford University Press, Inc., 1965.

Brustein, Robert. *The Theatre of Revolt.* Boston: Little, Brown & Co., 1964.

Butcher, S. H. *Aristotle's Theory of Poetry and Fine Art: With a Critical Text and Translation of the Poetics.* Rev. ed. New York: Dover Publications, 1955.

Clark, Barrett H., ed. *European Theories of the Drama.* Rev. ed. New York: Crown Publishers, 1947.

DeMetz, Peter, ed. *Brecht — A Collection of Critical Essays.* Englewood Cliffs, N. J.: Prentice-Hall, Inc., 1962.

Downer, Alan S., ed. *American Drama and Its Critics.* Chicago: University of Chicago Press, 1965.

------. *The British Drama. A Handbook and Brief Chronicle.* New York: Appleton-Century-Crofts, Inc., 1950.

------. *Fifty Years of American Drama: 1900–1950.* Chicago: Henry Regnery Co., 1951.

Eliot, T. S. *Poetry and Drama.* Cambridge, Mass.: Harvard University Press, 1951.

Esslin, Martin. *The Theatre of the Absurd.* Garden City, N. Y.: Doubleday & Co., Inc., 1961.

Fergusson, Francis. *The Idea of a Theatre.* Princeton, N. J.: Princeton University Press, 1949.

Gassner, John. *Masters of the Drama.* 3rd ed. New York: Dover Publications, 1953.

------ and Ralph S. Allen. *Theatre and Drama in the Making.* Boston: Houghton Mifflin Co., 1964.

Harsh, Philip Whaley. *A Handbook of Classical Drama.* Stanford, Calif.: Stanford University Press, 1944.

Heffner, Hubert. *The Nature of Drama.* Boston: Houghton Mifflin Co., 1959.

Kronenberger, Louis. *The Thread of Laughter.* New York: Alfred A. Knopf, Inc., 1952.

Krutch, Joseph Wood. *The American Drama Since 1918.* New York: Random House, 1939.

------. *The Modern Temper.* New York: Harcourt, Brace & Co., 1929.

------. *"Modernism" in the Drama.* Ithaca, N. Y.: Cornell University Press, 1953.

Lawson, John Howard. *Theory and Technique of Playwriting and Screenwriting.* New York: G. P. Putnam's Sons, 1949.

McCollom, William G. *Tragedy.* New York: The Macmillan Co., 1957.

Myers, Henry A. *Tragedy: A View of Life.* Ithaca, N. Y.: Cornell University Press, 1956.

Nicoll, Allardyce. *The Theory of Drama.* London: George G. Harrap & Co., Ltd., 1931.

------. *World Drama.* New York: Harcourt, Brace & Co., 1950.

Olson, Elder. *Tragedy and the Theory of Drama.* Detroit, Mich.: Wayne State University Press, 1961.

Peacock, Ronald. *The Art of the Drama.* New York: The Macmillan Co., 1957.

Prior, Moody E. *The Language of Tragedy.* New York: Columbia University Press, 1947.

Stuart, Donald Clive. *The Development of Dramatic Art.* New York: D. Appleton & Co., 1928.

Thompson, Alan Reynolds. *The Anatomy of Drama.* Berkeley, Calif.: University of California Press, 1946.

------. *The Dry Mock.* Berkeley, Calif.: University of California Press, 1948.

Also:

Bentley, Gerald Eades, ed. *The Development of English Drama.* New York: Appleton-Century-Crofts, Inc., 1950.

Bradley, A. C. *Shakespearean Tragedy.* Rev. ed. London: The Macmillan Co., 1949.

Brooks, Cleanth and Robert B. Heilman. *Understanding Drama.* New York: Holt, Rinehart & Winston, Inc., 1948.

Brunetière, Ferdinand. *The Law of the Drama.* New York: Dramatic Museum of Columbia University, 1914.

Chandler, Frank W. *Modern Continental Playwrights.* New York: Harper & Bros., 1931.

Clark, Barrett H. and George Freedley. *A History of Modern Drama.* New York: D. Appleton-Century Co., 1947.

Dickinson, Thomas H., ed. *The Theatre in a Changing Europe.* New York: Henry Holt & Co., 1937.

Egri, Lajos. *The Art of Dramatic Writing.* New York: Simon & Schuster, 1946.

Feibleman, James. *In Praise of Comedy.* New York: The Macmillan Co., 1939.

Flexner, Eleanor. *American Playwrights:*

1918–1938. New York: Simon & Schuster, 1938.

Freud, Sigmund. *Wit and Its Relation to the Unconscious.* Intro. by A. A. Brill. New York: Moffat, Yard & Co., 1916

Gallaway, Marian. *Constructing a Play.* New York: Prentice-Hall, Inc., 1950.

Granville-Barker, Harley. *Prefaces to Shakespeare.* 2 vols. Princeton, N. J.: Princeton University Press, 1946.

Harrison, G. B. *Shakespeare's Fellows.* London: John Lane, 1923.

James, Henry. *The Scenic Art: Notes on Acting and the Drama.* Ed. Alan Wade. New Brunswick, N. J.: Rutgers University Press, 1948.

Macgowan, Kenneth. *A Primer of Playwriting.* New York: Random House, 1951.

Maeterlinck, Maurice. "The Tragical in Daily Life," in *The Treasure of the Humble.* Trans. Alfred Sutro. New York: Dodd, Mead & Co., 1903.

Mahr, August C. *The Origin of the Greek Tragic Form.* New York: Prentice-Hall, Inc., 1938.

Millett, Fred B. *Reading Drama.* New York: Harper & Bros., 1950.

Raphaelson, Samson. *The Human Nature of Playwriting.* New York: The Macmillan Co., 1949.

Selden, Samuel. *An Introduction to Playwriting.* New York: F. S. Crofts & Co., 1946.

Sper, Felix. *From Native Roots: A Panorama of our Regional Drama.* Caldwell, Idaho: The Caxton Printers, 1948.

Young, Stark. *The Flower in Drama.* New York: Charles Scribner's Sons, 1923.

PLAY PRODUCTION AND DIRECTION

Boyle, Walden P. *Central and Flexible Staging.* Berkeley, Calif.: University of California Press, 1956.

Brockett, Oscar G. *The Theatre — An Introduction.* New York: Holt, Rinehart & Winston, Inc., 1964.

Chekhov, Michael. *To the Director and Playwright.* Ed. Charles Leonard. New York: Harper & Row, Publishers, Inc., 1963.

Cole, Toby and Helen Kritch Chinoy, eds. *Directing the Play.* Indianapolis, Ind.: The Bobbs-Merrill Co., Inc., 1953.

Dean, Alexander and Lawrence Carra. *Fundamentals of Play Directing.* Rev. ed. New York: Holt, Rinehart & Winston, Inc., 1965.

Hatlen, Theodore. *Orientation to the Theatre.* New York: Appleton-Century-Crofts, Inc., 1962.

Heffner, Hubert C., Samuel Selden, and Hunton D. Sellman. *Modern Theatre Practice.* Rev. ed. New York: F. S. Crofts & Co., 1959.

Jones, Margo. *Theatre-in-the-Round.* New York: Farrar & Rinehart, Inc., 1951.

Kernodle, George R. *Invitation to the Theatre.* New York: Harcourt, Brace & World, Inc., 1967.

Shaw, George Bernard. *The Art of Rehearsal.* New York: Samuel French, 1928.

Smith, Milton. *Play Production for Little Theatres, Schools and Colleges.* New York: Appleton-Century-Crofts, Inc., 1948.

Sprague, Arthur Colby. *Shakespeare and the Actors: The Stage Business in his Plays.* Cambridge, Mass.: Harvard University Press, 1944.

———. *Shakespearean Players and Performances.* Cambridge, Mass.: Harvard University Press, 1953.

Watkins, Ronald. *On Producing Shakespeare.* New York: W. W. Norton & Co., 1951.

Whiting, Frank. *An Introduction to the Theatre.* Rev. ed. New York: Harper & Bros., 1961.

Wright, Edward A. *A Primer for Playgoers.*

Englewood Cliffs, N. J.: Prentice-Hall, Inc., 1958.

Also:

Brown, Gilmor and Alice Garwood. *General Principles of Play Direction.* New York: Samuel French, 1937.

Crafton, Allen and Jessica Royer. *The Complete Acted Play.* New York: F. S. Crofts & Co., 1943.

Gilder, Rosamond. *John Gielgud's* Hamlet: *A Record of Performance with "Notes on Costume, Scenery, and Stage Business"* by John Gielgud. New York: Oxford University Press, 1937.

Houghton, Norris. *Moscow Rehearsals.* New York: Harcourt, Brace & Co., 1936.

Hughes, Glenn. *The Penthouse Theatre.* New York: Samuel French, 1942.

Knight, G. Wilson. *Principles of Shakespearean Production.* 3rd ed. Evanston, Ill.: Northwestern University Press, 1964.

Nelms, Henning. *Play Production.* Rev. ed. New York: Barnes & Noble, 1958.

Poel, William. *Shakespeare in the Theatre.* London: Sedgwick & Jackson, 1913.

Stanislavsky, Constantin. *Stanislavsky Produces Othello.* Trans. Helen Nowak. London: Geoffrey Bles, Ltd., 1948.

————. *The Sea Gull Produced by Stanislavsky.* Ed. S. D. Balukhaty. Trans. David Magarshack. New York: Theatre Arts, Inc., 1952.

See under ACTING: Gassner, *Producing the Play;* Young, *Theatre Practice;* AESTHETICS: Dolman, *The Art of Play Production;* Selden, *The Stage in Action.*

SCENE DESIGN AND THEATRE ARCHITECTURE

Adams, John Cranford. *The Globe Playhouse: Its Design and Equipment.* Cambridge, Mass.: Harvard University Press, 1942.

Altman, George, Ralph Freud, Kenneth Macgowan, and William Melnitz. *Theater Pictorial.* Los Angeles: University of California Press, 1953.

Appia, Adolphe. *Adolphe Appia: A Portfolio of Reproductions.* Zurich: Orell-Füssli, 1929.

Burris-Meyer, Elizabeth. *Color and Design in the Decorative Arts.* New York: Prentice-Hall, Inc., 1935.

Burris-Meyer, Harold and Edward C. Cole. *Theatres and Auditoriums.* Rev. ed. New York: Reinhold, 1964.

Cheney, Sheldon. *Stage Decoration.* New York: John Day Co., 1928.

Friederich, Willard J. and John H. Fraser. *Scenery Design for the Amateur Theatre.* New York: The Macmillan Co., 1950.

Fuerst, Walter R. and Samuel J. Hume. *Twentieth Century Stage Decoration.* 2 vols. London: Alfred A. Knopf, Inc., 1928.

Jones, Robert Edmond. *Drawings for the Theatre.* New York: Theatre Arts, Inc., 1925.

Kepes, Gyorgy. *Language of Vision.* Chicago: P. Theobold, 1944.

Komisarjevsky, Theodore and Lee Simonson. *Settings and Costumes of the Modern Stage.* London and New York: The Studio, Ltd., 1933.

Leeper, Janet. *Edward Gordon Craig: Designs for the Theatre.* London: Penguin Books, 1948.

Nicoll, Allardyce. *The Development of the Theatre.* Rev. ed. New York: Harcourt, Brace & Co., 1947.

Oenslager, Donald. *Scenery Then and Now.* New York: W. W. Norton & Co., 1936.

Philippi, Herbert. *Stagecraft and Scene Design.* Boston: Houghton Mifflin Co., 1953.

Pope, Arthur. *An Introduction to the Language of Drawing and Painting.* 2 vols. Cambridge, Mass.: Harvard University Press, 1929–1931.

Sheringham, George and James Laver. *Design in the Theatre.* London: The Studio, Ltd., 1927.

Southern, Richard. *The Open Stage.* New York: Theatre Arts Books, 1959.

———. *The Seven Ages of Theatre.* New York: Hill & Wang, Inc., 1961.

Watkins, Charles Law. *The Language of Design.* Washington, D. C.: Phillips Memorial Gallery, 1946.

Architectural Forum. Theatre Reference Number. September, 1932.

Also:

Beaumont, Cyril W. *Design for the Ballet* (Special Winter Number of the Studio). London: The Studio, Ltd., 1937.

Bel Geddes, Norman. *A Project for a Theatrical Presentation of the "Divine Comedy" of Dante Alighieri.* New York: Theatre Arts, Inc., 1924.

Craig, Edward Gordon. *Scene.* Oxford: Oxford University Press, 1923.

Fry, Roger. *Vision and Design.* London: Chatto & Windus, 1920.

Graves, Maitland E. *The Art of Color and Design.* New York: McGraw-Hill Book Co., 1941.

Isaacs, Edith J. R. *Architecture for the New Theatre.* New York: Theatre Arts, Inc., 1935.

Jacobson, Egbert. *The Science of Color.* Chicago: American Photo-Engravers Association, 1937.

Luckiesh, Matthew. *Light and Shade and Their Application.* New York: D. Van Nostrand Co., 1916.

———. *The Language of Color.* New York: Dodd, Mead & Co., 1918.

Macgowan, Kenneth. *The Theatre of Tomorrow.* New York: Boni & Liveright, 1921.

——— and Robert Edmond Jones. *Continental Stagecraft.* New York: Harcourt, Brace & Co., 1922.

Munsell, A. H. *Color Notation.* Baltimore, Md.: Munsell, 1946.

National Theatre Conference. *Are You Going to Build a Theatre? A Bibliography.* Cleveland, Ohio: National Theatre Conference, 1946.

Scholz, Janos, ed. *Baroque and Romantic Stage Design.* New York: Herbert Bittner & Co., 1950.

Selden, Samuel and Hunton D. Sellman. *Stage Scenery and Lighting.* 3rd ed. New York: Appleton-Century-Crofts, Inc., 1959.

Silverman, Maxwell and Ned Bowman. *Contemporary Theatre Architecture: An Illustrated Survey.* New York: New York Public Library, 1965.

Simonson, Lee. *The Art of Scenic Design.* New York: Harper & Bros., 1950.

Teague, Walter Dorwin. *Design This Day.* New York: Harcourt, Brace & Co., 1940.

Zinkeisen, Doris. *Designing for the Stage.* London: The Studio, Ltd., 1938.

See under AESTHETICS: Craig, *Towards a New Theatre;* Simonson, *The Stage Is Set.*

THEATRE HISTORY

Antoine, André. *Memories of the Théâtre-Libre.* Trans. Marvin Carlson. Coral Gables, Fla.: University of Miami Press, 1964.

Beckerman, Bernard. *Shakespeare at the Globe, 1599–1609.* New York: The Macmillan Co., 1962.

Bieber, Margarete. *History of the Greek and Roman Theatre.* Rev. ed. Princeton, N. J.: Princeton University Press, 1961.

Brown, John Mason. *The Modern Theatre in Revolt.* New York: W. W. Norton & Co., 1929.

Campbell, Lily B. *Scenes and Machines on the English Stage.* Cambridge, Eng.: Cambridge University Press, 1923.

Cheney, Sheldon. *The Theatre.* Rev. ed. New York: Longmans, Green & Co., 1959.

Clurman, Harold. *The Fervent Years: The Story of the Group Theatre and the Thirties.* New York: Alfred A. Knopf, Inc., 1945.

Dubech, Lucien. *Histoire générale illustrée*

du théâtre. Paris: Librairie de France, 1931–1934.

Flanagan, Hallie. *Arena.* New York: Duell, Sloan & Pearce, 1940.

Flickinger, Roy. *The Greek Theatre and Its Drama.* Chicago: University of Chicago Press, 1918.

Gilder, Rosamond, Hermine Rich Isaacs, Robert M. MacGregor, and Edward Reed, eds. *Theatre Arts Anthology.* New York: Theatre Arts, Inc., 1951.

Grube, Max. *The Story of the Meininger.* Trans. Ann Marie Koller. Coral Gables, Fla.: University of Miami Press, 1963.

Guthrie, Tyrone. *A Life in the Theatre.* New York: McGraw-Hill Co., Inc., 1959.

Hewitt, Barnard, ed. *The Renaissance Stage: Documents of Serlio, Sabbattini, and Furttenbach.* Coral Gables, Fla.: University of Miami Press, 1958.

———. *Theatre USA.* New York: McGraw-Hill Book Co., Inc., 1959.

Houghton, Norris. *Advance from Broadway.* New York: Harcourt, Brace & Co., 1941.

———. *Return Engagement: A Postscript to "Moscow Rehearsals."* New York: Holt, Rinehart & Winston, Inc., 1962.

Kernodle, George. *From Art to Theatre.* Chicago: University of Chicago Press, 1944.

Langner, Lawrence. *The Magic Curtain.* New York: E. P. Dutton & Co., 1951.

MacCarthy, Desmond. *The Court Theatre 1904–1907.* Ed. Stanley Weintraub. Coral Gables, Fla.: University of Miami Press, 1966.

Macgowan, Kenneth. *Footlights Across America.* New York: Harcourt, Brace & Co., 1929.

——— and William Melnitz. *The Living Stage.* Englewood Cliffs, N. J.: Prentice-Hall, Inc., 1955.

Mantzius, Karl. *A History of Theatrical Art.* 6 vols. Trans. Louise von Cossel. London: Duckworth & Co., 1903 ff.

Nagler, Alois M. *Sources of Theatrical His-*

tory. New York: Theatre Annual, 1952.

Nemirovich-Danchenko, Vladimir Ivanovich. *My Life in the Russian Theatre.* Trans. John Cournos. Boston: Little, Brown & Co., 1936.

Odell, G. C. D. *Annals of the New York Stage.* 15 vols. New York: Columbia University Press, 1927–1949.

Sayler, Oliver M. *Inside the Moscow Art Theatre.* New York: Brentano's, 1925.

———. *Max Reinhardt and His Theatre.* New York: Brentano's, 1924.

Smith, Cecil. *Musical Comedy in America.* Rev. ed. New York: Theatre Arts, Inc., 1961.

Also:

Agate, James. *These Were Actors.* London: Hutchinson, 1943.

Anderson, John and Réné Fülöp-Miller. *The American Theatre and the Motion Picture in America.* New York: Dial Press, 1938.

Atkinson, Brooks. *Broadway Scrapbook.* New York: Theatre Arts, Inc., 1947.

Blum, Daniel. *A Pictorial History of the American Theatre, 1900–1950.* New York: Greenberg, 1950.

———. *Theatre World, 1946–1947.* Annually thereafter. New York: The Stuyvesant Press, 1947 ff.

Carter, Huntley. *The New Spirit in the Russian Theatre, 1917–1928.* London: Brentano's, 1929.

Cheney, Sheldon. *The Art Theatre.* New York: Alfred A. Knopf, Inc., 1925.

Craig, Edward Gordon. *Henry Irving.* New York: Longmans, Green & Co., 1930.

Deutsch, Helen and Stella Hanau. *The Provincetown.* New York: Farrar & Rinehart, Inc., 1931.

Freedley, George and John A. Reeves. *A History of the Theatre.* Rev. ed. New York: Crown Publishers, 1956.

Gielgud, John. *Early Stages.* New York: The Macmillan Co., 1939.

Havemeyer, Loomis. *The Drama of Savage*

Peoples. New Haven: Yale University Press, 1916.

Komisarjevsky, Theodore. *The Theatre and a Changing Civilization.* London: John Lane, 1935.

LeGallienne, Eva. *With a Quiet Heart.* New York: Viking Press, 1953.

McPharlin, Paul. *The Puppet Theatre in America. A History: 1924–1948.* New York: Harper & Bros., 1949.

Moses, Montrose J. and John Mason Brown. *The American Theatre as Seen by Its Critics, 1752–1934.* New York: W. W. Norton & Co., 1934.

Nicoll, Allardyce. *Masks, Mimes and Miracles.* Rev. ed. New York: Harcourt, Brace & World, Inc., 1964.

Reed, Joseph Verner. *The Curtain Falls.* New York: Harcourt, Brace & Co., 1935.

Reynolds, George Fullmer. *The Staging of Elizabethan Plays At the Red Bull Theatre, 1605–1625.* New York: The Modern Language Association of America, 1940.

Roberts, Vera M. *On Stage — A History of the Theatre.* New York: Harper & Row, Publishers, Inc., 1962.

Rothe, Hans. *Max Reinhardt: 25 Jahre Deutsches Theater.* Munich: R. Piper & Co., 1930.

Simonson, Lee. *Part of a Lifetime.* New York: Duell, Sloan & Pearce, 1943.

Stevens, Thomas Wood. *From Athens to Broadway.* New York: D. Appleton & Co., 1932.

Vardac, A. Nicholas. *Stage to Screen.* Cambridge, Mass.: Harvard University Press, 1949.

Williams, Harcourt. *Old Vic Saga.* New York: MacDonald & Co., 1950.

Winter, William. *Vagrant Memories.* New York: George H. Doran, 1915.

Woollcott, Alexander. *Enchanted Aisles.* New York: G. P. Putnam's Sons, 1924.

Young, Stark. *Immortal Shadows.* New York: Charles Scribner's Sons, 1948.

Zucker, A. E. *The Chinese Theatre.* Boston: Little, Brown & Co., 1925.

See under ACTING: Stanislavsky, *My Life in Art;* AESTHETICS: Gorelik, *New Theatres for Old;* Simonson, *The Stage is Set;* SCENE DESIGN: Altman, et al., *Theater Pictorial;* Macgowan and Jones, *Continental Stagecraft.*

OTHER ASPECTS OF PRODUCTION

Adix, Vern. *Theatre Scenecraft.* Anchorage, Ky.: Children's Theatre Press, 1956.

Barber, Philip. "The New Scene Technician's Handbook," in *Producing the Play.* Ed. John Gassner. Rev. ed. New York: The Dryden Press, 1953.

Barton, Lucy. *Historic Costume for the Stage.* Rev. ed. Boston: Walter H. Baker & Co., 1961.

Bellman, Willard F. *Lighting the Stage: Art and Practice.* San Francisco: Chandler Publishing Co., 1967.

Bowman, Wayne. *Modern Theatre Lighting.* New York: Harper & Row, Publishers, Inc., 1957.

Burris-Meyer, Harold and Edward C. Cole. *Scenery for the Theatre.* Rev. ed. Boston: Little, Brown & Co., 1948.

Corson, Richard. *Stage Make-up.* Rev. ed. New York: Appleton-Century-Crofts, 1949.

Davenport, Millia. *The Book of Costume.* New York: Crown Publishers, 1948.

Fuchs, Theodore. *Home Built Lighting Equipment for the Small Stage.* New York: Samuel French, 1940.

———. *Stage Lighting.* Boston: Little, Brown & Co., 1929.

Gillette, Arnold S. *Stage Scenery: Its Construction and Rigging.* Rev. ed. New York: Harper and Row, Publishers, Inc., 1960.

Halstead, William Perdue. *Stage Management for the Amateur Theatre.* New York: F. S. Crofts & Co., 1937.

Komisarjevsky, Theodore. *The Costume of the Theatre.* New York: Henry Holt & Co., 1932.

Laver, James, ed. *Costume of the Western World,* Vol. 3. London: George G. Harrap & Co., Ltd., 1951.

———. *Drama: Its Costume and Décor.* London: The Studio Publications, 1951.

Martin, John. *Book of the Dance.* New York: Tudor Publishing Co., 1963.

McCandless, Stanley R. *A Method of Lighting the Stage.* Rev. ed. New York: Theatre Arts, Inc., 1958.

Motley. *Designing and Making Stage Costumes.* New York: Watson-Guptill Publications, 1965.

Napier, Frank. *Noises Off, A Handbook of Sound Effects.* London: Frederick Muller, Ltd., 1936.

Plummer, Gail. *The Business of Show Business.* New York: Harper & Row, Publishers, Inc., 1961.

Prisk, Berneice. *Stage Costume Handbook.* New York: Harper & Row, Publishers, Inc., 1966.

Rubin, Joel E. and Leland Watson. *Theatrical Lighting Practice.* New York: Theatre Arts Books, 1954.

Smith, Milton. *The Equipment of the School Theatre.* New York: Bureau of Publications, Teachers College, Columbia University, 1930.

Strenkovsky, Serge. *The Art of Makeup.* Ed. Elizabeth S. Taber. New York: E. P. Dutton & Co., 1937.

Walkup, Fairfax Proudfit. *Dressing the Part.* Rev. ed. New York: Appleton-Century-Crofts, Inc., 1950.

Also:

Baird, John F. *Makeup.* Rev. ed. New York: Samuel French, 1941.

Bernheim, Alfred L. *The Business of the Theatre.* New York: Actors Equity Association, 1932.

Dabney, Edith and C. M. Wise. *A Book of Dramatic Costume.* New York: F. S. Crofts & Co., 1930.

Edson, Doris and Lucy Barton. *Period Patterns.* Boston: Walter H. Baker & Co., 1942.

Eustis, Morton. *B'Way Inc!* New York: Dodd, Mead & Co., 1934.

Evans, Mary. *Costume Throughout the Ages.* 3rd ed. Philadelphia: J. B. Lippincott Co., 1950.

Factor, Max. *Makeup Pamphlets.* Hollywood: Factor Co., n.d.

Goe, Ida Mae. *Historic Costume Plates.* Evanston, Ill.: Northwestern University Theatre, 1948.

Hake, Herbert V. *Here's How!* Evanston, Ill.: Row, Peterson & Co., 1942.

Jones, Leslie Allen. *Painting Scenery.* Boston: Walter H. Baker & Co., 1935.

Lane, Yoti. *Stage Make-up.* Minneapolis: Northwestern Press, 1950.

Liszt, Rudolph G. *The Last Word in Makeup.* New York: Contemporary Play Publications, 1938.

Mitchell, Roy. *The School Theatre.* New York: Brentano's, 1925.

Nelms, Henning. *Play Production.* Rev. ed. New York: Barnes and Noble, 1958.

Sheringham, George and R. Boyd Morrison. *Robes of Thespis.* London: Benn, 1928.

Smith, André. *The Scenewright.* New York: The Macmillan Co., 1926.

Strauss, Ivard. *Paint, Powder, and Makeup.* New Haven, Conn.: Sweet & Son, 1936.

Urban, Josef. *Theatres.* New York: Theatre Arts, Inc., 1930.

Ward, Winifred. *Theatre for Children.* Rev. ed. Anchorage, Ky.: The Children's Theatre Press, 1950.

Whorf, Richard B. and Roger Wheeler. *Runnin' the Show.* Boston: Walter H. Baker & Co., 1930.

See under SCENE DESIGN: Selden and Sellman, *Stage Scenery and Lighting.*

ANTHOLOGIES OF PLAYS

Bentley, Eric. *The Classic Theatre.* 4 vols.

Garden City, N. Y.: Doubleday & Co., Inc., 1958–1961.

[Vol. I: Six Italian Plays; II: Five German Plays; III: Six Spanish Plays; IV: Six French Plays.]

————. *From the Modern Repertoire.* 3 series. Bloomington, Ind.: Indiana University Press, 1949–1956.

[Series One: from Becque and Büchner to Brecht and T. S. Eliot; Two: from Grabbe and Ostrovsky to Giraudoux and Mac-Neice; Three: from Büchner and de Musset to Cocteau and Anouilh.]

————. *The Play, A Critical Anthology.* New York: Prentice-Hall, Inc., 1951.

[*Cyrano; The Importance of Being Earnest; The Miser; Twelfth Night; Othello; Antigone* (Sophocles); *Ghosts; The Ghost Sonata; Death of a Salesman.*]

Block, Haskell and Robert Shedd, eds. *Masters of Modern Drama.* New York: Random House, 1962.

[Plays by authors as early as Strindberg, Kaiser, Schnitzler, and Pirandello; and as recent as Brecht, Becket, Ionesco, and Frisch.]

Caputi, Anthony, ed. *Modern Drama.* New York: W. W. Norton & Co., 1966.

[*The Wild Duck* and *The Three Sisters* to *Desire Under the Elms* and the *Henry IV* of Pirandello.]

Cerf, Bennett A. and Van H. Cartmell, eds. *Sixteen Famous American Plays.* New York: Random House, 1941.

[Important American plays, principally of the twenties and thirties, and ranging from *They Knew What They Wanted* and *The Petrified Forest* to *The Little Foxes* and *Our Town.*]

————. *Sixteen Famous British Plays.* New York: Random House, 1942.

[British plays, comparable to those included in the previous entry, though covering a somewhat wider range in time; from *The Importance of Being Earnest* and *What Every Woman Knows* to *Victoria Regina* and *The Corn Is Green.*]

————. *Sixteen Famous European Plays.* New York: Random House, 1943.

[From *Cyrano* and *The Dybbuk* to *Tovarich* and *Amphitryon 38;* includes *The Weavers, The Wild Duck,* and *Six Characters in Search of an Author.*]

————. *Thirty Famous One-Act Plays.* New York: Random House, 1943.

[Includes Ibsen and Wilde, Lady Gregory and Lord Dunsany, Strindberg and Galsworthy, O'Neill and Millay.]

————. *Twenty-Four Favorite One-Act Plays.* Garden City, N. Y.: Doubleday & Co., Inc., 1958.

[Mostly plays published between 1943 and 1958, though Chekhov, Wilde, and Yeats are included, as is Susan Glaspell.]

Clark, William Smith, ed. *Chief Patterns of World Drama.* Boston: Houghton Mifflin Co., 1946.

[From Aeschylus to Anderson, without Shakespeare or Shaw; includes *The Second Shepherd's Play* and *Nice Wanton, The Miser* and *The Man of Mode, Hedda Gabler* and *The Sea Gull, The Life of the Insects* and *The Hairy Ape.*]

Dickinson, Thomas H., ed. *Chief Contemporary Dramatists.* Boston: Houghton Mifflin Co. Series One, 1915; Series Two, 1921; Series Three, 1930.

[Series One: includes Jones and Pinero, Bjornson and Strindberg, Fitch and Moody, Galsworthy and Synge. Series Two: includes Benevente and Schnitzler, Drinkwater and Dunsany, Maugham and Guitry. Series Three: includes the Quinteros and von Hofmannsthal, Kaiser and O'Neill, O'Casey and Pirandello, Molnar and Howard.]

Duckworth, George E., ed. *The Complete Roman Drama.* 2 vols. New York: Random House, 1942.

[Includes twenty plays by Plautus, ten by Seneca, and six by Terence.]

Durham, Willard H. and John Wendell

Dodds, eds. *British and American Plays, 1830–1945.* New York: Oxford University Press, 1947.
[From Bulwer-Lytton and Robertson, through Ibsen, Pinero, and Jones, to O'Neill and Odets; includes *The Playboy of the Western World, The Admirable Crichton, Strife, The Circle, Juno and the Paycock,* and *The Adding Machine.*]

Gassner, John, ed. *A Treasury of the Theatre — From Aeschylus to Ostrovsky.* 3rd ed. New York: Holt, Rinehart & Winston, Inc., 1967.
[Part I: Periods of World Drama. Twelve plays before Shakespeare, who is represented by *Hamlet;* thirteen plays from Jonson to Turgenev. Included are *Oedipus, The Frogs, Everyman, The Way of the World,* and *Faust.* Part II: The Range of Western Drama. Fifteen plays arranged according to form, including *The Bacchae, Life is a Dream, The Cid, The Beggar's Opera, Hernani,* and *The Thunderstorm.*]

————. *A Treasury of the Theatre — From Ibsen to Ionesco.* 4th ed. New York: Holt, Rinehart & Winston, Inc., 1967.
[Thirty-nine important modern plays, including two by Ibsen and two by O'Neill; others represented are Lorca, Brecht, Sartre, Shaw, O'Casey, Odets, and Williams.]

————. *Best Plays of the Modern American Theatre.* 5 vols. plus supplementary vol. New York: Crown Publishers, 1952–1961.
[Series One: plays published before 1939; Two: before 1947; Three: 1945–1951; Four: 1951–1957; Five: 1957–1963; Supplementary volume: 1918–1958.]

————. *Twenty-Five Best Plays of the Modern American Theatre.* Early Series. New York: Crown Publishers, 1949.
[Plays published and produced earlier than those in the preceding entries, ranging from *Paris Bound, Saturday's Children,* and *Broadway,* to *Front Page, They Knew What They Wanted,* and *Street Scene.*]

Grene, David and Richmond Lattimore, eds. *The Complete Greek Tragedies.* 4 vols. Chicago: University of Chicago Press, 1960.
[Volume One: Aeschylus; Two: Sophocles; Three and Four: Euripides.]

Hopper, Vincent F. and Gerald B. Lahey, eds. *Medieval Mysteries, Moralities, and Interludes.* Great Neck, N. Y.: Barron's Educational Series, Inc., 1962.
[Two mysteries, including *Second Shepherd's Play;* two moralities, including *Everyman;* two interludes, including *Johan the Husband.*]

MacMillan, Dougald and Howard Mumford Jones, eds. *Plays of the Restoration and Eighteenth Century.* 2nd ed. New York: Henry Holt & Co., 1938.
[The principal English dramatists of the eighteenth and of the late seventeenth century are here represented by twenty-five of their most important plays.]

Mantle, Burns, ed. *The Best Plays of 1899–1909, 1909–1919, 1919–1920,* annually thereafter. Boston: Small Maynard & Co., to 1919; New York: Dodd, Mead & Co., 1920 ff.
[Summaries and extracts from the ten most successful plays of each year, with critical reviews, statistical data, and the like.

Moody, Richard. *Dramas from the American Theatre.* Cleveland, Ohio: World Publishing Co., 1966.
[Begins with the eighteenth-century "dialogues" and reaches to *The New York Idea* and *The City;* includes *The Contrast, Metamora, Uncle Tom's Cabin,* and *The Drunkard.*]

Noyes, George R. *Masterpieces of the Russian Drama.* 2 vols. New York: Dover Publications, Inc., 1960.
[Griboyedov, Ostrovsky, Pisemsky, and Mayakovsky, as well as Gogol, Turgenev, Tolstoy, and Chekhov.]

Oates, W. J. and Eugene O'Neill, Jr. *The Complete Greek Drama.* 2 vols. New

York: Random House, 1938.
[Seven plays by Aeschylus, eleven by Aris-
tophanes, nineteen by Euripides, three by
Menander, and seven by Sophocles.]
Quinn, Arthur H. *Representative American
Plays*. 7th ed. New York: Appleton-Cen-
tury-Crofts, Inc., 1953.
[Twenty-nine plays, ranging from *The
Contrast* to *Winterset,* and including *Fran-
cesca da Rimini, Secret Service, Shenan-
doah, Hazel Kirke, Rip Van Winkle, Fash-
ion,* and *Sun-up;* O'Neill, Barry, Crothers,
Sheldon, Thomas, Fitch, and Dunlap are
also represented.]
Rowell, George. *Nineteenth Century Plays*.
New York: Oxford University Press, 1953.
[*Caste* and *Ticket-of-Leave Man,* plus five
earlier and three later selections.]
Tucker, S. Marion, ed. *Twenty-Five Modern
Plays*. Rev. Alan S. Downer. New York:
Harper & Bros., 1953.
[Ibsen, Strindberg, and Chekhov to
O'Neill, Riggs, Auden, and Isherwood;
such plays as *Cyrano, Riders to the Sea,
Liliom, Gas, The Plough and the Stars,
The Infernal Machine,* and *Command De-
cision* are included.]
Warnock, Robert. *Representative Modern
Plays: American*. Chicago: Scott, Fores-
man & Co., 1952.
[*Beggar on Horseback, The Late Christo-
pher Bean, Biography, Mourning Becomes
Electra, Valley Forge, Waiting for Lefty,
The Glass Menagerie, Death of a Sales-
man.*]
————. *Representative Modern Plays: Brit-
ish*. Rev. ed. Chicago: Scott, Foresman &
Co., 1964.
[*The Admirable Crichton, The Doctor's
Dilemma, Loyalties, Riders to the Sea,
Juno and the Paycock, The Constant Wife,
Blithe Spirit, Murder in the Cathedral, A
Phoenix too Frequent.*]
One-Act Plays for Stage and Study. 9 vols.
New York: Samuel French, 1924–1938.

INDEXES, BIBLIOGRAPHIES, AND WORKS OF REFERENCE

Baker, Blanch M. *Dramatic Bibliography*.
New York: The H. W. Wilson Co., 1933.
————. *Theatre and Allied Arts*. New York:
The H. W. Wilson Co., 1952.
Bates, Mary E. and Anne C. Sutherland, eds.
Dramatic Index. Published annually. Bos-
ton: F. W. Faxon & Co., 1915 ff.
Firkins, Ina Ten Eyck. *Index to Plays, 1800–
1926*. New York: The H. W. Wilson Co.,
1927.
————. *Index to Plays,* Supplement. New
York: The H. W. Wilson Co., 1935.
Gamble, William Burt. *Development of
Scenic Art and Stage Machinery*. New
York: New York Public Library, 1928.
Gilder, Rosamond. *A Theatre Library*. New
York: Theatre Arts, Inc., 1932.
———— and George Freedley. *Theatre Col-
lections in Museums and Libraries*. New
York: Theatre Arts, Inc., 1936.
Hartnoll, Phyllis, ed. *The Oxford Com-
panion to the Theatre*. Rev. ed. London,
New York: Oxford University Press, 1967.
Hyatt, Aeola L. *Index to Children's Plays*.
Chicago: American Library Association.
1931.
Logasa, Hannah and Winifred Ver Nooy. *An
Index to One-Act Plays, 1900–1924*. Bos-
ton: F. W. Faxon & Co., 1924; 5 supple-
ments, 1932–1965.
Mersand, Joseph, ed. *Guide to Play Selec-
tion*. 2nd ed. New York: Appleton-Cen-
tury-Crofts, Inc., 1959.
Rigdon, Walter, ed. *Biographical Encyclo-
pedia and Who's Who of the American
Theatre*. New York: James H. Heineman,
Inc., 1966.
Santaniello, A. E. *Theatre Books in Print*.
Rev. ed. New York: Drama Book Shop,
1966.
Enciclopedia dello Spettacolo. 9 vols. Rome:
Le Maschere, 1954–1966.

International Federation of Library Associations. *Performing Arts Collections: An International Handbook.* Paris: Centre National de la Recherche Scientifique, 1960.

The Player's Library (Catalog of the Library of the British Drama League). London: Faber & Faber, Ltd., 1950; supplements, 1951–1956.

Acknowledgments for Photographs

Frontispiece

Photograph: Joseph F. Scharrer. (*J. B.* at Ohio State University. Director, Charles C. Ritter; designer, Jerry R. Emery; costumes, Joy Spanabel; lighting, W. M. Schenk.)

Plates

1. Photograph: Vic Haines.

2. (Above) Photograph: Frank Chong.

4. (Above) Photograph: University of Miami Photo Center. (Below, left) Photograph: University of North Carolina Photo Lab. (Below, right) Photograph: Richard W. Purdie.

5. (Above, left) Photograph: University of Miami Photo Center.

6. (Above) Photograph: Photograph Laboratories, University of Minnesota.

7. (Above) Courtesy of American Museum of Natural History. (Below) Courtesy of Hans Jacob Nilsen, Director of Folketeatret, Oslo.

8. (Above) Courtesy of Henry B. Williams, Dartmouth College. (Below) Photograph: Kay Coull.

9. (Above) Agne Beijer, *Slottsteatrarna på Drottningholm och Gripsholm* (John Kroon, 1933). (Below) Courtesy of James Laver and the Victoria and Albert Museum, London. Crown Copyright.

10. (Above) Courtesy of the Victoria and Albert Museum, London. Crown Copyright.

11. (Above, left) Harvard Theatre Collection. (Above, right) Mezzotint by Green after Zoffany. Photograph from the Harry R. Beard Collection, Little Eversden, Cambridge, England. (Below) Harvard Theatre Collection.

12. (Above) Courtesy of George Freedley. Crown Copyright. (Below) Courtesy of Theatre Collection, New York Public Library.

13. (Above) Courtesy of *Theatre Arts Magazine*. (Below) Courtesy of Penguin Books, Ltd.

14. (Above) Courtesy of *Revue d'Histoire du Théâtre, Vol. I, i-ii, 1948.* (Middle) Photograph: Walter H. Stainton.

15. Photograph: Ouradnik, Ann Arbor, Mich.

16. (Above) Photograph: Vandamm. (Middle) Photograph: Menasco, Shreveport, La.

17. (Above) Photograph: W. B. Nickerson. (Below) Photograph: Ouradnik, Ann Arbor, Mich.

18. (Below) Photograph: Eileen Darby. Courtesy of James D. Proctor for Kermit Bloomgarden.

19. (Below) Photograph: Stanley Young.

20. (Below) Photograph: Squire Haskins, Dallas, Tex.

21. (Above) Photograph: Marty Nordstrom. (Below) Photograph: Douglas Spillane.

23. (Above) Photograph: William Nelson. (Below) Photograph: Photo Science Studios, Cornell University.

24. (Below) Photograph: Richard W. Purdie.

25. (Above) Photograph: James Lioi. (Below) Photograph: Walter Barnes Studio.

26. (Above) Photograph: S. Buck Michaels.

27. (Above) Photograph: Brugière. Courtesy of Theatre Collection, New York Public Library.

28. Photograph: Peter Smith.

29. Photographs: Ouradnik, Ann Arbor, Mich.

30. (Above) Photograph: Ouradnik, Ann Arbor, Mich. (Below) Photograph: Eileen Darby, Graphic House, Inc.

Index

Abbott, George, 386, 447
Accent, color, 306; costume, 272, 273, 275
Accentuation, pictorial, 416; vocal, 372, 388, 411
Accessories, 272, 274, 277, 511
Accretion in design composition, 316–318
Accumulation in design composition, 316–319
Acoustics, 176–179, 181, 220. *See also* Auditory stimuli
Act curtain, 185, 186, 187, 189, 194
Act division, 21
Acting, 6, 79–144; characterization, 125–135; historical style, 410; movement and gesture, 85, 87, 90–110, 113, 114; naturalistic, 165; perspective on the whole, 136–144; preparation, 86–88, 142–143; purpose, 79–84; study and memorization, 88–89; systems, 84–86; and thought expression, 60; voice and speech, 111–123. *See also* Auditory stimuli; Visual stimuli
Acting areas, 363–366
Acting script, 472
Action, 15, 16; effect on setting, 243–246; expanding and narrowing, 260–261; intensifying, 368; localization, classified by staging types, 148–166; recording of, 347, 349–350, 351. *See also* Bodily action; Gesture; Movement
Action plot, 244–246
Actor, and audience, 63, 136–138, 147, 149, 151, 155–156, 161, 162; auditory stimuli provided by, 372–390; and costume, 275–276, 279–285, 370–371; and director, 451–455; dual nature, 82–84; influence of design on, 354–371; objectives, 80–82; physical requirements, 109–110; relationships with other actors, 142–144; responsibility, 95, 99; task, 79; and teamwork, 142; temperamental needs, 453–455; thought, 60; visual stimuli provided by, 340–354

Actualistic staging, 148, 157, 161–165, 166, 415
Adams, Maude, 461 n.
Administrative function of director, 324–325
Aesthetic acceptability of character, 30–32
Aesthetic balance, 138–140
Aesthetic distance, 151
Aesthetic illusion, 136–138
Aftereffects of drama, 67–70, 75
Albright, H. D., 88, 109, 128, 140
Alienation effect, 206
Alliteration, 42–43
Alternation, in composition, 314–316; of gay and serious scenes, 411–412; of movement, 353; of speech rate, 386. *See also* Variety
Amplification, 176, 382
Anachronism in historical dress, 283
Analysis, by director, 326–335; period in rehearsal, 464–468; role, 126–130
Anderson, Judith, 241, 446, 461 n.
Anderson, Maxwell, 334, 380, 414, 428, 430
ANTA-Washington Square Theatre, 219
Antioch Shakespeare Festival, 213
Antiphonal speech, 389
Antithesis, 44
Antoine, André, 163, 323
Aphorism, 54, 61
Apostrophe, 53
Appia, Adolphe, 205, 206–207, 241, 323
Appropriateness of design, 234–237
Apron, 159, 189, 190, 214, 344
Arbor, counterweight, 194
Arbuckle, "Fatty," 366
Archaism, 47
Architectural stage, 205–206
Arena staging, 147, 148–149, 166
Arena theatre, 106, 137, 177, 209, 211–212. *See also* Open theatre
Aristotle, 17, 47, 50, 125, 151
Arliss, George, 417
Armor, 270
Articulation, plot, 20–22; speech, 112–115, 373, 383–384, 411

Asbestos, 185, 189, 194. *See also* Fire curtain
Aside, 161
Aspirate quality, 382
Assonance, 43
Astaire, Fred, 390
Atkinson, Brooks, 213, 416 n., 458
Atmosphere, 128–129, 143, 409, 411–415, 435
Attention, means of attracting, 345–346; on speaker, 397–399; through color, 300, 301–303; through light, 298; through line, 287–291; through movement, 350, 352, 357, 437
Attitude, actor responsiveness to, 119; author, 8–10, 328–329, 334; bodily, 342–344 (*see also* Position; Posture)
Audibility, 111–115
Audience, and actor, 63, 136–138, 147, 149, 151, 155–156, 161, 162; comfort and safety, 179–180, 440; and director, 448–451; and drama, 63–76; responsiveness, 143–144
Auditorium, 173–180, 246–248; Elizabethan, 156; Greek theatre, 151, 152; shape, 159, 176
Auditory effectiveness, 41, 42–44
Auditory rhythm, 331, 332, 385, 427–429, 430–431, 433
Auditory stimuli, and climax, 419; patterning, 394–435; provided by actors, 376–390, 393; provided by other media, 390–393; and role of director, 372–393; in voice and speech, 376–387
Auslander, Joseph, 117
Autonomous composition, 8
Auto-transformer dimmer, 199
Ayers, Lemuel, 304

Back reference, 117
Backdrop, 194, 202, 203
Background, 361–368, 412; analysis by director, 333–334
Backing, 182, 200
Back-lighting, 297
Baker, George Pierce, 454
Bakst, Leon, 70, 237, 304, 312

Balance, 319, 397, 417–420, 435; aesthetic, 138–140; of character relationships, 126; occult, 412, 418, 419; repetitive, 43; symmetrical and asymmetrical, 290, 292; visual, 418–419; vocal, 419–420

Balconies, 159, 173, 178, 247

Balcony scenes, 257, 348

Bamberger, Rudolph, 446

Bankhead, Tallulah, 425 n.

Barrymore, John, 242, 314, 333, 341, 458, 459

Barrymore, Lionel, 341, 425, 458

Barton, Lucy, 271

Batten, 194

Beards, 280–281

Beaton, Cecil, 314

Beats, 432–433

Beaumont (Vivian) Theater, 170, 214 n., 217–218, 221

Belasco, David, 164, 166, 262, 323, 455, 459, 468

Belaying pin, 193

Bel Geddes, Norman, 192, 205, 238, 357, 418

Belief, arousing, 121–123; in characterization, 133–135

Benois, Alexandre, 237

Berlin, Irving, 431

Bernhardt, Sarah, 283

Bipolar scenes, 227, 246, 256–258

Beam lighting, beam projector, 198

Bobbinet, 204

Bodily action, 85, 87, 90–110, 113, 114

Boleslavsky, Richard, 466

Bolger, Ray, 390

Bon mot, 53–54

Book of flats, 200, 202

Bookholder, 468, 476, 478, 487

Borderlighting, 197, 198

Border, 200, 203; cloth, 202

Box set, 163, 200, 201

Boxes, 159, 173

Boyer, Charles, 333

Boyt, John, 227

Bracing, 182, 184

Bragdon, Claude, 293

Breakaway, 265–266

Breathing, 111–112

Brecht, Bertolt, 10, 206, 338

Bridging, 119, 122

Brown, Gilmor, 211, 389

Buckmaster, John, 343

Budget, 449, 514

Building codes, 174, 179–180, 196

Bulwer–Lytton, Edward, 54

Burbage, James, 460

Burke, Billie, 385

Burlesque acting, 329, 333, 341, 390, 410, 447

Business, 340, 343, 416–417, 443, 467, 469. *See also* Gesture; Movement

Business rehearsal, 471–474

Butterworth, Charles, 390

California, University of at Los Angeles, theatre, 169, 211, 213

Camp, Paul A., 465

Campbell, Mrs. Patrick, 427

Carriage, 194

Casting, 325, 331, 378, 381, 382, 416, 447, 450, 460–463

Catharsis, 151

Cavea, 151

Celastic, 270 n.

Chaney, Stewart, 304

Channing, Carol, 390

Chaplin, Charlie, 390

Character, aesthetic acceptability of, 30–32; analysis by director, 330–331; consistency, 30, 31, 34–35; contrast and conflict, 38–40; development, 80, 83; generalized, 31, 129; identification, 32–34, 230–231; irony, 27; key, 327, 397; motivation, 35–37; particularized, 31–32, 129; relationship with other characters, 131, 227, 330; revelation, 30, 37–38; super-objective, 131; types, 14, 32–33, 35

Characterization, 14, 15, 30–40, 59–60, 83, 125–135; analyzing a role, 126–130; completeness, 125–126; enrichment, 131–132; imagination and belief, 133–135; by make-up, 519, 522; by pantomime, 94–98; and posture, 342; selection and adaptation, 130–131; and speech, 381, 382, 383–384; and volume, 377

Characterization rehearsal, 476

Chekhov, Anton, 31, 37, 138, 227, 233, 378, 381, 411, 450, 464

Chiaroscuro, 157, 204, 293

Chichester Festival Theatre, 216–217

Children's plays, 66, 366

Choral speech, 388–390

Chorus, 13, 14, 21, 22, 60, 61, 149, 151, 389

Christians, Mady, 459

"Cinderella" change, 38

Circus theatre, 209, 211–212. *See also* Open theatre

Claire, Ina, 461 n.

Clarification by design, 226–228

Clarity of performance, 80

Clark, Bobby, 353, 390, 424

Classical drama, 10, 33, 148, 411. *See also* Greek drama

Climax, 327, 375, 378, 419, 431, 433

Closed position, 344

Clurman, Harold, 460, 472

Cohan, George M., 333

Cole, Edward C., 182, 185

Colloquial prose, 49

Colloquial speech, 384

Color, and atmosphere, 412; attention through, 300, 301–303; in costume, 275, 510, 511, 512; in design composition, 298–309; harmony, 303–306; hue, purity, value, 299–301; in lighting, 199, 306–309, 369; perception, 311; selective reflection, 306–308; visibility, 301, 302; warm and cool, 303, 304, 305

Colored light, effect, 306–309, 369, 511, 517–519. *See also* Light

Comédie Française, 161 n., 188

Comedy, 9, 25, 31, 37, 66, 68, 128, 133–134, 154, 155–156, 161, 293, 328, 330 333, 353, 369, 376, 377, 380, 383, 385, 386, 411

Comedy scenes, 327, 329, 411–412, 413, 414, 448

Comic appearance through costume, 284–285

Comic exaggeration, 390

Commedia dell'arte, 94, 148, 150

Communication, as director's goal, 337; of meaning, 115–117, 119, 337, 380

Community theatre, 168, 219, 450, 485

Comparison, of plays, 69–70; in poetic imagery, 45

Completeness, of characterization, 125–126; in design composition, 239–240, 318–319; as mark of work of art, 299; of production, 323

Complex plot, 17–18, 312

Complexity in production design, 312

Composition, dramatic, 3, 5, 7–16; and attitude, 343: elements, 14–16; formalities, 11–14; kinds, 7–11; for open theatre, 251; structural coherence, 141. *See also* Design; Direction; Script

Composition in design, spatial, 286–309; temporal, 225–226, 234, 286, 310–319, 395, 418

Compound plot, 18–19

Concealment, by costuming, 513; by make-up, 517; psychological, 367

Concentration, light, 298

Conflict, of characters, 38–40, 102, 103, 127; plot, 22–24, 27, 327

Confrontation, 102, 103

Congreve, William, 133, 138, 392

Consistency, in atmosphere, 412; character, 30, 31, 34–35; in costume and properties, 406; in direction, 385

Constructivism, 205–206

Context, factor in speech, 119–121; and learning, 89

Continental seating, 174, 179

Continuity, open theatre, 438–439; variations, 313–316

Contour curtain, 186

Contrast, characters, 38–40; in direction, 330, episode, 22; for focusing attention, 399; harmony of, 303–304; of movement, 353; pitch, 378, 379; speech, 117, 121; speech rate, 386; vocal, 383, 390; volume, 376–377

Control, body, 109; breath, 112

Controlboard, 163, 199

Conventionalization, pantomime, 94–98

Convergence, line, 287, 288, 291

Conversational quality, 122

Cooper, Charles W., 465

Copeau, Jacques, 205

Corneille, Pierre, 10, 21, 154

Cornell, Katharine, 73, 227, 230, 353, 358, 425, 451, 460, 461 n., 475

Corpulence, simulation of, 283–284, 513

Costume, 267–285, 407, 508–515; and actor, 275–276, 279–285, 370–371; and atmosphere, 412; clarification by, 227; fast changes, 275–276; and make-up, 512; mobility, 275–279; for open theatre, 220, 253, 515; period, 409–410; "real," 162; style, 240, 267–275; tragic, 161, 414; variation by changing, 313

Costume rehearsal, 480–481

Counterweight system, 194

Court theatre, 159

Coward, Noel, 328, 428, 447

Cowl, Jane, 319, 461 n.

Cradle, counterweight, 194

Craig, Gordon, 206, 207, 230, 314, 323

Creativeness, actor, 453; director, 335–336, 426

Credibility, 121–123, 133–135

Critical function of director, 326, 336–338, 426, 478

Criticism, by director, 453, 454–455; by newspapers and magazines, 334, 486, 487

Crosby, Bing, 390

Cross coloring, 308, 309

Cross-lighting, 198–199

Crossing, 104–106, 113, 114, 352–353

Cue-line link, 439

Cues, 481; co-ordination, 441; picking up, 386, 479

Curtains, 162, 173, 180, 185–186, 187, 189, 194

Cutout, 202, 203

Cutting a script, 443–445

Cyclic sequence, 319

Cyclorama (cyc), 163, 188; cloth, 196, 202; drape, 200; plaster, 188; trough, 197

Dailey, Peter, 387 n.

Dance, 15, 110, 148, 149, 354, 432, 457

Dane, Clemence, 54

Dean, Alexander, 340, 397, 415

de Loutherbourg, 162

Delsarte, François, 94, 340

Design, 6, 15, 192, 193, 205, 207, 225–319; aesthetic factors, 234–242; analysis by director, 334–335; costume, 267–285; defined, 225; and director's interpretation, 236–237; and individuality, 235, 237–239; interpretation through, 234, 446; modern, 207; nature and function, 225–233; for open theatre, 221, 251–255; physical factors, 243–285; realistic, 162–164; and script, 235–236; setting and lighting, 243–266; spatial, 286–309; influence on actor, 354–371; temporal, 225–226, 234, 286, 310–319, 395, 418; and visual unity, 239–242

Designer, relationship with director, 455–457

Detail, in design, 262–263; in motion pictures, 174

Deus ex machina, 14

Dialect, 384–385, 409, 411

Dialogue, 50–52, 111; linked, 13, 51–52; poetic, 151

Diction, 47–48, 122

Dilemma, 24–26, 27, 28

Dimensional action plot, 244, 245

Diminishing effect of visual sensation, 310–311

Dimmers, 199–200

Direct conflict, 23

Direction, 323–488; auditory stimuli, 372–435; of crosses, 352–353; for open stage, 436–441; visual stimuli, 339–371, 394–435

Direction of illumination, 294–297, 298

Director, and actor, 451–455; as administrator, 324–325; and audience, 448–451; and composition, 251; as creator, 335–336, 426; as critic, 336–338, 426, 478; and designer and production heads, 455–457; first reading by, 463; interpretation by, and design, 236–237; as interpreter, 326–338, 464; as leader, 317, 325–326, 338, 486, 487; as playwright, 442–448; relationship with associates, 442–457; as student, 326–335

Director's design, 163, 335

Dishing of auditorium, 176, 178

Dissolve, 265

Diversity of design elements, 260–262

Docks, 182, 193

Dolman, John, Jr., 139

Dominance, 348, 368; by elevation, 400; by lighting, 368–370, 399; by position, 345, 346

Donnée, 34

Double-casting, 462

Double conversation, 389–390. See *also* Bipolar scenes

Downstage, 188, 344

Drama, 3–76; as art, 3–6, 137; characteristics, 3–5; elements, 5–6; quality tests, 73–76; the word, 3

Dramatic composition. See Composition

Dramatic language. See Language

Dramatic structure of play, 327

Dramatic time, 12–13

Drape, drape border, drape cyclorama, 186, 200

Draped costume, 268, 269, 270, 275, 412, 513

Draperies, 276–277, 278

Draw curtain, 185, 187, 189

Dress rehearsal, 457, 482–485

Dressing rooms, 197

Dressler, Marie, 341, 461 n.

Drop (curtain), 186, 187, 189, 194, 202, 203, 204; tripping of, 160

Dryden, John, 410

Duration, in design composition, 310–312; of speech sound, 385–387

Eccyclema, ekkuklema, 151, 190

Echoing, 117, 420

Educational theatre, 337–338, 358, 449, 450, 451, 454, 462, 470

Effect machine, 163–164

Effects of drama, 63–76; after-effects, 67–70, 75; changes, 70–73; immediate, 64–65, 68; and levels of perception, 65–67; tests, 73–76

Electronic dimmer, 199

Elevations, 367–368, 399, 400; as factor in attracting attention, 345; and movement, 357–361

Elevator, elevator stage, 174, 175, 180–182, 190, 192, 193

Eliot, T. S., 66

Elizabethan drama, 148, 154–157, 227, 275, 314

Embellishments, 55

Emotion, and color, 298, 303; confined to audience, 135; and pitch, 378

Emotional tone of a production, 128–129, 412

Empathy, 139–140, 352, 461

Emphasis, in design composition, 317; on groups, 399–402; by lighting, 298, 368–370, 399; by make-up, 516–517; by movement, 100, 104, 354; nature, 117–119; in patterning visual and auditory stimuli, 395–402, 435; pitch, 378; position, 345–346; on silent actor or inanimate object, 399; on speaker, 397–399; in speech, 368. *See also* Dominance

Enclosure, in line composition, 287, 289, 291

Enrichment of characterization, 131–132, 143

Entrances, making, 95, 387, 436–437

Entranceways. *See* Openings

Environment, response to, 374

Epic Theatre, 206

Epigram, 54

Epilogue, 14, 60, 161, 318, 319, 420

Episodes, 19–20, 127, 329–330; variety and contrast of, 22, 313

Ethical conflict, 39–40

Ethical motivation, 35–36

Ethical viewpoint, 57

Eurhythmics, 110

Euripides, 14, 54

Evans, Maurice, 366, 370, 444, 446, 447, 460

Exaggeration, 447–448; comic, 390; and costuming, 513–514

Exercises, sense, 109

Exposition, devices in composition, 13–14; gesture, 349; pantomime, 427

Expression, motivated, 373–374; as phase of interpretation, 326; of thought, 58–62

Expressionism, 206, 348

Extensive drama, 10, 11, 31

Familiarity, changes due to, 70–71

Farce, 9, 56, 155, 294, 328, 333, 353, 369, 376, 377, 390, 408, 411, 430, 474

Ffoulkes, David, 231

Fields, W. C., 380

Figures of speech, 45

Fire, dramatic appeal, 254; stage, 259–260

Fire curtain, 173, 180, 185, 189, 194

Firelight, 297

Fitted costume, 268, 269, 270

Flats, 200

Flipper, 193

Float, 160

Floodlight, 195, 197–198

Floor, auditorium, 176, 178; gridiron, 194; stage, 188–190, 204

Floor plan, 335, 341, 350, 361, 362, 363, 456

Flown (flied) scenery, 193–194

Fly loft (flies), fly galleries, flymen, 193

Follow-spot, 198

Fontanne, Lynn, 370

Footlights, 160, 197, 297, 518

Footwear, 273, 275, 282–283

Forced perspective, 158, 190

Foreshadowing, 349, 376, 387

Forestage, 189, 190, 205. *See also* Apron

Form, unity of, 241–242

Formal prose, 49

Formal staging, 148, 149–153

Fortuny System, 188

French curtain, 186

French drape, 186 n.

French scenes, 329–330

Front curtain, 185. *See also* Act curtain

Front lighting, 198, 247–248

Frontality as factor in attracting attention, 345

Frost, Robert, 428

Funding, 64, 65

Furniture, 361–368, 399, 406; open stage, 439. *See also* Properties

Galantière, Lewis, 329

Gallows, 259

Galsworthy, John, 66, 378, 429

Garrick, David, 162

Garwood, Alice, 389

Gas-table, 163

Generalized character, 31, 129

George II, 163

Gerard, Rolf, 425

Gesture, 85, 87, 90–110, 113, 114, 348–349, 452; styles in, 406

Ghosts, 437

Gielgud, John, 70, 238, 392, 446

Gillette, William, 82

Giraudoux, Jean, 445

Goe, Ida Mae, 318

Goldoni, Carlo, 392

Gorki, Maxim, 411

Grand drape, 186, 189

Grand pause, 116

Granville-Barker, Harley, 323, 334, 444

Graves, 258

Greek drama, 33, 53, 61, 148, 150–152, 190, 227, 231, 238, 259–260, 272, 353, 378, 389, 414, 456

Greenroom, 196–197

Greenstreet, Sidney, 352, 416

Gridiron (grid), 183, 185, 193–196

Ground cloth, 174, 204, 252

Ground row, 197, 202, 203

Grouping, 397, 436, 438; costume, 271–272; emphasis on, 399–402

Guard rails, 185

Guiterman, Arthur, 428, 431, 444

Guthrie, Tyrone, 171, 220, 254; Theatre, 171, 173, 217

Harmonic effect, choral speaking, 388–389

Harmonies, color, 299, 303–306

Harris, Jed, 343, 364

Hart, Moss, 328

Hauptmann, Gerhardt, 338

Hayes, Helen, 284, 416, 451, 452, 461 n.

Head block, 193

Headgear, 273, 276, 280, 281

Hearn, Edward G., 169

Heavens, in theatre structure, 154

Heffner, Hubert, 478

Hellman, Lillian, 331, 414

Hepburn, Katharine, 427

Heteronomous composition, 8

Highlights, 271, 297; in make-up, 520–522

Holland, Joseph, 446 n.

Hope, Bob, 390

Hopkins, Arthur, 341, 425, 458, 468

Horizon strip, 197
Horner, Harry, 193
House curtain, 186
House lights, 199
Howard, Leslie, 70, 304, 446
Hue, 299, 300, 301, 302, 303
Hughes, Glenn, 211
Hutton, Betty, 390

Ibsen, Henrik, 75, 138, 232–233, 338, 378, 414, 464
Identification, 9, 30, 32–34, 230–233, 328
Identifying speaking character, 438
Illumination. *See* Light; Lighting
Illusion, aesthetic, 136–138
Imagery, 44–46, 61, 62
Imagination, audience, in supplying setting, 262; in characterization, 133–135
Imitation, avoiding, 121, 238, 422, 452, 464; and behavior, 139
Immobility, effect of, 352
Impact, 64–65, 229–230; in design composition, 317–318; devices for increasing, 13; unity, 424–426
Imposed movement, 99, 100–103
Impression as phase of interpretation, 326
Impressionism, 206
Incidents. *See* Episodes
Individuality of design, 235, 237–239
Individualized character, 31–32, 129
Inflection, 379–381, 411
Inherent movement, 99–100
Inscenierung, 225
Integrating rehearsal, 434, 480–482
Intelligibility of speech, 111–115
Intensification, by light angle, 297; in design composition, 228–230, 317–318; of dramatic action, 368; of suspense, 330
Intensity, of composition, 311–312; dramatic, 298; of perception, 64, 74
Intensive drama, 10
Intercut, 265
Interest, continuing, 81; intensifying, 230
Intermezzi, 157
Interpretation, by design, 234, 446; by director, 128, 236–237, 326–338, 444, 445–446, 452, 464; by drama, 4–5
Intersection of lines, 287–290, 291
Invocation, 53
Intonation, 379–381

Irony, 26–27
Izenour, George C., 194, 197

Jack, 202
Jackknife stage, 182, 191, 192
Janauschek, Mme., 417
Jeritza, Maria, 343
Jessner, Leopold, 357
Jessner treppen, 447
Johnson, Albert, 192, 193
Johnson, Samuel, 8
Jones (Margo) Theatre '47, 212
Jones, Robert Edmond, 228, 229, 237, 238, 242, 247, 279, 282, 283, 314, 316, 341, 357, 401, 425, 446
Jonson, Ben, 75
Jouvet, Louis, 205

Kabuki theatre, 190
Kaufman, George S., 328, 331, 447, 458, 468, 472, 478
Kaye, Danny, 353, 390
Kernodle, George, 154, 155, 158
Kerr, Walter, 425
Kerz, Leo, 358
Key (inflection), 381–382
Key character, speech, or action, 327, 397–399
Kiesler, Frederick, 205
Kingsley, Sidney, 328, 378
Kjerbühl-Petersen, Lorenz, 86, 135
Klieglite, 198
Kortner, Fritz, 425
Kruger, Otto, 346
Kyd, Thomas, 156

Lahr, Bert, 353, 390
Langham, Michael, 220
Langner, Lawrence, 428, 431, 444
Language, 6, 13–14, 15–16, 41–55; changes, 73; as channel of thought, 60–61; forms, 50–55; poetic and prosaic, 44–50; requirements, 41–44; rhythm in, 427–428; special uses, 331–332; study by director, 331–332; of various nationalities, 44. *See also* Speech *and* Voice
Laughton, Charles, 461 n.
Lauterer, Arch, 194
Lawrence, Gertrude, 343, 415–416
Lead voice, lead group, 389
Leadership function of director, 317, 325–326, 338, 486, 487
Leading lines, 397
Leg drape, 200
Leg drop, 202
Legerdemain, 263–264
Lekolite, 198

Levels, 357, 412. *See also* Elevations
Lewes, George Henry, 98
Liaison in plot, 21
Light, and balance, 418; colored, 306–309; cross coloring, 308, 309; variation of episode by, 313
Light and shade in design composition, 293–298
Lighting, 160, 162, 182, 188, 243–266; and atmosphere, 412; changing color, 369; and costume, 271; for emphasis and dominance, 368–370, 399; equipment, 195, 197–200; and make-up, 516, 517–519; "natural," 163; open theatre, 198, 220–221, 252–253, 308; tragedy, 414
Line in design composition, 287–293, 314, 397
Lines (rope, cable), 193
Lining, in painting scenery, 204
Linked dialogue, 13, 51–52
Listening, 342–343, 397
Literary prose, 49
Living Newspaper, 206
Local color, 262–263
Locale, identification, 231–233; influence on style, 408–409; singularity of, 12
Localization of stage action classified by staging types, 148–166
Loft blocks, 193, 194
Lorre, Peter, 352, 461 n.
Lowlights in make-up, 520–522

McClintic, Guthrie, 468
McCollom, William G., 137
McElvy, Carl C., 169
Macgowan, Kenneth, 174
Machinery in scenes, 259
MacKaye, Steele, 192
Maeterlinck, Maurice, 381, 411, 412
Magical property changes, 440. *See also* Legerdemain
Main, Marjorie, 461 n.
Make-up, 280, 281, 516–522
Malapropisms, 55
Mansion, 153
Mantle, Burns, 334
Marlowe, Christopher, 155, 156
Marx Brothers, 353, 390, 393
Masking pieces, 182, 200
Masks, 276
Master dimmer, 199
Maugham, W. Somerset, 66
Meaning, communicating, 115–117, 119, 337, 380; interrelationships of, 116–117

Melodrama, 9, 10, 259, 293, 370, 376, 386, 387, 392, 411, 447
Melody, 379–380
Memorization, 88–89, 462, 474–475
Memory rehearsal, 474–476
Meredith, Burgess, 451
Metaphor, 45, 62
Meyerhold, V. E., 205, 447, 448
Mielziner, Jo, 170, 229, 232, 238, 241, 258, 313, 319, 397, 425
Miller, Arthur, 59, 331
Miller, Gilbert, 452
Miller, James Hull, 168, 211
Mimesis, 4, 5, 15
Mise-en-scène, 225
Mob scene, 374–375, 388, 389, 474
Mobility, costume, 275–279
Moeller, Philip, 473
Moiseiwitsch, Tanya, 167, 171, 214, 215, 217
Molière, 10, 21, 37, 59, 75, 138, 227, 231, 354, 392
Mood, 228–229, 298, 381, 411–415; contrasts of, 39. *See also* Atmosphere
Moore, Victor, 390
Moral viewpoint, 56–57
Morality plays, medieval, 153–154
Morris, Angela, 454–455
Motion pictures, comfort at theatres, 179; detail afforded, 174; music and dialogue, 391; naturalism, 164
Motivation, character, 30, 35–37, 39–40, 131–132; and inflection, 380; for movement, 348, 350, 356, 358, 367, 415–416; "natural," 415; role, 348; for stage position, 346; and vocal expression, 373–374
Motivation rehearsal, 476
Movement, 85, 87, 90–110, 113, 114, 349–354, 361, 362, 363; ascending, descending, 357–358, 412; and color, 312; improved by costume, 282–283; inherent and imposed, 99–103; lighting of, 297; motivated, 348, 350, 356, 358, 367, 415–416; "natural," 366, 398; on open stage, 106–109, 436–438; rules, 103–106; tempo, 246; in tragedy, 413; ungainly, 284. *See also* Action; Gesture
Multiple staging, 148, 154–157, 314
Music, 14, 15, 335, 390–392, 457
Musicals, 212, 390–391
Mystery plays, medieval, 153–154

Nagler, A. M., 190
Naive soliloquy, 33, 55
Nasal resonance, 112
Nathan, George Jean, 333, 334
Naturalism, 164, 165, 166, 376
Nazimova, Alla, 427
Noel, Craig, 212
Nonillusionary style, Greek theatre, 151–153
Nonrealistic scenery, 206
Noton, 293

Obligatory scene, 24
Odets, Clifford, 338, 428
Oenslager, Donald, 362
Olivier, Laurence, 216, 353, 446
O'Neill, Eugene, 10, 58, 75, 235
Open position, 344, 346
Open theatre, 147, 148–149, 166, 167–171, 208–222; advantages and difficulties, 219–221, 440–441; buildings, 214–219; combined with proscenium stage, 221–222; and costume, 220, 253, 515; design for, 221, 251–255; direction, 436–441; influence of Shakespearean festivals, 212–213; lighting, 198, 220–221, 252–253, 308; movement, 106–109, 436–438; open stage, 209–212; thrust stage, 106, 147, 148, 167, 177, 213, 214, 253; voice projection, 115
Opening (doors, etc.), 352, 354–357, 358, 412
Opening night, 485–486
Opening out, 104–108
Opening (beginning) of the play, 340–341, 395. *See also* Prologue
Opposition of lines, 287–290, 291
O.P. side (opposite prompt), 186
Oral effectiveness, 41–42
Oral and orotund quality, 382–383, 411
Orchestra (in Greek theatre), 150
Orchestra pit, 174, 175
Order in design, 286. *See also* Composition in design
Ornament (in setting), 290
Orth, Gus, 168
Outdoor theatre, 255–256
Overlapping sentences, 389
Overlapping sequences, 265
Overtones, 382

Packs, 182, 193
Pageant-wagons, 153
Painting scenery, 157–158, 204
Pantomime, 349, 402, 427, 431–432; conventionalization, 94–98;

nature, 90–94. *See also* Action; Gesture; Movement
Pantomime rehearsal, 478
Parallel episodes, 22
Parallels, 202, 204
Parker, Dorothy, 458
Particularized character, 31–32, 129
Pathetic conflict, 39–40
Pathetic motivation, 35, 36–37
Patterning visual and auditory stimuli, 394–435
Pause, 116, 387–388
Payne, B. Iden, 212, 352 n., 428, 437
Pearson, Talbot, 451
Pectoral quality, 382
Pemberton, Brock, 458
Penthouse Theatre, 211–212, 219
Perception, of color, 311; intensity, 64, 74; levels, 65–67
Performance, 485–487; elements, 79; objectives, 80–82; place of, and setting, 246–256; preparation *versus*, 86–88
Periaktoi, 151
Period style, 409–410
Personal viewpoint of playwright, 338, 447–448
Personality contrasts, 38–39
Personification, 46
Perspective, 287, 418; forced, 158, 190
Pictorial action plot, 244, 245, 246
Pictorial effect, 100, 101, 106
Picturization, 397, 415–417, 435
Pinakes, 151
Pinrail, 193
Pipe batten, 194
Pirandello, Luigi, 59, 66
Piscator, Erwin, 206
Pitch, 378–382
Pitts, Zasu, 390
Plaster cyclorama, 188
Platea, 153
Platform, 149, 202, 204, 344, 358, 359, 360. *See also* Elevations
Play, selection, 448–451; type of, and style, 410–411
Playwright, attitude of, 8–10, 328–329, 334; first reading by, 463; purpose of, 7–8, 235–236, 332, 333; treatment of material, 10–11
Plot, 6, 14, 15, 17–29, 125, 127; action, 244–246; analysis by director, 327–330; articulation, 20–22; conflicts, 22–24; dilemma, 24–26; double, 330; episodes, 19–20, 22; irony, 26–27; kinds, 17–19; suspense and sur-

prise, 27–29; and thought expression, 58
Poel, William, 208, 212, 214, 428, 437, 459
Poetic language, 44–48, 428, 430. *See also* Verse
Pointillage, 204
Polishing rehearsal, 478–480
Porter, Cole, 431
Pose, 342, 344, 397
Position, 343, 344–348, 400; effects on acting, 87, 93, 98–103
Posture, 282, 342; styles in, 406, 410
Preface to play, 334
Presentational action plot, 244
Presentational play, 137, 138, 392, 456
Producer, 236 n.
Production curtain, 186
Progression, 426–427, 431, 435; in composition, 290–293, 314, 315
Projection, pantomime, 91, 92–94; voice, 115, 478
Prologue, 13–14, 60, 161, 318, 420
Prompt side, 186
Prompter's box, 188
Prompting, 441. *See also* Bookholder
Pronunciation, 122–123, 384, 411
Properties, 262–263, 361–368; and character build-up, 97; magical changes, 440; open theatre, 220, 253, 440; in rehearsal, 481. *See also* Furniture
Proportion, 420–424, 435
Prosaic language, 48–50; rhythm in, 428
Proscenium arch, 147, 157, 158–159, 172; equipment, 183, 185–188, 189
Proscenium steps, 190
Proscenium theatre, 172–207; auditorium, 173–180; combined with open theatre, 221–222; general structure, 172–173; revolts from the pattern, 205–207; stage, 248–251; stage house, 180–205
Proskenion, 150
Proximity, in colors, 303, 512; as factor in attracting attention, 345
Psychological concealment, 367
Puns, 55
Purity of color, 299–301

Quality, of light and shade, 294, 298; vocal, 382–383, 411

Racine, Jean, 10, 21, 66
Radio City Music Hall, 186, 193

Raking, auditorium floor, 176, 178; stage floor, 158, 188
Ramps, 357. *See also* Elevations
Rapson, Ralph, 171
Rate of speech, 385–387
Reading, first, of play, 463–464; for meaning, 115–117, 119; at tryouts, 461–462
"Realism," 153, 244
Realistic staging, 162–165, 166
Reality, levels, 137; and truth, 133, 134
Recording stage action, 347, 349–350, 351
Redman, Joyce, 283
Reed, Florence, 446
Reflection, on a play, 68–69; selective, of colored light, 306–308
Refraction of light, 198
Rehearsal costumes, 370
Rehearsals, 142–143, 458–488; business, 471–474; characterization and motivation, 476; costume, 480–481; dress, 457, 482–485; integrating, 434, 480–482; memory, 474–476; polishing, 478–480; running, 476–478; scheduling of, 468–471; study of, 434; types, 471–485; visitors at, 484
Reinhardt, Max, 192, 205, 209, 323, 330, 357, 447, 459, 471
Rejoinder, 54
Renaissance theatre, 148, 152, 157, 160
Repertory theatre, 188, 212, 214, 218, 252
Repetition, in design composition, 290, 295, 318; in language, 43–44; and rhythm, 429, 433; of stimuli, 420
Representational action plot, 244
Representational play, 57, 137–138, 391–392, 399, 456
Resistance dimmer, 199
Resonance, 112, 382
Responsiveness, actor, 109, 119; audience, 143–144
Restoration drama, 66, 148, 158, 160, 377, 408
Revelation of character, 30, 37–38
Reviews, newspaper and magazine, 334, 486, 487
Revolving stage, 182, 190, 191, 192–193, 202
Rheostat, 199
Rhythm, 46–47, 290, 353; language, 331, 332, 385, 427–434, 435

Rice, Elmer, 378, 414
Rigging of curtains, 186
Right-left stage directions, 186, 344
Ritchard, Cyril, 425
Robson, Flora, 446
Roll curtain, roll drop, 186
Romantic drama, 353, 376
Romanticism, 411; in staging, 162. *See also* Actualistic staging
Rosenthal, Jean, 194
Rosse, Hermann, 205
Rouge in make-up, 520
Running rehearsal, 476–478

Saarinen, Eero, 170
Saroyan, William, 428
Sartre, Jean Paul, 445
Satire, 9, 35, 36, 54, 57, 66, 328–329, 370, 428, 445, 447
Saxe-Meiningen, Duke of, 163, 323
Scene curtain, 186
Scenery, 200–205; for depicting locale, 157; Elizabethan, 155; fast changes, 265–266; flied (flown), 193–194; Greek, 151; nonrealistic, 206; painting, 157–158, 204; shifting, 158, 164, 182, 190–196, 254–255; standardized, 204–205; units, 184, 200–204; wing-and-drop, 202, 203
Schiller, Friedrich, 410
Scrim, 204
Script, 7; adaptation, 442–448; analysis by director, 326–335; appropriateness of design to, 235–236, 256–266; cutting, 443–445; revision, 326, 333
Sculptural action plot, 244, 245, 246, 251
Seating plans, 152, 174, 176, 177, 178, 179, 214, 215, 217, 252
Selden, Samuel, 265
Selectivity, of amplification, 382; in characterization, 130–131; in lighting, 399; in realistic staging, 164, 166; of reflection, 306–308; stage pantomime, 92
Sense-awareness, 109–110
Sequence overlapping, 8, 265
Sequential conflict, 23–24
Serious drama, 9, 26, 37, 68–69, 376, 377, 411, 417
Set speech, 52–53, 423
Setting, 243–266, 367; diagram, 344; divided, 389–390 (*see also* Bipolar scenes); effect of activity, 243–246; effect of place of performance, 246–256; effect of script demands, 256–266; fragmentary, 265; and stage move-

ment, 359, 360, 361, 362, 363, 365. *See also* Scenery; Staging

Seyler, Athene, 134

Shadow, from lighting, 369, 370; in make-up, 521; in theatre structure, 154. *See also* Light and shade

Shakespeare, William, 8, 11, 17, 21, 22, 32, 41, 42, 46, 54, 59, 71, 75, 80, 81, 133, 137, 154, 155, 156, 165, 231, 332, 352 n., 353, 354, 369, 376, 380, 392, 428, 443, 444, 450, 467

Shakespearean festivals, 212–213

Shaw, George Bernard, 66, 75, 80, 133, 208, 232, 334, 338, 410, 420, 445

Sheave, 193

Sheridan, Richard Brinsley, 392

Shops in stage house, 196

Sides, 464 n.

Sight lines, 104, 176, 220, 257

Silhouette, 267–271, 272, 297, 437

Similarity, harmony of, 303, 304

Simile, 45

Simonson, Lee, 98, 182, 207, 230, 238, 242, 260

Simple plot, 17

Simultaneous speech, 388–390

Simultaneous staging, 148, 153–154

Sinking stage, 192

Skene, 150

Sky dome, 163, 188

Sky drop (sky cyc), 194, 202

Slice-of-life drama, 244

Sliding stage, 180, 190–192, 266

Small parts, 325–326, 333, 421 n., 460, 468, 475

Smith, T. V., 117

Snatch line, 194

Soliloquy, 13, 33, 54–55, 161

Sophisticated soliloquy, 55

Sophocles, 21, 59, 75

Sound effects, 392–393

Space, actor's position in, 87, 93, 98–103

Spatial composition. *See* Composition in design, spatial

Spectacle, 174, 263–264

Spectrum band, 300

Speech, 111–123; audibility and intelligibility, 111–115; characteristics, 372–373, 376–387; in context, 119–121; and credibility, 121–123; emphasis and, 117–119; and irony, 27; reading for meaning, 115–117; sectional, 408–409; style, 411; in tragedy, 414

Split stage, 401. *See also* Bipolar scenes

Spontaneity, 81

Spot-flood lamp, 198

Spotlight, 195, 197, 198, 248, 297, 399

Sprague, Arthur Colby, 334

Spreader, 193

"Stab," 318

Stacking, 193

Stage, architectural, 205–206; arena, 106, 137, 147, 148–149, 166, 177, 209, 211–212; moving, 180–182, 190–193; open, 209–212; proscenium, 248–251; thrust, 106, 147, 148, 167, 177, 213, 214, 253; wagon, 192; wrap-around, 177–211

Stage floor, 188–190, 204

Stage house, 180–205, 250–251

Stage screws, 188

Stage speech, 384, 411

Staging, actualistic, 148, 157, 161–165, 166, 415; arena, 147, 148–149, 166; formal, 148, 149–153; multiple, 148, 154–157, 314; simultaneous, 148, 153–154; theatrical, 148, 157–161

Stairs, 357–358, 447. *See also* Elevations

Stanislavski, Constantin, 84, 122, 134, 135, 163, 166, 323, 434, 459, 460, 466

Star, 421 n.

Stereotypes, 32–33, 94, 460

Stevens, Thomas Wood, 212, 437, 459

Stewart, James, 431

Stichomythia, 13, 51–52

Storage in stage house, 196

Stratford (Ontario) Shakespearean Festival Theatre, 167, 173, 213, 214–216, 219

Strickland, F. Cowles, 470

Striplight, 197, 198

Stuart, Marion, 477

Study, by actors, 88–89; by director, 326–335

Style, 405–411, 435, 446; costume, 267–275; mixed, 425; unity, 240–241

Subordination, 402–405, 423, 435

Subplot, 328, 386, 424, 427, 444

Substitution, in costuming, 514; in poetic imagery, 45

Summary speech, 53

Suspense, 27–29, 387; heightening, 330

Swanson, Wesley, 465

Switchboard, 163, 199

Symbolism, 61–62, 153, 416, 446–447

Symmetrical balance, 418

Sympathy, audience, 330–331, 416, 422, 460–461. *See also* Empathy

Synthesis, 5, 6, 207

Tableau curtain (tab), 186, 187

Tableaux vivants, 154, 190

Teamwork in acting, 82

Teaser, 186, 189

Technical crews, relationship of director and actors with, 456–457

Technical rehearsal, 481–482

Telephone conversation, 389

Tempest, Marie, 448 n.

Temple, Shirley, 426 n.

Tempo, 246, 385–387

Temporal composition. *See* Composition in design, temporal

Temporal nature of theatre art, 3–4, 5, 235

Terminal devices, 14

Terminal dilemma, 25

Texture of costume, 271–272, 511–512

Theatre, 147–222; common inadequacies, 250–251; structure, 147–173. *See also* Open theatre; Proscenium theatre; Staging

Theatre-in-the-round, 137, 211. *See also* Arena theatre

Theatrical gauze, 204

Theatrical staging, 148, 157–161

Theme, 6, 128, 228. *See also* Meaning; Personal viewpoint; Thought

Thickness, 163, 200

Thought, 6, 14, 56–62, 127–128; analysis by director, 332–333; expression, 58–62; nature, 56–58

Thought group, 115–116

Throw, 188

Thrust stage, 106, 147, 148, 167, 177, 213, 214, 253

Thyraton-reactor dimmer, 199

Time, dramatic, 12–13

Timeliness, 71–72

Timing, 143, 393

Tip jack, 202

Tone color, 382

Tormentor, tormentor doors, tormentor tower, 186, 189, 198

Tragedy, 9, 12, 14, 17, 25, 31, 35, 53, 56, 57, 68, 69, 150–152, 156, 161, 238, 259–260, 272, 328, 353, 369, 370, 378, 385, 411, 413–414, 456

Transition in line composition, 290

Traps, 190, 441
Traveler for curtain, 185–186
Treadwell, Sophie, 458
Trees, 259
Trimmings, 272, 277–279, 510–511
Tripping backdrop, 160
Truth and reality, 133, 134
Tryout, 461–462
"Turning worm" change, 38
Twofold of flats, 200, 202
Type characters, 14, 32–33, 35, 129, 460, 463

Underplaying, 390
Understudying, 462–463
Unifying devices in composition, 11–13
Unison speech patterns, 388–390
Unit setting, 240
Unity, 424–426, 435; of bodily action, 92; of design, 235, 239–242; of effect, 11–13, 19; of style, 406
Upstage, 188, 344, 346
Urban, Joseph, 176, 179, 193

Value, color, 301, 308; as property of light and shade, 293–294, 298
Values, meaning, in lines, 119, 120; of a play, 74, 103
van Druten, John, 331, 401
Vardac, A. Nicholas, 164

Variety, in design composition, 312–316; and emphasis, 401; of expression, 451–452; in patterning visual and auditory stimuli, 435; of speech rate, 386. *See also* Alternation; Contrast
Vaudeville, 387 n., 430, 431
Vega, Lope de, 17
Vernacular, 49–50
Verse, 13, 51, 137, 151, 156, 337, 427–428, 430–431
Vestris, Mme., 163
Viewpoint, ethical and moral, 56–57; personal, 338, 447–448. *See also* Thought
Visibility, of actor's features, 280–281; of color, 301, 302; and light and shade, 294, 297; under colored light, 308. *See also* Sight lines
Visual balance, 418–419
Visual rhythm, 429–430
Visual stimuli, and director, 339–371; patterning of, 394–435; provided by actor, 340–354; provided by influence of design on actor, 354–371
Visual unity, 235, 239–242
Vitality in characterization, 30–31
Vitruvius, 151
Vocal balance, 419–420
Vocal stimuli. *See* Auditory stimuli

Voice, 111–123; and atmosphere, 412; balance, 419–420; characteristics, 372, 376–387; rhythm, 430; style, 406, 410; variety, 451–452
Volume of speech, 376–378

Wagon, 182, 185, 204
Wagon stage, 192
Water on stage, 260
Webster, John, 58
Webster, Margaret, 402, 417, 420, 424, 445, 447
Welles, Orson, 237, 446 n.
West, Mae, 425 n.
Western Springs (Illinois) Community Theatre, 168, 219
White, Emily, 431
Wigs, 280
Wilde, Oscar, 54
Williams, Tennessee, 10, 32, 75, 409, 414
Windt, Valentine, 473
Wing-and-drop scenery, 202, 203
Wings, 158, 188, 202, 203
Women disguised as men, 284
Woolley, Monty, 461 n.
Wrap-around stage, 177, 211
Wright, Frank Lloyd, 205
Wynn, Ed, 390

X-ray border, 198